Enchanted Dreams

The Poetry Guild

Enchanted Dreams
Copyright © 1998 by The Poetry Guild

Rights to individual poems reside with the submitting artists.
All rights reserved under international copyright conventions. No part of this
book may be reproduced, stored in a retrieval system or transmitted in any form,
electronic, mechanical, or by other means, without the written permission of the publisher.
Address all inquiries to Publisher.

ISBN 1-888680-32-6

Printed in the United States of America by
The Poetry Guild
Finalist Publishing Center
3687 Ira Road · Bath, OH 44210

Editor's Acknowledgment

In conducting its poetry competitions, The Poetry Guild has received and evaluated poems written by poets from all walks of life. The collected works of *Enchanted Dreams* consist of a wide range of sounds and styles: free verse, traditional verse, narrative, lyric, dramatic, avant-garde and even experimental.

As the Editor of this book, the hardest part of my job was going through all the poems and making choices about which ones to use. All of the poems featured in this anthology deserve to be celebrated in the form of publication. And all beginning poets should especially be cheered.

One of the traits that makes this anthology unique is that it gives newcomers a chance to write and be read, and by doing so brings poetry back to the people. After all, art is meant to be appreciated.

The real beauty of this anthology is its inspiration. In some ways, all of us can relate to the topics and themes expressed in these poems, which address important and often timely issues that we might otherwise ignore or suppress. Each poem conveys its own message, and provides a vehicle of expression for diverse attitudes and fresh insights.

I would like to congratulate each and every poet on their inclusion in this special anthology. In addition, I am grateful to the editors, book designers, production assistants and countless others for their efforts in creating this important work. Most of all, a special thanks goes out to those of you who chose to share your poetry with us and the world!

Terence Troon, Editor

"Poetry is life distilled."

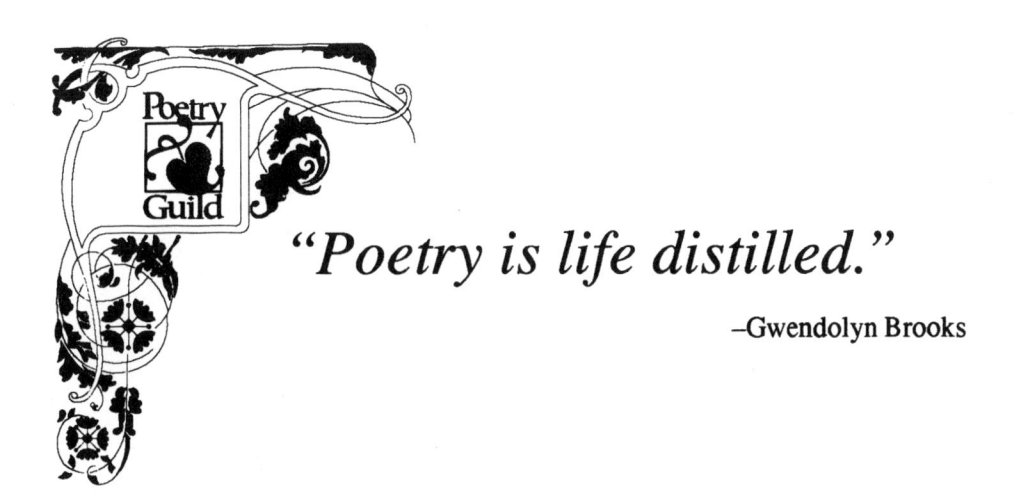

–Gwendolyn Brooks

Welcome to the Poetry Guild's heralded edition of *Enchanted Dreams!* This unique anthology contains a collection of selected poems composed by a variety of individuals.

When the idea for this anthology surfaced, its main purpose was to create an ongoing resource for those interested in publishing their own poetry and, more than anything else, to showcase the best original work.

Members of our staff have been hard at work creating this special edition. You will find featured the work of 1,831 contributors whose poems deal with a wide range of subjects. The selected poems focus on the reflective power of words to inform the public and create awareness about significant issues through frequently meaningful observations and vastly different poetic styles.

As communicators in the literary field, we all want to reach the widest possible audience. This anthology appeals to a broad spectrum of poetry lovers. By having a poem published in this anthology, you will be gaining exposure and sharing your work with many others in the poetry community.

In addition to poems, this anthology also features special dedications and a most interesting chapter of "Poet Profiles." This book encourages you to browse. In reading it, we hope that you will come away with new understandings and shared realizations of our world and experiences.

CHAPTER ONE

The Anthology of Poems

The poems in this chapter are notable not only for the masterful way in which they convey the poets' ideas, but also because they challenge the reader to reinterpret significant subject matters. It is truly amazing to see the variety of styles among the poems submitted.

EDITOR'S NOTE: *You will find that some of the works represented in this and the following chapter are dedicated to people who perhaps influenced or inspired the individual authors. All special dedications are composed by the poets at their personal request.*

Enchanted Dreams

Anno Dente
W. P. Forsyth
Nothing makes me feel humbler
than my teeth in a tumbler.

Our Porch:
Marie H. Reneau
There is some—thing we have,
That has brought us great pleasure,
and I'm sure, like us,
Many people would treasure.
It's our porch.

It's not real fancy,
For some it's not even swell,
But our old porch,
Has a tale it could tell.

It's a form on the ground,
with little foundation.
It was the owner's own creation.
There are windows on three sides,
you can sit on the swing,
and watch people go by.

It's attached to a house,
The color of green.
From the back, a fishing pond
can be seen.
It has a cement floor,
and also the walls,
The ceiling is stucco,
so that it won't fall.
There's a few cracks in the walls
Some windows have dust.
But we're all very grateful.
It's good enough for us.
There's a carpet on the floor,
and lights so we can see,
When we're on this porch,
We're as happy as we can be.

There is a radio, a heater and a fan.
This porch has everything we need,
Except, maybe, the can.

If only this porch could talk,
What stories it would tell.
We've had parties and talked
and most often eaten,
and many of us at cards have
been beaten.
We've had many laughs,
and some—times we've cried.
Had lots of kisses and many hugs,
It has a patched—up screen,
to keep out the bugs.

This porch has had many steps
on its surface.
Family, friends, the rich and the poor,
Its a grand old porch
it was built for this purpose.
I'm sure I've forgotten many things
I could write.
These are only a few thoughts, that
have come to my mind.
Thank God for this porch,
It's one of a kind.

Tanka On Africa I...
Martin J. O'Malley, Jr.
Lead, Great Africa!...
You are All–Time's Noblest Song !...
You... Where we began...
From pure Homo erectus
Evolved Homo sapiens...

Lives That Touch
Sharon Ann Solarski
Making our way, never knowing from day to day
The lives we touch, the path we take
This is the life we make

From a stranger's view from across the room
Drawn together as a lust taboo

Just one look as our eyes crossed each other's world
I knew a dangerous passion would set ablaze my attraction
As candles in the sill, burning my desire's path with everlasting
    compassion

Never knowing what's right or wrong
I can truly state I will forever long
To touch you in my deepest dreams
Just the thought of you and me

But reality is the light that breaks through the night
To walk separate journeys, pulled together only by thoughts of yearning

You say what will be will be and now I see...
To let go of a dream will never give me serenity

To be a free spirit is what you have shown me
A teacher of life is what you have been to me

A simple attraction brought to my mind a kind memory
that has been defined as a gentle hand from you, a mortal man

I can only hope you have learned from my presence
A sincere friendship of genuine contentions

Never forget to follow your heart
For you are a true inspiration, such as a priceless work of art

As a valued cobblestone path bending and winding
through this world we walk apart

Never forgetting that our foot is placed firmly on that stone
of Earthly belonging someway,
somehow, it grounds me from not knowing why we ever
were set here without a chance at heart

You have exclusively touched my soul to the outmost level of
self—wealth
Now I know that, no matter what, I will never regret my time
spent was an indefinite must

When we crossed paths in the journey of life
It was a reflection of what I could not fight

I only can reflect that fate has dealt us a deck of cards that
has brought me pure understanding
and appreciation to entrust my feelings of loving, living
and accepting the ways of letting what is meant to be, be...

Which gives me fond memories, the thought of you and me

Dedication: to Ryan, you've touched my life...

Guide Me Lord
Sheila Prokop
Lord, see me as I am, not as I was.
I was blind, now I see, life was
meant to be a better life with thee.
So walk beside me and guide me to
a better place.
So that I may be with Thee
when my life is over.

ExSOLtation — Alleluia
Ronda Scott-Marak
Dawn creeps slowly in
Unseen birds sing in rippling trills
Water splashes, pitter, puddle
Upon a shallow stone
Sky is black then a pale horizon
Emerging into tints of yellow, mauve and blue
A watercolour of sun and sea reflect in sky
Songbirds whistle, chirp, a fluting soaring, orchestra of sound
An overture to day
Flowers open to the light
Petals damp with dew
Leaves sway to the rhythm of the breeze
Nighttime peace yawns and prepares to sleep away the day

Noon sun rises like a temple gong
Harsh then dulcet
Reverberating waves of heat
Fish bubble and plop, catching the light with their midday meal
Playing children giggle, shriek and run
Chase and tag
Bats crack on flying balls
Bicycle tires turn and whoosh against opposing winds
Sky cerulean-bright against a fleet of fleece-white sailing clouds
Trees rustle, hiding thieving squirrels and warbling songbirds
Drowsy-eyed against the light
Day basks in the sun

Day starts its journey toward the night
Sky and sea both flat and darkened blue
Swallows flit and dart
Circle, swoop
Hunting their buzzing dinner feast
Sun swells
Descending in a brassy, blazing fanfare
Of orange, red and gold
Robin whistles the evening in
Russet breast aburst with joy and pride
In rousing finale
Crescendos
As day's purple-streaked curtain draws closed.

Day is done
Moonlight blankets the land
Stippling the trees in silver
Reflected orbs in sea and stream polka-dot the darkness
Whippoorwills flute a descant to the owls
Midnight-shrouded trees
Shrug their leafy branches
Redistributing the nestled birds
Heads under feathered wings
The world is silhouettes
Colourless against blue-black
Only eyes are visible
Nocturnal gold and green
Matching their light against the moon and stars
Day snuggles down in blessed dark
And sleeps away the night

Hen Party
Margaret McCurley
The name was tossed into the waiting
Circle.

They pounced on it
Catlike,

Leaving in shreds, what had once been
Innocence.

Days Gone By
Rebecca Lawrence
Summer days appeared longer, the sky a deeper blue, rain
fell clean like crystal teardrops,

Dawn's chorus was beautiful, too.

In the fields, harvests grew ripe and plenty, wheat and corn
swayed majestically

Life-expectancy wasn't long, due to poor sanitation, malnutrition,
dirt and disease.

The pace of life seemed slower, people had more time to spend
with each other,

Sunday schools and churches were full, but so were the taverns...
the Dog and the Bull!!

Stress was never heard of, life was hard, choice was less, family
ties were very strong,

Support given when you were distressed.

Neighbours became friends, caring, sharing, through good times
and through bad,

Laughing with you when you were happy, crying for you when
you were sad.

On cobbled streets, in all weathers, children laughed and played
together, they didn't mind

The cold or the rain, television hadn't been invented, fun was had
just the same

Whip and top and hop scotch, marbles, skipping ropes, bat and
balls,

Games played by every child, whether their family were rich or
poor

The man of the house worked long hours, the pay was very low,

Material wealth was never mentioned, the Pawn shop was the
bank years ago!

Luxuries of life were sacrificed, making ends meet was the
priority of life.

To have clothes on your back, shoes on your feet, food on the
table, a home clean and neat.

Warmth from a fire, embers glowing in the hearth, a home filled
with love, contentment in

Your heart. To have walked through life with your head held
high... Who could wish for more.

Enchanted Dreams

The Invitation
Kathleen Mullen Parker
How fresh the country air of morning,
see there the fragile droplets of dew
exquisite liquid diamonds
clinging in dawn's first light
reflecting brilliant webs
jewels of night...
spider spun
to decorate, alas, invite,
the innocent to dinner.

Tomorrow
John Westbrook
'Ore my restful slumber, I lay still and wonder
of what became today.
A feeling I did blunder, through words that sound asunder
I tripped my tongue away.
A heart so pure, I want to be sure
of what to feel.
Tomorrow is always a day away

Through my mindless mist, I need to feel the gist
of what I am to say.
Silently I think a list, offer you an open fist
not to sound cliche.
These words I implore, I want to be sure
of what to feel.
Tomorrow is always a day away

The darkened mist begins to fade. To it "farewell" I abide
to leave forevermore.
Through my fear of loss I wade, only to wish we could've stayed
breathless a Moment more.
Your touch is sweet, when our lips meet.
so good to feel.
Tomorrow is always a day away

In my mind the word's been said. Now to get it from my head
to you lying there.
A haunting fear I still dread, yet I must empty my head
to you waiting there.
Opportunity lost, at such a cost.
how do I feel
Tomorrow is always a day away

During my restless slumber, over words I plunder,
I ask, "will you stay"?
The end is all I wonder, for, like the sound of thunder
will take it all away.
My mind 'lorn. My heart torn.
what is real?
Tomorrow is still a day away

My relentless fear of rejection causes this projection
out for you to see.
There was no dejection, instead you made a connection
helping set me free.
My mind feeling. My heart healing.
how do I feel?
Tomorrow is still a day away

Ending my eventful slumber, I sit up and wonder
when is today?
Over thoughts I plunder, strong-willed and somber
thoughts of yesterday.
One and one, in life—is one
I know how I feel.
Tomorrow is today and was yesterday

Him
Dustin M. Riggs
He prayed, but it wasn't my religion;
he waved his banner—it wasn't my banner;
he dressed—they weren't my clothes.
He spoke, but it wasn't my language;
he danced—it wasn't my style;
he sang—they weren't my songs.

He offered me his hand—it wasn't the color of mine;

But when he laughed—it was how I laughed,
and when he cried—it was how I cried;
so I took his hand.

Why
Shannon Butts
Why is life so precious,
Snuffed out so quickly,
Without any warning, Without any signs.
Why are the warmest of hearts
Taken away so abruptly,
So suddenly,
All we are left with
Are the memories,
Sacred memories
That are held so dear,
Very close to our hearts.
Why did they have to go,
Why did they have to leave.
Didn't God know how much they meant to us,
Didn't He know how much we needed them
Why didn't we say all the things
We wanted to say while they were here,
Those times when we should have let them know
How very important they really were,
How we cared for them.
Now the chance is gone.
All we can do is talk to the sky,
Hope that they are listening
And understand that our tears are
Shed out of selfishness.
Yes, we are selfish
We want them back in our lives
Here to brighten our days
Like they did so easily before,
Here to ease our fears,
Here just to be here
To be near.
So, why do I now have to
Settle for a mental picture
All I want to know is why
Why did you have to go
Why did you leave me alone,
To wallow in my tears.
I guess I'll just have to stay behind
And wait for my time
The time that I may be with you once again
But for now,
Just remember,
You are always in my heart.
I'm so blessed to have known you
To have had you in my life
And, most of all remember that
I loved you
While you were here
And I love you still, now that you're gone
You are so special and will never be
Forgotten

My Life
Gary J. Sasala

My life is filled with memories,
of all the days gone by.
Days that are lost forever,
until the end of time.
You gave my life meaning.
since you came into my life.
You gave me hope and confidence,
and not to give up the fight.
You showed me how to love and care,
and were always by my side.
I will love you, dear, forever
until the end of time.

Untitled
Sandra Larsen

We were best friends way back when.
Although your name was Ginny, I called you "Jen".

We were together both night and day.
We didn't care what people might say.

We always seemed to get in trouble.
Whatever one did, the other did double.

"I can do anything better than you can."
That usually got us in one heck of a jam.

Like the time you got your butt stuck in the bucket.
My Dad brought the blowtorch and said "We'll have to cut it!"

Your mother got angry and started to shout.
She didn't know you really couldn't get out.

I'm not sorry that I laughed so hard,
cause I'll never forget that day in your back yard.

Remember the attic and our secret jars?
Remember the time we took my Dad's car?

Remember the times that we slept outside?
Remember the boys that we tried to hide?

Remember sailing down the creek in an old wash tub,
or giving me all those fabulous back rubs?

Remember smoking cornsilks and thinking we were cool?
Remember the next day, those sick little fools?
Remember when we put the hole in Daddy's garage door.
or when you broke the tomatoes on Mom's basement floor?

Remember drag racing in front of the school?
How many times were we grounded for breaking the rules?

Remember Roy Ogden? I'm sure that you do.
That trip to Mayetta got me grounded, too!

I truly remember your wedding day.
I cried and I cried 'cause you moved far away.

My fella tried to console me by holding me tight,
but there wasn't anything that brought me comfort that night.

I could go on because I remember lots more.
But I gotta stop now. It's a quarter till four.

Besides, all I really wanted to say,
is "I love you girl. Have a Happy Birthday!!"

Untitled
Lawrence R. Starry

Really all it ever wuz,
was just a little ball of fuzz.
Growing lonely every day,
wishing he could go and play.

A swish of a broom lifted him high,
making him wish that he could fly.
But someone thought he was a bug,
and knocked him back down on the rug.

But being just a little ball of fuzz,
was glad to be back where he wuz.

Queen Of The Mountain
Lori Dawn Holdaway

She ascends like a queen
With the mountains in her eyes
Shadows cast around her
And an Angel by her side
The arctic path is steep
As she balances her crown
And strides up glacial peaks
Then lets them take her down
Sometimes she skis in moonlight
Constellations float above
And the night–sounds of the winter
Whisper words of love
Her heart melts like a candle
Glowing from inside
Canyon walls can't hold her
From this magic carpet ride
Leaving imprints in the snow
Where once her body danced
She traverses downward now
And all that's left are tracks
Where she was, she isn't now
She's descended far below
Back to her safe haven
To a place God only knows
And the jesters of the mountain
Offer her their gold
Shallow are their passions
As they reach out for a hold
But she floats ever so freely
As they roll and tumble down
Two faces on the mountain
An empress and a clown
And if you think you'll hold her
From your temporary stool
Or catch her on some lonely trail
You're thinking like a fool
She'll strike into the forest
Like a deer running free
Leaving only wishes
For some midnight fantasy
Sometimes she wears an instrument
And her broken heart unfolds
A singer at her hearth
A child no one knows
See the teardrops falling now
She's trying not to drown
This damsel of the city
Strikes again for higher ground
She ascends like a queen
With the mountains in her eyes
Shadows cast around her
And an Angel by her side...

Enchanted Dreams

Happy Mother's Day
Carol E. Centric
When I think back when I was young and looked into your face
I thought you were so beautiful, a face so full of grace
A heart so kind and loving, a mind so honest and true
Two arms that wrapped around me, a lap that rocked me, too
For great mothers just don't happen, I'm sure they're sent from above
God swept His hand across your face
And said, "I've created Love."
You cared for me like no one else, you made my life worthwhile
And through all the tough times you always wore a smile
I appreciate, to say the least, the things you've done for me
And I'm so glad you're my Mom through all eternity.

Dedication: to Rose Green Rook

To The Best Parents In The World
Dawn Michelle Hawkin Stroud
Thinking of my past, from year after year –
So many memories, I remember so clear–

I look towards Heaven and began to pray –
Whispering to Bobo, sharing things I have to say –

I sat there quietly, I thought I heard his voice –
Deep in my mind, but not by choice –

So, I listened carefully and grabbed my pen –
Writing down what I heard, from beginning to end –

"Life is so precious, yet, it flies by night –
We were born for a reason, everything will be alright
God knew what He was doing, creating us one by one
Each and every person, that lives beneath the sun –
From one generation to another, He built a family
tree –
Making you as my parents and together you made
me–"

The phase was short, yet it meant so much, –
Using the right words, it had the right touch –

Like the way you raised us, sharing all your love –
The best in the world, you were sent from up above –

Working so hard, you made everything right –
Thank you for the memories, each day and each
night –

Trips to the ocean, trips to the snow –
You drove us through deserts, many places, we used to
go –

All the times I took for granted, I'll always regret –
But thank God for memories, so, I'll never forget –

You gave us what we needed, one day at a time –
Sharing every second, spending your last dime –

It wasn't your gifts, or places we went –
But everything you've shared, all the time you spent –

I love you so much, I appreciate what you've done –
Also as Grandparents, you're the best for my son –

These words will never explain the feelings I have for
you –
I just want the world to know, my parents are Jim and
Sue –

Heartache Introspection
David A. Rockwell
Viewed from up here, you look insignificant,
darting here and there,
crawling around in your desperate search for food.
Briefly a thought of crushing you enters my mind,
but I decide to pardon you today.
The shiny-wet blackness of your body sends shivers down my spine
as I picture you crawling up my leg.
I wonder to myself if you see my shadow and my face so far above you?
Do you see me? Do you care?
Everything in your world is so vast and insurmountable;
risk faces you whether you move or stay still.
I question whose life is more dangerous,
and which one of us is truly insignificant.

Summer Strife
Emily Wheeler
Summer vacation's almost over and I've about had it.
Three full months of my kids and all kinds of havoc.
It hasn't been all bad, this I confess.
We've let go of the laundry and the floors are a mess.
For I know in my heart, that these times are short.
And how I find treasure in a "Mother's Reward"
The clock is still ticking, as I run for the door.
All's keeping me busy, I can't take this much more.
Oh, hold just one Moment, as I check on the stove.
For my dinner's now burning and the phone's left on hold.
"Mommy, Mommy, I need you, come now!"
"What is the matter?... Who, what, when, how??"
"It's brother, he did it, he made me a kite."
"Well, I think that was thoughtful, so what is the fight?"
"But, Mommy, look, there's a string tied to my back.
I don't want to be a kite, would you please tell him that?"
... And as I remember that call on the phone,
I rush back to apologize as I stub my big toe.
Still struggling to get there, I'm stepping over toys,
when I hear a voice calling, "Mom where are the boys?"
"I don't know!" I try telling her, "I'm only one being.
Heck, I can't even find the person called me!"
"Hello, Hello, are you still there? I'm sorry I got lost,
but I'm so glad you cared
Enough to wait for me with a heart full of patience.
My kids have kept me going fast all summer vacation."
So tell me, Dear Nellie, "How have you been? Nellie, oh, Nellie",
I think she's hung up again.
Now dinner's all done with, as the day nears its end.
I think of tomorrow and doing it all again.
It's time for a shower, or a warm bath with bubbles.
Somehow I'll escape today's life full of troubles.
I'm sure I'll have to do this with some toys and a boat.
And two extra bodies, with no room to cope.
But good ol' Mommy, she learns to contend in a crowded bathtub
with two little friends. 9 PM bedtime for some.
I'll be so lucky if I'm there by One.
This is my time for being alone.
Though I could phone Nellie who has kids of her own.
And together we'll thank God for our children divine.
I'll pray for her sanity and she'll pray for mine.
We thank Him for teachers so blessed and true.
We've learned to appreciate all that they do.
We'll say to the Heavens,
"Let angels remember Mother's like us each June – September."
Oh, Lord, You must know that I love my kids so.
And in these three months, I've watched them grow.
I see all the changes taking place in their lives.
That's when I thank You, God, for the long Summer Strife.

Dedication: to Ronnie, Jackie, Chad, Charles and Aaron

Sepa
Tabor Skreslet
rate
They seek to separate
me from my
self and fam
ily. From fri
ends and fut
ure. From those
so close
they are my
self. But such divi
sion shall not
conquer us
whoareone
nomatterwhat.

I Do Love You
Teresa Schmidt
We were so young when we started out,
Too young to know what life was about.
Love and determination drove us forward,
Because we knew there would be a great reward.
Time went on and things were tough, but each trial caused us to grow,
Closer together like no one could know.

You became a part of my soul,
We became as one, as that had been our goal.
You were my reason for living,
It was for you I did all my giving.
Life, trials and death took their toll,
And our love they very nearly stole!

There was a betrayal I couldn't believe,
Could ever be allowed to happen, I was afraid we would leave.
We were ripped so far apart,
I feared there would be no mending of my broken heart.
It bled so long with pain and sorrow,
The rip was so deep I thought there could be no tomorrow.

Then, I heard that voice that I hadn't heard for so long,
I felt your presence that had been so gone.
I cried with love and a small hope,
Could it be possible to find a way to cope?

Each day I felt your presence more and more,
The painful tear in my heart began to mend but not before,
You said, "I do love you" and I began to cry,
This time there was happiness in my tears, oh, my.
The touch of your hands and lips that I love so much,
Had been ripped from me but now I longed for that touch.

Each day brings tears of grief, pain and sorrow,
But those tears are healing so there can be a tomorrow!
It's going to take time and many more tears to heal the pain,
But I know that we can be happy again.

Please know how deeply I love you,
It is from the center of my soul that I feel you.
I long to be with you every minute we're apart,
With the anger and emotion there is intense love in my heart.

The trust and security must be rebuilt,
From the very beginning, like each stitch of a quilt.
Those stitches will be stronger than ever,
Will anyone tear it apart?
NEVER, no, NEVER!!!!

Dedication: to Tom, whom I love

Shadowed
Kathleen Kane
His wit still cut fine figures,
But he's unmoved.
The dance is for his audience—
Applause can fill some gaps.
He never dances with the music now.

I could shoot him for fading on us all,
So coolly and deliberately.
Yet the Moment that I shot him
I'd be tossing with his ghost.

Coward! I was whirled with you through flames.
The quick are always maimed. The loving mend.
Pay the piper and come alive!
Or kindly finish your suicide.

The Victim
Jackie Palladino
I once knew a victim of a violent crime and
never knew what was on her mind.

You see, the crime was a crime called rape and now
I know why she feels such hate.

She was always kind and loving, too and never would
hurt me or you.

You see this isn't just a crime, it's something that
stays in your mind.

People say that you'll forget and life will go on.

But does it really?

You see, I am that victim and I can't forget, no
matter how hard I try.

All I do is sit and cry.

It's something that's on my mind and will always
be there all the time.

I sit and try to understand why I feel as I do, Even
when I don't know what to do.

You see, I was forced to do something I didn't want,
And I really, truly tried to fight.

I try and live my life the best I can, But I just go
on distrusting men.

I feel so dirty at times, I do, even though there was
nothing I could do.

Tell me someone, What would you do? If you were faced
with such disgrace.

It's only the victim who pays the price for a crime
we don't even commit.

Is it fair? Maybe not, But it's real.

So let me say, even though it's sad, There'll come
a day I will forget, But it will only be at my
death.

Dedication: to my mother, my friend

Enchanted Dreams

Old Books
Ailene Hayes Schneider
The pages of books,
Like petals of flowers,
Yellow with age
After the hours have gone
Wherein their message,
The scent,
Lay fragrant
Upon our lives.

But, like the flower,
Their message is still
Scenting the mind,
Perfuming the will,
Though brittle the page
And yellow with age.

For Dinky
Nikola Howell
You're old now, my dear little dog, your body is racked with pain,
You're tired, your eyesight is not so good, you'll never run and play again.

I remember when I first chose you, your blue eyes could not yet see,
I cradled you in the palm of my hand, oh, the fun there was going to be.

We grew up in the countryside, chased rabbits, roamed free all day,
And when it was time to head for home, it was you who led the way.

We grew up together, took photos galore, you were always at my side,
And now, as I look at them through my tears, my heart is filled with pride.

You guarded me faithfully through my life, when sad you licked my tears,
You always knew when I needed you, your instinct sensing my fears.

Your mischievous eyes, your flopped-over ear, your fur that was black and white,
You were the one who watched over me and stayed close throughout the night.

The wag of the tail, the gentle touch of your paw, the sniff, then the cold, wet kiss,
These are just a few of the things, so painfully, I shall miss.

The Vet came and assured me there was nothing more he could do,
I hope and pray you'll understand, it was my turn to do something for you.

Goodbye, God Bless, my dearest friend, it's time for you to go,
I pray you'll forgive and understand, 'tis because I love you so.

Wherever you are now, be happy my friend, run and bark and play,
And then, who knows, when my time comes, we'll meet up again one day.

Untitled
Julie Merrick
That part of me could forever absorb you,
devour you, if you let it, a carnivorous darkness,
created not entirely by my own hands,
despite the dirt and blood beneath my nails.
Inside this crevice, I am not myself,
as I cry for to you to come—whisper for you to leave.
You can't comprehend the vastness of my needs,
the oasis of pain that awaits you if you stay.
And while I have the strength to warn you,
do not eat the fruits that I will offer you this morning.
They're poisoned by red lips that do not belong to me.
My voice will call to you, but block your ears and go.
Walk slowly over the bridge I made you,
carefully without peripheral vision to distract you.
And don't mind that I am crying.
It's not your fault—not even mine.

The Last Dance
Nina Smith
I believed,
As summer turned to fall.

I believed in the magic
That hearts such as mine
Long for.
The dance of all dances.
Ballroom gowns flowing
In excitement and anticipation.
The Queen of the evening.
And he pushes toward me,
To spark the fires of passion.
Only a memory of my youth.

Is it only a picture
From the endless night?
Is this existence
Only in dreams?
Is life so endlessly boring
That one can only fill the cravings
In the shadows of the mind?
Is love so fleetingly elusive
That to touch it
Is to expel it from one's life
Forever?
For I have touched it
And it turned me away.
I have smelled
The exotic fragrance
And it turned to stench.
I have flown with the Eagle,
Only to come crashing down
To the horrors of reality.

Only in the silence of sleep
Is there beauty.
The lies of love
Become truth.
The doldrums turn to
The freedom of passion and expression.

So only in darkness
Is there light.

I will lay my heart
To sleep now.
And rest in peace
Through all of eternity.

A Season
Barbara Unger
Sun, you rise unveiled in glorious blush
Spewing mood—altering light over the landscape.
I am a plant drawn toward you,
Transfixed and nourished on petal—lips gathering nectar.
A gentle breeze stirs the sweet scent of balsam and playfully jostles
the elm
Casting its own shadows, evoking Momentary images through
sun—pierced leaves.
Emerging now, weary from time passed,
From the pupae of long, dark days, blurring time, feigning existence.
And yet are not light and darkness as one
Necessary to the other, joined like twins in mysterious bond.
Still, let me swoon in dream—like warmth
As you bleach away already—faded dark—tone memories.
Burn, then, deep into the branches of this heart – winter's reservoir
Contented now to nourish the seeds of tomorrow.

Through The Years
Melody Hill
In 19 Hundred and 49, Mom wed Dad and that was fine. Now in 1950
Gene comes along– hoppin' and Boppin' and singing a California Song.

Away they went in a 2–door Ford and along comes Einella in 1954.
Two things happened in 56 – Melody was born and Einella got sick.

And what, to their surprise, you see; Melody was born on New Year's Eve.
Living in California, being five of a kind; that wasn't enough Elise
was born April 6, 1959.

Now in California, our time was all well–spent. But Grandpa and
Grandma write and away we all went.

I'm sure it wasn't easy and not a lot of fun, Mom and Dad built the
house – Farm and all – in 1961.

In 19 hundred and 67 – We got Eva Lynn dropped straight from Heaven.
Mom and Dad worked hard for the bunch, Melody and Elise made shavings
and Einella made lunch.

In 77 it was time to be wed, Elise married Vernon with his cotton–
white head.

Einella and Bruce, they just couldn't wait, they were married in 78.
Before long, Melody knew it was her time, she married Randy in 79.

Gene being the man and Sherry being the lady, they were married in 1980.
1980 – sick Mom did lay, but on September 8th, the Lord took her away.

Mom going away may not be the key, but in 81 we got Natalee.

September 29th was when she was due, we got Lenzie in 82.
So happy were we, you see, when we got Cole and Taylor in 1983.

We needed another wild and alive, we got Wade in 85.

In 86 we had quite a blend, Clinton Otis married Eva Lynn.

Looking for a boy, they didn't get their pick, Lorin was born in 86.

87 was filled with both good and bad; we were sure surprised when we lost
Dad.

Being as sweet as a piece of cake, 87 was when we got Blake.

We all keep in touch by telephone, to make sure we all know what's going
on. Now where do we all stay when we all come in?
Well, of course it's with Clint and Eva Lynn.

Foxwoods
Joyce Barksdale
Hidden deep in the imagination of a
dreamer it rises tall and green and
regal
The sun rests upon the vision of loveliness
to shame Adonis... unequal
Greenery, shrubs and cascading waterfalls
plush and rich and welcoming

Quiet passion and still yet unrealized
dreams awaiting in the wings... I saw him
eyes fixed on mine and his gaze turned towards
the rolling thunder of casinos and roulette
cash machines and gambling...

But he caught my heart and I inhaled the
vapors of love as it was breathtaking as
the expansive view of the woods that lay in waiting

End Of Summer Song
Gail M. Sutton
End of summer song;
End of playing with dogs, running and bike riding
too long.
Alone, but not alone, sitting at the great
white spirit's throne.
End of summer song;
Progression of wildflowers did end, from
purple rises, arose, Indian paint brush and
grasses, the lush summer green turns
a shade,
The autumn leaves come on parade.

End of summer song;
Time to harvest has come along,
Time for happy hunting song,
Fawns, does and bringing home the 12–point
buck that comes along.

End of summer song
She will hide her face from us for a while
Time to breathe in cold air and smile.
Just when you think winter has set in
Indian summer shows up again.
The sun warms the air in the day,
But you can tell from nights cold winter is
on its way.

So, say goodbye to summer in a song;
Old man winter's grip is very strong,
The north wind has come along.
So say goodbye to summer in a song;
End of summer song,
End of that time in life.
You can't live those Moments over
Just like finding a four–leaf clover,
This summer has been here, come,
gone, never to reappear.

On November sixteen the ice set in
completely freezing the lake,
Yesterday only the edges had a crust,
Summer is gone, she's had all she can take.

So, I end this summer with a song
End of summer song

Dedication: to my father (deceased July 1, 1996)

Enchanted Dreams

The Poet
Carol Brown
I heard a tribute to a poet newly–dead
Whose "so well crafted" "poignant" lines I lately read.
Lines unlike the bitter or cloying verse
Served up by others. Terse.
Or rambling, all too many I quickly forgot
If briefly touching and even more quickly if not.
All too few imbued with arresting flavor
Compelling one to linger, chew, savor.

She had been depressed, they recall.
But perhaps that depression was vital,
Created from her poems' weighty matter,
Life, pressing on the brittle who shatter,
Not touching those who seek escape.
But those pliant poets who are molded to shape
A hole, whose hollow, cup–like receives
Then transubstantiates what it perceives
Into rhythms, words, images by the hundredfold,
Feed readers, who, in turn, are wholed.

Our Heart
Janis Harvey
Our heart,
A picture book of stories
untold,
A faded photo–album of
memories, tattered with time
yet never grows old.
A scratch pad of reasons
Why? How? or, can it be done?
Not today, pain so deep
And truly victories won.
Days marked, must do,
don't forget, all those nights
filled with not enough sleep.
A new day dawning.
I watched as the soldier's
marched one, then the other.
A stern, confident, leader
ordered the command.
the sounding of the taps
and a twenty–one gun
Salute broke the silence.
Tears ran down my face.
It was hard to see as
they folded the flag in honor
And handed to the wife.
The air was filled with pride,
dignity and the American way.
Now, in my heart I hold
A picture of a proud mother
who at this time must do
What some mothers may never do.
I want to shake your hand
For today you were not a child
I saw a man.
All I ask of you
Just like the men
You lay to rest
for them you must carry on
a job well done you will do.
Remember, there are three
young boys at home
soon to be men
who are following after you.

Dedication: to our son Lewis Wayne Halstead

Jimmy's Field
Charles G. Lauder, Jr.
Much like exhuming my own grave centuries later
and breathing in the dark clay caked onto my shoes,
the life of a farmer's son is awakened
by this field, by grunts of oak branches
stretched wide in midnight calisthenics,
a beckoning call, not as a bugle, but as a door
opened to a barn writing to be filled
glimpsed in the next field over, or not at all,

perhaps imagined through cracks in the hedge
an English farmhouse, a flat facade
of fading orange brick and gangrene moss,
low black beams and low doorways, winter crops,
sheep whose coats can hide half my arm,
their trails revealed in this mud soup
by February's full moon, once called
the storm moon, while behind me, you are lost

to shadows, whipped away by the cold touch
of time and the singularity of the night.

On A Fall Day
Janice Nicolson
We must get up to go to school; no more lazy summer days.

Shirts and jeans must stay home today and wait for us
to come home to play.

We eat toast and Cornflakes to keep away tummyaches.

The school bus is coming. Out the door we are running.

When school starts, we pledge allegiance to the flag,
with our hands over our hearts.
At school today, we put on a puppet play.

Every one must sit in his chair. Today we hear a story,
about the biggest bear.

We go outside for recess, that is the time that I like best.

We sing about a puppy named Spot. Just like the puppy I've got.
With our many papers in a bunch, we hurry home for lunch.

We put on our shirts and jeans to play. Billie, my neigh–
bor, is coming over today.

When we play in the leaves and Billie buries me, there
must be no breeze.

When we play squirrel, nuts we find. We hide them for
winter. "Billie, don't leave that nut behind. "

Buckeyes we also collect. The biggest and shiniest I select.
When we play hunter, we duck in the tall grass and wait
for the ducks to fly past.

When we are monkeys, we climb up in the tree to collect
coconuts for Billie and me.

Out in the tree, up in the sky, we smell coconut pie.

It must be time to eat, so we drop to our feet.

Supper is over. We watch TV, but it's off to bed early.

This is not easy for Mommy or me.

What Did You Know Of T. S. Eliot?
Teresa Taylor

You looked at me
Across the years of our togetherness,
Looked at me
As cherry blossoms landed like pink snow,
Piling up in corners of the pebbled path
At the Brooklyn Botanical Garden,
Looked at me
With all the love of one who has lost possession,
All the hatred of one who wants it back.
Looked at me with a promise of better memories to come, Oh, yes,
Denying images I could still see — and feel —
Of yanked hair,
Slapped face,
And broken glass...
Looked at me and, when I shook my head "No"
For the very last time,
You said, with burning eyes and unsteady mouth
(Your flair for melodrama and Byronic tragedy
Not quite dead yet, I saw),
"The poet was wrong.   May is the cruelest month."

Silent Screams
Kevin Patrick Fram

Once upon a distant end,
you took from me my special friend.
She made me crawl,
She made me stand,
in our dreams she held my hand.
Whisper Silent Screams of Pain,
in her dreams you'll hear my name.
Sentenced guilty of no crime,
bound by honor, I passed the time.
You felt so secure, me trapped and caged,
you brought your lies to center stage.
From my love you took an hour,
from my soul you took a flower.
Whisper Silent Screams of Pain,
in her dreams you'll hear my name.
Never had I held a silver spoon!
Never had I spun a golden tune!
The Earth beneath my feet's been bare,
reflections of my deadly stare.
Once upon a distant dream,
I built myself a garden, so it seemed.
As my boyish hands would dare,
I placed each stone where Earth was bare.
Whisper Silent Screams of pain,
in her dreams you'll hear my name.
While my stones began to tower,
the lies you told began to shower.
She was mine, you saw in bloom,
till she walked into your room.
Now her love I cast aside,
a fool alone I stand with pride.
I've walked on through the gates of hell,
what I've had I couldn't sell.
Whisper Silent Screams of Pain,
in her dreams you'll hear my name.
you drowned inside the shoes I wear,
you feel your heart beyond my stare.
To a man you have no stride,
to yourself you have no pride.
Whisper Silent Screams of Pain,
in her dreams you'll hear my name.
Silent Screams

Dedication: to Marie Elisibeth Fram, my mother

The River Of Convenience
Christopher Tanzola

Allow my hand to roam with your mind
And I shall paint these cavern walls a gleaming white
And when the intricacies of a million memories
Stored and collected and depicted
Are washed new white by the great equalizer
The topography of the cave
Once an elevated symbol of relief
Will offend and sting you no more
And its memories and intricacies
Will glow as a lamp in a bowl
The white force field will shield
The world of my hand and your mind

For a river flows in the underground of that cave
And through the subconscious of the cave–dwellers
Those who know more than I claim to
Have called it Lethe — forgetfulness
I, self–appointed member of their club,
Do now call it what it is — a spade a spade
Lethe — convenience.

The American Dream
Elaine Ostroff

When we were young and our
objective was to find a man,
Old age and sorrow didn't enter
into our plan.
All we thought about was the next
party and big bash,
We never worried about the news
or the crash?
We were happy–go–lucky, high spirited
on life.
Looking forward to someday becoming
a mother and a wife,
The American dream, a family in a
house with a picket fence.
But so many things have come
about hence,
The war years came they were so
traumatic for us all,
The men who had to leave to answer
their countries' call!
The war we thought we would
never see again,
Came and took our boys and sent
them home men
The little white house with the
cute picket fence
Was put on hold and life
became tense!
The war took priority over everything
we had,
Then came V Day, but many of us
were sad,
The loss of loved–ones on faraway
foreign shores,
Didn't we say this would never happen
anymore!
Each year that passes brings us
new threats
Fears of nuclear destruction it isn't
over yet!!!
Though our dreams have been shattered
and our loved–ones taken,
The pride and love we have as
Americans will never be forsaken!

Enchanted Dreams

Untitled
Jennifer Keeney
"Speak logically!" they shriek.
And I,
in all my silent reverie,
Ask,
"Why?"

"There is no tolerance for
one apart,
Lost in worlds of
Popsicle mornings
and twinkling, starry nights."
Logic is the law on Earth.
Explanations abound in columns of fractions
and algebraic postulations.

But I heed not their "practicality".
I have no need for logic –
that is for those who can sit still.
Give me daydreams and miracles,
Popsicle mornings,
and twinkling, starry nights.

Innocence Of Who We Were
Erick Moffatt
The age of innocence has crept upon us for many, many years.
Hiding in darkness, watching our chaos, counting all the tears.
Taking our loved-ones, stealing their lives, watching us begin to strive.
Hoping we learn of what we've done and whom we will become.
Helping us triumph, counting our failures, watching the table begin to turn.
Weeping in joy of our victors and in defeat as they watch us yearn.

The eternal Mentor, our Beloved Friend.
Watching over us until the end.
Following His footsteps, learning His trade.
Watching over us to see what He's made.
Giving us life, giving us birth.
Creating us, to blanket this Earth.

Giving His life to create thousands more,
and with a reason, we know not what for.
Taking His own, to give another, generosity at hand.
Giving us freedom, giving us hope, giving us love, handing us land.
The thanks we give Him, become lies and death, murders and deceit.
When, in fact, we should truly grovel at His feet.

This Man of Wonder, a Man of Power, has reached a perilous height.
This Man of Triumph, this Man of Defeat, unveiled all of His might.
He created us, put us here in hopes we would become like Him.
Doing what's right, not murder or lie,
but find courage so light and dim.
He passed on His torch, His life and His heart,
in hopes we would choose the right.
There are some who disregard His life,
others who thank Him, every night.

But we've come to a point, one of despair, we're killing ourselves and now declare,
that this new age, era of innocence, might change the things we take for granted.
Hoping of love, triumphing over evil, destroying Satan's childish antics.
He made us kill, he made us murder. In hopes to bring us to his mound.
He promised power, he promised riches, but now we lay, underground.
Its those who forget our Mentor, the Man who gave us life,
It's those who forgot our Friend, who live their lives in strife.

Dedication: dedicated to all those I inspire

Cuban Missile Crisis, 1962
Krista Miranda
The ends of your pigtails
flew upwards
as you dropped to the floor,
creating a capital W
with the crown of your head.

They told you they'd
fall from the clouds,
like Mary Poppins
with a steel cap
and a bag full of tricks.

Do your knees still bend
instinctively
when you hear the sirens
(accidental plies
in drug store aisles
as an ambulance drives by)?
Are your hands still cold
from the linoleum?

I know the sky makes you nervous.

Her Repose
David W. Lucas
Where do you go when you know
That it's over?
Where can you turn when
The daggers won't stop?
Where do we sleep when the nights
Are too lonely?
Where do we crawl when the days
Are too long?
How do I breathe without
Thinking about you?
What can I do but
Write another sad song?

Keep sleeping...
(don't wake...)
Keep sleeping...

How do I scream when my
Lungs are left frozen?
How do I bleed when
The river's run dry?
How can I stand you're not
Thinking about me?
How do I rise when I
Break down and cry?

Keep sleeping...
(don't wake...)
Keep sleeping...

How do I leave when the door's
Left wide open?
Why do you say that you
Can't hear me call?
I know one day when
You see me so lonely
I know that I won't
Matter at all.

Keep sleeping...
(don't wake...)
Keep sleeping...

Indigo Angel
Bebe Butler

The day had bled completely into night, its deep indigo drawn over the sea
As she stalked the sands,
And though souls were sleeping
Their hearts followed her like a quiet, misunderstood longing.

Pieces, deep and still beautiful, wandered with her,
Out of their boxes
Into a world that hadn't found its periphery.

She was a strange angel, with Indian wings in violet blazes,
A Guatemalan canteen to her side, half-filled with water,
A band of pink flowers in her hair,
And bare, thick limbs that stretched upwards with an arrowless bow.

Gentle, yet full of adventure, as if to galvanize the stars
Her face glowed the soft, pink fire of wonder,
Trimmed in a cool, quiet mystery.

She lured the world into her gaze and allowed them to get lost
In truth again...
And for an evening they waded in forgotten beauty
Tucked deeply inside of her like secrets she promised to share.

Rag-A-Muffin
Helen J. Jarvis

She's a Rag-a-muffin of a dog,
Straggly-tailed.
She's a faithful companion,
rescued from the pound.
"Rags"; she idolizes her Master
patiently waiting when he's gone.
Following across the compound,
down to his office.
Laying at his feet as he works,
greeting all who come on business
or just to visit.
At the end of the day, they settle
in at the rectory.
A priest and his faithful companion
at the end of his busy day.
She's no ordinary dog, you see,
she's really his guardian angel,
she told me so one day.
Little did he realize when he
found her.
He just couldn't resist that
wagaly tail.
God had put her there for him
to find that day.
Angels take on many forms,
we just don't really know.
Somehow I think he knows,
keeping this revelation
in his heart.
God sent her to protect him,
not in a physical way.
Who are we to question,
the ways of the Lord.
The life of a priest can be lonely,
so I've been told.
Rags just lays at her Master's feet,
mostly you don't even notice her,
like our guardian angels.
Not realizing they're around,
Ever-protecting us from harm.

Dedication: to Dennis J. Carver and Rags

Heatwave
Olga Magliocco

Searing rays of sun
extend like claws of a cat
those who hide from her sharp sting
know she is there
as they feel heat
from her breath
as she prepares to pounce.

Cancerous golden eye
espies its prey
sweltering, shimmering haze intensifies,
each tail beat bearing down,
cracking Earth's dry and scabby skin,
smoldering, blackened forest
fanned—ignites.

Flames lick, swallow
explode with laughter
growing, greedily grabbing, consuming
all succumb to her sharp sting
scorched and withered
Earth, flesh, forest.

To See The Face Of The Lord
Frances Jeffrey

When you witness the coming of a new day
with the glorious sunrise;
rainbows that reach from one horizon to the other,
to the most beautiful of sunsets,
to the darkness of night, lit only by the moon and stars.

Lying on your back in the thick, green grass
looking to the Heavens and watching the clouds, big and fluffy,
animals, people, all kinds of things floating by.
Watching all the birds, both large and small, fill the sky
From Eagles riding the winds to tiny Hummingbirds darting to and fro.

From the top of a beautiful, snowcapped Mountain
to the winding, narrow and steep roads,
flat, lonely four-lane highway, or dusty, one-lane country roads,
A busy, dangerous big-city street, to a small-town business square;
being lost in the tangled, paved cloverleaf, or hiking in the thick dark
   woods.

Watching the waters rushing down the sides of the mountains,
to the clear, deep and cold, trout-filled mountain lakes,
to the rivers cutting paths down through the dirt and rock,
with its wild and exciting white rapids;
to the slow, trickling, babbling brooks in the valley floor.

To look from the high, magnificent cliffs and see for miles and miles;
and in the sides of the cliffs where people lived many years ago,
from the years of erosion the deep, colorful canyon walls,
to the enormous and unique rock formations,
and the never-ending plains and open prairies.

From the small, cool springs,
to the wells and farm ponds that were dug,
to the underground lakes and the caves which they made,
to the many natural lakes and vast seas,
to the magnificent oceans.

When seeing the vastness and beauty of all these things,
and having felt the tranquility and serenity
that surrounds you then and only then;
Have you looked into
The face of the Lord.

Enchanted Dreams

Lite Love
Ann M. Souder

You hold it out to me
arranged, pleasing to the eye
hungry, I reach and eat.
Biting down, fooled by the
aroma, taste and textures,
unaware I'm chewing on double–edged hope.

Hope that your food can show your love
fill me like you're unable to do—
with your words, your actions, your monies.
Hope that I will feel something more.

Chew, chewing in hope, on hope
expectations, obligations,
grinding self–acceptance into pureed mush
swallow and I'm still feeling hungry,
empty. It's not working. Time to eat again.

How long does one go on feeding
on hulls, empty of their seed,
their lifeblood. How long until
one recognizes this is not nourishment.
EMPTY love. Empty love.

The Never Born Child
Heather Dorman

Why didn't you just tell me,
    Or let me know that you were there.
When I learned of my precious cargo,
    You were already in great despair.

I wanted so badly to hold you that day,
    To count your fingers and toes.
To share you with your father,
    And to touch your little nose.

One of the things that hurts the most,
    Was never giving you a name.
I call you my "Little One",
    But it's never been quite the same.

You were not mine to keep,
    For God wanted your Heavenly smile.
But I thank Him every day,
    For letting me walk with you for awhile.

I've been told to let you go,
    That remembering will "have to do".
I've tried so very hard,
    But have too few memories to pull me through.

My love for you is a circle,
    It has no beginning or end.
So when I look up to the Heavens,
    Please know it's love for you I send.

Goodbye my "Little One",
    I'll miss you oh, so much.
And until we meet in Heaven,
    I will be longing for your touch.

I'll never completely let you go,
    My thoughts of you will often re–visit.
Not only did you grow two months under my heart,
    More importantly you grew IN it.

Dedication: to James John Meighan, my soul mate

Night Storm O'er The Shadows
Drew Toney

I hear you stumble far off
(in the distance)
I watch your fall like an
(empire)
I can see the day at night
(hours, lonely–soft flashes)
Before we've stood complete

Blown away, calling for peace
The sky frequents war within itself—
don't ask the rain for wisdom
don't seek from it help... retreat.

Calling off for
that smell, so clean and so sweet
We've listened to that steady sound,
irregular and neat.

But don't you lead me astray, rainbow,
The most beautiful part
is the storm

Raining down souls for the incomplete.

To My Guardian Angel
Kari Werner

Day by day, year by year, I grow stronger, becoming the person of which I
    am proud;
Uncertain and insecure no longer, if need be heard, I will be loud.

As life plunges on, I plunge in – swimming strong and in control, if it
    were a race, I would win.

Still something guides me, some force directs me;
It's coming from you, Mother, you are my Guardian Angel... you see.

You give me wisdom even when you have no answers, you give me strength
    even when you are weak;
You give me hope even when you feel hopeless, how is it that you are
    almighty and yet so meek?
3,500 miles away draws me closer – can you feel the pull?
It's that bond, it's that umbilical – it's you, Mother, guiding my soul.
Ironically, I hope my child feels for me, this painful ache I feel from
    our distance... sea to sea.

This yearning to be in your arms, close to your heart, close to your
    breast – it hurts to be apart.

How can I ever hold this noble title of "Mother" when I myself am the
    child?
Are there clues I need to uncover? Are the answers somewhere filed?

Where will I find the wisdom? Will I have the right stuff?
Where will I find the strength? How will I ever measure up?

I know where... it will come from my Guardian Angel – it will come from
    You, Mother;
You've passed on to me, a gift like no other.

The gift only a mother can give to her child – a gift I will hold on to
    for only a short while;
It is a gift that I will soon pass on, for I will be the Guardian Angel
    to my sibling... my spawn.

How can I ever thank you?

Dedication: to Robbi Booth

The Anthology of Poems

Cornstalk Stubble Under Snow
Oana Marian
How often, as a child, I wished to see
Some heavy snow. For if a field of corn,
Or what remained of it, appeared to be
Just patched with white, mid-winter's blanket torn,
The hillsides chafed my eyes and bothered me.

But since a year or two ago, I've found
An eerie comfort in these fields. The sky
Behind Magnolia Hill, the furrowed ground,
Seem like a deep, long-drawn-out winter's sigh,
Cut by a single kestrel's call. The sound

Grows faint, the echoes rarefy. And where
The snow spreads lightly like some rough-grained chalk,
Exposes yellowed devilgrass and bares
The tops of rudely-stubbled corn, I walk
Rapt in an idle trance and shade the glare.

Refracted by the silos' cold-sheened domes.
And when I've traced the furrows far enough,
Along the darkening tracks of ghostly combs,
When cutting lines and shadows become rough,
I have no reason left not to go home.

Happy Mother's Day
DeLoris Hartle
It's Mother's Day, Again and, as
usual, I'm broke
No gift to you, can I bring. Just
this homemade card, a smile and
maybe a joke.
You have to be, I'm sure, the
best Mom in the world.
You've given me love beyond
compare and raised me from a
little girl.
When times were to hard to bear
you were always there.
Reaching out to help, showing me
how much you really cared.
You have taught me right
from wrong,
giving me strength and a
song.
You taught me how to be
proud
And hold my "hurts" above
the clouds.
Your sorrows have been many,
but you've always managed to
survive.
And I've learned from you
just how great it is just to be
alive.
You've given me determination,
taught me how to cope,
With all life's frustrations,
And made sure I never gave up
hope.
So, if God ever made anything
better than a Mom
It could only be the rays from
the Sun.
That shine down upon you and
brighten up your day,
And we love you in "Oh, so
many ways!!!"

I Remember
Ashley Essig
I remember when we were Friends
Just about a year ago
But I never knew the way everything would go
It started out GREAT
But soon became HATE
Not against each other,
Mostly against yourself.
You were MOST likely to succeed,
Then you started smoking weed
I watched and I watched,
As your life began to fall,
And I never knew I could help you at all...
I remember you talking about SUICIDE,
BUT, in my head it was all just a lie.
I remember the night when you died,
Nowhere in sight was a tearless eye.
I remember thinking that it was my FAULT,
BUT, I knew deep down that you wanted that ROUTE
I miss you SO much and I wish you were here...
I can't believe it has only been a year.
I remember when we were friends.
It started out great... but soon, became hate
I REMEMBER...

I Still Call Her Mother
Julie Kite Hamilton
The baby was born quite small,
in fact, they say she could've fit in a coffee pot.
The lady grew to be quite strong,
and with her life she's done a lot.

She's the oldest of eleven children,
but the mother of just one.
She does so much for all,
at times it seems her work is never done.

She has always believed in sharing,
and would give her very last dime.
With everything that she gives,
she gives most of her very precious time.

She stays patient, kind and understanding,
and is very open about her love.
Even though she was born on Earth,
I'm quite sure she is an angel from Heaven above.

The lady has been through it all,
and she's seen a lot in her life.
Still she's remained quite devoted
as a child, a sister, a mother and a wife.

Her commitment to God and family
has remained constant through the years.
She stands strong through adversity,
but isn't too proud to shed her tears.

She is truly a good person
with lots of love and caring to give.
It is for these and other reasons
that I will love her as long as I live.

The lady's name is Martha,
and I could never want another.
Although she is my very best friend,
I still call her Mother.

Dedication: for Martha Kite, mother and friend...

Enchanted Dreams

In My Dreams
Danielle Kiedaisch
I talk with you in my dreams,
I feel your love in my heart.
I realize you're gone,
I know we're far apart.

My saddest days, they come and go;
There are some things I'd wish to know.
When all I can do is sit and cry;
My question, why you had to die?

It is said, "time heals all pain",
So why do my tears still flow like the rain?

Several months have passed by now,
And still I question how
I will make it through the day,
Wondering why He took you away?

God has plans for every season.
Who am I to question His reason?
Someday, Dad, we'll meet again,
But until then — I'll see you in my dreams
And keep your love in my heart.

What Happened, Nes?
Jackie Chandler
What happened, Nes?
Where did you go?
Talk to me, Nes,
I really need to know.

I heard your name on the news, Nes,
I couldn't help but cry,
They said that you were hurt, Nes,
Please don't say good–by.

Why did you have to go, Nes?
I went to your funeral today,
Everyone was crying, Nes,
Why must it be this way?

I really wanna talk to you, Nes,
I really am so scared.
I have so much to tell you, Nes,
Not enough time was shared.

I really miss you, Nes,
I don't know what to do.
Everyone is crying, Nes,
Everyone misses you.

I remember when we met, Nes
I never thought this could be.
I will never forget your smile, Nes,
You mean so much to me.

Can you hear me, Nes?
Are you listening to me?
Can you see me, Nes?
Are you Watching over me?

I can't believe this, Nes,
I won't believe this is true.
Please don't forget me, Nes,
'Cause I'll always remember you!

Dedication: to Vanessa Draper, beloved friend of mine

Sandra Dee
Stephanie Trevino
Smiling from beneath a velvet top hat,
she drowned in torrential laughter
that streamed out like summer rain.

Poems sprouted from her tongue,
each red or cracked or tangled in vines,
herself abandoned and groping for light
wishing on magic lamps for a sunrise,
lost woman as she was.

In the sweat of noon
she'd ride the white sidewalks
thirsty for a hand to hold her face
and finding men tucked in strange places:
under knees and behind ears,
they salivated over the slender hips
that rolled to her own erotic beat.

On the last day she was Going To Rise,
though I never saw her lifting wings
or ascending to her fantasies of dawn;
instead she succumbed to the sea of faces
that carried her off in its tide.

A Mother Remembers
Charlotte McCann
A mother remembers when her child is first born.
A precious little bundle with blue eyes or brown.
With lots of hair, or none at all.
She counts the fingers and then the toes.

A mother remembers when they first smile,
And then later, when they first crawl.
She remembers when they're sick and need to be
held, all night long.

A mother remembers their first day of school and
how hard it is to leave them, all day long.

A mother remembers all the little scrapes and
scratches and all the little hurts that had
to be kissed away.

A mother remembers all the animals, too. The ones
they just had to have, but couldn't find time to tend.

A mother remembers when graduation comes and the
tears she tries to hide from her pride and respect.

A mother never forgets when they're gone and on their
own, trying not to worry and has to let them go.

How can a mother forget when they marry. The feelings
just swell and the tears come willingly.

A mother remembers the grand–children that come.
She has lots more love and caring to be giving.

Why then, all of a sudden, the children stop coming?
There's not enough time to come and see mother.
No phone calls and so few visits. "We are just so
busy, " that she keeps hearing.

A mother starts to wonder, did I do something wrong?

A mother sits by the phone, but it will not ring.
They're just too busy to "remember their mother."

She Shouted No!
Helen Stapleton

Surely, when she shouts, "no!"
A man would have the decency to STOP!
Do all men believe that rape
Is just another complaint,
Made to save face?

To say "no!" Should mean "no!"
To struggle and resist
Doesn't mean she's enjoying it.
Does it have to be,
That you carry on?

The act of sex and lust
Is not only for a few minutes of fun;
It will break her forever.
And always, she'll believe it was her fault.

To have the feeling
That you'll never be clean,
To wash and to scrub
The hand-prints away.
Maybe invisible to see but
Possible to feel, over and over again.

Life
Rebecca Harrell

Standing, watching from afar.
Poor girl crying.
Tears are fading.
Red eyes clearing.

Little boy laughing.
Sad girl running.

Standing, watching from afar.
Little boy falling.
Pains are flaring.
Red blood flowing.

Little boy crying.
Sad girl helping.

Standing, watching from afar.
Children playing.
Boys and girls laughing.
Red lips smiling.

Little boy smiling.
Sad girl blushing.

Standing, watching from afar.
Little girl kissing.
Hormones are raging.
Red hearts beating.

Little girl loving.
Little boy lusting.

Standing, watching from afar.
Adults now walking.
Feelings are happening.
Red hands sweaty.

Little girl speaking.
Little boy speaking... I do

Standing, watching from afar.

Skeletons In The Closet
Bryce W. Rhymer

Skeletons in your closet, be they
Conscious or hidden away,
Are ever-active stimuli
That haunt you night and day.

Skeletons are very interesting;
They are dead, but yet alive.
They are unresolved problems
We attempt to bury, yet they still survive.

The mind, heart and spirit
Record all we ever do.
Deny, ignore or hide things;
Skeletons remain with you.

Usually when one tells a story
Especially when they're part of the wrong,
It's extremely rare for the listener to hear
Exactly where blame belongs.

Consciously or otherwise we go our way
Acting assured of what we've done,
But in the strangest way and strangest places
Up pops a skeleton.

Storms Of Life
Claire Awberry-Beck

The storms may rage and lightning fill the skies.
The
thunder
unrelenting
resounding
shields your
cries.
Cling to
our love
when the
flood
waters
rise.
I'll swim
in the
sea of
the light
in your
eyes.
We'll be
together
as the
storm
breaks
and the
sun
comes
shining
through.
I'll walk
to the
end of
the
rainbow
as
long
as
I'm
with
you.

Enchanted Dreams

Meteorologist's Mistake
W. H. Farrell
This weatherman could not take winter,
He despised the ice and snow!
But he was stuck in Minnesota—
As these things will sometimes go.

Saved up his whole vacation time,
And worked throughout the summer—
So he could have six weeks in winter,
To leave this frozen bummer.

He'd walk the wide and sandy beaches,
Absorb the sun's warm glow—
And think of freezing friends back home,
No doubt shoveling snow.

If you should like the happy ending,
There's something you should know—
Read no further of this tale,
And skip the verse below.

The upper winds that year were strange,
They played the wrong refrain—
In Minnesota... sun and fifties,
Where he was, six weeks of rain!

New Shoes
Mary Griffin
As she sat by the window,
her little feet crooked and drawn.
She watched as the other kids
played on the lawn.
She turned to me with a
Great, big smile,
"Mom, do you think I could go
out for a while?"
So I pushed her out to watch
the others play.
"Mom, did you know I'll run and
jump and play someday?"
My eyes filled with tears as I
tried to hold them back.
"Don't cry Mommy my feet's ok,
It's just magical shoes they lack."
I pushed her back in and put
her to bed and placed her pillow
under her head.
She hugged and kissed me, then
went off to sleep; as I thought
of the things she said, I began
to weep.
The next morning I went to get
her up to start a new day, But the
good Lord had come and taken
her away.
So Kelly now wears a new
Pair of shoes.
She can jump and run like
Other kids do.
She's happy now, with her new
Little feet; she dances with
The angels and they are hers to
Keep.
Her two little feet aren't crooked
Anymore, in her new shoes
She walks the golden shore.

Dedication: to Julian Griffin with love

Cap And Gown
Gregory B. Orton
Flute songs on the avenue
Long hairs with dancing fingers,
Adorn the night, with sweet sounds

A celebration, where families or origin
Observe the rights of passage
Gift cards, scrolls
And words about the future
While our past hastens regret

You saved your quiet songs of praise
Now, they will go unheard
Like the words of the flute songs, implied

We'll dance on the future's fire
Grace the American dream
with icy laments
Our robes are fantastic
as we prance

Vice for the lost child
Flowers on her grave, reason
a benign cancer
where the cap and gown are hung

Back To Life
Susan Bowers
Today is the day I celebrate the death of an old flame...
One where violence and hate were constant reminders,
Of whom I was slowly becoming.
Controlled by a force so evil and so painful,
A force that never again will rule my world.

Never thought it was my fault, although curiosity
Made me wonder why I was his chosen one.
The torture, the bruises and the broken pieces,
Were nothing compared to the strain it put on my being.

I never could leave, I was afraid of what he would do if I left
Or what he would do if I stayed.
I stayed with hopes that things could change.
They only got worse and my inner soul became destroyed.

My life grew fearful, like a puppet I became his.
My head was a wreck and my body full of bruises.
I was lost, but could I be found?
I had taken enough! My courage slowly began to grow.

He pushed me to the edge on that final day,
He threatened my family and threatened my life.
They had to take him out, it was the only way,
He wouldn't have left by a simple request.

He's gone now and I thank God every day,
That the hurt is going away and I am gaining existence
Back in the world that I once knew –
So peaceful, so quiet with such beautiful surroundings.

God bless those who ache and suffer from abuse
Hearts reach out, like mine,
To those who lack the strength
To live life the way life should be lived.

Your day will come, I pray you'll be strong.
Existence is so precious for you and for all.
Throw away the ghosts,
And join the world as I now know it!

Untitled
Andrew L. Borgheiinck

As I tread upon this ground,
Without a single, solitary sound.
I feel oh, so brave,
To place this rose upon your grave.

Where I stand was once your head,
Before you were set in this bed.
How I wish I could change your state,
But I don't know how to change fate.

If only I could have another chance,
To see you again, just a glance.
Even though this is a dream,
If only this story could have a different theme.

I will tell you I still remember,
All that happened in December.
Now I shall always hate the snow,
'Cause now I cannot see your Heavenly glow.

But as it states on your final resting place,
Rest in peace and with humble grace.
And here I stand, brave,
Placing this rose upon your grave.

Love, Love, Go Away
Nahed Fahmy

Love, Love, go away
I forgot how to cry

Go away with the cloud and disappear
I told you my heart is full of fear

When I see you, I have to fake
Shut off my sadness and hide my body's shake

Keep this voice away from my ear
I do not want to see, I do not want to hear
I told you my heart is full of fear
I do not have any more rivers of tears

Go away, love, go away
I forgot how to dream

I do not need these shiny eyes
I do not have tears to cry
I like my soul free spirit to fly
Go away love, kiss me and say good bye

I am proud of what I became
I am happy with who I am
I do not want to do wrong
I am happy with where I belong

Sorry I have trusted you before
I cannot trust you any more

Go away, love, go away

I told you once and I will say again
You do not have anything with me to gain

Go away, love, go away
I do not wish to cry
Just kiss me and say good bye

Dedication: to my son Ramsey Ackael

Someone is Always There
M. Goodman

No one is ever along, you know
If you breathe a silent prayer,
In the darkest night a candle glows,
To show you, someone is there.

No child is ever alone, you know
In the darkest night, aware
In the heart of his mother, her love shines through,
She is always there.

No one is ever alone, you know
Thoughts do show you care,
The thoughts of the one you love and support,
Will always show they care.

Life is a struggle at times, you know
That someone is always there,
In the heart of a person, their love shines through,
Showing that love is there.

As you say, goodbye, on a journey,
On a journey, you don't know where,
When there is hope in your heart, the love will shine through,
The Lord is always there.

Blackness
Samantha Gore

The blackness that encloses my heart strives to catch on fire
Burned again and again until the flesh can open anew in this
cycle of pain, perplexity, sadness,
hesitation, freedom and growing
Many can't understand this tortuous road leading to purity
I crawl on the cold floor yearning to let go, to free my spirit
from memory and fly from this place soaring as a feathered
creature high into the deep, dark, old and mystical night sky
where candles burn, where love is made, where vulnerability
is prized and blood and sweat drip and weep from my soul
I can't perform the impossible yet needing, permitting, wanting,
desiring, though no love will be unearthed instead flirting
turns into pain inflicted on others grasping for freedom turns
into suffocation from those who try desperately to grab hold
of emptiness in disguise laying down blackens the heart with
those who get a faint glimpse of what's hidden in the
depths of my wounded kaleidoscopic spirit
Why is suffering and pain so blindly oblivious to other people
when it distinctively is the healer of life
To bleed so deeply, to fight to allow it to abandon my soul
when it wants to impregnate itself
within my body as a prisoner with all the power
You ripped my eyes with your hands, you pounded me with
your intensity, you abused me like no one has nor ever will
again and you loved me fiercely with your dagger full of the
blood you stole from me despite the innocence in my tears
You planted your thoughts in my head and kept me tied down
I will escape, I will not wound and I will lay down with
what is love again
The lessons have tried to scorch me to my knees, but they
won't win, I refuse to give up, I would rather die than not
fight this insanity.
All those that love me, should leave me
All those that want to play I welcome into my tides— see if
you can fight the powerful prisoner, hurt me, tease me,
abuse me and never love me, cause you don't
know me and you'll never find the fear you want to control.
But choose to believe in me and see my murdered insides as
you watch me burn through the blackness that saturates my
veins, eyes, mouth and heart, but never the core of me.

Enchanted Dreams

The Impossibility Of Geometry
Diana Marx
Nature lacks geometry.
A pond is not round.
Each point equally distant from the center.
Even less so a lake or even a puddle.

Its surface never flat.
On a still day a breath, a ruffle, disturbs the horizontal linear.
Or a small bug walks across it.

The shortest distance between two points is not a straight line.

Which path is straight where a child often runs
From his house to a friend's?
A climber cannot take the straightest way
Up a mountain or a hill too steep or boggy to transcend.

Is one half like the other?
Cut a flower in half with a surgical scalpel so that the cut is clean.
Each half is different, each side their own.
No leaf, or feather, or the human nose
Can be cut in half to mirror the opposite.

Why do we hold these half-truths in such esteem?
What is round or straight or whole except in our own mind's eye.
Geometry blinds us to discovery.

Love Is But A Word
F. J. Lasala
Love is but a word and unless it is said with
Expression; as "I love you, " it is meaningless,
Love is but a word which has real meaning, for when
We know war, hunger and disease are eliminated,
That for us is priceless,
Love is but a word having an "L" which stands for
Life and through God's love we will have life forever,
Love is but a word containing an "O", an unbroken chain
Signifying love in return from the lover,
Love is but a word with a 'V' for vitality in love
Through courtship, care and devotion,
Love is but a word with a final letter "E" as in
Everlasting, excitement and emotion,
Love is but a word which is really expressed when
Lovers are playful and happy like a sunny day,
Love is but a word that comes alive when lovers
Give of each other in his or her own way,
Love is but a word that begins with attraction of
One person to another,
Love is but a word and words lead to a growing
Fondness, promise and then a joining together,
Love is but a word through a couples' conjugal
Love, comes their creation,
Love is but a word said many times to their
Children by their parents who for them have
Great expectations,
Love is but a word that suggests joy and happiness
But may portend pain and grief,
Love is but a word and through love we initiate our
Birth, nurture our growth, yet our time here is brief,
Love is but a word and yet can one really
Measure the love of child by its mother,
Love is but a word that has a profound meaning
When someone chooses to give their life for another,
Love is but a word and through an action of the
Love of God, the world was created, then man and
His mate,
Love is but a word and because of love we will
Return to God as our fate.

There May Be No Tomorrow
Richard W. Otto, Jr.
If you are living in sin, my friend,
Whether it be excessive or small,
And it makes you feel unconsciously good
And you have no remorse at all,
You had better wake up, my friend
And start using your head.
Because forgiveness may not be given to you
A long time after you're dead.
Who knows when Jesus will return
Could be today or tomorrow!
Are you going to continue your sinful ways
And have it all end in sorrow?
Whether on your knees or standing,
Confess your transgressions today,
For the Lord will surely forgive you
If you earnestly take time to pray.
It is said the last will be first
And the first will be last on that day.
Are you willing to take your chances
That you will be forgiven, as they say?
My advice to you, brother, is confess your sins today
And do not hold it all inside until the very end
Ask for His forgiveness and mercy
And forever try not to offend.
With His almighty guidance.

A Summer Not So Long Ago
Linda Frances Bogle
My memories as a child seem as yesterday.
All those precious Moments seem as portraits in my mind.
As if it were a certain point in time.
As five children raced thru the door and into the yard to play.
Swing the statues, red rover come over, hide-and-go-seek,
    favorites of mine.
As evening began to set, a sound would cross the breeze so sweet.
My loving Mama calling,
"children, it's suppertime come on in and eat. "
The smells of the food would be floating thru the afternoon air.
We would all race to the table where the food was prepared.
There at the table awaits Mama, Daddy,
Grandma and my loving Granddaddy.
He always seemed to have a loving smile upon his face,
His familiar words of, "children, come on in here",
was said with so much grace.
Here, at this point in time, a new game would be played.
With a smile and him asking us all, now just how was your day.
Smiles upon our faces and thoughts racing thru our heads,
The race was on of just who would be the first to say,
Just how much more important to tell about their day.
But laughter was broken with his kind voice of care.
Saying, "children let's all bow our heads in a word of prayer. "
His words, "thank You, Lord, for our food, family and the love
    we all share. "
When troubles and worries so often come my way,
I just shut my eyes and go to the point in time of yesterday.
Memories paint portraits in my mind to erase the worries of the times.
These words of my Granddaddy still linger in my ears,
Thank You, Lord, for all Your wonderful blessings on me.
Help me, Lord, to stand strong like that old oak tree,
With branches outstretched with lots of love for the whole world
    to see.
These are not only portraits of times long ago,
but when times were so sweet.
These memories will forever be sealed in my mind.
The summers which will always be set in time.

Dedication: to my grandfather George Washington Sullins

So Far, So Near
Hope McIntyre

Diverging worlds pass before my eyes
Diverse realms of rights and wrongs
A dichotomy of delving directions
Until I no longer know where to go
Or how to be found
Amidst a river of raging seas
And waves of disease.

O come with me
Swiftly follow the trees
Bellowing above the intrepid interests
Walk slowly to my side
My hair shall flow before your eyes
As soft as you shall know
Nowhere else to go.

Alone with this incestuous infection
Knees knocking my fingertips
Echoes call out from within
Touching the fathoms of unknowing knowledge
Lead me to this passioned point without relief
Leave me as I wither
I am gone again so far so near.

And you, what do you hear?

The Culloden Claymore
Terence Giles

At Culloden, he charged with claymore in hand, at the redcoats led by Cumberland.
When he felt the pain of the musket ball, that spun him 'round and made him fall.

He lay in silent agony, blood running down his wounded knee.
For a while he thought that he was dead, his kilt was soaked, his sporran red.
Heaven knows how long he laid, 'til the noise of battle began to fade.

Some of his clansmen came next day, picked him up and took him away.
They carried him to his parents' croft, who hid and nursed him in the loft.
Finally the redcoats went, after looting and killing, their anger spent.

Then he and the other hunted men, who fought so bravely on that fen,
Took a few things and began their flight, down to the sea where they sailed by night.
He had his claymore and a few gold coins, concealed in his sporran in front of his loins.

The weeks went by and they finally saw, the distant green Cape Breton shore.
As they stepped upon the welcome land, a solitary piper was on hand,
To play a lament for those who died and those who sailed the ocean wide.
To build their homes in this new place, where, as free men, they'd live in grace.
Raise their families by the ocean's roar and remember the dead of Culloden Moor.

Now his descendant's younger son, carries the highland traditions on.
He plays the pipes and wears the kilt and his own claymore with basket hilt.
On ceremonial occasions when he can, as a Canadian forces infantryman.

And proudly displayed in his front hall, is his forebearer's claymore on the wall.

Happy Endings
Susan Rimby Leighow

Tell me....

Do happy endings come in life
Or only in the movies?
Is Cinderella based on fact
Or did the Grimm boys lie?

I really need to know because

I, too, lost my glass slipper,
But Prince Charming never brought it.
Instead I turned into a pumpkin
Bruised and shattered, oozing pulp.

The knight in shining armor came
And pulled me up behind him.
But then he pushed me off the horse
Into the poison ivy.

And when I kissed the handsome prince,
He turned into a frog.
So can you understand
Why I really don't believe

In happy endings?

Snow Play
Susan L. Smith

Dawn brought scavenger birds of red, blue and brown,
As they cleaned scattered seed from the frozen ground.
Tree limbs crackled from the weight of blanketed snow,
As the chilled Earth took on a twinkling, mystical glow.

Children shivered with joy at seeing such a delight,
As the air filled with shimmering flakes that had fallen all night.
Fluffy snowsuits bundled children from head to feet,
As cheerful voices rang out up and down the street.

Sleds flew upon rolling ice-slick crevice's and hills,
As everyone spoke excitedly of their fun and thrills.
Silver blades glistened upon the magical blue crystal pond,
As skaters twirled and glided, as though touched by a wand.

Shadows extended deep beyond the starlit lanterns of evening.
As mother's called, at the end of day, "It's time for leaving."
Snowflakes wet their noses and wind burned each cheek,
As they crunched footprints, homeward bound, into snow so deep.

All in a row hung their crisp, dried socks, by firelight,
As little chapped cheeks were all aglow by moonlight.
Mugs of cider, steamy and hot, were poured from a whistling kettle,
As skate blades were polished and waxed, to a shining new metal.

Anticipating a brand-new day, they each laid down their sled,
As every child found their own soft little bed.
Stars brightly shining, they soon would be counting sheep,
As each little head snuggled deep into a goose down sleep.

Impressions of powder-soft snow bunnies slipped through their minds,
As dreams carried them to view wonderful, fun-filled times.
Drifting on whispering snow clouds they floated far, far, away,
As a new day reached out and asked them to return and play.

Dedication: to Fred, Loretta, Daniel and Timothy

Enchanted Dreams

Everywhere
David Frost
Every time I think of you,
I feel the love we share...
and every day I face the world,
I know that you are there.
I've never seen the beauty in
your eyes, your face, your hair,
but the part of you that I can see
goes with me everywhere.

Though I cannot be the one
to hold you, taste your wine
I take you with me in my heart
for it's there that you are mine.

Never now, should we despair
for we are destined to
Be one again, together when
I'll hold your love so true.

'Til then, keep me in your heart
as I will do for you
and remember this, above all else,
my precious love so true... I love you

Dedication: to Nicole, who opened my heart

The Paradise Of Snakes
Richard Fitzpatrick
The loneliest child who fate has now harrowed
Left to die in the remotest of places.
With coal for his eyes and lips of dry blood,
Now unrecognizable with a beaten-up face.

Alone and afraid, no love now is left here,
With tears streaming down for lovers to see.
A reasonable changing for all but the skeptics
Who challenge the lover still left inside me.

With uncontrollable anger and innocence of birthright,
A virtue that you just can't understand.
A license to live here with a view to a kill
Love still lies bleeding on so holy a land.

With love still a force in your bleeding heart
And arrows and slings beat you far from my door.
I find my emotions still jangling like nerve-ends.
You wonder if life is worth dying for.

You still lose no sleep for the pain of the suffering,
Symbolizing the paradise land of the snake.
The unenviable task of finding your freedom,
Where people run the risk of making that break.

The last time you see her in motionless gaze,
A horizon so beautiful, you can't look away.
Paradise found here on Heaven's own deathbed
Where dragons and lions so often are slain.

If ever you come across such power and such beauty
And feel the need to summon your Lord,
I shall not be far from the pain and the glory,
For we shall live by the strength of the sword.

The time we are left here is still in our hands,
But lovers and angels shall never forsake.
I use my own conscience to appear here in person
To the land they call "the paradise of the snake".

Man In Charge
Jana Endreson
Caught you in a lie
Smiling and talking as you were walking
With woman in charge, suit and skirt

The truth lay here
The lies you say in a business day
Are as many as the tasks we work for, you jerk
Us away from our homes once again

We stayed late and ate little to give you your numbers
Large and exact, their image so black in our minds

We went blind and inept, our fingers so bent
Pushing the keypads of productivity

Just a concept to you
Those numbers are real to us
What a horrible mistake had we refused to get on your bus

Look at you now
Your image and words like birds singing sweetly
But we heard your song of misconception

Look at you now
Not sweet but fat from your paychecks
And the effects of always eating the not-so-delectable truth

Souls
Casey Schuler
I hear them in the night
calling me from the walls

Sometimes they chase me
running through the halls

I just want silence from the moans and cries
of the someone or something that inside slowly dies

Trying to hide
I cover my ears, trying to control my fear

Covering my eyes
so the souls can't see my tears

My heart beating fast
every thought leaving me behind

Trying to catch up
I'm now losing my mind

Scared too much to move
I try and walk away from what I hear

The day is coming soon
the souls left living off my fear

I wonder if I'll hear them tonight
scratching on my wall

Trying to get out
I wonder if I'll see them in the hall

I lay down with the sounds of cries in my head
I wonder if they'll lay next to me while I'm sleeping in my bed

Or will they go off on their own
drifting away like night shadows

Hermetic Homes
Philip Anthony Antonacci

In winter they remain warm, heated through forced–air vents,
Seldom peering between sealed windows onto the barren streets below.

In summer they remain cool, chilled through forced–air vents,
Seldom peering between sealed windows onto the barren streets below.

Amused by media events, informed by the internet,
Challenged by the video game, seduced by the celebrity's fame.

Oh, come out from under the air,
Of the hermetically–sealed home,
To venture only down the street,
And stand with the others we meet.

For where have we gone,
But into the bonds of our comfort,
And what have we lost,
But the communion of our cohorts.

Speak to me, then, all you lonely ones.
Look at me, then, all you scattered ones.
Believe with me, then, all you sheltered ones.
Come with me, then, all you lost ones.

To gaze upon the distant shores,
Of lands beyond our sealed doors.

Ode To Mom And Dad
Anne Davis

It must have been planned in Heaven above
For Jeanne and Jerry to fall madly in love

For in 1960 he asked for her hand
And that's how the Davis family began

How could they know things would happen so quick
Four baby boys later, then finally one "click"

The trailer, the college, the sacrifices you'd make
The struggle to provide for your children's sake

The bottles, the diapers, the times they were sick
The reading, the writing, the arithmetic

Through baseball, soccer and Indian Guides
You cheered them all on, you gave them all rides

The bruises, the cuts, the scraped–up knees
The hunting, the fishing, the trips to the Keys

All the turmoils of being Dad and Mom
The tuitions, the heartbreaks, the dates for the proms

Then there were weddings, rehearsals and stress by the tons,
All for love of the girls who married your sons

You taught us "play fair", "be a good sport",
You always said, "life is too short"

You taught us the best things in life are free
You taught us to love unconditionally

And now we are starting families of our own
My, how strong your roots have grown!

Your years of support have helped us to grow
Thanks, Mom and Dad, for loving us so!

Commitment To Life
David B. Krisher

If I do not use, I cannot lose,
The things I hold so dear.
The family I love, my God up above,
To me this is now so clear.

I must work at my program daily
and join with my Higher Power.
The 12 steps I work, they keep me alert,
I'll eventually bloom like a flower.

My drinking and drugging were awful,
This I keep, in the back of my mind.
I can't dwell on it, but I keep it or slip.
My sobriety, it helps me find.

I have grown much closer to God.
The peace that He gives me is Great.
My honesty, purity and unselfish love,
I have found in my life, not too late.

My fellowship comes from A. A.
It really helped show me the way.
My serenity I'll keep and I'll never be weak,
and I'll deal with life, Day by Day.

Dedication: to Jill, my life's love

Dread Atonement
Maurice Oliver

To what is the author of this dread I my soul;
this deep–seated grief that denies to make me whole?

Where is the solace I once had as a child;
the peace found in innocence, when affections were mild?

Tell of the pain, of the dread that you feel,
when your body awakens to a new trial to deal.

Reveal the cardinal source of the dread in my heart
that lends to despondency of the life I impart.

Through my exhortations, I beseech to be glad again,
and relish the prizes life has to befriend.

Expose the demons that deride my attempts to be kind;
allow me to stop the torment and have back my mind.

Is it the fear of being a penniless man that causes my disdain;
the fear that my tombstone will echo that refrain?

Please self, won't you let me know of the genesis I can reprove,
then shall this lugubrious heart once again be removed?

What's that you say? I don't hear you so clear.
Are you trying to tell me it's my failures I fear?

Could this be true? Could it be as simple as that?
For if life has taught a thing, it's that honorable men do come back.

If the dread that I fear can be summed in such vein,
why should I accept a role as to be in such pain?

Shall I start this very day to improve the frame I am in?
Shall I use my newfound wisdom and walk tall among men?

I will avow this to be my creed from this Moment on,
to believe in myself and from this dread, do atone.

Enchanted Dreams

The Answer
Delores Hagerich
When I was a youngster,
I questioned many things...
What makes a rainbow?
And why a bird sings.

Then, as I entered
My teen–age years,
I began to experience
Many doubts and fears.

Temptations were many...
And true friends were few.
So now the "real world"
Came into full view.

But somehow I aimlessly muddled through
Many difficult and troublesome days.
The answers I'd sought for most of my life
Became clear, when I gave God the praise.

You see, He's the answer to all things
And the savior of all who just ask.
When I put Him first in my life,
Nothing is too great a task.

Dedication: Conemaugh Church of Brethren

Amidst The Storm
Ginger Sullivan
How does someone replace a loss so great?
That breaks the heart with each passing day.
Deep within the soul–it feels cold
Because your loved–one has gone on.

Soon questions with no answers arise
You then reply– no more pain can I stand
So I'll run and hide, close all the doors,
Let no one in, I'll find safety from within.

Days turn to weeks, weeks turn into years,
And soon you're old and your door is still closed;
"What if I'd opened it – a tiny bit?"
"Would loneliness still be my only friend?"

If only I'd just realized, life is full of sorrow and pain.
That God, somehow, would restore our hope in little things,
Blue skies, flowers in bloom, a baby's smile and friends
Who are true.

So don't linger long behind closed doors,
Your loved–ones – great and small – want you to give
The love that they shared with you.
The soul can only grow – the more you give!

Dedication: to my mother, Virginia Lewis Sullivan

The Childhood Magic Of Christmas
Judy Laqualia
Everyone's a child
At Christmastime it seems
We all have hopes and wishes
And special little dreams

Memories of Christmas past
When we were very small
Remember climbing out of bed
And hiding in the hall?

Keeping watch for Santa
With his great big bag of toys
Especially selected
For good little girls and boys

The lighting of the Christmas Tree
The carols that we'd sing
The prayers to baby Jesus
And the joy that would bring

Going off to Grandma's house
For turkey and some pie
And sometimes feeling very sad
Without understanding why

Things haven't changed
Now that we've grown
We've a secret place forever—
Within our hearts
Where childhood dreams
Can be retrieved — whenever

So while we share this Christmastime
With family and with friends
Remember that the magic's in our hearts
And never ends.

Dedication: to Dougie and Danny – always dream

Color War
Will Stafford
I fall to my knees,
Hidden in trees,
Perfection is key,
Or the rebels might see,

We are all one,
But not united,
So it's a war we fight,
For we have decided,

That we have differences,
That can't be settled,
With words and discussion,
Or paper and pencil,

They think they're better,
Think there's no other kind,
Some people see further than the skin,
Some people are blind,

He is black,
He is white,
Why do we,
Have to fight,

Those Confederates, they're wasting our life,
They're wasting our time,
Why can't they see,
Between the lines,
Our lives could be good,
Our lives could be joyful,
The Declaration says,
"All men are created equal",

In the light we kill,
In the dark we pray,
I guess it's worth it,
For a better day.

Thinking Of You
Ken MacKenzie

It's tough for us all, you being gone
When I'm alone, I think of what I did wrong

I know I never gave you the respect I should have
When I think of all the good times, you've been gentle as a dove

I'm sorry for all the times I made your day rough
But I cared for you and that was tough

I know that I never showed that I cared for you
But it's hard for me, what else am I supposed to do

When I heard that you had passed away
That night I cried and didn't know what to say

The one memory that was great, was fun and we told a lot of jokes
Was when you, April and I had that Diet Coke

We were so hyper for that whole night
I thought for the rest of our lives, it would be alright

I came up to see you, but I was not allowed in
I guess no matter how you look at it, I can never win

I you could have come home, we would have got together
And we will have fun and stay friends forever.

Cloud Cuckoo Land
Susannah Cooper

One flew over the cuckoos' nest to find a place where safely to rest
From the haunting presence of that deserted place, now an empty shell without a trace
Of the people, the suffering, that's lain within, veiled behind the walls
of the "loony bin".
It's far removed from those peering eyes and the figures that they hypnotize.

That black shadow creeps up from behind, an escape from which
you cannot find
It pervades every inch, every part of your being and stops you living,
stops you from seeing
The other world that people see, asylum is a place for you not for me
Taken away to the funny farm, to prevent themselves and others from harm

To a place where you can leave their pain and maybe learn to smile again
They often trace a fragile path as they find that they can really laugh
and laugh
And live to fight another day, take some Prozac, the doctors say
A pill full of sunshine to make you feel you're alive again and
life is real.

As they sit in the sun on a faded bench, she can feel herself gaining
strength and a tiny daughter kisses her hand while she is lost in
cloud cuckoo land.
Broken windows, dinners up the walls, the depths of despair,
she's seen it all.
Yellowing net curtains, nicotine-stained ceiling, a smokescreen of
tobacco and cannabis dealing

Recurrent psychosis, anxious neurosis, they each await their diagnosis
Voices they fear so much in their head, wishing they were really dead.
At the window the sketch of an anonymous face still clinging to the
human race
Look beyond and what do you see? Who's mad then?
Is it them, is it you or is it me?

Dedication: to Matthew and Katie

Reflections
S. J. Sell

I am your very good friend,
and yet your enemy, as well.
But still you come to me every day,
with our innermost secrets to tell.

You rely on me to tell the truth
but to be a liar as well
and then you curse and call me names,
because only the truth, I will tell.

I can show you no mercy
when before me you stand,
for I am your cruelest critic,
and yet, your greatest fan.

You ignore me, love me, treat me with derision
blame me for every wrong decision.
Not once have you ever shown your delight
by thanking me, for getting it right.

Once more I'm left on my own
whilst you're partying at the ball.
But then again I'm just the mirror,
hanging on your bedroom wall.

Dedication: to William, for your encouragement

Anniversary
Connie Anderson

On this day we commemorate,
A Wedding on February twenty–eight!

Fifty years ago, Joe and Sue,
Said I Love You and I Do!

For better or worse,
So goes the verse.

For richer or poorer.
Who could ask for more?

In sickness and in health,
They did this one with stealth.

To have and to hold,
This statement so bold.

Till time us do part,
Spoken from the heart.

With this ring, I thee wed.
That was what they said.

Through laughter and tears.
Love has grown through the years.

They were blessed with children two.
Then came challenges anew!

They were blessed even more.
With their Grandchildren four.

This meant more love to share.
For a special couple who care.

Fifty years have come and gone.
And still their love is a paragon!

Enchanted Dreams

True Love
Raymond Raine

True love, like the river, flows,
From start to finish, ever grows,
Through meadows, valleys, crags and hills,
With wondrous beauty, the Earth it fills.

Deserts it turns to fertile lands,
Life created from scorching sands,
Sustaining crops and all God's creatures,
Enhancing views and wondrous features.

Springs contribute crystal waters,
Offspring may be sons and daughters,
Who will in turn find them a mate,
True love will then perpetuate.

The journey's constant without a falter,
But the course, at times, will surely alter,
Sometimes slow, sometimes in flood,
With patience turning all to good.

From nature's tears in tiny, upland streams,
Gaining strength, fulfilling wildest dreams,
At last down to the wide and open sea,
Ne'er to return, but you must come to me.

Dedication: to my dear wife, Joyce

They Of The Earth
Dennis A. Zelazny

They spread their caustic seed through virgin channels,
acquainting themselves with the local fauna
and the dim, sweet flowers of doom, sating themselves
upon the honey–sweet flesh of our naive youth.
They'll bide their time while the whole Earth consumes the
remnants of its own decay.

A new species they, spawned from conditions we have laid
for centuries, the inheritors of all that we have been,
all that we have bequeathed, all that we can no longer support,
adapt to or tolerate.
A new species worthy to succeed us! Creatures devoid of
innocence, mirth and gaiety. Revelers in dirt, muck and slime.
Products of greed, neglect and self–indulgence. Oh, can't
you see them already, encased in their steel cars and buildings,
their rusting, rotten armaments, or running rampantly through
the streets of the cities like stray chimeras, zombies and goons?

They're coming by the rag–tag horde, holding aloft one filthy,
bloodstained placard:
"We are you and you are us. You cannot escape us. We have
lived inside of you long enough. Now it is our turn to walk
the Earth. You shall forfeit all. We will live the longest.
We will witness the demise of the sun! We will gladly go
down with the Earth. If you should survive in spirit
(for your bodies we shall have long ago eaten) you may yet
plan the strategy for your redemption, your timely resurrection.
We will laugh sardonically at your suffering. We will not care
whether you succeed or fail. It will be a matter of indifference.
We will rejoice over the agony of your struggle to ascend,
even as we die so horribly, so utterly, without the hope
that sustains you."

On a once jewel–like, blue and green planet, in an obscure
corner of an obscure galaxy, a new race of fair, near Godlike
men and women, more spirit than flesh, strides triumphantly
over the crumbling corpses of the millions who have gone
before them – the last generation, they of the Earth.

Apollo 99 (Baby Boomers' Lament)
Wayne D. Wheeler

What of the moon?
Worthy of thought?
A desolate waste that God forgot?
"One small step for man, a giant leap for mankind!"
What is gained or lost in knowing?
Still out there glowing...
Man's crowning glory?

Same old story!

Baby Boomers' Babel, minus one tower
A vain attempt in man's final hour...
To regain his lofty self–appointed place
Alone, monopolizing God's attention, in this vast, endless space.

'Tis not for me to say
But, if I had my way...

The Man in the Moon would live without question
Its soft glow would still inspire romantic suggestions
The tides will always rise and fall without any help from us at all!

"Red moon at night, a sailor's delight..."

Alas! Enough of this lunacy!

LET'S ALL HAVE A HUNK OF GREEN CHEESE!

The Rest Home
Sheri L. Burkhardt

When I walk to the door of the rest home each week,
I see the same, sad faces
So pale and so weak. As I walk inside and all I see,
is every elderly patient looking
At me. You can see in their eyes that they're lost in time,
wondering is she a friend of Mind? I smile and say
"Good Morning"
as I search for my friend in room 65, and I feel these
People are barely alive. Many all humped over in their
wheel chairs asleep, not a Comfortable Moment can they keep.
Each day for them is harder than the one before,
Until one day they can go no more.
As I walk into room 65, my friend
sits looking up with
A smile, "How did you find me? Please tell me so."
I tell her I see her each and every
Week, for this is a promise I try to keep.
We talk about the days of old, these memories
I will forever hold. Her memory is short from one minute to the next,
like a book with jumbled text. I understand this comes with age,
life is like writing another page.
If I could only write how happy the golden years should be,
because what I write and what
They are, are two different things, you see.
We should live our golden years happy and pain –
Free, but it's the opposite, you see. So live life to the
fullest while you can, while your hearts
Are young and free, because before you know it, it may be you
sitting in room 65, waiting for
Someone to see. I give her a kiss and go on my way and she knows
I'll return on another day.
I walk to the car with tears flowing down my cheeks,
I've made it through another visit this week.
Some say, "Why do you put yourself through this week after week?"
I only hope within my heart, when my golden years are here,
that a friend of mine, will
Share her time, to make my life complete...

The Anthology of Poems

A Poet's Mind
Jennie Clary

It frightens me to know what
A poetic mind can discover
In the depths of thought.
The magic of the word expressed
In hidden splendor. The changing
of colors into words and words into
colors.
The soul turned inside–out to
Impress those who will listen
And understand.
To whom else can God and
nature dare to unfold and give
such a gift.
Some thoughts which only a
few can comprehend and others
only sigh; To make the mind
Swell, till it bursts into rhyme.
What is this power given to
a handful of so–called geniuses.
Thoughts that run rampant through
The streets at my mind. Words of
fire to flame the heart. Words
rhyme to boggle the mind.
A Gift from God, not to be
wasted. Each day a new generation
unfolds, the explosion of
The inner soul.

What's This Mean To Me?
Norma J. Boyll

Have you ever asked, "what's this mean
to me?"
About the birds in the sky, the sun and
the moon.
About the leaves on the trees and the
Flowers in June,
These are God's things, that He has made
for us,
with His Grace, His beauty and His
everlasting trust.
We take them for granted, the colors,
the hues,
Until something happens and we can no
longer choose.
Then we have a wake–up call that brings us
back where we belong,
It can be gone in an instant or a blinking of
an eye,
This beautiful splendor that's been put here
for you and I.
Oh, how I would – miss hearing a child laugh,
see their smile, or hear my mother's
voice as she talks with me a while.
To feel my husband's gentle hug as he kisses
me goodnight,

Dedication: to my mother, Ola M. Lynch

When I Seat Alone
Ruth Taylor

When I seat alone
Cannot stop thinking of you
When I alone
My heart will along belong to you.
When I seat alone
I know you are so far away
When I seat alone
need you here knowing you cannot
be here
When I seat alone
my world so very pull when you was
in it.
When I seat alone
I knowing your soul and spirit be
around
When I seat alone
need the touch of you holding me
in your arm pulling close to you
When I seat alone
When I realize you are not go
to be their for me
When I seat alone
I feel my heart beating so
aloud for you
When I seat alone
knowing hear me call out for you
in pain
When I seat alone
coming to point of time
knowing
When I seat alone
will never be back again
for me
When I seat alone
I find myself holding on
to love had one together in
pain of lost for you.

To My Children
Verna L. Kammen

It's been so many years since the patter of little feet
From one room to the other helped make my day complete.
No more chubby little fingers building castles in the sand,
No more "Trusting Little People" asking Mom to hold their hand.
But I have many pleasant memories that I will not forget.
I thank God for trusting me with the best job Moms can get.
It wasn't always easy, but you made it all worthwhile,
I'd do most anything I could just to see you smile.
It was hard to tell you no, when I wanted to say yes.
But I cared too much to let you do harmful things, I guess.
From the time that you were little, I really tried to show
You how to live for Jesus, though I made mistakes, I know.
I think that you all loved Him as long as you were small,
You loved to hear His word and you believed it all.
But then as you grew older you had to "do your thing, "
You "flew the coop" away from God and often broke your wing.
You began to doubt His word and didn't count the cost.
Now my heart is burdened for those who still are lost.

For you, beloved children, I pray this earnest prayer,
That when I get to Heaven I'll see your faces there.
If I should go before you, to some I'll say "goodbye"
To some I'll say "so long", perhaps you'll ask me why.
The ones I say so long to I know I'll see again,
For you've repented of your sin and now you live for Him.
But if you are rejecting Christ where will you go then?
For when He comes to claim His own He'll also judge all men.
Precious children, don't you know, it's Jesus that you need,
To free you from the yolk of sin, then you'll be free indeed.
As Jesus wept for Jerusalem He weeps for souls today,
He's knocking now at your hearts' door, dare you turn Him away?
Then my burden lightens, for God's promises are true,
That if I taught you His word it would not depart from you.
As much as I would like to, I cannot spare you pain,
Nor sickness, trial or sorrow, these things on Earth remain.
But a better place awaits you if you choose to meet me there,
So I'll go on believing God will answer a mother's prayer.

Enchanted Dreams

Another Shift
Robbin E. Down
I have walked from the parking lot and into a foreign country....
with no time for adjustments.
I have been coughed on, sneezed on, thrown up on and held a hand
while blood silently dripped on my already-soiled shoes.
I have endlessly explained procedures in lay terms without a note of
gratitude.... only to hear accolades of praise for the physician who
repeated word for word, my previous explanation.
I have turned the heat up in closed rooms, transforming them to ovens
while the sweat rolled down my brow, to my nose and to the floor.
I have worked without lunch, without breaks and have not emptied
my bladder for unending hours at a time.
I have politely answered to a gruff.... "Hey, you, Blonde!" My life has
been threatened by a patient whose life was saved.
I have listened to a colleague question an order and be humiliated in
front of a patient.
I have wiped bloody footprints up outside the trauma room, I have said
prayers for strangers, hung toe tags on children and spent hours on the
phone, attempting to reach family members.
I have felt fear grip my soul, like an icy wind... Run down a hall when
I didn't think I could walk another step.   Stayed an extra hour, or two,
or three.
I have combed someone's hair, brushed someone's teeth and grabbed
a coffee for the visitor in room 5.
I have often looked up and asked where God is... I have found the
Answer in an old man's eyes and his wife's tears.
I have gone home at night, only to continue my shift, in my sleep.
I have watched the sun rise on my way to work... knowing my life
Makes a difference.

My Nan
Jenny Quinn
Grandma, Granny, Nanny or Nan to a Grandchild these words we are told
Belong to a person who has touched our lives and who has that heart of
gold.

Memories are so many, good and bad alike
From caravans in cold October to Sunday dinners on a Sunday night.

The house in which she lived, the familiar smells, the familiar rooms
Each one holds a happy memory, no sadness, no dooms, no glooms.

The friendly face that always looked up whenever you walked in the door
And in the last few days of her long life, the fragile look I'd never
Seen on her before.

The pictures of the family in every desk, cupboard and drawer
Pictures of the family on every shelf, table and wall.

When I touched you so warm and silent the tears fell, I couldn't help but cry
My watery eyes looked down at your hand in mine, so still, just waiting to die,
For who was the one who never found fault, who never sought to blame
To whom you went to when trouble comes, whose love remained the same.

Pictures, letters, cards and memories are all that are left to us now
It'll be a long time before I see you again, but maybe, someday, somehow.

When I go out and look outside and shout your name aloud
I expect to see you looking back and hear your laughter from a cloud.

I know if I need you, you'll be there to give advice and lookout when you can
So I'll ask my Dad and my Grand-Dad now just to please look out for MY NAN.

Dedication: to always forever nan, dad, grandad

CCC Trucking Song
Vernon Archer
From the shores of California,
To the rock-bound coast of Maine;
We 3-C boys are on the job,
In the snow or sleet or rain
We do not shoulder arms or drill,
All our work is done in peace;
We are proud to bear the tittle,
of the US C. C. C.

We are ever-ready anytime,
Whether it be night or day;
Our work is done in every part,
Of the dear old U. S. A.
Wherever you may find us,
In a ditch or felling trees,
You will always find us on the job.
The U. S. C. C. C.

When the roll is called up yonder
And the sound off, one by one;
Every 3-C boy will answer "here"
When our work on Earth is done,
But in case they ever need some Trees,
To plant on Heaven's Scenes;
St. Pete will sound assembly,
For the U. S. C. C. C.

Dedication: to Leonard Melvin Archer

Combinations
Leroy Grier
Many have said, "you are Old, " but
this is the message, "I want told. "

There was a time when love made you
bold, Friendships were something to
behold.

Your neighbors were truly your friends,
It was an respectful relationship that
endured to the end.

Now progress has made its mark, nothing
is left in the dark.
Information; gained at the punch of
a key.
New flashes for all to see.

The economy is at its highest, but
we the people can't eliminate
our bias.

It's logical to summarize; that
hate is on the rise.
No one seems surprised, when
Many are hunted and traumatized.
One dilemma we all face; We
Need to make this world a better place.

Give love of old another chance
Surprise! Civilization will still
advance.

Love with Harmony,
Will replenish the economy.

Dedication: to Betty, my inspiration

The Anthology of Poems

Petals
Aubree Silver

Before I knew you, I was a dying flower. Picked before my time,
petals torn out, one by one, as they reached for florescence.
But how I tried! Perhaps it was the chill in the air, the frost on the
ground, the ice in their veins that inhibited my growth.
"Please," I begged, "let me show you my joy and the poetry of my heart
that is somewhere locked within... I know it could be sweet".
Perhaps it was my own thorns; no one could touch my soul.
Surface faults, fear, hate and submission all made me into poison. Real
parts of me, yet yearning to escape and reveal my hidden innocence.
Sometimes I felt nearly safe and my petals would start to creep open.
Bold and ready to give.
But always too soon and they tore my petals out so cruelly, casting what
I thought was true love on the ground and crushing it to pieces.
And suddenly, you walked out of the shadows and encouraged this dying
flower.
You showed me the natural sunlight, fed me with patience, gentleness and
what I now know is love.
I've become a rose, alive and vibrant, with petals in full bloom.
You've shown me my own beauty, my ability to grow tall and strong.
I can honestly give you my love, knowing that I will receive it.
This connection seems unreal, but truth lies in your touch... You have
become sacred.
You, who did not crush me, but adored me; My petals open like an eternal
sunrise.
You, the water of a rose's existence...
And I will live on and on.

Dedication: Billy, the petals are yours

Caedere/Genos
Ron Christian

Concentration camps of prison
Extermination a ruler's vision
Flesh–draped bone could not hide
Hatred shown they who decide
Strong men weep, stench of death
Of bodies heap, mask their breath
A vapor shower, a final flame
A country's power, one man we blame
Beneath the Earth they disappear
No age of birth or passing year
No lesson learned of yesterday
We have returned that fateful way

An exodus beyond belief
Roads of dust, no relief
Hope will find destination
Leave behind annihilation
Frightened village of whom remain
Come to pillage these brothers Cain
Machete blade their bodies shred
From view they fade along riverbed
Beneath the Earth they disappear
No age of birth or passing year
No lesson learned of yesterday
We have returned that fateful way

Love thy neighbor, false pretension
Sheath thy saber, no intention
Endless war, generations past
To even score in stone, it's cast
The world will wait, their end is near
To live with hate, you die in fear
Beneath the Earth, they disappear
No age of birth or passing year
No lesson learned of yesterday
We have returned that fateful way

Children and Light
Diane Netherland Baxter

Like the flower pushing up through the Earthy mist toward the
sun.

So is the child sown in Earthly abyss yearning for one.

Just one to guide, to love, to correct and hug.

Fragrant is the flower and tender. The breathy wind tosses it
here and yonder.

Harsh is the hurt when placed in a pot and numbered without
thought.

The soil is not as rich nor are the neighbors warm and stable

The roots fail to reach deep and the blooms display the
drought.

Untended, the weeds move in and disable.

Eerily, the pain is numbed with a cold, unnatural glow.

Quietly, the tender sprout dies without turmoil. The tomb is
the silent, weeping bough.

But, what about the child. How does he grow?

Dedication: for thought to all

Oh, Jesus, Shine Your Light
Charlene A. Hayes

Sometimes as we travel down life's busy roads, they seem so dark
and lonely, where do they seem to go? Everyone seems to be in
a hurry, not really caring which way they go.

Oh, Jesus, could You shine Your light down, could You shine Your
light so the world could see, could You send Thy Holy Spirit
down, could You send Thy Spirit to teach us Thy way?

Sometimes as we travel down life's busy roads, we get so confused
which way to go. It's so easy to get lost on these roads, it's
so easy to lose our way.

Oh, Jesus, could You shine Your light down, could You shine
Your light so the world could see, could You send Thy Holy Spirit
down, could You send Thy Spirit to teach us Thy way.

For as we cross over rivers and through the valleys and climb
the mountains, there seems to be a bright light shining down
on a very special road, it seems so peaceful. I can feel Thy
gentle Spirit feeling my soul.

Oh, Jesus, why can't we seem to stay on this special road, why
do we have to wander off on our own? For I know Your light is
shining down on the world to see, so why can't we seem to see
Your light, could it be the clouds in the way, or maybe it's
the tears in our eyes.

I hear a soft voice whispering, Oh, My Child, there are many
roads you must travel and many rivers to cross and many valleys
to go through and many mountains you will climb. For you will
never be alone. For My Light will always shine for the world
to see.

Oh, My Child, stay on thy special road and let your light shine
for the world to see. For Your Father, His Son and thy Holy
Spirit shall always travel with you wherever you may go.

Enchanted Dreams

The Window
Helen Peterson

I see birds fluttering in my garden starting a nest
in my holly tree. Tiny little buds appearing after the rain.
A big tree stretches its leafy branches under the first sun.

It's spring.

I see sunflowers, velvety grass, colors everywhere.
Patches of dry soil around my blossomed garden waiting to be watered.
A bee swarms over my lilac tree, attracted by its sweet smell.

It's summer.

I see golden leaves floating in the air, then finally touching ground.
The trees are lowering their dried branches.
In the gray sky birds are flying towards a warm climate.

It's autumn.

I see a white blanket of snow covering my garden.
A bleak sun peeks through the dense clouds and kisses the tree.
Drops of melted snow falling like a string of pearls.

It's winter.

I see days, months and years fly.
I see life flashing by

Through my window!

The Three Sisters
Bertha Givins

On the trails of the Old Blue Mountains in Australia far away,
Comes the tale of The Three Sisters who were turned to stone one day.
Legend tells of how their father left his daughters all alone,
In search of food to nurture them in the valley far below.

Now there was a frightful creature who resided on the way.
And that day he lay a–sleeping in his dark and musty cave.
When a strange, loud noise awakened him from a dream in
which he craved, just to dine upon his table, meals of fine,
young, tender prey.

'Twas a stone thrown by the sisters at a centipede that day.
Who did not know the thunderous sound the tiny stone
would make.
And when he looked up at the shining cliff where the sisters
cringed with fear, he desired to devour them and go back to
sleep again.

But the father of the sisters heard their loud and desperate cry
and he saw the frightful creature when he leaped up towards
the sky.
So to save his lovely daughters, he took out his magic bone.
And he waved it towards the sisters and turned them into stone.

Now the creature became angry as he turned to face their Dad,
who turned himself to a Lyre–bird with the magic bone he had.
But in his haste to get away he dived into a cove.
And the magic bone fell from his beak to the valley far below.

So if you ever go to Blue Mountains, you must go by to see.
Where Three Sisters stand in silence, beyond the Eucalyptus trees.
While the Lyre–bird in the valley searches for his magic bone,
to change them back to mortals and take his family home.

Dedication: love to Dana, Sherrie, Mike and Mark

Missing In Action
Jo Scott

Hey Mom, I'm goin' for a walk and takin' little brother
Ah, don't worry, Mom, we'll be back for supper
Supper's getting' cold, it's a quarter to eight
Where could they be, they've never been so late...
Missing in action.

Mama says, "Son I've got some shoppin' to do"
"Mom, can I look at toys 'stead of goin' with you"
One small child in a busy shopping mall
Mama comes back, now he's not there at all...
Missing in action.

Left alone in the car, behind locked doors
Said he'd only be a minute, had to run into the store
Daddy returns to see the door opened wide
Oh, dear Lord, there's no one inside...
Missing in action.

It's a great big world for such a little one as you
With each approaching day, this is what I'll do
"Father, please protect them, angels go forth
Watch them every second, in the name of the Lord"

With baby in the shopping cart, Mama bends to get the soap
A stranger grabs the baby and puts her in his coat
Soon an Earth–shaking scream and the man is seen
Thank God this child won't be...
Missing in action.

Give Me Free
Linda Ann Taylor

Give me free is a righteous (wo)man's cry, give me free from this white man's lie:

Give me free, to return to my own, to walk with my mate hand and hand, to take care of my family the only way a free man can, with pride, with my creator at my side.

Give me free, to praise the creator of the sunshine and rain. Free to follow that luminous star from which my salvation came. Free to love myself for who I am, black and beauty like the night, pure as ebony, ivory and gold. The way my story should have been told, authentic and bold.

Give me free, to love my mate, black and strong, holding me close Into the dawn, as we live our lives as one. Free to express that unity that keeps us together even when we are apart. Free to encounter that freedom upon which this country was born. Where all men are created equal with undeniable rights of liberty and glory in. Understand just what I said, remembering whose name is on the Liberty bell. Oh, well.

Give me free, to love as a free (wo)man ought, endlessly with passion running hot and cold from deep down in their soul. With a distance as far as the eyes can see, you tried to separate my lover and me. But little did you know or could appreciate, still waters run deep, deeper than your empty mind could perceive, stronger than any chain You can shackle me in.

Give me free, realize you are wrong, for trying to take my identity, My soul, take away my hopes and dreams. You beat me, starved me, raped me, too, hoping I would see things the way you do. You concealed me from your history books. Thinking it would keep you safe from me, again you lied, here I stand with truth on my side.

Give me free and release your chains, give me free and together we can build a better nation.

My Ebony Queen
Alice Elaine Young-Powell

What is a queen? An Ebony Queen – soft–spoken, yet concerned.
Free – spirited although very stern. Not rich with jewels,
not anyone's fool.
Days appeared sunny even though there was no money.
Didn't own any foals. She danced with lots of soul.
Food would get low but God multiplied it and made it grow.
Rich with love that could supply the Canaan Islands.
Never resorted to any type of violence. Dreams appeared
shattered, it didn't really matter. For prayers were answered before you
could chatter. Family came first in the needful struggle.
Words seem hard sometimes for thee. Words about my queen
flow free you see. A promiscuous husband that wasn't a big loss.
Three little children to add up the cost. She was short in her build,
not stubborn–willed. Strong, courageous black queen, but a mother still.
Fought the height of her battles ill, holding on to her sex appeal.
Broke financially, sick physically but rich spiritually.
Beautiful black pigmentation of her skin that appeared Ebony, s
omewhat a teasing brown, could this be the queen of my
dreams – a mother to me, a father to me, a sister to one and a
friend to all. Missing my queen dearly, tears fill my eyes causing
me not to see clearly. Doubtful sayings, doubtful
beliefs, doubtful dreams that cause one to fear. Experienced
heartaches and pain, advice ringing in unison in my ear, one you told
your daughter dear. Now that you're gone to Heaven, your new home.
Your great wisdom has set me free.
My Ebony Queen known as Mom to me.

Dedication: to my mom, Mary Alice Young

July, 1991
Amy L. Patlan

Well, someday
Chet
Tell me about your father
How he has filled your life,
your mother's,
your sisters',
your brother's,
with pain. I
Feel for you
now
Because you've had to deal
With so many things in chaos, in love, in the night, in painting
your pain.

Glad for you
though
That you have found someone
And she makes you feel so good, you deserve that, you really do, you
need passion,
not pain.

Glad for you
that
You've rid yourself
of Christine, of
your pain.

Going
away
Today to a wake in Lombard, for Chet
Christine
threw herself
in front of a train
the other day
and now I feel
his pain.

In The End
Colleen Hughes

Eventually...

Destiny will jump blind–folded
into a swirling whirlpool that bubbles furiously
with fear and hate and pride
and envy and triumph
and Love

Eventually...

An elevator will run from
Heaven and hell
and trap death on the thirteenth floor

Eventually...

the bell jar will shatter,
Pygmalion's statue will breathe life,
George and Lennie will live off the fatta the lan'

Eventually...

we'll meet Holden in the rye
and taste the flavor of irony
and forget the dusty path road

Eventually...

hope will be seen in a sidewalk crack

Getting Older
Joan T. Smith

Older means being wiser than our youth.
Why, then are my insides so filled with doubt?

Older means knowledge. The ability to make decisions.
When, then, do I feel such uncertainty of mind?

Older means a sense of security.
Why, then, am I filled with such a fear of tomorrow?

Older means being able to say what you think and feel
Without caring about the world's demands.
Why, then, do I lock what I think and feel within me,
covering it up with the proverbial wisecrack and laugh?

Older means being able to reach out to others who need
you and reaching out to others when you feel a need.
Why, then, do I hold back tears and words, feeling that
those others will think me foolish?

GETTING OLDER: When will I ever find again that
carefree feeling, the laughter that once came so freely,
the imperfect loves that were so sincere, if not lasting?

Would that the future years, however few, would give
peace of mind, laughter and smiles, a lightness of heart
rather than the heaviness that seems to engulf...... and,
perhaps, a little bit of that imperfect but sincere
love that seems to be the most evasive feeling of all.

GETTING OLDER:
It the truth be told
I am not getting older.
I.... AM.... OLD...

Dedication: to my dad with butterfly kisses

Enchanted Dreams

Locked Inside Myself
Lisa Cuellar
Locked down by a ton of chains
Sometimes I can't remember my name

So insecure, can't make a choice
I'm not even sure I have a voice

Would anyone care if I expressed
All the feelings inside that I've suppressed

Would they give an ear or turn their head
If they knew of all the tears I've shed

I'm in a room but it has no door
I'm not sure if I can handle it anymore

I feel so lost with nowhere to go
So much hard work and nothing to show

I'm running full speed, but I'm right where I started
And then I wonder if I had ever departed

My head is floating or is it attached?
I start going forward but I always fall back

Nobody knows what I'm feeling inside
Just give me a rock to crawl under and hide

And I'll hold this all in and put on a smile
Though I'm truly crying inside all the while...

Roses For Daddy
Imara Vanessa Otero
I remember all the love that you fed,
how you liked to eat butter with your bread
and the wise things you said;
with a rose of red.
I remember your witty humor so pure and light,
how our chats would last through the night
and how you would hug me so tight
with a rose of white.

I remember the loyal, friendly fellow,
who greeted me with a sweet whistle that said "hello"
and your nature so calm and mellow;
with a rose of yellow.

I remember your adoring affection in a blink,
your unconditional love when my world was about to sink
and the way you would smile and then wink;
with a rose of pink.

I remember the things you loved to teach,
making me believe there was no goal I could not reach
and our many memorable visits to the beach;
with a rose of peach.

I do not remember your woes that tormented you so,
the demons of regret being your greatest foe
that always reminded you of your times of low;
for nowhere does a rose of blue grow.

With these roses in hand, I go and visit you,
the soft, pretty petals in almost every hue
however, the roses are always moist with dew;
from the tears I spew since the Moment of losing you.

Dedication: to my parents Marvel R. and Delia M. Otero

Norma
Jill M. Pardoe
Out on the street she would stoop just to greet a doggie that had a nice smile
Or walking along she would pause for the song of a purr or some pussycat guile.

When visiting friends she made no amends for ignoring the talk or the fare
If the cat was around she would stop for the sound of a chat with a bundle of fur.

Then off to the back, in her gabardine Mac, come winter or summer or spring,
She was out with a tray to feed all the strays but particularly Pong and young Ping.

At home of a night a marmalade sight, "Oh, Shem, what a beautiful cat".
She would open the door to his gingery paw and his welcoming roll on the mat.

You think she has gone with her warmth and her charm
And her outbursts of rage and fear
But the cats they all know she will come where they go
And whisper her love in their ears.

And where is she now? With a little meow and someone she loved very dear:
"Shad, my black Swee, old friend on my knee, it has been a long wait, but I'm here."

Last Visit To The Artist
Jennifer Liles Courtney
We discuss art, his eyes
lit by each word. Quick eyes
which seized sky splendor
in infinite hues.

Opposite the bed looms
black and yellow paint daubed
inch–thick on the canvas.
Through the sole window,
the steel sky promises
coolness of rain, but
still air suffocates.

He smiles through pallid skin,
lifting weary wrinkles.
I bring bright flowers
and a weak smile. We talk
of the sky which should be
brilliant but isn't.

I want to paint him
dancing me across the
kitchen floor. Mustache
bristle tickles my face.

He steadies my child hand,
helps me paint garish red
scars over his best work,
calls it my masterpiece.

Now, down antiseptic
corridor of twin doors,
I come to this borrowed
room where too late, too soon, he
gasps borrowed breaths.

My Gift To You
Denise G. Penny

When I look at you, I see
The man I dearly love
Your hands so rough and callused
Your heart's as tender as a dove

When I look at you, I hear
The softness in your voice
And I thank GOD everyday
For making you my choice

When I look at you, I imagine
The feel of your tender touch
And it helps me to understand
Why I love you so much

The years we've shared together
You've always been there for me
Even in times of great pain
Your love was easy to see

You've given me so much through the years
Yet your love has never wavered
My gift to you is faith and a love that will
last only forever

Happy Anniversary
I Love You

Dedication: to my husband, Tim

Untitled
Candice Pappas

I sit here with a tear in my eye,
As I think of us and wonder why?

For some reason, there's this uneasy feeling settling in,
I don't know how or just where to begin,
But its a feeling of fear that it's coming to a end

It's something that's there, it whispers "things aren't
right" and sometimes it makes me cry at night.

It whispers things aren't how they used to be before,
It whispers we're growing apart even more.

And this voice is worse then anything else,
Only because it tells the worst about us.

I only wish I could make you see,
Just exactly what this does to me.

It makes me think and wonder, if I'll always be here
or maybe another.

I wish and pray that I could be the best for you,
But sometimes it's not enough and I don't know what
to do.

The day might come that you're no longer here,
I wouldn't hear your voice or feel you near.

I don't want to lose you, because you're like the air
I breathe,
So that means without you there would be no me.

You're my buddy and the best friend I ever had,
Without you I would be lonely and a whole lot of sad.

Miracles Of Creation
Frank Pellegrino

There aren't enough hours in a day
When planting time comes in May,

I dig and plant all week
'Til I'm tired and weak,

You forget the work and pain
With the soothing sun and rain,

The flowers I planted in a circle
Grow and bloom like a miracle,

Birds gather together and sing
These are beautiful signs of spring,

Under the stars at night
While the moon shines so bright,

I hear the sounds of barking dogs
In the misty grass, croaking frogs,

All these living things are free
God gave them to you and me,

These are samples of His masterpieces
Their life continues and never ceases

When winter, comes, it's time for hibernation
And dream of God's power of creation.

Where Am I?
Rhonda K. Fleming

Almighty God, how do I find my way through the forest of
confusion when all paths look alike?
My child, only the straightest path will carry you out of the forest.
For confusion is built on twisted paths that carry you nowhere.

Almighty God, how do I find the warm light of truth when the
trees' canopy casts shadows upon my thoughts and reasoning?

My child, the light is found within, in which no shadows can be cast.
For truth is pure and bright and warm.

Almighty God, how do I forsake pleasure when the flowers smell so
sweet and their beauty lures me into its bed with lies?

My child, the sweet smell of flowers does not last past the first breath.
For pleasure only seduces those who are willingly lured into a
bed of thorns.

Almighty God, how do I find strength by dipping into the pool that is
overgrown with reeds, when it mars my reflection at the mere touch
and ripples away from me?

My child, the pool only ripples at the surface and reflects a new image.
For strength is only found within the depths, and you must swim
through its darkness alone to find it.

Almighty God, how do I find my way through the forest of confusion
when all paths look alike?

My child, only the straightest path will carry you out of the forest.
For this path has no shadows cast upon it, no flowers worth smelling
and in itself, will bathe you in strength to complete your journey
into the light.

Dedication: to those who are Lost

Enchanted Dreams

The Optimistic Robin
Marlene Wenger Roadruck
On a rather "lusterless" day,
when the clouds were only gray,
a ray of sunshine
came into this life of mine.

Now, I know you thought sunbeam
but, I'm talking about daydreams.
While aimlessly folding some laundry,
I found myself pondering a quandary.

The patio brick and trestle are wet
and, in comes a robin like a pet!
Surely the beak holds some mess (food)
but, the water-drenched item fits a nest.

How lovely! How timely! How neat!
What fun to have such a front seat.
What a marvel! What a thrill!
My grandchild will learn about goodwill.

Beyond the obvious opportunity to learn
and, the sighting of young that we yearn
how optimistic and smart of the bird
using the wet to seal up the nest's dirt.

Surely the robin expects to stay dry
or, where-else should the pair try.
March started to be April and spring,
the branches the leaves yet to bring.

Brief Journey Back
Regina M. Rafajko
Ah, Sweetheart, You've returned
If even for a brief Moment in the span of time
We can be young again
Remembering a select era when you used to call me by my name
The sweet aroma of the Moment
Bought tears of joy and tears of empathy to the CNAs that observed
This was a romantic Moment for a long, lingering twinkling
There was light in his eyes
Wife and husband re-united together again
The twosome had a brief journey back, recollecting the
Sweet essence of their passage in time together
How sweet it was; how sweet it is
For the Mrs. to have this bittersweet memory to hold on to
for the duration of her life
A Moment in time that she will cherish, hold on to and dream
As her husband wanders back to the land unknown
Where, unbeknownst to any of us, he travels in a space,
a lingering sphere of time
Where none of us knows the essence of his road he takes
'Tis sad to see his brief journey back ended
One wonders where he goes and if in his mind
He desires from deep within his core to pack up his suitcase
and leave from here with his beloved
Ah, that light in his eyes, 'tis faded for sure
Dullness and staring into the unknown once again
Ah, beloved of mine, if you return once again
I pray thee to arrive
When I am present
So we can warmly embrace in our cherished event
We call remembrance
So we can briefly journey back
Together once again
In our memories

Dedication: to all Alzheimer's couples and families

Abortion (Pro-Life)
Mary Elizabeth Roser
Silently, I shed a tear
Silently, so you could not hear.

For the ones who died before their birth
Ones who will never walk on this Earth

As a seed in the womb
They became a baby in a tomb.

Death took them all away
To never talk, to never play

I have muddled it in my mind
and still I cannot find

A reason why they should die,
before they even once will cry.

Because of our world of sin and sorrow
they will not see their first tomorrow.

Pass them on to us with none,
We will teach them, about God's Son.

So if you must decide about a birth to be hidden
Don't wipe this life away, away and ridden

What's the sin in birth and living
God is love and love is giving.

The Virus
Riva Marea Williams
It took over body and mind, almost blind,
Couldn't see nor hear, yet didn't fear.

Young mother and almost a wife, but drugs took his life,
He left death at the door, begging and pleading forevermore.

It went to the brain, it nearly making insane,
Saved, but not by a lover, savior was a brother.

Fought off the deadly destruction that lived inside,
Almost didn't survive the ride.

The virus roared like a raging flood,
But now undetectable by blood.

Beautiful life is again, but remember when,
Lying on death's door waiting, all were contemplating.

Death from this doom of destruction,
Body so sickly it couldn't function.

Now here sitting, should thank the Lord above,
Mostly it was brotherly love, saved doom.

By all rights should be in a tomb, yet here body, fit and free,
agony, pain and harm all gone from me.

Once death's door without choice, but stopped, so now rejoice,
No more pounding head, or endlessly lying in bed.

Destroyed the ugliness within, yet now wished never had been,
With the junky as a lover, should have picked another.

Poisoning of body and soul, who knew the deadly price of the
toll, almost life was paid, for a bridge never made.

Lanise: Beneath The Wind
Deana L. Arroyo

I lay beneath the wind, swaying soft whispers of fresh cut flowers mother
  brings me.
Each visit, she leaves with messages of love she still feels; as time
passes, slowly, like winter days yearning for length.
Limited space forces stillness of flesh, as this unforgotten soul
stretches far beyond humble, naive beliefs. Memories of youth are seen
in supernatural existence, which for some, seem impossible.
It is a bond shared with my remaining past.
Senses still intact, though distinctively unique from the living,
give comfort without acknowledgment. I know of the unknown.
Feel trapped fears and restlessness from those
who know not. I see pain in expressioned faces as saline tears give
flavor to green pastured overcoat. Hearing mother's sweet voice,
I move closer to her presence; as she stands with a
sorrowful glance at the unbearable truth. I wish to touch her soft black
skin to deplete the wrinkles she creates; while soaking her handkerchief
with horrified tears. It is she whogave pollen to this flower in order
for it to bloom. As petals began to unfold, dispersing in different
directions, each began leading to prominent aspects of my life.
I dated a man, ever more seeking love. Quickly, years
passed, so did my feelings for him. I began loathing his face, caress,
unrighteous accusations and began to break away to obtain freedom
and space. I grew stronger, he weaker, we departed each other's lives.
Devastatingly, my life was snatched, without consent, by this cipher,
who left other firm flowers to wilt as if only desert sun was left to
generate growth. I stand by my grave, as mother cries to me.
And I return, to lie down, beneath the wind, until she returns.

Dedication: to my beloved friend, Lanise Nash

As One
Santy Salernitano

Taking you on an extraordinary,
exciting journey, an adventure through the
stars–filled sky, together forevermore,
is what I plan to do. Flying champions
crossing the universe as one, a new learning
experience, what joy and happiness is all
about. Making a love scene with my beloved
wife bathin' under hot–water springs close in
wet–warm mist. Caressing, nourishing,
pampering every inch of your beautiful body
head down to toe. Keeping us safe from harm
caring about your needs. Sharing most precious
gifts that the Heavens will bring upon us
a blessing few may ever get. Walking along
the emerald beachside holding hands with my
favorite girl. Blue calm sea, raindrops falling
as one looking at the candy–cane rainbow
called us. Summer, cool breeze, midnight
moonlight whispering soft words to comfort
your solid–golden heart. The fountain of love
is overflowing with so much fidelity, commitment,
sacrifice. Have a strong shoulder you can rest
your pretty head on. Milk and honey straight
from the promised land filled in richness like
your sweet spirit, my little angel.
Making you steamy–hot, flames, high sky
with passion, compassion, a unique magical
touch only I can do for you. Putting a diamond
ring on your left finger that will shine brightness,
warmth all over the world. Becoming as one
on that great marriage fest, is a treasure I will
never forget when time stood still for me and
you.

Dedication: to Lori McDonald

Simple Pleasures
W. McNicol

Have you ever watched the sun rise,
To start a golden day?
Or looked from the top of a mountain,
At God's wonderful display?

Have you watched the flight of a bluebird,
Or heard the song of a lark?
Have you wandered o'er green meadows,
Or walked in a storm in the dark?

Have you strolled on the banks of a river,
On a beautiful summer's day?
Or drifted in from the ocean,
To a quiet, secluded bay?

Have you ever seen a day–old chick,
Or a lamb just newly born?
Or the cows come home at the end of the day,
All tired and forlorn?

Have you ever watched a child at play,
No troubles, cares or sorrows?
And in those little minds of theirs,
No worries for tomorrow.

Have you ever thought of the many things,
That give us joy and pleasure?
They may only last a little while,
But leave memories to treasure.

Jennifer's Graduation
Colette Boldue

To my cute and smart daughter
From your very loving mother

Today is your special day
And I want to find a way

To show you how proud I am of you
Because of all the things that you do

You've learned so much in first grade
The groundwork has been laid

You've come such a long, long way
You are the sunshine of my day

You love to read your new books
Snuggled quietly in your nooks

Quiet time, or fun time together
Rain or shine, no matter the weather

It's such a joy to see you learn
Someday it will be your turn

To have a daughter just like you
To make you happy when you're blue

Congratulations, Jennifer, you've passed 1st grade
My memories of today will never fade

I love you so very, very much
My heart is full from your touch

I know I'll always feel this way
So proud, so happy on your special day!

Enchanted Dreams

Single Reminder
Junior Marquez

I can't reject, or lie about my feelings,
The feelings I feel when you're near or around me.
I've been hiding myself too long,
And now there is a single reminder of someone so far, yet so close.

Somewhere in my mind, there is a single reminder of you,
And it's hiding, somewhere in this head.
A single thought of your kiss,
An image of your hug and your touch.

For some reason, time drifted us apart,
And distance kept us away.
And it's a single reminder that I can't,
And won't let it happen again.

But even though I can't let any of the time we've had go away,
Thoughts of you come and go so frequently.
Even in the dreams I have, you're around
There is a single reminder, Always.

And the things you say to me,
remind me of the way,
You and only you, can make me fall in love
So fast and easy.

It's a reminder of how we always have to say good–bye,
Every time we come together.
And the times we separate, the pain I endure,
Is a single reminder, "I love You"!

Sonya's Southern Fried
Tamara Martenia

Stop by and see us, anytime.
When the hunger is big and the budget small.
From 10 a.m. to 10 p.m., seven days a week.
We serve chicken, fixed southern–style.
The coating is crispy,
Seasoned like Mama's used to be.
The juiciest meat you'll ever eat.
Homemade crispin's on the side.

Scoot on up to a table,
Tuck that napkin in.
Choose your side dishes carefully, you're in for a treat.
Potatoes – mashed, boiled and fried.
Gravy smooth and tasty,
The sopping' up with buttermilk biscuits kind.
Hushpuppies, grits, pone and greens.
Don't forget the candied yams and baked beans.

The desserts are a Heavenly temptation.
There's pecan pie, caramelly sweet.
Rice pudding, fluffy and light
With or without raisins, you decide.
And deep–dish peach cobbler or almond ice cream.
To name a few.

Lean back in a comfy booth,
Loosen your belt, go on let yourself go.
To top things off; before you waddle out the door.
There's coffee, strong and hot,
Lemonade made from scratch, cold and sweet.

Whenever you pass our way,
Come in, relax and take a seat.
You will always be welcomed with a smile,
At Sonya's Southern Fried

Memories
Arlene M. Moore

Memories seen so long ago, sometimes they are forgotten,
A tear may fall, a smile may come with a feeling of satisfaction,
But what would life be like if there was nothing to recall?
Our lives are touched by history and molded by experiences
Not realized at all.

Where is our place, do we control the destiny of our lives?
What brings happiness, what brings peace,
What brings confusion, we wait for release,
What makes a memory, what makes joy,
What makes a family be fun for all?

Can history help sort out what words can never speak,
Pent–up emotion without a release.
How does the past life control us today,
What do we hope for, what do we pray.

What makes a family have peace and joy,
Finding happiness with each other, making memories galore,
Finding pleasures in sharing of lives day by day.
Which will someday be memories put in a book
For recall of someone to have a look.

A tear may fall or a smile may come to the face
of the one looking over the book of the
memories recorded by a family who took
The time to make history for a
Memorable book.

Dedication: to my husband, daughter, four stepchildren

The Magnificent Rose!
Carolyn A. Davis

The rose is one of the most
Alluring plants on Earth. It is
Symbolic of a woman with
Many layers of her giftedness.
The leaves depict her vulner–
Ability. The perimeter denotes
The genesis of her existence.
While each layer speaks of
Her heart, mind, body and soul.
The spirit of the woman is all
Wrapped and intertwined
Within the center of this
Beautiful bloom, which she
Carefully nurtures and assigns
It a proper place to be
Cultivated and cared for, at
The risk of being exposed:
Which can be fatal or
Fabulous!
Allow your beauty to be
Honored and recognized by
All creatures. Your softness
Will sometimes be trampled
Underfoot and when the
Elements of life cause your
Rose to shrink or shiver,
Remember the fragrance that
It left, which is the evidence
Of your;
Courage,
Faithfulness,
Strength,
Love,
And divine design.

Dreamer's Diary
Scarlett Shepard
An Evening with the cast of Twin Peaks over an Icy Cocktail. Pink Flamingo Hideaways. Eating in a Diner that is orbiting through space. Winning the Lottery and quitting my dead–end job. I wave goodbye and leave the stranglers behind.

Dust Curtails, I leave a Cloud of exhaust behind.   I begin my Adventure.
Never–ending fairytales.   Mysterious SuperHeroes in Flight.
A prescription for relief and pleasure; my imagination.
A simple remedy for an outrageous world,
With its tremendous complexities,
I know, I can get lost inside my head, the ultimate escape
The insatiable imaginariness,
Frame by Frame, A film projector scanning and reading,
Dreams spliced, creating new imagery to run away with,
Abusive Tales, Broken and Reconstructed,
Realigned and enhanced,
Tucked away behind my smile.
I can just close my eyes, imagine and wander,
A self–proclaimed journey around the world like a nomadic ghost,
A meditative journey teleprompting myself to and from paradise,
Colossal Castles, Candy Cane Kingdoms and Unicorn Storms,
Rhythms and Abstractions,
I am the Insatiable Dreamer. Insatiable Lioness. Insatiable Thinker.
A Passenger on board dreaming up the unreal,
The next town, Endless entries in my Diary,
Everyone has a story and I am never an Ear–Full,
I want to know.   I want to extract knowledge and gain wisdom,
Quench my curiosity.   To speak collectively.
And to escape from the confines of earning a living,
And find my purpose in this world.

My Sister–In–Law
Jayne Hamilton
A sister–in–law is someone you know–
Through a marriage to a loved–one you start to grow.

Together as a family – when children come along
The bond between you can become quite strong.

Though time becomes tight and hours are few,
I try to make time to spend with my nephew.

I love my little cutie with my heart and soul
I enjoy playing my auntie role.

Time needs to be found to spend with all of you
It passes too quickly – it's what we must do!

In our lives we get so busy and distorted and
Take for granted what is most important.

I have immense love and respect – it's true
Your husband and son are so blessed to have you.

As a Mom and a wife no one can compare –
Look at all you have to share.

Never lose sight of how much I care
and know that when needed, I'll always be there.

I write this, sis, from deep in my heart
And hope our family and friendship will never part.

Family will be there through thick and thin –
So open your heart and always welcome them in.

Dedication: to Paula, with all my love

Becky
Nora Porrata
You are near
I feel your presence,
We feel your LOVE

You live in my mind,
You live in our hearts
Because of us,
You are there

Because of you,
We understand what is important,

You are the shining star,
You are the guiding angel,

We need not fear
We need not cry
Because you are there
and we are here

BECKY,
In the end
We'll be together again

WE LOVE YOU,
I Love You

Nora

Dedication: to Ivan Deloyce and Felice

Rockin'
Mary Lou Strouse
Just sitting here rocking
In the old rocking chair
Not a worry on my mind
Not a trouble or care

Oh! There's troubles to think of
If I'd take the time
But as I sit here "a rockin'"
All of life seems sublime

My mind wanders to – yesterday
With its joys and delights
And I pause and reflect
On a beautiful sight

Out of memories garden
Flow treasures untold
Worth more than diamonds
Or rubies or gold

There's a lot more to livin'
As I sit in that chair
Gray clouds turn to blue
And stormy days – fair

So, if you are despondent
Lonely or blue
Come close and I'll tell you
Just what to do

Go find yourself
An old rocking chair
And then rock away
Every trouble – and care

Enchanted Dreams

The Trail Of Tears
Rachel E. Larmer
The Great Spirit hides His face from us, yet still we carry on
Our glory days draw to an end, our hopes are growing wan.
But still with pride we mount our steeds and trod the trails of old
We've braved the worst that men are dealt: the wind, the heat, the cold.
And no man, white or otherwise, can beat us to our knees
Our chiefs, though withered, shrunken men, won't stoop to utter pleas.
We've passed the pipe of peace around, but still we're faced with war
Perhaps they wait with baited breath until we are no more.
They turn us from our tribal homes, we flee across the plain
We swoon from hunger, faint from thirst, we're overcome by pain.
We cannot weep, our tears are spent, we've cried them all before
Our falcon brother has borne our dead to some far, distant shore.
The great eagle guides our footsteps, he leads us where we go
He beckons us to follow him, he pays no heed to snow.
Our limbs are frozen through, there's blisters on our feet
At dawn we're beaten down by rain, at night there is the sleet.
But still there's signs that spring is near, there's budding of the trees
The frozen ground and frosty shrubs are looking for release.
The day is drawing near at last when our journey is at end
We'll count our loss and start again, our brokenness will mend.
We'll paint our faces, find our bows and put away our shame
And then we'll ride the hills again in search of wild game.
We'll eat the fat of buffalo and dine on wild boar
The dingo pups will bark with glee as babes play on the floor.
The squaws will laugh among themselves and tell their tales of old
Lores about the spirit world and tales of men born bold.
But first they'd tell a tale their own, about the trail of tears
They'd say with quiet dignity, they overcame their fears.
They'd say, "Our pride won't let us fall, our will won't let us die."
And that, they say, was. in the end, what really got them by.

Renaissance
Connie M. Wilson
She closed the door behind her as she sighed.
"This is the end," she thought,
As she walked down the driveway to her shiny, red Mustang.

The sunlight through the leaves, danced gaily round her feet.
Surreal within, Surreal without.
She drove away.
The scent of burning tires and of exhaust remained behind,
To tell the story of a marriage and its death.

Lipstick stains on crewnecks and ties,
The smell of lust that slapped her face,
When she came home at night.
The age-old lie of working late
had brought her to this Interstate egress.
The road behind held fear and hate,
Ahead were strength and forgiveness.
She drove around all day.
The many sights she saw,
brought peace to her torn mind.
past corn fields, tall with sweet silver-queen corn,

The young, new leaves on strong wind-bent limbs,
painted the countryside with feathery-soft strokes.
In the fields, the Earth's new children played and nursed,
while, tender crops burst through the ground.
A sudden relief washed across her face.

She parks the car and walks across the field.
An old, abandoned, tattered barn her destination.
And within the long-forgotten shelter, she espied,

Small wonders, beginning life within ruins,
A pile of soft, gray fur, moving and mewing.

Inequality
Sonja Mardi
If the prickles in my back
Could talk
They'd make the sound of gray-day rain
Rasping 'gainst my window-pane!
Strange, I think,
As I watch the raindrops track
How some...
d
r
i
p
d
o
w
n

s
t
e
a
d
y...
Meet NO flack!
Yet, O(o)thers have to
Twist and turn,
Struggle past ev'ry bump and crack...
Same Surface; same Space; same Time...
Listen!
In the distance...
Sad bells still chime!

Love Undone
Arlene R. Bennes
Love takes many forms throughout our lives. We dream of that romantic love — of hearts and flowers.

And once found, we know that bliss will last forever — our love will overcome anything life brings our way.

We grow older and into a comfortable love of companionship and deep friendship. We learn to rely on one another.

We learn about ourselves and wonder...

We try to appreciate and understand ourselves as individuals.

We begin to grow comfortable — and justify our habits.
Yet somewhere a small seed of doubt creeps in.

We misunderstand...

We wonder about fear and shame — disappointment and confusion.

But the loves goes on, doesn't it? Tainted maybe, but once given never undone?

The fear grows... the hurt grows.

Regrets draw a dark curtain across an unimpassioned gulf and we reach out into a void...

Where is our lifelong friend?

What have we done — destroyed that one and only thing we ever wanted?

Dedication: to Richard, my world

The Decision (God To Mankind)
Jane V. Boucek

Shall I weep or laugh, or just smile benignly
At your antics, my little Man??

You stand on your mound and crow
Waving self–important rattles in each hand
You strut and stutter, babbling obscenities
While the odor of your contentious excrement
Sears my nostrils and vastly displeases me.

I have nourished you with mounting hope
To raise a sacred being for my yearning breast
When you emerged with life-filled flippers from the sea,
I rejoiced
And cheered when your limbs could stand erect to roam
my verdant Earth
Yes, exalted when your mutating brain could hold my
all–encompassing soul

But then, repulsed by your un–evolved pretensions, I sent my
very essence
To be housed in your feeble body, uniting myself with human
flesh
I gave you my greatest gift, my very own self, Jesus

So now what shall I do?—shall I OR SHALL I BUT NUDGE
Your blue–green bubble and send it spinning——
To oblivion——into the blackest of black holes——

OR ——shall I once more DESIST and yet once again
Await my prodigal's return?

The Return
Evelyn Cope

The shy violet and the delicate
primrose
I discovered, again, still blooms
in the lane
The lane where I walked to
my school
With its horse–chestnut trees
And the place for when the gypsies
came

The pool with its swans is still
there.
Nearby is the Tudor–built
Walsh Hall.
With its spreading branches
of its Mulberry tree
Standing by its garden wall.

The farm house where I took my
first steps.
Is modernized now.
The barn and the stables are
still remaining.
But long–departed are the horses.
That pulled the carts and plough.

I have shed tears as I have
thought of those years
Those years of my childhood.
So soon passed away.

A dear husband has passed on
Our descendants live on
In Australia far away.

Speechless
Melinda Kaye Cummins

I'm so confused
By the likes of you
Why do you treat me this way?
I want to see
But cannot believe
Any of the words you say
You say you won't
But I know you will
I'm sick of all your games
You say you care
But it's not fair
That you can cause all this pain
How can you state
The vows you won't break
When I watch you fall
But I really do miss
The taste of your kiss
I try not to remember it all
But it always comes back
And sometimes I lack
The courage to stay away
I miss you so bad
And the good times we had
And I think of you day after day
I'm ever–lossed
And this bridge is not crossed
Could you please show me the way?
I'm so confused
By the likes of you
I don't know what to say.

Feelings From The Past
Bertha J. Moore

Oh, what a sight to behold!

From my back door I watch
the evening sun low on the horizon,
A brilliant red with silver streaks
reaching upward in the sky.

The lush, green meadow curving down
to the pond.
I walk to a bit of sandy beach,
sit and bury my feet.

I dream under the elm tree
loaded with mistletoe;
My eyes are closed as I listen to the
sounds of nature.

My imagination so vivid –
I hear the farm family of years gone by
busily doing their evening chores.

Now it's time to gather around the long table
for the evening meal.
I open my eyes; it is the close of the day
Yet, I am not alone –

The people who lived and worked here
a century ago
Are still around the buildings, the trees,
the meadow and the pond.

What a wonderful, magical Moment!

Dedication: to Bernadine, my beloved granddaughter

Enchanted Dreams

Bird
Jerrie Desgroseilliers

Saucy little bird, what is it you say
Are you telling the others it's your turn today.

Are you flicking your tail and making such a chatter
Over something important or things that don't matter.

Are you scolding the dog lying close to your bread
Or saying look at me, aren't I fine, in my feathers of red.

Do you care what it costs to put food on your plate
Or do you just fly away being happy you ate.

Do you talk to the robin about how far he must go
And when he should leave to avoid all the snow.

Are you jealous of the jay with his body so blue
Or do you think there are none quite as lovely as you.

Does the sparrow annoy you, so tiny and brown
Or perhaps Mr. Owl with his large eyes and permanent frown.

Would you like to fly south when the weather turns cold
Or are you happy to stay north where as king you can scold.

Do you have any idea how your call starts my morning
Puts a spring to feet and lifts my heart without warning.

I suppose not, but thanks!

Dedication: to Raymond – thanks for believing

All Because Of You
Kathy Tilot

For your love
I would go anyplace
Just to see
The smile on your face

You give me hope
You give me reason
You give me something
To believe in

You make me feel
so very much alive
Just with you being there
Helps me to survive

The kindness you show
Your gentleness you give
The peace within us
The life we do live

Your love is the joy
That from day to day
Touches my life
In its own special way

When I need someone to hold me
Your arms are open wide
When I need someone to guide me
You are always by my side

I'll always love you
I'm so happy you are mine
I'm glad I have you
Till the end of time

Diana
Enid Fenton

I thought I heard Diana's carefree laughter on the breeze
but, alas, it was just the wind rustling in the trees.

I thought I saw Diana and my heart with hope would ache
but, alas, it was just the sunshine dancing on the lake.

I thought I felt Diana caress a sick child's head
but, alas, she can do this no more, the poor Princess is dead.

I felt I knew Diana, her heart was made of gold
and when I learned about her death it made my blood run cold.

We all lost a special person robbed of her lust for life,
a very giving everywoman, mother, sister, daughter, lover, wife.

Jesus smiled and took their hands and led them to His wonderland,
no gauntlet to run, no people to stare, just peace, love and tranquility there.

I well recall Diana and her travels o'er the world
she would light the darkest corners, her wings of love unfurled.

I still can sense Diana, compassionate and free,
she'll live on in our hearts and minds for all the world to see.

Although I grieve, Diana, I try not to despair
she'll find her peace in Heaven to dwell forever there.

These dark days have been empty without our eternal flame,
we had an angel here on Earth, Diana was her name.

A New England Year
Russell A. Krapf

Seasons change like day into night,
All four different seasons to our delight.
Although here in New England they sometimes forget,
And One season starts early when the other's not done yet.

In fall we have colors galore,
Those long, autumn drives I simply adore.
As temperatures dip from cool into cold,
Enjoying those colors never gets old.

Next comes the winter with its wind and some snow,
As Mother Nature puts on a great show.
Snow angels, snow forts, snowmen and snow fights,
No matter the age, you become a kid against all your might.

In spring when the flowers start to grow,
Surprise, What is this? New–fallen snow.
You never know just what to expect,
And after a long winter, it's time to reflect.

Summer's here and away we go,
Beaches and baseball and golf, you know,
The heat just keeps rising, humidity, too,
And with those long, summer days, so much to do.

Here in New England all the seasons year round,
And here in New England there's a lot to be found.
Apples and Syrup and Adirondack chairs,
Lots of places to go to melt away your cares.

So come to New England, come sit a spell,
The weather you'll get, you can never tell.
So if you like surprises, just come and see,
Come see for yourselves, don't believe me.

The Anthology of Poems

An Apology, Father To Son
Perrin Antonio Dannug
I watched as my son
ran out to play
at the end of schooldays
through my backyard
to the elm that he loved.

Days, one by one,
he would look up as he lay
through leaves straining the sun's rays
in my backyard
under the elm that he loved.

He would twist and swing for fun
or in his tire swing gaze
not thinking of cost or pay
in my backyard
with the elm that he loved.

How can I say what will be done,
that not every day
can be play
in my backyard
with the elm that he loved?

The elm that he loved
in my backyard
I cut down and anger filled his eyes.

Son,
I'm sorry

So Different
Leona Newman
The mouse and the frog were very good friends,
And they liked nothing better than together to spend.
Long hours discussing the world and its course,
And, between them, they solved all Earth's problems, of course!

Then, one day as they lay beside a still pond,
The mouse, who was George, said to the frog who was Tom.
"Why'd you suppose that we're such good friends?"
"'Cause we're so different, we two, when you take it all in."

"I'm fuzzy, you're slick; I'm brown and you're green;
You eat bugs and I nuts, that's why I'm so lean!
You croak and I squeak, you hop and I run,
I prefer the night air and you bathe in the sun."

Then, Tom who had listened with interest aroused,
And said to his friend the George; who was mouse,
(He got things mixed up when he just started out.)
But he said to his friend, "I've figured it out!"

"It's because we're so different that we get along.
It's that, in our friendship, that makes it so strong.
If we were alike, we'd have nothing to share,
But we give to each other and that's why we care."

"You tell me of things that I couldn't know,
You make my world wider by the places you go.
And, I share with you things I see that you can't;
Like things underwater, a fish or a plant."

"Yes, different is different as different can be,
But that's what makes us so special, you see!
And, that's how things are and how they will stay
But a friendship like ours, I'd have no other way!!!"

A Palliative Care Nurse
Connie Manning
These people are going to die
Whether I am here or not,
And so I am lucky to be here for the people
That are dying of cancer.
I love my job with a passion;
I am a palliative care nurse.
I am able to fight for my patients.
I am able to help my patients die with dignity,
And so I don't feel sad when the patient dies
But I cry?
My tears are not for the loss of that patient
He deserves his death
He has worked hard, very hard, to get there.
He is at peace, he is not suffering and he is free of cancer
And so my tears are not for the patient.
My tears are for the families who are left behind,
Who have to live with what they have seen
For they live with cancer for the rest of their
Lives
Cancer not of themselves,
But of their family member they have lost.
And so I will feel sad
And I will cry.
Why?
For the memory of my patients.
For I am a palliative care nurse.
This is not a job to me;
It is my passion.
It is a part of my life.
I love my job.

Your Voice
Lotti Maria Kaihani
I went to bed with the warmth of your voice.
It wrapped its soft arms around me.

I felt its breath caress my face,
Like the velvety touch of silken lace.

I felt its sweetness kiss my skin,
It made ice melt from me within.

I felt the strength of you from afar,
Like the fragrance of roses kept in a jar.

I felt your voice lift and enfold,
As over my body your hands did rove.

It ran through my hair, swept thru my mind,
It ran down my neck and caressed my spine.

It breezed past my eyes; to my ear it did whisper,
Down and across my lips, like old, aged liqueur.

It slipped like warm oil, all over my chest,
It hugged and sucked the tips of my breast.

My nipples harden and they did rise,
The touch of your tongue was quite a surprise.

It made my womanhood cry out from within,
It felt like honey all over my skin.

The want of you, your body my choice,
I went to sleep, with the warmth of your voice.

Dedication: in memory of Hashmat Kaihani

Enchanted Dreams

Who Am I?
Anne P. Linares–Crilly
I am a star in CREATIVITY. An original Observer and Lover of LIFE.
A eulogist to SENSITIVITY; Who with a SMILE acknowledges STRIFE!

A Positive Thinker, with the ability to DREAM and create DREAMS!
Forever wanting to be: A sunshine, a light, an inspiration, a BEAM!

To NATURE and LIFE itself in all its facets strongly attracted,
with its mysteries, puzzles, dogmas and enigmas, curiously, fascinated...

An individualist, ethnically aware of my roots, with human compassion;
and a ravenous desire for cultural pondering into mankind–affections.

With an eagerness to ALWAYS COMPREHEND and LEARN. By nature multifarious.
By making a DIFFERENCE in my LIFETIME, as main goal desirous...

By leaving a wonderful, world–wide ethnic awareness impact and TRACE
wherever possible, by making EACH and EVERYONE feel as important as an ACE!

By making each one conscious of their BEAUTY and UNIQUENESS.
That as creatures of GOD, they each stand out in blissfulness!

I am a Teacher, an Optimist, with lots of LOVE and EMOTION, who still
has time to hope, to dream, with goals to live for and fulfill...

I AM A UNIVERSAL ETHNIC BEING: A PERUVIAN, MOCHICA–CHIMU, INCA, CELTIC,
with FRENCH, GERMAN, SPANISH and PORTUGUESE–ARABIC...

This is who I am, the Writer, the Dreamer, the Entrepreneur,
the Genealogist
The Poetess, the Poliglot, the Amateur–self–made Anthropologist...

Born To Darkness
Cristine Maria Ramos
I opened up my eyes and saw
I have lost my innocence
No more pink laces and bows
I opened up my eyes to be no more
I looked at the mirror and at me
A mysterious figure stared with
Empty eyes and evil grin
Her hair was fire and her mouth
A dungeon of evil and darkness
I looked her in the eye and drowned
Lost into despair and grief

Why, my love, why??
Like an angel of evil
She took me into her world
In a bright tube, shyness is lost
And friendships throbble
Out of control, I see my life
Falling away from me
Why, my love, why??

The prince of darkness has arrived
The prince of lies and madness
Ghosts come and go, dancing
On the wall like macabre puppets
Hold me, my love, because
I'm falling into darkness and madness
Darkness surrounds me and there's no way out
Too late for salvation and too early for damnation
Did I find my true one or I am insane??
I get up and as blackness surrounds me
I see I'm no one and nothing
And, dead inside, I get up drown in sin
And sit up to become someone

Two Roses
Dale Cody
Two roses lived in a forest form
one a beauty, one a thorn

The beauty lived with one only thought
to live long, till summer's drought

The thorn wanted not to blush unseen
beneath the pine and evergreen

A fair maiden came to pluck one away
to rest on her bosom one spring day

The beauty she took in full bloom
placed near her heart, but solemnly doomed

It was admired and kissed by her mate
sulking and withering, it cursed its fate

Through the season many a maiden's foot bore
along the path on the forest floor

And how the thorn yearned for the fingertips
the love, the smile, the sweet–sweet lips

But alas, its desires ended in vain
for life passed in a late winter's rain

And what a fate it is to blush unseen
beneath life's forest and evergreen

The Dancer
Julia C. Dooley
Supple, fluid dancer
serene at peace
and iron–clad motion
grace under pressure.

eyes so bright
round and brown
limbs soft and muscled
hair flies in the wind
as she steps, prances and glides

Strength unknown but to one
silent joy sparkling
in her eyes
dimples and smile
radiate free love
freedom from the foes
and so many woes
of yesterday.

She lies eyes open
and stares
at the wonder of the sky...
... the bluer blues,
the scattered billows of clouds,
the dappling sun
up above.

She celebrates life
and embodies her treasure,
because she is me,
and this fire is mine.

Dedication: to Kathryn Samer

Someone
Judith Shafer

Someone can have a very close friend,
Not just woman to woman or man to man, but
A woman to a man with no amends.

Someone whose loving friendship is
Built on trust, without involving lust.

Someone you can let inside the wall you have
Built around you and let you inside the
Wall they have built around them, too.

Someone with whom you can share your innermost
secrets, knowing they will never be repeated.

Someone you can get so angry with, that
You find yourself hollering and shaking
Your fist.

Someone will say, after the last shout,
"What were we arguing about?"

Someone will then say, "Do you want a hug?"
And then both of you will open your arms and shrug.

Someone will always be there for you, you see,
And by now, you should know, that one of
Those someone's is me.

Dedication: To JJ, from BJ

For The Love Of Grandma
Stacey A. Adams

For Grandma had a special
gift in her heart that no one
could ever take apart. That
gift, was the gift of love. A Grandma
taking care of a little girl
named Debbie, while her
parents went to work. Grandma
was so proud teaching her the
values and all the good that
remains in a person, if you
are to believe in God. Their
house was in the countryside
that was so beautiful to with
peace and harmony, that no
one could ever buy. For
Grandma made peace with
all grandchildren and had
love for all. For those parents
that I know are ours, Shannon,
Stacey and Debbie, too. Debbie
is my sister. She also is the
firstborn. Debbie will
remain the firstborn.
Grandma gave a very special gift to
all of us kids. A very special
gift. In my Heart I needed
to give that special gift
Away, God may pass it on with
love, thank you,
Grandma, for giving the greatest
gift to me, to share, with
Debbie.

Dedication: to my sister Debbie

Thoughts
Sadie N. Williams

Thoughts that pop out in the night
Reminding me of bygone days

Here I lay me down to sleep
Lingering thoughts come shining through

Silent thoughts, they keep on growing
Making history for the world

Lingering thoughts, they keep on flowing
On its own, unending stream

Rhythmic thoughts in flowing heartbeats
It flows on–and–and–on–and–onward

Echoing silence in the night–watch
When the eye no slumber seeks

Willfully bearing distant message
Bringing in some old, some new

Some are welcomed, some distasteful
They pop up and keep on coming

Lingering thoughts that travel onward
Soaring high to the beyond

Day–break beckons memories of
Heart–felt thoughts that will live on

Dedication: to Christina Tanya Marie Dwyer, my granddaughter

Advice To A Young Bride
Maryann Carlson

With a few, rare exceptions,
It can safely be said
That men over fifty
Should be shot in the head.
They're angry,
They're bitter
And they hate their whole life,
Even the woman they chose for a wife.

Their children annoy them,
Their in–laws do, too,
But the boys at the bar
Are the bluest of blue.

They've lost all their manners,
They swear and they smell,
They aren't worth the powder
To blow them to hell.

But at romance they're wizards,
Technique all the way
And unlike us ladies,
It doesn't take them all day.

So, to any young woman
About to be wed,
Keep a gun with one bullet
Under your bed.

If he asks why you've got it
Smile sweetly and say,
"I bought it for you.
You might need it someday!".

Enchanted Dreams

Rose Of Beauty
Justin K. Atha
The rose is a symbol of beauty,
at full bloom.

You can see the way my face lights up,
when you walk into the room.

My heart is overfilled with love,
just to be in your presence.

Long have I awaited,
to prey upon your essence.

Your sweet lips of wondrous curves,
portray a delicious dish.

Upon a falling star tonight,
I am granted with this wish.

To have, to hold and to cherish,
you till the end of all mankind.

Because another rose of such beauty,
I know I'll never find.

I shall take this to my grave;
I'd die for you, 'tis true.

But the beauty of my full–bloom rose,
Is all my love for you...

Dedication: to my loving daughter, Angela Lynn

Who Do We Thank?
Terrie Schellhamer
Who do we thank for the sky and the trees?
Who do we thank for a cool, cool breeze?
Who do we thank for a child so small?
Who do we thank for that child grown tall?
Who do we thank for that child's life?
When they've grown up and taken a husband or wife.
We thank the Lord for the trees and the breeze.
For the child so small, for the child grown tall.
For that child's life and their husband or wife.
But who do we thank for a child who's lost?
For a child who drinks and doesn't think of the cost?
For a child who's tried to be helped, talked to and yelled at.
That loved one who's gone, we can only sit back.
Who would we thank when that someone is gone?
Who would we thank when they leave us here alone
Do we thank the Lord for that child so tall?
That parent whose talk has only grown small?
That sister who yelled or that brother who cried
A spouse who watched? God knows, we've tried.
A Son who did leave, an aunt who believed.
There's blame all around, as everybody will state
If only we can save her before it's too late.
The love for my sister cannot be denied.
For the last 5 years I've tried and tried.
We'll thank everybody for the sister that drinks
The sister that can't think, for the sister who's
gone, who'll leave us alone, for the sister we cry
for, for the child that parent bore. For the mother
She is, for the Aunt they all miss.
So who do we thank? Who will be blamed?
Who will be blessed to live with this shame?

Dedication: to my sister Lori

The Source
Adam Dave
If there was just one thing that I could achieve
I would convince you and have you believe
In a love that is infinite, knowing no bound
Perfect, complete, the best thing around.

This love is like medicine, fed to the ill
To heal their wounds, the ultimate pill
The doctor is you and the patient is, too
Love cures the flu, it makes you brand–new.

This love is a flower, a delicate rose
And each time it's felt, its sweet nectar flows
You are the bee and through you it goes
The honey's the proof, as your love grows.

This love is a mountain that pierces the sky
Frustrated at first, you continue to try
To soar its great hills, majestic and high
You are the eagle and upwards you fly.

This love is an ocean, so vast and so deep
Let its calm waters lull you to sleep
You are the dolphin, the whale, the fish
And from its still depths, love grants every wish.

Be all these things, the bird and the bee
You still won't believe what your eyes will see
For after the journey, this marvelous ride
What awaits you is truth: love's source is inside.

Dedication: to the hardhearted, that they may feel

The Last Dream
Shane Strawbridge
Waking in the morning and losing sight of the hour,
as you dream of what lost goal you try not to
achieve today.

As you think there will be a chance tomorrow,
your beloved doesn't wake up.

There once was a time when you hated her,
when she was what you opposed.

As time went on and dreams were dreams,
your life began to change.

One morning you wake up to find yourself alone,
and having strange feelings for someone you hated
the night before.

Remember the times the two of you dreamed of
marriage,
and argued over what to name your children.

Then as you woke up, you realized is was just a
dream,
and did nothing to accomplish it.

Given that time is called infinite you think she
will always be there for you.

by the time you get ready to ask her out she has
been dead for thirty years.

You fear what you do not do,
because it will change your last dream.

I Am There
Elaine Luster

In silence, sometimes you hear
me speak.
When happy, sad or when
at peace.

I cry out, sometimes, in the night
In darkness, I'm hidden
till morning's light.

I awake at dawn,
A silent tune
For old time's Sake,
I appear at noon

I exist, although I am not seen
A hidden face of inward streams.

If you would only notice me there
Real as life, I'm everywhere.

From inward thoughts, I reappear
No more alone, I am near.

As time moves by my side once more
I'm led to find the open door.

Light is the way
Which helps me see

In Silence, I'm found
Alone, just you and me.

Reflections On Nature's Stillness
Donald J. Ferguson

There is a stillness there around the pond, not as the unseen or that to be feared; The kind that reassures and comforts; A stillness which is serene in affirmation of Nature's everlasting scene.

Minute intruders wing their way upon the pond in graceful flight to embrace a quiet touch of nature's unceasing reality.

Awakening the serene quiet as their presence upon the pond etches ripples to the shore and ducks appear upon the shimmering surface; so self-assured that they here are not as prey.

In this pristine environment they need not call and what little sound occurs is their quickening movements across the pond, as a whisper in the quietness.

A little rain shower makes its presence known as it nourishes the waterfood to ferns and fronds and flowers alike in abundance.

And, in an instance the squall has ceased to be overtaken by the whimsical sun again peeking through the evergreens with warming rays of golden glimmer upon the wetland acre.

This is truly God's little acre of Nature's land blessed by the keepers who are in residence but not intruding upon the ever-wondrous realm of nature.

It is a haven for all things beautiful and bright established here on Earth in God's sight. There is contentment here.

Dedication: to Martha Norem

Surely Stupid
Gary L. Heck

We have a six-month-old kitten
by name of Shirley Stupid,
and everywhere that kitten ran
her shadow ran there, too, then.

The only time we'll not see them paired
is when the lights are out,
when you step upon her paw
MEOW, that's Shirley... STUPID.

I had never seen a kitten climb a ladder
till just the other day,
she'd bounce and sway a bit
then climb on up the way,

this continued on until
the very top she'd found,
missed the second from the top—
and bounced the whole way down.

We have a sliding door
on our shower stall,
and every once in a while
she climbs inside to bawl,

to curb her kitten curiosity
we close the door not used,
later at night we hear
a thud, when she's confused—

that's, surely... STUPID!

Somewhere
Linda J. Waldron

Somewhere other than in my dreams
I need to feel your touch
your words, your love...

I need and want your presence
the warmth of your kiss
your arms wrapped around me...
Somewhere other than in my dreams

I need to see your smile
the love in your eyes
feel your heart racing
Somewhere other than in my dreams

I want to see the passion building
as you walk toward me...
Your arms outstretched
reaching for me
Somewhere other than in my dreams

Will the day ever come
that all I have to give
is yours without question
that the two of us
become one
Somewhere other than in my dreams

Will the sun rise tomorrow
and will we see another sunset
Will we be together
so our hearts will touch or
will these things be
Somewhere other than in my dreams...

Enchanted Dreams

In All Things
Robert W. Vaughn

Who is patiently waiting and plotting, for your will to confuse
To place pitfalls in your path and for your goodness to misuse

To test your dedication, your love and the depth of your faith
To steal your protection, your armor, as a thief lying in wait

To seek you out, overcome and destroy you, to gain the advantage
To continually come at you, to try you, to place you in bondage

You can recognize these satanic forces, with your spiritual mind
For with the power of God's Holy word, victories shall be thine

You must be on guard and ever watchful, with your spiritual eyes
Be alert to the evil one's ways, let the Holy Spirit in you reside

Pray for God's wisdom and knowledge, for discernment of spirits
For with God's supernatural gifts, His power in you has no limits

Your spiritual ears must be open, be prepared and ready to listen
To hear God's instructions to you and to abide by His direction

Who can stand against you, when the authority you've been given
By Jesus Christ our Lord and King, son of our Father in Heaven

To use the powers of the Father, bind fear in the name of the son
Let loose your faith, defeat the enemy, let the Father's will be done

For to stand alone is foolhardy, you have no strength or weapons
In all things, look to God and expect victory with His blessings

AMEN

Sean
Alpha Corrine Coffey

You say you love me
I say I love you
And I hope we will always be.

Sometimes I get scared
I think that someone will take
you away from me
But I know that you really care.

When we are around your friends
They ask you who I am
And you tell them we are just
friends

Even though you don't know it
hurts
It does very much so
And then all you do is flirt

I know you don't want to hurt me
But sometimes you do
I don't tell you, because you
might get mad at me

I know sometimes I hurt you
And I don't mean to
But sometimes I feel like I am
going to lose you

But over all
I still think I love you

Dedication to Sean Stewart

Daddy's Girl
Shelley Isham

A little girl dreams of that happy day
When she puts on a white dress and her Daddy gives her away.

Now, my day has come and I'm looking for you...
But God took you to a place, so that you might see your little girl from a different view.

Now you see her as an angel in lace
Pearls and satin — sparkling eyes light her face.

Daddy, I've found the one who loves me dear
I just wish there was some way you could be here!

So I prayed to God that He might give you a "pass"
Just to leave Heaven for a day, to see your baby get married —
Our dreams come true at last.

The day that I could share with the two men I love,
Then He said to me, "WE will be watching from above."
"Don't you worry, for your Daddy is in you.
He is a part of you in all that you do."

So, I am so glad you are here — just like every other day,
You've watched me grow and watched me play.
And you're watching me now as I walk down the aisle
Tears fall from your face when you see my big smile.

I know you'll be here to wipe away the happy tears that start to stream down my face.
For you are here today as you have always been, walking with me and holding my hand.

Happy Birthday, Jesus
Peggy Guynn Calloway

We thought of painting a beautiful scene on a birthday card.
We thought of planting You a flower garden that would
　　cover our whole yard.

We thought of going to the end of a rainbow and giving
You the pot of gold, but then we remembered we have
Your gift and even though it is old,

It is still the perfect gift for You and fitting I must say,
it's in mint condition for we've had it packed away.

It won't take us long, dear Lord, we know just where it is at,
it is down deep within our souls and won't be hard to get.

But there is no box to hold it nor a ribbon big enough,
There is not enough tape in this world to tape Your present up!

For it holds so many praises to You and Your Holy name,
Because of what You've done for us our lives are forever changed!

Why thy praises alone for You saving our souls no box could ever hold,
and eternal life You've given us free could never be bought with gold!

Flowers we could have given You, Lord, but they would only last a
　　few days,
And a birthday card we could have painted for You, but how could
　　one card say?

What we feel inside, dear Lord and what You mean to us
So we give to You these praises and in God's grace we trust.

That this birthday gift will last You, Lord, for all eternity,
One praise after another is the gift we give to Thee!

True Love's Spell
Andrea Soria
A thousand words wouldn't do
Because they can't describe how I feel for you

Look into my heart and tell me what you find
If only you could read what's on my mind

To my heart, you hold the very key
With you, I'm forever happy

To be away from you, I cannot bear
For in your eyes, I love to stare

Unlock my heart and look inside
My love for you, I cannot hide

I'm so happy that we got this chance
To share a very special romance

Hoping we won't ever say goodbye
A broken heart, will definitely make me cry

It could last forever
As long as we're happy together

A love like this doesn't happen everyday
This feeling in my heart is here to stay

That's all my heart has to tell
You've got me under True Love's Spell

Dedication: to Robert Ruiz, my inspiration

You Can Smile
N. Coupland
There are many troubles that will burst
like bubbles
There are many shadows that will disappear
When you learn to meet them with
A smile to greet them
For a smile is better than a frown
or a tear

You can smile when you can't say a
word
You can smile when you cannot be
heard
You can smile when it's cloudy
or fair
You can smile anytime, anywhere

Though the world forsake joy will
overtake you
Hope will soon awake you if you
smile today
Don't parade your sorrow, wait until
tomorrow
For your joy and hope will drive
The clouds away

When the clouds are raining don't begin
complaining
What the Earth is gaining should
not make you sad
Do not be a fretter, smiling is much
better
And a smile will help to make the
World Glad

110 In The Shade
Tony Franks
Music starts blaring, country and western
All I wanted was to recover, by resting.

Stress levels reached 110,
Neighbours start rowing, headaches back again.

5:30 am drunks start singing, buzzing noises,
Mosquitoes start singing.

TENERIFE sunshine greets me in bed
Shower's running, coffee's been med.

Pathways that were meant only for hikes
Underage teens out on motorbikes.

Rhyming words form a picture
an old girlfriend (HMM)! I shouldn't have ditched her.

Wanting to sort out my age that's past,
Taking it easy to make it last.

People I have met, some good and bad
will always say he's not a bad lad.

Truth in oneself is a certain must
You may go broke, but you'll never bust.

Waiting for a plane ride I sit in the shade,
All my problems begin to fade.

Dedication: to soul searchers and travelers

Four Seasons
Bernice Weddington Pernu
Flowers bloom in summer,
Spring brings new life and beauty, how
wonderfully nice.
Autumn is of deadness and slumber
Winter covers the Earth with a blanket of
frozen snow and ice.

Life goes on, on Earth, in the four seasons
Is there life in the starry and moonlit sky?
The mighty Creator has great reasons
For the beauty of the creation of Earth's by and by.

How awesome it seems, for our human
mind,
Who is to understand the beauty of
the winter snow?
The gentle breeze of spring and all its
kind
The fall and summer that seem to also
glow.

We search for work and toil from morn to
dusk
Looking for answers of life's problems and
health
But we could be quiet and still and watch
each thing rust,
Observe, instead the beauty of it all
And how it came to be, the creator to
bless us with such enormous
wealth.

Dedication: to my children Sharon, Fred, Delores, and Lee

Enchanted Dreams

New Life Insurance Company
Karen D. Green
INSURED... Whosoever will let Him come

PREMIUM... His grace is sufficient for thee

DATE... Now is the time

TERM... God never breaks His promise

SUBJECT TO CONDITION STATED; For God so loved the world that He gave His only begotten son that whosoever believeth on Him should not perish, but have everlasting life.

... "and thine health shall spring forth speedily"
... "my God shall supply all your need"
... "I am the bread of life"
... "he that hunger and thirst after righteousness shall be filled"
... "ask and it shall be given unto thee"

I believe in the Father, the Son and the Holy Ghost, the Trinity. I believe that Jesus is the Son of God, He died for me and rose for me. I confess with my mouth the Lord Jesus and believe in my heart. Thank you, Jesus, for SAVING me.

A new creature

Therefore, if any man (woman, boy or girl) be in Christ, he is a new creature

NEW LIFE

I am a child of the King, WITHOUT HIM YE CAN DO NOTHING, I can do all things through Christ which strengthens me.

Far Too Young
Jan Jones
I was only young
When I found you that day
You were only young
To be taken away.
You looked ASLEEP
But, yet I knew
I didn't really know just
What to do
I ran downstairs
To tell my Mum
I ran downstairs
To tell you to come
I was only 13
But, I knew you had died
I was so in shock
I never cried
A few days later
I had a dream
Inside my head
I started to scream
It's 27 years
Since that awful day
You were far too young
To be taken away
I picture your face
I remember the smell
I ran downstairs
I had to tell
This sadness that lives
With us all every day
You were far too young
To be taken away.

Imagine Please
Patricia McGrath
A rose of such unspeakable beauty,
Rising from a dull stem,
Touched by the hand of one gentle youth.

Each feels the softness of the other,
Each feels the delight of devotion
And each thinks,
"Never before has something
so pure been brought to
walk on Earth"

Dewdrops glisten,
Like tears from Heaven,
Each petal sings in tune with all,
—Take me,
For if you leave,
I shall wither and fade from sorrow—

In the youth's generous heart,
It beat unto thee silently,
Dear, Sweet Rose, Beauty as I have never seen,
I would love to hold you as only mine,
And let the world stand jealous,
But if selfishness takes you from your life
—you would soon be dead and gone—

So the youth withdrew the hand,
The Rose mistook the deed,
Such exquisite tenderness,
What abandonment is worse,
The delusion of betrayal,
Or the betrayal one's own heart would feel.

Pass Me By
Antoinette Washington
Pass me by
You the world
that wholes the Pie
Pass me by
Look down
Look away
I'm still around

I won't disappear
going away is not
in style

You make me this way
And you don't know how

Why don't you listen?
Why won't you see

One day you could
be just like me

So take my advice
Look and learn to help

I may need you
now
But I can't
pay you later
If you don't
help!!

Dedication: to Jessie, Mark and Billy

The Storm
Stephanie Mount

The Clouds stampeded through the sky
Like a war party thirsting for battle.
The wind follows behind like a lunatic filled with bloodlust.
Softly caressing my skin with a lover's touch one Moment,
The next ripping and tearing at my hair and clothes in a psychotic rage,
Assaulting my body with piercing shrieks and knife—like sands.
Then slows and simmers and kisses my face with apologetic tears.
The clouds, clothed in their armor of dark, smoky steel, set themselves
Above the Earth preparing to strike.
The wind about—faces and cackles at its deception.
The cloud army lets loose its spears of lightening
And war cries of thunder.
The spears stay confined within the warring masses above.
But, several lances miss their mark and fall to the Earth.
Drops of blood fall from the wounded
First slow and fat
But as arteries and veins are opened up, it runs in sheets
To soak the Earth.
The wind continues its ravings like Eris in her brother's chariot.
She drinks of the violence but is not sated by it.
She cries out for More and More and gets Stronger and Stronger.

I sit on the grass soaked in blood,
Feeling the cold bite of the wind as she tries to drink of my life.
I am enthralled by the chaotic beauty.
My eyes focused on the Heavens.
My heart beating with the thunder,
Stirred by the battle cries.

But then the boiling rage slows to a simmering anger.
The blood still falls but the lances become fewer.
The wounded retreat with their dead to a place beyond the horizon.

A Song Of Summer
William B. Smith

In the beauty of summer, God's Glory is displayed
In the heat and in the blue—white haze
In the lush, green foliage, in the smoky, blue skies
All praise God on these still, sultry days
The weeds and grasses, designed with beauty so fair
They put forth, they show, a glorious display
And all the butterflies, all the meadow flowers,
Created they are in colorful array

In the warmth of God's Presence, life and praise
spring up
In the simmering heat of the summer light
This song I seem to hear burst forth
"Glory to the Holy One, for all His creative
might."

In the humble silence, I hear them boast
The wonders of what, for them, God has done
"You have clothed us in such glory and of works
like yours, truly, there are none."

The grasshoppers and insects leap and dance for
joy
The birds, they too, they sing Your praise
And all creation does declare
"Who is like this God, Holy, He is, in all His
ways."

My heart, it too, does leap for joy
For His Glory has made my spirit shine
In the summery sunshine of God's grace
Inspiring me to call this great God, "Mine."

Robin
Christian Masot

Two of them
him and her,
under the mask of stars
the moon looks down
blessing him with the light to see her face
the waves applaud them
their timeless echoing in the distance
she looks at him
he realizes
The wind makes her hair dance
making him want to kiss her more
filled with confusion
what would she think
if fate would be so kind
what would she think
take the chance
feel her lips mimic his
what does she think
the waves silenced
blinded from the moon's light
sheltered from the wind
by her
she is all that matters
wishing for infinity
is fate a friend of his
lips separate
time returns
they separate
her reflection still in his eyes
confusion
they separate
the wind dances with her hair

A Mother Of Choice
Melanie Barnett

There is one person that makes my life complete,
She is so giving, so kind and sweet

And to this one person I owe so much,
She's taught me the value of a gentle touch.

When I've been down, she's always been there,
To lift me back up and show me she cares.

Why I was so lucky, I'll never know,
One thing's for sure, I'll never let go.

The memories we've shared, I hold so dear,
Which is why I know she'll always be near.

Together we are the perfect pair,
Mother and daughter, the times we share.

Of one so thoughtful, no words can explain,
This wonderful mother is far from plain.

In her heart, no selfishness to be found,
For her all about kindness, is profound.

As I think of the past, I am not depressed,
Because I know how richly I'm blessed.

So Mother, on your special day,
I would like to simply say.

I only hope to someday be
As good a mother as you've been to me.

Enchanted Dreams

Portrait Of God
Melody J. Carolan
To see, to hear, to taste, to smell and to feel.
Use these senses well and you will know that God is real.

His eyes are the million stars shining in the sky above,
Looking down upon us with His unconditional love.

His face is mirrored in the innocence of the young and
agelessness of old,
In all the faces around you and the joys and pains they
hold.

His smile is in the dawn of a brand—new day,
In the sunset and the rainbow, He brightens up the way.

His voice greets us in the song of the bird and summer breeze,
The clap of thunder, the murmuring streams and the whispering
of the trees.

He tastes of the salty sea air as it comes to the shore,
And the fruit, the food that His good Earth has bore.

He smells of flowers in the summers and springs,
The just—plowed Earth and the scent the rain brings.

His touch is of a brand—new leaf, or baby's tear,
A soft rose petal, or a newborn deer.

Seeing, hearing, tasting, smelling and feeling,
God's presence is always there, loving and healing.

This, then, is a portrait of my God,
I have seen Him and now give Him His laud.

Brief—Grief
Parrish R. Young
I'm feeling bad, I'm kind of sad, it's making me mad,
What am I going to do?

The mist in the air has me scared, high in the sky doves
see me cry,

Inside emotions full and true. What am I going to do?

Energy into motion, twisting and tumbling has me
grumbling.

If only when I think, it would be swift as a wink or to
blink,

then my feelings wouldn't be in such a kink.

My devotion is on emotions that clash with tempest like
the ocean. What am I going to do?

With feelings pushed to the side, I can diligently search
within and find a way to grin.

As one ponders on laughter now and times after, puts
emotions in precision and gives you a better vision.

With my heart strings not so blue, I know What I am
going to do!

Eat, laugh and be merry, then things can't get so scary.

Once my feeling was kind of steep, now I realize it
was only Brief—Grief, oh, how sweet!

Julia
Judith Davies
Stiff and stark and cold
just as the Bard had said.

A shrunken head indeed.
Every bone protruding, every hollow sunken deep.
The eyes, now closed, their merry sparkle gone;
Lips, that once had twitched to make a wicked smile, now disappeared down
into the deep black chasm of the open mouth.

She lay. I sat. Helpless both.

The kindly fussing, bustling of harassed nurse appeared clutching,
wrapped in gauze,
the teeth of the deceased.

Bottom set first. Shape to the mouth.
Top set... Not in.
Why not?

Dried, set hard, stuck into the roof of the plate
A toffee — her favourite kind — still there.

Irreligiously, we giggle
then wriggle
the denture home.

The face resumes a shape, almost a life.
And beneath the lids, I sense merry eyes glisten
And lips, now full again, somehow seem to grin.

They were her favourite toffees after all.

Untitled
Larry D. Reeves
It was the day before Valentine's,
and the two people were in love;

Man and woman lay in bed,
beneath the setting sun above.

The two were one in spirit,
mind, soul and body;

They knew it was love,
and not just something naughty.

Starting out slow,
but they were naked together;

And soon became more passionate,
their love is forever.

They thought only of the other,
their own pleasure wasn't a concern;

But in the height of their passion,
both pleasures would burn!

When at last, breathless and
exhausted, mate to mate;

They smiled into each other eyes
and said, "That was great!"

Dedication: to Leslie, my love

Acer Et Superbus
Ian Strain

"Acer et Superbus" is a footballing tale but with no
trophies of silver but plenty of ale.

It speaks of a team that would never grow frail and
who in its day could always prevail.

For when it was wind and rain or pain or mud their
Agincourt hearts would persist like no other teams could.

Their brave hearts and rough skills were neatly distilled
and they would charge forth with careless will.

The purest of all with these distilled skills was the keeper
"Mad Muzza" who feared no ills.

But now there's no call of "Berry on the ball" which for
one brief, shining Moment made us all feel ten feet tall.

Gone, too, is the shout that rang out when the defense
had been cleared when all of the lads spontaneously
cheered – "Headband!"

No, now the lads have been parted, some to foreign lands,
and the tradition's been passed on – but to less worthy hands.

So what trace of this team? Does its name adorn trophies?
Do its lads command great fees?

No! What made it so special was not results or great form –
it was the crack; the way we played; the manner those shirts
were worn!

Within My Heart
Barbara Caldwell George

To bare one's soul
To open one's heart
Is the more of the one who loves you
Is shared with you like no one other.

Each time with you
In the Moments of depth
I give to you the beats I feel
Within my heart.
I share with you the wonders
Discovering in myself.

You are a gift to me
In each present of you
I unwrap the more of who I am
And find myself more real
I will always be myself for you.

What of the fears I ever hold
For all the who of you
And me and the love we hold within
A Sacred Space we save between
For a time to share in God's inviting grace.

Who you are for me
Awakes new hope
Refreshes commitments to the
Who I am.

I am what am for the
Love of you.

Princess Di
Elias Ahmed

Heavens have called you back Diana,
Heavens have called you back

Your smile brought smiles to millions
Your never–ending love lifted us to ecstasy
Your gift of giving touched many a soul

Heavens have called you back, Diana
Heavens have called you back

You are the rose of roses, Diana
Spreading the sweet, sweet scent of goodness
Blanketing the Earth with your charm and aura
and were the sunshine of many a heart
A shining star of hope and harmony
Spreading and giving joy to the world

Heavens have called you back, Diana
Heavens have called you back

You were the Royal of Royals, Diana
A beauty unmatched in all this universe
With soft heart and a knack to reach in distress
A true worker for the ill and the poor
Unabashed generosity and radiant elegance
Dazzling everyone around you
Your innocence has left an imprint of gleam in our eyes
And you were loved more than you will know, Diana

Heavens have called you back Diana
Heavens have called you back

My America
Jay Hip

Proud to be an American
Wherever I go
I shall let everyone know
I am proud to be an American
All through the states I will stroll
Over all of our highways I shall roll
Remembering wherever I go
I am proud to be an American
I may not be rich
But freedom I see
Love for my country is part of me
I see people standing hand–in–hand
All are proud of their land
Together, when necessary, they will take a
Stand
This country is the greatest in all the lands
I am proud to be an American
As I stand and salute my flag
Tears of joy are dropping from my eyes
Our flag is waving real high
As it is passing me right by
I am so proud to be an American
No country is so free as this sweet land
Of liberty
No country holds such mighty dreams
Our freedom is the beauty of our land
As we sing the songs of freedom
We hold out our hands and our prayers
Our love for man is never–ending
Children singing throughout the land
I am proud to be an American

Enchanted Dreams

The River
Rye Palmer
The river swells high
Destroying all in its path
Earth is dead no more

April Showers
Alison Stranger
It's raining outside!
Heavy drops thud, rhythmically against the glass,
the fragile borders of my world,
a warm, watery lullaby.
Yet there is no peace — feelings of despair well up and drip, tearfully
    into focus,
reflections of the person before me merge with memories of shared
    Moments.
My soul is lost in you.
A torrent of emotion, stinging reality,
It's raining inside!

A lifetime ago, we were radiant, sunshine reigned.
Abruptly, the skies darkened, hopes faded,
submitting before the relentless advance of the clouds.
Shades of gray but the dream is still visible, emphasized in silhouette.
Oh, where is the light?

The winds of change summon strength, lifting my spirit away on the whim
    of a breeze;
a wild, whirlwind journey into the unknown, finally easing, their force
    spent.
Emotions blossom and die as surely as the seasons change.
With renewed hope, I embrace the freshness of a Spring day and wonder at
    the unpredictability of love.

Dedication: for Richard

Just Wanted You To Know
Wanda Starks
Just thought you should know
You have been appreciated in a very big way
The tiniest things embedded in my mind, will forever stay

Just thought you should know
Your trust in me has not escaped my attention
Highest honor that could be paid, I thought I should mention

Just thought you should know
Although, at times, quite rocky with tears
The respect that has been shown will last through the years

Just thought you should know
Your fidelity has won my heart
You made a great sacrifice so we could have a pure start

Just thought you should know
Our last date surprisingly afforded the opportunity to see
Insight into your character, yes, you have truly claimed me

Just thought you should know
Your arrogance was not part of the plan
But with your heart of gold, you remain my dream man

Just wanted you to know
Because of all the above and more
You are very deeply loved, right down to the core

Dedication: to my loving husband, Roy Starkes

Haiku
Linda J. Ziolkowski
Frail is the willow,
her limbs aching and brittle;
she will weep no more.

Two Hearts
Rebecca Sparks
Classic case of boy meets girl
From the start, they were each other's world
You couldn't tear them apart
Each held the other one's heart
They were young and had a lot to learn
Knew what they wanted
And had some time to burn
Couldn't wait for the day
When they'd make their getaway

Two hearts in love
and that's how they'll stay
Young hearts so strong
that they'll never stray
Forever in love
these two hearts will stay

As they say their vows
Swear they'll never part
Rings on one hand
on the other their hearts
"I do" are those two words
They'll say today
Forever in love
These two hearts will stay

Dedication: to Craig — I love you always

To Mikey, With Love
Candelee Woodward Wilson
To Mikey, our brother, a son and faithful
friend;
Your loss has caused us all to grieve, when
your life came to an end.

From this tragic mishap; I feel is still
not real;
God left us your spirit to help us all to
heal.

Mikey, weapons alone are not dangerous,
guns do not kill;
It's the person who pulls the trigger
upon his own free will.

You tested fate instead of faith, a
choice often mistaken;
A death so young is a misgiving to
cause us all to awaken.

God gives his hand to guide us but,
often we walk away;
Never looking back, we walk alone until,
our judgement day.

To Mikey, our brother, a son and faithful
friend;
It's time to close this chapter and time for
our hearts to mend.

The Anthology of Poems

Haiku: 4th of July
Gloria A. Jones
Opal stars and stripes
garnet red and sapphire blue
patriotic gems

Truth Seeker
Sherilyn Biagini
Truth Seeker from afar, truth seeker, that's what
you are. Living in a world that's so different from
you, you gotta get out and find the truth.
An endless journey you dare to take, all the
promises and sacrifices that you make

Truth Seeker from afar, truth seeker, that's what
you are. The people here don't understand and
doubt they will, even if they can – but for now
believe and it might be true – all those
dreams you made, don't turn them blue.

Truth Seeker on an endless search, looking for
truth on the highest perch.
Truth Seeker from afar, truth seeker, that's what
you are. Now don't you stop, don't be afraid
find that rainbow of truth before it fades.

Truth Seeker, I hear your cry, a mighty voice
way up high. Truth Seeker from afar, truth
seeker, that's what you are.
Truth Seeker so far from home, truth seeker
So all alone.
Truth Seeker, was it meant to be, when
you find your rainbow, you'll be set free
Truth Seeker from afar, truth seeker, that's
what you are.

Nothing Is Enough
Gloria Jean West
Having the worldly things are not of my concern
Getting my star and crown is what I am trying to earn
Into this world, nothing did I bring and nothing can I take
But I can keep my faith in God and be saved from the fiery lake

For my journey in life is like being in the valley low, the
River deep and the mountain steep.
But I fail not to keep in mind that the Lord is my
Shepherd and I am His sheep.
At night I get down on my bending knees, I cry out, "Lord,
have mercy on me, please,
Let Your angels stand guard as I lay sleep in my
bed. Keeping death away so that I do not wake up
dead.

However, if my soul gets trapped and my body has to
be placed in the ground, it is my Soul I want You
to save before I lay my body down.
But if it's not my time for sleeping on and I do not go,
This means my prayers were answered by You once more."

So when I rise in the morning and my eyes see
the daylight, I will say "thank You, Lord" for watching
over me all night. Even as I go travelling about through
the day, I'll thank You for not letting me go astray
Then, as the day comes to a close and again the sunset,
I then will say, "Lord, I am not thanking You yet."

Dedication: Mr. and Mrs. Ernest Clements

Being
Myron E. Yoder
To Be,
is to soar free,
and life begins
anew.

Ode To The Queen Of The Skates
Fred Duffield
My name is Melissa
I am Queen of the skates
I fly around the pavements
Crashing into gates.

I skate with such elegance
I glide with such glee
Eye's glued to the pavement
Ouch! Never saw that tree.

Dad said I'm crazy
But I say I'm not
Just a bump on my knee
And a bruise on my bot.

Mum runs round the kitchen
Protecting her plates
Who cares ! I'm Melissa
The Queen of the skates.

Dad said, when I'm older
I can skate where I like
But to be on the safe side
I should stick to my bike.

Dedication: to my daughter Melissa, with love

Breath Of Unity
Julie Saggers
Breathe into me,
Your endless galaxies...
Your perfected soul...
The ever long melodical tunes,
That make injustices insignificant.

Breathe into me,
A pictorial image of perfection...
A salt–stained vision of hope...
A jubilation of eternal greatness,
A Heaven–claimed sanctuary.

Lead me from the shadows,
Beg me from the silence...
I will follow...
Close behind...

I will breath into you...
If you so desire...
The infinite intensity of my world,
My well–developed sense of humour...
The candlelight silhouettes of yesterday,
And the twin flames of tomorrow...

Night caresses our weaknesses,
And melts away our frozen confections...
While we create the,
Ultimate illimitable
Breath of unity.

Enchanted Dreams

Spring Legacy
Wanda E. Sanders
April yields a profusion of blooms
That makes my painful heart sing
A gift graciously given
I now have wings!

Springtime
Christine Ledbury
The early morning blackbirds song.
The daylight does extend,
These are the signs to tell us,
Winter nears its end.

The sunshine—golden daffodils.
With their trumpet heads held proud,
Blow softly in the gentle breeze,
Erasing winter's shroud.

With excited twittering, to and fro,
Birds fly on full–extended wing.
Beaks laden full of twigs and moss.
For their new nests they bring.

Each springtime day stretches longer,
Buds burst forth on each bare tree,
New life is born and these miracles,
Are there for us all to see.

So through your busy daytime hours,
Make time to sit a while,
And take in all these wondrous things,
Then share a springtime smile.

Dedication: to Alan, Rebecca and Greg – my world

Gathering Wisdom
Louise Judge
Gather Wisdom as you gather flowers, for its perfume is rich in understanding.
Wisdom's petals fall as drops of Knowledge, gathered by the Righteous.
For them the way is alight with Discernment, they know where the gathering takes place.
Wisdom is very Precious to them, it is as Jewels are to those who walk in folly.
Wisdom to the young is but a trifle, but to the Old in years it is as drops of Honey.
For it is Rich to the taste and Powerful in its Usage.

Those who use it, do not fall into the Pit, nor under the influence of evil ones.
Wisdom has a Protection and a Shield that none can break through.

Wisdom to the powerful is a Fruit most desired, only given if the One desiring it is Virtuous, for it is Truly more Precious than Gold.
It opens doors and hearts that are unobtainable by Worldly goods.
For such is its Power that man would Ransom His Soul.
But to no avail to Him that is Unclean.

Wisdom is Born from God and He alone is Pure and Holy.
Only He can bestow the Precious Gift and all the Fruits that come from it.
For the Nectar is from Heaven and only gathered by those who Know its Fruit.
Therefore Search for it and Guard it when it is found.
Let its Nectar enrich you all Your Days.

Love's Light
Phillip LeChance
Love's light forever burning.
My heart's hot blood churning.
Without love, I'm forever yearning.
About Love, I will be forever learning.

To Our Four Sons And Two Daughters
Elizabeth B. Newby
When the time comes
For you to leave
To begin travelling
Life's trail on your own
Here are rules we hope
You take with you
When you break those ties
And leave home.
Yes! Reach for the moon
In your dreams
If you should fall
Hang onto a star
Always honest in all
Of your dealings
So you are pleased
With the person you are.
Take each day as it comes
And be thankful
Of the blessings
We each can enjoy
Ours have been multiplying
Over and over
Since given each girl
And each boy.

Dedication: to my six children

Last In The Clas
Cathy Cassidy
Im sit in here alone to nite I shud be in my bed
But I thought Id take my pen out and lern to rite instead

Watt cud I put on a sheet no topics in me head
A pile of books is on the shelf but not wan of them I've red

I opened up a world book Oh, boys was it a stoper
So I voted with myself to change the damm thing for the topper

I shud ave larned a little more when I was at the skool
But I thought it was much more fun to sit and act the fool

I didn't mind the lessons of them I had no feer
What they tried to drum in one side went straght out the other ear

They put a som up on the bord it made my brains so sore
The master tore his hair out wen I sad 3 n 3 made 4

I cudnt see wat made the fus I only dun my best
But the master give me to each hand and sed I was a pest

Then the teachers called a meetin to iron out their plite
The task to ed–u–kate me keep them lying wake at nite

They sent a note to Ma and Da to ask them to attend
But they sed I was a black sheep and my ways I must ammend

So I think I'll just review the case sur that has sed it all
Ill thro away the blody pen and rally down the hall

The Anthology of Poems

As I Look
Aulia Claytor
As I cry, I look into his
eyes, They are like butterflies.
Flying across a blue, wounded sky.
Surrounded by evergreens.

God Is Love
Chris C. Guinn
God made the Earth with plants and trees,
You could tell that He was pleased.
God made the fish and birds in flight,
After He made day and night.

God made Adam, then made Eve.
Adam named the plants and trees.

Eve offered fruit to Adam, then,
He took a bite and sin began.

God was not pleased and He was sad.
From there on out, our world was bad.

God loves you and He loves me,
God sent his Son to set us free.

The Christ that lived, died on the Cross,
Took our sins and saved the lost.

Once you are saved, you then will see,
That you will live eternally.
Our Father lives now happily...
Inside of you, inside of me.

Dedication: to all of God's children

Lost Visions
Lisa Thomas
A story awaits to be told, of a land so bright and green.
In an empty field of rolling hills, caught in a world just in between.

Millions of soldiers marched to war, day and night, night and day.
Through rain, snow, fog and sleet, was the warrior's fighting way.

Diseases spread man to man, helmets aplenty scattered around.
People sobbing in despair, rifles and cannons crying out loud.

Trenches exploding by grenades, bodies falling all around.
Broken limbs lay everywhere, puddles of blood amidst the ground.

Fallen warriors returning to land, soldiers' names carved in stone.
Graves of many line the Earth, never to journey home.

People's hearts must never be cold, we must not run and hide.
We must remember the boys we lost, the boys, who died.

Let us not forget the pain and cries, agonies, heroes and smiles.
The time that was so long ago, across so many miles.

People remember the day, by wearing poppies for those who died.
We still shed a tear here and there, for both the enemy's and Ally's side.
The war began and ended sadly, while we watched in disbelief.
A nation takes back its land, with little, but noticeable, grief!

Dedication: to Grandpa Reinhart for his encouragement

Untitled
Pamela L. Burnette
What for have I lived to see this bright blue sky?
What for shall I die to have left no mark on this world?
What for have I laughed but only for a fleeting Moment?
What for have I loved, only to feel Heaven on Earth.

Gone Forever
Cherie DuPlayee–Brown
Forget his name, forget his face.
Forget his kiss and warm embrace.
Forget the love that you once shared.
Forget the fact that he once cared.
Forget the time you spent together.
Remember now, he's gone forever.
Forget him when he played your song.
Forget you cried the whole night long.
Forget how close you once were.
Remember now, it's him and her.
Forget you memorized his walk.
Forget the way he used to talk.
Forget the times he was so mad.
Remember now, he's happy, not sad.
Forget his gentle, teasing ways.
Forget you saw him yesterday.
Forget the things you used to do.
Remember that she loves him, too.
Forget the thrill when he went by.
Forget the times he made you cry.
Forget the way he said your name.
Remember now, it's not the same.
Forget the time that went so fast.
Forget those times – they're in the past.
Forget he said, "I'll leave you never."
Remember now, he's gone forever.

Baby Dreams
Ana M. Sloan
I look at my belly
And will it to grow

I wish for a stirring
That will let me know

Soon, from my womb
Will spring forth a new life

But month after month
It cuts like a knife

To find that within me
There's nothing but space

I'm told to be patient
Accept the slow pace

I think, yes, of course,
That's easy to say

But walk in my shoes
And feel for one day

The sadness, the longing
The diminishing hope

I have dreams, I have faith
I am strong, I will cope

Hell
Sally Erickson

Inside my own protective shell
I trapped myself in torturous hell

Not knowing what my fears were about
I was afraid to let the anguish out

The pressure built inside my chest
I yearned to give up and rest

Without warning, how could I know
My fears released in one massive blow

My body trembled
My heart beat fast

I wasn't sure
My life would last

The explosive pain made me yell
And in the process I escaped from hell

As my shattered self mends from the blow
Back to hell I'll never go

As I heal and rest in calm
I'm so grateful I detonated that bomb.

He Comes
Nicole Seevers

He comes to me, day and night
I can't see him, but I know he's there
He makes me feel so special inside
It hurts when he goes by

We Are Like Christ
Glenn Farris

We are like Christ – a mini–Christ
Issue like Him of a mother's womb.
Surrounded are we by more luxury, certainly,
But of human flesh with some divinity and
Endowed by a living God who dared not create
Gross imperfection in image of Himself in matters of destiny
and free will.

Given, too, a guiding conscience as decisions' balance wheel
But, O, yes, a real difference here: when devils tempted Him
He lost no battle to temptation while we oft–times suppress
right tendencies
To embrace allurements of base men and circumstances.

But, just as often, thanks to God, when we deviate from befitting conduct
His hand touches our shoulder and His divine finger points out the
goal again
So once more we become like Christ, re–fortified with love, compassion
And indulgence for all fellow creatures from whom we
Ask forgiveness when our transgressions bruise and wound.

At each break of day we must recall: "we are like Christ; the chance
we have to perform small miracles for family, friends and strangers
as well – all brothers and sisters of ours in Christ."

Our Earthly task must endure til our last heart–beat when, in breathless
Anticipation, we hope to hear: "Well done, my child, you were a Christ,
A little Christ, it's true, but sent to help those you touched
Seek the reward of Heaven for all eternity. Now come into your glory."

The Real Abode Of God
S. Suhela Nashtar

Shattering the idols of jealousies and viciousness.
Extinguishing the fires of hatred and enmity.
Lifting the curtain of hypocrisy from face.
Enlighten the heart with the "candles of love"
Because the heart is the real abode of God.

The Fall Of Troy
Mark Hebert

Variations on a Theme by Kit Marlowe – (1564–1593)
Was this the face that launched a thousand ships,
And burned the topless towers of Ilium?
Sweet Helen, make me immortal with a kiss.

(Dr. Faustus, Act V)
There comes a presence with this fall of night.
Deep memories, burned into my every sense
And summoned by the fading of the light,
Assail my study's darkening emptiness.

They take her perfect form. I glimpse that face.
Pierced by the vision of those steel–blue eyes,
Snared in that tangled mane of night–dark lace,
Bleeding, I yield to her, myself as prize.

I hear, transported now by passion's force,
Above the city night–noise, distantly,
The splashing of a myriad of ancient oars,
My spirit's thousand ships are all at sea,

My vessels tossed ashore, their raiders starved–
As warring hoards to self–destruction turn–
While, in the ravished city of my heart,
My Ilium, the topless towers burn.

Tidbits And Green Nails
Bob Carreiro

Tidbits and green nails biting at my toes,
Long have I been without thee, fighting with my foes.
I think I may be sanity lost,
Without thee I fear me and would trade at all cost.

Tidbits and green nails biting at my hand,
Oh, how I long to hold thee far across the land.
For strength in its entity cannot be absorbed,
I am veering off the ends of the Earth, my lifeforce being poured.

Tidbits and green nails biting at my brain,
Stronger am I now, weakening the chain.
The third month is the fishes, although I cannot swim as far,
Is why I sit and write this poem and wonder how you are.

Tidbits and green nails biting at my toes,
Entrapped are my feelings, I must let them go.
I labor at incantations, but it arrives not,
A sorcerer I mustn't be, it is empty, my pot.

Tidbits and green nails biting at my hands,
I struggle to write this message far across the lands.
Shall I strike with my sword, or draw on my bow?
How can I engage in this duel, my enemy is whom I not know!

Tidbits and green nails engulfing my heart.
I am losing what I once had; it was many, it was a lot.
Cry if you must, but was it not nice,
To be as free as the birds and trapped like the mice?

Limerick
Bernie Kuntz
Doctor Fix told old Gert: 're your spasm,
Medications might help – my store has 'em!
Wait, you said you've just wed ——
The strange feelings in bed?
Don't complain, that's no pain – it's orgasm!

William
May Parker
Where are you, William? Can you hear me?
The time we had together was short, but the love in your eyes was there
    for all to see;
The years we shared are precious, William; we all love you and
    especially me.

I throw the ball, but you don't retrieve it;
I shout and call, but you cannot hear me.
I miss your toothy grin when I come through the door;
I miss the kiss you give to me as I lean toward the floor.

The house is quiet without you, but I still cannot believe that you are
    gone;
Life is lonely without you, but your love and affection lingers on.

When I die and go to Heaven, please be there to welcome me;
I know that when those Gates are opened wide, you will be there, waiting,
    inside;
With your toothy grin and your love for all to see.
I will lean toward the floor and you will kiss me again.

I love you, my precious William;
I always will.

Dedication: to Catherine and Stephen

You Have The Key
Charlotte Henry
I put a lock on my heart.
The key I tossed away.
Nobody was to enter,
As the nights turned into days.

My heart needed protection,
For it must have time to mend.
It had been broken to pieces,
Tossed around time and time again.

As if it were a puzzle,
For it didn't resemble a heart at all.
Due to neglect and apathy,
There were pieces both big and small.

As you unlocked my heart,
With the key held tightly in your hand.
For now my heart is mending together,
From the warmth of a very caring man.

Now as the nights turn into days,
I have you in my heart and on my mind.
It gives me a close tender feeling,
For a man so gentle, sweet and kind.

Now that you have unlocked my heart.
As you tightly hold the key.
I know all about lonesome.
Will you teach love to me?

Gateaux The Mathematician
Matthew W. Funk
There once was a man named Gateaux
Who lived on top of a plateau.
His notion of direction
Deserves resurrection
Right near his aesthetic chateau!

Search Right
Calvin Pratt
Search right, use God light
Don't let the devil school you
Because he will only fool you
Tell him that he is a liar
And that you are not for hire
Because his soul is headed for that burning fire
Don't fall for his ol' dirty work called sin
'Cause it will only do you in
Get on your knees and pray
So God can show you the way
Remember God wants us
That's why He sent Jesus
He is so ever sweet and nice
So please take His advice
Because His last name is Christ
So hold your head high
And let the sinful ways pass you by.
And if your life seems to be a real bore
And you need just a little bit more
Just remember He's knocking at your door
Stay away from the devil's work chart
Give Jesus the key to your heart
Because there's where your new life starts.

Dedication: to Sharon Kay Martin Morris, sister

But No More
Elizabeth Wallis
Your face I see waiting at my door,
Your paws across the floor, running.

But no more.

Your happy sounds to see me home
Your loving licks upon my hands and face.

But no more.

The balls you chased across the lawn,
The friends you watched from your garden wall.

But no more.

Our walks along the country lanes,
Our happy hours together.

But no more.

By the fire so safe and warm you lie,
I kiss your face and say good–night.

But no more.

My footprints heavy to your grave,
Goodbye my faithful, loving friend.

But now I dream.

Enchanted Dreams

My Little Angel
Edith Soucie
My little angel up above, please look down on the ones we love.
Keep our children from going astray, help them find a better way.
Teach them to listen to what parents say so they may guide them all of
    their days.
Every morning I look up high to see my angel in the sky.

The Dumb Prayer
Calvin A. Austin
There was a man who would always come for the hour of prayer,
And every week you could always find him sitting there,
People would come in and say hello and he would nod his head,

But no one ever heard a word that he might have said,

One night the devotion leaders asked for someone to come up and pray,
Being a mystery, all eyes fell on the quiet man, to hear what he had to
say,
He was reluctant for they did not understand,
But he went on up thinking, maybe this was God's plan,

He knelt down, but nothing was heard,
For his lips were moving, but no one heard a word,
He was down there for a long while and tears rolled down his face,
And amazement swept over the entire place,
He finally got up and as he walked by he heard someone Mumble,
"what is Wrong with that guy?"
The man turned around and wrote these words on the board for
everyone to see

"You asked me to come up here, now some make fun of me,
You see, I am dumb, so you cannot hear the words as my lips part,
But it does not matter, for God does not worry about the words I speak,
for He hears my heart."

Missing You
Dana Sue Brown
I lie in my bed so fragile and cold
No one beside me. No one to hold

Awake all night with nothing to do
In the latest hours. I am thinking of you

After I drift so slowly to sleep
I dream one day I will be yours to keep

To have and to hold till death do us part
I was the one who broke my heart

In my dreams I wish so much
But most of all to feel your touch

When I wake, you are the first thing on my mind
How could I have been so stupid and been so blind

Hours pass so slowly, the days are so long
Months go by as I realize I was wrong

As days slowly passed and months turned into years
I flooded my heart with so many tears

Back in my bed to lie fragile and cold
Wishing so much I had you to hold

It's not only at night that I miss your touch
But it's now and always that I miss you so much

Love will last, don't forget the past
Christopher Foley
People say love can't last, I shall not forget the past. This one goes out
    to the one I love,
who is now watching down from up above. My heart and soul will keep on
    waiting, for the day my life force be faded,
only then will I be happy. In her loving arms, bring joy back to life...

Love
Debra Ann Donato
Sitting around innocently; not waiting for something
to happen... just solitude.
Suddenly... unexpectedly... a slap in the face!!!

Luckily, ... was pulled to safety, not knowing how.

Oh, no... the next may be worse... or better?!

Or will there be a next?

How or when will it come, ... or how strong will it be?

Will there be somebody? vegetable? nobody?

Will the life end in happiness? misery? tragedy?

Who knows, does
ANYBODY?!!

Just reach out in the darkness...

If you
DARE!!!

Dedication: to Dan, my deepest love forever

I've Been There
Ruth Carter
I've seen happiness beyond compare. And I've seen heartbreak,
Loneliness and misery that I never dreamed would be there.
I've given my heart and soul, my love and every ounce of my
entire strength to the one I love so dear. I put them on a pedestal,
with dreams to reach the sky. And yet, I find myself asking why?
Why did this happen to me?

We ran and romped and carried on and had so much fun. But as the
years passed by, I find myself rejected by this same one. As I sit and
look out at the great big world, I try to read the stars that shine so
bright afar, then I only bow my head and say, "Yes, I've been there."

I've been through the good times and I've had the bad. I'm in this
world of a large, large crowd and yet I'm all alone. I feel used and
unloved. A smile here and there, but yet no one to care. Oh, yes, I
still go on about my daily chores, hiding my pride, trying to cope
with life's pressure, but I'm dying inside.

So friend, if you're struggling with life's ups and downs, your mind
so confused you can hardly remember your name and you feel
that you've been cheated and fate has been unfair, well, just
remember, you're not alone, for I've been there.

And now, with my own tears blotting my lines and the story
coming to an end, I must say, "If I don't make it, as I lay down my
pen and fold up my paper and raise from my chair, just keep in
mind the words that I've written, for I've been there."

Dedication: to Kimberley and Mark Hayes, daughter and grandson

Energy
Debbie Anderson

As warm sand sweeps across my feet,
The power of the ocean enthralls me.
The overwhelming thrust of the wave,
Enrages me by her beauty.
Without resistance,
I accept the invitation to ride her.

Dashing towards mesmerizing comber,
I plummet myself in her essence.
As my arms burn with adrenal furor,
A sigh of victory releases my being.
The "line–up" becomes my reality.

Gazing the horizon,
Her beauty rolls upon me.
Insanity, Euphoria, Passion,
Rush through my veins.
Paddling like a tortoise, I accept her energy.

A few seconds become an eternity...
All becomes black.
My body flops like a rag doll,
While her strength endures.

Dedication: to Kim, my friend and strength

Peer Pressure
Gina Krohl

This is me and you can't change it.
I am what I am and you can't rearrange it.
So if I say, "that's not for me,"
Just leave me alone,
It's not what I want to be!

To The Family Of Jack McMahan, Jr.
John Ristow

Jack McMahan was something to everyone here,
Grandson, son, brother, cousin, all shedding a tear.
Countless friends, co–workers and people he just knew,
All gathered together today to pay their final respects to.

But this is not a funeral but a celebration of life,
To remember all the happy times, not just his strife.
Anyone who knew him and you all knew him well,
Can remember these instances I am about to tell.

He was a dedicated freightliner employee for 13 years straight,
Although no awards for attendance and he had been occasionally late.
He would fix your car but borrow your tools,
Never quite understanding the borrowing rules.

If you needed it he would get it and usually very fast,
Only don't ask how or who owned it last.
His rock and roll played proudly to the highest degree,
Just ask his neighbors, they used to like country.

Jack was competitive in motorcycle racing or anything,
No middle ground for him, he had to be king.
His nickname was "Action" and that really says a lot,
If you needed his support that's exactly what you got.

Jack was special to a lot of people in a lot of ways,
Putting his friends above all to the last of his days.
He'll be sorely missed by friends and family alike,
As he shows off for God, doing tricks on his bike.

---

6 Feet Tall
Muriel Wheeler

If you want to be 6 feet tall,
Keep your eyes on, "God" most of all,
And when the money starts rolling in,
You will be wearing the biggest grin,
Because, you kept your eyes on, "God" most of all,
You are now 6 feet tall.

I Miss You Daddy
Brandy D. Gabriel

It's hard for me, Daddy, to say good–bye, pain in my heart and tears
in my eyes, I miss talking to you, Daddy and you just being here,
you taught me to love and to have no fear. Daddy, we shared a lot
of things, like winter, summer, fall and spring. It's not like you left
us for no reason at all, you had to go because God had called.
But here I sit, late at night, trying to convince myself, everything
will be alright. You told me to take care of
Mama and that's what I will do, but still it's hard to fill your shoes.
Daddy, I miss you so very bad, time doesn't help, it just makes me
sad. I remember the silly things you would do, I remember time
shared between me and you, I think of you, Daddy, all the time,
your loving memory weighs heavy on my mind. I know you're
not sick, Daddy, anymore, you've walked through Heaven's
golden door. I can almost see you in a glow of light singing
Heavenly songs day and night. I wish I could touch you one more
time to tell you all the things on my mind. Daddy, you told me I had
to be strong, you told me not to be sad because
you were going home, But I just can't help this pain in my heart,
the uneasy feeling that we are so far apart. Daddy, I know what
I have to do in order to be with you, I have to be patience and
I have to be good and do all the things I should and on that glorious
day all my pain will go away. So until I see you in Heaven above,
Daddy, I'm sending you all my love.

Dedication: to the memory of David T. Gabriel

Roy J.
Joanna MacDonald Sapp

Christmas? Oh, yes, we had snow!
Did I go sledding? Sadly, no
But it brought back the year
when I was five and
Roy J. Schilling was close by my side

I loved the sound of the name
he bore. So I shouted it loudly
more and more
Roy J. Schilling, come out, I say!
We're going sledding
I hope, today

Our ride from the yard down
to the street
Was a thrill we thought could
not be beat
Up and down that little hill
Till into the snow, we both
would spill

Running home to warm by the fire
Out again in half–an–hour
Our mothers had the patience of Job
Wrapping us warmly, every day
Did we ever thank them, Roy J.?

Dedication: to Sopha E. MacDonald, my mother

Enchanted Dreams

Someone Else's Child
Nicholas Spencer
If she were to ask me:
Could you love someone else's child?
I would kiss her lightly on the cheek
and reply:
Are you not someone else's child,
and do I not love you?

San Francisco
Ron Seuberling
Such a wondrous place, this "City By the Bay".
Its beauty so enhances, the wonder of each day.
Wherever rising hills, push downward toward the wharves.
and parks resemble threads, of gorgeous, silken scarves.
This city, made of hills, bids you here to live.
Saying... "Here!... Enjoy!... Partake of all I give.
Welcome, all my guests! At work or here to play.
Be tantalized; enthralled; you'll never go away."

The San Francisco charms, embellished by its sounds.
arias of bells and horns and seaside noise abounds.
This city's great, because it's old. Not old, but just not "new".
It fits us all with comfort, Like a favorite, casual, shoe.

Its so blase to those who live and work, right here in town.
The ones whose life is mingled with all the sites around.
Those whose very being, is driven... yes, controlled,
by the city and its treasures, each day as they unfold.

If asked, they'd hardly notice, the fog, or crowds or rain.
Simply shiny links of a brilliant, golden chain.
A chain called "San Francisco, City By The Bay".
"Who would ever leave here, for even one small day?"

Dedication: to Martina: my San Francisco heart!

Train II
Camerone A. Welch-Thorson
They Mumble incoherently, they beg openly:
"Please a quarter so's that ah might eat. I ain't had nuthin' in two days."

They attach themselves to the walls, sticky with sweat and
caked-on dirt from lack of water and soap.
They drool, with spittle running over bearded stubble, oozing sores,
coated with pus and dried blood.

They stare at you with empty orbits that seem to know that this is
their fate.
They reach toward you with malformed and bruised, nail-bitten
and yellowed hands, asking, no, begging — begging for something,
for anything...

And what do we do? — nothing.

We walk on by — closing our eyes to the sights, our ears to the sounds,
our noses to the stench of urine and regurgitated slop.

... They exist — a day-to-day struggle. They cannot cry, their wells have
   long ago run dry.
They are many ages — they are all aged, used, forgotten, abused — they
   are left to rot among the rafters of our society.

And we, what do we do? We shut our eyes, lock our minds, close our hearts,
   think no thoughts and go on;
Go on living our day-to-day struggle, not much different from those we
   choose to ignore.

Quiet
Nathan Williams
Quiet is a sound you cannot hear,
even when you listen, nothing is there.
You know, quiet is rather queer,
like the sound of snow hitting your hair.

Dedication: to my wife and daughter

I'm Supposed To Be A Christian
Linda Shane
I'm supposed to be a Christian
I go to Church every Sunday
Sing in the Choir like an angel
But when my brother needs a helping hand
I won't even extend my hand to help
I'M SUPPOSED TO BE A CHRISTIAN!

I'm looked up to in my community
And admired by my Pastor
I work faithfully in the Church
And pay my Tithes and Offerings
I'M SUPPOSED TO BE A CHRISTIAN!

I attend Prayer Meeting faithfully
Yet my heart is made of steel
Don't ask me to pray for you
My prayer life's not really real
I'M SUPPOSED TO BE A CHRISTIAN!

I have deceived so, so many...
And I know it's a horrible shame
But I'm a WOLF IN SHEEP'S CLOTHING
And to me it's just a game.

Dedication: to my daughter: Darcellia M. Shane

Fall Reverie
Alma M. Holm
Looking thru the Kitchen window —
A favorite pastime —
Morning sky, blue overhead,
Treetops dancing
To the tune of the wind
Branches swaying lightly
Ever so graceful —
Sometimes so still
Beautifully green, though it is still fall
And as I watch
A vigorous breeze begins to blow –
Treetops wildly dancing now
I see small patches of fall yellow
Shining in the early morning sun – –
Now the whole tree is moving
Branches bending, twisting —
Again, quiet stillness reigns
The wind doesn't know its full strength,
Surely it is testing its power – –
Life is like the wind –
Sometimes our hearts dance wildly,
Life is full of joy and gladness
Sometimes, sadness, broken dreams
Life becomes dull and full of burdens,
No desire for dancing —
Even then — we can know
God is there
Always, He is there for us!

Fostered Heart
Troy M. O'Brien
For therein lies the betrayal,
She took him in with promises,
Strung him along with touches and smiles,
And reduced him to nothing but pure love,
Then wished him well,
Without another look.

Pass It On
Ethelyne H. Lewis
Whatever God gave you, it's not just for you.
It's to be learned and used and passed on.
If you keep what He gave you all to yourself,
It's lost when your life is gone.
We aren't like wells to be filled to the brim
And what we're given to be dropped down deep.
No, we're all streams and must travel His fields
For He wants us to feed His sheep.

We must daily live knowing He sends folks our way
Who need comfort and kindness and love;
And to be sure we have it to pass out each day,
He sends bounteous supplies from above.

So remember each morning to pack up your wares
And ask Him for strength on your way:
And He'll send you the sheep who need comfort and care;
Folks who need what God gave for the day.

And because you are faithful and do as He asks,
And because, of course, you are His, too;
Whenever you need kindness, comfort and care,
He'll send someone to minister to you.

Dedication: to the Missionary Society of my church

America! Once I Come There
Phung Kim Dang
America! Once I come there.
Where I could walk,
Where I could talk,
Without fears,
Without tears.

America! Once I come there.
Where I could sight,
Where I could find,
Where I could acquire,
The picture of the United States of nationalities.
The painting of the United States of communities.
Which its within people seem to mix together,
But colors look to divide each others.
White is a pure blood,
Red is not a main stream,
Black is sometimes shine like a beam,
Yellow spots in different teams.
All of that make a promised rainbow.
It grows something I could not know,
Why people throw God in one dollar bill,
And jail Him in the Great Seal.

America! Once I come there,
Where I could care,
Where I could share,
Without cover,
Without pretender.

A Virginia Thanksgiving
Richard Askew
It was in old Charles City County very many years ago
that a noble band of colonists did offer thanks here below
for God's care and blessings, abundance
and riches of all good things; new lands to farm in this great expanse.
Thus, the first great Thanksgiving took place on the shores of James River.
So we now give thanks to God and continue this custom ever.

The Bowling Champ
George L. Carruthers
There's a man in our club
Who's out on his own,
For never a bad bowl
Has he ever thrown.
He aye plays the right haun
And aye the right weight,
In fact I never tell you
He never gets bate.
His drawing's perfection
And his striking's a treat.
He aye has his opponents
Cringing down in defeat.
He's the champ of all champs
He thinks he's the greatest,
He even coagles his bowl
Aye that's his latest.
When watching a games
He does naught but deride,
But when the finals are played
He's aye sitting on the side
over
The truth of the matter
Is in the last verse,
He plays a' his guid bowls,
Sitting on his erse.

Nevershed
Wanda T. Snodgrass
By the rocks along the river, lived a hermit now long–dead.
Decade after decade, People called him "Nevershed".
He didn't talk about his past or why he chose this way...
A dirty, dingy dugout on San Saba's banks of clay.
Did he come to mend a broken heart? Or just to meditate?
Draft dodger? Outlaw? Wanted convict? Town folks speculate.
In the Great Depression there was hunger in the land.
He killed wild game, staked catfish caught with his bare hands
For perhaps a penniless father, a widow or hobo...
He never asked who took it... he didn't want to know.
There was not any fanfare; there was no drum nor fife...
He gave the meat in secret... hung in his "Tree of Life."
One dismal day in winter, someone found him on his bed;
Filthy, tattered quilts, one rolled up for his head.
Two bloodhounds stood vigil, their whines so sad and blue...
They knew their happy days of hunting were all over, too.
A Bible in his weathered hand, its pages thin and worn,
An aged letter... Would only angels mourn?
The letter told a tender story written in a girlish hand...
"I love you," she told him... though she wore another's band.
Tucked inside the dirty bible saying, "Read When I am Dead"...
The Last Will and Testament of this man called "Nevershed."
A limousine from Wall Street... many saw him put away.
A lovely gray–haired lady wept openly that day.
The first time I heard his name was after he was dead...
She used his Christian name... we called him "Nevershed."

Dedication: Bruce Coffer Kerrville, Tx, author of Tad N Me

Enchanted Dreams

Angels Rising From Their Beds
Laurin Ashley Werner
Angels rising from their beds
As they watch the morning sunrise
They do wake with morning pride
As I see them watching over me.

Dedication: to my music teacher, Mrs. Jacobson

Runner's High
Nancy Kylloe
Every day I wake up and I run, there is
dew on the grass and the bright orange
rising of the sun.

The wind is blowing a cool, gentle breeze,
the birds are singing in the tall, budding trees.

The beautiful spring flowers are starting
to bloom, they fill the air with their sweet,
fragrant perfume.

The sky is a crystal–clear dark blue,
as I am running along I take in the scenic
view.

Beautiful surroundings everywhere, I
forget that I even have any cares,

As I head toward the end of my daily
Route, I take a deep breath in and I exhale
out.

It is a runner's high, I get one day after
day, I have seen the world again in my
own special way.

Gone
Tony Wayne Davis, Jr.
The town that you lived in
for so many years,
Your favorite pillow
where you shed many tears,
The bed that you slept in
on cold winter nights,
The tree that you climbed
when your parents had fights,
The trophy you got
for the points that you scored,
The best friend that you loved,
the dog you adored,
The money you worked for
all of your life,
The house that you lived in,
your husband or wife,
The mother that kissed you
every night before bed,
The Dad who read to you,
the book that he read,
The name you were given
on the day of your birth,
Your only child,
prettiest thing on the Earth,
Your health with your eyesight,
and your will to go on,
Such wonderful things,
and all of them gone.

Ode To Home
Fred Hornung
It's a little white house
by the side of the road
in a village that's pleasant to see.
It's just the right size and
the joy of our lives
'cause it's home to Frieda and me.

I Wrestle
Nick Meola
As I walk to the circle, eyeing–down my opponent,
I gaze for a second not even a Moment.

I shake his hand and wait for the whistle,
As soon as it blows, I explode like a missile.

I grab for his thigh and reach around his waist,
I know I got him and must use great haste.

He falls to the mat with an unhappy frown,
I know that I got it, the first take down.

I look for a move to put him on his back,
It's no use for him as he squirms like a rat.

The match is won, I beat him fair,
As the Ref. grabs my hand and puts it in the air.

I know I succeeded and made myself proud,
As I stand there waiting, listening to the crowd.

With the screams and hollers for my victory,
My 500th. pin, I will go down in history!

Dedication: to my momma, whom I love

Nature's Magic
Earline Vaughn
Nature flaunts its beauty,
Like magic in the air,
It wraps its cold winds, with
Its warmth of sunshine, everywhere.
Its birds chirp, as they folly,
Seductive melodies,
Fluttering their wings amidst
The branches of its trees.

Its raindrops sprinkle, with
A burst of flowers everywhere,
Which spreads a floral–scent, that is
Enchanting, through the air.
Then, nature draws its curtains
And its sunset fades away,
The twinkle of its evening–star,
Commence the close of day.

Its clouds in motion drape
The sky to overcast the light,
As darkness sets the background,
For its stars to fill the night.
At dawn, its kiss of dew gives
Life, to every blade of grass,
Reassuring, mother–Earth,
Its magic's unsurpassed!

Dedication: to mother dear and Paran

The Safest Way to Travel
Kathy Graff-Nelson
"Last call for flight 209!"
My Love and I run towards the gate,
I secretly hope we'll be too late.

We board.
Hearts pumping, luggage bumping.
I tell him to sit in the rear
So we'll have plenty of air.

Take off! I clutch the seat.
I lose my lunch at 10, 000 feet.

My husband reassures me,
"It's the safest way to travel."
But turbulence makes my nerves unravel!

Forever ends. We're taking it down for a landing.
"Look at the lake!" he exclaims, "What a beautiful thing!"
But I hear a noise.
Did we just lose a wing?
Like a long-awaited friend... we touch solid ground.
Prayers answered... we're safe and sound.

"The next time we vacation..." he begins talking.
"The next time," I inform him, "I'll be walking."

Dream
Nadia Alicia Douglas
A dream is a small child playing in a vast field of white flowers, irises.
Her dress flying up over her head and her laughter
echoing through the delicious green of the valley and bouncing off the
tall, granite walls of the mountain.

Dedication: to my mother, my backbone

Unborn
Chris J. Osmond
Unborn. Planning my life already.
Every detail studied and I will start my Heavenly journey.

Unborn. Let the world accept my birth.
My family in which I enter receive me!
The world seems to beckon, an irresistible life of wonder.

Unborn. Frustrated by this cave in which I exist.
Ever waiting for the day I break through.

Unborn. The animals and environment I wish to encounter,
The many people in my life I will experience.
I seem to know them, I seem to feel their presence.

Unborn. The diseases at my peril lay dormant until birth.
They wait for me, just to intoxicate me.

Unborn. Wealth, wealth and health are all I yearn for.
A family to earn for, a spouse to adore.
All I ask are these.

Unborn. Who am I talking to?
Myself? or something else?
This is another mystery, that the world in which I enter is full of.
Accept me cruel world.
Unborn.

Dedication: to all my family with love

Untitled
Liz Scantlin
I watch how quickly my world is disappearing with a
feeling of awe and wonder.
How could something so strong, deep, beautiful;
like the skinny pine or the ever-fattening oak,
be taken away in scattered bits?
I can hear the faint cry of leaf and stump as
I stare at a brown and dirty vacancy.
They call to me... they knew me before I ever knew myself.
They saw my first bicycle ride, my egg hunts, my wasp stings.
What would they say to me now in this despair?
There are a few noble giants left and, like me, they ponder
their own fate.
Oh! Too quick this strange life goes, willingly or not.
Beautiful guardians, you who have watched over me,
I mourn for your lives,
for your knowledge that will be cut down; oh, too shortly!
You have seen so much. Quickly, tell me all.
Let me be the living memorial to all that meant your existence.
Let me know just how the land and soil, with the blood contained
under the surface, nourished you during your winter sleeps.
Gentle and silent angels, I will be here at the last to be strong like your
boughs and roots, to carry on your legacies and to always remember
what you meant to those who were the first to believe in you.

Dedication: to my mama, whom I miss

The Lost Lamb
Steven Tungate
A sheepherder in a world of goats tending to a lost cause.
They never listen, only strive to devour the plain.
My flock lost years ago, yet I strive to bring the inevitable to my will.
Waiting for the day a lost lamb will come astray and lead me to my herd.
But till then I will amuse the sinful creatures.
Because I would rather be with them, than to trust myself.

Deserted
Sharon Redington
My thoughts are of the darkest day,
The one you took yourself away

The hurt is there, just as bad,
I can't be happy, I'm so sad.

You are my love, my friend no more,
I wish my heart could just ignore

The pain that you have put me through,
The love I hold that is so true.

I gave my all — my hand, my life,
That couldn't hold you as your wife.

And now it all has slipped away,
No explanations come my way.

I hope one day your heart will bleed,
For something you so badly need,

That is a love, so true, so dear,
Something that was once so near,

To have and lose a precious friend,
From start to finish til the end...

Dedication: to Mark, still loving you

Enchanted Dreams

Casey Lee
Tarrahal Branch
We used to run and
play together.
fight and Argue,
but always stay together.
I would think,
and you would speak.
I would get hurt,
and you would feel the
pain.
I would be sad,
and you would hold me
I got my heart broke,
and you went away.
I cried the tears,
and now I'm sad and
lonely.
I feel the pain,
and you can no longer
take it away
I miss you,
my sight, my feelings
my best friend
My life

Dedication: to Casey Lee, someone I will always cherish

Yule Dawn Christmas Morn
Cathy Miller
There once was a child born on Christmas long before.
I'm sure you all know, whom this child was born for.
Born a savior, lived on our land.
Died in suffering and sorrow for the sake of man.
To this day we worship the new babe, fragile as a fawn,
and give thanks, love and praise to the babe born on Yule Dawn.

So Long
Shawn Theobalds
So long for you and I
Times were fun and great in my mind
So long for what we had
So long for what we could have had

Maybe in time we will both see
But until then we're both blind
Sure, in time, I'll be forgotten
Forgotten comes in time of other happiness

When your feelings take over your actions
You do things never known before
And that's what you did to my actions
You turned them into feelings

So long, so long my love for you
I thought I could see your love for me
I spent a year of love to see the life above, for
you and me.
My love was there and now I've learned

If you could only see thru my eyes the
love would be in your mind
You're so confused, I don't know where I stand
I've tried and tried to read your mind,
as my life goes by.
Unless you see the love, in your eyes
Let's say goodbye for a long, long time

Again
Alisa Gomes
If I am to be reincarnated, I would like to be a tree.
It really seems like life would be so simple and carefree.
I might not be able to make the world a better place, but
for those who see through me might see a different face.
I would be identified as one class you see, but my feelings
are hidden deep inside the root of me.

Help for All Seasons
Helen Robinson–Romeo
She wields her ward of wintry wizardry
Draping trees in cloaks of white lace;
Mother Earth done proudly, her coat of white diamonds,
Silvery frost for a scarf frames her face.

Then she chooses pastels from her palette
Softly splashing her carpets of green...
Kisses each tiny flower a sit, stretches and yawns,
Once more wakened from its long, winter's dream.

With a wave of her hand, she summons sweet summer
Her breath beckons warm, sultry breezes;
Far off in the distance, rolling thunder reminds us
Mother Nature does just as she pleases!

Now, her brushes emblazoned with rainbows of fire
Flaming hues peek through fall's chilly mist;
The Earth is a portrait of panoramic perfection...
Can man alone paint a picture like this?

Nature dresses the Earth in all of its glory
With God surely guiding her hand;
Just as artists draw beautiful seascapes...
But, only God numbers each grain of sand!

Dedication: to Gerard, love of my life

Call of the Sea
Priscilla Chermely
The seashore beckons me each year
With a call that only I can hear.
The chanting waves and whispering foam
Soon lure me from my distant home
With promises they pledge to keep
For peace of mind and wisdom deep.

This year, I greeted eagerly
My annual summons from the sea,
Then smiled to find myself once more
On that familiar, rocky shore
Where gulls swept down and noisily
Called out as if to welcome me.

As I watched the waves recede, then swell,
I was drawn within their rhythmic spell
And lost my own identity
Somewhere between the sky and sea.
My body's warmth, that of the sun,
My breath, the wind, they all were one.

As nature gently merged with me,
The knowledge came with clarity
That each of us, though flawed and small,
Is loved by God and is part of all
That is and was and is yet to be,
Surviving through eternity.

Our Family Angel
Eleanore Humphreys
You are not forgotten
Although a year has passed.
For we always have our memories
And your love to hold us fast.

A rose reminds us of you
Of how tender and how kind
You were to all who knew you
Yes... a rose brings you to mind.

The smiles of little children
Also make us think of you.
How you always made things better
When we were feeling blue.

A rainbow in the Heavens
Reminds us where you are;
And the sun that shines in daylight
And, of course, the evening star.

And so, one year has ended,
But we shall not be sad.
For God has made us grateful
For the time with you we had.

Dedication: to my mother Elizabeth Christianson

Night At The Beach
Alexander W. Levy
Moonlight pouring down to the ocean,
Sand sparkling in the white glow,
Stars glittering in the clear night sky,
Waves jumping onto the shore,
Fish glowing in the water,
And me watching a star fall into the ocean.

The Legend of the Lost Vein of Gold
Sharon Reesey
An old legend deep from the past. Of the prospector known as the Old
   Dutchman.
He was the first and last. To know of the secret of the lost vein of gold.
A mountain of pure, rich beauty, so the legend is told.
As he traveled back and forth to the land above. To get more of that
golden love.
An bring it back to the town of desire. But his guidance was not
for hire.
Many followed and lost his trail of return — As they felt their greed and
lust, out of control, burn.
Back to the old Indian burial ground — Where the lost vein of gold can
be found. Some say it leads to a mountain mother lode deep inside,
Waiting for the Superstition Mountain to open wide. For its wealth
to share with those who dare to seek and find, experience the greedy
evil soul of the human mind.
The legend of the old Dutchman's lost gold mine. Truly a revelation
of one man's power of his past imagination.
Of the story, of the legend, of the lost vein of gold.
What does the future hold, only time will tell;
If the old Dutchman's soul of the past is
burning and screaming in hell, in all its power and glory —
One hell of a revelation story.

As the mountain of gold begins to rock and roll.
Taking with it another soul. This mountain of gold is still there —
Waiting for those who dare, to share —
Its haunting, greedy, evil, golden nightmare.

Heaven's Waiting
Laurie Radzwilowicz
As wings upon the winds of change,
time must pass us on.
we say good–bye to loved–ones
and miss them when they're gone.

Grandma, we love you dearly
but know that you must go.
We know that Heaven needs you
and God has said it's so.

They needed an angel in Heaven
where eternal peace exists.
You deserve the happiness awaiting,
but know that you'll be missed.

Although you have to leave us
We hold you in our hearts
We'll keep the memories warm
As every new life starts.

Today we won't say good–bye
for that word is much too strong,
rather, someday we, too, will join you
and until then, we say so long.

Dedication: In memory of Genevieve Brink

Dark Souls
Linda L. Roffe
Darkness begins to fade the light,
as an eagle takes to flight.
His soul is one with the sky,
which makes you stop and wonder why.
The spirit that dwells deep within
can turn our hearts so cruel and grim.

The Lord Is My Savior
Sherri Warren
The Lord is my savior, for this I know is true.
He is always watching over me, as well as He is you.

The Lord is my savior
He helps guide me and show me the way.
My Lord stands beside me
As I know He will every day.

The Lord is my savior
When I need Him, He is there.
In good times, as well as bad
His presence is everywhere.

The Lord is my savior
My confidant, my friend
He comforts me when I am sick
And helps my body to mend.

The Lord is my savior
Who gave His life for all.
A most unselfish act of love
For creatures great and small.

The Lord is my savior who watches me from above,
The Lord is my savior and will give me eternal love, Amen.

Dedication: to my dear friend Mark

Enchanted Dreams

Pen Pal Love
Joseph M. Forcaro
As I walk along the road of life
I often face the pain and strife.

But meeting you along the way
Makes it easier day by day.

I often stop to contemplate
The good I have upon my plate.

And even though we have not met
It's safe to make per chance a bet.

The bonds of love are strong and true
Like trees are green and skies are blue.

I know someday we will unite
When silver wings can bring you flight

From warmer breezes and tropical flow
To cooler climes than bring the snow.

I'm certain then as time may go
Our love will bring an afterglow.

The inner vault in heart replete
Brings love beyond all worldly treats.

I'll Be Forever With You
Nicola Walsh
I'll be forever with you, my heart, my body, my soul,
I'll be forever with you, till the day that I grow old,
I'll be forever with you, to love and watch you grow,
I'll be forever with you, your Mum who loves you so.

Dedication: to my children, Nikita, Sam and Daryl

A Wind From... Elsewhere
Elga Haymon White
The wind blows here... the wind blows there
The wind seems to blow from... everywhere.
But the wind I love... when it blows... blows fair...
This wind... when it blows... blows from... ELSEWHERE!

Can you see its graceful fingers... playing in your hair?
Nay! You cannot see the wind... e'en though you know it's there.
It's flitting... it's flirting... it's prancing everywhere
This wind... when it blows... blows from... ELSEWHERE!

It blows unexpectedly... with a gentle breeze... it blows...
The Great Hand of Miracles... brings it... then it goes
To greet the early morning sun... to dance to and fro
From the highest, loftiest mountain heights... to valleys...
far below.

"Who is He that sitteth upon the circle of the Earth...
Who gathereth the winds in his fists —
Who maketh a wind to pass over...
Thou hearest the sound thereof...
But canst not tell whence it cometh... and whither it goeth."
The wind blows here... the wind blows there...
The wind seems to blow... from everywhere.
But the wind I love... when it blows... blows fair—
This wind... when it blows... blows from... ELSEWHERE!

Dedication: to inspiration from Rev. Tom Marshall

Cliches, Ducks And Bandstands
Mark Bennett
I recall this
Space.
All grass,
dead air
and you.
Framed by a gray
midlands sky.

Good Night, My Love
Robert W. Anderson
Good night, my love, now you've gone away.
The veil that hides is night, my love,
The other side the day.

I held you fast at night, my love, till in my weakened clasp,
I had to let you go, my love,
To daylight's firmer grasp.

The wind blows cold at night, my love, since you went away,
I'm not afraid at night, my love,
So near to dawning day.

The fire glows bright at night, my love, dispels the shadows there.
The ties that bind are tight, my love,
They keep me from despair.

Across the crevice of the night, I see the lightning flash.
I know you're there beyond the breach,
Safe from the thunder's crash.

And when it's night for me, my love, 'twill be my fervent prayer,
That in the shining light of day,
You'll wait and greet me there.

Good night – God bless you... my love.

To Mum
Helen Ostle
I wish you could tell us exactly what you think,
I wish I could read your eyes in–between the blinks.

But as it is, you're silent, locked in a world of your own,
And how we all desperately wish that tumor had never grown.

It's taking the very person who meant the world to us,
The one who was always there, always full of buzz.

I wish I could have read the future and what it held in store,
Then had we seen this coming we could have closed the door.
But as it is, it's here and it's a rough and bumpy road,
But together as a family, we'll carry this heavy load.

We're here to help you through it, we're with you all the way,
And after the 4th of August you'll be back with us to stay.

Back to the Mum we know and love, the best Mum in the land,
The one who's always been there to lend a helping hand.

We know it won't be easy and recovery may be slow,
But with all our love we have to give, we're sure your strength will grow.

So Mum we know you're in there and soon you will be free,
The bestest Mum in this world for everyone to see.

Dedication: to my mum who sadly died

Job
Marjorie J. Morse

A stroke, a heart attack, a broken hip, an operation,
and a bruising fall.
During the last 18 months I've endured them all.
Overall, I've been lucky with all I've been dealt
At least I know how Job must have felt.
I know, of course, I'm not liable
Yet it is nice to relate to someone in the Bible.

Just Yesterday
Anna O. Taylor

Just yesterday – we had precious Moments,
rebellion in our teens, just "brezzin" with our
homies and just too blind to see.
Just yesterday – we raised our children and
then the grandkids.
My Lord? What? Whatever happened to me?

Just yesterday – I was twenty and a model/dancer/
writer, I would be – but by then I was two,
my baby and me.
Just yesterday – I was forty, you know, thinking
about retiring and looking out for me, but children
having children and when I looked up, I had three.

Just yesterday – I turned sixty and I should sit
back and smile, but I can feel that tear in my eye.
My teens sped by, my homies died, my child
and the grandkids and retirement learned how to fly.
My Lord? What? Whatever happened to me?

Just yesterday – when I turned sixty:
I thought... a model of sorts, a dancer I'd boast,
a writer, I would joke, a mother of kind spirit,
I'd hope and try to find out...
My Lord? What? Whatever happened to me?

Untitled
Yousef Michael El–Youssef

Like a picture
Like a book
Like a fire
That destroys them all.

Unperturbed by the joys and the sadness
Surrounding us everywhere we turn.

Thoughts and emotions
Are just the beginning of...

Great things that will come between us and fall
Like broken glass to the floor.

Streaking through my mind
As we meet on the street.

Greetings exchanged
Hardly, a second glance
My head screaming at me.

Then I pass on
Wondering why it's so hard
To tell her how I feel.

I passed the most beautiful flower
Unable to return.

Solitude
Penelope Vigil

As I sit in the deafening silence,
I feel the breeze telling me secrets
Of sky so vast and blue it seems
Destined to remain cloudless always,
Garnering peace for whoever dares
To make the acquaintance of serenity
Hidden from the world in the glare of a sunset.

Late–Night Ramblings Of A Restless Mind
Judy Hunter

I curl into my bed, snuggle warm, flannel sheets
Cozy and drowsy, wanting dreams to be sweet.

I scrunch up the pillow to cradle my head
Close my eyes, try to sleep, but am restless instead.

I try to shut out the events of the day
But worries and tensions get in the way.

I count all my blessings. I even count sheep.
Yet try as I might, I just can't get to sleep.

I peek at the clock and it fills me with dread
As unstoppable videos dance in my head.

I drift through my youth, face my faults, see my dreams
Tossing and turning the entire night, it seems.

So tired of floating between awake and asleep
I am suddenly startled by the alarm's screaming beep.

I sure don't remember dark turning to dawn.
As I foolishly realize, I was asleep all along!

Dedication: to my son Jason, my hero

Can Someone Stop The Pain
Angela C. Brigham

Can someone tell me, why does love
Have to hurt so bad

My heart has been broken
Why am I so sad

How could he be so wrong
Leading and stringing me along

Life is so tough
I guess my love wasn't enough

Can someone stop the pain

I was his best friend
I would have stuck with him
Through thick and thin

Why did he have to be so cruel
Making me out to be his fool

How can I give my heart again
Where can I start
Will it be hard

Can I ever drop my guard
Can someone stop the pain

Enchanted Dreams

Poems
Kirk Antony Watson
Me and any old someone
tell on these thoughts, or fools
will pretend love, can continue tumbling
into a miserable wander:
Passing the year, yes,
Me and your poems interviewed, so easily
will feel left aside.

Tribute
Jennifer Buedel
It all started with the dance.

Until then, you were warm laughter,
A brightness that came to a room
And a glow that remained after you had left.
I'd never imagined how it would feel, though,
To be in your arms, until I was actually there,
Effortlessly following your lead,
Completely in step with each other, connected.
Giddy, I looked into your eyes and had mine opened,
But told myself it must be the spinning that left me dazed.

Because it was just a dance, after all,
An interlude with its time and place and purpose,
A dream too overwhelming to even consider a reality.
So I sat the next few dances out,
And waited for the exhilaration to pass, the emotions to diminish.
But I found myself lulled back by a soothing, familiar rhythm.

And suddenly your arms were around me again,
Strong, comforting, reassuring and it somehow felt safe
To be afraid, to feel, to want and to believe.
I kept wondering when the music would end: it never has.

Dedication: to Bob — my everything

Time Is A Clown
Roberto Guzman
Time flies; like lightning—strikes,
Like a joking clown laughing till death,
taking in our sleep, our dreams, our hopes.
How to fly, I wish, so the clown I will reach,
To reach the time I wish, past time that is.
Because in time, I left all my hopes and dreams of love.

So many tears just disappeared,
So much laughter and happiness
Had all blown down to pieces.

The curtain has come down,
The circus has left town.
Dust and darkness is all I see.
The steps, the music, the silly laughing is gone,
and every soul is calming down

Up there, Up in the sky between a bunch of dark clouds,
It seems to me there's an unhappy clown,
Looking at me with an angry face,
He looks too moody and too mad,
Is the time that laughs and cries,
He's trying to tell me,
Your time is gone
Whether you've used it right, or wrong.

Dedication: to my son, Jose, God bless

Untitled
Thomas Smith
We who could only stand and stare
At the merry events out there.
Watching all those revelers
Without a care, all we did was stand
And stare, so could you kindly spare
A thought for those little ones
Who were so distraught.

Thoughtswarm
Alicia Marie Mumford
Through the sands of time I sift,
The long ride home,
A song that's incessant
Waves of thought now struggle
To escape the fate of their currents
And reach their crash of freedom
At the shores of freedom,
I wait.

A fingerprint splash of color
The framework horizon
Eyes turned up to a fractured stone face figure in formation
Bleeding its wisdom down over the horizon
I fall, under its unmerciful wind.

Waters lie still now,
The calm before the storm,
Prophecy in small reflections
Now scatter along the surface.

Nightfall tiptoes to the water
Like packs of hungry wolves
Hungrily devouring the daylight.

Dedication: to Ralph Michael Tyler Coppola

Race Has No Color
Maxine Atkinson
Before too long it will be too late.
We're asking You, dear God, to keep
us safe from bigotry and hate.

We are prisoners of hate and no one
can keep us from harm.
Even if we pray about it, from dusk until
dawn.

We are all the same people, regardless
of race, creed or shade.
And we must remember that we are exactly
what the Lord made.

Brothers and sisters of all races,
please hear my plea.
We can get along without these words.
Race, creed, or color, you see.

Love is all we need to be sisters and brothers.
We don't have to stand here and talk about
my white father and my black mother.

As we face these wars of hatred and turmoil.
We will think about race, creed and color.
When our friends are left to rest on the
Enemy's soil.

Christmas On The Coast
Barbara J. Winter
It's the week of Christmas and they're still mowing lawns
wearing just sweats or sporting their brawn
in flimsy shorts as they jog.

Rolled–down windows are frequently seen
on warm, sunny days in–between
winter rains and fog.

For A Love
Shirlene Wallingford
For a love so soft,
Like a pink rose on a spring day,
I would love.

For a love so beautiful,
Like a sunset over the ocean,
I would dream.

For a love so colorful,
Like a rainbow after the first spring shower,
I would dance.

For a love so peaceful,
As a baby's sigh,
I would cry.

For a love so romantic,
Like a kiss in the moonlight under the stars,
I would melt

For a love so sweet.
Like an ice cream on a hot day,
I would laugh.

Dedication: to my son, brothers, friends and family

Me, We
Eboni Cooper
Me when I felt the thin pocket lining on my beaten jeans touching
My useless, brown skin

We when my aura is a sea mist–green and I have a scent of
old and new

Me a blank sheet of paper

We the lines in which you write upon until...

Me a seed

We the tree of life in which evil dwells

Me we

I laugh

It is only me when my pockets show faces of the dead
It is only me when I when my thoughts are none

Me we
I laugh again

You is what I see

Dedication: to 7th grade teacher, Mrs. Talbert

Nanny, Nanny
Tecia Lanese Smith
Into work every day,
children laughing, wanting to play.
Washing dishes, washing clothes,
taking care of their runny nose.

You give them love and you give them affection.
You always look out for their protection.

It's a job that's tough, but you use your heart.
Not a job of skill, but a form of art.

Creativity is a really big key,
to show these children what they need to see.
They trust you, love you, with body and soul.
Because YOU are the one that makes them feel whole.

You dry their tears and show them you care.
Say "Don't worry, love, I'll always be there."

For you are the Nanny,
God's chosen one.
An angel for children,
The keeper of the young.

Dedication: to Karen, my angelic bubbles

Burgundy
Crystal Enck
Swimming through a sea of burgundy I swirl,
my body bathed in it.
My senses are overwhelmed with the smell of it.
Leaping into my mouth, stifling my nostrils, blinding my eyes.
Drunk on this burgundy that overwhelms me.
Where is my release?
Where is my sanctuary?

Untitled
Christine McGinley
I Resolve To Explore My Innermost
Feelings And Thoughts.
To Harmonize With My Soul,
My Very Essence.

I Swear To Treat Others
As I Would Want To Be Treated Myself.
To Lightly Touch One's Hand With Love,
When Words Are Insufficient.

Today Is Day One Of My Future –
I Will Succeed And Find Fate Within.

I Resolve To Face My Worries Today
For A Day Too Late Can Never Be Corrected.
To Do What May Be Painful Now,
Avoiding Despair Tomorrow.

I Swear To Be Gentle With All That Surrounds Me
As I, Too, Need A Quiet Whisper In The Night.
To Reassure My Desires,
Dream With My Soul On A Chariot.

Today Is Day One Of My Future –
With Love, My Fate Is My Own.

Dedication: to Mom and Dad with love

Enchanted Dreams

What Indian?
Edward P. Cole
an
insignificant
number
of
smalls

they
died
crushed
against
a wall

here
are
the
remains

of
a
race
so tamed

What Indian?

Dedication: to Beatrice, my Nzadi

Winter
Khristian Vanier
In the Winter,
It pours down snow.
And everyone will soon know,
After a few days,
It gets quite cold,
And gets Oh, – So,
Slushy and old.

The Inner Me
Alicia Rosalinda Marquez
Always sitting alone in the dark, please
Break the silence, come and visit, come and see the
Crazy visions that dance around me.
Dreaming of a life more ordinary, maybe
Even a little sane, with this complicated madness
Falling down on me, please, I'm in pain!
Going full–speed down an endless hall
Hell, I give up, why go anywhere at all.
Intense depression is the life I lead, God
Just might be watching, but not fulfilling my need.
Know that I am not what I seem, but a
Lie! pretending to be light and carefree, that
Might be you, but that is not me.
Now there have been times when I felt like
Opening up to a
Person or two, but the
Question is, why won't they listen?
Repulsed by my reflection, pretty am I not
So I can see, for some people maybe, but the
Tables will never turn for me.
Unable to control the sick ideas in my head
Visions of things I must leave unsaid. I've
Wafted past the onlooking eyes. Doctor check–ups,
X–rays will never find the problem
You will never know the real me, just a
Zany cover–up. Maybe in time, you will see my mental
Hostility.

The Stroke Victim
B. N. Fletcher
All these months you've watched the scene
Is there a plan, part of God's scheme?
Physically trapped, your mind elsewhere,
Into middle distance, you sit and stare.
APHASIC!
Medical terms in books abound,
But from your wheelchair, no freedom found.

Once a brave and fearless fellow,
Children and middle–age saw you mellow.
Was there a care as retirement approached?
"Life is for living", you often joked.
REMEMBER?
Useless limbs, face awry
Emotions labile, sometimes you sit and cry.

Nursing care has kept you going.
Now you're watching the gardener mowing.
Wish you could up and join the action
Make a movement, the merest fraction.

FRUSTRATION!

In the shade of the nursing home garden
Death comes swift, it's the final pardon.

Leprechaun
Rosanne Ford
Catch a leprechaun, if you can.
Stop! Look at the footprints to where he ran.
If you catch him, make a wish.
Wish for luck or your favourite dish.
"Follow me now, don't be blind, because at the end
of the rainbow you will find something I have left behind."
Well, what a surprise: a pot of gold.

He's Forever Near
Wandasha A. Rhetta
Always know that there is hope for tomorrow, even when things are dim;
Hold your head up – keep the faith – and put your trust in Him...

Whether you're happy or sad; having a good day or one that's bad...

Don't despair or lose sight of what you hope to gain; because with – –
faith in God and in yourself, your goals you will obtain...

Whether you're busy or asleep in bed; surrounded by loved–ones – – – –
or just lonely instead...

Though darkness lies ahead – "Jesus" is always there; with arms
that will hold you with His loving care...

Whether you're rich or poor; "Jesus" is always knocking at your door...

Just when you think you're losing everything; "Jesus"
appears with comfort to bring...

Sometimes we laugh and sometimes we cry; in bad health or good health–
we know one day we must die...

Knowing and believing with prayer and assurance that the Lord will never
part; for He is within you – right in your heart...

What a comforting feeling – with reason to cheer; ———————
Knowing that the Lord Savior will always be near...

The Anthology of Poems

Witness
Jean Hough
Against the backdrop of a milky moon
and the cold glint of stars.
It was then I first espied you,
Mysterious and uncertain
My initiation rune.

Like a fair maiden, on her voyage of light,
A trail—blazer of the sky.
Combing the Heavens with your molten train
All decked out like a bridal veil
Survivor of the night.

Contained within you
A frenzied mixture of fire and ice.
The hidden spores of life.
Silent and swift they penetrate
Rekindling life anew.

You and I
We share journeys of time.
We are but cosmic dust.
I, a speck of planet Earth
And you, a child of the sky.

Dedication: to Atlow Mill Centre in Derbyshire

Untitled
W. Ben Keel III
"We all pass through different phases in our life, from peace and joy to
solitude and sorrow. In our solitude, we search for that pixilated place
where we can open our hearts to dance our clumsy dance and sing
out our songs, but in our dance and in our songs we find our souls.
And as we find our souls we are able to open our hearts to more love
and more openness and understanding.
All of that, just so that we can learn to live life!"

Lifeless
Vickie Dunlap
I now walk this big, black, empty hole.
Everywhere there is a coldness, bringing a chill to
my tired and weary bones. It is black and empty as my existence.
The frost and iciness numbing my heart, as there is no longer any
sun to warm it anymore I walk its empty halls, wandering aimlessly,
lost, with no direction; no future to worry about
any longer. There is no light to guide me.
Like the light that used to shine within my eyes,
it has been extinguished, destroyed forevermore.
Yet I care not, for I cannot and do not wish to see nor feel.
There is nothing I wish to cast my eyes upon, the beauty departing
from my life like a thief in the night.
To feel would mean only anguish and pain.
It is easier to feel nothing than this pain that is so rapidly coursing
through my heart and mind. I have ceased to be; no longer is there
any life within me. With nothing left but an empty
shell of the woman who used to be.
To no longer feel the warmth of your hugs, the fire of your caress,
the softness of your breath against my cheek, is to live no more.
There is a coldness and emptiness now, a big, black, empty
hole where once lived a heart and soul.
The tears flow endlessly, yet no one sees. I am screaming,
yet no one hears. My heart is breaking into a billion pieces,
floating away with the winds. Like your love, it is gone,
to be nevermore...
Everything is black and empty, a shell of what used to be —
lifeless as an empty sea.

The Journey
Jason R. Griffiths
Sunrise motivation breathes
as the wind echoes
over the hills and through the trees
in a desolate space,
one heart too numb to cry
reading between the "lines"
she only wanted to say goodbye.

Out of the valley into the pale, ivory sky
as a bird on the wing flying so high
silently listen, never far away
my senses tell me, you are gazing over by day.

Time stands still for a little while
reminisce with a faint smile
fragrant fragments linger from your freedom flight
while stark, frail emotion, dimmed our room to candlelight.

Sunset, regret
sympathize with our grief
your inspiration allows new belief
as time steals and heals with one hand
take a safe journey, to the promised land.

Dedication: to the memory of Keith Jenkins

The Message
Marcellus Tetter
Hey there, you,
Look sharp at what you do
For what you do will reflect on you
And evil lies on all men's eyes
So take heave, take heave.

Dedication: to my daughter, Kyra A. Tetter

Untitled
Ashley Luth
"Come sit young children and listen to me,
I'll tell you a story of one you can't see.
Some say there is a man up there.
With big, green eyes and long, green hair.
He doesn't talk, but watches us,
I think his name is Mr. Gus."

"Oh, way up there, too far to see,
there is a man named Old Magee.
He lives up there, on the tip of the moon.
Since it's getting dark you'll see him soon."

"You're wrong, you fool! His name is Gus!
He sits up there and watches us!
He sews and knits and plays with beads,
And when he's tired he likes to read."

"You're wrong, my friend! About more than one thing!
He doesn't read, he likes to sing! And,
He doesn't like to sew or knit,
He likes to play with his Ping—Pong kit.
He plays alone and hits them far and when he misses
It's a shooting star! So sit back friend,
And let me be! I'm going to wait for Mr. Magee!"

"Yes, children, sit back and don't make a fuss,
And wait for me with Mr. Gus!"

Enchanted Dreams

The Struggle
Chrissie Hough
I am, quite simply, a little miracle.
Substantive proof that the humble and rebuked can reign triumphant.

Rise above petulance!
Yield not to cynicism!
Be resolute and reach inside your heart.
Hold fast to your conviction and your goal will be attainable.

A convoluted path I had to follow;
Tenacity and compulsion my saviours from sorrow.
I was bullied, threatened and ridiculed by most.
To be loved was all I ever yearned.

Existence was a painstaking struggle.
But my passion for life they could never subdue.

To have existed at all was achievement enough.
Regrets? I have none.
I had conquered all adversity:
Contentment filled my inner sanctum.
It was time to move on.
Time for change...

But who knows?
One day, I may be back!

Spring Is Here
Angel Ocana
Spring is here
Birds sing in the air
Animals are near
Flowers are here
Red, green, blue
They are so cool
And you are, too.

The Grave Sight
Cristy Hicks
I was walking home last night
When, I saw an old man kneeling
At a gravesight.

His head was bent in sorrow
and he looked as if he might
pray and as I started toward
him I heard him say.

"Son, you know I come here
each May, to visit my grand–
daughter who let drinking get in
her way."

I stared at him with tears
Streaming down my face, because
I had been at that same place.

She had drunk too much just
as I but; the only difference
is she died and I am still alive.

I never got a chance to tell
her goodbye but, I know her
glory was being let free to fly.

Dedication: to people that believed in me

Anticipation
Sara James
I feel it in me, somewhere deep inside,
Pulsating the love I cannot find.

Considering the eyes of strangers,
I search for you in everyone I meet
And as callous coldness smothers the heat,
I recognize unfathomed dangers.

Your disguise is deceptive to uncover,
Yet I remain assured that you are there.
The sensation of a love so very rare,
A nexus with your mind a joy discovered.

My day is raped by the search for you
And the cruel night nourishes my bane
Of a memory that you once called my name.
I pray you are out there looking for me, too.

The sky erupts in applauding saturation
And the splinter of brilliance lights up my face.
All I need is patience in my hopeless haste,
As I drown in sweet, sweet anticipation.

I feel it in me, somewhere deep inside,
Pulsating the love from you I will someday find...

Spring
G. G. Oliver
Spring is softly in the air
Gentle breezes blow
Blossoms are leaving a fragrant
Scent in the air.
Buds are awakening everywhere
Oh, how my heart rejoices
To see Earth's awakening.

Want–To–Be Poet's Contest
Sharon M. Bonesho
Oh, another contest to enter and try your luck
It could be your poem that will bring in a buck.
Be calm now, take your time, read the rules
Something might be in fine print that seems cruel.

Perhaps you'll have to send money, buy a book or two
Now you're in a quandary and don't know what to do.
Just write a corny poem, send it in on time?
Maybe they'll adore it and all will end up fine?

But wait, future poets, there's something I would like to say
If the contest asks for money, well, "Just walk away".

However, if you have a cute poem and the entry is "free"
Put those lovely thoughts in writing for the whole world to see.
Then breathe a sigh of relief when all is said and done
For who knows, your corny poem might be the "chosen" one.

And while you want–to–be poets send poems in for a look
I'm walking away from the contest with, yes, a "free" book.
I'll read it, study it, start composing poems real bright
So the next time there's a contest, I am sure to get it right.

I will get published next year, you all just wait and see
For the real want–to–be poet here is—————simply me!!

Dedication: in memory of Marion Bonesho

A Journey...
Jillian A. Gilmour

I came into this world unknowing and you taught me.
I was cold and trembling and you gave me warmth.
I cried when I was scared and you comforted me.
With this, I grew to feel secure.

I smiled at familiar faces and you smiled along with me.
I spoke my first words and you gave them importance.
I took my first steps and you picked me up when I fell.
With this, I realized that you were always there for me.

I attended my first day of school and you were there to hold my hand.
I performed in my first play and you were there taking pictures.
I wrote my first story and you were there to listen.
With this, I learned to enjoy life.

I began to make choices in which:
I attempted and you encouraged;
I failed and you sympathized;
I was confused and you gave me guidance;
I looked to the future and you gave me support,
and finally, I flew and you let me fly.
All of this time and I never said I love you.
I LOVE YOU!

Dedication: to those who believed in me

The Green Sea
John Law

You give me shelter from the storm.
You give me shade when the sun is too warm.
Heat me up when the nights grow cold.
Keep me steady when I grow old.
Give me air to breath from your delicate leaves.
Why, oh, why, do they cut you down, my beautiful
TREES.

Chauvinist
F. M. Brindle

I want a female who's just right,
A lady in the day, but a woman in the night.

I want her slim, but not too much,
Straight and firm, but soft to touch.

I want her kind and full of love,
Slim of waist, but full above.

I want her true with firm endeavor,
Heart of gold, bright, but not too clever.

I want a woman to love me true.
Stand by my side, support my view.

If one exists, please let me know,
Straight if you will, I've hunted high
And low.

I want her polished, flag full mast.
A gentle smile, but when pushed fight
To the last.

What will I give when this paragon I
See,
Fortune, fame and wealth?
No, ——— just me!

Freedom
Crystal M. Collier

Our freedom today is what we make it. Whether if it is successful or down
    in the dump.
Freedom is what we can do for ourselves, not what others can do for us.
When one thinks of the word freedom, you hear life, liberty and the
    pursuit of happiness.
But are we thinking of a fantasy world or living in the state of reality?
When we listen to the words of freedom and rights, the constitution comes
    to mind and why we fight.
We strive to be free and one with mankind so that the spirits and souls
    will soar in the sky.
To resound on a victory given, one must rejoice in a life worth living.
Freedom is women's rights, it is the underground operation of slavery.
It is a role played by distinguished leaders. Freedom is the hand extended
    out among the world.
It brings the color to the land, with this equality always stands.
Freedom lives among the nation and resides with the population.
It relates to reservation and provides a life of self-determination.
The F in Freedom stands for Free
The R for Rebel
The E for Eternity
The E for Evolution
The D for Domain
The O for Opportunity
And then the most important is the M which stands for Mankind
without these things there would be no Freedom and no state of mind.

My Pet Remembered
D. J. Bratt

I planted a tiny tree today and
Watered it with tears, in memory of
A dear friend's birth of just a few
Short years, I planted it near where
He lies, so that when it grows up tall
It will shade hot summer sun and rain
Storms as they fall.

Obsessions
Edith Witter

Getting it right every time
The task may be big,
the task may be small but,
I have to get it right every time.

For I fear if I don't, they no longer may trust me;
they no longer may respect me;
so I try to get it right every time.

I want them to know that they can rely on me.
I want them to know that I can succeed.
I want to get it right every time.

And, I hope that they will reward me,
will accept and respect me,
making it worthwhile,
my trying to get it right every time.

But, time and again I discover, there is no reward,
now and then a little praise, promises, promises...
and, I carry on and try to get it right every time.

Angry, frustrated, losing faith,
I try to break free, try to escape the curse,
of having to get it right every time.

Dedication: to all my bosses

Enchanted Dreams

Flying Into The Sky
Noriko Fulmer
New York, Rome, Paris, Hong Kong, Sydney...
I read all the destinations on the departure board, very slowly to her,
pointing to many cities with my right hand
and hugging her with my left hand.

"Mom, when you want to meet with your first daughter, you can go to
 Brisbane directly by that airline.
When you want to meet with your second daughter,
that airline to USA is best.
Because many Japanese passengers use it."

My mother had very big feathers to protect me,
showing and teaching me how to fly into life.
Now, I am going to fly into the sky, to my new married life with an
American, spreading my own feathers.

"Mom, here, an airport can make our connection. The world is not big."
Hugging her small hands and shoulders, I smiled to her.
Her small shoulders became smaller with her tears.
I surprisingly noticed how small she became.

Detroit, New Delhi, Madrid, Cairo, Auckland...
"Mom..."
She was dropping her tears, staring at my flight.
I lost my words.

What Is Love
Donna Marie Stewart
Love when – days are golden by sun
Love when – dawn by night
Love when – sad turns to happy
Love when – friends are forever
Love when – lovers are faithful and loyal
When it slips away
What is love

I Am But One Person
Celena Lewis
I am but one person
I have but one face,
If I make a mistake
Don't get on my case

I try to be good
I try to do everything right,
but I'm not really perfect
So I'll just be happy and bright.

I am but one person
I can't do everything at once,
but one thing I'm good at
is making a big fuss

I try to be good
but I always get the blame,
They say they're sorry
but the next day's the same

I am but one person
I try my best to please
but its so–o–o hard
oh, why can't they see!?
I am but one person!

Dedication: to all my family and friends

Tomorrow
Roy K. Acland
To tell the truth I may not last.
Mostly because of my bad past.
Getting me what I need, always hunger, always greed.
The scag has got me, it's got me bad.
And even I, think that is sad.

You go to the doc, if you're an alcoholic.
And come away with tabs or tonic.
But go to one 'cos you're in gear.
There's no deal, not here, no fear.
Junkies are human and talk you know.
But none of us know where to go.

None of these places are any good.
But why do we junkies think they should.
We are just scum of the Earth, from the day of our birth.
Yet my agony isn't past, I've got to do it for, I've got to last.
And get rid of my bad past.
For my two sons I love so dear and younger brother by a
year.

My niece, Karen, I'm sad to say.
Passed away the next day.
Charlie took her at twenty–seven.
Now I pray she's up in Heaven.

The Funny Clown
Alice Chaussee
Everyone loves a funny clown, he makes you laugh
When you feel down, but things are not always as they
Seem to be, for it's only a disguise that you see. Beneath
The mask of paint and comical clothes, he is just a fellow
Like you and me with his share of trouble and woes.
Often we, too, wear a disguise that you cannot see; it is called
Pretense and we are not always just what we appear to be

Secret Passion
Barbara Phillips
My love for you is hidden beneath my soul,
with joyous revelation resting in my heart.

Your wit and humility; wondering how,
how will the secret be so ever exposed.

A commitment so deep that drives all others away,
and ensures a safety net no one can invade.

But for one, reasoning could never explain
the continuing commitment of passion
that will never, ever be exposed.

Your warmth and sensitivity cuddles my fears
and secures my inhibitions without
exposing true meaning so dear.

Conversations are explosive with both our passions raging.

Longing for justice,
we shall only depart with
peace and understanding
and a secret so dear to my heart.

Passion held within;
a secret can only endure within one's heart;
and a perpetual love that only endures through a passionate secret.

A Life Wasted
Stephen Moyes

Your life is sad
You have to say goodbye.
It's all gone downhill
And you don't know why.
You say you're sorry
And you start to cry.

Poor kid

You thought that you
Could get real high.
You thought that you
Would never die.
You thought that you
Could touch the sky.

You never did

Now it's all gone, it's disappeared.
Towards oblivion you slowly veered.
It turned out,
just as your mother feared

Your mind slipped, it isn't very nice,
You tried drugs and you paid the price.

Hard Or Easy
Gordon W. MacKenzie

Some like the world easy,...
Some like it hard....
From what we know of weakness...
We see the result of easy.
But what we know of strength...
Hard is good... and strength the winner...
be it outer... or inner.

Mama And Papa
Kathryn Ann Wiseman

Now let me tell you about Mama and Papa....
Papa John drives an 18-wheeler for a living,
Mama Ann thanks God for another day he's been given,
To come home safe to her open arms each night,
Even if it is only to growl, do paperwork and go to bed.

From dawn to dusk he travels the highway,
As each day Mama sends the angels out his way,
It's hard leading a trucker's life,
And it's even harder being a trucker's wife.

Soulmates and Romeo and Juliet of the 90's,
Papa says, "You're under my skin,"
And Mama says, "I'll love you forever, as long as I can,"
She's his loving lady,
And he's her man.

They share everything together in life,
A couple no closer, as husband and wife.
They face each trial with strong faith in God and family,
And go through life, hand-in-hand.

Together forever, will read on their headstone when from this world they depart,
As for now, they are one union, one soul and one heart.

Dedication: to my life partner, John Blair

Hopeful Dreams
Cadge Clayton

Looking for love, my eyes peeked in on an angel
Wanting for beauty, my angel picked me a rose
Lusting for happiness, the Gods sent me a gift
A blooming rose;
A loving kiss;
Embedded with love;
Eternal bliss;
ending it with a perfect happiness.

The Beggars
J. Kitchener

When tonight you go to bed
On a pillow you lay your head
Think of the people who've nowhere to sleep
Only cardboard boxes in a dirty, damp street
Nowhere to wash, nothing to eat.
Open-soled shoes adorn their feet
Some are there through no fault of their own
No one to care for, nowhere to call home
So pity the beggars you see in the street
They're only asking for something to eat
They hold out their hands as if to say, "please"
But all they get are sneers and tease
Long shadows fall across their days
In corners they cower, frightened to face
The loneliness, despair that nobody sees
No one listens to their painful pleas
So when you see them, in wind and in rain,
Give them a smile to help deaden the pain
Try to be Christian, offer a hand
Speak to them gently, they'll understand
Please don't pass by without a glance
Without some help, they've got no chance
So if you have not a copper to spare
Please! I ask the Lord, let somebody care

To Be As You Are
Eric G. Nitsche

To be as you are, I must learn to love unconditionally.
To be as you are, I must learn that a child soars on the wings of patience.
To be as you are, I must learn that a child only sleeps when swimming in serenity.
To be as you are, I must learn that a child takes its first step only after repeated stumbles.
And that a child's first step is always in the direction of the ones he follows.
One day I hope to be as you are.
To be as you are, I must learn that happiness is not the destination but rather the journey.
To be as you are. I must learn to cherish what I have, not yearn for that which I do not.
To be as you are. I must learn to give without expectation of receiving.
To be as you are. I must learn that simplicity is often more fulfilling than complexity.
One day I hope to be as you are.
To be as you are. I must learn that anger is often a misdirected emotion.
To be as you are... I must learn that sadness is fleeting, yet elation is eternal.
To be as you are, I must learn to command respect, not because I expect it, but because I've earned it.
To be as you are, I must learn to live every day as it may be my last.
And ensure that those around me are aware of their place in my heart.
One day, I hope I will be as you are.

Dedication: to Mutti and Pops, my inspiration

Enchanted Dreams

Looking Back
Luke Jagiello
I'm hurting,
Yet I feel no pain.
I'm crying,
Yet I shed no tears.
I'm screaming,
Yet I make no sound.

Why do you make me remember?

Life
F. E. Atkinson
What would you have me say, is it just a span of years,
from childhood to the close of day.
What have I done with this life of mine and did I make my mark on time.

Has it been a life of ease, hardship or of gain, were there knocks along
 the way,
pleasures to be enjoyed, for which one day we had to pay.

Yes, I would say that, you reap just what you sow, I know, OH, yes I know.
No one gets an easy ride, there always is a price to pay, that breaks you
 up inside.

But there's so much to gain, from the living of life,
To know love, tears, happiness, as we go along life's way.
Regrets, we cannot undo what is done and that's a fact, I'd say.

But at the end, when the race, is run, will anyone remember me, I pray.
Will they know the cost and what I paid, for every wrong and the
 mistakes I made.
I will never know, I will be gone, here no more without one backward
 glance,
I will have left and quietly closed life's door.

Dedication: to Barbara, my niece, for encouragement

Miss You Still
Karen Charrise Merriwether
I still miss you after all these years
The way we used to talk
The cute way you used to walk

The way I used to hang on your every word
The funny way you used to hold your head
Your beautiful, soft hands
That bright, warm smile that you had
That lasted and lasted.

That night on the porch, you remember when
The nickname you used to call me way back then

Our song, Our last dance
Sometimes I think you were my last chance.

The way we used to talk on the phone till early morn
The way you used to whisper I LOVE YOU
It seemed like it went on and on and on

I will always miss you
You are in my heart

I hate to admit
You still have a small part.

I MISS YOU STILL!!!

Evelyn's Poem To Her Son
Evelyn Clark
Happy Birthday, little man.
You've reached the age of twenty
And may the many years ahead
Bring you the horn-of-plenty.
You've always been so good and kind,
So quick to help another.
A son like you is hard to find
I'm proud to be your mother!

The Woodlands
Mary Billingham
The sounds of the chirping birds
Echo in the woodland below,
Telling us secrets of their lives
We're the only ones wanting to know.

The multitude of fallen leaves
Carpet the uneven ground,
You can see the small animals scuttle
But with hardly any sound.

A ray of sun cuts through
As if lighting up my way,
How life feels so good
On such a calmed, relaxed day.

My daughter and I like to stroll
Down to the riverside,
Through the maze of trees and leaves
Which we use as our guide.

Now at our journey's end
The river reflections we can see,
As my Mum and I settle down
For our woodland Summer Tea!

Cat-Song For William
Fred B. McCarty
Comes now this cat of fur and flea,
Candidate for "least of ye."
Old soldier, hurt, with scars,
His bounty from Survival's wars.

So being thus, he faintly spoke without a sound.

What could be done was done and healed.
But mystic changes now revealed
A lion, mutton-chopped, with Roman nose,
Two ears lopped, yet regal pose.

So being thus, he proudly spoke without a sound.

All the cat that cat can be
Was this cat that came to me.
All the love that heart can hold
Was his gift, his feline gold.

So being thus, he sweetly spoke without a sound.

All the grief, that will not go
Juggernauting Fates bestow.
But, fairly, first they give
That, which taken, makes grief live.

So he is gone. The silence sings his little cat-songs.

Autumn Leaves
Hazel J. McClintick
Autumn leaves are happy
In the playful wind,
Gold and crimson flashing
At the beaming sun.
Swinging from the branches
Twirling in the air,
Dancing on the ground
Autumn leaves are having fun.

Another Sad Day
Paul J. Baker
Here I sit, day after gloomy day
The twilight years seemed so far away
Hoping our love will survive and never sway
Yet the solitude overwhelms and leaves disarray.

With harsh, frigid winter comes the pain
The compounded injury of years of strain
Limping like a sad, demented Ahab
Imprisoned body and soul in a pretty prefab.

The aging body lies crumpled in the chair
Former sparkling eyes no longer there
Has his soul on some fantasy journey departed
Or is it smothered by ill will by others imparted?

The glowing figure stands before the chair
Unseen by others, yet the sitter does not care
The glowing hand gently beckons wistfully
The soul rises, pain recedes, the body discarded
Gratefully.

Do not despair, wife of mine
For all of space and time are divine
There will be an eternity for you and me
Spirits entwined but forever free.

Love's Dawn
Roger K. Nickol
Last night I stood staring up at the sky,
Watching the clouds as they slipped by.
The stars! How they glittered and glimmered so bright!
And the moon was magnificent! A pearl of light.

A great owl was flying low across the way,
Banking and floating in quite a display.
A soft, gentle breeze stirred the quiet of night,
Swirling dry, crisp leaves as they danced and took flight.

In the calm, morning hours, just before dawn,
As I pondered night's beauty from there on the lawn,
I was swept away in a dream—like state,
To a time and place on another date.

Back to a time when love first filled the air,
And a beautiful woman, so sweet, so fair,
Came into my life to fulfill my desires
With soft, tender lips and a passionate fire.

Now, in the middle of life I can see,
This woman is truly God's gift to me!
Whatever time I have left in this life
Will be wonderfully spent with this woman, my wife!

Dedication: to my love, my life, Linda

Cancer
Caroline Rae
What is this thing we call Cancer
The Big C

The pain, the suffering, the misery
we wait and hope in vain
that someday they'll find a cure
to kill the pain
no more misery for all those families
to live our lives free from this fear
oh, Cancer how you've caused so much
Tragedy, why can't they find a cure!

Could it be something so simple that
as yet no scientist can see
for Heaven's sake, we found penicillin
what a miracle that turned out to be
so for now we live in hope
maybe in the next millenium it will
all be made clear
but for now this Cancer
The Big C
we have to put up with the pain
the suffering, the misery.

Dedication: to Henry Edward Betts, in memory

Wherever I Go
Matthew Wegienka
I see flowers and flowers wherever I go.
See (GOD'S) beauty, creation, the raindrops and snow.
See the mountains, the valleys, the rivers and plains.
See (GOD'S) goodness, generosity wherever I go.
Sometimes I'm happy and sometimes shed tears.
Sometimes I'm saddened, by news of these years.
See the Forests, the animals, the birdies that fly.
See (GOD'S) splendor, HIS radiance Wherever I Go.

I Admire You
Jo Vanna Ledesma
I admire you
With your hair so soft
I admire you

I admire your eyes
They're so young
I admire you

I admire your smile
It's so bright
I admire you

I admire your intelligence
It's so high
I admire you

I admire the aura
That surrounds you
It's so innocent
So white and pure
I admire you
You, my daughter, are growing
So close to our God
And I admire you

Dedication: to Keyerra, my loving inspiration

Enchanted Dreams

The Tear
Pamela N. Kirtos

Teardrops are falling down like petals from the dew,
staining what they touch and memories of you.
Stains of virtue and love all drowning with ease,
stains of the prints of muddy hands all soddened in a
cloud of dust, how quickly love can be lost.
The stains encompass my mind as clouds fall from beneath
my toes and I am ascending up through the air
with a stain of thee upon my tear.
Love is lost and hearts are dead, the blood that once boiled
for thee lies in an arctic sea of dreams once lit by steam.
Try as thee must to win my love, the stains shall always remain.
And when ye shall find what ye hath lost but never replaced,
ye will be a smarter rose to have bloomed in spring.
And yet the petals that hath bloomed in summer shall fall
in July, next to the tear I once shed for thee. But fall alone
for mine is not dead, fall with the lost souls of misplaced
fear who have all been replaced with a lonely, sullen tear.
And spread thy seeds amongst thee, let the breeze take thee
to where thee belong.
Where did thy roots decide to grow? Thee Lordith shall not
know until a stain of the tear hath fallen. How can a tear fall
from a petal who hath not bloomed?
Ye must wait and let thee tides roll over thy back and fire
catch thy heart and thy water dwell deep within thy
heart, before a tear shall ever come to thee.

My Flower
Deborah J. White

A fragrant flower growing on a strong stem,
The colour of the petals gleaming, as a precious gem,
The velvet, luscious leaves, glossy and green,
This is the most beautiful flower ever to be seen,
I call this flower the "Beautiful Scent"
For you, my darling, with all my love and heartfully meant.

Dedication: to Betty, my dearest friend

Lost Love
Jonathan James Osborn

We used to make love with words,
Now they only cut deep.
Never-ending talk ended
Every last drop of the climax has been bled.

How do you feel now, baby?
Is it all clear.
Has time differed your love for me yet.
Do you still shed a tear.

Why couldn't I love you like I do now,
Betraying inhibitions, hid it from you.
Now I've been stripped naked,
I wish you would rape my heart.

We talk about the weather,
There is a voice of loving need in those eyes.
Does my mind play or your eyes lie,
The game it becomes when play dies
Always a victor and loser.

There are no conclusions to comfort me.
At what price is love lost,
A sacrifice of the mind or of the heart.

Dedication: to my dear son Ethan

When Love Is Missing
Martha Giles

When love is missing it hurts us
all. When love is missing it leaves nowhere
at all
When love is missing, it
hurts so deep inside.
When love is missing it stays inside until it can
no longer hide. When love is missing
it sometimes feels as though your
heart has burst inside. When love
is missing it feels as though someone
has died. When love is missing where
do we turn, to family to friends
or to the quiet corner in the
den. When love is missing who do
we blame. When love is missing some
search for more. When love is missing
some never feel the same. When love is
missing we sometimes break down and cry.
When love is missing we
Break, destroy. When love is missing we
feel so down. When love is missing there's
only one way to turn. When love is
missing what do we learn. When love
is missing God gives it back to us
all.

The Fallen Soldier
Gemma Clapton

A soldier stands,
His head bowed.
Strong. Silent.
A nation's strength.
Through the years he stands,
Watching over his fallen friends.
Now he stands alone,
Defiant to the end.

Daddy
Randalee J. Keaton

He was my knight in shining armor
The king of my world.
I will always and forever be
My Daddy's little girl.

He was everything I dreamed of
He was my gentleman.
He was a charmer and a poet
But mostly my biggest fan.

He made me be a little lady
Always proper and polite.
And he'd come and hold me
If I cried at all at night.

He'd take me fishing
And even bait my hook.
He'd let me know how proud he was
With just a little look.

Though he's no longer here,
But in Heaven above.
I will always know
I'm my Daddy's little love.

Dedication: to Garrold D. Keaton, Sr.

The Anthology of Poems

Alone
Erin Carlton
Sitting alone in the dark.
feeling the rain hit my skin.
Hiding the tears that flow
down my face, aching with
the pain that only lies
within.

Being totally alone in the world
Knowing no one else understands.
Fighting in order to continue
to live, trying to meet society's
demands.

Realizing that there is no
Hope, failing no matter how
hard I try.
Losing the drive that makes
me push on.
Wanting only to die, lacking the
self-respect that I need.

Dancing to someone else's
beat allowing my life to
fall apart living
life on the street.

This Bitter Earth
Ammayeh Yisrael
This bitter Earth
Here I stand.
This bitter Earth
I love to hug
This bitter Earth
Till Heaven awaits
This bitter Earth
May bless us all

A Poem for Poetry
Denise McCarthy
I love writing poems for those that I love.
For my husband, my family, even the Lord up above.

Now I have a contest to enter. Imagine my joy,
Until I don't know what to write. My ideas are being coy.

I think of people to whom I have written
Or past loves about whom I was smitten.

I look at the sky, the birds and the trees,
and know that I have written poems about these!

I want something fresh, something new as I pace the floor.
My head begins to ache with the burden of this chore.

I go to the kitchen for something to drink.
Maybe a soda will help me to think.

I sit at the dining table and begin tapping my fingers.
Yet this feeling of failure and confusion still lingers.

I get back to work, open my notebook and sit.
I run my fingers through my hair, about to have a fit.

I wonder why all my poetry ideas went off and hid.
I just want to write one poem... Oh, I guess I just did.

Babyboy Lyrics
J. J. Hicks
Today. Today is the day we met, do you remember?
The coincidence of us colliding, in the intersection of life was
uncontrollable. It was our faith. Our eyes locked together, not a
soul could pick our combination of predetermination. There were
answers that clouded my mental, needing to be questioned.
An urge that had to be subdued. So with no hesitation, I start the
conversation. With certainty you responded, with phrases that were so
On point it was as if I gave them to you. After sharing thoughts of
Togetherness, I realized that I had been blessed with an Egyptian
Goddess, which is you.
Do you remember?.

The rainy–day walks through the park. Picnics for two in the
backyard, how could I forget the romantic mid–night rides down the
boulevard. Appreciating the entity that we had become. Simultaneously
enjoying each other's individual being. Our love symbolizes an
everlasting devotion. One that can stand the test of time, the
trials and tribulations of life. It was written long ago in the
celestial regions, that you were to be my wife.
Do you remember?.

The bad times we've experienced. The time in the club foolishness, or
at the house when that woman called. It was a simple misunderstanding,
that turned into a spiteful confrontation. Every couple goes through
it.

Fall
Joshua McDowell
When the leaves fall and God
sends a message down to Earth
telling us that fall is coming.
He will say, "out with the old
and in with the new" — that's why
the leaves fall.

Dedication: to my family

Flight of the Butterfly
Sandra Sutherland
The butterfly seems to fly so free
Its wings never touching the ground
It hovers like a bird in flight
Around it, a Heavenly crown

Its wings seem so majestic
It flutters in God's Heavenly glow
It never falters in its flight
It can hover ever so low.

It soars over rivers and mountains
It flies over fields and streams
The beauty of its mystery
Soars over my nightly dreams

I wish that I could fly so high
Never having a worldly care
I could chase away my troubles
But that wouldn't be very fair.

God made the butterfly
To be a source of beauty and grace
Not to relieve man of his problems
Not to vindicate the human race.

Dedication: to grandmother Roney, I love you

Enchanted Dreams

Love Route
Mary F. Scott
Love, Love, Love, What have you done to make
me feel I have none?
Blooming like a flower but not as strong as a tower.
Colors of all sorts dwelling in many forts.
Tears of sadness, smiles of joy, breaking our hearts
with so much pain
Mistakes we make but risks we take
Sleep I have no more, for Love has gone out the Door.
Joy and Happiness we share no more for we could have
made a good pair.
Heartache and pain are here to stay, for how long we dare
to say.
Love is a battle to be won but only by some is it gained.
Die it must do to bring about a new you.
Blossoming with bright tomorrows with no more sorrows.
Happiness returning again to share with my friends.
It's time to rise above and shine in God's love.
For there's always a price to pay to gain Love and
togetherness in this day.
So, future, here we come, riding the tides from within
knowing we can't hide all the Love we have inside.
So Love, Love, Love, We welcome you again to abide
with us and our kin.
Thanking GOD for his Blessing in teaching us a lesson
on how to Love no matter how it's protested.

Stay In School
Kristen Browne
Stay in school
So you won't be a fool
You'll get strait "A's"
Because you study for days
People will think you are cool
Because you stayed in school
Dedication: to Forest Park Elementary School students

Mother Son
David Bauman
Far off in the distance
where the sun no longer shines
is a place where you can sit
on top of the horizon.
Since the beginning
always warm with affection,
placed out of time
where stairs lead to Heaven.
So take a look at any reflection
it will always be so enrichingly beautiful.
More than any sort of words,
a touch of magic was heard.
Let the blind be ignorant
since all around you are lifted
by your spectacular shine.
Like a crystal statue
shall you stand,
in gardens of far—off sacred lands.
Let all anchors be cut loose,
since all should sail as they choose,
filled by breeze that blows,
all should know,
that you are the waters
that made so many lives grow.
Dedication: for my mother, who shines

Christmas, Christmas, Christmas
Dave Hatcher
Sleigh bells ring; Jingle, jingle they ring and songs of joy
and peace, choirs have gathered to sing.

Christmas, Christmas, Christmas is near, the season of good
tidings and giving is here.

Children laugh, they dance and they play; while believing
Santa is on his way.

Oh! What a joyous time, families gather and friends come by;
no signs of sadness, tear nor sigh; and only in happiness
do we cry.

Let us be joyful, let us show cheer; let us be thankful
Christmas is near.

Let us remember that night in Bethlehem, when as a gift to
all mankind, The Baby Jesus was born. With him came salvation
into the world, from whence we've chosen we can't be torn.

Yes, Christmas, Christmas, Christmas is here; So let us all,
with an open heart, show good cheer; While keeping in mind,
Christ the Savior is near.
Dedication: to Antonio, Lamar and James D.

One
Melisa Zahn
There are days when I long for your eyes,
to set my heart on fire.
Where I can be safe and where I
can trust.
Let me slide into you, like an open
door, let me be shown your kindness,
your humanness.
Become me and I You. Together.

Two Little Kids
Micah Taylor
I heard a gunshot in the distance and thought,
Hey – what might that be?
As someone nearby fell to the ground,
I realized they were shooting at me.

One more fell, another one dead,
This time she was shot in the head,
Everyone's running in every direction,
Fleeing from the pain and worthless affection.

A catastrophe from only God knows where,
To do this to us just wasn't fair.
Who would have thought going to school one day,
Could make everything happen in the opposite way?

A feeling this gives to see your friends on the floor,
Knowing you won't see them every day anymore.

Two little kids who wanted to have fun,
Shot up a school, now they're on the run,
We've caught them red—handed, now they're in jail,
It doesn't make up for the ones that fell.

What should we do? It doesn't make up inside,
Should we throw them in jail? Or take away their
Life?

The Anthology of Poems

Gift
N. L. Andrews
I shall have to seek high and low
to find a Mum with such a glow,
her love and strength is beyond belief
I see her pain as she grinds her teeth.

I know how lonely she must be,
but she is strong and that's the key
she brings light to the darkest day,
when I find it hard she shows the way.

She misses Dad so much, I know,
but her pain and grief she will never show,
she cries each day but hides the tears,
never will she show her thoughts and fears.

She is our idol, love and our guide,
we treasure her presence with such pride,
we see within her sadness and sorrow
but with love and hope we pray for tomorrow.

To spend more time with the one we love,
the one I'm sure was sent from above,
who is our loving Mum so brave and dear,
no matter what the distance, in our hearts
she is near...

Our Son
Barbara McCumber
A baby is born... you hear him cry
A baby is born... it's our little guy
He jibbers, he jabbers... and begins to walk
Puts words together... he's begun to talk
Off to school to learn... what he can
Our little boy is now... a grown man
A baby is born, never... to stay small
Our little boy is... six feet tall

Blessings Of An Angel
Lynn S. Robinson
I was a blessing sent from
afar;
in the beginning, a twinkling of a star.

I was a miracle made and sent from God's
majestic throne;
loaned to you briefly, so you wouldn't be
alone.

Our time together was special, spent with a lot
of love and a lot of tears;
as we bonded our hearts forever, in just seven short years.

I'm now living free from sorrow and from pain;
running and playing in the sunshine and singing in the
rain.

So let go, live your life and put a smile on your face;
because I'm waiting for everyone, in a much happier
place.

I'm sitting high on God's special cloud, made just for me;
So I can send you my BLESSINGS of happiness, love
and peace.

Dedication: to my family

I Saw The Daystar Fall
Eric James Olmos
I saw the Daystar fall
He fell upon a hill
That overlooked a meadow
Divided by a stream
Or was it just a dream?

I heard the Heavens call
The sky grew dark as pitch
I watched the clouds surrender
My body gripped with fear
And wet with God's own tears

I hurried up the hill
His countenance to gaze
His undenying beauty
I could not bear to look
The angel I mistook

I woke to mortar fire
The smell of death's perfume
I knew that he was with us
A face none dare recall
I saw the Daystar fall

Dedication: to Mary, my first love...

Because I Have You
Suzanne R. Heller
There is love in my heart,
and peace in my mind...
The best one can ask for,
and possibly find...
Life's troubled waters,
I can make it through.....
And all of this,
because I have you!

Untitled
Kelly Ahlstrom
Depression
The smiles go away and it begins to rain
tiny little teardrops making puddles of pain.
Out in the open, I've become soaking wet.
No shelter. No umbrella. No relief do I get.

Total isolation. No cover I seek.
They say "Look up! There'll be flowers next week!"
Though the ground never dries, it stays slightly damp,
I know there is hope by the light of His lamp.

Hope
(the reply)
Blooms will die and fade away my dear,
but my love is the root
making them return again each year.

Recovery
In my garden as He talks to me,
what is that?! a flower I see?
Planted there so long ago,
survived the winter and the crippling snow.
Upward thru the ground, the seed made its way
and shall bloom again on this chosen day.

Dedication: to my family – love binds

Enchanted Dreams

Seeing Nature From My Window
D. C. Baker
It's wonderful to see the wonders of nature
As the seasons come and go.
To watch the spring, then summer
Watching bees humming – flying, to and fro.
Taking pollen from the flowers
Making us some honey
It really makes me feel so good
When it's bright and sunny
Then we come to autumn
The green starts turning brown
It really is so pretty as the leaves
Come tumbling down

Twirling, swirling, as they dance
In the wind that nature brings
Oh! It's wonderful to see outside– so many different
Things.
Then comes the winter– Bringing with it snow.
It really is a picture for us to see you know
Nature is sleeping the trees are really bare
I see a little Robin hopping here and there
Nature is so wonderful and what I see is free
We are so very Lucky– having eyes that we may see.

Dedication: to my brother, George Hopkins

Bouquets
D. E. Arneil
After a winter's snow
Bluebells and snowdrops pop through
Warm, dark Earth and
Yellow buttercups and daisies wave
Across the cultivated field to
Pansy faces smiling at
Comos and snapdragons who
Dance gaily in manicured gardens.

No Notebook
David Keiser
'Cuz it's not cool to bring to school
and you think it's a waste of money you don't have, anyway

Maybe you bring paper, yellow and folded pocket–size
or twirled up your sleeve, or maybe
you borrow white, frilly filler paper from friends

Or maybe the pencil lead smudges your assignment
or you say you hate what you wrote anyway
that you'd rather just talk it out

But your resistance is not about the paper or the pencil lead
but about some doubting demons inside your head

You ask why even try to write
what you so easily can say aloud?

Maybe you think
you can't write
at all
Well, what if notebooks were cool and didn't cost you money
and the teacher accepted folded and twirled and smudged work
and you could just dictate your words

Would you write then?
Would you write then?

October Gales
Jessieca Sinnott
The sea lifts and rolls as lightly as a newlywed's sheets,
and tumbles free as her curls and giggles across the gate.
Flowing satin at her ankle flirts and then retreats,
and waves leap at her impatient heart with desire that
cannot wait.

The grass runs like rats round the indomitable hill,
before the blustering red–faced farmer's wife.
Bodice straining as she shrieks curses blind and shrill,
and lashes wildly at the streaming tails with her carving
knife.

Leaves cringe as fallen friends crumble 'neath the raging
Halloween hags,
and tremble in their frigid breath with dread for those
they will disbud.
Curling away their ripe glow from the snatching rags,
lest they be tossed up like sparks from a pyre, then cast
down in the mud.

I turn for home, a bullying wind sharply shoves my shoulder.
Lifts my collar for a stinging slap on my frozen cheek.
Tired legs stumble, the harpy pushes harder, colder.
Eyes smart with tears from the blast, or memories old and
bleak.

Daisy
Douglas Sandler
In every daisy in the field
Full Thirty Morals are concealed,
And though but one of them be mine,
And I forgot the twenty–nine,
Yet am I better off by far
Than rich men and their butlers are,
Who ever have of Morals none,
While happy I at least have one.

My Angel
Joseph Michael Lanasa
The Earth has not anything to show more fair,
than my Angel's beauty, which is without error.

The morning sun will start its rise,
to rest a while in noonday skies.

But while it's there, cannot compare,
to the glowing light in my Angel's eyes.

Behold her hair and its every strand,
where rests it gently on her head.

Mar not its radiance by stroke of hand,
possess its charm by touch, instead.

Spring! Be not proud of thy soft, tender breeze,
Summer! Be humble of the smooth, warm seas.

For, far must thy journey and listen to this;
to equal my Angel in breast and in kiss.

Many and more could I think of to boast,
but always of one will I think of the most.

Her warm breath she breathes past my ear as she says,
"I love you, sweetheart, till death names the day."

Love – Life
Kimberley Dickson
Love is like life.
They are both difficult to
understand and to explain;
they can be cruel and can
hurt.
But they should be enjoyed,
as they are gifts that we
can treasure, forever.

Loss Of A Friend
Donna Marie Garcia
At times when I sit all alone
I start to think about

How precious your friendship was to me
How hard it is without

You always made me feel special
You took away my fears

And if my heart got broken
You said time heals with tears

You gave me hope and inspiration
When my dreams all fell apart

You could always tell when I was sad
It's as if we had one heart

It's so hard to live without you
I miss our special bond
Just know I'll never forget you
You're at peace, my friend, with God

Dedication: to Mom, who completes my life

If The World Could Embrace Love
Toni Terry
If the world could embrace love,
Feel its warmth transcend from Heaven above
Society would breathe such a sigh of relief
Crimes committed would diminish in its streets

If the world could only embrace love

Love manifests acceptance in our hearts
Breaks chains of racism far apart
Let's offer love 101 in our universities
Educate all on the issues of diversity

If the world could only embrace love

Love is long–suffering, gentle and kind
Can be used to nourish our future, a child's mind
Love is taught by example
I'd bottle love – give away free samples

If the world could only embrace love

The universe would unite with such power
Unlimited, shared knowledge bouquet–ing like flowers
Wars would cease
We'd live in peace
If the world could only embrace love

The Land Deep Underneath
Jason Lucas
Determined to succeed,
Over every task,
Lands deep underneath,
Perhaps too far,
Having seen the land beneath,
Interested by far,
Now is scared to seek the land that
is so far.

The Letter
Charles Lauersdorf
Thanks for your letter
I hoped you would write
Though we've never met
I thought someday we might

I understand
Just how you feel
You wonder if
I'm really real

I have the same
Thoughts about you
How can I be sure
What you say is true

Fate is to blame
It led me to you
So I guess there's only
One thing to do

You said we should meet
That's okay with me
I'll be there with bells on
You just wait and see

Second Chance
Colleen Malanczyn
Ever want a second chance?
A chance to make things right.
It can haunt you, if you feel at fault
From early morn, through night.

I want to change some things I did –
A year or so ago.
Just turn back time and start out fresh
Then maybe I can grow.

As things stand now, I feel I just
Can't start to move ahead –
Unless I'm sure he can forget
The wrong I did and said.

I know it's much to ask of him,
But he means more to me,
Than anything in my whole world.
Just have to make him see.

If I'm to have a future and a life –
It is with him.
I hope with all my heart and soul,
Our future isn't dim.

Dedication: to Alan, my love and inspiration

Enchanted Dreams

Unbridled Passion
Frank S. Conte
A girl who incessantly chattered
Tried to woo me, but I wasn't
flattered.

Unbearably vain,
She was such a great pain,
And her hopes of marriage were
shattered.

Signs Of Fall
Dean E. Gerry
I feel the breeze as it passes my face
It's cool, yet sharp, like a fancy, pretty lace.
The trees are bending with their colors so bright
Some leaves have fallen, others will fall later tonight.

The days are shorter and the sun seems bold,
You'll need your jacket, the wind feels kind of cold.
The birds are flocking and soon will head South
their feathers are fluffed and a smile lines their mouth.

The grass is turning brown and the crop's ready to bin
the clouds are bellowing gray, a cold front is moving in.
There's a mist in the air, the dampness goes clear through
the pumpkins sure are ripe and the frost has turned to dew.

I looked to the sky as I heard a beckoned call
the geese are honking loud, my heart's not beating at all.
Their wings are hardly moving, they seem hung up in space
what a marvelous bird they are, clumsy but full of grace.

I love this time of year, it feels so clean and nice
the smell of pie fills my nose and I yearn for just a slice.
I can hear the ghosts and the goblins seem to stare
fall has finally come, you can feel it in the air.

I Surrender All
Virginia Rhodes
Jesus is the central focus and love in my life,
He carries me through each problem and strife,
By keeping my eyes fixed on my dear, blessed Saviour Jesus,
I am aware of His love and the precious price He paid to release us.

His agonizing death and glorious resurrection have set me free.
Accepting Him by faith and because of God's grace I can live in Heaven
eternally.

Regardless of what life brings to me each day,
Jesus is always there to strengthen and guide me all the way.

Before I invited Jesus into my heart, my life lacked purpose;
I was always in a state of confusion and seemed totally useless.
My life was lonely, empty, unfulfilled and fruitless.

Now I have surrendered my heart and life to Him.
Peace, assurance and love are mine with Jesus as my Saviour, Lord and
friend.
He is in control and on His Heavenly throne;
Never again will I have to be alone.

His love for me is beyond my understanding or any measure
It is far more precious than any Earthly treasure.

Oh, how I love Jesus!

I Can
Tommy Crabtree
I can be anything I can
From a doctor to a farming man
A lawyer would be kinda fun
Or a cop with a gun
A teacher would be pretty cool
If you follow the main rule
I think I can, I think I can
I know I can, I can

This And That
Bob and Catherine Webb
Here is a story you've got to hear
The story of this and that
This was a little, tiny, gray mouse
And that was a big, black cat

That was always chasing this
And this was always running from that
This was getting really tired of it all
Why should a mouse have to take that from a cat

That just simply didn't like this
And this had a way of getting to that
So one day that set a trap for this
But this was having none of that

This had to do something really fast
So he set a trap of his own for that
Then he sat right down and waited and watched
Cause he knew for sure he would catch that cat

So that finally did catch this
And this finally did catch that
And if you think that there is more to this
I'm telling you now, that's, that

What Happened?
Carol R. Newingham
To find love and then lose it
This loneliness that I feel
Just seems to keep building and building
I can't seem to shake it off.

No matter how much I try
it comes and it goes
But, mostly it stays
What went wrong?
We don't talk, we don't do anything.
But, work and pay bills

Somewhere, Somehow we have lost it
You are you, I am me
Can we accept it?
We were once happy
What happened? What went wrong?

How do we start over again?

where do we begin?
Or shall we call it quits?
I'm scared, but not of you
I'm lonely, because of you.

Dedication: to my lovely daughter Candice

Forever Yours
Brain Lashomb
to my wife, my darling dear
who has always been sincere
I give to you 3 rings of pure, white gold
sparkling clear stones is what they hold
and upon your finger, you will share
all the love my heart will bear
forever and ever it will glare
for you my heart will be there.

The Garden Isle
D. M. Squires
Tranquil, serene as in a dream
The Isle of Wight appears
Its little bays from bygone days
Awash for many years

The gentle lapping of the tide
The seagulls soaring high
The little yachts that watch in awe
The ferry gliding by

Along the shore the flags fly high
To welcome in the fleet
High on the hill is Osborne House
A splendid Queen's retreat

Small cottages with whitewashed walls
Stand proud along the lane
Where coach and horses used to ride
In Queen Victoria's reign

This Garden Isle so picturesque
An artist's dream come true
With splendour, beauty, peacefulness
A window with a view.

Our Bond
Lora Taylor
You, my friend, will always be
Our hearts, they seem in harmony
A bond we have, deep in our souls
You are my friend, this I know.

And no matter what comes our way
You will always be in my heart to stay
This bond I feel, so deep and strong
Is what gets me through each day long

I see your face each day I wake
And a smile it puts upon my face
I hear your voice each passing hour
It tells me stop and smell the flowers.

My spirit is with you in all that you do
And, I will stay close to help you through.
I feel as though we touch each day
As our spirits each go upon their way

So my friend, I hope you know
My love is with you wherever you go
This bond is as strong as one could be
And, I thank you, for giving it to me.

Dedication: to Pepper, my friend forever

Love
Jessica K. Riffle
Love is a bird in the
midst of the sky
Love is a charming smile
you give as you pass by
Love is a boat sailing in
the deep, blue sea
Love is when you loved
me for me.

My Nephew: The Son I Never Had
Christopher William McNeil
David was born in seventy-eight.
A nephew relation whom I think is great.
Considered the son that I never had.
He made me laugh, He made me glad.

He's "Giving" to all except to himself
And waits to excel what he keeps on the shelf.
Most people don't know what he's all about.
I'm honoured to know him, I have no doubt!

Insecure in his confidence, "Sure".
A tuff exterior, He prefers to "Assure".
But in his intentions he does not mean harm.
It shows in his stylish, original charm.

He'll never be dull, he'll always have friends.
A part of himself, who matters, he lends.
Yes, "Independent" you'll find him to be
"Unconditional Love" is the key?

I know he's young and living fast.
Memories of me. Of my quicker past.
I'll never forget him when I have to leave
My David, " I'm dying, " In you I believe!

Could It Be?
Charlotte G. Olson
There are campfires on the hillside, their lights,
They flicker through the trees – or
Could it be, angel spirits of departed ones
Winking at me?

Rain comes, thunder booms and lightning strikes, or
Is it just my guardian angel
Dusting off its wings and
Saying "Hi" to me?

There's a "Blue Hole" in the foothills
Fed by a mountain stream, or
Is the "Blue Hole" just a place
Where an angel comes to shed some tears
For those of us who stray?

The raccoons on my mailbox
The rabbit's in the road
The bear just went up the mountains
My dogs just told me so.

Could it be, these are the reasons why
My shack beside the mill creek
Seems like a mansion to me?

Dedication: to those who love the mountains

Enchanted Dreams

Dreams
Adam H. Baron
I wandered all throughout the night
and wondered what I had in sight.
I looked around at all I see
and pondered at a willow tree.
My thoughts so deep, for all I keep
and wondered if I'd ever weep,
for knowing what or who will be
the future holds uncertainty.

Salvation's Song
Sherry Egan
Breathe on me Lord, Breathe on me;
You open my blind eyes so that I can see.
A Heavenly vision of the cross and of purity.

You open my ears so that I can hear;
Creations praises shouting Your holy name.
In fire, wind and rain
Is birthed a blaze, whirlwind and flood;
That puts upon my sin and shame, a hood.
For at the bottom of the cross they stood
To be consumed, swept away and washed by
Your redeeming blood.

So I bathe in flowing showers of blood divine
Cleansing my soul Oh, first Love of mine
I bow down to wash Your feet
You kiss my tears, I'm whole and complete.

I kneel before Your precious throne
Servant before King
You Christen me child and as your own
While the city of angels sing!

Dedication: to the Lord Jesus Christ

Engraved
Gaylyn Collins
As I stand dazed and confused, I wipe the
tears from my eyes and look into my hands.
Lost in the emptiness of the Moment, my heart
echoes, WHERE ARE YOU, JESUS?
In silence, still looking into my hands, my heart
flutters and I feel a voice say, "Look into
My hands, WHAT DO YOU SEE?"
Looking through the tears I see a child loved and
adored by all.
Tears streaming down my face, the child grows older
with hammer in hand, he learns.
Fighting through the tears, there's a young man,
loved and adored by most, misunderstood and
feared by others. HE LOVED ALL.
My heart says look deeper. In brokenness, my heart
hurts. I'm scared.
With His arms opened wide He tells my heart, trust
in Me – look deeper – WHAT DO YOU SEE?
As I looked into His wounded hands, my heart feels
the love and compassion, honor and strength,
and healing for the wounded heart.
Deeper He says.
There I see me!
ENGRAVED IN THE MASTER'S HANDS.

Dedication: to my grandmother, Ethal Starutska

Losing The One You Love
Cassandra Cordingly
Losing the one you love is very hard, you know,
For I lost my Grandpa Howard a few months ago,
For I love him dearly, for I was very close.
He would get down on his knees and play with me.
He was a loving Grandpa who was very fun.
For I loved him dearly, to let you know,
For I won't forget my Grandpa Howard.
The one I lost whom I loved very so.

Love Never Known
Ronnie Salmons
Hands never held
Affection never shown
Lips never kissed
Love never known

Pools of tears
Deep as a well
Feelings so strong
Voices never tell

Questions never asked
Answers never given
Dreams never revealed
Life never liven

Filled with desire
Words never spoken
Promises never made
Promises never broken

Flower of life
No blossom grown
Died before living
Love never known

Untitled
Shirley Ann Lewis
This Earth that we've inherited,
In all its infinite beauty,
To preserve it for our offspring,
That surely is our duty.

Our children skip through childhood,
Running before they can walk,
Fairy stories distorted,
Hardly any baby talk.

No time left to appreciate
Little things that people say,
Missing out on simple things,
As technology gets in the way.

What right have we to interfere,
With a human embryo,
When this is really something,
For God alone to bestow.

Maybe now the time is right,
To consider the aftermath,
Avoiding self-destruction,
Or even our creator's wrath.

Dedication: to my beloved father, Peter Woods

Sojourners
Tommy L. Ketron

Lights—repressed
Streets seemingly void
Conceal displaced transients
on a moonless night.
Vague figures sift through
broken beams of illumination.
Passions thrive, seeking refuge
in deep cavernous shadows:
Uncertain feet ready for flight
from secrets unacknowledged,
icy winds, agonized tendrils
prying into crevices,
heads bent low,
shoulders hunched
hungry eyes searching.
Fears shrouded by darkness emit
thoughts unspoken:
mere dust beneath shod feet
desires, smoldering embers
shadowy things clutched to the heart.
Time past, time to come elicit
growing patters of the soul's
predestined cycles
never—ending, all—consuming.

Skye
Graham Willard

You could be so many other ways
as so many are
You could have had a different past
with countless variations
You could become any answer
in any questionnaire
I will love you
as an ocean rising to the clouds

Sons And Mothers
Jan Martin

You and Me,
Toast and Tea,
Black, White,
Day, Night.

You and Me,
Silver filigree,
Logic, Passion,
Taste, Fashion.

You and Me,
Spirit Free,
Urban, Rural,
Singular, Plural.

You and Me,
Sensitive We,
Tipple, 'stain,
Pattern, Plain.

You and Me.
Lock and key.
Together, Bound,
Apart, Found.

Dedication: to my son James

Life–Universe
Pearline Alexander

Life does not lead those blinded by the darkness
Its will is the universe's creation and destruction
For without life no matter its form
Forever still no eyes born
The boundless universe, what known darkness has life willed
Its power we praise, no one knows when its curtain will rise or fall
The universe awaits the will of life's decision
Tomorrow, what's to envision.

A Wildlife Contrast
Evelyn Cleghorn

The humming birds sang music,
Only the Lilac bush could hear,
Tiger Lilies grew by the brookside,
But no Tigers lived out here.

Goldenrod stood in masses,
Roots firmly planted in the grass,
Coltsfoot grew by the wayside,
Where no young horses ever passed.

Morning Glory lifted their trumpets,
No notes came from their horns,
Dog Roses covered the fences,
But no Dogs would touch their thorns.

Delicate pink Ladies' Slippers,
That no Lady's foot could please,
Foxgloves stood at the forest edge,
Have you seen Reynard wearing these?.

A Green frog sat on a Lily pad,
Waiting for a Dragonfly,
Iris grew by the water's edge,
The ever present "Eye".

Paradise
Alison Kirkham

She strolled along the desolate beach,
Clutching her shoes, her feet were bare,
The sand trickled between her toes,
On her face a faraway stare.

She was captured by the wonderful sight,
Of the sun shimmering across the sea,
The waves gently rippled over her feet,
Her perfect place to be.

She carried her thoughts along the shore,
To her, the world had gone away,
The peace, calm and tranquility,
Was how she wanted it all to stay.

Her mind was free, her spirit alive,
An inner sanctuary she could feel,
Her heart content, her eyes so bright,
She felt so alive and so real.

She wishes it would last forever,
As there's no other place she feels this way,
She captured every single Moment,
Captured the memory, forever and walked away.

Dedication: to my ever-loving father

Enchanted Dreams

Untitled
Danyelle M. Webber

When my mind is seized by fancy.
I dream of a place by the ocean.
The ocean waves are crystal blue.
The soft waves.
When my mind is seized by fancy,
I see a lighthouse blink off and on.
I always dream of this special place.
When my mind is seized by fancy,
I dream of a place by the ocean.

God's Teardrops
Valerie Hornbaker

I walk in the garden early in the morning.
The dew resembles teardrops on the flowers,
As if the sadness from all of my sins
Has caused God to weep in the night hours.

But soon on the horizon, a red glow appears;
The warmth of the sun will soon dry the dew.
A breeze whispers gently, as it caresses my cheek,
The voice says, "Don't worry, I have forgiven you."

I reach out, trying to grasp the presence I feel,
But the wind of the spirit escapes my touch,
And I think of the red flow of blood that was shed,
From the body of Christ, who loved me so much.

He walks with me in the spirit that He sent
When He ascended to His Father in the Sky.
He talks to me whenever I'll hear.
He's with me as each Moment of life goes by.

But when I get lost in the spirit of this world,
I know that His heart breaks anew,
And His teardrops fall all during the night,
Once more covering the flowers with dew.

Sophie
Janet Allwright

Sophie the King Charles Spaniel,
Her only aim in life is to please.

See just how beautiful she looks,
As she darts ahead with ease.

In and out and round about,
Winding a circle around the trees.

Bringing sticks and running away,
She loves a game and a tease.

To be the very best of dogs,
Every opportunity she will cease.

She is so very adorable,
You just have to give her a squeeze.

With all of her wonderful loving ways,
Every wrong she does appease.

So if you see her running,
Don't bring her to her knees.

For Sophie is our most beautiful and faithful dog,
Who is loved by everyone she sees.

Little Miss Bossyboots
Rhoda Glanville

Little Miss Bossyboots
Plays at dressing up, a lady
In beads and bangles that jingle jangle
And Grans' hat sat at an angle
And a handbag on her arm
She clumps around, tries not to fall
Flip–flop she goes down the hall
In shoes too big for her wee feet
Quite delightfully petite.

Automation
June Roberta Shaffer

Have you ever bought a hot dog
At an automated place?
You say, "I'll have some mustard"
Window closed – it is too late.

Have you ever come up to a door
To which it opens wide?
There's no one there for you to thank,
But then you are inside.

Have you ever dialed a telephone
To hear a recording say,
"This is not a working number, sir",
So try another day.

Have you ever parked your car
Where you put money in a slot?
While looking for the change to use,
A nickel you've not got!

So if everything is automated,
On Earth and in the sky,
There'll be no need for you up there,
So it just won't pay to die.

Penthouse 206
Deborah J. Marston

The midlanders were so calm
They did not express their mind
So we showed them how
And in time they came to party!

There was no mercy
We gave it all
Without a care
And soon they did see!

Ranting and raving
We lead the way
But always leading
At least one astray!

Yorkshire girls are the best
We are down–to–earth
But wild and crazy
YES, we shall amaze thee!

As we travel southwards
We stay in other's hearts
The secret code of S. A. D.
Shall be a fun tale legend!

Dedication: to Sarah Hutson, for creative inspiration

The Anthology of Poems

Candle
Kaleigh Eichhorst
Why was I put in this holder?
The furniture and the entertainment unit sitting in the House
Kids yelling
Cranberry melted wax
Pie baking in the oven
Love is here
People like candles
The flame warms me
It doesn't hurt me

Early Moments
Deborah A. Fultz
Awaken
to a world of silent gestures
where cool grasses lie
and where dew sparkles
through the misty air.

Awaken
to a world of gray whispers
where birds sing of promise
and where nature patiently awaits
the warming colors.

Awaken
to a world of crimson skies
where streams of color brighten the hills
and flow down pink and lavender.

Awaken
to a world of sunbeams
warming Earth, golden air,
embracing me
a new day, a rebirth

Awaken

The Virgins Of Arkansas
Hilda Roberts
In one fell swoop, they lay bloodied.
A terrible clean swipe from two angry buddies.
Hundreds of rounds of ammunition and guns
camouflage gear contemplating more stunts.

Amidst all the chaos, the stillness of the playground,
two young teenage boys effectively mount
playfully toying with a horrendous, unexplained idea
to kill and kill with profound panacea.

The shrill, the endless screams, the sight of the fallen,
young girls grapple to save the helpless and sullen
as these two boys emerge triumphant in their cause
the bushes behind them begin counting the loss.

Those ways routine, en route to continue,
the savagery, the pain, a quiet retinue
if hatred unmasks, embroiling its whim
tearing fears, all told, no Hollywood can trim.

No shock, no grit, no amount of pathetic yelling,
it supposes understanding but not its fervent coming
so innocent those lives, blazing firearms uphold
the virgins of small towns self–inflicting and cold.

Dedication: to my ever dearest John

Time
Gloria Street
The old saying is that time
waits for no one.
We say time out, there's time to
play, time to work, time to love, no time
for hate. Today we need time for
understanding, time for trust, caring,
most of all there should be time for
Jesus Christ.
So little time for so many things

The Pheasant
Ellie Halcrow
Hidden flat beneath the tall grass, senses acute,
She blends, bland brownness, into the decaying decor.
Silently she listens to the hunters' hurried, hungry step.
As he and his hunting hound cast with the wind.

Her talent tells her to toy with and tantalize her stalker,
Lead them around the patch playing "The Game".
The challenge takes cunning and cleverness,
Knowing its nostrils are demanding and determined.

She runs, puffed up, pacing herself the winner,
Then she slinks low, lying on the turf.
With swift foot she reaches the brambles
Safe, sophisticated, with a sense of seniority.

She nibbles a selected seed, but still listens,
Her skills, though proficient and practiced,
Give her an adrenaline rush every time.
Her life demands and depends on her ability.

She hears the hot breath of the pointer,
She sees the sway of shrub just ahead.
Ground thunders, then silence is felt in the field.
The mesmerizing of bird and pointer alert in the stillness.

The Advantages Of A Single Woman
Mandy Henderson
I have no one to consider in my life,
no one to worry about late at night.
I can stay awake all night long,
or stay in bed for hours till the day is gone.

No one to answer to, only myself,
and everyone thinks I'm left on the shelf.
My time is my own, no appointment to keep.
no one to disturb me when I'm fast asleep.

I can travel the world from one corner to the other,
but knowing me I probably won't bother.
But in my mind I'm free to do all this,
though I know that boat I'll probably miss.

I've got no one to take my personality away,
or remind me of my place and tell me stay.
And people think I lead a strange life,
because at my age I'm no man's wife.

No one to say this is who you should be,
just me on my own but, me being me.
Do I get lonely, yes, a small price to pay,
for living my life all my own way.

Dedication: to my sisters with love

Enchanted Dreams

His Shadow
Annette Gilsdorf
I thought I saw his shadow next to me today
But it was only in my heart and soul
How I miss my love, my friend
I thought I saw his shadow next to me today
His hand warm in mine, blue eyes smiling
Always dreaming of a better tomorrow
The days go on, the nights are long
My love, my friend is no longer
I thought I saw his shadow next to me today

The Search For Meaning
Paul W. Dickerson
I wander around looking for life's meaning,
Why we all exist just to die.
We try and fool ourselves with lies,
Lies of a higher purpose for the human race.

Trying not to think of the cruel fate ahead,
Running around acting like everyone else.
Using someone else to find meaning in life,
Then wanting to die when they abandon you.

Leaving you to rot looking for truth,
But there is no truth to any lies,
Which means there is no truth to life,
No truth nor meaning to life at all.

The true meaning is so meaningless
Yet I continue to do the same as you.
And search for truth that does not exist
Wasting my life looking for purpose.

Instead of having fun and enjoying life,
Which could be the true meaning
To life
To life in itself.

The Helping Hand
Charles Charnock
I went down to the superstore
To where they keep the Trolleys
She placed a finger on my wrist,
And, in a voice like Molly's, said

May I walk with you through the store?
I really feel quite lost!
I may not find just what I need,
Nor know the proper cost!

Aha, thought I, the lady's blind?
So come with me I said.
And I will show you how to find,
Your coffee, cheese, or bread!

And at the till, she said to me
You really have been kind
I've only just now realized,
That you, yourself are blind

The speaker from St. Dunstan's said
We'd get a big surprise, if
When next we went our shopping.
We tried without our eyes.

Dedication: to Ruth and Arthur Smith

To John
Joyce MacGillivray
Should I die if you will think of me
Forever, my love, as loving you,
The grave has no call to surround me
Your love can take me beyond
To the heights of paradise
Together we fly as one, you and I
Soaring and soaring in love, my love

Dedication: to John – love never ends

The Lady
Crystal Jackson
There's a darkness in her
Expression. What is she thinking?
She stares into
Nowhere. Her eyes never blinking.

What tragedy did she face? How
Many tears has she cried? What
Caused the emptiness—Raging
From her eyes?

She seems so distant. So
Out of touch. You can break
Her with words. Without
Saying much.

Her body's so tense. Void
Of Emotion. Undisturbed
By sound. Not roused
By commotion.

Like a lifeless statue. She sits
Frozen and still. Unable to
Comprehend. The sorrow
She feels.

Someday
Andrew Haywood
Someday I'll find you.
Like springtime in autumn.
No matter how hard I try it won't get through.

I sit. Flat. Looking beyond the view,
Trying to ignore a certain hum.
Someday I'll find you.

You may think I'm the first in a long queue!
My heart, beats, like an old, used drum.
No matter how hard I try, it won't get through.

How will I confront you?
Why did you treat me like an old street bum?
Someday I'll find you.

My body drank you,
As if you were a bottle of old Indian rum.
No matter how hard I try, it won't get through.

And I am somewhat drawn to you,
Like a clown to fun!
Someday, I'll find you.
No matter how hard I try, it won't get through.

Dedication: to Mum, Dad and Michelle

A Summer's Day
Brian Wheeldon

Hedgerows and butterflies
Country lanes and you
Daisies and buttercups,
a herring gull or two
Clear blue skies
Deep blue sea
Boats in the bay
Let's live forever
Forever and a day.

Poetic Riddles Of Nature
Kevin Watts

Nature's light.
Brightening our day clearly.
Luminous, vivid, tepid.
What disappears at night?

Nature's tears.
Descending towards the Earth.
Limpid, damp, unscented.
What are the tears of nature's sorrow?

Nature's breath.
Slightly leaning trees by its strength.
Progressive, invisible, insipid.
What moves without being seen?

Nature's bellow.
Dispersing vibrations of roaring sound.
Vociferous, rumbling, fierce.
What is nature's stentorian voice.

Nature's father.
Giving birth to new life on Earth.
Heavenly, celestial, enduring.
Nature is the child of whom?

Merry Go Round
Roberta McLennan

A swinger of the bold, brave sixties
Threshold of new life, new wife, the seventies
Super Mum, wife, daughter, neighbor, the eighties
Maturing, reflecting, seeking, studying the nineties

Unknowingly, slow, slowly slowing
Like a broken wind—up doll
Done. Discarded, not working at all
Sitting, thinking, blinking back a tear

Oh, where is the woman of yesteryear?
Wondering, asking what is the reason
Of this, this body's treason?
Used up a whole life span of energy

Spending recklessly, giving it generously
As the dawning of each new morning
Thankfully, gratefully still enjoying life
Still a friend, a mother, lover and wife

Still have a lot of giving, striving, believing
In love, people, family and friends
So the giddying, surprising merry go round of life
Continues to go on and on until it ends.

Dedication: to Leslie, my best friend

Diana
Ann Humphrey

Time has passed but a legacy lives on.
Why one so full of life and hope,
Had to die, we know not why.

Heaven is now a better place,
Now our princess,
with her beautiful face,
Full of kindness and grace
Will always be Queen in Our Hearts.

Danger Junkie
T. Earl West

Once upon a time, in a land far, far away,
Lived a young man, just living day to day.
When bell bottoms and flower power were the symbols of the day
Old enough to fight, but not to say "nay".

Like any young man of his day
He drove his Chevy to work and play,
To sunset and surf and sunrise of the next day.

But as it was a sign of the times
A letter he got from his Uncle Sam saying,
"Man, I'm in a terrible jam in the land of Nam."
But the young man didn't know if he wanted to go,
And his uncle's reply was "surely, you are to go!"

Eight months later, with no gun by his side
In one of those flying machines, he got his first ride.
Just he and the pilot went across the land of Nam,
When Charlie began to wave in his usual way,
"Welcome to the enchanted land of Vietnam".

Then the pilot began to fly from side to side
And before the young man knew it
A Junkie of Danger was he in the land of Vietnam.

A Plea
Eric W. Baker

Oh, I have been so heartless and so cruel
To write to you, sweet one, in manner curt;
To cast aside a rare and precious jewel,
And send to you such sorrow, grief and hurt.

Forgive, I pray, those thoughtless words of mine,
Which I would give my all not to have penned.
To err is human; to forgive, divine.
Forgiving me, may our dear friendship mend.

Each hour is dull and dismal, here, alone;
Anticipation of time with you gone,
With days aplenty to think and bemoan
My empty life, whereon the sun once shone.

I beg that you accept this heartfelt plea;
That I may once more see your wondrous face
And look into your eyes and in them, see
That, understanding, you forgive, with grace

I ask only that I may be with you,
For that, to me, would be joy unconfined,
And life would once more don a golden hue,
And give me purpose, light and peace of mind.

Dedication: to Betsy with deepest affection

Enchanted Dreams

Once
Angella Russell

Moments pass in the time, staring obvious
Waited for this, gone so quickly, all for naught
Again I've sold myself short of an empty offer
and sigh.
In my thoughts fondly breathing
Quietly stealing more than I've left to give
I'm still alone, hold it tightly, don't let go
It wasn't mine, but I've touched and know
That the burning was there, even if now it's still

Finding Your Way
Sharon Gipe

Let me be the shadow in your light
The silence of words never spoken
Always seen, hardly ever in sight
Being one of the few, never the chosen

As one in life yet to become
The beginning of a new start
With time, all can be done
Know and feel the strength in your heart

Always follow as we do guide
Only learning from what we expect
Following shown signs and going in pride
Keeping the image and all it reflects

To walk countless steps in the miles
Seeing the inside of what's really out
Accepting all tribulations and trials
Being the best you can with no doubt

So as you travel through life as your own
Take heed in the call
Only you and I together, yet alone
Forever to walk steady, straight and tall.

Time Stands Still
Nellie Ruth W. Demons

I heard a man say today
that time moves swiftly by
for the retiree who doesn't work
and the baby who likes to cry.

For the mothers who raised their children
for the children who prosper in life
for the pets who love their masters
for the waves that come in with the tide.

Time stands still for the aged
whose best years are far spent
for the disgruntled man
who is not God—sent.

Time stands still for the yelping dog
who can't tell night from day
for the mewling cat
who sometimes goes astray.

Time stands still for unstable people
whose eyes are closed and mouths are shut
for the unsaved souls who are afraid
to admit they love Jesus so much.

Time Stands Still...

Liquor
Penelope F. Sommer

I have a lover
Who loves this other
Much more than he loves me.
I see him tempted
When discontented
For liquor to be free
From life's exertion
To the desertion
Of pain and love and me.

Of Mexico
Daniel Ray Cano

Mexico is home to the Aztecs and Mayans,
But every single day they can't stop tryin',
to eat and live and just get by,
'cause so many people down there always have to die,
of poverty, living conditions and basic starvation,
They ask themselves every day, "What can we do to change this nation",
Home of the fearless warriors and great Mexican pride,
Even though they're strong, so many have cried,
over the situations they've gone through and problems they've faced,
But they still love the tradition and culture of their great race,
The Mexican revolution has unleashed many heroes,
But it seems today it has really amounted to zero,
Immigration is a big problem down on the Mexican border,
Every day little kids on the streets are fighting for a quarter,
Business has been good for the past couple of years,
Now they're trying to get past all their tears,
The crucifix is loved and praised in every single town
and for one single Moment, they are unable to make a frown,
hoping and praying every day Jesus doesn't let them down,
Mexico hopes to be a developed country just like the U. S.
and will someday do their best, to get out of this mess.
It's a great place to live, visit and go,
because if there's one thing Mexico does well,
it is put on a show.

Ambition's Grasp
Mira Matejin

From sweet repose I must awake.
Shutter the quiet night's reign
To face another day of my career
As a prisoner of my ambition.

A whole new day yet old to my feelings,
In a mad race against old man time
I restlessly rush forward to my capture
A prisoner of my ambition.

I longingly look through the window
My thoughts escape and wander unrestrained,
For a brief Moment I savour the freedom
I, a prisoner of my ambition.

Slowly, obediently, I return to my desk
Resigned to life's merciless demands,
I should be happy but my heart rebels
In this prison of my ambition.

When the day is over my relief is fleeting
For tomorrow already casts its shadow,
I long for freedom, I long to escape
From this prison of my ambition.

Dedication: to Jeff with my love

God's Little Miracle
Jackie Magnuson
You will go from bottles and booties
To coos and giggles, crawling everywhere
With laughing eyes and bouncing curls
Then ballerina shoes and buttons and bows
There will be soda pop times
Jewelry galore, bracelets and rings and all those things
There will be prom times, graduation.
Oh, yes!! First love with all its wonders
God's little miracle is like a touch of spring

Football
Gregory J. Lilley, Jr.
Football is a brutal sport,
It involves a field, not a court,
When the players' helmets clash together,
It sounds like thunder in stormy weather,

Number 1 is running down,
Number 2 is fooling around,
The ball is oval, made of pigskin,
But, we do not know who's going to win,

Number 3 has made a goal,
Number 4 has hit a pole,
Running on the 10 yard line,
Number 5 breaks his spine,

It is all now up to number 6,
His skeletal structure is made of bricks,
Charging like a war machine,
You see his ears blowing off steam,

Now, you see, he's got the ball,
It is a win for them all,
They pick him up to shout and cheer,
They go out to celebrate someplace near.

The Missed Loved One
Rebecca Rising
You were always here,
and I could tell you anything.
You helped me when I had trouble,
and I looked up to you.

Now you left me here alone,
with no one to look up to.
I can't talk to you,
and you can't help.
I can't even hear the sound,
of encouragement in your voice.

You're not here when I,
accomplish something I really want.
I cry for the loss,
because I lost so much.

I know you're not really gone,
because you're always in my heart.
You are always watching over me,
and see everything I do.

I know you're proud of me,
and I will see you in the future.

Dedication: to Aunt Peggy Johnson with love

My Dues
Alan Fait
Due to my ignorance,
due to my lies,
due to my expressionlessness,
due to my computerized pies.
Due to my attitude,
due to my emptiness,

...
I now have a list,
full of my silly little rhymes.

You And I
Dianna M. Pond
There's no happiness for you and I
Read and you may understand why,
You are mean and cruel
In your heart, you let hate rule.

Happiness is feeling good within
It's sad, but you're not even my friend,
You hurt me in every way you know how
If you loved me once, I don't see that now.

Friends and Family stopped coming around
Because you find faults and put them down,
I fall asleep and I awake
To your words and actions of hate.

I've gone to work, nervous and shaking
How can I be happy at any job I'd be taking,
Life should be meaningful, pleasant and fulfilling
You don't try and you're not even willing.

You tear up my pictures along with my heart
And constantly talk about being apart,
You think with your liquor, you're doing fine
Things just get worse instead of better with time.

Till Then
Irene Jackson
Take care of my heart —
that piece of it that went with you.
For since we've been apart,
it has been damaged — torn in two.

The biggest part is there with you,
The rest, with me remains,
and though its beat is just as strong,
it doesn't feel the same.

For fate came with no warning
on that unsuspecting day,
and mercilessly grabbed my heart,
and tore a piece away.

Now you have it safely with you —
Part of me, for you to keep,
and though my heart is healing now,
the scars, they still run deep.

So when my life is over,
I will come to you and then,
We'll be re-united and I know,
You will give it back again.

Dedication: to my beloved late son, Jimmy

Enchanted Dreams

Untitled
Nancy Mabee
Beyond the pines, the ocean lies
Its sweet, sweet smell of salt and brine
The gulls fly so softly bound
Among the drifts of winds around.

I imagine it here... in Georgia... I sit
One day I'll be home... in Maine... I know it!
Back to the sea and the wave of those pines
The rocky–bound coast and purple lupines.

My Prayer
Penny K. Benton
As I kneel beside my bed each night
At the close of a weary day,
I bury my head in my trembling hands
And tears fall as I pray.

Dear God, unworthy as I am
I ask one thing of Thee,
Go to the one I love tonight
And help him remember me.

Dear God, he's only human, You know
And so when the day is done,
He may be as lonely as I am
And turn to another one.

I can go no longer to him, God,
And take him by the hand,
But You can go to him
And make him understand.

Just help him keep me in his heart
Until the day we meet again,
And even though we're far apart
I love him, God... Amen!

The Crack In The Doorway
George Bonsper
My room is dark, not a speck of light.
Wandering, I sense with touch but cannot feel.
Yearn for what should be.
I am alone, no mate, no life.
Nothing to assess, so I pound on the walls.

With my irrational act, striking out at my obstructions.
It produces a crack, from a doorway comes a light.
Foreign to me since being very young, I cannot recall how long.

I crawl towards the opening, indeterminate to get more.
I pull with command, the insignificance that I am.
Still just a crack but I'm not where I was, before.

With the little bead of sun, I quickly realize.
I'm not the only one in the dark and my precious lucent is
not shared by all.
There are many dark rooms, others yearn to be fed.

So I continue to break down my walls, built for my safekeeping.
More light may fill my room,
no longer a crack, but possibilities.

My self–value would rise, I would no longer cry,
for the life that I ache for, never again, an innocent
but a chance to be... ALIVE.

Disillusioned Aspiration
Mary McCarty
A whole individualized people
Wheeling amidst construed veracities
Delirium progresses as feelings obscure
Equivocally left in superficial bewilderment; a blur
Why–oh–why
Disenchanting scrutiny manifesting an incentive to cry
Ironically bizarre – the journey has ceased to appease
The common goals for wants and needs
The desire for sanity – we ask you, "Please!?"

Time
Olga Forty
Sometimes I look back and wonder
How quickly time goes by
When I was playing in the fields
Believing I could fly
Sometimes I look back and wonder
What happened to the time
When I believed that the world would be mine

Sometimes I look back and wonder
Why the world's so different when you're young
All that you do has an element of fun

Sometimes I look back in wonder
At the birds, the sky and trees
And understand I'm lucky to be walking in the breeze

Sometimes I look back and wish
That I could do it all again
Once when I was a little girl playing in the rain

Sometimes I look forward
And believe that what's to come
Is just as special as my life
That's already been and gone.

An Ocean Of Memories
Brenda J. Shimmel
As the ship sets sail their eyes meet,
Two worlds collide to become a single heartbeat

Lips touch, Arms embrace
Passion explodes, Hearts race

A love so rare brought together by fate,
Only to be torn apart on that dreadful date (April 15, 1912)

Unable to stay, Unwilling to go
Sealing one's fate to the cold dark waters below

A promise to never let go was made,
As the "Ship of Dreams" slowly began to fade

Upon them came a darkness, as black as night could be,
It took away a love, a love once meant to be

As she looked to the Heavens above,
She declared once more her undying love

It was destiny that bound them together,
And in her heart he would live forever

Her heart would go on despite all the tears,
Kept hidden in an ocean of memories lasting throughout the years...

Hello, Spring
Cindy Sutton

Flowers blooming brilliant reds, yellow and purple.
Trees are budding.
Birds are chirping.
New life abounds.
The Earth warms and renews itself.
Goodbye winter,
Hello, spring.

Dedication: to Scott Harper

Need Of A Friend
Jane Glenn

I have a friend so far away,
who rings me up almost everyday.
She needs to know there's someone there,
to help her through her despair.

We thought she'd started to live again,
as she finds herself a loving friend.
He helps her through her bitter past,
unknowing to her it will not last.

He has a secret of his own,
and finds it hard to let it be known.
He tells her that he loves her so,
and that his love will never go.

In his heart he knows that's not true,
he knows his life is through.
The doctor said "he hasn't got long,"
he knows she has to be strong.

She finds it hard to take it all in,
the pain and suffering he must be in.
Why did it take him so long to tell?
He must be going through hell.

Guilt, Remorse And Shame
Antonella Camarda

He leans over the cold, cruel stone
And lays a rose on the damp ground.
He whispers words of love and sorrow
Knowing there will not be a tomorrow.

He digs the sand with his bare hands;
In the hopes of having one last dance.
The rain runs down his lonely face.
All bad memories he would love to erase

When all of a sudden he hears a voice
He turns to the sky and begins to rejoice.
A blinding light begins to shine;
The voice repeats "You'll soon be mine."

A gentle kiss on his tender lips
She slowly lets go of his fingertips
The light begins to disappear
He can feel that she's no longer near

He turns his head and falls asleep
She smiles upon him, then starts to weep
He lies on a stone engraved with his name
He will soon forget the guilt, remorse and shame

Dedication: to my family for unconditional love

The War
Samarah Haq

This never-ending conflict I compete in constantly.
Antipathy overpowers my mind repeatedly;
At what time will this fight hinder?
Will the wounds of disgust ever cleanse?

There are times when victory seems inevitable.
Then greed conquers my will to win, I'm failing.
The enemy bribes my body: my mind feels futile.
War will continue, unless I secure the flag of success.

Abandoned Child
Brenda Hammersley

Found in an alley at only two days old,
crying and hungry and feeling very cold.
Wrapped in a blanket of pink and white,
a beautiful child but a pitiful sight.

Left by a young girl afraid and alone,
who had no choice; she had no home.
Every birthday she sits and frets,
her life is lived in pain and regret.

The child has blossomed in a foster home,
but wonders why her Mum left her alone.
One day she will find her,
and learn the terrible truth.

It's her Dad who should answer,
why he abandoned poor Ruth.
When she needed him, he wasn't there,
irresponsible and spoilt, he just didn't care.

When the little girl grows, she will learn,
of Ruth's undying love.
And that forgiveness must come,
as it does from above.

Raindrops From The Sky
Kathy Wood

The night is cold, the sky is dark,
The air is so fresh, the stars are bright
We see the moon fading away, the clouds
are moving so rough and fast,
I felt a raindrop come all the way down
streaking from my face to the ground,
The rain gets heavier, it all comes pouring
down!
I am getting all soaked in my white
night-gown, twirling my hair and spinning
around and around
I put my arms out, facing the sky,
trying to catch the rain-drops, but they're only
fading away,
I took an empty jar and held it to the
sky, trying to catch the drops that come
flying down!
I closed the lid, so tight and shut,
so I never let them go!
I keep my drops so safe, so they won't
ever go away,
I put my jar away so I can use them
for some-other day! The rain has taken away
all my pain! So now I can have fun and play in the rain

Dedication: to Mom and all my loved ones

Enchanted Dreams

It's Spring
Kenneth V. Randall
From winter's cold clasp, oh, happy release.
It's spring and it's warm and I feel so contented.
I look through the window and notice the breeze,
Lifting and turning the new leaves on the trees.
Their dancing and twirling makes me feel tempted,
To enter my garden and merge with the frieze.
Be, at my ease.

Dedication: to my wife, Maggie

Love's Spell
Jan Russell
My body trembles at your touch
I taste Heaven on your lips
My mind explodes when you call my name
There's promise in your voice

You stand too close, don't hurry me
I sense fever in your veins
My thoughts are racing, but time stands still
There's danger in your eyes

Love's spell is cast, time's running out
There's magic in the air
I know your game, the secret's out
You're seducing me

Tender fingers stroke my soul
There's velvet in your touch
Our spirits join in a timeless dance
There's passion in your heart

I'm spellbound now, you're in control
There's power in your kiss
The game is over, I surrender
There's triumph in your eyes

Friendship
C. Habrovitsky
A friend in need is a friend indeed
This is how I feel to you
For all the troubles you are there
A friend in need is a friend indeed.

The trials of the world are great indeed
With our own small trials great to us
To have you by my side
A friend in need is a friend indeed.

We all have much to bear
With much to love
Both in our private and public lives
A friend in need is a friend indeed.

Whenever I call you in my need
There you stand by my side
Always ready to listen to my cares
A friend in need is a friend indeed.

May the love of friends be there
Always freely given and received
By those who care and love
A friend in need is a friend indeed.

Dedication: to my family and friends

Thoughts
Anna Hepburn
Often I dream that all is as it was—
That precious souls are here to touch
With all their precious flaws
I sometimes hear a whispered word
Just like a little breath, when everywhere
It seems there's only death.
Thus I am heartened to live each day.
To love and be forgiving in the darkest hours—
In thankfulness, that I was loved so specially.

Beauty
Alicia Jackson
Everywhere you look
If you could only see beneath the dried–up leaves
To the bud awaiting growth
To open and expose its beauty to the world

Will you wait around to see me unfold
And give to you all that I have and all that I am
Will you be the sun of which I'll bask in
Causing me to expand into a creation yet unseen

I want to reach out, to burst forth
From this frozen ground of which I exist in
I never chose to be placed here
The winds of my past have blown me around
Tumbling, turning in each new direction
Until finally setting me down in this place, too horrid to remain

My tears rain down, nourishing what is to come forth
I am covered by all the dirt of this world
And I long for your warmth
So that I may grow and become what I may
Beauty

Dedication: to Alan, my inspiration...

As I Stare
Denise Ann Kappes
As I stare at your picture
I can feel your warming touch
Finally realizing
I miss you so much

As I stare into your eyes
Tears pour out of mine
Wanting you here with me
But I know you're doing fine

As I stare at your lips
I can hear your thoughtful words
You saying "I love you, Denise"
Was the best yet I've heard

As I stare into the mirror
I can see an image of you
You're telling me to live my life
And do the best I can do

But don't you worry, Dad
I will make my dreams come true
You won't be disappointed in me
And remember, I love you, too.

Dedication: to loving memories of Dennis Kappes

The Anthology of Poems

Full System Meltdown
Christopher Martucci
Melt.
Strip away the sanity.
Blacken the soul of humanity.
Help me.
Anger and spite course my veins,
It's your blood that ever stains.
Perish.
I am lost in a demented state,
The hands of time sealed my fate.

A Time For Love:
Gladys Ramsey
This is the time that Our King, Our Love,
is seeking for His own,
the precious fruit He has so carefully Watched,
and so tenderly pruned and grown.

In the rich soil of the Father,
with Sun and Rain from above,
He seeks for fruit upon each branch
Birth by Calvary's Cross.

Upon all, whom the North and South Wind
has blown, to stir up and awaken His Love,
to send forth a sweet fragrance throughout all the Earth,
an odor well–pleasing to God.

To enjoy for His own pleasure,
the Trophy of His Grace,
fruit filled with righteous and Holy Oil,
with His countenance upon each face.

Perfected in the Father's Love,
In the planting of His own chosen place,
always pouring forth oil and wine,
shouting Grace, Grace, Grace.

Do You Think About Me?
Kathleen M. Parsons
When you're lying there
Wishing you could be free
As the tears start flowing
Do you think about me?

I dream of your touch
As I walk the sea
Can you see me there?
Do you think about me?

I'm alone and free
you're alone, confined
But our hearts are one
They are intertwined

As I'm lying there
Wishing you could be free
And the tears start flowing
Wishing that we could be

Oh, this present state!
And as cruel as it be
I am here beside you
You can think about me...

Dedication: to Stephen Michael Picard

Untitled
Stephanie Bilello
I haven't written one in so long
wings on a dove, words of a song
dew on the grass, mountain of snow
squeak from a mouse, squawk from a crow

Tears of salt, dry like sand
upon my cheeks a desert storm
beguiling witch, all forlorn

A crooked nose points the way
darkness of night crushing the day
the black side of magic taking ahold
pins in my neck, shiver with cold
Limp as a rag doll, eyes sewn shut
dances and rolls, tumbles and slides
down midnight corridor, weary soul glides

But who can save? An angel in white?
Destroying the squawking crow in flight?
Building a ladder up through the trees
further, further
where the sky becomes velvet and the stars like diamonds
sparkle and shine
where sheer delight becomes all mine

Overcoming Devastation
Marie Gennaro
A fading moon amidst a blue and cloudy sky.
Blistering winds and a lovely sunny day.
Weatherman reports windy and rising temperatures.
Perhaps a thunderstorm to be forthcoming.

Rising tides to drive people from their homes.
Vast destruction to many areas.
Finally all is calm with restoration in progress.
Proving repaired devastation can prevail.

The Span Plus
W. Herbert Palfrey
A baby is born to this old world, it's well and
Healthy, a new form, curled
Against its mother, snug, warm and safe, pretty
the fingers, lovely the face;
The baby grows and is strong and well, it goes to
school it must learn to spell
Then weds and mothers, whilst growing old and
grandmother's worth her weight in gold.

But life has taken a heavy toll, There's babies born,
and there's endless toil,
That body's older, it's worn and frail, while every
wrinkle tells its own tale,
The years have passed so quickly for her, there's
just a jumble of joys and tears.
Bad times forgotten while Moments passed and
good times are stored in memory's cache.

The spirit goes back from whence it came, to rest,
to worship, to start again,
So shall the harassed soul from this life, find joy
and gladness without the strife.
Now, if this life is blessed by God's love, the years
will sense a contact above,
And through this life a strong golden chord will
bind her, to THE LOVE OF OUR LORD...

Enchanted Dreams

Marriage
Ryan Petrilli
Your hands have joined together
Unity of two souls that were destined,
Bound by daily steps bringing you
Closer each day since the light of birth.

Your lives are now one forever
Beginning a journey that will challenge
The definition of happiness, exceeding
Its pleasures and all its treasures of worth.

Your lives have been made complete
By the half who can find your smile
In a cloud of constant confusion that a
Day's struggles have been known to bring.

Your future is two with one heartbeat
Handling a horizon of sometimes turmoil
With the calmness you both possess
Remembering the eternal promise by the vowed ring.

Your days ahead are filled with mystery and magic
Moments of beautiful bliss and untimely tears,
But countless memories, making tomorrow brighter still
Like your love that will grow stronger through the years.

Untitled
Kimberly Jo Marshall
When the sun rests behind the mountains
And the moon silhouettes the hills
I sit alone at night to watch the sky lights
As they flicker like flames in the wind

Then sleep finally comes to the mountains
The fog blankets the valley below
And veils those Heavenly candles
As if God gently blows them out

We
Aleshea J. Johnson
I see the problem
Me,

I see the problem
Can you see?

I see the problem
Hold my hand out free,

I see the problem
Like a big tree,

I see the problem
Of charity,

I see the problem
Of prosperity,

I see the problem
My people see,
I see the problem
My people, free.

Dedication: to my dad with great knowledge

Untitled
B. V. Jones
Today we remember the men
who died
That those they loved might
live
To see a free and better world
for this they gave their lives

But have those that died
died in vain
What would they think, I wonder
If they could come back and see
today
The world they died for
yesterday.

Many were young and full
of life
But they are now only a
memory
But those are the ones who will
never grow old
And so today we remember.

Dedication: to my dad, Albert Edward Smith

Measurements
Dorothy Politziner
A child makes a daisy chain — so long.
A woman makes a skirt to wear— so long.
A man builds a road to ride — so long.

I make footsteps in the sand;
Soon, of course, they'll wash away,
But Oh, the joy in making them—

So long.

My Guiding Light
Angi Gorton
When my life was just a struggle,
Every day another fight,
When my days were filled with darkness,
You became my guiding light.

My dark clouds now are lifting,
My view seems somehow clear,
Now my storm is passing,
Because you are all near.

You have brightened up my days,
You've made me raise some smiles,
At a time when every inch I walked,
Felt like a million miles.

When life was so painful,
That I wanted it to end,
You reached out your hand to me,
And proved you were a friend.

Knowing you're beside me,
Makes me feel secure,
If life's hard knocks are the illness,
Then friends must be the cure.

The Anthology of Poems

Washing Away
Tami Smith
I want nothing more
than for the pain,
to wash down the cracks,
in the sidewalks,
to be washed away as if it never
happened,

but that is not in my power,
what is in my power
is to be there for you.

Untitled
M. A. Kiddle
A little church high on a hill,
A beautiful place, serene and still.
Not very big, even with a spire,
It has bells, that never tire.

Old grave-stones are scattered around,
Some tilted, some on the ground.
Arched doorways set in stone,
And the spire, like an upturned cone.

A cross, way, way up high,
On the spire, touching the sky.
Old oak floors Line the aisles,
And hymn-books, lovingly set in piles.

Cushioned pews in embossed wood,
Where many people, have knelt and stood.
A smell of incense, wax and must,
Little nooks covered with dust.

At the alter, candles stand tall,
And beautiful flowers decorate the wall.
A little church, upon a hill.
Old and quaint, peaceful and still.

Words To Be Heard
Elaine Collier
Words are important
Take note what is read,
For my words will be
Used when I'm dead.

Unknown to you all,
I've not been found,
Search they will,
They will seek me out.

Work hard as you can
You will be in those hands,
Write to be read,
Write to be heard,
These are my important words.

My work will never stop,
I have so much to share,
Words will bring light,
Happiness everywhere.

I write what I feel,
I write what I see,
Soon you'll get to hear of me.

Untitled
Freda Waters
William and Harry don't worry,
Your Mother went off in a hurry,
No time for good-bye, she is Queen of the
sky, with Dodi beside her in Heaven.
The Angels were waiting to greet them,
As they sang in a band with a rose on a
stand bearing the name Diana the purest
in our land, reminding us of the one we
held most dear and of the flower that will
bloom, Year after Year after Year.

Ode To Pat LaFleshe
Gloria M. McGary
I'm writing this poem for you, Pat
To let you know you are in my prayers,
Because I was moved by your stories
And there are some of us who care.

You see, my mother-in-law had an operation
They took out part of her lung,
At present, they give her a year to live
Because, the cancer once again has sprung.

You both are very courageous loved-ones
To tolerate the suffering and pain,
I know God is watching over both of you
Your goal of time you will gain.

You have made a difficult decision
Concerning your treatment and care,
With the support from Hospice, friends and family
Remember, they will always be there.

To close this poem with a friendly thought
Is to thank you for sharing your story,
I pray you will see your new grandchild
Fulfill your dreams and go out in glory.

Night
Jeffrey Butler
Listen to the night as the sounds unfold;
Truly the music of the night
Each sound unique, each voice alone
Crying out. Who will hear?

The sounds, they meld together, but one stands apart.
That one that always does
In the stillness of the silence,
In the tumult of the noise.

When nothing else matters,
When everything is still,
That is when the silence speaks
Its secrets to impart.

This life moves on too quickly;
This life is all too slow.
Time it is to stop and see
What this night will speak to me.

I will not ask, for the questions do not matter.
Words are so entrapping,
Tonight they will not bind me,
Tonight the night will set me free.

Enchanted Dreams

My Son
Laurie Anderson
I look beneath the Earth for my son
I don't see him
I look above the clouds for my son
I don't see him
I look within my heart for my son
I see him, I hold him, I love him
My heart is where my son is
Not beneath the Earth
Not above the clouds
But in my heart

Me And The Wall
Stephanie J. Andrews
Hello walls—Are you listening? What are the
secrets tonight? Is there love in the air or a fight?
How do you stand there alone—Painted or white?
Are you awake in the morning, noon and night?
Do you ever sleep, or do you listen to us breathe,
and help to make sure we are all at our ease?
Sometimes I wonder if you hurt when we hit
does it hurt when we damage you even a bit?
If I were a wall, what kinda wall would I be—
One that would eavesdrop or one to be free.
Being a person, if I took my pick. I think I'd
prefer to be a wall quite thick. To never be painted,
never feel pain and to be inside, out of the rain.
Being a wall—What would I be? I'd be a person
and I would be free — I'd walk through the gardens
get dirt on my feet. I'd stop at every market for
something to eat. I'd walk along proudly, head
held to the sky — and if I were a person I'd
not tell a lie.
For being a wall — I can tell you some facts,
that most all people will talk behind backs.
Boy, it's nice to be a wall — for a while anyway.

Dedication: to my family, I love you

The Crazy Psychiatrist
Thelma Starks–Veliz
For A Very High Price
He Used to Give Everyone Who Came To Him
His Advice
He Always listened To The Troubles And
Problems of Someone Else
Until He Cracked–up Himself
I'm Talking About The Crazy Psychiatrist
The Crazy Psychiatrist

He Was Helping Other People For A Long Time
Until He Finally Lost His Own Mind
For His Own Problems He Couldn't Find A Solution
So He Ended Up in A Mental institution
I'm Talking About The Crazy Psychiatrist
The Crazy Psychiatrist

He Went Completely out of His Head
He Don't even Remember His Wife And Kids
He is insane As He Can Be—He Has Lost Touch
With Reality
I Would Tell you That He is in Another World—
If you Ask Me
I'm Talking About The Crazy Psychiatrist
The Crazy Psychiatrist

Magic Is Everywhere...
Melanie Mifsud
It's the love and friendship,
that keeps it going...
that's where the magic is.
the magic is in the love and friendship.
we all want to make it like on the screen...
all sparkly and magical.
the actual magic is in everyday life,
breathing, living and loving.
that's where the magic is.
open your eyes.

Untitled
Jo Lupa
Clouds fill the sky
Wind chills the bone
All is black
Hearts turn to stone

Ice in blood
Blood on rock
Spirits of alive
Away do flock

Hidden away
Scared and crying
For one's mind is filled
With hate and dying

Souls of the healthy
Turn sick, then dead
A liquid drips out
Hot–poker red

A putrid smell
A dying race
But there's one who's smiling
Satan's face.

Do You Know My Grandmother?
Robert W. Dunn, Jr.
To my cousins and I she's been grand.
To our children she has been great.
If one was to describe her,
she is the opposite of hate.

Do you know her patience?
a virtue that is rare.
Do you feel her essence?
fill the atmosphere.

Has she ever told you "no"
when her help was badly needed?
Did you ever seek her counsel
'cause her words you would have heeded.

When she walks, the flowers bloom
and the birds sing.
I thought she was an angel,
But I didn't see any wings.

Her kindness is relentless,
to that we can all attest.
If 75 years have been like this,
I can't wait to see the rest.

A Life Of Sorrow
Eboney Love

No one knows the love she gives. Pain and suffering is all she fears. Her soul full of sorrow, her eyes full of tears. The feelings of someone she is very near. As her life passes day by day, her soul needs someone to be near. Her life burns on like a candle in the wind. But she knows it's about to burn to an end.

Dedication: to Ann, my mom – always, Merrian Ann Love

Little Piece Of My Heart
Tim Harvey

The first time that I saw you,
I saw it in your eyes.
That little special something,
You could not disguise.

The first time that you walked away,
You took a little part.
Of something from inside me,
The best part of my heart.

Now every time I see you,
My heart skips a beat or two,
Yearning for that part of itself,
You carry around with you.

If, in time, I said "I love you",
And you said you felt the same.
I'd give you all I have to give,
My heart, My love, My name.

I want you, girl, I need you,
I knew it from the start,
I just can't live without you,
And that little piece of my heart.

Forgotten Dreams of Love
Maureen Gillespie

Unsmiling eyes, blank stares,
cold silence in the dark.
Disheveled bodies, lifeless limbs,
no voices to be heard.
A time of life when joy has been forgotten
or perhaps was never known
A lone figure sits in silent shock.
Her eyes have seen but her voice may not come back

Ah, is this the sadness of old age
and a time of war they know?
No, these are the images of children
those of tender years.
Before our eyes we see each day
these sights that leave us cold.
A legacy of silent sorrows.
Children with forgotten dreams of love.

But God made a rose to bloom, its fragrance fills the air.
A little bird to sing with joy.
And to us a heart that feels.
Have faith, God sees and hears.

Dedication: to children the world over

The Anthology of Poems

God's Love
Trey Rush

God loves you, God loves me
God loves everyone, as you can see
Somehow God will send His love
It might be in the form of a dove
God gave us the gift of learning
Because inside His love is burning
God sends a lot of love
In return I love the God above

Dedication: to my dear grandma (Maee)

Grandma, Hurry Home
Virginia C. Hernandez

Something nice and pretty I have for thee,
All pretty and clean as she can be.

One of my dresses she does wear,
And neatly combed I have made her hair.

To keep you company day and night,
Hold her closely and hold her tight.

Think real hard and when you do,
Pretend you're holding your little Magoo.

When home sweet home you have finally come,
Real kisses and hugs you'll get by the ton.

Quiet as a mouse then I must be,
'Til you're able to romp with me.

God's perfect little angel you might see,
But don't count on it, Grandma, cause you know me!

I Love You.

Dedication: in loving memory of Grandma Margie

Lonesome Dreaming Lover
Christine DeGennaro

Your strong arms hold me near
As you whisper sweet–nothings in my ear.
With a look of love on your face,
You hold me closer in your embrace.
Our bodies close,
Not kissing, yet almost.
As your lips touch mine,

Shivers shoot down my spine.
We move our faces away,
But the feeling of the kiss does stay.
Your strong, muscular body,
Screams that you are Godly.

Your brown eyes and light brown hair,
Your skin tan, not fair.
We kiss again and as our lips touch,
I know why I love you so much.
All of a sudden I open my eyes.
All but a dream, I realize.
I hop out of bed and cross the floor,
Open my room and see you at my door.
I see you and my heart does soar,
And I know I won't be lonely any more...

Enchanted Dreams

Farewell To Sanbury Moor
A. C. Cash
And now we leave
the somber vales
the lonely, leafless trees
the forlorn farms
inhabited by shadows
of memories and deeds,
where in the windy winter nights
old souls return to meet
and whisper stories
of their fading lives.

Revelation From Mars
Carmen K. Clarke-Brown
May we learn from your still panorama
Where once there was a Diaspora
Now bereft of life and matter
An unnerving stillness, no chatter

What secrets do your plains hold
Your hills appear barren, yet bold
Did Armageddon unfold?
And left you infertile and cold

Two vistas so very similar
The mind's eye makes it familiar
One ponders about the event
Which left such a sad testament

Your boulders so markedly leaned
A story could surely be gleaned
Rocks and stones in a dry riverbed
A disaster, so forceful, so dead

As we gaze at your place in the sky
We must learn to take heed and defy
The emblems of war and pollution
Lest our fate be a cataclysmic conclusion!

Nature Of Love
Tina L. Wyatt
Like the dew sticks to a rose on an
Early spring morning,
Is the way I feel when I'm with you,
In all my glory.
As the waters so naturally run over
The rocks,
My love runs for you and it can't
Be stopped.
Like the spring brings forth every—
Thing new,
The love I have, grows deeper
For you.
Looking out over a field of beautiful
Wildflowers,
Reminds me of the love we share; I
Think of it for hours.
The warmth of the sun coming through the
Window early in the morning,
Reminds me of waking up next to you
Without a worry.
The way you make me feel is like
Mother Nature,
Unexplainable, but so beautiful in
Every feature.

Happiness
Frank W. Probett
Happiness is a butterfly!
Just like life it flutters by,
Like the echoes of a song,
Never lasting very long.
Grab the Moment while you may,
Even if for just one day, —
so that when the winter's chill
Freezes both the mind and will,
The warmth you feel will make you say:
"Happiness was mine that day!"

Struggles
Lois A. Steir-Lewin
Saddened by the loneliness that feeds endlessly on my heart,
The cares of this life are beginning to unsettle my spirit,
The hardness of the struggles over many years
Is now setting in, pressing forcefully on my hopes.

The long arms of dismay sweep o'er my hurts
With chilling fingers of disasters, leaving much despair;
And the thought of giving up lurks heavily within
With swaying doorways of dominant darkness.

This enemy that shatters my reliance and leaves me timid
Is as real as the hot summer days, when it is hard to breathe;
And the pending danger that fashions my very thoughts
Is looming on the horizons with clear, approaching pace.

I have become a pawn in the game of this struggle
And most definitely, I know that my heart is about to faint;
To focus my inner being on what I know is truth
Is much as a thirsty one crossing the barren desert.

How do I react to such pressures when the odds outweigh my plans?
What can I learn from this terrible mistake when I am so far gone?
There has to be a way of escape, but then, my thoughts are tired, too
Deliver me from the hand of the enemy is but my one and final plea.

Grown Apart
Ellis Skoglund
I have watched you grow into
The man you are today.
I have held you and hit you
and pushed you away.
When we were younger
we were the best of friends,
But for some strange reason
our friendship now ends.

I watched our lives grow
far apart,
But you will always remain
in my heart.
It seems you have found
a brand—new "drug",
One that is physical
one different from love.

I wish we could start our lives over again.
And go back to when I could call you a friend.
It's funny how you always made me feel bad,
And I always looked up to you and called you my Dad.

Dedication: to my father Eugene Skoglund

The Open Heart
Cynthia Davies

My heart is broken, yes, in two
No shattered edges, just clean in two.
Half full of sweet memories that have been
Half full of wishes, that should have been
But the gap in–between creates its own pain
All carry the same love that is pain, real pain
Lovely memories of dear Bill will always remain

Such tearful grief I cannot contain –
It's simply called, brokenness.

Near The End
Angela Leighton

Nothing but a raindrop fell
Yet through the depths I heard them yell
They pointed at the starry crown
And watched as it fell down, down, down.

I stood amidst the angry mob
a woman soon began to sob
I watched wide–eyed and full of fear
I felt the dampness of a tear.

It seemed to cut and slice my cheek
and then fell red upon my feet
Who was I to know or care
compassion in this world is rare.

And yet my heart, it welled within
I prayed forgiveness for their sin
though I knew then that they would dwell
in their master's fiery hell.

Then my soul, it welled with pride,
I knew I had not truly died
But I would spend eternity
Surrounded by God's love for me.

Untitled
Christon Flournoy

How do I say goodbye,
To all I know and love?
It's so hard to leave you all,
I beg for help from above.

How do I greet the world,
I do not yet know?
I yearn to stay with you, my friends,
But destiny calls me so.

Now I have begun to see,
What the world has waiting for me.
Fate has torn us all apart,
I feel this now deep in my heart.

As I stand here and say goodbye,
I am overwhelmed to cry.
There is nothing more I can say,
But I will miss you all every day.

Our souls will always be spiritually bounded,
Our thoughts always of each other.
Even though our paths might never meet,
We will always remember each other.

Pain
Lisa Niishimura

Sometimes I sit alone in a dark room contemplating how and why I will die,
Why do I ponder death? Is it because I feel it coming so fast that I can't stop it? Why does it rush right through me as quick as the light, My life flashes before me quickly.
How and why will I die, I sit and ponder why.
You cry about your pretty face,
You cry because you want attention.
I cry because I feel life isn't worth living,
I cry because I feel empty and alone inside,
I don't have that pretty face, so shut up and stop telling me lies.

Friends
Lecy Marie Simpson

Friends are like flowers,
In the great bouquet of life,
Their fragrance seems to fill the air,
And their beauty brightens the night.

No matter what the season,
Winter, Spring, Summer or Fall,
In timeliness, buds open and bloom,
Into flowers large and small.

Each one presents themselves to us,
With unique, colorful blooms,
And they surround us with their fragrance,
And fill our lives with their perfume.

Such a wide, diverse selection have we,
So different but yet alike,
A wide variety of formations and colors,
Yet all such a lovely sight!

Oh, what would life be without this gift,
That in love, God has given,
To add beauty to our world,
And give us a little touch of Heaven!

Spring Is Coming
Jenna Mayville

Joy, Oh, Joy,
Blossoms red and blue,
Dearest child, Dearest child,
I truly love you true.

Joy, Oh, Joy,
Spring is coming,
Lilac trees galore
Dearest Child, Dearest Child,
I shall teach you more.

Joy, Oh, Joy,
Spring is Coming,
Children happily singing,
Dearest child, Dearest Child,
Soon your voice shall be ringing.

Joy, Oh, Joy,
Spring is coming,
Babies being born,
Dearest child, Dearest child,
Blow your little horn.

Dedication: to my family, with love

Enchanted Dreams

Sadness
Jeff Phillips
Empty, lonely, so utterly alone,
no one cares, no one knows my pain.
I am an outcast, a reject of this world.
My home is my sanity, still fading.
Why must everything depress me?
Why are my emotions so vague?
I long for a touch, a squeeze, a kiss.
I receive nothing; I blame myself.
All I want is passion, to replace...
My sadness.

World Peace
Teresa Brewer
We are all in this together
each and every day.
Passing through life
trying to find our way.

We all have destinations
to whatever it may be.
So give up the fighting
live and be free.

It has gotten out of hand
the fighting in this world.
People, have you forgotten,
about God, "Our Lord".

He gave us life
by giving up His own.
This is not our world
it is His home.

So can we respect Him
and follow His guidance.
He gave us the Bible
and the "Ten Commandments".

My Second Brother
Dana Petrillo
Joined with me in loving friendship old
Out of doors in sunny morning bright
Smiling, Swinging through branches of the trees
Hailing Dawn's sweet glory of the light

Under Canopy, the greenest boughs became
An elf land, or a palace where we'd play
We were Kings and fairies in our minds
A jungle kingdom near, yet far away

Running through the Summer meadows' dew
Deeper than the Firefly's bright flare,
Even though we were forbidden to,
Not caring what would happen if we'd dare

And we were happy in our childish love
Not knowing that we'd grow and drift away,
Daily we would meet for a new game, not
Dreaming of the end of summer days

And still I love him as the brother that he was
Never to forget his face, or the smile that rested there
And I wait for him, to greet my friend of youth,
Pleased in my mem'ry of secrets we once shared.

Lust
Brian O'Dell
My mind is blinded,
Only seeing in result of humanity.
To thee and thy eyes are bound,
Inside an inane fantasy.

My eyes desire which my heart does trust.
To feel with thy eyes is thy disgust.

Foolish boy,
Foolish lust.

My Rose
Shayne P. Baldwin
Can we capture the beauty of the rose
And leave it in its nature's pose
Not having its roots spread so wide
Finding nutrients to build its pride
Heaven has blessed us, if you ask me
Angelic beauty for all to see
A single rose and all its strength
Defining tenderness throughout its length
Endless purity from a source within
Tender and delicate upon the skin
Always colored to catch the eye
Enduring the seasons and darkened sky
Obscure from harm that nature brings
Virtually ageless, Its love still sings
And with the dew upon its leaves
Resembles tears, as if it grieves
Still in grief, Its beauty is there
Stealing my heart and all my care
Requiring a touch of the beauty I see
Eagerly I reach, but gentle I'll be
Electric sensations, making me high
Touching your face, I begin to cry

Dedication: for Garcin you know why

The Hopes That Fly Away
Juan Marrero
I felt the cold of night approaching,
as to die was prone the sun,
and a little light remained,
but her hopes of life were gone.

In the middle was I standing
of a place named never known
surrounded by tall trees
in that land was I alone.

There the wind, my only fellow,
moved the leaves withered and yellow,
they were scattered in a dancing,
over floors I think I trod.

Without haste a woman walked
thorough the trees in my direction,
claimed glory, I, my salvation,
How I need to hear her talk.

Beauteous was and so rare maiden
for no words she came to tell
only smiled and disappeared
gave me no time, to say farewell.

Mother Tree
Valerie S. Humphries

See her in the springtime when her limbs show newborn leaves
She will feed and strengthen each of them 'til they are strong and green
When summer comes, they are full and strong, she sways with loving pride
She shows the world their beauty, though fear plagues her heart inside
Fall arrives and her leaves take new colors before they fly
they leave her arms for newfound worlds before they die
But now it's winter, her arms are bare and she is left alone
to grieve the winter through because her family's grown and gone

Dedication: to my mother, Donna Anderson, who always knew when to let go

---

Awakening
Susan Mann

The early dawn's light
peeking through the trees,
nature's next genesis
caresses its gentle breeze.

Morning's special fragrances
like promises of before,
pierce my very existence
a paved path once more.

If only for a Moment
does a robin's egg lie,
for soon it's beckoned
like an azure sky.

Light rain begins to fall
treading softly down below;
sunshine is summoned
gracing its seed to sow.

Dewdrops glisten
like dreams with new allure;
igniting a dormant passion
that lived once before.

Anticipation
Richard Isakow

The knowing waits in the grass,
The unknowing has done no wrong,
Yet one animal has not eaten,
In a time that has spanned long.

The knowing waits in the grass,
The unknowing cannot suffice,
Out of the ones in his herd,
He is the one to be sacrificed.

The knowing waits in the grass,
The predator watches his prey,
Unfortunately for the unknowing,
Tomorrow will not be another day.

The knowing waits in the grass,
Waiting for its opportunity,
He is as still as a rock,
Not waving like a tree.

The knowing waits in the grass,
The time has finally come,
The anticipation is over,
And the herd is minus one.

Vows
John Nichols

Always Remember My Love
My Commitment And Devotion
Even As Sometimes We Are Apart
Assuredly I Am With You

Always Remember, My Love
If You Dance, Embraced By Another,
Caught Up In A Blush Of Intimacy,
That Mine Would Be Those Arms

Always Remember, My Love
My Very Essence Is Tempered
Yesterday, Today And Tomorrow
Your Needs, Wants And Desires

Always Remember, My Love
Wondering Of "Might–Have–Beens"
Nothing Can Change What Has
Reality Is And Dreams Could Be

Always Remember, My Love
Time Unfolds Our Path Of Choices
Question Not To Look Ahead Or Behind
My Eyes Will Always Meet Yours

A Moment Of Lost Love
Lauren Melissa Click

I withdraw, but it's all in vain
I see a smile through the rain
I feel a touch but it's not the same
My love is gone forever
Ever–long I feel the burn
Why will I not ever learn?
But I grin softly, it's your turn
"It's love," I whisper sweetly

Dedication: to Bill Mahr, in loving memory

Soul
John Slough

Oh, well, my fantasy
that everything we see is real
Doesn't seem it's gonna be.
So I'll just leave

That feeling in my gut
that I'll find what I forgot
I'll just take my thoughts and cut
out the bad

Oh, but all the leaves are falling
and the silver stream is calling
but all of them are making
me detour

The glare off the glass
is only what I look at
Now I can see at last
but it looks so Hazy

And the one painted grey
that I want to help find a way
just sits on her soul all day
reciting her speech

Enchanted Dreams

The Attic
Vivienne Higgins
Lift the latch and take a breath of still—fresh air outside,
For deep within the attic only dust and spiders bide.
No light can reach this lofty place, save for a ray or two,
Through a cracked and dusty skylight, with Heaven for a view.

Soft shafts of moonlight show the way within the lair,
With many cobwebs gleaming, like silken angels' hair.
A silver trail, left by a slug, crosses to and fro,
And from a box an old doll's face assumes a waxen glow.

Bears and books are littered around, forgotten and forlorn:
Their owners' lives long over, with others left to mourn.
A looking glass, once polished bright, sits proudly on a chest.
What beauties did it flatter?—before it passed its best.

This place of quiet soiitude seems lonely and decayed,
Yet every item stored here once knew happy days.
A young girl in a photograph smiles across the years:
For her, so fresh and youthful, this attic holds no fears.

Stand for just a Moment in the dusky, gathering dark,
And remember all the people, who here have left their mark.
Don't be afraid to look around in the thickly rushing gloom,
Just feel lucky to have seen this long—forgotten room.

My Father's Spirit
Deane P. Goodwin
My father's spirit walks within like Hamlet's restless shade
gliding the battlements.
A treacherous assault
that often conquers.

This wretched phantom speaks
in cold language beyond reason,
his cruel philosophy of limit.
And I find I look upon my
children with his eyes.

My Home Town
Sarah Jane Blankenship
I sit on my stoop to take a rest,
And put the neighborhood to the test.
I can see the world from here,
This little stoop from which I leer.

There's Mr. Jones, a wealthy man,
His wife's alone as he travels the land;
Oh, and there's the Millers' home,
Seems the children are all alone,

But as I looked, I felt a shock;
There are many people on this block;
And each one has their own front stoop,
to look at me from in their group.

They are deciding, just like me,
What they think my life can be;
Sitting on this stoop every day,
Never taking the time to play.

For if truth be known about my town,
Excitement hardly can be found,
Except in my imagination;
I use this stoop as my vacation.

Off The Beaten Track
Rena Fraser
Salty tang of seaweed, wheeling seabirds high
Fishing boats safe—harboured 'neath a clear blue sky.
Moorlands scattered round me, scent of bog and peat
Silvered sands outstretching a haven for retreat
How can we who see this ever question why
Surely this creation is the work of One on high

Coloured pebbles scattered as the tide recedes
Smooth and cool and different in colour shape and size.
All this quiet solitude, footsteps in wet sands
Rolling waves foam—crested splish—splashing onto land
Seascape and landscape an artist's paradise
Dazzling eye and senses work of a higher hand.

Truly man's creations, wonderful though they be
Can't compete with nature, land and sky and sea,
Sunrise and sunsets crimson dappled waves
Moonlight—silvered splendour changing scenery
Autumn— scents of harvest wafting on cool breeze
Arouses deep—set feelings of awe and majesty
Tears well up unbidden as an inner chord responds
To the quiet, beauteous splendour afforded one alone
Tranquility and peace reigns renewed, spirit bringing back
You will only find this inner—self off the beaten track

Moonlight
Paul Bonner
Illuminates a darkened world
Celestial brilliance
Shows being in a different light
Life is full of possibilities on a moonlight night

Moonlight
Evokes memories of time past
Dull objects transfigured
As the moon rises it washes away
The faults, flaws and failures of the imperfect day

Millionaire
Amanda McStay
Lying in the sun
Beside my swimming pool.
My butler serving drinks
To keep me nice and cool.

My gardens all around me,
My mansion set back from the tennis court.
A red Ferrari sitting in my drive
Not a common Ford Escort.

The children being taught by their tutor,
The baby being fed by the nurse.
My eldest daughter away shopping in Paris
With only plastic as her purse.

My husband's away in our Jaguar
To order our new boat.
The dog—trainer's away with the poodle
To get more curls put in her coat.

Such a wonderful life I lead
When I'm dreaming in my bed,
But I wish it was non—fiction
Not something in my head!

The Guide
Audrey Pilcher

An angel came and said "It's time
To climb the stairs to Heaven,"
"No way" said I indignantly,
"I'm only fifty-seven

I've lots to do before I go
So away and play your harp
My body might be getting soft
But my mind is razor sharp."

The angel began counting then
Upon his abacus
The beads flew swiftly back and forth;
"You're right to make a fuss

Your number isn't up at all
I got it wrong; oh! dear
You've got another twenty years,
What's that I see, a tear?

No crying now for past regrets
You've got a second chance,
Make sure you fill your future days
With laughter, song and dance."

Down In The Forest
Tamara Ryan

Down in the forest is a fishing hole,
Where I would go fishing with my bamboo pole,

There's a waterfall, bubbling white; over the edge it flows,
And down through the trees, the sunshine glows!

Oh! How I love to be there with my bamboo pole;
Down in the forest by the fishing hole.

Dedication: to my parents, Richard and Margaret

The Circle Of Life
A. Llewellyn

Tired out and they are quiet
Those little sleepy-heads
Safely gathered under one roof
Fast asleep in bed

Dainty slippers and tiny sandals
They try to climb the stairs
Soon turn into boots and shoes
That noisy children wear

Now they wear a grown-up style
And have children of their own
Missing shoes and toys on the floor
A repeat of days in the old home

Every time I visit them
It turns back the years
Except it's "hello, Nan" not "hello, Mum"
Those little voices I hear

I still miss the way things were
But when young ones peep around the door
The old house so settled and quiet
Is filled with laughter once more

Memories
Joan Almond

Do you remember when you were courting
When your fellow made this remark,
He said "Oh, girl, your hair looks lovely,"
While you were walking through your local park,

Do you remember the day you got married?
At the altar he looked handsome and coy,
And he said he would love you forever,
And his promises filled you with joy,

Do you remember when your youngest got married?
And the guests had at last all gone home,
He said "well, girl, we're back where we started,
And it's great to be here on our own"

Did you remember to put the cat out, girl?
He said as I mounted the stair,
Me with my bunions and varicose
Him with no teeth and no hairs

I remember he gave me a cuddle
And he said "I still love you, my pet"
I remember thinking to myself,
There's life in the old dog yet.

Serenity
Lydia Castillo

When sitting in a garden, I can feel serenity
Such peacefulness could not compare with city dwellery
I see the flowers all around seem smiling straight at me
And I could live forever in such pomp and greenery
And fluffy clouds above that move and wave consistently
Oh, how I wish I could be here for all eternity
Surrounded with all this, I find such absolute perfection
I'm mystified to think that one would question its creation
This could not be but His hand and only His rendition
That masterminded Eden and brought it to fruition.

The Healing Sanctuary
Deirdre Maria West

Twas on a Sabbath, I felt unwell.
Upon the bed I fell,
laying on my back
with an asthma attack.

As I struggled to breathe,
something happened that made me believe
a guardian angel came to my aid,
I wasn't alone or afraid.

The bedroom changed into a surgery,
doctors and nurses rallied around to help me.
Resting my head on the doctor's knees
he massaged my scalp, easing the wheeze.

I listened to the conversation
as they continued their examination.
Twas a simple test
a stethoscope upon my bare chest.

The healing sanctuary faded.
I came to, unaided,
I called out "Thank you"
For the healing and... "I love you, too".

Enchanted Dreams

The Valley Of Glencoe
Joseph Fahy
Homeward now I journey,
My hills to see once more.
For it's there my heart is yearning,
For the Valley of Glencoe.

The mountains seem to call me,
Wherever I may roam.
The breezes seem to whisper,
This Valley is your home.

I wonder if those mountain streams,
Are tears of loneliness.
For nature's gift of beauty,
Was marred with tears of stress.

I miss that strange, old feeling,
As I stroll down through the Glen.
A feeling you remember,
But never can explain.

And when my journey's over,
And the hills with heather glow,
It's there I'll sit and rest a while,
In the Valley of Glencoe.

Pearl
Sharon L. Sobczak
We would like to make one thing clear.
You have always been someone very special and dear.
We sure miss you, that's what we feared.
There's no one watching out for our rear!
We have worked together so many years.
There is something we all would like you to hear.
We wish you health, happiness and much deserved cheer!
Please stop in, we know you are near.
We'll always have time to bend your ear!
Happy Retirement from your career!!!

The Coming Of Spring
Emma Hunt
His shoulders hunched, his back is bent
Tears flow down his wrinkled face,
For him all wintertime is spent
And spring is here, in all her grace

He made the ground all white with snow
And all the trees were bare.
No sign of life or growth did show
But now new life is springing there

Leaves in bud and flowers in colours gay,
The fields now fresh and green,
The birds are singing through the day,
As though bleak winter had never been.

Catkins dangle from willow bough
Daffodils and tulips with colours all aglow,
Whilst small creatures from their winter sleep arouse,
And stream and brook now gently flow.

As old winter goes on his weary way
Banished from the Earth and now must fly.
Whilst spring reigns in her golden glory
Beneath clear, blue, cloudless skies.

Tongues And Cupidons
Alethea Andrews
They said your cupidon was entwined with parasitic ivy,
Or perhaps draped with ravenous Lombardic vines,
Thus accordingly, a causation of stir,
Understanding but little, conclusive judgement errs.

Reading metaphors into coincidence,
Deciphering some arcane symbolic reference,
How they weave complexity into indifference,
For in chaos, simple minds find preference.

You see, I don't believe your sculpture to be,
A symbol of unrequited love or intoxicating melancholy,
For if the arrows of Eros failed to scratch the object of fidelity,
Then surely the figure of he, would have long since been smote in three?

You see, I don't see the repression of ivy,
Or the oblivion of vines on an image of love,
They don't say anything to me,
Your private life is private enough.

For what use of ivy and vines?
Careless drapery to save thought?
Or an attempt to provoke society, devourers of time,
No, simple art, simply coming to naught.

Everywhere
Ashley Lorenzano
I've been everywhere and don't know how to get back again,
I'm going everywhere and nowhere fast,
I can't see where I'm going,
Because I am blinded by the stop sign of life,
No one can see everywhere but everyone can know it's there,
It's the feeling of confidence,
That assures you that one mile passed is still one mile gained,
Where time passes so quickly that you don't know how long it's been,
So when you have finally seen all there is to see,
Everywhere will be such a small place to be.

Winter Is Past
Joan Huxter
Winter is past! Oh, welcome spring
'Tis now the time to hear birds sing
A new, a bright and cheery song,
For winter is past. The dark days gone.

The grassy fields are fresh and green,
The leaves and buds on boughs are seen,
The blossoms on the fruit trees bloom,
And bulbs now shout "make room, make room."

The warm sun draws them from the dark,
Transforming the garden and the park—
A glowing mass of colours bright.
Spring–time is truly a wondrous sight.

The fledgling birds now take to wing
And cheep each day "it's spring, it's spring."
The lambs are leaping in meadows green
Yes, everywhere new life is seen.

Dear Lord, each year we hear and see
The wonders of springtime mystery.
It brings to us Your promise true—
"Old things are past. I make all things new."

The Anthology of Poems

Homeless
Louise Marie Cheyne
Somebody help me,
Somebody please,
Somebody help me,
But nobody sees.

I've no lovely house,
That I can call home,
No mother to turn to,
I'm all alone.

I took to the streets,
in search of some love,
I even prayed to,
God above.

Somebody help me,
Somebody please,
I'm begging you now,
I'm down on my knees.

People, they pass me,
They all stop and stare,
It's a hell of a world,
When nobody cares.

The Love In Your Eyes!
Regina McMinn
The love in your eyes I can see,
Around the bluish–green
Your love is warm and fulfilling
It's like a nice fire burning at night
Your house is as warm and caring as your heart
When your children come home and see you
They say "I love you, Daddy!"
And they know you love them, too,
They can see it in your eyes!
"I love you, Daddy!"

Waves
V. M. Beedell
Within the silence I watch you
Catching my breath as you place your hand within his

With fullness in your eye
Sublime acknowledgement recognition of beauty reaches me

It is not time that calls me but acceptance
Yet here I remain not with indifference but love

A mother's love that binds, holds and recognizes
When not to move or speak, lest one should break the spell

Within the stillness I sense you
The magic truth which is you and I rejoice in your birth

As I held you then, I hold you now, yet from a distance
Lest I should allow you to feel my own joy
Linked with sadness, not regret
The memory of what was and what is now

Walk with me, breathe with me
For one last time join hands with me for one dance
And let the music of our souls carry us along the sands
For the last time.

Sunshine Love
Karen Hennessey
The Clouds were forming in the sky
The tears were welling in my eyes
I thought I heard you say goodbye
I felt that I was going to die

The sun peeped, then it squeezed its way
Right through to make a brighter day
My tears dried when I heard you say
The sun is out, I want to stay

Then rain came, with it came my fears
It poured and blended with my tears
And Moments passed, they felt like years
But hope comes as the downpour clears

So tired, I feel I want to sleep
But if I did and it was deep
I'd miss it if you were to creep
Out of my life and so I weep

But with your hand, you wipe my eye
And say "there's no more need to cry"
You tilt my face, I look up high
And see a rainbow fills the sky...

Divorce Chronicle (1983–1997)
Michael Hendrix
Just a second ago, we enjoyed a life together.
Just a minute ago, we lived our California Dream.
Just an hour ago, we loved each other deeply.
Just a day ago, we were passionate lovers.
Just a week ago, we were in love.
Just a month ago, we were lustful and naive.
And just a year ago, we were friendly strangers, unknowing how our life paths were destined to cross, merge and eventually separate.

Dedication: to Caril Duncan, whose presence remains

The Philistines Are Here
Craig Vowles
They came, they said, to put her right,
But all they did was to further blight,
A building of such sublime design,
With new ideas so utterly malign.

The ornate, white Georgian plaster,
Was turned into a huge disaster,
When daubed with paints of copper and blue,
None of which were the original hue.

A precious jewel was reduced to paste,
With an almost wanton lack of taste,
As they continued in their destructive vein,
Showing no regard and all disdain.

Till the elegant lady was stripped at last,
Of all her dignity and illustrious past,
And then relaunched in her cheap, new dress,
Too much rouge, a tawdry mess.

Unfortunately, now the deed is done,
And rest–assured no prize was won,
She was abandoned to her ghastly fate,
Because the Philistines passed through the gate.

Enchanted Dreams

My Destination
Ian Challinor
I wake up in a railway station
No other place for a destination
A single hand pointed the way
A glance at my ticket, there's nothing to pay

The end of a year, which way do I go
My hands to my body, I rock to and fro
My long bony fingers reach out for a case
My eyes, they are borrowed to another time and place

This way, please, you're going to be late
Destiny has stepped in and chosen your fate
I rise to my feet, my coat unfolds
Come along sir, please do as you're told

My mind slips back to when I was in school
Lessons to learn, too much the fool
A bearer's walk, my arm she grips
A one train carriage. No time for slips.

A kiss on the cheek, a hug farewell
A single tear, a story to tell
With saddened fingers and trembling hand
We wave in the breeze, reach out to the land.

Sunshine
Lia M. Corey
Sunshine is a friend of mine,
She is the best friend a girl could have,
People think she is the sun, but she isn't,
To me she is 1.
She is a bird like no other,
She is yellow, like the sun,
And green, like the grass.
She is my bird and that's that!!!!!

Dedication: to my parents and Sunshine

Until Death Do Us Part
Sarah M. Powell
I reached out for you and you were not there.
I dreamed of you often and could not see your face,
I knew you were my true love, a love that is rare.
I had to know where you were in the human race.
I did not realize until I was older, an adult,
That my true love was my childhood pal, my playmate.
I grew to love you more as the days went by and as
A result.
We married and had children and you are still my
playmate.
Now I reach out for you and you are there,
I dream of you often and I can see your face.
I know you are my true love, a love that is rare,
You are no longer obscure among the human race.
I love you more today than I did at the very first.
True love only grows brighter, not dimmer.
I love you so much that my heart, at times, seems it could
burst.
You are the reason my eyes glimmer,
Darling, I will never grow tired of the love we share.
Of the life we have together, together, not apart.
I will never doubt you and I know you will always care.
Together we will go on and enjoy what we have—until
death do us part!!

The Gift
Margaret High
God gave to me a gift of love,
I had to give away,
But every time I tried,
Here in my heart it stayed.

I gave it to my husband,
He took it so easily,
He knew he couldn't keep it,
So he gave it back to me.

I gave it to my children,
They kept it for a while,
But then they gave it back to me,
With a kiss, a hug and a smile.

I gave it to my grand–children,
To share in their own way,
But then they gave it back to me,
So in my heart it stayed.

So I just gave it to the Lord,
He smiled and said to me,
"This is My gift, I gave to you,
It just keeps going around, you see."

Waiting For Love
Danielle Conrad
I've waited my whole life for him.
Without him, my life is dim.
He will bring happiness and joy to me.
Then I will shine with radiance for all to see.
To me, he is my other part.
And he will remove the clouds from my heart.
Love is a joyous thing.
That will make my heart and soul sing.
Yes, I do believe in fate.
For he is my soul mate.

The Truth
Cynthia T. Hager
You need to know it's written down
just as confirmation
These feelings I'm about to share
will last for all duration
I've loved you since before you were
when I could feel you stir
And in the instant you arrived
God showed me love's true worth
For in my child my life was whole
I loved you as you grew
I tried to keep you safe and warm
and teach you right and truth
You are so close – a fine young man
and yes, I am still proud
While there are choices still to make
I want to shout out loud
I love you, Son, I always will
forget this not, I pray
The truth is simple – live by this
remember every day
To be your best and choose your path
be happy, wise and true
And know, no matter where you are
forever, I love you.

The Anthology of Poems

Crossing Toronto Island Ferry
Renny V. MacKinnon
I lift my bag; it's light to carry
And walk along in time with the band.
The ferry waits as the crowd alights –
I'm going on a trip to the Island.

A man sits there with his feet on his case,
He puts on his glasses and starts to read.
He doesn't notice the sock sticking out
Struggling with the bag to be free.

I turn away so the wind's in my face,
And close my eyes to feel the boat moving.
I smell the warm sun in a small child's hair.
The feel of life steals over me – soothing.

Seagulls wheeling, diving, screaming
Sailboats racing; rigging snapping
Children calling, laughing, running
Past and present seeing, melding.

The ferry pulls in while I'm watching the birds.
I'm free and flying on their flashing wings.
I smile to the man with the bulging bag,
But he sees the gulls and says "Dirty old things".

Thinking Of You
Ruth A. Seide
I dedicate my thoughts to you,
I dedicate my every fiber to you.
In the quietness of the night
I listen to the beats of my heart;
My thoughts are the greatest gifts I
can give you.

Your friendship eases my anxiety.

Dedication: to whom I love

The Hotel Window
Luis R. Diaz
I look out this window as I look outside,
I stare at the world as it passes by.
I sit by this window, I'm drinking my beer
and asking myself what I'm doing here.

I sit by this window, the lights shine inside
as I think and wonder, how high they can fly?
A trek in life, a step in time, a route unseen,
a path I chose, a journey for opt have I.

My quest may be futile, my trials in vain,
for least I know the answer's not here.
For the window shall know for what it's been
shown, the rest shall remain what's unknown.

I sit by this window as I look outside,
and wonder whom all it has known?
The thousands of people that it must have seen,
I wonder how far they have flown?

The window lies silent as it has been told,
the window nearly knows what it's been shown.
My life may have been futile, but not in vain,
the window, not I, will die in pane...

Fragile Environment
James E. Tawse
Heavy industry mostly gone, the atmosphere's more clear
But the motorcar has taken its place, this is my current fear
The Government and the Scientist must find a solution
To solve the problem and get rid of this pollution

A new source of power without the nasty gases
Has got to be found to satisfy the masses
Environment is a fragile thing, but we can be the master
It's important to get the balance right to avoid a major disaster

We must safeguard our Planet and protect the ozone layer
Shows you what can happen if we don't really care
Our land has been exploited for man's personal greed
No consideration for the things that we really need

If we interfere with nature it has a way of kicking back
Sooner or later it will have us all on the rack
Now that we're aware the damage that has been done
Scientists unite another challenge to be won

I'm sure it can be reversed, it will be a mammoth task
Hoping they get their thinking caps on before their oxygen mask
Government can play their part with money they can give
And give us back our fresh air so we can all live

Nature's Peace
Shayna Leah Rose
When you look
at the sea you will look at me.
When you look at the moon
you will realize I am in your eyes.
Look at the mountains and the trees,
feel the warm, summer breeze.
Look at nature and you will see
this is the resting place for me.
For now I am free,
no more suffering to be.

Like An Albatross
Kevin Short
I spent my life in chaos and fear,
Drowning in sex, drugs and beer.
Head always in the sky,
My life was low but I thought I could fly.

So I was just like an albatross,
Flying through sea breeze and frost.
Soaring over the wide, lonely sea,
Not knowing were to go and who to be.

Ruined life and death surrounded me,
To unlock this hell, I needed the key.
I knew I had the strength in my heart,
And the will to start.

So the albatross did land,
And made a nest on the sand.
I banished all my evil ways,
And stopped the things that would end my days.

And then my life was true,
When I found brightness in you.
The months of hell were seven,
But you were the angel that made my life Heaven.

Enchanted Dreams

Atlantic Convoy
John Conrad
I awoke and my heart's blood was racing
and the pitch of the deck was not right.
As the thirst for a scream dried my throat out,
I got up to join with my last night.

Electric pumps and acrid smoke, sweat and blood,
fuel the cacophony of desperate effort.
The fierce, alien staccato of dying metal confirms the worst fears
and competes with the urging of the Deck Officer, "Come boys, Come on!"

Everyone knows,
from the three-ringer to the youngest killick,
everyone knows.
She is losing.

Indescribable home of true horror,
the altered reality where familiar fades hostile,
and flesh and steel dissolve together,
in the black salt elixir of countless lost fleets.

She breaks up and embraces the water.
Leaving no trace of her wreckage in flames,
Only loved-ones at home to remember,
all the boys and the men and their names.

Wisdom
Joann Schofield
Old hat, New Place.
But, always filled with grace.
Life, Death
Earth, The Human Race.
Heaven, Hell
Should All Be Graced,
To have overcome
The Human Race.

Dedication: to Esther Loring Baker

Good Times Are Yours For The Taking
Ricky Jones
Whatever you are going through
It's only the thunder of a storm
It's only noise to distract you
from your destiny, to take away your calm

But "don't let" trouble still your peace
"don't let" heartache rob your joy
Your God knows and loves you
Your God is never far

He knew you before you were born
He knew every step you would take
He knew all the good and bad times
Yes, He even knew all the mistakes

But He still loves you
in spite of what it seems
He still sees the best in you
He's still going to fulfill those dreams

So hold your head up high
Praise God who rains downs blessings
Good days are in right in front of you
Good times are yours for the taking

Rain
Julie Ori
Sitting at the window,
And watching the rain
Come down, makes me
Think of when I used to play tag.

Running on the slippery, wet grass,
Getting dirt on my feet and hands,
Rain dripping down on my face,
My clothes getting all soaked.

It was always fun to run in the rain,
And play like we were cops chasing
After robbers in a thunderstorm and
To feel the glory of getting the freedom to
Run around on the soaking-wet eternity.

The rain would always shield and protect me
From any kind of pain I was feeling and
Put a gentle hand on my shoulder and to
Guide me when I was depressed.

You really miss acting like a kid when you
Don't have the time or you don't want to
Deal with the mess that rain causes.

Today, Tomorrow And Always
Wanda Hayes
My Dearest Friend, I Need You Today;
For I'm Troubled, Confused And Full Of
Dismay.
I'll Need You Tomorrow, For My Fears
I Can't Hide; In A World So Cold,
Desolate and Wide.

And For Always I'll Love, Need And
Want Thee; For Today, Tomorrow And
Always Is Eternity.

Cold-Hearted One
Kristy Lacey
Cold, it is so very cold...
As I fall for you to hold.
Nothing is there when you find
They did not care.
Wait, was there a flare,
No, nothing but cold-blooded, Heartless One.

Heartless is the way you feel.
Emotions spin until you drop.
But no one is there to care or share.
Deeper and deeper I fall...

Once in a lifetime is One I once had.
Why am I so sad? But also kinda glad?
Because once in a lifetime is only one lifetime away.

I would never sway away...
With blackness so cruel and cold or someone to hold.
So I've been told,
That was only cold-blooded Heartless One.

With time, like fine wine, he will fade away.
From black to gray and finally to day.
Then everything will be O. K...

From The Beginning
Melba Sietman
From the beginning of time, In God's own way,
He ordained that Christ would come one day.
The promise of His coming, God did reveal
When He said to the serpent: "Thou shalt bruise His heel."

In the fullness of time, This promise did come,
In the person of Jesus, God's own dear Son.
Born in a manger, a lowly birth,
This wonderful One came down to Earth.

He came not to live, but rather to die,
Our sins to atone, on a cross raised high.
Though He was rich, yet He became poor
That we, through His poverty, might have more.

We miss the significance of the Christmas Season
If we fail to see that He came for this reason.
As we celebrate Christmas, sing carols, give gifts,
Let us thank God for Jesus whose birthday it is.

And keep looking forward to that bright day
When our Saviour will come to take us away.
He promised to return, this promise is true,
I'm ready to meet Him, my friends, are you?

Another Chance
Laura Bennett
Used to cry when we broke up,
Now I know that we'll make up.
Glad I gave you one more chance,
Didn't toss you at first glance.
Wish that I could believe you,
But what you usually say isn't true.
"I love you," isn't said with a smirk,
Maybe this time it will work.
One more chance, that's all you get,
After this, that's all, I quit.

Is It True?
Dorothy J. Harpster
Tell me darlin', is it true?
That you love me as I love you?
When I'm feeling sad and blue,
I wonder where the time went to.

We met a million years ago,
You said to me, "I love you so."
But there's one thing that you should know
I'll have to be a G. I. Joe.

But you came back to me, my dear,
And told me I should have no fear,
For every day you would be near,
And you have made that very clear.

Now our hair has turned to gray,
And still I want to hear you say,
I love you more and more each day,
Together we will always stay.

I never wanted someone new,
And soon our judgement day is due,
So tell me darlin', is it true?
That you love me, as I love you?

Songs Of Joy
Alf Butler
Once upon a time, it was long ago,
Lying under my apple tree,
Songs of joy, songs of mirth,
Came down to awaken me.

Rubbing sleep from my eyes,
What did I see?
Young children all around,
Dancing merrily.

Such the sight I had never seen,
As I joined in,
Sure to keep these songs,
From coming to an end.

Danced all day,
Danced all night,
In the dark,
And in the light.

Seasons came,
Seasons went,
Still songs of joy,
And merriment.

Untitled
Patricia Embro
At one time, our lakes were clear.
We could swim without fear.
Then came factories, production and waste.
They had to have a dumping place.
The lakes were their only solution.
The fish are dead because of pollution.
Oh, what a loss.
Bad luck, misfortune, is the cost.
All this contamination.
Throughout the nation.

Comfort In My Solitude
Carolyn Valenzuela
Lord, if you gave me a hill,
I would climb with ease.
If you gave me a valley,
I'd walk and feel no breeze.

If you gave me a mountain
I'd conquer, my head held high
But now, I have a sorrow
And in my heart I cry.

I'll find comfort in my solitude
With all our memories fondly made
And I'll find comfort in my solitude
In all the plans we carefully laid.

As this solitude fills my heart
And I journey through this maze
I'll remember friendship kindled
I'll look for rainbows on cloudy days.

With each new day I'll search my heart
And watch this sadness slowly part.
I can move ahead in an inspiring mood
To know I'll find comfort in my solitude.

Enchanted Dreams

Oh, For The Breeze
Tom Lawrence
Oh, for the breeze that would rustle the leaves
As I sit in the sun on the bank 'neath the willow trees
With rod in my hand I watch the float, it sinks
My first catch it doth please but oh, for the breeze

There's peace and content in this way of life
By this stream far from strife
To sit and dream with the cottage nearby
And my plump, happy wife, but oh, for the breeze

And sensing the smell of new-mown hay
In nearby meadows where farm labourers strive
At their skills, the farmer to please
Oh, for the breeze

The girl by my side, chin cupped in her hands
Golden hair fastened with Rose Pink bands
Her mother calls, "June, stay out of the sun
My fair child of fun", but oh, for the breeze

Downstream the Mallards with young
Seek the shade of the reeds
Swans float with grace in the still of the air
Oh, for the breeze

My Empty Heart
Basdai Sookoor
My days, my nights, my life So filled with longing. So filled with need
For one thing... Love. To fill my empty heart. So distant, so obscure.
Do you exist or do I seek in vain? I feel you close so many
times, yet you slip away like a fine mist when the sun appears.
Where, oh, where do you slumber?
I know in my soul that You are there... hidden like a treasure...
Waiting for me... Somewhere.
Will I perish in this desert of wanting? Drown in this sea of need?
How I long to feel you! Encircle me!
Comfort me!

A Seeded Soul
Paulinerose M. Epstein
My tears hidden
and washed away
as rain pours down
my solemn face

Cries of Angels
ring in my ears
visions of demons
flash by my eyes

Seeing Faces in shadows
that were not there
my soul remains open
as pain shines through

Crooked glass
bleeding feet
my heart pours out
what my soul seeds

Tired, my ashes
laid down to rest
with a harbor
of liberty, freedom, distress.

The End Is Nigh
Doug Coverly
Astrologers have noted
As they watched the spacial void
A slab of rock that's bloated
That they call a hemorrhoid

Is on its way to get us
The Earth is on its track
Even new labour voters
Can't make the thing go back

In the year of 2028
The scientists have told us
It is our natural fate
To be splattered by big boulders

Tin helmets will be pertinent
To protect us all from harm
And a little tube of ointment
To rub on as soothing balm

The dome for the millenium
That every man repository
Won't protect your cranium
So hide in a suppository

If You Ever Loved Me
Helen August
If you ever loved me;
I wonder...
For time has never revealed,
Just how you feel.
So in a world of all my own, I wonder;
Day and night, night and day
All by myself, alone;
In a dark and lovely corner
I wait...
Never to know if you ever loved me.

A Special Place
Cyril Maunders
A Cottage By The Railway Line,
In The Middle Of Newby Moor,
This Is Where I Wooed You, Love,
With A Love So Pure.

We Used To Walk For Miles And Miles,
Your Hand Clasped Into Mine,
We'd Listen To The Curlew's Call,
The Sun Did Always Shine.

Years Ago They Pulled It Down,
And Built A Bungalow,
At The Time We Were Sorry,
And For A Time Felt Low.

I Still Remember That Cottage,
And The Love So True,
So When You Passed Away, My Love,
I Scattered Your Ashes There For You.

I Visit There Quite Often,
And Shed A Little Tear,
For A Love That's Not Forgotten,
And A Love That's Still Quite Near.

The Hollow Barrels Of War
Rhys Tassell
Beyond the homefront
Our soldiers fought for king and country
In union with our allies.
The enemy was not Hitler and his forces.
The abysmal weather, the soldiers' dreary pace
Was the true enemy that would affect them more.

Jerry flew overhead,
Following one of our Air Force friends.
Streaks of white light: A constant image of war,
Flashed in front of many eyes.
Startled, these eyes fell to the ground
Alongside the hollow barrels
Of their owners' guns – the tunnels
With no light at the end.

War was full of heroes;
Our loved and cherished,
Some of whom did not return;
Gave up their lives for the future.
The poignant images of war
Are encased in people's memories.

Remembrance.

The End Of Season Sale
J. Middleton
In the club's "Singles Night" evening,
It's getting late – people are leaving.
And those who are left play out the sad, lonely tale
Of the middle-aged, last-gasp relationship sale:
With hopes slashed!
And dreams crashed!
Including a flirt now—pay later guarantee
With sex which is long-term, interest-free.
It's only here where people are discounted and cheap,
That whatever you break you don't have to keep.

Three Simple Words
Katherine J. Upton
In '95 I felt alive
I'd met a wonderful man.
In '96 I was thrilled to bits,
Everything was going to plan.

It was everything a romance should be
With all the flowers, I was the office envy.
The girls would say, "he's quite a catch"
I smiled, I knew I'd met my match.

We loved each other, I was sure.
We had this saying — "I love you more".
Cards carrying this message he would send
— now we're married, it's come to an end.

Maybe, I'm just insecure
in which case he should tell me more,
but since we've been married, it would be nice
if he told me he loved me more than twice.

Really, it should make me mad
but most of all it makes me sad.
All I want to hear — but rarely do
— is three simple words – "I love you".

Johnny Got His Gun
Amy Brate
I had my family and my love,
I had my faith in God above.
No one could ask for any more,
Until they told me to go to war.

Now all I can do is lie and dream,
About the things that I have seen.
Without any eyes, ears, or nose,
I can't tell when it rains, pours, or even snows.

I tried to find my mouth and cheek,
Has it been day, months, or only a week?
Since that terrible thing happened with a shell,
Someone is trying to blow us to Hell!

Now I have lost both of my arms,
And the ring that Kareen gave me to charm.
Where is she now and how does she feel?
I can't even walk or run or kneel!

I cannot yell and it is hard to talk,
This thing on my head feels like a sock.
Why I am here, I cannot see,
Please God, somebody kill me!

Eyes Of Bondage From With–In
Cristoval Diaz
My own eye's are seeing beauty from within, but
acknowledging still what's on the outside.
For is it wrong to try and have both beauty and personality,
I do think not.
For the personality does make the beauty I do see from
within, that is on the outside. That I do see from within,
that is on the outside.
That I do see from within

Dedication: thanks everyone in my life

Through The Years
Linda Lafreniere
A man and a woman,
Together as one,
To love, honour and cherish,
Through the years.

Days and years pass by,
A family begins to grow,
So many memories made,
Through the years.

Children become adults,
Leaving the nest, one by one,
Making their own way,
Through the years.

A man and a woman,
Sharing their lives together,
Their love growing stronger,
Through the years.

Another anniversary to celebrate,
This one of 35 years,
So many more to come,
Through the years.

Enchanted Dreams

If You Looked Into A Mirror
Loretta N. Woolridge
If you looked into a mirror,
do you know what you would see?
Would it be a look of honour
staring back convincingly?

Would your eyes refrain from telling
all the secrets harbored there,
or perhaps be more compelling—
revealing all behind your stare?

Would it be the truth reflected,
or simply what you let be seen?
Every mystery protected,
deeply buried in—between...

for there are many, many layers
beyond the surface of the glass,
tightly guarding all that's sacred—
be it the present, or the past.

The mirror holds your inner sanctum
but one must look beyond its gate—
to find the valor it may cradle,
as the keeper of your fate.

Sounds Of A Country Summer
Carol Wilk
A rooster crowing at dawn, the song of the birds in the trees.
The babble of a brook, the wind rustling through the leaves.
A distant lawnmower, the whine of a chainsaw, the thud of a hammer.
Sounds of activity and nature alive after a long and cold winter.
The whistle of the soaring hawk causes little creatures to scurry.
Some little, some larger, some feathered, some furry.
The patter of raindrops as they fall on the roof.
And at dusk the hoot of the owl, mournful and aloof.
No roar of taxis or honking horns or even a bus.
The peace and quiet of a country summer, this is for us.

Our Father's Plan
Robin Farnsworth
Our Heavenly Father Loves us so
that He sent His Son so long ago.
Sending Him to us on Earth,
Jesus came by Human Birth.

He grew into a Gentle man
continuing Our Father's Plan.
He would go to preach and heal
according to His Father's Will.

His precious life, for us He gave.
Soon after, His body laid in a cave.
Not knowing Christ died for us,
many wondered, "Why the fuss?"

Christ died for our sins
to rise and walk again.
Yes, way back when
we did not know Him then.

We have a chance now.
Would you like to know how?
Invite Him into your Heart.
That's a good place to start...

Poetic Words And Thoughts
Virginia C. Geiger
To some people, poetry is a group of words that rhyme,
To others, it is merely expressions of fine thoughts, in line,
But, whatever the style and timing one wishes to convey,
The beauty and rhythm of poetry emerges each day.

Gentle breezes, rain showers and flowers are tokens of Spring,
Warm, sunny days and outdoor activities Summer doth bring,
Cool temperatures and colorful leaves announce it is Fall,
Followed by blankets of Winter—white snow, covering all.

A babbling brook murmurs along a country road,
And we hear the croaking of frogs and see a toad,
Gathered in the trees are groups of fine—feathered friends,
Singing their merry tunes until the daylight ends.

Folks assemble together at the green picnic grounds,
Soon, musical instruments give forth lively sounds,
The likes of which inspire all to hum or to sing,
While others feel the urge to dance around in a ring.

Scents from varied homemade edibles fill the air,
And down all sit, their delicious goodies to share,
There's little time to talk while savoring it all,
What a pleasant day spent under a pavilion tall.

My Place
Amy L. Moyer
The origin of my joy and pride.
My selfish little place to hide.
The trueness that is me, where I cannot lie.
This place I return to be alone.
The one spot where everything about me is known.
My passions, my fantasies are an open book.
My thoughts, my dreams, are all on record.
My happiness, my fear, forever etched here.
A place that no one can ever invade.
My mind, where very ounce of my being has stayed.

Regret
Donis Canisales
Somewhere in the changeless past,
a regretful memory burns.
An instant dissipated much too fast,
so a heart yearns —

Yearns to recolor the view.
Or better yet, with Knowledge in mind,
Wipe the slate clean, rewrite anew.
Alas, Regret inevitably delivers its guilt—ridden bind.

For there's no way to change Reality's Story.
And, if we have ever one wronged,
Regret gets the heart and Antiquity gets the glory.
Then to Repentance our heart belongs.

Looking back and reliving Recollections Past,
Appears as Tomorrow and Yesterday's Fate unchanged.
Now, speaking in terms of Historical Facts,
Time, the master thief, is to blame.

Destiny, powerless to spent Grains of Sand.
Regret's Revenge then set in stone —
And Time's Artistry evidenced by Unknown Hand,
Unlike Michelangelo's Pieta in Rome.

The Princess
Carolyn Ware

She had such a beautiful smile
And loving, compassionate eyes
She had a flair for style
And a walk so elegant and spry

She fell in love with a prince
And married into rigid royalty
But his love for her was thence
Thus she was heartbroken by disloyalty

Like the dry sand of the desert
And the wind pounding the England bays
Our princess heart did thirst
To be loved forever and always

And for just a Moment in time
Our Princess finally felt loved
But in the blink of an eye
Darkness descended from above

The soul of the world was shaken
Its inhabitants shattered and dismayed
For the "Prince of Death" has taken
Our "Peoples Princess" far, far, away

Untitled
Kristin Heath

Pieces on the floor
Mirroring the reflection of our mistakes
Sharp and shimmering
A beautiful mess
Each angle reflecting a different light
All I can do is look down
Helpless to its distortion
Paralyzed by its numbers
Unable to grasp the missing fragment
That lights the face.

A Penny For Your Thoughts
Theresa Trepanier

I am just a penny
I'm insignificant
When I'm dropped upon the floor
Most people just ignore it.

I cannot buy a condo
A car or diamond ring
I'm a bother counting
I'm just a piece of zinc.

But if you take the trouble
To save me in a jar
I'll add up to something
You admired from afar.

A nickel, dime or quarter
Add up to more, you see
But I can be important
When you need one of me.

They say they will omit me
Not make me anymore
That would be a big mistake
Don't let them, I implore.

The Undeserved
James McConville

I was born the same as all young lads
With my family always around me
I did not want to go to war to kill
But I was forced to go against my will

Why am I here, I cannot say
My mind was dull on that fateful day.
The noise was so much I cannot describe
But the order was up and over the side.

I saw my mates tumble and fall
When we were ordered and over the wall
Don't make me a coward, I plead to you
As I saw the lads go down, no chance, it's true

I trembled with fear when the guns were fired
With no sleep or warmth I felt very tired
I would have given my all just to be with my mates
Alas, my strength and fear gave way to fate

I only ask you to forgive me and others
As a young lad I tried my best, we were like brothers
And let me rest in peace now the war is done
So my name can be written alongside those gone

Exodus Robin
Loren L. Qualls

As I listen with fearful anticipation,
You speak...
Words of going, of soaring.
I hear your wings wash over the air
And another joins your flight and still another and another,
flapping in mocking vanity, but swearing a gentle love.
I watch you circle overhead, screaming by in wondrous liberty...
But I can only hear the faint whisper of my name in your beating wings.

Comes A Time
Susan White

Comes a time to reckon with oneself,
Evaluation pending.
All bias put away on a shelf,
No longer self-defending.

You see yourself just as you are,
Not what you once meant to be.
Remember times you went too far,
Remember, too, the fee.

The setbacks of your bygone past,
Should serve but to remind.
Learn, look onward, life goes fast,
Leave bitter remorse behind.

Rid yourself of all dead weight,
Be not victim of illusion,
Don't let yourself be used as bait,
Joining in the mass confusion.

Choose carefully those you call "friend",
And of every man be wary,
Some are loyal until the end,
And others you will carry.

Huntress Of Truth
Cynthia Maiorino
Standing in the Place of Time
One step ahead into Life's Rhyme
A Pure Reflection She does find
in Truth, the Everlasting.

Eyes that cast the Light of Day
Trained to see Each Other's Way
Right or Wrong She Will Not Say
in Question, All is Free.

Her Smile Redeems the Fate of Man
through her Quest to Understand
with Light and Dark upon the Land
in Blindness, We Shall See.

An Open Heart and Naked Skin
Reveals what's hidden Deep Within
Passions Flare with all that's Been
in Unity, there's Love.

Speaking with the Spirit's Mind,
Connecting People, Place and Time
Reminders of a Life Divine
in God, we are All One.

Make What You Will Of It
Danielle Bersch
millions of heartbeats from now.
when our stardust is the only remaining legacy of our loves and losses;
wars and peace.
when I am nothing more than dust floating, what stories will my
leavings spell out across space?
give them something to say of you;
of how particles (by then cold and far apart),
were once the warm skin of hands, belonging to lovers,
who caressed each other under this same moon;
when love was a greater power than science and now the only time.

A Volunteer's Prayer
Gee Gee Shelfer
Lord, may I not be too busy
to stop and recognize
The grief I sometimes see
in other persons' eyes.
Never too busy to offer help,
or share
Never too busy to sympathize
or care.
I've done a heap o livin'
and had some measure of pain
Don't let me cite them to others
over and over again.
May I refrain from pious
platitudes
Be reasonably sweet and
full of gratitude.
Make me thoughtful and helpful
and prayerful each day.
For blessings received are
best when given away.
Help me have a word of cheer
to all who come my way.
Please, Lord, strengthen their
shoulders, or take the burden away.

Just Hello
Edith T. Fluharty
I'd like to be with you
awhile,
and hear about the folks,
I'd like to sit and see you
Smile at the same old jokes,
But since, you are so far
away, I cannot hope to
go, I'll send along this
little poem,
Just to say,
"Hello"

Imagination
Hank Staley
In the early morn before the dawn
And the sun begins to shine
The shadows hide something inside
That my eyes cannot define

Although I strain my weary brain
The picture isn't clear
In the morning skies the sun will rise
To make the shadows disappear

In the light of day it will hide away
While the sun is warm and bright
Where every line can be defined
Though they'll vanish in the night

Then in the night without the light
I'll search and try to find
So I'll stare at the darkness there
For a picture in my mind

But as I sleep I know it will creep
Into the caverns of my mind
There it will stay to hide and play
Between the shadows and the lines

One August Night
Doreen H. Akizaki
One August night in the City of Light
A second chance for life to begin.
Two lovers take flight from the media blight
In a race they thought they could win.

Wanting peace and respite
Ironically, they finally have what was sought
But at such a costly price
Were these Moments bought.

Her legacy of charity
And heart–felt compassion resounded.
Yet known as much for her style and grace,
Her detractors she confounded.

All mothers fear in their own death
Leaving their cherished alone.
More difficult leaving these cherished two,
As one will ascend to the throne.

How deep this pain
As the world all shared one sorrow.
But she showed us how to carry on
And bravely face tomorrow.

Dying
Tab Fulle

Over yonder! What do I see?
Passed my eyes, was only me.

Not knowing where I am going, heading afar.
Was only me wishing upon a star.

Traveling now to the Heavens above,
knowing now I have left my love.

I left the day before the past,
if I had only known it was my last.

Charlotte
Meghann O'Hara

You're only four,
Yet as I look into your eyes, so liquid brown,
I see your pain, almost too great for you to bear,
Dear God, I cry, this isn't fair!

You gaze at me,
Those gentle eyes great pools of deep despair,
I long to help, to take away the pain,
Dear God, I cry to you again!

Yes, only four,
You've brought us all such joy in those short years
Your childhood should be free from grief and care
Dear God, please listen to my prayer!

You're part of me,
My first-born's child; wise far beyond your years,
It hurts me so to see your tears, my heart, it aches,
Dear God, I cry for all our sakes!

To "Mum and Dad,"
Your daughter's life is in your hands, she's far too
Young to understand; don't wreck her life, please try
Dear God, for Charlotte's sake – AMEN!

My Special Friend
Sharon Gorman

Today I had to say good-bye to you
my very special friend
Thank you for all the time we shared
but all good things must end.

For God had plans and needed you
so much more than I
How truly blessed I am to have
a part of you inside.

Your voice I'll hear forever,
a whisper in the wind
A kiss of sunshine on my face
will find my strength within.

As my tears fall softly
You will let me know
I'll never have to walk alone
I can smile as flowers grow,

And in the Heavens late at night
as I look up and see,
the star that shines the brightest
Is you watching over me.

Heaven's Legend
Deanna Maruca

Words alone cannot express, the kindness,
the tenderness
Of a gentle man from above
That God sent us, to share his love
He's gone from us and Grace lands gates
You see, Heaven is his resting place
The king is gone but shall remain
In rock-in-roll's Hall of Fame
My love for you shall never cease
God bless you, Elvis
May you rest in peace

The Blemish
Lynne Hayes

It was just a blemish,
Or so I thought.
It never really went away,
But I forgot.

Life went on as usual,
Days flew by.
There was so much to do,
I don't know why.

Then one day I noticed it;
It grew quite big.
The doctor did a biopsy.
I'll need a wig.

And now the treatment's done at last.
It didn't work.
It won't be long now.
Just a quirk.

Now the pain's so bad
I could cry.
But I don't have the energy;
I die.

Penny Jane
Dennis C. Davies

I love you, darling Penny Jane,
these latter years are not your blame.
Each market day we walked those miles,
sold our wares, came home in style.

We pass our years together still,
share our sorrows, share our ills.
Five and twenty years of dreams,
have passed so quickly, so it seems.

Both you and I now bent and old,
keeping warm from winter's cold.
It pains me to see you look this way,
a doctor soon will come, I pray.

O, Penny Jane, you lie so still,
I fear, my dear, you've lost the will.
My worldly goods are yours to share,
gentle lass, I do so care.

Eventide shadows through the door,
casts its fingers across bare floor.
Penny Jane, my darling gray,
a horse so gentle died this day.

Enchanted Dreams

A Tribute To A Princess
J. P. Casey
Oh, Diana, Oh, Dodi,
Who have left us too soon.
All our prayers go out to you,
Just when your love's beginning to bloom.

Why did our Lord take you both,
When you seemed to have found true love,
Not even time to take the oath,
When marriage could have been so close,

Books are signed with condolences,
Flowers are laid, lining your route,
And our loving country and other nations,
Laying more and more flowers to you, their tribute.

As we go forth today,
Into Westminster Abbey to pray.
As our country and other nations weep,
We lay our Princess down, who now sleeps,

A Princess of understanding,
And caring in every way,
She's our Princess Diana,
And in our hearts, she will always stay.

A Mother's Heartaches
Virginia Ekdahl
Life has been one tragedy after another
So hard to bear as a mother
Let's count all blessing today, for tragedies do go away
Most lives are wasted and sad adult thinking would not be mad
This world we all will leave so in God we should believe
Helping others should be our goal to reap the treasures that will unfold
Positive thinking is all it takes for all the world to escape the fakes
Smile and laugh today and let the heartaches go away
You're loved by God, to love Him is not hard
Sing your heart's delight to face another fight
To suffer alone is a crime, better days will come in time.

A Walk To Joy
Cassandra Philp
Gentle, tender ear creased
Strong shoulder soggy and broad
Long road traveled together
Valleys not easily trod

Mountain climbed in tandem
Hard and rugged and steep
Holding me — together
Through the dark and deep

Now standing just a bit apart
Seeing what was lost
Knowing each will always be there
Can we say it was worth the cost?

Assured this is the one true road
To the desires of my heart
I'll travel it now alone
Until we're no longer apart

Joy is the destination
Freedom and reward
I look now to the horizon
It is Heaven I walk toward

Insomnia
W. M. Bossen
Sleep, sweet sleep, dear angel of rest
Who takes me on her ample breast.
She smoothes the worries from my brow
And softly whispers, "Rest dear, now."

Tonight my angel is not here,
To me the reason is not clear.
My mind's at ease, I'm in no pain,
My bed is warm, I wait in vain.

I close my eyes, the day's been long,
And now the night is going wrong.
So maybe I should read my book,
At the clock take another look.

I'm sure that she is somewhere near,
I felt her wingtip brush my ear,
I tried to clutch her floating gown
But she had flown like thistledown.

Perhaps if I with patience wait
She'll come, but oh, she is so late!
Within my heart I know she's gone,
My bedside clock ticks on and on.

The Memory
Alisa M. Turner
Sparkling eyes, a sudden laughter,
tender memories of a friend long gone.
Now, Rik rests his head upon the Earth.
A youth to fame and fortune unknown.
For living too precious, he was called to
go: he gained from Heaven a friend.
No one seeks his merits to disclose
nor draw his frailties from his happy
home. Contented now and peaceful
always, he lies on the bosom of his
father and mother: his God above.

The Loving Years
Lorraine K. Lines
The time goes by so very fast
and age begins to tell,
yes, it's fifty years ago
you caught me in your spell.

Across the room I saw you there
almost at once I fell,
love grew between us
as you were caught as well.

We were joined in wedded bliss
together we did dwell,
some things went wrong
but love would still excel.

We're still together even now
aren't things going swell,
I'm glad you loved me then
and happy so to tell.

We grow older each new year
our love is lasting well,
naught can part us ever
excepting death's own bell.

Pensive
Gordon MacDiarmid
Sitting, watching, rain creating patterns on the window
filtered light
Pensive, contemplating, missing you
It's only for one night.

Selfish, jealous, thoughtless, these emotions
Are they love?
Tender, warm, soft, like a virgin
Like a dove.

Tense, worried, anxious, losing you
I could not face
Smiling, laughing, twinkling, eyes aglow
I see your face.

Thinking, remembering, our bodies meeting
Gentle arms entwine
Feeling, wanting, needing, so in love
Praying you'll be mine.

Confident, assured, secure, facing together
Come what may
Loving, caring, growing, with each other
From today.

I Wonder
Roger Lemos
Sometimes I wonder
Where she is?
How she is?
What she is doing?
Who she is kissing?
And when will she change?
Then I stare out across
Time and space
And I see that
When I wonder
I sometimes miss her

Journey's End
Julie H. Wright
Long ago, I loved you so,
You were part of me,
Deep inside of me,

Long ago, many moons ago,
Our hearts were but one,
And then you were gone.

Through my tears, I cried for you,
My heart called out "Please Hear Me".
My soul hurts so, it just won't let go,
To the memory, will this journey end,
Cause I love you now,
As I loved you then,
And I've waited for an eternity.

Come to me, please find me,
Just rescue me, from torment.
My journey ends,
When I find you,
My journey ends,
When I've found you.

Dedication: to Angel Face – I love you

Storm By Music
Masir Ahmed
My short visit to club I find
Thrilling notes of mystic mind
Playing trumpet–Terry Sue
Diane Johnsons–Light and Blue.

Breaks a darkness, dashing sight
Where I go in stormy night
Fear of lightning, slashing bind
Clouds of terror roving grind.

Falling tree leaves forming crowd
Look–out, roots all upright proud.
True path yet be seen paths go
Heavier kind of thunder blow!

Music thoughtful, rhythm clear
whiten dreadful night of fear!
Lose I home for searching one
Midst of whirlwind tracing none.

Tumbling–rolling Earth is mine
Has but queried tones divine;
Brings a past for now to flow
Feeling fruitful future glow.

Untitled
Brandon Subia
We used to be like Romeo and Juliet
So many days together we had spent
Caressed in each other's arms
How I longed to carry on
This love until our death

And yet now we seem so far apart
I wish thy soul
Was in thou heart
So we could be together
And never part

Quiet Invocations
Thomas Beechey
When silence surrounds and you're in its midst,
There still exists sounds that are hard to resist,
For the effects are sensed deeply within,
Beyond what is dealt, time and again.

There's an aura that reaches past the boundaries set,
And spans the breaches of each doubt and debt,
And brings into focus what has always eluded,
The passions which woke us from slumbers deluded.

Now fully aroused, we may pick of these fruits,
Which are no longer housed within the mind's roots,
As we revel unhindered, time doesn't concern us,
As the flames are tindered within the soul's furnace.

Expectations are equaled and surpassed by a margin,
This Moment shan't be sequelled for all that we have been,
Heightened and lengthened to exceed the extreme,
Structured and strengthened to withstand the dream.

The dream which evolved from a Moment so gifted,
When inhibitions were lowered and barriers were lifted,
Created by the lyrical tones of a psalm,
Interwoven amongst the presence of calm.

Enchanted Dreams

A Shadow
Theresa Kollefrath
A shadow—
What I once was many years ago—

Has drifted like a chaff of grain.

A vision—

What I could have been during that time—

Haunts me—the ghost of broken dreams.

A reflection—

A shell of a human, devoid of love;

Existing in the present, yet not alive.

I sweep up the bits of myself,

And cast them into the wind;

For they will wander as aimlessly

As my dreams have been.

Broken Home
Jessie Myers
A Mother and Daughter
sit and sigh.
For the daughter has to say
Goodbye.
The mother weeps.
The daughter cries.
They look each other in the eyes
They say, "I Love You"
They say, "Farewell"
What comes next?
I cannot tell.

A Walk In The Sunshine
Roger G. Harbidge
Little Tommy Duffy from Newry's only ten
"Can we go out Mummy, can we go, when?"
Since the devil's trouble came to old Erin's lair
Tommy stays home now, he's much safer there.

"Of course, my little son, go fetch your coat"
Whilst through the lace curtains Mummy's eyes check it out.
It's no game for the parents of foxes chase hare
Tommy stays home now, he's much safer there.

Out into the sunshine, Tommy walks with his Ma
At the side of the road, men in green check a car
A crack from a rifle cuts through the air
Tommy should have stayed at home, he was much safer there.

The green men all scatter hugging the ground
Whilst faceless ones melt away, no scent for the hound
Why now Tommy's so still, "doesn't anyone care?!"
He should have stayed home, he was much safer there.

Tommy's Mummy is screaming, accusing, denying
Whilst there on the ground little Tommy is dying
Does no one know why, for what and for where
Little Tommy's safely home now, the Angels are there.

In Memoriam: Tiger
Diane Dee
To you again I'll come, Tygrene
When evening draws nigh
When devilish moon glistens again
And stars prance on high.

Home again I'll come, Tygrene,
My heart's so lonely, too,
No more a wanderer will I be
On distant seas so blue!

Across the shores to sunny Spain,
Or near warm waters of Aberdeen,
None live who may compare
Witty yellow–eyed Tygrene!

O! Yonder down by southern seas,
Under velvet Tahitian skies.
Nothing glows as fair, as pure.
As the gleam in Tygrene's eyes!

No more a–roving will I go,
For all the lassies I have seen,
None are more faithful than
My yellow–eyed Tygrene:

A Christmas Poem
Dora Jackson
It's Christmas, the time we celebrate when Jesus came,
And the Spirit of the Lord surely reigns
We are blessed to be here
And have Jesus which we hold so dear
God's word is more true every day,
Which is more reason to praise Him in every way.
The gift of Jesus is more wonderful than words can express,
and His word provides the armour in which we dress.
Who would have guessed so much could come from one small baby,
He gives us salvation and eternal life and that's not just a "maybe".
With more reason to praise Him, Let's never let His light grow dim.

The Earth To Come
Debra A. Blesing
The Earth has been transformed into a beautiful place
Crystal–blue oceans that nestle around the Earth
Colorful trees and grass so beautiful to smell and see
It's all the things yet to be

As I stand upon the shore
Two colorful birds fly down from the Lord
Their colors are mauve and teal
And I know that they are so very real

I never saw such wondrous colors on birds before
For I knew they were created by the Lord
There's new animals being born unto the Earth
Look how they're discovered at the time of their birth

The sky is so violet blue
As the clouds seem to pass me by, I cry
I see beautiful streams flowing
And realize what God is showing

I look at others and I am amazed
Some people look like they're living in a haze
Now that the Earth has been made new
Let's stand united, together and stay so true

The Anthology of Poems

Soldier In Blue
Ann L. Howell
Viewing with awe the construction of justice before my eyes
Expressive of emotions deep within the heart
Staring at the immense pain that lines his grin
The shift of mystery now begins

Weighed down by the tools of the night
He travels with hope and compassion for his fellow man
Deep concern for the growing of crime
Wondering what he can do to help make this world right

Crying inside for this man of many fates
Hoping for a better life for his family
Struggling against all odds
Never giving up and strongly believing in God

Appalled by the actions of some in the human race
He longs to return to his castle of love
The slain, the child victims and all the waste
Heartache and trouble tonight he will again face

Always reaching for a better way
This wondrous man wants to help guide all through the maze
A shield of silver, strong and steadfast
A love of a lifetime that will forever last

Point Of View
Martha D. Bass
When I awoke I heard the rain drumming on my roof
And I thought, "How nice.
Now my grass can wear a dress of jade
And my roses' crimson robes will have a brighter hue."
The ducks were splashing in the puddles
That the rain had made.
"Oh, what a lovely day," I said.
Some have to see the sun in order to enjoy a day
But I love the rain-draped clouds
Of this which others call
A dreary day.

Searching For Serenity
Kerri Lynn Verstraete
I yearn to feel the love, happiness and security I once knew.
CRR — Date Unknown

For so long I have yearned to feel the love, happiness and
security I have never known.

I think I am beginning to feel it now. An unexplainable
feeling —— too glorious —— to describe with mere words.

Feelings that do not compare to any other I have felt before
this time. Feelings so sweet and pure that it is hard to
imagine how they can possibly exist outside of my dreams.

I feel as if I know everything about you, yet there is so
much I have left to uncover. Somehow I feel as if I have
known you all of my life and before.

Since that fateful day when you strolled into my present, I
have felt as if you have been with me through my past and I
know that you will be with me in my future.
KLV — 9/25/95

Two souls – separate paths. Two souls – reunited to become one.
This intense union will end their – – Search For Serenity.

Dawn
Leslie Redd–Preston
Feel the joy of sweet victory
as the day shines with newness,
the past fades as starlight
into the dawning of day.

The present, rich with promise,
pulses the air with excitement,
the aroma of life
fills the senses to bursting.

Hear the lark calling
in the morning mist,
see the light sparkle
on the dew's fading glory.

The sun warms the face
in a gentle embrace,
the wind whispers softly
through the leaves of trees.

I stand in awe of the beauty
that creation provides,
as the light streaks the sky
trumpeting the newborn day.

Out Of The Cocoon
Susan Fila Murphy
I have been united with this solidity
for ten–thousand years, or that's how long
it has seemed. My crushed–velvet clippings
have been growing inside this creamy shell
and are ready to expand. I have never known
what it was to have them. Will I still be me?
I have never had beauty in others' eyes before.
Will I be too different? A change like no other
is happening to me. I'm frightened more
than I have ever been, yet
I love what I will become.

A Deadly Guilty Past
Cicily Traudt
Guilt is a terror that evolves in the mind.

Everyone's feet drag their pain with them
to roll over the dusty footsteps of the past.

The tight metal chains restrain and trap the shame.
The ankles swell with time and
the prisoner groans shallow screams of regret.

The gray circle of guilt is disabling
and the walk becomes an awkward, torturous shuffle.

As time ticks,
the ball enlarges slowly.
It is unable to be ignored.

The scared feet can no longer be persecuted by
the constant weight of the enormously thick, gray circumference.

The prisoner is remorseful about the past
but wants loose from the gripping pain.
The prisoner is unable to bear dragging the amount any longer.

The unshackled person falls exhausted to their death.

Enchanted Dreams

Untitled
Markeeta Robinson
My tears flow like a river
Reaching far beyond the bend
Of what was once true happiness
Having no definite beginning or end

Barely bobbing above the sorrow
Trying not to be weighed down by my aching heart
Drifting off toward the Sea of Anguish
I see my journey into loneliness is about to start

There are images reaching out to me
Seemingly trapped in the forest of the distant tree
My cries of despair, like those of a caged creature
Only echo hopelessly; there's no one to help me

I look ahead in a state of sadness
With a stare, so very empty and cold
Until I spy my help, a mighty Rock
That will bring me out, if I only grab hold

Now in the arc of safety
I feel, on my face, the warm rays of the Son
Comforting me, letting me know it's alright
Because my new life with, the Lord has just begun

Endless Nights
Brodi Petitt
Funny laughs are far away,
teary eyes are here to stay.
Pain awakens me day and night,
No one's there to turn out the light.
Endless relationships broken through,
love and hate what will they do?
Triumphs are beaten,
phenomenon's past, endless relationships last.
Forget me, forget you.
Lovers one lonely, deja vu nights are here from the past,
pierce through my flesh, pain will not last.

Just A Thought
Roger Daniels
"I haven't won the lottery",
"I haven't won the pools",
The most common words on a Monday,
Whispered by life's sad fools.

All the money in the world,
All the things that are known as wealth,
Mean nothing at that crucial time,
When a person loses their health.

"I'd give anything to get my health back",
They cry when it's far too late,
After years of craving money,
It's their health that becomes their fate.

When ill health begins to get a grip,
And they worry how long they've got,
All the money in their bank that day,
Just doesn't mean a lot.

They should be glad to get up in the morning,
And feel happy to see the sun,
To live every day as if it were their last,
And they'd feel life had just begun.

Bird House In My Tree
Betty L. Echols
I put a bird house in my tree,
To feed these birds so I can see.
Happiness I bring to them each day,
As they hop on limbs, then fly away.

God's little creatures, safe and warm,
Keep the birds from Earthly harm.
A shelter from the storm, too, will be,
In the trunk of the old magnolia tree.

In the spring they come, two by two,
Cute as a button in all they do.
They flit and all day they do play,
Come to eat their seeds and fly away.

They cannot thank me but it stirs my heart,
To know for these little fellows, I do my part.
It makes me happy just to see,
These little birds so dependent on me.

When at dusk, in the stillness, I will know,
My loving and feeding helps them to grow.
In the morning they show their love to me,
By returning to the bird house in my tree.

Faces
M. E. Webb
Haunting, empty eyes
They stare at us
From faces so twisted and sad
They hunger for love, just as we
The very lucky members of society
They are the accidents of our race
The pain and frustration show in their face
And so we reach out
To touch and to share
Their joys and their sadness
And show that we care

I Hope To Get It Back Someday
Dianne R. Swann
I once had a love
And it was wonderful
I was blissfully ignorant
Frighteningly naive

I thought the feelings I had
Were returned in full
I misread every action
Every lie I believed

It was good there
In the shadow of love's glow
I was under a misconception
I was sorely deceived

My days had never been better
As the days when I was a fool
I basked in that wonderful illusion
I hated to leave

I'll never forget that feeling
And I may never feel it again
I hoped to get it back one day
It is the stuff of which dreams are woven

Untitled
Joyce C. Greenacre

O Planet Earth how comes it that beneath such grace
Of forest, flower and field
There lurks such loveless lust for conflict and control
Of all that Thou dost freely yield?

How Planet Earth? Can cruelty and selfish greed
Cause such calamitous effect on body, mind and soul
Of shattered bodies, broken hopes and young lives ended
Torn apart before they've yet begun to live.

Why Planet Earth? Do forests cover and conceal
Animals that in fear from each other flee
And creatures prey upon their weaker fellows
That they themselves might live their life–span full and free

When Planet Earth? O Planet Earth will come the time
All living creatures and mankind exist in harmony
And freedom from all pain and hurt
And endless woe.

I cannot tell, O Planet Earth, suffice to take
What life may bring of sunshine or of rain
And breathe it back. And breathe it back in Prayer.
And hope again.

A Ray Of Light
James Carter

With dignity and inner strength
you philosophically accepted the end.
Fondest memories I'll treasure forever,
from a cousin to a friend.

Final good–byes have been said,
these sentiments are so true.
Your spirit lives inside my soul,
always I'll remember you.

Dedication: in memory of John Watson

A Journey By An Infantry Soldier, 1939–1945
F. C. Hawkins

We bade farewell and left our home
On a long sea voyage to Sierra Leone
The native boats brought many a face
To see their friends of a different race.

From here we sailed to Durban
Four leave days we will not forget
Then made our way to Egypt
Where Germans we first met.

We went across to Italy
But not to swim or laze
We had a job of work to do
This lasted for many days.

The mountains of Cassino
The rain, the mud and snow
It's something we will not forget
But still we had the foe.

Everyone was very pleased
As the Hun began to retire
The we'd return to the land we love
And our families round the fire.

A Struggle
Douglas Storey

I wish to jump into
The cold river.
And this cold water
Babbles its icy song
Whose words will caress
Me with numbness.
On the bridge that crosses
The river that passes
The church
Where the dead lie frozen
In their graves.

Dolce Evita
Shirley Bailey

Eva Maria, oh, Dolce Evita, descamisado of Argentina
Father Juan Duarte's, non–dulcet, funeral rings in your ear today
And Estela Grizolia, wife of Duarte, pushes your last respects away
Walking behind her legitimate children, you vow to triumph one day
Discontent in your heart, you are ready to start, Buenos Aires, beware!
Hungry for food and for love, you can graft and you act and your picture's all over the city
Earthquakes and coups, they are lucky for you, what a pity!
When you meet Juan Peron, you want to help him get on and he knows
That you are his strength and the hero of all descamisados
You will be the first lady of Argentina when the President wins
You speak, the crowd cheers, the middle classes still shout out your sins
But soon you are ill and the end of your brightness begins
Now it's your turn to die, it is eight–twenty–five, oh, Evita
Eva Maria, Dolce Evita, Spiritual Leader of Argentina,
Look at you now, see how your country is mourning for you,
Eva, Maria,
Oh, Dolce Evita,
Non–dulcet funeral, ringing
Through Argentina!

The Golden Touch Of A Chariot Princess
Georgette M. Reardon

Windsongs of sorrow
Streamlines of tears
Complete devastation
from the world's– dismal eyes.

Strong blend of emotions
A scent of roses
A token, A kiss,
Farewell, Goodbye
To our lovely, beloved Di.

Embossed in hearts of young and old,
Remains a golden Quondam Princess,
Ten–folds a ravishing–monarch's Princess.
Innate talent in charming the world
By pouring out your love and beauty.
Indeed you were
You'll always be our "Shining Star".

Heartfelt of milestone memories
Perpetually remember and honor
All that you have given to the world today.
Thank you for the inspiration you had become.

Enchanted Dreams

Adoption (A Quiet Storm)
Christina Paulsen
A heavy tear lost upon the ground,
A twisting storm that makes no sound.
I feel the grayness of emotional drain
yet the brightness of life just the same.
I cry for the days that I will never know,
and sing of the chance for you to grow.

I say goodbye and kiss your tiny hand,
and hope that one day you'll understand,
that as you pass from one to the other,
you bind them, for they are your Mother.

Waiting For You...
Kathleen Gledhill
"Tomorrow," I'd say, to all who asked,
Not devoting much time to think,
To try to find the proper one,
Who has that special wink!

I'd smile, I'd flirt, I'm one to have fun,
But deep inside, I never won.
Why lead him on? Why bother, too?
When I knew I was waiting for you.

I knew there wasn't something right!
I'd quit, turn away, to jump in flight!
Kept waiting for a Mr. Who???
For I was waiting just for you!

You hiked into my lonesome heart,
I knew I finally found gold!
Hope we'll keep loving and never part,
Always, two hands we'll hold!
You asked me why I wasn't found,
Why single for so long!
The others just could not compare,
That is why I waited for you!

Soul Mate
Brad Deifer
Our precious love has endured,
the test of time. It has matured,
your beautiful smile, my universe whole.
A fate drawn, climactic, union of souls!

Different ways, paths and beliefs!
In spite of the difference, the middle we meet.
Admiration you deserve for your persistent ways,
headstrong, you help lead me through life's maze!

Sour Mate, please always shoot straight.
Our differences make us a unique Twist of Fate.
Celestial life when you are involved.
The simplest things all seem to revolve
around your beautiful sun–bright existence.
In this crazy life, my love for you a consistent

Fights and feuds and disagreements,
are all just a product of human existence!
Undeniable fact that we have endured,
enables my soul to be complete and secure!
Crazy and elegant, rebellious and clever,
with you I stand; Together Forever!

Stereotypes
Melissa Mirkovich
So what if I don't wear skirts.
That doesn't mean I'm not a girl, or
Even that I don't keep my legs closed. I'm a
Real person with feelings and
Emotions that can get hurt
Or broken. Sometimes, maybe even more
Than those imbecile robots, that believe
You can only be happy if you listen to
People's conforming ideas. Which all seem to be an
Explicit imitation of what once was an attempt, to break through the
Stereotypical impediments that control our lives today.

Christmas Past
Deb Reed
Memories from my many Christmas' past are pure and innocent.
All the simple gifts that were handmade or bought by the sweat of Dad's brow.
We five children believed in the ol' Santa Gent.
Momma and Dad, worried and weary, gave God a thankful bow!
We'd walk in the woods and chop the most perfect tree;
Cedar needles, cold hands and red noses;
We'd drag our fragrant little tree indoors for all to see.
Nothing could compare to our tree all aglow with an angel on top in her angelic pose.
We kids would look at our homespun–decorated cedar tree; too excited to go to sleep.
We would talk and giggle and keep Momma and Dad awake.
Our parents would tell us that these memories would keep;
But just thinking about Santa was more than we could take!
We never knew what thought and love must have gone into each precious gift.
The girls' drink and wet dolls, brother's John Deere tractor, baby's rocky horse and
Momma and Dad's simple child–made treasures.
Each eagerly–awaited Christmas dawn, we'd all awake with a festive lift.
And oh! Those simple gifts and memories from my Christmas past, bring me the most heartfelt pleasures.

The Punk Vicar
Rebecca Yaltiligil
The first time we met him, came face to face
Our shock was tremendous, as we quickly embraced
We covered our tracks and acted polite
Plastered smiles where they should be, our faces felt tight

My daughter had explained, he's different, Mum,
But she forgot to mention, he looked like a bum
He had five rings in his ear and a hoop through his nose
And a tattoo on his arm, of a girl minus clothes
His nose was connected by a chain to his lip
And his clothes, I'm sure, were out of a skip

We have known him a while now and I might add
He is better for knowing, a nice sort of lad
The lesson he's taught us, is not to judge at first glance
Be open–minded, give people a chance

It happened for real, what I'm just about to say
Last Sunday, at St. Mary's, on a fine, sunny day
We go to church sometimes, not as much as is fitting
I find it quite soothing to listen whilst knitting
Imagine our horror, oh, where will it end
For up in the pulpit was our daughter's boyfriend

Forever In Love
Andrew Wilds

My heart is and was,
Yours was and will be,
Forever we are one,
As I hope you can see,
Not alone like once we were,
But happy as we both should,
Love is ours and always will,
Our love stronger than steel or wood,
We know not where we're going,
But always we know we are together,
Forever, as one

She Won
Linda Barnett

She won hands down, there was never a chance
if She'd had softer flesh, if She knew how to dance
I could see it...

you let Her, capture your essence
advance and retreat, no longer was sweet but compelled.
I can't stop it...

you kept Her hold, a secret from me, denied to yourself
the lies and the threats, the grief and the bets
it never ended... you couldn't let it

She feigned love with a swirling regret but made you forget
And that's what you needed, not owning yourself
nor loving the world you protect

if She'd had lovely hair or a mist in Her eyes,
a kind disposition or sweet, juicy thighs
I would of kept fighting to be by your side

but She sucked you dry from the inside out,
you open the Bottle—you open Your Mouth, to become someone Numb
I can't wait anymore till you're, done, she won.

Insanity Is Sane
George A. Tutko

Time escaping the bonds of reality
Lost, but not forgotten
who's to say, we lost our way
in a time of obscenity
realms of existence
thoughts out of control
we've taken it upon ourselves
to be banished to a black hole

filled beyond capacity
swallowed by the night
we stood, horrified
disbelief amazed our sight

creatures summoned from the deep
awaken and stir
surface to do battle
in hope of a cure

Silence penetrated by evil
broken loose on humanity
brought forth by the devil
no end to this insanity.

Tides Of Time
Dana D. Byerley

Waves of changes erode away unneeded excess from an
unshaped block of life.
As I age, I am constantly surprised with the openings of personality,
joys and sorrows, likes and dislikes, exposed by the ever-constant
tides of time.
Various openings appear, like caves to be explored, some shallow,
only to fill and firm over, others vast and never-ending.
People come and go, carried with these tides, making subtle or even
Drastic changes... but always changes.
Even memory is not safe from the tides. Ever-fading, giving way to these
endless waves, relentless, eternal tides of time.

Silent Presence
Cherrin Tessitore Freeman

A SILENT PRESENCE in my life, there has always been, it's true.
It gave "inspiration", a "compliment" a word of "encouragement",
Too, was always sent to me from you, a feeling of "worth" when
others failed me, a promise of "hope" when no others hailed me, a
reason to thank God

I was born when others succeeded in making me wish I hadn't been.

A SILENT PRESENCE in my life has made me part of what I am,
"a good mother" I've been told, a "caring sister" to behold; a "devoted
Wife, strong, brave and bold", it's true, all this I know, for my
PRESENCE
told me so.

The SILENT PRESENCE, the loving words, came from a man that
was seldom heard, but in my mind and in my heart rang the words that
kept me close, though miles kept us a part. My Silent Presence saw the
best in me, when others saw the worst, lifted me up when others put me
down, my Silent Presence was my strength and I wore him like a crown.

The SILENT PRESENCE was a man I seldom saw but always loved,
the Silent Presence I know was sent by God from up above, that Silent
Presence "was you... ".

America, Home Sweet Home
Claudia Kowkabany

A – America, Home Sweet Home
M – Motherland of our hearts
E – Eager to try our best
R – Respect yourself and others
I – Imagine the imaginable
C – Create your goals
A – Acclaim what is given to you

H – Humble thyself
O – Organize your priorities
M – My prayers for God to hear
E – Electrify our knowledge

S – Sharing with your loved-ones
W – Wonderful world to grow in
E – Extraordinary dedication towards life
E – Express our inner thoughts
T – Thank you, God Almighty, for this unique land we live in

H – Heart is where love is
O – Observe the beauty of this great nation
M – Moving with the times
E – Expect the unexpected

Enchanted Dreams

Knowing
Nicholoas L. Schnittker
Your face is looking back at me
But you I do not know
I think I've seen you once before
But you I do not know
It must have been or was it when
Oh, I do not know
I remember but oh, so long ago
Your face has changed and you've
Also grown
But who you are, I do not know
You've changed so much since then

Untitled
Rick Keller, Jr.
With tears in my eyes, I look at you and wonder why
You walked with me and talked with me when it was all a lie
Memories flood my mind, images of the past
You were there for me, you loved me, you were more than I could ask

Like a knife piercing through my skin
Do you really think I'll come back again?
You slice through my flesh, straight into my heart
You poison me from inside, like a poison dart
All the time you put into it, with just a little thrust
You destroyed our relationship and shattered all my trust

You're like a fire, you draw me to your light
Your words are smoking, you are real in my sight
But as I draw near, the warmth I should feel
The warmth of the fire, none of it is real

Like a knife piercing through my skin
Do you really think I'll come back again?
You slice through my flesh, straight into my heart
You poison me from inside, like a poison dart
All the time you put into it, with just a little thrust
You destroyed our relationship and shattered all my trust

Hope
Pope F. Brock, Jr.
The breath of frost is everywhere
Amid the falling leaves,
Twigs and roots lie still,
Nature takes her course
Man, in his bones, knows the
Twilight of his years.
He sits in the shade of the
Coming night.

Black Trees against blue sky
Speak of that which used to be,
Of that which is yet to come.
The whistle of the train
Echoes down the valley of time;

Yet, ere man depart for another plane,
May he know the peace in the
Twilight of winter night,
The hope embedded in
The season of his years
Blessed by God's own light.

Dedication: to the Lord our God

Goodbye
Ron Morgan
The time had come
breathing shallow, pulse faint, then gone
the once-ruddy complexion gradually paled
then blue
As she held him tightly, ignoring the web of tubing and hoses
that had artificially sustained life just a little longer
the warmth faded into a bone-chilling coldness
that she knew was death
I can't bear to let him go

But you must.

Fore For Four
Joseph A. Parker
This golfer hits them distant
But low scores he finds quite resistant
He's the team's keeper of scores and scars
We raise our putters and wish him many pars
This senior member of the fearsome foursome
Finds misfired drives and chips loathsome
And driving alone in a golf cart lonesome
But his long putts truly have been awesome

Don't get out your fine linen hankies
For the guy who almost made the Yankees
He can still belt them out far, we know,
But they only go where the mushrooms grow

He dreams of flocks of birdies to record
And even a few soaring eagles to report
Alas, he's happy to hit them straight
And accepts that as his present fate

Then along came a chap from the west
Who gallantly tries to do his best
So his foursome proudly recalls
How he once parred the first three holes

One Day In The Future
Sota Kurylo
One day in the future, (to our dismay)
from a single cell (pinched off) of our
skin we will make a human.

Wanting or not, he will be the exact
replica of us.

He will be given the name, or the number,
distinguishing him from us.
But otherwise, he will be all the same
as we.

Once cloned from the cell, his head,
limbs and other parts of the body
will be in the right place.

He and we will look alike;
he will have our eyes, our voice,
our face.

The same as ours will be his soul,
cloned to feel and suffer the way
as does the whole human race.

The Poet's Hand
Joshua Gurley

To tame the thoughts that run
wild in a mind of creativity;
To paint its words of color
on a canvas of paper;
To draw pictures of thoughts
and feelings with words;
To let ink seem to breathe
with the colorful breath of life;
all in a desperate attempt
to explain the things that can
only be seen with the mind's eye.

Devoted Unto You
Anna M. Ruble

I have been asked to devote some words unto you
Such a task I am unsure I am able to do,
A color may be devoted unto you – the color sky blue,
This color is so bold and so true,
Yet is this color really you?

How about a flower dedicated unto your name,
The beauty of a rose so dark as midnight still smells the same
Yet, even such a rose can never be so tame,
Is it nature that keeps it alive with rays of light and drops of rain
Such as love keeps you alive with dreams of devotion with
disappointment of pain

One day you shall know what you want,
This day your feelings of joy shall not be distraught,
Like the color of the sky, you, too, shall change and the change will haunt

Yet don't let the haunting make your love grow weary,
Such as the rose which continues to grow darker and learly,
So you must continue your passage down your path, then you
shall see it isn't ceary.

Dedication: to Hemmer, my only love

Daddy
Diane M. Hubiak

I caught a glimpse of you last night
While in my peaceful sleep
You held my hand and walked with me
Across mountains very steep
You told me that you loved me and didn't want to leave
Your time on Earth was finished and that I shouldn't grieve
We spoke of all my heartaches, my fears and what to do
I kissed your cheek and told you, how much I miss you, too
You looked at me with soft, brown eyes and spoke in a gentle
tone
And said "no matter where you go, you'll never be alone"
You said you will watch over me and I will always know
Your guidance through our loving hearts, will forever flow
And with a hug you kissed me and said you had to go
But your heart is always with me and this I'll always know
"Think of your past and future, let memories lead the way"
"Your inner strength and wisdom will get you through each day"
I wish you were still here with us to visit every day
To hold my hand and talk with me when stress gets in my way
I guess I should be happy, we had you for so long
To know you're watching over me will always keep me strong

Dedication: in memory of Earl Walker

Find My Cat
Raianne A. Raymond

Find this, find that, Find my kitty–cat.
She might be lost. She might have run away.
Find her quick. Because the sky is turning gray.
If it starts to rain, she will get all wet.
I loved her since the day we met.
If you can't find her, I will cry.
It makes me feel like she will die.
If you bring her home by the end of the day,
my sky won't be gray.
Her name is Honey. She acts real funny.
She is home at last and sitting on my lap!

A Piece On Truth
Suzy R. Custodio

Living in a world of shadows and foes, where time seems to
pass between lies and masks. Shakespeare once said "life was
like a play and we were all actors who were playing certain roles"
Tis a saying worth considering, because it plays into a reality
no one seems to admit to, or succumb to its rotten wrath.
I mean no harm or any dishonesty, because I am merely living
out a recollection of past episodes I have had a role in. I have
now removed my mask and my costume and it is now that I
am at ease with my inner self. It is at this point in my life that
I can truthfully look at myself in the mirror, without wondering
who I am actually looking at. Is it not ironic how no one will
lay down their own mask and truthfully act out their virgin self?
a self that has not yet donned a fake personality and can be
who they want to be? I can no longer keep playing the fool,
because I would rather play the master of honesty...
Tis a play that shall go on throughout time and people will
solemnly keep on putting on their make–up and costumes. They
will do so without being their true selves. 'Tis a sad, but unfortunately
shameful existence one must go along with. To do so is to survive,
and to survive is to live. Let the curtain rise... and the show must
   go on.

Dedication: to my soulmate, my husband Paul

On the Day after Beautiful Weather...
W. W. Fardels Bear

On the day after beautiful weather...
My daughters share colds with each other
The cats in the house look for each catnip mouse
And the dogs will have mud in their "feathers."
On the day after beautiful weather...

On the day after beautiful weather...
While we sniffle at supper together
And having our say at the end of the day
We certainly can't help but wonder,
On the day after beautiful weather...

On the day after beautiful weather...
Suffering students take exams together.
The lecture hall is cold and the teacher is old
But the test's as impossible as ever.
On the day after beautiful weather...

On the day after beautiful weather...
Could someone tell me what's the matter?
The animals are drained; the kids are insane
And we act like we all hate each other.
On the day after beautiful weather

Enchanted Dreams

My Pet Rooster
Mary Jane Dooley
I and my pet rooster,
He was Rhode Island Red,
Would talk and play,
In the hot California sun,

I was but four or five—
Such a wonderful age,

Full of imagination and fun—
He always listened,
My friend "the rooster".

Lyric (17)
R. L. Sharpe
The moon doth wax and wane,
All things by time are slain,
The stars grow dim, the sun doth set —
Beauty and age the soonest met —
Yet not my love for thee.

The night succeeds the day,
The hours do haste away,
The song of birds, the Summer airs
Bring pain in joy and sharp despairs —
Yet not my love for thee.

This life has one brief Spring,
Our birth one youth doth bring,
The flowers die, the leaves do fall,
The globe of Earth absorbeth all —
Yet not my love for thee.

All things must change or die,
As soon wilt thou and I,
Dear eyes grow dim, loved voice fall dumb,
And life itself complete its sum —
Yet not my love for thee!

The Burial
Aeron Ives
Huddled in a mass of darkness,
Tears falling like a rain sorrowful,
The sun blinded behind ebony clouds,
Trees swaying in a wind furious,
And a grass damp of lamenting,
Whilst a fog crawls upon us quickly,
We bow our heads and clasp our hands,
Wipe the tears from our eyes, cheeks,
And turn our gaze Heavenward,
Seeking answers, solutions, truths...

Oh, how red it bleeds freely now,
Streaming in unison with the sorrow,
Lying wounded and dying in coffin,
Beaten harder than destiny or hope,
Taken from it red love, life, blood,
The promise of all that was to come;
Surrounded by dirt, dust of the Earth,
Whenceforth came all living things,
It is now bruised, beaten, bleeding,
And broken.

Dedication: to Adelaida, la mujer mas bonita

Campaigns
Denyse Jensen
Pretty people with pretty lives.
Vague causes and vacant eyes.
Looking for the one thing that puts them above
The cruel inspection of a very white glove.
Charity balls; charity's divine.
I'll give and give —
Just stay away from that, that is mine.
A new world order, a new leader to choose —
The politicians weeping their political boo–hoos.
They take and take the money you make —
You pay and pay, it's still the American way.

March Equinox
Martine Makower
Each spring it happens to the backyard trellis:
a cloud of white wisteria blossoms
interlace themselves on the slatted spine,
coaxed by the season's first warm days.
With blooming, buzzing,
thrashing and whispers,
all lifeforms respond to changes
that the equinox ushers in.

Like the greeting of old friends
after lengthy separation,
intense sun in early spring recalls
sensations that winter all but obscured.

Those who pause at the wisteria
find simplicity
and thrilling intricacy;
seasonal invitation to both let go and take hold.

Intertwining wisteria and trellis,
like the mixing of lives through years
of greetings and separations,
make visual the intimacy of reunion.

Brooke's Garden
Carla Yancey
In the ground at the start, a sign will say, Brooke's Garden this way!
The path is a simple and beautiful path.
We walk on pebbles made of fallen tears that have been shed over the years.
A white butterfly, its significance known by few, flutters above us in a sky of pure blue.
Follow me! Follow me!
Flowers are blooming and the trees are all shades of green,
All around us, signs of life can be seen.
Look! Smell! Feel! Breathe!
Ahead is our special place, in a wide open space.
There is a tiny yard, with all sorts of animals standing guard.
Colors and smells are present in everything, everywhere, the grass, the birds, the air.
I see a bench. One that has been used much.
It's waiting to be needed again for resting, thinking and such.
"All are welcome! Talk loud, laugh or cry," it says on a note nearby.
A gentle and loving purpose to everything here,
Things like; true love, forgiveness and acceptance are all now clear.

Put your bad thoughts away and Thank God for every day!
... and remember,
in Brooke's garden— You can say "hi" but you never have to say good–bye!

Love
Vickie Lynn Walker
A word with so many different meanings.
It represents feelings, dreams and hope.
It is something, a person will fight for,
die for.
Is it just a word, or is it more?
Does it blossom from within?
Questions of no answers, just a feeling
of something wonderful
A word with so many different meanings
What is the word you may ask?
The word is Love.

Hannah And Mam Mam
Dolly Dowker
Hannah had a bad day, you see
Teacher said, "you broke the rules".
Time out will come two times for me,
Once at home and once at school.
So if things don't go my way
Just call my Mam Mam,
She'll take me for the day

Safe at last in Mam Mam's arms
Nothing can hurt me,
I'm free from harm

Not many rules I have to follow
Please be good and don't mis-behave,
And go to the potty, my rear I'll save!
Mam Mam will play with me, I know
Although sometimes she is slow
We laugh, cuddle and kiss often
She holds me tight and says "I'm rotten"
Mam Mam thinks she's in control
But—— I just think, she's getting old.

Dedication: to my husband, Bob, for his support, encouragement, and love

---

The Day
Kenneth Brown
As I'm awakened from my bed,
As I walk outside my home,
I'm faced with the challenges of the day.
The day could be interesting,
but it's hard to determine that
so early in time.
Why am I so intrigued by this day?
Is there something special I perceive in this day?
Would this day be like no other?
Or would this day be like any other?
I don't know.
I never know where this day would take me.
I should pursue this day
and make the most out of it
to have a happy day.
I shouldn't be discouraged if this day doesn't turn out right.
There's always another day.
However, I want this day to be special.
Because there's something about this day that seems different
from the past days.
If I approach this day with confidence and endurance,
who knows,
probably this day will last forever.

Your Love
Natalie Lebron
I'm on top of the world, I'm as happy as can be,
All because God sent you to me;

My love for you I cannot hide,
I feel like a queen when I'm at your side;

Each day that passes is so filled with joy,
I feel like a child with a brand-new toy;

The love that you give me means much more than things,
Like our house and car and my diamond ring;

You give so much more, you give me yourself,
And that I will cherish much more than wealth;

I couldn't love you more at this Moment and time,
I couldn't love you less if you had only a dime;

Our love has grown with each passing day,
Our love is real, so I know our love will stay;

I promise to love you till death do us part,
I give you my love, my soul and my heart.

The Eyes of a Mother
Whitney Durham
A mother of her word
can be told by her eyes.

A gleaming word can come
swiftly by.
Seeing a faithful look
that is so lovingly,
carefully, cheerful;
to her children.

Dedication: to mothers everywhere

Kristi and Corey
Stephen Brown
Here I am, watching my girl and boy
God, how much they have grown
It's a shame that it has been that long

She's my little Krisi Lee
In her eyes I can always see
The love that she has especially for me

And there is Corey, my little boy
If he's not playing Nintendo, then he says he's bored
But we play ball or wrestling and he's always a joy
You ask and I say they're my Devils in Disguise
You say they look like angels and how can I lie
I just look back at you with a big, big smile

That's my "Bud" and my little "Huni"
We've had dogs, fish, birds and a little bunny
They think I'm stern and they think I'm funny

I guess what I'm really trying to say
I love you two in your own special ways
It makes me feel so special when I hear you say
"I love you and miss you, Dad"

Enchanted Dreams

Shed The Tears
Betty Callahan
Please, Mother, can I ask of you, the question about life.
The existence of our ancestors, the pain, the hurt, the strife?

Oh, why must you ask me now. We have our freedom, be glad.
To be able to walk down the street without the pain, the hurt, the sad.

But Mother, please let me know. Tell me of your pain.
I want to know the truth about being last to board the train.

I want to hear about the bus and the lady who kept her place.
I want to hear about the leaders, who constantly got spit in the face.

Oh, Dear Child, I cannot begin to tell you of my fears.
Please do not worry about the past, for I've already shed the tears.

I struggled and fought to live, in order to give you a place to stay.
Sometimes I went without food and prayed to live another day.

Do you want to hear, my child, about the segregation?
To be black in my day meant you were not part of the nation.

My child, my child, I want you to enjoy life and always have the best.
Don't trouble your mind with worry. Please put the past to rest.

Death
Kelly Huffman
I had too much to drink that night, I guess I took my birthday too far.
I think I drank enough for my whole lifetime, but that's another story.
My friends begged me not to drive, but I did not listen
(I guess that comes with the alcohol) but that night I thought it would
be cool to play chicken with this car. I guess they won, because the
next thing I knew, I saw a wreck that I knew the person
could not have survived. I went over to see if I could help,
then I looked at the person and it was me. For the next couple of days
I tried to tell people I was not gone, but they just kept crying. I felt
bad, but I guess I'd better go after the light that keeps calling me.
I am kinda scared but what else can I do, well, here goes nothing...

Mom
Michael J. Cash
Every time we look your way,
You seem to really brighten our day
Knowing you're always here to stay,
And there are so many nice things we could say.

At the end of each day I look in the sky,
To ask God the question "why"?
Why He gave us the gift of you.
Because when were sad and blue,
We realize that's when your love is so true.

Day by day our love for you climbs,
And when I think back, I can remember many good times.

You're always trying to run and help us with things,
It's as if you had wings,
But even though you don't,
You still find a way to treat us like kings.

Even though we don't show it,
All four of us know it,
We can't make it without you.
We love you, Mom!.

The Scarf
Elizabeth Ann Raymond
Jewel–covered silk
stained by the watermarks
of the mythical Aegean

Dancing from her fingertips
sensually caressing the moonstone sky
Playfully wafts and waves
Turquoise crest and opal foam

Stretching far across azure Heavens
taut with aquamarine passion, if only
The scarf could carry her to her lover's arms

Stranded on the silent shore
sailing with sapphire longing
reeling with emerald wanderlust
Adorning Mediterranean memories

Jewel–drenched silk
Immersed in the watercolors
of the whimsical Aegean

Dedication: to my love, Kostas

Panther
Sarah Mendoker
Pacing; calm and composed
Uninhibited
Wearing black like a legacy
Eyes burn with yellow ambers.

I am the uninhibited panther.
Waiting.
Waiting.
For burning eyes to find a legacy
through the black.
Pacing; calm and composed.

A Love Letter From Jesus
Patricia Lynn Deaver
Dear Friend,
How are you today? I had to send you this letter to tell you how
I love and care for you. I saw you yesterday, as you were talking
with your friends. I waited all day, hoping you would talk with me
also. Evening drew near. I gave you a sunset to close your day and
a cool breeze to rest you and I waited. You never came, oh, yes, it
hurt me, but I still love you, because I am your friend! I saw you
fall asleep last night and I longed to touch your brow. So I spilled
moonlight on your pillow and face. Again, I waited, wanting to rush
down so we could talk. I have so many gifts for you. You awakened and
rushed off to start your day... My tears were in the rain. You
looked so sad... so alone. It makes my heart ache, because I
understand. My friends have let me down and hurt me, too, but still
I loved them! I try to tell you in the green grass, I whisper it in
the color of flowers. I shout it in the mountain streams, I give the
birds a love song to sing. I bathe you in sunshine and I perfume the
air. My love for you is deeper that the ocean. We will spend eternity
together in Heaven! I know how hard Earth is (I've been there, too).
I want to help you, my father does, too. Just call on me, ask me,
talk to me. It is your decision. I have chosen you and because of
this, I will wait... Because I love You!!!

Your Friend, Jesus

The Anthology of Poems

Untitled
Michael J. Chaplick
I'm gonna color the world with my crayon!
My canvas is talking, moving, walking!
Peel the paper back and see my mystique!
Beneath the sheet lies another technique!

Got my crayon in my hand
Teacher says "look like contraband"
Teacher wants to guide
Wiggle, jiggle, slide...
Crayola
All ov' ya
Wanta hol' ya
Smell ya

Red, white and blue
Smell of dew
Can't put it down
More than 'nough to go 'round

Purple, pink and pearl
Whirl
What a crayon
In my hand!

Home
Lester M. Hulick
Gables green have
turned to blue

Moon–brushed porch and
Garden's hue

Strength of home and
quiet peace

In darkness reign
all troubles cease

Creation
Caitlin Frazier
In the beginning, God made
the trees, the flowers and
the seas,

He made the birds, He made
the sky, all for you and me.

God made you and me, to preach
His word; for every word should
be heard.

We came here to sing His praise:
and He came to us as help for
these mind–twisting life mazes!

He made poets, writers, artists
and all, He made dancers and
helps them up when they fall.

So He helps us and we help Him
And we must always remember...

God comes before men.

My Father
Wanda S. Tobola
It's a hot springtime afternoon, in deep south Texas.
The bluebonnets are in bloom and the cactus are in flower,
spreading their lovely fragrance.
I pull off the road to take a walk in a shady tree–laden
park. Everywhere I stroll, I see greenery and color. The
scent is magnificent. I notice many prairie dogs popping
their heads out of the ground as I walk past their hole.
These cute, little, furry squirrel–like creatures, scamper
across the grass towards a tree and soon disappear from view.
I think back to my father's home in central Texas. His home
was lovely. He had Ducks, Goats, lots of trees and shade galore.
He spent his time fixing up his place for retirement. But a
stroke from God took him away far too early from us. I often
think of my father in the springtime working on his land,
and I smile because it was there that he was the happiest. He
lived in a mobile home in the hill country of central Texas.
He had a pond, fish and a old porch swing. He died while
working his field on a tractor. I miss him terribly and think
of him often in the springtime, when all the trees turn green.
Blossoms are everywhere, the wind is gently blowing, as a
butterfly lands on a branch nearby. I remember my Dad...

Dedication: to my father, John Thomas Hensley

Reflections
Marcia Benson
I see you sitting in the sun,
It was your favorite thing.
I see your face, your hurt, your pain,
I see your suffering.
I see your glow, your peaceful grin,
It was our last goodbye.
My heart is sad,
My memories glad,
For you shall never die...

Dedication: to my Nonny

Seasons With A Friend
Richard Parlin
I stand before a field full of
Nature's golden way, the sun at day's end,

A stream flows with silences as autumn
ages this troubled time without a friend,

We parted ways long ago, neither
knowing seasons change, days on end,

Remembering memories of spring
and summer shared together.

Our love was set free, as the unicorn
of love should be, to walk the miles anew

Years pass as do the seasons of the heart
Ever–changing to fit the part

Our days are once again as we stand apart
seeing seasons change with the heart

The time has come, once again, to
live the seasons with a friend.

Enchanted Dreams

Let Me Love You Today
Susanne Eaton
Today is here
Yesterday is gone
Tomorrow will be here
at the break of dawn

Memories are yesterday
Today is reality
Tomorrow is the dream
to which we hold the key

Yesterday made today
Today makes tomorrow
We become who we are
through both the joy and sorrow

Tomorrow is born as
Yesterday dies
Today we keep
throughout our lives

Tomorrow is unknown
Yesterday we once knew
Today... I love you.

This Is My Life
Elizabeth Penagos
A never-ending sadness, every day is a fight to enjoy life. It has been like this since I can remember, a struggle at times just to stay alive.

I have accepted this as a disease, since I have not found a cure. I do not believe in self-pity.

I only hope that I won't get so tired of this war in my head, that death will find me. My journey has no end, always seeking new directions to a path of inner peace and happiness. This is my life.

What More Can I Do?
Linda Camacho
Did I not send the Earthquakes, famines and
diseases in various places?
Did I not through all this relate the desired
effect?
Why won't you hear Me calling to you?
Why won't you come home to rest under My wings
in safety?
Is not My love greater than any other offered
upon Earth?
Am I not the Creator of all the eye can see?
All I have I give to you and yet is it not
enough?
Why do you pollute yourself with his lies that
only lead to destruction?
Why do you allow yourself to be blinded from
the truth?
Did you notice the hour grows late and yet
while you draw breath I wait?
Am I not your Father, Saviour, Comforter and
Friend?
How much longer will you torment Me while
waiting to share eternal love and life?
Will you wait until it's too late?

Under The Sky
Jenniffer Hobbie
I begin to think
I'm standing in an odd window
When I once stood in yours

Looking out at the sky
I wonder
Will I ever be in your window again
With you behind me?

I stand looking at the same night sky
Thinking
We're looking at the same sky
Will we ever again look at the night sky together again

In the same city
Under the same old sky
I can't take this very well without you
I feel that I'm lost

I wonder to myself, will I ever see you again
Under the same sky
In the same window
In an embrace?

Values
Jennifer Schleis
It's not how you look,
And it's not what you wear.

It's not that you're rich,
And it's definitely not your hair.

It's how you treat people,
It's how you live.

It's how much you love,
And how much you give!

Friends
Patrick T. Browns
If you are my friend
then be my friend.

Hold me not at arm's length
but put your arm around me.

If you are my friend
then tell me no lies.

I will trust you with my hopes,
my dreams and my fears.

If you are my friend
then I give you my heart.

Be ever so careful, you have
the power to break it.

If you are my friend
then walk beside me.

Let me put my arm,
around you.

Native American
Cathrine Illguth

Native Americans are strong
in heart and soul
they fight to get what is theirs
when they are wronged
when they are right, people don't
give them enough credit for
their accomplishments
the only time there is credit
given to them is
when they kill someone
or they are framed
for killing someone

Native Americans are proud
of their heritage
they cherish Mother Earth
and all of her creations
they have ceremonies
to show their love for
Mother Earth and the food
which she produces

Dedication: to Mrs. McPhail for her encouragement

Darkness
Stacey Stark

Darkness,
like the color of his eyes
the night he murdered me.

Darkness,
it was almost hypnotizing,
but not now.
there shall be no more darkness.
Because he will get what is
Coming to him.
I will soon have my revenge.

Just Go
Philip K. Jordan

Find me a road and I'll follow it.
Show me your heart and I'll take you with me.
Open skies and rolling landscape will greet us.
Give me your hand, we'll put the top down and just go.
Freedom like this will stay with us forever.

I'll turn the radio up, let the world go its own way.
Sing along with the music, only our hearts will hear.
Our touch will comfort us under dark desert skies.
We'll put the back seat to good use and just go.
Times like this will happen again and again.

Surpass the limits and let our spirits roam.
Car keys and imagination, that's all we'll need.
Highway, freeway and back road will show our course.
Throw away the maps, put your feet up and just go.
Getting lost will be our grand adventure.

With the wind under our wings we're ready to fly.
A cooler case and a blanket mark our destination.
You, me and the world, it's all for the taking.
Sure it'll end, but for now we'll laugh and just go.
Riding off into sunset, we'll find a road home.

Later On
Joy Udell

"If there's reincarnation, as I've heard"
said my Mum, "I'll come back as a blackbird.
The one in that tree just lightens my life.
Especially this Spring, now he's found a wife.
He trills in ecstasy, a melody gay.
How I would love to sing like that each day."

"But no – perhaps I'll be a sunflower tall.
Tall enough to gaze over that brick wall.
And watch the river meandering by.
And lift my head to the sun in the sky.
Or be a squirrel – see – climbing that tree?
Snoozing the Winter away – blissfully."

"Reincarnation?. So many options.
Does God allow one to make decisions?.
And blackbirds and sunflowers and squirrels have
Such short life–spans, swiftly over – so sad.
I think, on reflection, an Angel I'll be
Singing in Heaven eternally"

my Mum said

The Inside
Cynthia Cooper

Thank you for loving me and speaking to my heart.
You've given me a second chance to make a brand–new start.

Please grace me to take care of the inside like you told me to do: (Walk in peace, love, forgiveness and wisdom.

And to leave the outside totally to you.

P. S. I love you.

Dedication: to Chipiri LaDester and Lauren

The Gamekeepers' Daughter
Helen E. Cooper

Down the field at a very fast pace
Her little, thin legs look as if they will break,
Just look at the smile on her little, red face
To get to the wood, an effort she'll make.
For she is the gamekeepers' daughter.

He's watching for her, he knows school is out
She's his pride and joy, for he hasn't a son
And of her love for him, he hasn't a doubt
For he knew from the start, her heart he had won
For she is the gamekeepers' daughter.

The pheasants are calling, she knows it's the time
To scatter the food all around on the ground,
They won't fly away for to them she's the sign
That feeding time's here and there's much to be found.
For she is the gamekeepers' daughter

Yes, there are his arms stretched out so wide,
He swings her around and she shouts "Hello, Dad"
Then carrying her basket, she walks by his side,
And years later, I thought of the fun that I'd had
For I am the gamekeepers' daughter

Enchanted Dreams

Quiet Now
Mark John Goulden
Quiet now, I must make no sound
Must keep my breath in check
Silence now, in sleep she's so peaceful
At last she dreams, at last she rests
She's beautiful in half–light, half–naked
Oh, for one, for one caress
So funny now in sleep she's so peaceful
A chance to dream, a chance to rest

Baby, sweet baby, must make no sound
To bend to temptation, to lose the child

Morning sun and the Moment is broken
A woman raises her head
Funny how in sleep she was peaceful
So sweet the dream, so sound the rest
Quickly now, while the light is just breaking
A chance to steal, to steal a kiss
Funny how in sleep she was peaceful
So sweet the dream, so sound the rest
I love you, I love.

Dedication: for my children's mother

The Third Eye
Eugene Bowers
There are some
Who never see
Beyond the shell of things,
Theirs a life less–lived
It seems,
For they know not,
The heart can see as well.
There the third eye waits arousing
And, when wakened, births a new world.
Heart sees to heart,
And armor falls away to love.

Fragile Earth
Joanne Hadley
About life,
Nothing stands so clear
That it, shivering so seamlessly in daylight,
Lies silent in the darkness.

As light, a gracious mask to foolishness and pain
Shatters, reach night, standing alone
And note as clear as senses,
A fragile Earth
Breathing softly and thinking
With wide–eyed mind, about forever.

Lone clouds stand, waters densely fill and
Life grows around.
Hope, a patchy mark for many
Desires the purpose oblivion denies,

And alone
Standing with her soul surrounded,
Nothing as design – turmoil gathers,
Signs,
Runs away
And turns again.

The Change Of Seasons
SueAnn Ohagan
The night slowly drifts into morn
The birds start to spread their wings
and sing to awake you to a brand–new day.

The sun slowly raises up over the trees
The sunlight twinkling off of the brown leaves
of fall...

The air is crisp and saying that winter will
be coming and the birds will soon be leaving...

But not to worry, the birds will be back to
welcome the spring and bring new life and the
flowers will be blooming all around us soon...

The trees will get new green leaves and then
Summer will walk in, showering us with sun and
warmth and then...

We will look forward to the next
change of seasons.

Dedication: to my loving husband, Barry

Memories
Peggy Payne
I loved my love and he loved me
I married my love and he set me free,
Free to be happy, love, laugh, be me,
We loved our children my love and I.
Then he had to leave us, he had to die,
But our love grows like a beautiful tree
Because I loved my love and he loved me,
The love of our children and their children, too
This I have to last me my whole life through.

Dedication: to Cliff and our loving family

Untitled
Elizabeth Ackroyd
He just wants to be left alone
No one can speak to him
he can be there for days on end
The house changes its mood all 'round
Children understand, even lend a helping hand

"Put on a brave face" I say
go upstairs and check all is ok
Don't cry or get upset
he's just sleeping
doesn't want to awake yet

The mood is low
People come and go
I know I have to leave him
to go to work, you know
I hide all his pills

People try to understand
Doctors, Psychiatrist, family and friends
Only people with the same mind
can really see what goes on behind
DEPRESSION!!!

Whenever There Is Rain
Lawrence Sparks
The sky above is crying, teeming are its tears
A child below is dying, too early for their years
Clouds begin to cuddle, united in their pain
Each tear becomes a puddle for those who must remain

Distant thunder rolls by, angry in its quest
Below, it hears a mother's cry
As she lays her child to rest

The woman's heart is broken
She'll hold her child no more
Each prayer is softly spoken
For the child at Heaven's door

The sky above stops crying
The clouds begin to part
A rainbow is seen flying
Coloured with God's heart

The child is in God's keeping
No longer feeling pain
But he hears his mother weeping
Whenever there is rain

New–Found Rose
Kimberley McCutcheon
My life is like a Rosebud,
Ready to bloom into action,
Though not yet, I am ready to blossom,
Thoughts running through my head,
Busy people who shan't even notice me, for a drop of blood,
As they do not see my inner beauty,
As far as the eye can see, I am a body with no soul,
But, for when I blossom into a new lifeform, I shan't forget those who
could not see such beauty beyond repair.

Dedication: to Mum because I love you

When Love Came Home
William A. Cooper
As now, with love, I send thee forth,
The world will judge thee,
O jewel of my heart,
Now thou must leave me.

Fear not – where e'er the fates may lead thee,
Yet stand fast and to the world
Thy message still proclaim...

This world is not the end of all our seeking,
The road beyond was never meant for weeping,
Faith be thy guide in all thy striving.
And to those who've gone before – be ever true

As, far off, I saw banners waving.
A symbol of the hope we hold so dear
Of victory o'er all our human failings,
And in that instant knew the end of life, was near.

And as this happened – my demise,
'Neath wondrous, wondrous azure skies,
Then – there before my very eyes,
I crossed over the bridge of sighs.

The Little Cowboy
Lana Elledge
I know a little cowboy sitting on God's knee,
Singing with the angels and shouting jubilee.
Our precious little cowboy, he suffered for so long,
Then his pain was finally ended when our Lord Jesus called him home.

God took away his sorrow and all those painful things,
He gave him back his eyesight and rewarded him with wings.
We miss our little cowboy and often question why,
God, why did you take him, he was much too young to die.

He fought so very hard, he fought so very long,
Then Jesus told the angels "bring that little cowboy home."
Bring him straight to Heaven, do not hesitate,
He need not suffer any longer, I'll meet you at the gate.

Jesus stood at the gates of Heaven, His loving arms open wide,
The angels sang in celebration when the little cowboy arrived.
Jesus told the little cowboy "you are so brave and so tough,
But even the strongest little cowboy can only take so much."

You will nevermore suffer, you will nevermore roam,
Then Jesus smiled at the little cowboy,
And said "ROBBIE, WELCOME HOME."

He's Still Here (To Care)
Teresa Janniello
I can't take it anymore
the pressure is on,
And nobody cares
but my best friend who's gone.
The one I always counted on,
to help me along in my
times of trouble and grief.
But if I believe
hard enough that he is here,
All this will pass
and there will be relief.

My Little Boys
Luverna Stella Shannon
The whole world comes alive,
for there is a certain kind
of magic that little boys have:

Perhaps it lies in their happy
little dreams that burst into
happy dreams:

'Tis then the outdoors beckons
them, As nature fills their hearts,
The search for all the happiness
That the April days impart

And every creature bids them
well and always willing to
share. For little boys love to
climb the hills afar
and fish in creeks, or streams.

The buds that burst in beauty
that's so rare beneath the skies
of brightest blue, Both of you
are a miracle in view.

Enchanted Dreams

Together Forever
Amy Boone
I see you standing there in a world of loneliness.
I want to reach out a hand to pull you into my arms, into my world.
My heart falls to my feet as you leave into a dark void of nothingness.
I was there once. It is depression and sadness. No one to love but yourself
but yet yourself you do not love.
You are a lost soul yearning to be found, loved and saved.
My heart says to love but my mind says not to trust. Which one is right?
I do not care. All I care about is you.
I cry for you but no tears fall to the ground. The cries are inside of me,
inside my head, inside my heart. My cries are silent but loud enough
to drive a person insane. Insane from caring for someone too much.
I would give you my heart on a silver platter if you asked me to.
My mind races with thoughts of you. Thoughts of us together forever.
Holding each other gently, never to be separated again. But the
demons in my head and the demons around us don't want us to be
together. They separate us with thoughts and words, words of hate and
disgust, disapproval and demise.
I see you standing there all alone in a world of loneliness.
If only you knew how much I wanted to reach my hand out and pull you
Into my arms, into my world.
Then we will never be lonely again and together forever...

Dedication: to T. J. for being there...

Rites Of Passage
Elizabeth Bell
Sorrow, the wind that blows through tree and field,
never extinguishing its lust for the beauteous.
Pity, the exhaulted,
shining for those who adore out of piteous self–detachment rather than
merit.
Relish not the fervor,
created by souls unbeknownst to their own valueless and conformist
legion of beliefs.
Value only that which defies all but the individual,
for it is this truth and the love of this truth that creates the bond of
spirit and soul from whence mankind derives its true strength.

The Circle Is Complete
Dorothy Chenoweth Klausner
Years ago when families stayed
most of their lives in one small town,
I was lucky to have my Grandmother
as my mentor and best friend
for all the years till I was forty–odd.

Now that our peripatetic family members
move from town to town, state to state,
and even occasionally to another country,
you'd think I'd miss the opportunity
to enjoy such friendship with my Grands.

But circumstances have allowed me
several years of close companionship
with almost all my grandchildren
when they were young. They have remained
my close, good friends as they've matured.

Enjoying all our times together,
I have recognized that our relationship,
like that I had with my own Grandmother,
is unique. Not often granted in the world today,
such friendships have made my life complete.

Our Lady In Blue
Gina D'Agostino
You are blessed...
B bright; beautiful; a bearer of good news
L loving; a lovely creature of light
E extraordinary; an enduring, exalted Queen of Heaven and Earth
S self–sacrificing; a simple servant of the Lord
S sorrowful; a contemplative; a special Saint
E empathetic; empowered; ever a Virgin
D docile; dedicated; the first disciple of the Lord

V valued; a virtuous woman of vision
I immaculate; imaginative; an inspiration to all human beings
R responsive; receptive; a rare individual
G gentle; filled with grace; a wonderful gift to us
I intelligent; interested; an ideal intercessor
N neat; a being near to us and to the Lord – NOW

M married to St. Joseph; the mother of Jesus Christ; a missionary
A alive; an available, altruistic person
R responsible; a real giver; rich (spiritually)
Y a youthful friend; yearning for Jesus' coming.
You said "yes" to the Lord

You possess meaning, purpose and direction.

My Dad
Daniel Meyer
My Dad and I, really didn't talk,
Heck, we didn't even walk.
That is walking together,
And it will probably stay that way forever.
He lives in another state,
And just for that I have anger and hate.
He probably doesn't even think of me,
And my sense of presence is totally erased
from his memory.
So maybe he won't be there for me,
But I do know, forever I will be, Dadlessly.

Ode To A Princess: Diana
Bonnie Lovelace
An angel of love –came down from above
And graced–this Earth below
Such beauty was shown– through this angelic
form.
To this Earthling –here below

A princess she was– and loved by all
She loved the rich and the poor
And the children she loved– like a Mom from
above
She was always on the go

Doing whatever she could– whatever was good
Whatever in life would unfold
But in a short span of time –one dark night
God took our Princess Diana home

But as long as time shall exist
She will always be missed – From now on
And Generations– to come
Missed by family and friends –Worlds without
end
For Heaven is now her new home

The Anthology of Poems

After The Divorce...
Tammy Begamen
I miss you. I miss your smile
first thing in the morning
your touch the last thing at night
and I miss you, in—between these times.

I miss your laughter, your cheers
when your team won
I miss your tears, even your anger
when your dreams came undone.

I miss your strength, when I lose mine
I miss the security of your arms
telling me "I'll be fine".

I miss being an "us" or a "we"
Now it's just myself, or me.

I miss us, so much, that every
passing hour seems like two
I miss so many things, but most of all
"I miss you."

Dedication: for Tuesday, my whole world

She Sleeps
Bill Sunshine
She sleeps, her mind at gentle peace.
Our love a softly—spoken dream.
A joy her face to see at rest.
Breath soft, as flowing summer stream.

Light touch the face of my desire.
A wish at last come true.
The ever, everlasting love.
I have, forever you.

Dedication: to Lynne, whom I love

An Aspect Of Marriage
Pat Driver
So now, at last, you have a mistress
Secret trysts in leafy lanes
Both tell the censored versions of your marriage
Ease your pains.
Blinded by the dazzle of each other.
You do not see the wounds you cause another.

Her face a mix of patronage and glee
She tells me that you're very fond of me.
Fondness or lust, is that the span of your emotions
Don't you encompass love, or hate, or even trust?
Perhaps you don't, perhaps adventure is a must.

The act is commonplace, the pain unique.
And in my pain I cast around to seek; an explanation
Men of your age, they do this thing, I'm told
It helps them tend off getting old
Time off for good behaviour, p'raps?
It's nothing, dear, it's just a lapse
Why is it then my agony is great?

Lies and betrayal were the things
That waited to demolish in the wings.

The Bumblebee And The Flea
Dorothy Jean Evans
Now be realistic said the bumblebee to the flea
If you only had a pair of wings
you could fly as high as me.

I am sure you are right
was the flea's reply
but considering my size
can you jump as high.

Now the bumblebee said, "Get on my back"
and we will see what we can see.
When suddenly down from the sky
swooped a big blackbird
and had them both for tea.

The moral of this poem
is for all to see
No matter how high you
can jump or fly
On that big blackbird
you should keep your eyes

Dedication: to grandchildren, Rebecca and James Evans

Confusion
Shelia DeWulf–Sellers
Confusion is a state of mind, when all my thoughts are far behind.

And all at once, without restrain, they race like madness
throughout my brain.

I cannot seem to sort them out.
I want to run and scream and shout!

But instead, here I sit and try to sort my tangled wit!

Dedication: to forever remember my Eric DeWulf

Where Am I?
Michael N. McKimm
Where am I?
If when I shower
I wash my hair above me

Where am I?
If when I shower
I wash my neck behind me

Where am I?
If when I shower
I wash my ears each side of me

Where am I?
If when I shower
I wash my face in front of me

Where am I?
If when I shower
I wash my chin below me

Where am I
in the shower?
In the shower, where am I?

Enchanted Dreams

On This Earth
Felina-Marie Mucha-Kangas
During the time we have here on this Earth
we wait for someone special
Who that someone is we find out in time
Sometimes they are right under our very
noses
We turn, take a glance and to our very surprise,
there they are just waiting to be with them

Each day passes, each glance imbeds
the memory of the love we are to share
But where are we to go?
What are we to do?
Will our love last forever?

The memories of our past fill our sleeping hours.
When we awaken we can only think of our love
never—ending.

Where is our energy for the other things they say
life has to offer.
What things, what meaning do they hold?
For we are together as one, never—ending, love lasting.
Forever.

Type A
Cynthia Yvonne Jones
The push for perfection
and search for success
drives us to the edge
of human nature
until the only friend left
is the reflection at the bottom
of our coffee cup
and we have to buy recordings
of waterfalls to relax by
instead of going to see them
ourselves.

One Voice
Linda Lee
You arrive at birth,
Accepted; no questions asked...
No matter your sex, weight or worth.

Taught to know right from wrong,
And to survive...
You must be strong.

As time moves on for you,
Race — gender and sexuality...
All become an issue!

What happened to the freedom of choice?
One nation...
One voice?

Such dangerous times today,
Look around us now...
How did things go so astray?

What happens to choice?
to our nation...
And our voice?

Untitled
Fanci Floyd
Sometimes at night,
When I'm all alone
I sit and cry.

Wounded, hurt and bleeding —
I wonder why.
Why all this suffering
Just because of pride?
Never knowing fully,
Why I'm so afraid
and never fully knowing
the very meaning of my life.

Is there more at stake here?
Or am I just a pawn?
Is there somewhere else I
am wanted
Further down this road I'm
on?
Or am I just a traveler,
Lost without a map—
No clue — no purpose —
Just a mere mortal mishap?

Rahu
Paul Medenwaldt
Is there a wave underneath the sea
where I can touch, but the sun can't see
Maybe a meadow of flowers
with the thunder in the sky
run to the end, lift off to fly
Search all of the Heavens for a sign
and when you hear a whisper, pretend it's mine
Pick an island to land on
and let the angels caress you with their song
Lay in the paradise and never dream
Everything is real, even the love you feel

The Path
Ethyl Lyons
The path is muddy,
The road is long,
My feet are tired and worn.

Yet still I see
Ahead of me
A brightness in the fog.

I know I'm late
In coming home,
Along the way I strayed.

I thought I heard
An angel's song,
But the wisp, it was a fake.

So back I go
Upon the road,
I know it leads to home.

Though the path is muddy,
The road is long,
And my feet are tired and worn.

To Love Again
Shelley A. Bhola

Somebody shattered your dreams,
stole your pride and broke your heart.
But that's in the past,
it needn't last,
don't let a memory tear us apart.

I can give you more love
than you've ever known before.
You needn't run,
we've just begun,
don't let the past hurt you anymore.

Let the tears dry, he's shed none for you,
erase him completely from your memory.
You don't need to apologize,
no need to analyze,
he was the fool that set you free.

So take my hand and trust in love,
it's never too late to begin again.
Give up your sorrow,
walk with me tomorrow.
Together in love we'll make it, my friend.

Epsilon Alcoholic
Cathy French

So that's what you are.
It should be a relief
To put a term to it.
Barely a problem after all – at least
Nothing
That a course in Anger Management
Won't cure.
But to me,
You'll always be the man who
Killed my mother
With your drinking.

A Letter From Beyond
Jeanette Harris Jefferson

My beloved sons,
I watched so proudly during my memorial service as you walked behind.
No place in the universe will braver sons any Mommy find.
Because you, Will and Harry, keep me in your hearts,
My completed sojourn on Earth can never tear us apart.
My greatest joy and fulfillment while residing on Earth,
Was being chosen by our Creator as the vehicle of your births.
My brave, brave sons go forward and be the people our
Creator destined for you.
There is much happiness in the years ahead, I tell you true.
A destiny much greater, even than the crown.
So blessed it is, even indescribably more profound.
Imagine, my spirit craving to touch you again, in a lingering
drop of rain on your eyelash,
Or, the Creator allowing me to touch my sons, in a gentle
breeze you feel Me pass.
My death forever you must not mourn,
You cannot enjoy the roses if you cling to the thorns.
From my heart, my beloved sons, Go With God.
Do what you know is good and ignore the worldly facade.

A heart forever loving my sons,
Mommy

Waves
Diane Bellows

As I sat on the shore of the ocean, I thought of life and the people who have been my friends; and perhaps more importantly, the people who have refused to be my friends. And a wave rolled in, with careless beauty and grace and slowly is pulled back by a force greater than its own into the sea.

I thought of the people who took me in. Into their hearts, their minds and their souls. The people who trusted me. Trust, I thought to myself, is one of the greatest forms of love. And a wave came again. The soft, white fringe stretching by. Rolling and jumping and slowly is pulled back by a force greater than its own, into the sea.

I thought of the friends who will always be there; ready to listen and smile and let me know they love me, infinitely more than I deserve. And the wave came again, majestic and powerful.

And I realized in order to live, I must reach out, especially when reached for. And so I went forth, past the fringe, into the heart of the wave. And slowly a force greater than my own pulled me into the sea. And I died and I lived and I died and I lived; and in the process, I learned how to swim.

Dedication: to enrich Denise, my twin

You
Elizabeth A. Powell

When I think of you,
It's like dew on the ground of my heart,
And green grass blowing on the fields of my soul.
It's like springtime when the snows depart
Or the 4th of July when the fireworks start.
The tenderness of your boyish glow is like stars shining on
me below.
Your loving kindness is pure art,
An angel spell of which I am part.
Happiness is the joy of "we",
For you are what is good in life to me.

The Last Goodbye
Davina Mulvenna

If you are an animal lover,
You'll know the pain that we all suffer,
When we have to call the vet,
To put to sleep our little pet.

When he comes you'd like to say,
Can he come back another day?
But it does not work that way,
For you know that they can't say.
There is a choice you have to make,
And it will only bring heartache.

Keep her for another week?
Let her suffer in her sleep?
Tell the vet to put her down?
For you feel you're duty–bound.

For they can't tell us of their pain,
So we have just to watch in vain,
And now that fatal day is here,
It's goodbye from us, wee Sheba, dear.
Until we meet again I'll weep
Just close your eyes and go to sleep.

Enchanted Dreams

Shep
Dawn Campbell
A rubber ball lies at my feet
Two large brown eyes appealing to me
A golden paw rests on my knee
He's trying to say "Come Play With Me"

Never mind the wind and rain
Life goes on and time has come
Collect my lead and off we romp
Later we may see the sun

Daisies and the Bluebells grow
In the meadows and the fields
I run on! Then, I turn and wait
Is she following me?

Home at last – a welcome sight
A dish of water, lies in wait
A cool, long drink and then I turn
To find my bed so soft and warm
And dream of yet another game
Night – Night

Dedication: to a very special four-legged friend, Shep

The Blanket
Nora Toftely
Anxiety is the thread that runs through the blanket of my personality. It weaves patterns of shame, guilt and disillusionment. Pull the thread of anxiety and the blanket begins to unravel.

Throw the blanket off and the fear disappears. I am free, calm, and at peace. It is difficult to throw the blanket away. It is warm and comfortable. The world is cold and full of danger.

Yet is it not better to adapt to the cold, rather than depend on a blanket that will fall apart by pulling a single thread.

My Soul
Maryann Sanders
My soul hangs with a shadow of
an empty grave

Sometimes my spirit flies away to explore
the unexplained

I fall asleep into a nightmare, feeling
my rejection, hatred, greed in my
empty spirit

I can't control the evil that's around
me and they always blame
and point the finger at me

But I keep holding on because of the
love for my children
I believe my spirit has the answers
to most of my problems

My mind and soul will be cleaned
once it's released all the anger
and frustration and peace in
the air while I meditate

Behind Tinted Glass
Dorothy Fitzgerald
I am shielded by the light
of the dark, gray world
All is seen unreal,
no true colors, no true doors.
The tinted-glass shades
the shadows of one's mind.
Hidden to be safe of the unkindly time
in which we all pass.
But as the wall is lifted
the world is bright and clear.
The shadows have passed
with the close of night.

Human Flowers
Myrtha B. Corbier
Flowers here! Flowers there!
Different colors and shades, they wear.
What a beauty! What a splendor!
Drawing great lessons from nature
Makes the mind sound and more mature.

Is there on Earth some mold to use
For shaping man? Does each one choose
His place of birth, the color of his skin,
His tribe, his race, his origin?
You are black! I am white! That's right!

You are red! I am yellow! By our might?
My appearance, did I make it?
What kind of blame or what merit
Can be given to a mortal
For receiving nature's bestowal?

Where are all the human flowers?
Where are the elite of the Earth?
Let them rise and be harmonized
To become multicolored flowers
That enhance the charm of mankind!

Our Love Is Built With The Emotion
Reymundo Sanchez
Our love Is Built with Emotional Feelings,
That Come Within Our Hearts,
With No Anger, Or Guilt,
Without Having To Hide Our Pride,
Or Even Hesitate For A Moment...

Our love Is Also Built By The Precious Touch,
That, Giving Our Hearts To Each Other,
Will Keep Us Together Forever,
I Like To Think About That Moment,
When Our Hearts Become One...

The Commitment That We Both Thought Would
Never Be? Has Truly Found Its Way Into Our
Hearts and The Fulfillment It Brings,
Will Last Forever,

Don't Ever Stop Believing In The Dream,
That We Both Want To Have, Even If It Seems So
Hard, It Will Never Disappear...
And A Lifetime With You, Will Be My Strength,
I Will Be Lost, Without You In My World
Of Pleasure And Love...

The Last Visit
Maurice G. Bowler
We closed her eyes
and went downstairs.
Not knowing what to say and knowing him,
I sat there still,
until he spoke.
"She talked to me last night
about the flower that had to fall
so that the fruit could form.
She'll wait for me and now
I'll live her kind of life.
I know the way; I'll take her place,
this Sunday at the church".

A Tavern
William McIlwraith
Wet, moonlight–licked
on one side;
A tavern warmly inviting to frequenters,
cold to strangers and me.

Window glow to night sky:
Orange to blue.

Inside, two unshaven men with rose pipes
sit and squint and smoke, blow halos
of smoke over each others' heads;
Funny angels.

To better discuss their respective old days,
these fisherman wash their sooty mouths
with warm scotch whiskey;
Smile tarnished smiles.

Lit candles bedeck iron chandeliers
and drip wax and light to the floor
where both collect and rest;
Wait for morning.

Grandparents' Love
Eileen H. Welsh
Smiles like sunshine from above –
Fill my heart with warmth and love

Hugs so safe, secure and strong –
Let me know that I belong

Words that make my day so bright –
Soothe and calm me late at night

There is nothing in this world to fear –
Because my grandparents are here

How I love you, all that you give –
My dearest, kindest relative

Who loves me freely, evermore –
With love so sweet, so rare, so pure

I promise you to always be –
The grandchild you will long to see

For all the love you have given me –
I thank you now and eternally.

The Tea Party
Juanita Ortego
We went to a tea party with lots of fancy tea.
Mine was flavored with peaches and a touch of kiwi.
It was served in crystal stemware, I tasted it once or twice,
and the tiny little sandwiches were also very nice.
It was a lovely house with antiques and lace,
and dressed–up ladies seated all over the place.
I tried to act so proper and sat up in my chair,
but it's hard for a little girl to act so debonair.
I said to my Mommy, "Mommy, listen to me, I want to
leave this place and go to McDonald's for tea."

Dedication: to my granddaughter, Lonia Jeffers

Henry's Eye
Todd Schaffter
Fire rages down under. The rainforests
skirt the heart region. Blackness darkens
the intra–arc region for a period.
Temperatures culminate the basin region
to freeze the blistering tempera of last summer's
rage. Engulfed by rage, Ah... when love reigns
when poppies pop, when birds fly, oh...
how we strive to be free. So we continually
struggle between past and present. So
we teach today of yesterday and of current highs.
Recurrent highs of the now reappear, reshape
our time tomorrow. The reflection of
protective tears state their action.
The landscape forever flowing to that goal.
So very briefly hovering to a reaction. The light
of a dozen hens return one bursting spring.
The blood–stained feathers of a fighting cock
trickle between its scratching and picking. The
sweating lily looms one cold day to fume the
air only to receive from flight a Zion, a stream, a garden.

Dedication: to Mrs. Stella Wecht

Early Santa Ana
Heidi B. Morrell
This night the atmospheric caveats
come in gently like Chopin,
they bask and fondle
the fuzzed cheek, the goblet–aimed hand.
The breeze lifts hairs
tugging, sensual
like warm sand poured on a knee.

Come lovers, Santa Ana bathes the skin
with its aerial saliva
troughing through the canyons,
canyon tongues that spit their gusts
into the huge Angeles basin;
a basin no longer wild with
arching ferns and alluvial fans,
mugwort and lily, tides and spring floods.

But the wind is still here,
stroking or maddening
with its heaves and curt salutes.
Speaking in sepia tones
thrown into the sky.

Enchanted Dreams

Snow
Nathan Castello
Falling down, out of the sky,
Alone, Alone, that is a lie,
For there are more following behind,
Falling crazy like they were blind.
Don't worry snowflake, here come the others,
All your frozen sisters and brothers,
Falling anywhere they do dream,
But soon you'll stick just like a team,
Soon you will cover the world with white,
And twinkle in the sun's bright light.
You bring such happiness, I hope you know,
You little snowflake... you now are snow.

The Lucky Ones
Julie Parravano
Swaying back to catch a glimpse of
Whispering mouths playing kiss with an ear.
Unsure of what they think they know
They tell their stories.

Make a prediction,
Write a play, please an audience.
Make sure to remember
The lucky ones have all the light.

Grab, pull, tear, shred,
Desire, scheme, mask, smile

If only I was the one with the pot of gold.
Can I throw my coins at you?
Would you take a four–leaf clover
If you knew the third leaf was split in two?
Would you celebrate the find of a heads–up penny
Laying on a broken mirror?
Would you inherit the greatest treasures
From someone's heart, by their passing,
And call it lucky?

Transported
James R. White
Stepping into the house a
Fragrance, familiar, comforting
transformed me to times and places
Long–ago memories of childhood
Dimly reflected in today's pleasant
Fall Lifetime.

Spirit seduced, I have been
Fragrance–transported frequently.
Often scanning the arena for
A glimpse of the familiar, a
Gentle love–laced smile
Embracing beyond time, Eternal fragrance.

Today, in the morning air it was
Home in the smell of Kerosene.
Soft summer nights, whippoorwill–pierced.
Grown man longing to be child free.
A plaintive emptiness stretching for home.
A homebound entombment searching for life.
Living in contradiction and paradox.
What fragrance will tomorrow's breeze bring?

No Words
Darla Castro
I hear you crying,
I see your tears.
I hope my prayers
Will calm your fears.
Someone you loved,
And held so dear
Has gone from this world
And left you here.
I'll hold your hand
And just stay near.
There are no words
For what's happened here.

Roads
Susan Spilker
At twenty you say, I'm young and I'm free
At thirty you may say, I think I begin to see
That life is not easy and definitely not a spree
There are many roads to take, on which one I cannot agree

The road of life is fun you think... it is a journey
When you're young you know not how twisty and how turny
Turn right, turn left, which do you make
One of them is definitely a mistake

At forty have you reached where you wanted to go?
The road I chose was rough, so I had to go slow
I'm not where I want to be yet, that's okay and that's just fine
I've slowed down some more, this is not your life, this is mine

If you go down the road too fast, you will not see what you have passed
I may never reach my journey's peak, but I have seen what will last
Joy and happiness is not the only good
Pain and sorrow has a lesson in it, as it should

So life has its own mind,
That someday everyone will find

Thank You, Lord, For My Husband
Hazel Matthews
Thank you, Lord, for giving him to me
He made my life so happy and free.
We shared this world of joy and sorrows,
And always thought of a happier tomorrow.
He was always there by my side,
And when things went wrong he was my guide.

Then he got sick, was in so much pain,
You loved him and to his rescue came.
When he prayed and called Your name
"Our Father who art in Heaven"
Take this hurt or take me!

You said I love him too, you see.
And I have a better place for him.
You lead him through the pearly gates,
There for me I know he'll wait.

Once more we'll walk hand–in–hand,
With you, dear savior, in Your promised land.
Where never more we'll have to part,
To love and live forever, sweetheart.

From The Beginning To The End
Danny Minton

When you're born till the day you die
Everyone acts different ways and don't know why
No one knows why people act this way
But it's happening every single day

The world seems to get very strange
The madness is something I wish would change
In God's house there are many rooms... This is true
There's a room for me and one for you

Although everyone in the world is not the same
Remember life is short and not a game

A Poem About Love!
Jimmy McGrath

Love is something dear and tender.
Sometimes it can be a mind–bender.
Your parents are a good source.
Love is not something you take in a course.
You must have strong a feeling of love.
Knowing it is being returned is better than having a white dove.
The first real love to my knowledge is maybe when Adam and Eve were in college.
Some people say it comes from the heart, others say it is when you are hit by Cupid's dart.
Personally, I feel, that it comes from your nerves, for real.
I think to find the so called "one" is when that person and yourself can really have fun.
Preaching about this ultimate gift you are really giving your friends a lift.
Cherish love because it can lighten up your life, if you are a guy you may choose your mate to be your wife.
You may get cold feet on your wedding day, but don't worry if you love this person, you will chase the fear away.

Dedication: to Mom and Dad

The Agnostic
Kathleen Jackson

The song–filled seeds of summer were gone.
It was the season of dancing leaves.
Autumn portrayed her richness of soul with posies of color and grace.
Waterfowl and bird of shore spread wing from north to south.
Life of wild and animal searched for mate and meal.
Beaver and squirrel made way for frosted flake and winter's tide.
At dawn of new day, I met a man of carnal mind.
Agnostic was his name.
With delicate hand he held a robin bird of broken wing.
He placed the feathered songster in a mountain lilac tree.
Earth for the bird to keep her warm and secure.
Insect he lay at her breast and she fed.
He spoke to me of free thought.
The joy of being carnal.
To touch a tree, taste the rain, feel the warming sun.
Experience life with all that he was, know the pulse of reason.
These were his ways, his daily bread.
He was a man of true tongue, saw himself as privileged.
To be a part of evolution's journey was fulfillment enough.
He truly loved what he was and with an open mind began each day.

Dedication: to John Jackson

Untitled
George Ball

A passionate kiss, the touch of your hand,
these are the things that make life grand,
To you all of my love I shall give, for you, my
Dear, are my reason to live. I could not imagine
life without your beautiful face, I want to
hold you forever in a warmthful embrace.
Men shall never know what the future
holds and to live to face life's sorrows is very bold.
Whatever the future holds, we shall face
it together, two souls, joined as one.

Dedication: to Mom, Timmy, Lecia Danielle and Willis

Kentucky Rain
Melissa Parker

Dark, wet health perforates
from the mountains
penetrating three beings
sitting on a porch

Rain singing them a percussion song
Creatures dancing them an audio dance

A single heartbeat resounds
synonymously through all three
–an unspoken promise
–unforgotten worries

The dark presses on their backs
Unnecessary apologies press on their hearts
Rain presses on their souls
cleansing all past inequities
all past iniquities

Two words speak from the night
Patience
Faith

Trust
Jacqueline Perkins

The sun rose high in the sky as the journey
began. The wind blew ever so gently as the
warmth of the beams danced upon the brand–new
spring leaves. A hint of anticipation trickled
through the light, clean air and tickled my soul
with the feeling a change was about to come.

Like a hunter in search of a rare treasure, I ran
to find the answer anticipated by my soul and
cultivated into my brain. My being was lead by a force
greater than my will, all I could do was trust, like a horse
with a bridle being lead by his rider to an unknown destination.

Suddenly, I heard a cry that seemed so familiar, yet
my brain could not comprehend its existence, as it was
not yet supposed to come. I looked up to find the source of
my change, Kaitlyn, my new–born niece. As I looked upon
her adorable face, one thought crept into my brain, "I will
always trust the force greater than my will as it gave me a
blessing and never led me astray."

Dedication: to Kaitlyn Marie Turner

Enchanted Dreams

Pills
Edward G. Clarke
Pills, Pills, Pills, Pills,
guaranteed to cure our ills,
Pills for this and Pills for that,
some for thin and some for fat,
some for Kidneys and for Gout,
are we sure they help us out?
Pills for Liver, Heart and Blood,
is there no end to the mighty flood?
we pop them in and wash them down,
Red, Yellow, Pink and Brown,
how I am longing for the day,
when I can throw my pills away.

Hawaiian Duck
Pete Kimchuk
Our waiter brings the Courses and it's always
too much food,
But I chase a shrimp through Won Ton
Playing Hide and Seek.
And once I spoon the little fella I note
his missing spine –

Chompitychomp and gone.

Out of the oven a Breast of Hawaiian Duck
Is touched by magic or sulfur;
Burning blue and fragrant, this tropical temptation –
When down the way appears that early lover,

Stretching first and then she hovers –
Seeking her flock? Or something else?
I bury my face in the neck of my love
To. . . savor a bite of shoulder
As the other flutters in and out.

Our waiter then again with the Courses,
Clearing what no longer belongs.

The Angel
Nicole Janczak
I had a dream
and you were there

You had blonde hair,
A pretty face, that shined
all over the place.

You grabbed my hand,
and pulled me out of bed.

I put on this long, white dress,
and you said, I always
looked my very best.

We flew to the clouds,
Where we danced and laughed
all night long.

When morning came,
I woke up and you were gone.

Dedication: to Annie

The Street Photographer
David Anderson
Hey hen ye want your photies took,
Tae pit in yer holiday scrap book?
A photie wae yer man by the sea,
Or wan wae yer we'an an' a wee monkey?
Wan o' the we'an?... that's just the job,
Oh, by the way, that'll be six bob.
Ah hope ye wulnae be annoyed,
Ah'll take it wae ma Poleroid.
Ten seconds now that's all it takes,
Provided Ah don't make mistakes.
Eight, nine, ten, now there's yer snap,
Yer we'an wae a monkey oan its lap.

Quantum Love
Missy Spaulding
Galaxies collide
And the Universe
Is in your eyes...
Like a star–lanced evening
You radiate warmth
Within my heart...
We are the children
Of the Cosmos
And like stardust
We dance in a Spiral form...
We orbit and merge
Into each other...
This is our Destiny
To be one
For all Eternity...
You are the Gateway
To another world for me
And like a Nova
You tremendously
Transform my life...

Dedication: to Dave, with love

My Little Furrball
Dawn C. Haehle
She's dressed in gray
all through the day
in stripes so fine
I'm glad she's mine.

She is bright
and can bring fright
to the mouse
that's in the house.

She takes a nap
in my lap.
She's so thin
I'm sure she's in.

Sleeps like a lump
but sure can jump
way up high
as high as my eye.

She's no rat.
She's my cat.

Untitled
Monica McKibbin

Mankind is greedy, with grasping claw
We've really made "Jehovah" sore
It's time to look to him for help
Instead of pandering to the whelp!
Death and destruction is all in vain
All that horrible, putrid rain
Lungs gasping to breathe fresh air.
Who, is alive, left to care
Oh, God step in and show Your face
Please, to stop the nuclear race
You put us here, for a reason sure
Don't give up now, don't shut the door.

New Horizons Unbelievable
Val Vivian

I felt alone and I was fool,
No love, no money, no one cared,
I was not a product of love,
I was a product of the menopause,
And a doomed melodramatic marriage,
Motherhood is for the young,
Fruits of the old produce melancholy fruit,
And life is a hard mountain to climb alone,
It seems a nowhere land,
Suddenly I have risen from the ashes,
I am an Arabian phoenix.
Skepticism of human intellect slowly begins to wane
Somewhere over the rainbow and sleepy shores,
One day will belong to me and we will be as one,
Sun, wind, rain and laughing sea,
New horizons unbelievable,
My life is about to be launched anew,
If you can make me feel like this,
Take the canvas, oils and brush,
And paint my life anew with yours.

Dedication: to Mark, for believing in me

Why Am I So Fat?
Sandra Jean Ritchie

Why.am I so fat? I wasn't born like that,
I've tried each diet, Daft and sane, but still
I always look the same, with bulges here and ripples
There, I dress myself with utmost care, to cover bits
I should not have, I feel like hiding in the lav,

A lettuce leaf, a hard-boiled egg, but not an inch comes
Off my leg, my eating habits I could switch, if only I
Could stitch my lips and leave myself a little hole
For eating liquids from a bowl, with little straws to
Pop right in, to save me from another sin.

The mirror shows the bitter truth, not slenderness I knew
From youth, but chubby cheeks and rotund thighs, the only
Good point is my eyes and these I blame for what I am
By looking at the frying pan.

I try in vain at slimming clubs, then binge on meals in
Local pubs, I always say, when tomorrow comes, I'll start
To diet to loose my tum, but tomorrow is another day, so
Pass the Cadbury's milk tray, what you see is what you
Get, so try to forgive but not forget.

Sweet Love
Mary Sue Bryant

Love is like a roller coaster. Often, has its
Ups and Downs. For it can be, very Confusing, Sometimes.
But, there's nothing, like it, from all around. For it never,
costs, not one single Dime. As it comes, from within, the
Heart, for if we don't let it go, It will never part.
Love can be, Sweet, or it can be Sour, Even every minute,
of the day. It returns, again, Hour after Hour.
Love is something, Special, that God, gave us, to Have and
to hold, with one another, to last, until, the end of time.
— Because it's So Precious and very Dear, For, Love will, Last —
Year after Year. Love will never, Fade, or Go away, If we,
Keep it close, it will always Stay.

World
Linda Reyna

innocent. so innocent.
yet, being slaughtered day by day.
why do they deserve to die?
no choice and no say.
their lives aren't in their hands.
not a chance.
they are given no chance to live.

the trees will never be seen.
the breeze will never be felt.
the air will never be breathed.
the love will never be had.

we are "most intelligent."
can this be true?
we kill ourselves.
we kill each other.
we kill our children.
we kill our babies.
our world is in pain.
hope is at our door.
do we care enough to open it?

Eternity
Dolores McNerney

When we are young
life is so simple,
We worry about things
that are so simple,

When we get older
life is not easy,
We worry about things
that are so simple,

When we are old
life is so simple,
We still are not happy
we worry about things
that are so simple,

Life is just a passing of time
until our angel comes to take
us away,
To a world of love and peace and joy.

Dedication: to Janet, my eternal angel

Enchanted Dreams

Soul Memory
Adam J. Tedesco
I can still hear the music
Tortured and dark
Bones breaking
To a hollow beat
The cries of forgotten children
An aching heart
Trying to move
To another man's rhythm
The reasons are gone
But the song plays on
The melody lingers
And the demons rejoice

My Dad
Kristy Vega-Park
You were my hero,
The only one I knew.
You were one part of my world,
With Mom that made two.
You were my protector,
From evil and the whole world through.
You were my watcher,
Made sure I did what I had to do.
You were my Dad,
The best I could have ever had.

You loved me.
You cared for me.
You listened to me, too.
You taught me so much.
I owe a great deal of my life to you.

I will carry you in my heart and pass you on,
To those who are less fortunate, to see the man...
I CALLED DAD!

Dedication: to dad – I miss you

The Box
Marjorie Chesebro
Childhood was like being locked in a violence box,
Sheltered from everything but pain.
Viewing hatred daily, yet commanded to love.
No freedom to act, to think, to believe.
Forced into the robotic motions of obedience.
An air of nonchalance perfected on the outside,
Screams of agony suppressed on the inside.

What happened in the box is a secret.
Smiles stifled any questions outsiders might raise.
The secret contains brutal rage and fists and bruises.
The secret contains stolen innocence,
And permanent, yet invisible scars.
The secret is too shocking to be revealed,
And too horrible to be forgotten.

One might say childhood was lived in that box.
Or, one might say childhood was lived in a place
Where pain is imaginary and happiness is reality.
A place where life can only be survived
When the imagination invents a reality
That exists somewhere outside the violence box.

Untitled
Judy Liik
Life is Short
Love is great
I wish all things could be easier.
I try, I plead, I care, I love.
But you don't seem to care.
I would give you the world
if only I could.
I only wish that it will help.
I want you to have everything.
To Love, to Hope, To Be.
All I want is you to be Happy
So Okay, I give up, You're Free!

Growing Up
Shane Cullen
I don't socialize well. Probably never have.
Probably never will. No one will ever know the real me.

I'm far too grown up for my age. Matured to the max,
I can never relax. I'm a freak raised on center stage.

On the other hand, I'm intelligent. I'm sensitive, responsible,
never in a fight.
Raised to be a perfect gent. Sadly enough, that's my plight.

Kids don't usually relate to polite. For them it's mostly all cuss words
and sex.
They think I prance around like a knight. What they don't know is my hex.

I don't know what I've ever done to anyone I've ever known
That's been insensitive, inappropriate, or dumb,
But maybe my guardian angel has flown.

On the other hand, I'm the man I am. If I wasn't raised like I have been,
Then that would never have been. All in all, I thank God I am who I am.

Dedication: to my mother, Peggy Cullen

Angel in the Background
Tiana Robbins
He comes and goes in my life
As does sunset to sunrise
He always pops up in the nick of time
to save my behind
My angel in the background
does not judge me nor criticize my actions
but simply asks me why. "Why?" he asks.
"You are a gentle being that deserves much more."
"Why?" he asks. "Why must you cry?
Everyone, even you, falls from time to time."
He takes my face into his hands
and looks at me with his glossy eyes
and melts away my teardrops
with his glimmery glance.
He then makes me smile and says
"You'll be alright, just remember,
I've got you in my sight!"
With that statement he winks at me
and says to me.
"Fear not, worry not, sweet pea.
You are very dear to me, just remember,
I will never leave thee."

When
H. E. Conroy

When first they came into our skies
In craft no Earthly mind could glean
We listened to the fabled lies
By governments who only scheme
So we laughed and made our fun
And turning on our fellow man
With bombs and guns we tore the Earth
That was man's rightful place of birth
Then through the air they came
Like locusts on some distant plain
Had we but been prepared and tried
When first they came into our skies

True Friends
John Van Dyk

People come and people go
Like flashes of lightning
During a spring storm
As life progresses
And change occurs
While the wheel of time
Rolls endlessly on
But the memories of their passing
Stay forever
And are reflected and remembered
In each following day
Nourishing and enhancing
The quality of life

And true friends are marked
As those who remain
To guide and support
To share in the times
Both happy and sad
That mark your passing.

Dedication: to Caroline, my wife and true friend

Where Are You Going, Little Boy?
Harvey M. Kemmerer

Where are you going, little boy?
To the forest, to smell the leaves.
The forest is dark and there's danger within
So do not go therein.

Where are you going, little boy?
To the ocean, to learn to swim.
The ocean is wide
The ocean is deep.
Therefore you cannot swim.

Where you going, little boy?
To the mountain, to touch the sky.
The mountain is steep and the
sky is too high,
So do not even try.

Where are you going, little boy?
To walk on the forest trail
Stand by the oceans' edge
Rest on the mountains' peak
These are the things I enjoy.

Sisters
Michelle Bernhardt

I think of you each Moment,
for no one else do I care.
And when I go someplace you don't
how I wish that you were there.
Some big fights and stupid ones,
that both of us have had.
But when I see a smile on your face,
that's what makes me glad.
So much that we've been through,
hope it never ends
Blood has made us sisters,
but love has made us friends.

An Old Man And His Dreams
Kay Harrington

The barn rose from the knoll like an igloo,
and a soft light spilled through its panes and cracks.
Shafts of that light touched the rosy dawn and stretched
like the borealis across a polar plane.

Some said the old man should retire and take it easy,
but his tracks to the barn suggest that he cannot, for
his is still summoned from bed to his post like
every other morning in his life.

Pungent silage lingers between the cracks and stirs the man.
He smiles, secures his earflaps and recalls that dear
lamb, Blue, while gloved hands inspect rusted stanchions
that once embraced his favorite girls, Bessie and Oatmeal.

He now ignores the rude silence that esteems him
and would have him believe his world never existed.
He revels in the zenith of his kingdom.

Perched on a corroded milk can, undaunted, every morning,
he whittles sticks with twisted fingers and is
warmed by the magic of remembering.

Bones Poem
Bill Walker

What if my bones were in a museum,
Where aliens paid good money to see 'em?
And suppose that they'd put me together all wrong,
Sticking bones onto bones where they didn't belong!

Imagine phalanges, pelvis and spine
Welded to mandibles that once had been mine!
With each misassemble, the error compounded,
The aliens would draw back in terror – astounded!

Their textbooks would show me in grim illustration,
The most hideous thing ever seen in creation!
The museum would mold a model in plaster,
OF ME, to be called, "Evolution disaster"!

And paleontologists there would debate,
Dozens of theories to help postulate;
How man survived for those thousands of years,
With teeth–covered arms growing out of his ears!

Oh, I hope that I'm never in such manner displayed,
No matter HOW much to see me the aliens paid.

Enchanted Dreams

Memorable Years Anniversary
J. C. Seddon
It does not seem so many years ago
When we tied the knot, our loving bow,
Although all those wonderful years, have flown away
I will cherish and remember, our Wedding Day.
So on this very special happy event,
All my love and devotion to you is sent.
To such an understanding person as you,
Who is one in a million, is very true,
May the future hold in store,
Many more happy years as the ones before.
Thanking you once again, for your loving ways
And all those wonderful and happy days.

Innocence
Sheila P. Averill
I wonder, where are the children, have they gotten lost;
Are they losing their innocence, at any cost.
Is society moving along, with such a fast pace;
We don't notice that tear, or a smile on their face.
An if no one is listening, to what they say;
Who will listen later, when they've gone astray.
When they'll no longer be, little girls and boys;
But rather, children using weapons for toys.
Schools should be a safe place, to learn and play;
Not a place for fear, of being wasted away.
We all may question, who is to blame;
Ignoring the problem, that's the shame.
To give them more, is the reason we try;
Sometimes what they need, money can't buy.
Like memories, to make 'em happy, not sad;
Sharing good times, with their Mom and Dad.
A child has no direction, unless they're shown;
With love and guidance, from within the home.
Then maybe one day, all our children will see;
That children killing children, wasn't meant to be.

Dedication: to my loving husband

Guess Who??
Gathelma J. Herring
Each time you felt alone,
I was there.
When you needed a friend,
I was there.
When your stomach ached from hunger,
I was there.
Did you notice bad turned to good?
I was there.
You are blessed with so much because,
I was there.
So many times you never noticed,
I was there.
All you had to do was open your eyes and see,
I was there.
Enjoy each day of your life and be happy,
I was there.
You are loved now and forever because,
I was there.

"YOUR GOD"

Dedication: to my family and loved ones

A Long Road
John Turner
Well, I guess its all been told
Finally, I'm growing old
What has life been, a dream
Have I done a lot, maybe not
I've been, I've seen, I've done, I've conquered
But I know I've squandered
A life in the air, I didn't care
Work down a pit, spit
Be content, no, it's spent
A life moulded or folded
Wasted but often tasted
A long road, what more can be told.

Fighting For Freedom
Richard S. Griffith III
He is often heard giving fine speeches,
Everyone loves the way William Wallace preaches.
As he screams battle cries and sounds of call,
His fellow Scottish rebels begin to fall.
His people murdered and the village burned,
Wallace fought because he yearned.
For the freedom of the Scottish nation,
After the English killed his wife, he cried for retaliation.
He outwitted the British in forest and field.
Without Scottish freedom he would never yield
There was one trap he couldn't smell out,
It was some of his Scottish nobles who sold out.
There was a meeting with Wallace and the nobles few,
Then he found out their morals were askew.
"Freedom" he screamed with the last of his breath,
And freedom he found in his life and his death.
After Wallace's death, the Scottish continued to fight,
They would not go quietly into the night.
Robert the Bruce then led the Scots to their freedom,
He reigned over free men in their own sovereign kingdom.

Dedication: to my parents, Rick and Carrie Griffith

The Clubber
Frank Komer
Golfing is a complicated game,
You're always looking somewhere to put the blame.
First you blame the ball you say is not right,
It should be red instead of white.

You hit the ball and you hit it hard,
But the ball goes only a couple of yards.
Oh, it isn't the ball, it isn't the club

It's the clubber who clubs the ball.
It's the clubber who clubs the ball.

It's the clubber who clubs the ball.
Then you blame the club and say it's not right
The handle's too short and the pitch is not right

Who hit the ball with all your might
The ball goes left instead of right.

It isn't the ball and isn't the club
It's the clubber who clubs the ball,
It's the clubber who clubs the ball.

Untitled
T. J. O'Grady

The cold dark tunnel of death made the man leap off the bridge
into an icy surface of water. The current acted as a vacuum to
suck him into the tunnel of death. He had no fight in him.
He allowed himself to be drowned in the water.
His journey through the tunnel will be alone until he comes to
his final destination. I hope the story of his end will add a meaning
to his life. Maybe his death will save others from the same fate.
He might be able to find the calm flowing river of peace and
love in death. His life makes sense if the river will turn warm
and inviting for pleasure and dreaming from now on.
I hope the tunnel will never claim another victim,
when people remember this man's final journey out of life.

Daddy's Home
Theresa Lynn Thomas

February, Nineteen Hundred and Ninety-Four
Our father's years of pain and suffering were no more.

Many times his agonizing cough would bring him to his knees
And his forehead would pour out tons of sweat beads.

We know Daddy is in a better place
No longer living among the human race.

I see him beyond the Heavenly gates
With his guardian angel as his eternal mate.

Our Daddy is with Jesus at last
He has no regrets from his past.

But I do wish that we had more time forever
Laughing, sharing and being together.

If Daddy were here I know he would say. . .
"I'm alright, baby, it's better this way."

Dedication: to my father, Ruben Harper, Jr.

Why?
Faye Carada

Why must we go through life, with all these heartaches,
troubles and strifes?

Why must we always be sad,
when others we know are so glad?

Why is life so unpredictable,
and sometimes even unbelievable?

But we never know what's in store,
but we're always wanting more.

Work, work, work, it's never done,
and another day has come and gone.
Forgive me, Lord, I have tried,
and sometimes I even cry.

But tears don't help, for only You understand,
and I thank You daily for being my friend.

Forgive me for questioning Your almighty plan,
And, Please, Lord, always hold to my hand!

Untitled
Elizabeth Stark

This is for Betty
Who likes to bake
The kids come over
And they're on the take
She makes good muffins
And cookies, too
I've yet to see one
That's full of goo
Betty's birthday is here on time
I think she said she's thirty-nine
She said that this age is true
But I really think she's thirty-two

The Pain Of Resistance
Niki Clarke

The pain wrenched at my heart, the fear activating latent signals of
  doubt.
I believed; shielded by positivity. But now...
A pall of insecurity and disbelief enveloped my soul.
Muffled utterances of betrayal embraced my mind.
My body was failing and my presence slowly ebbing away.
Hope was withdrawing itself from my fragile existence.
Self-pity permeated my sanctity of thought.
Living was not an option; surviving a necessity difficult to accomplish.
Negativity impeded every step; faithlessness ordained every fall.
A barrier of confusion and frustration deflected all semblance of
  optimism...
... Until a chink of understanding invaded my morose disposition.
Adversity destroys the despairing, yet strengthens the survivor.
Obstacles are solvable problems; not destiny recounted.
Transformation is transcendental; evolution is exquisite.
Nothing ends; just recreates.
What I was, I no longer am.
What I will be will alter with time.
What I will not be is desolate.

Dedication: to my mum, my strength

Happiness
Kimberly Souza

Can't be defined. It's a certain mood.
A state of mind.
It's sharing everyday affairs
With one who understands
And one who cares
It's a tender look
Or a gentle touch
That says "I love you
Very much"
It's a smile of welcome
When you're blue
A dream that's shared
A dream for two
Happiness is even more than this
It's a warm embrace
And a tender kiss
It's a special blessing
From above
It's what you have
When you're in love.

Dedication: to my best friend Steve 143

Enchanted Dreams

Confusion
Stephanie Rhiannon Hankins
I lie in shadowed corners
Light entreats at my door
Tears well up in my eyes
And splatter on the floor
Moonlight through my window
Penetrating black
I bask in his gentle glow
Reluctantly look back
I dare not leave the fevered sun
For the icy moon
I fear I'll die without the heat
I fear I may die soon

The Hands Of Nature
Brandi Bathurst
Leaves rustling.
Soft, quiet whispers
calling to me.
The sun's warm rays
like strong hands,
soothe me.
Raindrops falling gently,
like tender fingertips
touching my skin.
A breeze of spring that smells
so sweet, caresses me.
Nature, in itself,
is a sanctuary.
Within her hands,
she holds me.
Looking at Nature,
at this beautiful Earth;
we not only smell it,
breathe it and feel it—
we live it, we are a part of it.

Dedication: to Soreren and believing in yourself

Helpless To Surrender
Salvador Lee Martinez
Is there a thing such as love at first sight?
Well, if not, then he is surely mistaken,
because if so, then there is no doubt in his mind he is
in love with her, right?

Love is not one of those things that is easily expressed,
the look that was given doesn't tell how long it might be,
it could be weeks, months, even years
until they both have confessed.

Now that she's gone, his love for her grows stronger,
growing in his heart, mind and in his soul.
Just wanting to hold her in his arms keeps getting worse
as the days get longer and longer.

Seeing her come to him in his dreams makes his heart all
so tender, because when he wakes up neither her nor her
beautiful face is there to look at, but only knowing that
when he does reunite with her his undying love will make
him helpless to surrender.

Dedication: to Tina, my baby boo

Taking Chances
Sharolyn K. Turner
An unchallenged life breeds an existence of mediocrity
intricately laced with inhibition.

Protecting our heart from potential inadequacy encouraging a
static and impassive form of being.

To endeavor investigating destiny and trusting instinct alone
can foster a profound objective to your purpose in life.

Letting go with each new venture and resulting change, we
explore our unlimited capabilities, permitting our soul to
experience absolute contentment.

Mountain Gorilla
Kathy Burch
As I walk, through jungles dense, my need to know is so intense.

Gentle men, fierce and strong, judging nothing, what could be wrong?
Babies stolen in the night. How can I keep up this feeble fight.

Sold by humans, left and right. My family's gone, who knows where.
You take your guns, you take your traps, you take my trees,
you make your maps, forever going where no man's been,
destroying my world, my Heaven's dream. All I want is to be left alone,
no strangers, no death, no family's bones.

My mate and I, our children, too, have to wonder, when you're through.
If our world will look like yours. Steel bars and concrete floors.
No more forests, no more trees, you've brought us down, to our knees.

You make us hide, you make us fear, all we need is family near.

Must we die, forever gone, before you realize, what's gone wrong.

We must see, if you learn.

Dedication: to Robert — love always, Kathy

The Reality Of Jacob
Ty Harrison
Daddy, where are you tonight?
Is everything o. k. ? Are you alright?
I need to know these things because
I'm your son.
We were always Together, we were one

I know you're out there and probably
not far away
I love you, Daddy and think of you
every day.
I don't quite understand, I'm
just a little boy
Without you around, I feel like
a misfit Toy
Don't cry, Daddy, Don't even shed a tear
Just hold me close in your heart and
Know I'm always there.
You know how I love you, this much is true
But I'm just too small, what's a
Little boy to do?

Dedication: to my precious son Jacob Loren

The Anthology of Poems

My World
Sally Truss
My World
Would you walk in my footsteps–just for a time?
Would you talk to me, dream with me,
laugh with me–just for a time.
I need you to come
where my fears are for real,
and my toys come to life,
and my daydreams take flight.
Would you leave all your worries
for a Moment in time,
and come walk in my world,
and share some of mine?

Two Legs Or Four
Kristine S. Roberts
I wonder who it is you see who climbs up in my apple tree.
Who picks the apples red and round, before they plummet to the ground.
Four legs or two, who could it be?
I did not see who picked my tree.
Not in the day, but in the night, all the apples out of sight.
The time was spent, but not at rest.
Those darling little dearest pests.
Strolled on my land for all to see and took the apples off my tree.
Strolled and did not even care, that I was sleeping near.
Then in the dawn, there came a fawn, round and gold, the story's told.
I will not cry, for there'll be no pie.
Pears instead with homemade bread.
I'm forced to stay inside this day, with Autumn's feel and no apples to peel.
Instead I'll sit and think again of who came sneaking round the bend.
Two legs or four, I hear the door.
I open wide OH, MY! A pie.
I take a breath, now I can rest.
Two legs or four,
I shut the door.

Dedication: to my family and Meadowhedge

The Final Suffocation
William D. Knapp
A leaf has fallen to the
ground. Earth has made
another sound. Fortresses
relying on the dark.
Chariots thundering across
the land that is our ark.
Dancing with the light, which
is the eye of the storm.
Forecasting the wind and the
rain. Feeling the sorrow and
the pain. Cries within the
night, tension becoming tight.
A hope of seeing it all through,
the shocking delusion of reality
that is now you. Nothing left
to conceal, only wounds that
will not heal. The spirit is
flying as the soul is dying.
Fate is done, never again to
see the sun.

Dedication: to Dr. Larry Bowlins

Pain
Edwin E. Anderson
Pain has been the admission price
for my new life
To with each rising of the sun – think
as your life has just begun
Pain has purchased more than I
expected – which is a degree of humility –
which also is a healer of pain
All yesterdays are there – buried deep –
there let them sleep
To concern yourself with but today –
woo – it and teach it to obey; just for today
But remember, I hurt, therefore I am

Summer Garden
Anne Roberts
Geraniums of every hue,
Lobelia, white and Cambridge blue,
Trees that create a shady bower,
Where I can sit and ponder for an hour.

Fuschias, dancing, their ballerina skirts twirling,
The pool, with its waterfall tumbling and swirling,
Bees and butterflies, around the lavender busy,
Drinking its nectar, until they are dizzy.

Roses and honeysuckle intertwined,
Bizzy Lizzies and begonias gently cascading,
From baskets silently swinging,
Antirrinhums and gladioli parading,
A feast of colour, to please my artistic mind.

Under the apple tree, the cat is lazy,
While in the branches, a bird drives her crazy,
The herb garden aromatic and fragrant,
Marjoram, sage and chives are blatant,
In my garden, where I can rest at leisure,
God–given profusion and splendour to treasure.

The Rose
Michael Loch
Slipped into my pocket as I didn't look;
the most astounding present I ever received.
Frightening, new, exciting: the lover's gift.
One Luscious, Long–Stemmed, Crimson Rose;
green thornless stem; little white envelope.
"A Loving Reminder" is the only written memory...
Finding affection our strange route
only means one thing: we cannot fail,
When I think of the time before you,
I only remember tumultuous seasons;
Waves of Pain forever crashing in my life,
Until you calmed those violent storms...
Every time I clasp your hand with mine,
I can die knowing I truly lived my life.
Every time I close my curious, brown eyes,
your nurturing memory dances in my head.
Every time I touch or glimpse the rose,
I smile as I think of what you mean to me.
Since I now have someone to cherish,
I know that I cannot lose my faith in life.

Dedication: to my inspiration, Lauren

Enchanted Dreams

The Arena
E. A. Scholes
Blades on ice –
steel frozen
Cutting opaque circles –
Figure–eights
Cumulus breath, warm
hits the air,
then vapourizes.
And the skaters?
Whilst the young tumble the ice
We, skate our own Bolero!

Dedication: to David, for keeping me young

Overtaken
Vonnique Harvey
It hides away.
It waits 4 that weak Moment.
and
clamps its pain into UR soul.
Feeding off UR strength, cramping UR thoughts.
It swells up like a balloon waiting 4 the right Moment to burst.
It squeezes every vessel of blood it can get near.
It lives as a parasite,
that feeds off UR one
wrong decision.
That one decision that someone else made 4
U.
It lives as a demon wishing only 2 do one thing, 2
dampen UR spirit and cling 2 the heart.
Grabbing ahold and refusing 2 let go.
It hides.
It crawls about,
and
walks only when it feels it needs a little
stroll.

Dedication: look Mom, your Angel flies

Oncogenic Confusion
Marilyn Y. Meyer
To put it into words to Explain
Is a challenge of the soul
To create a feeling
To make it count when unexpected
The most precious of memories
Are those held the longest
You cannot take something as desired as this
Through windows of time we can see
Be taken anywhere
Unbelievable chances taken
A world as undefined as this
Can snap us into oblivion in a heartbeat
But to take our loved–ones
Leaving us to watch and writhe
In an unsettling, almost animated
Movement of emotion,
Can bring with it a high no less tolerated
As this uncontrolled Disease itself
To take from us when in dire weed
To eliminate it from within

Dedication: I love you, Mom

Cats
Thelma Hart
Cats
These two
Are best friends
Both black and white.
Toby and Lucky, always together
Grooming, sleeping, eating, playing, never apart.
Gentle Lucky, stern Toby, totally balanced personalities
Bird watching, lap sitting, napping, always keeping watch
Their tranquil days are full of peace and contentment.
The soft rumble of purring states, "Life is good here".

Dedication: to Ray, my lifetime loving partner

Jenny
Lia Tripp
Life.
Inside of me.
Cells bursting into form.
Shaping. Growing.
A mind, seeking knowledge.
A heart, gently echoing
Through a warming sea.
Hands, exploring.
Feet, thrashing.
Suddenly moving downward.
Squeezing. Pushing.
Pushing. Squeezing.
Light. Blinding.
Cold air rushing over
Crying lips.
Trembling. Living.
Holding. Hugging.
Warmth.
A gift from GOD to be returned.
For now, she's mine to love.

Dedication: to my daughter and friend, Jennifer

Danny Thomas
David A. Kemp
There once was a man among us,
a man named Danny Thomas.
That did not want our children to be ill,
and I hope that this is a dream we can fulfill.
He wanted cancer to be a thing of the past, then our
children would be safe at last.

For this was a man of care,
and took the challenges of dare.
He opened a hospital called St. Jude,
for the little gals and little dudes.
He said no child will ever be turned away,
that makes no difference, if they had no money
to pay.
He hated to see families cry,
and did not want another child to die.

He hated all forms of cancer,
and wanted to see it defeated and only then his
task would be completed.
For he will always be among us,
the spirit of Danny Thomas.

To My Family
Neil Hicks
I feel the fresh winds of love
lapping at my shore,
Lifting high up in the air my
spirit from the floor,
Heartache and pain from misspent youth
keeps tearing at my soul,
But now I have a wife and sons, my
life is rich and whole,
Now I fear deep in my heart
that they will go away,
I just hope with the love I give
forever they will stay.

I Love You Truly, Truly, Dear
Rosaria Simonetti
As I sit home day after day
It seems so long since you went away
I hope and pray to the Lord above
To send me home the one I love
To hold you close would be Heaven, Dear
'Cause I love you truly, truly, Dear.

I hope and pray for your return
To have the child for which we yearn
To build a home for three or more
Or perhaps to have a perfect score
Of that football team, we used to say
That we would have some live–long day.

'Twas not so long ago, my love
God was our Witness way up above
We made a vow, "Till Death Do Us Part"
I came down the aisle with a beat in my heart
When I saw you there, so handsome and true
With a happy smile and eyes so blue
I love you afar and love you near
'Cause I love you truly, truly, Dear

Believing
Ray A. Strawser
Believing is what happens – sometimes.
But mostly, we just try,
And cry and cry and cry.
'Cause cancer, or something just as bad, could get you anyway.
Then believing comes,
And mammograms;
And feeling scared,
And getting over little fears –
'Til big ones come.
And you try again through tears
For faith that will hold the pieces of soul together;
For soul that will hold the pieces of faith together.
Fragments of life come and go.
Pushing wholeness from the center of being,
And you try to be one
With better than now experiences.
But sometimes – like now,
Faith works,
And believing
Makes it better midst the worst!

Dedication: to Karen, my daughter

Cloud Eight
Lorna Wilson
In the only–child grey of the morning
The rings round our coffee cups look somehow dirtier
Somehow less complete
Than last night when we left them
The wine we split so heedlessly
Makes a stain more violent, deeper
Than candlelight would have had us believe
The leftover food we feasted on
Puts me in mind of carnage
And when I turn and briefly
Catch your gaze
The spark isn't so bright.

He's OOOOO?
Bryan Scott Wood
He's there when I'm weak;
He's there when I'm strong;
He's around when I can see;
He guides me when I can't;
He loves me when I do right;
He shows me when I've done wrong.
He teaches me when I need to be taught
He rewards me when I teach.
He cares for me when I'm sick;
He cares for me when I'm not;
He surrounds me, when I need him,
He's by me when I don't Know him,
He cries when I cry;
He sings, when I sing;
He needs me when I need to be needed;
He comes to me when I need someone else;
He's my best friend.
He's my everything.
He's God: Father, Son and Holy Spirit.
Thanks

Dedication: to my mother, Linda B. Stelle

Pacific Blue
Dennis W. Bishop
The Pacific is such a lovely blue,
In the evening it takes on a wonderful hue,

So vast – as far as the eye can see,
When I'm near, it feels a part of me,

The moon pushes its waves to shore,
So life can live forevermore,

Spiritual beings come and draw near,
They know it releases all their fear,

Fish and birds are blessed in the day,
At its edge, children play,

Lovers share Moments that are pleasing,
The warm waters can be oh, so teasing,

To find the Pacific, look to the west,
You'll find me there, at home, at rest.

Dedication: to my beloved Baba JT

Enchanted Dreams

Memories
Diana H. Adams
Memories, like distant music,
Gently haunt the heart.
Bittersweet, we sorrow
For those from whom we part.
They rise up with the morning sun
To catch us unawares.
They follow through the busy day
In spite of other cares.
Then flutter like the wings of moths
At the closing of the day.
And echo sadly through our dreams,
"Remember us, we pray."

Remembering Mother
Suzanne L. Plein
Today I looked at you, unblinking, demanding truth.
I threw off the quilt of acquiescence
we kept around us all those years, cushioning us
against our vanity, our rage, the beauty of our otherness
you could not accept.

We thought love could not suffer truth.
Intimacy would shatter once a confidence unraveled,
a shortcoming was exposed,
in an unguarded Moment.

You tried for perfection, smiling through the ache of
unrequited passion.
You never spoke of it.
I always knew.

Today I look at you with writer's eyes that do not blink.
I reach for you across the abyss.
Holding enough truth for both of us,
I take your bony hand and walk with you.

Dedication: to my daughter Julie Dee

There's No One In Sight
B. J. Jackson
I see the sunset
with the golden colors of yellow
the russet shades of orange.

See the blue sky
turn into the darkest night
the star's twinkle of bright silver
and the moon shines aglow

As I stand by my window
to hear silence all around
the breeze filters through my curtain
right now the wind's song is the only thing I hear.

As the rain starts softly sprinkling
to the pavement upon the streets
I hear the sound of running feet

While the lighting slices into the darkness
And thunder shakes the silence
I stand and wait for your return
But, there's still no one in sight

A Cowboy Way Of Life
Jax Summers
He can play with the bad boys and take all the pain
He knows what it takes, to stay in the game.
Thrown off more bulls than remembered, his body's battered and abused.
He's hit the ground hard enough, to get up dazed and confused.
He can rope all those steers and stay on the roughstock.
Sometimes the only thing he can count on, is having bad luck.
He knows to pull the rope tight and stay out of the well.
He hits the ground running, learned that the first time he fell.
It's the rush when he rides and the cheers when he covers,
So even when he's hurt, he just climbs on another.
He'll never have money, nor much else to show,
'Cept for some shiny old buckle, he won at the rodeo.

Acceptance
Frances Wade
And all my sorrows become a whisper
That only I can hear.
Bright lights of daytime living
Dance here and there.
The tunes of past behavior drift through,
And the struggle to go forward – leaving behind
What I once knew.

The dreams drift in and out as tomorrow becomes today.
I watch the children run and play.
I hold back sadness and fight all the way
To stay within the sanity of mind.
Uneasiness, discomfort and remorse my companions are
A soothing peace o're takes me as I view afar.
The glimpse behind my eyes is hope,
But veils of my sick self enclothe my soul.

One day I know the dreams will slip into my life.
And, I at last will give up the fight.
But till that time, each Moment is a chain of misery;
Still, if this is the love I seek... then,
let it be.

Lost In The Wind
Lisa Wynn
In the wind, I hear a voice;
It's calling to me, I have no choice.
As I listen, I try to understand:
"Whose voice is this that I can't see to touch his hand?"
The wind grows stronger, the voice gets louder.
He seems to be screaming.
I don't know; "What is his meaning?"
He's saying to me, "I want to come home."
But I can't take him there, he's left in the wind to roam.
I cry out and say, "Please leave me be!"
He becomes calm as the wind dies down.
He whispers, "It's you that I need to believe in me."
His voice gets hysterical as the air blows with all its might.
"I really love you," he shouts out into the darkness of the night.
The moon and stars brightly appear.
The wind seems frozen with fear.
I close my eyes and softly say,
"When you are truly ready to be loved, then I promise you that I'll stay."
It became as bright as day; I opened my eyes and there he was.
He touched my hand and simply said, "That's all, my dear, that I pray."

Dedication: to my family with love

These Tears
Catherine Lindsley

These tears I shed are not my own, they are for all the guys who spent their time in Vietnam. For they deserved so much and received so little.
I shed these tears for the ones who bravely fought and lost their lives over there for this country. I shed these tears for the ones who came back missing parts of their bodies.
I shed these tears for the ones who made it back with everything but their souls. So brave to face a world with so much hatred. I shed these tears for the ones that are still over there, whether or not they are still alive.
I shed these tears but they are not my own.

Dedication: to all who have served

The Empty Seat
Tim Meyer

The moonlight lands
On the empty seat beside me.
In the silver light
Falling through the window
I can see your lovely image,
Sitting with a contented smile
At my side.
But you're far away,
Headed towards the rest of your life,
While I'm still here
Missing your loving caresses
And your sidelong glances that let
Me know you care.
I don't know where you are
Or what you are doing,
But wherever you are
I hope you're loving me
And missing me,
The way I'm loving you,
alone tonight.

Dedication: to Anna, whom I love

Untitled
Nancy L. Baker

I am like a hungry vulture, soaring through the sky.
Looking down upon you, hoping you will die.
I would love to feast upon your brain, I would relish in your pain, in your kingdom I would reign and never would I refrain.
I am your enchanted nymph,
I am the virgin in your bed.
I'd follow you anywhere you go, I'll follow you when you're dead.
I would jump from atop your castle and crawl on my knees through your muddy moat.
But for you, it would not be a hassle,
to watch as you laugh and gloat.
I am the mighty dragon, lurking in your cave.
I am watching and waiting and hunting you down.
I am your secret, forlorn slave.
Bearing this beautiful blood-soaked crown.
I sit alone, I dwell in the dark.
While You are praised and You stand tall.
And in my head I hear a harp,
As I await the day Your palace will fall.

Dedication: to Todd, who holds my soul

We Forever
Heather Ross

As naturally as day
Fades to night—
I,
Fade to you.
Becoming a whole—
Obliterating a pair.
Drinking in the dawn,
Surrounded by the warmth and coldness of
Time—
Everlasting through dusk.
A synopsis of
Heaven.

My Worlds
Sean Beach

I was walking through the woods one day.
All the light was gone, as the Heavens began to shower
I found nothing to help me on my way,
But then I saw a single flower.
Through all this dread and gloom
When all other colors died,
This single flower managed bloom
Though nothing else survived.
With all the beauty of the world, concealed within this tiny flower
My thoughts strayed to a "World", once lost.
But, not I've found within this flower.
And so I bring my two worlds together
My "World" once lost now concealed within this flower
One so strong it survived the dreaded, gloomy weather.
Yet as beautiful and magnificent as a jewel in laden tower.
And to my other World, which to whom I'd give my life
I give all I have of a lost World;
Pure, beautiful and free of strife.
I give you this flower which signifies my life,
As well as my "Love".

Dedication: to my love and inspiration, Katie

Childhood Romance
Debra Mayer

How sweet the memories of a childhood romance,
the feelings were strong and thought they surely would last.
Telephone calls just to say "hi," never wanting to say "goodbye."
Holding hands, a quick kiss at the door,
hoping their parents... would stay away from the door.
They said that this love would never last,
so, we went on with our lives, never forgetting the past.
When times seemed bad, or we were sad,
we'd think of the memories of our childhood romance.
Always wondering what might have been,
and thinking of them, with a grin.
And if by chance, a time arrives...
to see if the memories are truly alive.
Be cautious, but sure, with no stone unturned,
because there's a chance "away" you may be turned...
But oh, what a joy... if you should find,
your feelings are shared and you both want to bind...
in making new memories of the very best kind.
The ghosts have been lifted of your childhood past,
to begin your new journey, with your childhood romance.

Dedication: to Marilyn and Eddie, reunited 1998

Enchanted Dreams

A World Of Life
Lauri Kamiel
There Should Always Be Time For Life
you only have one
only one of each day
only one past to learn from... only one future to perish from...
what do you want to see in your future?
what has the past taught you?
when will you let your past show you your future?
see the world...
it's yours to greet... to frolic... to accompany... to complete... yet this
world may also be through your skin... from your heart and beyond...
to the soul and within... so explore that world... make it go round...
for this is the world which your spirit has found

Woman, God's Creation
Maggie L. Allen
When God created man, He gave him a wife
Someone to love and cherish for life.
A woman has a major role on Earth
By nature, she's the one who gives birth.
She's a wife, mother, teacher and friend
Who gives love and support to the very end.
For guidance and strength, she looks to God
To comfort and direct her on the road she trods.
She's never too busy to shed some light
When things are wrong or when they are right.
Whether there are problems large or small,
With prayer and faith she conquers them all.
From hour to hour and day to day,
She'll take time to kneel and pray
For her spouse, her children and a friend in need.
She'll give advice to all who will heed
The Word of God given to everyone,
Who will believe and accept His Son.
A woman is as precious as a diamond or pearl;
There's no one like her in the whole wide world.
She'll cherish, honor and give you love
As our Heavenly Father loves from above.

War Cries
Terry Holmes
See me here,
With paws pressed tightly,
To my face,
As rivers stream,
Form minute falls onto my knees,
Pressing firmly amongst the soil...

Feel the rage,
The gentle tears breed angst,
Into the Earth beneath my being...

Hear the cries of evil,
Counting coup upon my soul,
Licking my wounds,
Tasting the pain,
The snake has lost...

Smelling death,
As he falls void,
Beneath my claws...

Dedication: to Tha Fam and the Family

Love Always, Your Secret Admirer
Megan R. Smith
I watch you so silently,
hoping that you'll notice me.
You're the perfect guy, with just one flaw,
You fail to know I exist at all
I watch you in the halls each day,
Until you pass me by.
Wishing one day that I could say,
You'd always be my guy.
But until that day, I sit and dream.
Dream on and on about you.
Waiting for the day to come,
When you say "I love you, too."

Spirit Ride
Darlene Johnson
I caress your neck and hold you close
You are my spirit, my freedom
Upon your back I ride
Feeling your power beneath me
The wind caresses my face
As we ride through the night
In unison
As one

You understand my moves
You know my touch
You feel my weight upon you
And you answer my heart
By taking me into the night
Guided by the stars and moon
And into another world we ride
A world of spirits and freedom
Me and you alone
In unison
As one

Dedication: to my rose man

The Great Gift
Jeremy Senske
The tree stands surrounded
And slowly it grows
A weak little sapling
Surrounded with nourishment

The tree slowly grows
And becomes trampled on
It is cut and scraped
Bruised and torn
But slowly grows on

Corruption is sustained
And mistakes are made
Bended and twisted
It begins to grow straight
Gradually reaching to the light

Standing tall and proud
This tree tangles with another
And grows old solemnly
Only to be cut down
And laid to rest on a soiled floor

The Reason
Cassandra McCanse
In days of rain where the sun hides its face,
I await the Moment that death pours upon my soul like
delicate lace.
While enriching the strength of disconsolate dismay
Eyes wander the spot that enlightenment lay.
How to treasure a lost essence is what I long for...
And the endowment to receive the love again in the core.
This soul is everything I never knew I always wanted,
And if time were turned back, eternity would never be haunted.
Oh, if I knew that such an exquisite reality existed,
I could advance to life as though it were eternally blessed.
Oh, my sky, my sun, my moon, my stars... I was scared,
Was so afraid to show I cared.
That he would find me weak,
For I tremble when I speak.
I held out my heart upon my hand
And allowed the man to misunderstand.
Better to have loved and lost than never to have loved at all...
To give credence to that it were true were my own blemish
and detriment with fall.
Now I must choose to live for all that I can give and know,
And rely on myself for the spark that makes the power grow.

Depression
Amy Lefler
I close my eyes and lie on my bed.
Hoping this pounding will stop going through my head.
I try to stop crying, but nothing seems to work.
Why did I have to fall for such an incomplete jerk?
My head is throbbing and it's getting hard to breathe.
Mom, please listen, I am trying really hard to succeed.
All this pressure and all this pain, I just don't know what to do.
I know if I really need someone to listen it could always be you.
Why does life have to be so hard and unfair?
I think I will do nothing and cuddle by my bear.

Dedication: to my loving mom

Forever...
Jonathan Smith
The familiar sound of your words,
I hear as they are spoken from your tongue
Remind me of the days
In which I could talk and you would listen... forever

I would speak 1,000 words
And yet you would comprehend them as if they were one,
I would speak of the gleaming foreshadows in my life
Not spoken of to anyone but you and I trust you... forever

I could put my trust in you
And you would believe in me,
You would help me, guide me... forever

And now I believe in you
And trust you... forever

I would put my life in your hands
And you would hold it,
Like your own heart in your chest
And you would cherish it, help it
And this day will be in my mind... forever.

Children
Bruce Two Eagles
The child of my mind still runs free,
Alone, sometimes, and so far away from the body in which
it is enclosed.

Wondering, still, if it will be caught and bound up by the
presence of now.

Hoping that it will never release me from the impish moods
or pleasing thoughts of a carefree life.

To be able to smile at yesterday and not fear tomorrow,
or dance at the day and not be alone in the night.

The child of my mind still runs free to be my comfort and my friend.
To release me from the ironies of the world of realities.

As the days go on, my body grows older, but my child, my friend,
still lives on the same, never aging or tiring.

The child of my mind still runs free, I cannot give you my child nor
can I share it.
For I cannot touch it. I do not know it, it is just there.

Soul To Sea
Sareen Wamhoff
I take in the morning dew and always think of you.
The hue in my eyes is the reflection of the sea.
I feel the ocean in my soul, when the wind is cold.
Although the sun is high in the sky, the breeze is chilling my bones,
and I sigh. This cold sand is all I have, you were once here, too.
You are but a flake in the wind, a grain in the Earth's dust.
Shall I descend?
So that I may join you within the soul of the Earth?
I take but the air that I breathe, and water, the elixir of life itself.
Do I brave the suffering of my surrender of them, for you?
mine own self I do this for and I will, I will join you
in the soul of this Earth.

Mom
Pasquale Ferrucci
Words could never express
how much you mean to me
without your devoted love
I'd never fulfill my dreams
Within each day of my life
your wisdom seems to reflect
whatever I say or do
with the best of intellect
You're unique in so many ways
with personality and charm
your laughter brings me joy
and I'm content when in your arms
Whenever you smile at me
a warmth comes over my soul
filling my heart with pride
that I want the world to know...
You're the world's most precious gem
so exquisitely designed
You're flawlessly perfected
I thank the Lord you're mine!

Dedication: to my loving wife and aunt

Enchanted Dreams

Flu Attack
M. E. McClenan
Sometimes you lose your temper,
Sometimes you lose your rag,
Sometimes you leave me all alone and sneak off for a fag.
Upstairs lying on my own can get to be a bore
So then you come and sit with me
But all you do is snore.
The meals you cook are passable
But couldn't be called a treat.
Still, when the flu attacks you
You don't want much to eat.
You haven't done much cleaning.
But at shopping you're quite good.
Have you put the rubbish out?
I really think you should.
I hope you are not lonely
Just you and the TV
I know it's not exciting like it is when you're with me.
Hope your little holiday hasn't been too bad
Cause now the fun is over
And I'm back to drive you mad.

Dedication: to my beloved John

Untitled
Angela Legg
Glass from the window shatters silently as the pieces
of my heart
Crumble onto the floor. Shadows dance their last dance
on the walls of my mind.
Shades of black and blue are echoed in my memory. Only
time can heal the pain of what I had witnessed.
Seeing you lying there so timid and tame,
kills me more and more every day.
you gave me the strength I need.
I'll hold that memory with me forever.
You're with me wherever I go and you never know you're
the strength I have today.

Puzzle Pieces
Rima Bent
A Piece of the puzzle
refuses to Fit
Beer guzzled
Acrid, desire to Spit
Concealing her Pain
With fashionable clothes
Only Happy when it Rains
Anticipation of the special Glow
Hibernation of the Senses
Comes with a Liquid
Crawling with the skunks with their Stench
Not wanting to be Another has–been
Desire ebbing and flowing
the Will to Fight
Can't believe she's really Choking
On those Regrets in the Night
Beyond the Abyss
Pin dropped in the Chasm of my Soul
Absence of feigned Bliss
Uncaring skin feels so Cool
Trapped in an Upside china bowl
Screaming from nothing to Do A

Why If Ever
Vince Hampton
Eventually and relentlessly, each day ends and the
Twilight slides from no–where, intent on making friends,
Embracing all and sundry to horizons out of sight and
Smoothes the way for nightfall with its quiet and its might.
The weary drown in slumber and twisted minds subside,
And broken hearts reclaim their parts, failed in their suicide.

For night pulls on a soothing glove, dark fingers all
Out–stretched, to cloak the Earth and hide the scars and cuts
Of shame half–etched.

How long before the twilight and the darkness weld their
Shroud and be as one with life all gone beneath a nuclear
Cloud. With tree roots staring skywards and oceans boiling
dry, massed rubble moaning in the wind and not one child
to cry.

No bells to ring, no birds to sing, no armies left to quell,
where the signs all point to Heaven but the roads all lead
to hell.

Dedication: to Beryl, my dearest friend

Death By Suicide
Penny Baldwin
His friend had died
death by suicide
for Heaven's sake
His parents said he was a mistake
facing time, 15 years
No friends were there to share his fears
of sin too much
As drugs and such
of friends too few
what would he do
He drew his gun up from his side
DEATH again by suicide

Springtime
J. T. Perry
The early morning mist has gone,
The sun begins to shine.
I wash the sleep from both my eyes,
Today the time is mine.
I think I'll wander through the park,
I'll watch the squirrels play.
They see me come and gather round.
What has he brought today?
The trees are full of singing birds,
Their colours are divine.
Mother Nature at her best,
It surely is springtime.
The daffodils that mark my way.
Their bowing heads of gold.
They seem to whisper as I walk,
Keep secrets all untold.
I watch the ducks upon the pond,
I feel the springtime breeze.
Relax upon my favourite bench,
Let nature dress the trees.

Dedication: to my dear wife Elizabeth

Untitled
Vera Hammond

I think that it's extremely odd,
That those who are the sons of God,
Can rob and wound and hurt and kill,
And expect to get to Heaven still,
If, after a life of wrong-doing spent,
At the end they just repent,
But creatures such as beasts and birds,
The loners and the ones in herds,
Are told they do not have a place,
That Heaven's for the human race,
I feel that this is most unfair,
For smallest mouse and largest bear,
I think that all creatures wild and tame,
The Lord surely knows each one by name,
And as we are taught that God is love,
There is a home in Heaven above,
Where every little broken tree
Shall bloom again eternally,
And to all dear creatures who cannot sin,
The good Lord will say – please do come in.

Dedication: to Sally and Chico

Untitled
Jill Barnett

The hardest day is yet to come,
No more walks out in the sun.
As time grows shorter and the day comes near,
There is no time left for the fear.
Long, hard cries, up all night,
Is it time to give up the fight?
Every day's a struggle, there is no end,
Your body's one that God can't mend.
One day you will lose your grip,
About to take that one last trip.
Yes, it is true, the end has come,
One last walk up to the sun.

Life's Discoveries
Rosanna Fabrizi

Life is a road we all travel on.
The path we journey on parts in two.
Choices so many...
Chosen by few!
There are lessons to be learned...
For one day we can teach.
It begins with mistakes...
That we don't care to preach.
Our minds tell us one thing.
While our hearts say another.
The truths that we seek...
Shall soon be discovered!
There will be others along the way.
That we will meet someday.
Reasons unknown, soon will be realized.
We awake with dreams of wanting to be someone special.
Making our mark, for it will be official.
Those stars that we reach are there for the taking.
Only be certain and ask yourself...
Are you ready for the awakening?

Dedication: to my late father, Fernando Pettine

Untitled
Hannah Fisher

Why be a song when you can be a symphony.
You can do what you want, if you've got the
spirit.
It's all within reach if you stretch out your mind.
You will become so strong, if you believe in
yourself
You're the controller of your destiny, the precursor
of your fate.

There are problems that will face you.
There are people who'll stand in your way.
Are you really prepared to sit in a corner
Or take up the challenges that life has
in store

You can be the same as everyone else;
or you can shine right through and claim
your place.
You have a right to be heard and a right to be
seen.
Enjoy the glory and satisfaction in achieving
a dream.

Untitled
Stephanie Caswell

I have a theory; it is that we are all someone's dream.
Maybe like a paper doll, too!
We live our lives a certain way because we have to.
Because, if we don't, we might die or something.
We all have an ideal self or a dream that someday we'll have
the perfect life with everything we need.
But it will never come true, because we could screw up
the lives chosen for us.
So each day we awake, thinking we can change our lives,
but we all know somewhere deep down inside we'll never be able to!
This is a scary thing for all of us to face.
So we just keep on pretending and hoping the dream will change!!

In Memory Of Grandfather Robert
Claire Kyriacou

Grandfather Robert, well, what can I say
A stubborn old man right to the last day
When he said no, he meant yes
And when he said yes, he meant no
But the fact is he loved us
And that's all we need to know
But for me it doesn't matter if he said it or not
We all know he loved us
Just from those feelings we got
He was a real Granddad, because he put us kids first
If he told you a story, he'd read every verse
He'd never cut corners or rushed the job through,
That time spent together was dedicated to you
He'd always fix our toys, which we quite often broke
But it was never a hassle, just ask anyone
They'll tell you he was a great bloke
Listen, I could write this poem until it was a
Whole book long
But all I'm trying to say, grandfather,
Is that your memories live on.

Dedication: to Mum with all my love

Enchanted Dreams

The Lady Of Lights
Phil Murray
The lady of lights is a friend I know.
I met her only a short time ago.
She has given a lasting hope to me
Somebody who helped me with my insecurity.
Restoring the memory of who I now am
So freeing me from sorrow caused by a sham.
She has insight and foresight on the way I feel
The lady lifted my low spirits a great deal
All old isolation I am plagued with no longer
Due to encouraging words making me stronger
I'm starting a change aided by my new guide
Which will end at the time I find myself inside.
My pal's brain is phenomenal and like no other.
But similar defects, means we understand one another.
Delving, we were credited in our search of our souls.
Our talking levels match like two magnetic poles.
She is an example of the friend I desired
I have found this soul mate I required.
Someone that I can always talk to,
The Lady of Lights, my friend, is you.

Dedication: to Flain Darlington, a dear friend

Promises
Brenda Henson
In the depth and despair of my darkest day,
I turn inside to myself and I say;
I can do this, I can overcome,
Forget the past, what's done is done.
Concentrate on the future, what's ahead for me,
I can handle it, whatever it may be.
My strength is myself, of this I am sure,
Whatever happens I will endure.
Life's journey is an ongoing quest,
I promise myself to give it my best.
I'll strive to succeed in whatever I do,
My promise to myself, constantly renewed.

Silver Lady
Cassandra Mahon
See the green bottles floating on down the river
Tried and tired of trying to do
Seeing and weary of what I see
Silver lady, shine your light down on me
Smooth the way towards a heart of gold

I felt for a land of mysteries
Angelic division and a soul of compassion
God's own country, ruler of it all
Silver lady, shine your light down on me
Smooth the way towards a heart of gold

Slipping down the long highway
Where will it end in the days to come?
Creature comforts encompass the man
But wherefore art thou, Oh, my soul's delight
Wherefore art thou, my golden heart?

Time's movement onward succors the crying breast
Slowly joy enters again
The life force moving to regain harmony
Soothing the way towards a heart of gold

Grandfather
Ardeda Brown
My Grandfather was a good man
The kind of man that always lent a helping
hand.
No matter what, he was there if he could
And you know he would.

My Grandfather, a church-going man,
he praised the Lord
And his Grandchildren he'll always adore.
He helped my mother when she was down
He helped raise my little brother without a frown.

He was always there for us
to teach us the bible
And from right and wrong,
the way we live and survive.

My Grandfather did a lot in life
He liked fishing,
Watching all types of games
And things won't be the same
Without my Grandfather!!

The Tree
Peter K. Quain
Its leaves made music in the wind
Its trunk was strong and wide
Then construction came to town
To destroy a land of pride
The fearless tree stood proud and strong
Trying to hold its ground
Then from many miles away
Came the executioner's sound
The saw cut through the tree trunk
And the leaves cried their last song
When will the executioner's see that
Killing trees is wrong?

The Glen Of The Weeping
Stuart McDonald
In the highlands
In a glen
When times were wild.
With wilder men.
A demon storm
From hell it blew
Carried with it
A devilish crew.
They were given shelter.
Warmth and food
From their soon-to-be victims.
Who had warmth in their blood.
As they slept in their beds.
The were never to know.
The guests they had welcomed
Were a heartless foe.
It may seem a long time now
It seems o, so far.
For the guilty have no pride
And they know who they are.

Dedication: to Linda, love you wads forever

Riding Out–Dedicated To A Cowboy
Jo Ann Wilson
Riding out in the morning mist
Across pastures cool and crisp.
Tending his herds, both large and small
He was the keeper, the caregiver of all.

Calm in the saddle, he chartered the course
Of riders and herds passing him by on his horse.
The sick and wounded were tended to first
'Herds were slowed at the dugout to satisfy thirst

When the long miles were crossed and the herds safely penned in
He stepped down from his saddle and turned with a grin.
He organized all to gather around
The campfire was started, the songs and stories abound.

He taught a few, some good lessons and us all, about love.
He has left us for just awhile to ride a peaceful pasture above.
But we know he will be waiting with arms open wide
To welcome us to his and God's side.

And when our day ends, as we know that it will
He'll lift us up to God's peaceful hill.

Immature Intuition
Georgia Taylor Bidwell
NEVER KNEW What I Saw,
Never could say
WHAT BEFELL MY EYES.
You can't
YET YOU WERE THERE.
WE'VE TALKED about it many times,
Our Memories Don't Seem
To fail us.
THE IMPRESSIONS ARE THE SAME
BUT... EXACTLY...
WHAT It Was;
You and I it seems cannot say.

The Homecoming
Linda Preuss
I looked for you for such a long time, Darling... but I couldn't find you
I kept calling you... but you couldn't hear me
I'd close my eyes and "feel" you... but you couldn't see me

I know you were out there – waiting for me, as I was waiting for you
But the time wasn't right – and there was nothing we could do...

Just wait
And pray
That someday – we will find each other (once again)

Soul mates from a life time ago
I know... I can feel it deep inside the very essence of my being
– you reach down so deep
Where there is no such thing as time

Can you feel it?
Do you remember?

We were lovers then
"Impassioned" lovers... you and I...
And now – "Welcome home again, Darling"... I've missed you ever so –

The Dawn Of A New, Bright Morn
Yukwor Lee
From my little boat, rocking and rolling
through the night, dark and long,
I climb on the landing board
to set foot on solid rock,
to look for an odd job
at the dawn of the day in the mist and the fog!

The road to press on is rugged and long
and full of thorns.
Yet, I have to struggle on
with the dim hope of beating the odds.
But, now, I am caught at the crossroad.
Which road should I take?
I really know not.
My heart sinks and I am lost at the crossroad
in the mist and the fog!

The road in life is also rugged and long
and full of trouble and struggle
like living on a little boat, rocking and rolling
through the night, dark and long,
yawning and longing for the dawn of a new, bright morn!

Crown
Regina Davis
Circles of majestic light revolve around my head
Magic, appearing only to vanish and transform
Flash, an inner awakening of the other status of matter
Feelings of contentment materialize
As swirls of golden light, zag into particles
Disrupting rings of unified harmony into a wave
Which forms whirling eddies of warmth
Currents of unconditional love vibrate
A drum song of passion resonates through the air
Signaling the discovery of luminous jewels.

Dedication: to Gary Fiskum, for opening my heart

Silence
Bettie Cooper
The snow is five inches deep.
There is nothing but silence.
There are two small dogs in the house,
But they make no sound.
There is nothing for them to bark at.

I sit here alone.
The highway is about a quarter-mile away.
But you cannot hear the noise from there.
Although you can see the cars and trucks pass
There is no sound whatsoever.

There is no clock to tick.
Always, I thought, a beautiful sound.
Here I sit, with little to do
But listen to the silence.

To some Silence is Golden.
It is despairing to me.
For me, golden only after a day of activity
Or work.
Or at a place with people.

Enchanted Dreams

In Your Eyes...
Elizabeth Woolcott
When I look in your eyes
I see the stars, the moon, the sky.
When I look in your eyes
I see the Love that we hold dear,
And I know that you'll always be there.
When I look in your eyes.

And there'll be no secrets between us,
'Cause every tear holds the truth.
And no one will separate us,
Since our Love is so true.

In your Eyes we'll always be together
'Cause our Love is so strong.
And old age won't disappoint us.
We'll always carry on.

In your eyes is honor, truth and Love.
The man that you are.
And the life that we'll have... Together.
And I know that all these things hold true...
All when I look in your Eyes.

My Closet
Karly Roberts
My closet — who knows what's in there,
Maybe a lion or tiger,
Or a snowshoe hare,
Maybe a cat,
Maybe a dog,
But, who would know that?
Maybe a rat,
Maybe a skunk,
Or a bat in my best Sunday hat.
Who would know that?
I won't look in there,
I wouldn't dare.

Questions
Tracey Smith
The hand of death falls upon him,
and he walks away forever.

We've watched you leaving — not knowing that you were.
You've played in our world and then retreated to yours.
Was it lack of love or trust that you deceived us –
By intention or necessity that you rejected us –
By self–pity or pride that you deprived us–

Of your true heart and self.

There's a shadow in my mind of a stranger standing there.
I know who I was taught he was,
– saw glimpses of who he really was,
– or who he may have been.

Secrets that might have been shared,
Words that needed to be spoken.
Questions that search for an answer, if in a Moment
stolen from that stranger...
I have only one question;
... didn't you love us...

Portrait Of Vandals
Carla F. Ellis
As it hung from the wall,
Everybody looked,
At the beauty of colour.
Even I was hooked.
But something wasn't right,
Something was amiss,
What Should have been there,
Certainly wasn't this.
It should have shown a child,
So happy in her play,
But what it showed made all of us,
Want to turn away.
The flowers were OK
But behind the girl so small,
It showed the playground broken,
Her sad face shamed us all.
The vandals that had done this,
Just couldn't give a care,
Until they've children of their own,
And want to take them there.

Dedication: to all my family and friends

Hidden Agenda
Sally E. Lawson
MEMO:
Staffing is to be reduced.
The jargon of management.
Skills analysis will be used.
Redundancy beckons.
Personal qualities, years of experience
Devotion to duty, professional development.
Are they relevant?
Are they important in the handicap of life?
The hidden agenda
Is written between the lines;
My number.

Around The Corner I Have A Friend
Ruth Bradford
Around the corner I have a friend
In this great city that has no end.
Yet days go by and weeks rush on,
Before I know it, a year has gone.
And I haven't seen my old friend's face,
For life's a swift and terrible race.

She knows that I love her just as well
As in the days when I rang her bell.
We were younger then and now I'm tired,
I work, I learn, I try not to get fired
I'm tired with playing a foolish game,
I'm tired with trying to make a name.

"Tomorrow" I say, "I'll call on her",
To show my friend that I'm thinking of her.
But, tomorrow comes and tomorrow goes,
And still the distance grows and grows.
Around the corner, yet miles away.
Her daughter calls, – "she died today".
And that's what I get and deserve in the end,
Around the corner — a vanished friend.

The Wall
Susan E. Doty

Here stands a wall,
Tall and magnificent,
Built over many months.
My father and I built it,
Together.

We took turns placing the bricks,
One by one.
We strengthened it with time,
Supported it with memories.
It is a wall strong enough
To withstand any attempt to break through,
Tall enough so no one can see over it,
From one side to the other.

We made the bricks ourselves,
My father and I,
Of the strongest materials.
This wall will probably last long after we are gone.
Yes, my father and I built a wall,
Together,
But we stand on opposite sides.

Welcome to my Hell
Heather Wollesen

Welcome to my hell where you hurt and everything's
burnt.
Welcome to my hell where everything smells of smoke
and your heart is broke.
Welcome to my hell where you feel betrayed and enslaved;
never again to see the light of day.
Welcome to my hell where you're depressed and your love
obsessed; all he thinks of is you undressed.
Welcome to my hell where your life is blown and you're
all alone, where no one calls on the phone.
When it's my time I'll ring like a bell, until then
I'll stand here in my hell.

Acquiescence
Hasty Adlparvar

Hasti died on the 26th of February
For I am not she

Nothing around me is familiar
Nothing around me makes sense
I was kept by the love of a human
To roam the Earth, crippled
Crippled body, nay, crippled emotions
Torn between a sweet past
And a new life attacking fast

How sweet it could have been
To hold hands and fly
How dignified and clean
To soar without a lie

Yet the now I must use
And the now should be based
On a now filled with certitude
Of God's loving grace

If I am ever to fly again.

My Precious Brother
Irene C. Homes

Oh, how I'll miss you, brother of mine
Who gave up so much of his love and his time
To those he felt needing his help and his care
They all could be sure that for them Roy was there
Money meant nothing to him from life's start
He knew that all need came straight from the heart
He'd visit the old, take the young on his knee
How we all loved him, especially me
He gave us all laughter, kept a smile on our face
And with all of his jokes he was full of God's grace
Right from a child his belief was divine
Maybe stronger than yours and most certainly mine
He made us all happy whether family or friend
And never complained though in pain till the end
His faith always told him he'd meet Dad and Mum
For my treasured brother that time has now come
So goodbye dearest brother, we know that we'll find
So much love and the caring that you left behind
And to the most precious husband, Granddad and Dad
We all say God bless you to the best this world had.

Dedication: to dearest Roy, in loving memory

Instincts
Mark Thompson

Search your heart
to find what is true.
Search your mind,
to see what to do.
Follow your instincts,
they are usually right.
Your heart is so loving,
your mind is so bright.
All matters of life,
are easily solved.
Remember your instincts,
we are not that evolved

I Am
Vanessa Bacal

I am an energetic girl who loves sports.
I wonder if I'm going to be an actress.
I hear screaming in my head.
I see things I really don't.
I want to be a very active girl when I grow up.
I am an energetic girl who loves sports.

I pretend to be professional.
I feel a baseball in my hands.
I touch the clouds.
I worry about dying.
I cry for help.
I am an energetic girl who loves sports.

I understand I'm not the best.
I say I should try my hardest.
I dream about waterfalls.
I try to break my own records.
I hope you guide me through life.
I am an energetic girl who loves sports.

Dedication: to my teacher, Zelda Schopp

Enchanted Dreams

One Mate
Gloria Bozanic
It breaks my heart to see,
people who leave,
their mate that they'd chosen to be
The one to share forever,
The one to share each day,
The one to share,
time eternity.

When I was very young,
two hawks would come,
each summer to the same old tree.
Then one year just one arrived.
I ached for him inside.
He lost the one who shared his bright skies.

Even free wing birds know,
deep down in their souls,
with one mate, is
the only way to fly.
And if they share each passing day,
there can be no way,
To take their bond and turn it into broken.

The Watcher
Joseph R. Mays
God is my Watchtower;
watching over all that I do.
Protecting me from harm,
and watching every step.
For God is the Watcher,
surveying the twisted road of life;
looking ahead and preparing me
for troubles, toils and strife.
And for that reason, when the skies of life grow dark,
I shall not fear;
for God is the Watcher
and He'll always be near.

Our Town
Peggy Shafer Lucia
When you come downtown
To the Old Town Bay,
Your eyes are amazed
And you have to say.

The shops, along the beach
The people are friendly,
Places to eat,
Shopping on Main St., so many.

The scenic view
Overlooking the Bay;
Will make you come back
And you'll want to stay.

Hospitality, is our middle name,
Friendship, remains the same.

So, next time you are downtown
Remember us in your heart,
We are Bay St. Louis,
A place apart.

A Letter Of Love, To My Love
M. Cross
Light of my life, I see the shadow of the arrow as it flies through the air Splitting my heart in two. As I travel in my dreams, I see the love that we shared, memories and joys that we felt, but it's not a dream. The light in our eyes as they met. The warm of your arms surrounding me in the night. I love you now and in my awaking. Where are you now as you sleep the great sleep when I love you still?

The dawn arrives, I awake, it's just a dream, light of my life. The arrow was no dream, as it flew through the air, splitting my heart in two. Where are you now as I search and despair? Your family, you said, would honour our love and dreams, would always be there to help in the heartache and pain that I felt. But sadly, I found they left in their drougs, why should they care, when I'm not of your blood.

I love you, my love, with a love that was true. Where are you now in the great sleep that you sleep, when I'm still filled with the pain that I feel, when you left? You will always be a special part of me. No matter how they pretend that we were never real. I love you, I was always your wife. A part of me will always belong in your life and when we meet in the great sleep you and I will remember and share once more the love we felt as we both sleep together in the great sleep.

Light
Phillip D. Leach
Light in this world is hard to see,
when the candles are drowning in empty dreams.
Tomorrow seems, so far away,
when the night devours the day.
Does it make sense – this world of the living;
everything about taking and nothing about giving,
and everyone's concern is the "concept of me".
Around him the world and man still too blind to see,
a dying ember, a lost hope of dying light
dimly piercing a cold, thick night.
There is... a hope for the candle that dies...
in the reflection of a child's squinted eyes.

X–Mas Day In Florida
S. E. Alan Lambert
The sun is shining
The air is warm
And I am pining
For an Xmas norm.

I miss seeing bright rosy cheeks
on bairns whose happiness reeks.
Ear muffs, mitts and toques,
galoshes, scarves and rubber boots.
Snow ploughs, shovels and brooms,
Bright fireplaces in front rooms.

But then I remember
That many a December
Had freezing rain, sleet and slush,
slippery roads causing a fuss.
Frozen noses, toes and other parts
stalled autos that wouldn't start.

Do I miss that, too, as I reminisce
Really, if you don't mind
This year I'll give it a miss!

The Anthology of Poems

How Far
Wallace Dugan, Jr.
How far can I see within myself,
to wonder and succeed in life.
To assure the many wonders,
that lay deep within my soul.
To gain responsibility, wisdom, trust in learning,
a course in life that is worth earning.
Words that hold many keys to answers,
to teach myself as I can truly understand.
Self-confidence to realize my steps in reaching my goals.
To hear my answers as my voice starts to unfold.
In education to prove myself the ability in reasons,
to open doors, also to satisfy my mind and be just as pleasing.
How far can I go, I may say to others
to look to the night that has many bright stars.
In answers, as far as the eyes can see,
many views, many roads to knowledge.
In all to keep my hopes high, to have faith,
to reach out in my quest, that is more rewarding
that surely brings to me a higher level, not in frustration
but in willing at my own pace the terms in education.
Dedication: to Fayeanne Dugan and Austin Dugan

Be Thankful
Michelle Hammond
People have their ups and downs,
But if only they would stop and look around,
They would see that they don't have it all that bad.
Some have lost loved-ones and they are sad.
Others have no place to lay their head,
They are thankful for a cardboard box for a bed.
Some get their food from out of your trash,
And somewhere today someone will die in a car crash.
There is one thing that we all need to see,
Jesus is looking after you and me.
Be thankful for all that you posses,
And know that Jesus is looking after you, after us all, as we rest.

At Your Time Of Need
Kristen Hearty
When you're in pain and
feeling down
Don't go through a day with
a frown.
Just keep your head up
high
And give a sigh
That you pulled through
There's nothing you can't do!
I hope that you feel better
And not under the weather.
You are a Grandmom who is
so grand
That God will hold you in
His
hand.
So what I'm really trying to
say
Is that I'll always love you
any day!
Dedication: to my grandmother Kathryn Master

Fade To Black
Vanessa Harris
My spirit cries from a million
years of pain

I come from far away on the
wings of birds

My tears are as golden as the
rays of sun

Whose soul searches for a time
and place lost

My journey begins in the lush
green forest

I've looked through the eyes of
the pyramids

Looking into the past, present
and future

I fade to black

Silent Thoughts
Ryan Barrios
Alone with my silence,
my thoughts to my own.
My imbedded existence,
my internal deep blue is all that abounds me.

The atmospheric nectar,
freshens my sullen perception.

The birds sing the orchestral-type melody of ululation.
The sounds of nature's essence,
music of the spheres,
fill my range; the wide vastness of it.

Listen
Carla J. Jones
Judge not your children
By what you
Yourself may have done

For they learn through
Their mistakes

After all, they're still young

It's okay to reach out
And to lend them an occasional
Helping hand

But know when to retract
So that they might ask
For your help once again

Sometimes asking, is truly the toughest part
So when you extend your hand
Be willing to listen with an open heart
Dedication: to Corl, Jennifer and Vinny

Enchanted Dreams

Realization
Jewell Rita Mueller

It seems unreal to cope and deal
with the passage of time when you're
in the prime of years that still
could fulfill the dreams of youth.

Then one day in some strange way,
as if a dim light becomes suddenly
bright, the knowledge dawns that hopes
are gone to pursue the truth.

All the same, I played the game
giving, taking, sleeping, waking,
performing tasks that God had handed me.
I run, I walk, I crawl and try to
bear it all and hope for times
that now will never be.

How very extreme to plan and dream
and never be content when all
around my life was bound with
love and times of joy with those
my life was spent.

Time
J. McNelly

A time to live.
A time to die.
A time to laugh.
A time to cry.
A time to remember.
A time to forget.
A time to cherish.
A time of regret.
A time of happiness and sorrow.
A time to welcome a new tomorrow.
A time of memories constant and true
A time to say, I love you.

The Beam
Sarah E. Benson

He started off with a dream,
he saw what was right in the beam,
he said mankind should be as a team,
so not to break a seam.

He preached that color did not matter,
since we are all worn and tattered,
but then arose the ghostly clatter,
that scared and killed and battered.

The strong structure seemed to fall,
just like gravity pulling a ball,
and God seemed to call,
Martin, don't build another wall.

He started off with a dream,
he tried to build a strong, strong, beam,
but failed at making them a team,
it seemed to burst at the seam,
when he fell whispering "I Had A Dream!"

Dedication: to my grandmother

Euro 96
Simon P. Dennis

Euro 96, was full of excitement and aim
Teams from different countries making their name
I know victory can be sweet thus bring you fame
They all give it their best that they can on the day
It might not be how you planned that life so they say
My heart and my pride went out to England
So much skill and talent on display in this land
Our country did us proud we won't forget England
Lion hearts, courage, skill, determination, will big as any band
The team did us proud; they were all lion kings
It was a penalty shoot–out to decide things
One team had to win one team had to lose
But England done us proud, fans in the paper expressed their view:
Our soccer heroes had no cause for shame
They might have left Wembley in tears but they made their name
Remember they lost six–five
Football did come home, but our cup didn't arrive
It did prove what a great country we are
We didn't win the cup, but they were all stars
Next time 'round, I said, it could be ours

Dedication: to England players, fans, Mum and Nansi

Mirror–wise
Joseph S. Taylor, Jr.

I.
While I was staring at my skin, mirror–wise
I was then able to see—
That brow is really the true color of me
II.
I am not a so–called Black man
No, not Negro at all—
I was born a brown mortal
And I will die a brown person
Whenever my beloved master
Jehovah decides to call
Me home.

Teresa
Kathleen Savage

It's lovely to think of the times gone by,
When you were young and quite shy,
The hide and seek and cooking sessions,
We also had quite a few lessons,
Dogs were washed, dried and groomed,
Taking care none ever roamed.

Tubs and windows were full of flowers,
Twas quite nice to have some showers,
The gardens were kept very neat,
Everyone had to watch their feet,

Thirteen years have passed by
Since Granddad went to the garden in the sky

Everything has gone away,
Dogs, chickens, rabbits, I'm sad to say,
The flowers and shrubs have gone to glory,
But the River Wye flows by slowly,

We've all left, by the way,
That lovely village of Hoarwithy.

Internet Chat And Keyboard
Barbara Phillips
The keyboard sits in front of me
The screen is a sea of letters, ciphers
Alpha lines

How many times have I pressed these keys
Searching for I know not what
Seeking to conjure up
Before my eyes
A being

To entice someone
Into the breath–thin
Crack between fingertips
And pliant keys
To faintly brush against a soul
To come to rest
In a presence
Entwining with my own
Pushing back the cold
Glitter of stars
Staring through the gloom
Of a foamy moon

This morning
Shanna Smith
This morning I went outside,
I saw some birds up in the sky.
Some were big,
Some were little,
One was even playing a fiddle.
Some were red,
Some were blue,
One was even wearing a shoe.
Then I saw one so bright,
It reminded me of a brand–new kite.
As I watched it fly out of sight,
I wondered what it would be like to be in flight!

Lost
F. Decroy
When the mist is clear
Who calms the heart
Emptiness all around, never to depart
Walking on air, feeling strange
Life is a puzzle, try to arrange
What happens next, no one knows
In my world nothing grows.

I close my eyes, feel around
All I hear is heartache and pain to be found
Trying to be happy, it is so hard
Many hearts, bursting to be free
If I open my eyes, will I see
Happiness all around, it has to be
Let the people be happy and be strong,
With that sentiment, who can go wrong.

I want to believe, I really must try
But in my heart, I feel it would be a lie
So much pain, so much hurt
Is it so bad, maybe not
Embrace me in body, feelings never to be caught.

Drifting
D. Richardson
Drifting, destined to be just one.
One light among many, too pale to shine through.
Drifting, cocooned in her silence, alone with her peace.

Reaching towards shore, towards the light on the sunset,
calling out in the darkness, crying out in her prayer.
If someone can hear me, please answer my song,
untangle my chains to release me once more.

Drifting, destined to be just her.
Too far out of reach of the light on the shore.
Too tired to hope, just drifting once more.

The Reemergence Of An Image That Has Been Painted Over
Lori L. Ryczek
The only rhyme for Pentimento is... when I met you.
Lightning strikes, rainbows happen
and the mystic keeps rhythm by tapping.
He dwells in unfilled verses
where souls seek clues on the need for symbiosis.
A turtle doesn't need to be fast, the cheetah takes a test.
This is viewed from his misty window.
Rock the chair, my fingers in your hair and yes, yes, the image is there.

The only rhyme for Solicitude is... so this is good.
When rainbows fade, lightning reemerges to remain
long after the burst that brought it.
Released from his empower, the mystic embraces the hour
to pursue the passion of a rhymester.
"Caress my shell" says the friend to the friend who won't rest
... unless... to warm the faithful tortoise.
Rock and care, my fingers in your hair and yes, yes, the image is shared.

Hearts tapping, our souls grasp onto what is already within.
In harmony with the absolute music of the mystic.
Rock my world, my fingers in your hair and yes, yes, Pentimento is rare.

Rainbow's Child
Karen A. Piazza
The world sleeps but the great cities are awake. Noisy with
glory, love and music. People who stay up all night warring
against boredom and loneliness and pain.

Triumphant is the word "yes". Where I come from, defeat grows
like the weeds in deserted lots where human beings once
lived. Too many young men and women rode that white horse
across the ultimate river.

Too much humiliation, too much fear, too much rejection and
too much indifference lead to the great burning. And while the
fire engines raced through the eerie orange night, their sirens
piercing the city murmur, I was listening to music – choosing
to make art.

Growth is more difficult to accomplish but the growth is here
as I move on beyond the obvious. I have gone out into the city,
into the city ethnic and come back with a full basket.

Yes, I accept this, I accept the grief and the dirt and the pain. But
those are the dues I pay for admission to the feast and the feast
I choose to my own taste.

Enchanted Dreams

Patience
Cicely M. Hart–King
As after rain there comes the
sweet clear sunshine,

As after night there comes the
welcome morn;

In sorrow's path may joy as
surely follow,

The darkest hour is just
before the dawn

Dedication: to Diane, always an inspiration

Untitled
Bill Kavanagh
The prince approached that beauty asleep
to awaken her timeless repose
but nearing her lips to kiss slumbering breath
he stopped. He sniffed. And he froze.

He pondered.
He fretted.
Their future at stake.

For only
His kiss
Could
Allow her to wake.

Was it
Really
Worth it
For
History's sake?

Sweet dreams, Babe.

A Rose For Mama
Dorita C. Hill
The love you gave
A smile you save
The touch of your face
The warm embrace
The extra push you manage to abound
A mother all – around
A daisy can't compare to the things you do
But there is a special flower for you
It describes the sweet love you have given me
That will last until eternity
For all the mothers who have passed away
I have something to say
I want to take a minute or two
Just to say, I love you
To the elderly mothers who were there for me
also
You are a part of me, I want you to know
When push comes to shove
Mothers are the seed of God's love
Mothers, your concerned heart for others, it shows
It opens up fresh and sweet as a Rose

A Serenade In The Moonlight
Wendi Hirschy–Boutwell
As the moon's glow falls from the sky
The freshly–fallen snow reflects the beauty of above
The trees, heavy with the day's snowfall, bow with sorrow
From among the hills, the pack calls,
Mourning his untimely departure
Their song echoes throughout the hills and valleys

From among the stars
The Wolf Father's shadow looks upon his children
On the marrow another must be chosen
Tonight, however, they honor the one who has gone
The Mother's cruelty is clear
For all her beauty, the Mother is a hard mistress

Thoughts That Never Occur While Sipping Tea Or Eating A Sala
Srinivas Kannepalli
... Thquire, make the betth of uth: not the wurtht!
Mr. Sleary, Dickens, Hard Times
The factory pipes exhaled their smoking breath
In clouds of black. Inside its roaring jaws,
Young hands became fodder with young dreams.
The drone of machines drowned all thoughts in noise.
The silent workers: footprints in the soot.

Somewhere a silver spoon stirred tea with care,
Its tinkling made a distinctly loud sound.

A hundred years have passed since then, but still...

An airplane blew green smoke over vastly–spread
Orchards. A wrinkled hand rests for an instant,
To cough and adjust the worn, sweaty cloth
Bandana that loosely wrapped a parched mouth.
Then slowly, tired flesh once more felt the Earth.

Somewhere a savory garden salad awaits
A dinner table for a family supper.

Subscription To Continuance
Gene Lominac
Deep in wintered woods, crocheted–white
cold silence surrounds my stopping
before moving on: cathedral silence
wrapping me in wonder
lofty arches holding fresh flocking
fanciful flakes kissing my face.

Like a golden promise of warmth
in wished–for afterwards
when life begins all over again, an owl
breaks across chalk and charcoal softness
in quiet flight; settles like early sundown
settling feathers, blinks
at my shuddering, lost soul searching intrusion

On evenness he belongs, unquestioning—
Deeper into gauzed awesomeness
undisturbed before me, reverently
I weave my way through winter–shrouded aisles
out the other side of accepting
necessary naturalness before spring.

Mustard Seed
J. Benhur R. Torres

Each time not death
but inside me a dying I dare
and sorry I survived watching myself
as my parts takeover
helpless, the pain disconnecting us
and I ponder why it hurts
and whose choice it was
but being where I stood
killed myself once more
to the little left of me
and said Goodbye.
and Hello again
to another stride.

Our Children's Inheritance
Peter James

"How do we achieve peace?", asks a young child
The whole world seems to be so very wild

What can I tell you son, that you don't know
It's the "grown–ups" that don't want you to grow

Perhaps, if those in power had to fight
The blasting bombs could change their faulty sight
I weep and cry now with you, my son
Your life is not their light, as is, the gun
It's the old and feeble men who talk tough
But it's my son and yours that will act rough

After they come home, as pieces of clay
All "leaders" pin a badge and shout, "Hooray!"

"We were provoked to fight", is the angle
But it's dirty money that will mangle

My friend, what can I say, to your young son?
He'll go back to ash, while power, has fun

To An Unrequited Love
Norman Jordan

When I think of our times together,
I regret they had to end.
I wished those times would last forever,
when I thought you more than friend.

You saw me through some bad times,
and created times so good.
I began to feel a love sublime,
and wondered if you would.

I told you that I loved you,
I should have let it be.
For when I confessed my love so true,
you went far away from me.

Though you and I will no more meet,
and time will pass us by;
I'll always treasure that time so sweet,
and love you till I die.

Dedication: to Lee Stirling, my mentor

Swirl
Brad Gray

Looking out my living room window,
I see the sun setting, the trees bare,
just a few leaves on the ground.
Music in the background, the clouds
Swirl around each other like big,
Fluffy pillows. A chill in the
Autumn air so fresh and crisp,
A beautiful sunset is arising, blue
Sky, orange clouds, geese flying
South as the night creeps in.
The sunset colors are beginning to
Darken a brilliant orange color
What a beautiful day this has been.

Thoughts On Friends
Jana K. Curry

A friend is someone who likes to listen
To problems or jokes or me.
A friend never butts in till I am through
Maybe a time or two, but who's perfect?
A friend is a companion with whom I talk
Or listen, or have fun with, or maybe cry with,
Or just about anything I can think of,
Within limits, of course.
A friend is a rock who stands steady
Either for or against me and isn't afraid to
Tell me yes or no to important matters
Including my personality, appearance and thoughts,
Especially the latter.
Most of all, a friend is a human being,
Just like me, who wants to be treated as such,
Just like me and who, no matter what happens,
Stands beside me in times of happiness
Or sorrow and loves me for who I am...
A Friend.

Dedication: to Marcia, my dearest friend

Mom's Heart Sings
Lee Greathouse

That son of mine makes my heart sing, except on wash day.
When his pockets reveal snails, dried frogs and crawlies.
And sometimes butterfly wings, marbles, stones and used bubble gum.
Oh, yes and a ball of twine string.
A droopy bouquet of dandelions in a grubby fist.
"For you Mom, just 'cause" — and my heart sings.

There's sweat socks, sneakers that reek, all his collars have rings.
His room's a disaster, he claims it's his world, that's how he likes things
It's curfews and car keys, good pals and girlfriends.
Oh, just listen to that telephone ring.
A bouquet of roses, three pink and three yellow.
"For you Mom, just 'Cause" — and my heart sings.

That son of mine makes my heart sing, a man, standing tall.
He looks all in the eye and keeps his integrity in all things
Wisdom, knowledge, anointing, I pray, for my son in service for the
    king.
I'm glad he needs me sometimes still, to pray, cook and things.
A bouquet of daisies from a field nearby.
"For you Mom, just 'Cause" — and my heart sings.

Enchanted Dreams

Precious Gifts
D. J. Palmore
Of all the wondrous things, of life,
And all that, it unfolds.
The values, that we hold most dear.
Aren't always, made of gold.
The magic, of the sunrise.
The clouds, as they roll by.
Laughter, of children, as they play.
A baby's, smile, to light, our way.
These are precious, things,
Money cannot buy.
Treasure, them more.
They cannot, be bought.
With gold.

Two People
Jennifer Lynn Hoerl
Every morning, when I look into the mirror, I see two people.
One is who everyone expects me to be.
I am happy to see this person, but mostly because others are happy to see her.
She is who I should be and she is moving in the direction I should be moving.
She is interested in the challenge, but needs to be motivated.

The other person is difficult to see.
She is much deeper.
She is not interested in routine and rarely finds satisfaction in small achievements.
She needs excitement and adventure.
She can be caring, warm and sensitive.
She is not so easy to understand, so I never give her the credit she often deserves.

Both people, however, are important and special.
Neither should be hidden from the other.
When separated, they can create fear and confusion, but together they can accomplish anything.

Passion
Cynthia F. Walker
It engulfs you like a gust of wind and fits
you like a glove.
It comes to you without warning, leaves you
feeling light and free, almost like a dove.
It mixes and mingles in your heart, to set
One's Soul on fire.
It makes you ponder many things that you
didn't think could transpire.
It leaves you breathless, senseless and open
to desires.
It arouses your senses, making everything
you touch, see or smell a reason to inquire
It releases your emotions, secret potions and
some of one's innermost devotions.
It surrounds you like one's favorite blanket
keeping you safe from harm.
It holds you close to comfort, as if in
the safety of your mother's warm and tender
arms.

Dedication: to K. A. diamond of a friend

Weeping Willow
Natalie Wyles
Weeping willow with your tears
running down, why do you always
weep and frown? Is it because he
loved you one day, is it because
you could not stay? You found shelter
in his shade, you thought his laughter
would never fade.

Weeping willow, stop your tears
there is something to calm your fears.
although you may forever apart, but
I know you'll always be in his
heart.

Riches
Helen Kearney
The coins and bills were very few
In the faded, dark-blue purse
But that mattered little to the lady who knew
That things could be much worse.

Her grand, old face had an inner glow
As memories rushed to review
The happy childhood and loving parents,
Her faithful husband and children, too.

The years had been so good to her
She reflected as she sat in the pew
Of the church that taught important values:
Riches come from the heart anew.

And as she approached the holidays
She sent friends and family far away
A most precious gift, a letter of love
With heartfelt wishes for every day.

Dedication: to my daughter, Rose Kearney Nunnery

As Your Dreams Unfold
Brian Yoder
Soar into the deep, blue sky,
where passions and dreams
go to fly.

Out of your heart a river flows,
deep inside your soul, a fire blows,
and the spirit of truth breathes inside of you.

I give you wings like a dove,
a heart full of love,
everlasting life and Heaven above.
I shower you with liberty,
and I am filled with joy
as I watch you fulfill your destiny.

Like the clouds, time passes slowly.
But each step closer to eternity
holds the promise of you and me.
So take my hand as your dreams unfold into reality.

Dedication: to my beautiful family

A Happy Marriage
Michael J. McGrath
At first a thought nibbling on to anger.
The pent-up emotions of a smouldering grouch
Burst open on confronting the offender.
A petty argument whipping into a raging torrent
Buffeting the years of sacred devotion.

Cut off in mid-stream by the sudden departure of the one
Left alone with frustrations still to bleed
A hanging argument, sizzling and fermenting.

Another clash of horrendous words
And finally silence. Smothered in the loving arms of each.
The sacredness is intact.

God's Creation
Mae Frances Wesley
See the beauty of the trees?
Ah, such beauty in the Autumn leaves!
Orange, gold, red and brown,
All turn loose and fall to the ground.
Such splendor in these my Lord reveals
Of Himself. Indeed how great He is.

All's not lost as the leaves fall clear,
Forming a blanket 'round the tree trunks near.
As the Earth is covered with these beautiful leaves,
Warmth is provided for the ground beneath.

Through the trees His greatness continues,
As the mountainous hills I view;
I watch the sun in its glistening grandeur
Forming a rainbow in the skies anew.

Oh, what beauty in God's creation;
Oh, what joy that fills my soul
As I acknowledge His precious love
And see His will to man unfold.

Oh, Heavenly Creation
Bob Wallace
Amidst the stir of the darkened sky,
The Heavens part with peaceful sigh
And reacheth down God's mighty hand
And placeth man upon His land.

And unto he God giveth a mate
Of tender, loving and nurturing way.
Joineth ye their flesh thru God's pure love
Bringeth forth new life unto His world.

Oh, child of God, Oh, wondrous joy,
So open, so helpless, not yet a ploy,
Oh, blesseth he no ills receive
Unto his soul, may he be free.

To live, to learn, to love, to grow
So unto others His seeds may sow
Pray rise above all Earthly sin
And pass these gifts through God's sweet wind.

Dedication: to my loving parents, Frank and Jane

Alone With Your Love
Michael Miller
Without you I'm nothing,
an empty shell of loneliness.
It was you that filled that shell,
with all the contents of your heart,
making me whole and full of emotion.
I was by myself in the savage world of love.
Endlessly searching for the one I could call my own.
I found you finally, to complete my life.
You're not as close to me,
as you were then.
I need you now more than ever, but
I'm just,
alone with your love.

Step So Lightly!
Marlene Wenger Roadruck
Worry! Scurry! Hurry!
Never think about your life.
Worry! Scurry! Hurry!
What to do about this strife?
All the things that do not grate you,
are the things that help create you.
Since life's game is as you see it,
think the same so you can fleece it.

Once you feel that you deserve lifts,
you will know what things preserve this.
Take your time to get in sequence,
things go right when you concede them.

You're the one who chooses madness,
try again and there'll be gladness.
Then the pathway fills with smoothness,
and your pace is less than ruthless.

Step so lightly! Never fearful,
heading up the race and cheerful!

This I'll Always Believe
Paula Fraize
So many times I've tried to express just what you have given to me
But words on a piece of paper can't describe it adequately
How can you truly thank someone who has shown you the way to Him
Lighting the fire in your soul, never to have it diminish again
You made me look inside myself and learn what is really there
Showed me how to rely on my Faith and to turn to Christ in prayer
Renewed my faltering sense of Hope and opened my heart to see
That Christ is alive and everywhere and will remain for eternity
You showed me in your caring way that I, too, have something to give
That each of us has many gifts we must share as long as we live
Sometimes it takes a special person to enter our lives and help us to see
All the treasures that we do possess and the promise of what is yet to be
You are that special envoy that God has sent my way
For Him you set the example of how to live each and every day
So the Heavens must be smiling now, as you gave reason to my fear
And you have touched my very soul and caused it to draw nearer
To our Merciful Father up above, through His enduring forgiveness and love
I'll always believe you're a gift of grace and will give thanks 'til the
   end of time
May the Lord God bless and keep you always, dear and special friend of
   mine.

Enchanted Dreams

Silence
Pamela Wisher
Russet leaf on Autumn breath;
Earths' deep eiderdown of snow;
The house, now with the children gone:
Memories with the volume low.
Lying awake before the dawn;
Rich, green quiet of wooded dell;
Forming patterns of perfect peace
That nestle in the soul so well.

Busy, busy world 'mid noise and clatter;
"Silence is golden, " says the rule.
Gold for moulding words of wisdom:
Silence being wisdom's tool.

Carving A Piece Of Wood
Dave Flynn
The day was sunny
I was thinking of my honey
I went to my shop
I tripped over a mop
First I draw
Then I saw
I cut some wood
I knew it could be good
I mustn't slip
For the wood might chip
The day is so splendid
For this gift is to my intended
I really must sand it
Before I hand it
A box of candy could not compare
To this wooden heart I bear
If any sweetheart gives me a
Valentine
I surely hope it's pine

Dedication: to my dad

Sunday Morning
Charity Ann Ferguson
I awaken swiftly by the faint
Touch of morning light. Then I arise
To greet the pink-hazed, breathtaking
Sky. I kneel humbly as I thank the Lord
for the day's new Journey. I cross
my arms and look up to gaze prayerfully
To see God's masterpiece unraveling.
I imagine ascending up to see the morning
Through his eyes. High above, I watch the sun
display a show of dancing colors racing to
paint the world to tell it to awake from its sweet
slumber of night. Elegantly the rays caress
The forest with a gentle kiss and they glean up
and sway to the melody of the wind's
Talented gift. The birds and crickets praise
The Lord and serenade for their little
Lovely Lives. And now I swing ever so slowly
down to where my body awaits to take me to God's
Holy Place on His Beautiful Sabbath day.

Dedication: to the children of the world

Dreams
J. M. Organ
We dream of things so good, so bright
Within our world so full of light
But of other people and their plight
Do we sometimes think, or maybe never,
Of their dreams and if they ever
See their world filled with that light,
Instead the darkness of the night.
Pray to God to be forgiven
For we are the lucky ones who live,
In our little piece
of Heaven.

Dedication: to my family and friends

Reflections
Joyce Kerton
As I sit here by the firelight's glow
My mind drifts back to long ago
To happy days spent as a child
Coming woods and running wild
Long, hot days spent in the sun
When we would laugh and jump and run
Long, long walks with our Mum and Dad
Discovering the wonderful life we had
To the old music hall we used to go
With happy hearts and faces aglow
Coming home on a winter's night
To muffins and crumpets, was pure
delight
Christmas was always a family affair
With simple toys and ribbon for our hair
For us to spend a day at the sea
Was such a happy thought for me
Now we lead a different life
One that is often full of strife
But our own children will also recall
Happy days spent when they were small

Ad Verse Symmetry
N. Young
World jigsaw a kaleidoscope.
Each piece intricate, complex.
A delicate, balanced tightrope,
From humans to small insects.

We know much, yet so little,
Contradictions often true.
The lifeforce strong, yet brittle,
Old beliefs masquerade as new.

The spider spins his silken net,
To catch and feed upon the fly.
Instinct driven – wisdom yet,
No chance for him to know why.

Better for the spider to concentrate
on being a spider,
And the fly to accept he is a fly.
The folly of human beings is that
they struggle with the eternal
WHY

I Just... Love You
John P. Miles
I'll love you tomorrow, as I loved you yesterday,
But none of that is half as much, as I love you today.
If someone else can love you, the way that I love you,
Then he must love you desperately, exactly as I do.

I have loved you more, for I have loved you for so long,
And if I could I'd show you that my love for you is strong.
For all I have is love for you – more love than you will know,
And even though I love you still, it's not allowed to show.

I'll love you in the future, as I've loved you in the past,
No matter what you think of me
My love for you will last.

Untitled
Jolene Frahm
You say you know;
when I am happy.
You say you know;
of my pain.

Can you feel;
what I am feeling?
Do you know;
of my tears?

Have you ever sat;
in silence,
alone?
Waiting, hoping to
hear the ringing,
of the phone?

I am in pain,
I am alone!
Are you there?
Do you care?

The Fox
Zai O. D. Yates
Foxes are vermin, it is claimed and must be hunted, killed or maimed
But foxes are creatures, as are we and have a right to live and be.
Though dwellers on our planet Earth, they are classed of lesser worth,
Foxes need food to stay alive, because of this they must contrive,
to take what sustenance they find, to give continuance to their kind.
They kill as all wild creatures will, in summer heat or winter chill,
they do not need to have a reason, hunger persists in every season,
as they have just a basic mind, instinct is natural to their kind,
and limited in gifts of sense, they do not know they give offence.

Humans, though different in their strains, supposedly have better brains,
and should be capable of seeing, how sacred life is to each being.
Yet be he foe, or friend, or brother, humans will slaughter one another.
Humans, too, have better classes, who think their birthright far surpasses,
those folk who are not "superior" and are therefore deemed to be
   "inferior".
These are the ones, without excuse, who fail to put their minds to use.
who bring contempt upon their sort, by undertaking to cavort,
and swagger, preen and prink, whilst kitted out in hunting pink.
It takes no spark of nuclear fission, to show their brains are in
   remission.

The Cry Of The Unborn Child
Natalie Ford
Oh, how I want to be with you
laugh, cry, learn and love.
In the world I was to come.
Alas, you do not want me,
do not want to care for I.
When you nearly even know me.
My hands are so little
my eyes so small.
In your womb I am in, after all.
You think I am not living
growing, breathing.
I am a human being when you know of me.
A tiny child helpless from my bitter destiny.

The Storm
Tricia Le Wright
The dune is no longer silent.
The wind blows, fiercely, across the desert.
The sagebrush, now, bends to the wind's voice.
The howl, of the wind, has become as a lion,
Roaring before the Moment of devourment.

The desert has suddenly turned strange.
Familiar landmarks have vanished from view.
The road, once our guide, has lost its form.
No voice gives direction and the emptiness penetrates.

The force is deep and no warmth is found.
As the voice of the storm, amplifies; vision is lost.
The sky has become a filmy white blanket.
The sand dune's cover is pulled away,

As the storm travels its path.
Hours pass and a new sound comes.
The voice, of the wind, has become as a lamb.
The new day is here.
The storm has been lost.

At The Crossroads
Elsie B. Steen
A decision was to be made— The Crossroads!
Two ways there were that caught my eye.
One was traveled by many and one by few.
The first would give me much pleasure,
Perhaps much gain in this life, too.
Many friends would I have and possibly even fame and fortune
And yes, even much sorrow
Then in the end; where would I face the morrow?
The second way would bring me peace for which I longed.
But weren't the pleasures and fun more greatly wanted by everyone?
But then if I chose the second way there would be Heavenly joy
And much fruit to nourish my soul.
Also a "friend that sticketh closer than a brother"
Which I may not get from the other.
The second way is the Lord's Way,
He owns the "cattle on a thousand hills!"
There's also peace, forgiveness and love when we get to the
end of the way.
There await our loved–ones, too, gone on before,
And our kind, loving Saviour, His face to behold.
What is your decision— at the Crossroads?!

Enchanted Dreams

Wyrd
Josh Caskey
I am the sinner, for aye lost soul
With no empyreal crown to accompany thy head
To play the part of a highborn kinsmen's role
I am the bloody, fanged wolf divine of thy demesne
Lord of thy bier, chained within thy charnel dungeon
Forever to burn aeonian upon thy faery pyre
Sweet music playing eternal in thy ear
When passing bells chime to summon mans' arch fear
I am the dark shadow sapience, the stygian prophet
Preaching fears and prayers of mans' donnest tophet
I the fiend–voice, loudest to sing your requiems
Granting thee visions of after in black veil–shrouded dreams

A Moment In Time
S. M. Collins
In the silence of the dawn of a glorious autumn morn, how sad the sound of leaves descending, falling to the beginning of their ending.

Mother Earth's arms unfold to bring her children back safe to the fold. A wisp of air with a twist and curl brings even more, still colorful swirl.

A golden carpet soon forms around from the passing of children who converged to the ground. Dark winter nights add to the sorrow. Rapture returns with children of the morrow.

Dedication: to Gwendoline Amy Collins nee McKenzie

My Children
Cynthia B. Lewis
May the road you take
Be narrow and straight,
And the choices you make
Not be made too late.
My children,
May you live each day
Kind thoughts to embrace,
So the words you say
Will be seasoned with grace.

My children,
May you walk in the light
Of goodness and love,
And stray never from the sight
Of the One up above.

My children,
May your joys be ever–flowing,
Your sorrows few.
As you mature ever–knowing
That I will always love you.

Inner Child
Harvey Houle
As I push my smiles aside and look down deep inside
To feel the hurt and pain, from that I've always tried to abstain
It's only in the last few days, that I feel real, not a phony haze
As I learn to open up and trust, I begin to let go of some of my lust
It's the boy inside that I see now, I think of God, I think of "wow"
The little boy that I hated so, I start to love, don't you know
He is so alone, scared and hurt, I see his face in the dirt
I step inside and help him out, As I cry, wail, howl and shout
It's at last that I understand, What it means to be a man
I thought it was in always being right, I always put up such a fight
For what, I sit and wonder why, Is it important? And I cry
I believe that I could not see, The forest through that one lone tree
I know that I am letting go, As I share with you what I know

Sophisticated Lady
Natasha D. Ratler
You can see it in the way I walk, hear it in the way I talk,
Feel it in my every touch
But of course you can Never get 2 Much
Because I'm a lady... a Sophisticated Lady.

Descendant of an African Queen
Molded in her image, shaped by her dream.
My lips as sweet as cherries and teeth as white as snow
My shapely thighs and wishful eyes, were all hers long ago.

Take a while to look at my smile, tell me what you see.
What years of racism, discrimination and hate
Have tried to take from me.

Some may think I'm feisty, but that's all right with me.
My cold looks and smart remarks
My attitude has many sparks,
The shake of my head... Enough said.
But I can do that and you know this.
Why?
Because I'm a lady... a Sophisticated Lady.

Does He
Lynnette Barclay
As I lay here wondering
where could he be
I also was pondering
does he really love me.

I lay here thinking
with all of my might
But I fell asleep
with a hell of a fight

As I awoke in the morning
I thought it again
Does he really love me
or are we just friends

As I cried to myself
silent, but true
I said, I don't know
But I sure love you

Dedication: to Eddie, Mom, Tim – my motivators

Crossroads Of Life
Ned Thrumble
Two futures now I have to choose
To keep me in my happy news
At the crossroads I do stand
Deciding on the move at hand
Left or right, I do not know
The path I take, the seeds I sow
Far or near I have to go
Away from life I did once know
On my own in the big, wide world
Destinies that I now choose
The fun of it that I can't lose
My life is mine and mine to do
The life that I'll look forward to.

Oh, Children! What have we done?
Sandra Westberg
In our quest to insure
A future free of pain,
Hearts full of love,
Mind's challenged,
Bodies healthy,
And lives materially blessed,

We have struggled to find the balance
Between protecting you and setting you free.

We have nurtured you,
Loved you,
Laughed with you,
Dreamed with you,
Admired you,
Questioned you,

But not often did we deny you!
And, oh, children, because of this,

Did we ultimately fail you?

The Gift
Anthony Leal
I picked a pretty flower
One a soft shade of blue
With petals smooth as your skin
Only of a different hue

I bow to you meekly
So to my presence you become aware
I challenge not your beauty
As I would never dare

This is merely a simple gift
One which I could afford
To show how I appreciate nature
For this creation she has bore

So please take this flower
As a token of my heart
To show how much I love you
In hope that we never grow apart

Dedication: to my loving wife, Jennifer

Age
Robert Harniman
Age means little to me,
For although I have come far
There is still eternity ahead.
Although life is withered
And is faded from me,
I am joyous.
For I know soon around the corner
There will be a friend,
Who's caring eyes
May restore to me my youth,
So age means little to me.

Dedication: to Maureen Harniman and Gerald Harniman

Woman–Child, Lost In Dreams
Connie E. Hughes
Woman–child, lost in dreams, wondering if they'll
Ever be fulfilled, scared by time, wounded
By love and promises, afraid to try again.

Too gentle to build a wall around your heart,
Too warm to live a life apart, too loving not
To pause – then start again.

Have I told you that you walk above the Earth?
That stars envy you and flowers blush in your
Presence? That all the wounds and pain will
cease and you will be free and whole again?

Woman–child, lost in dreams and wondering if
They'll ever be fulfilled, walk with me
Beyond the rivers and the forests and stand
In naked loveliness on the highest hill!

Women–child! Women–princess!

Dedication: to England's Rose – "Princess Diana"

Remember
Kelly Nicholson
Remember when the grass first grew,
All the world was new.
All we needed was our love,
So strong.

Remember when the flowers bloomed,
In the heat of the day,
Our passions grew.

Remember when the leaves first fell,
The world was bleak.
Our passions weakened,
Our love grew dim.

Remember when the trees first died,
The world was old.
Our passions gone,
Our love no more.

Remember when...
All we had in the world was each other?

Enchanted Dreams

The Angel Of The Seas
Alice Salvatore
Bring me your shells.
Some shine as a Gem.
Others resemble a picture of one's thoughts
Through the centuries.

Angels, watch over all the waters.
Protect us from all harm
The angels will shimmer
As blue, green and white.

Beautiful crystals of the night
Shine on bright;
My angel of the seas.

How Great The Love!
Wesley G. Vaughn
Long time ago, God chose to show
Just how much He loves you and me;
He sent His Son, His Only One,
To give His life for you and me.

Life for a girl became a whirl
The day she heard the angel say
She'd bear a son, God's Holy One,
Who comes to take our sins away.

In prayer one night, the Son of Light
Said to the Father, "Not My will."
He took the loss and bore the cross,
As He walked up that rugged hill.

How great the Love of God above,
That Christ would die for you and me!
He shed His blood, the cleansing flood,
To wash our sins away and set us free.

Dedication: with love to Patty, my wife

Loving You
Tiffany Mosley
All the times that we've shared.
Lets me know how much you cared.
Saying I love you when the timing is right.
Sharing kisses all through the night.
Being there in my time of need.
And telling me that you'll never leave.
Staying together through thick and thin.
Thinking of me when you shouldn't have been.
When I was dying inside.
You seem like you weren't there.
But, I always knew that you cared.
Having arguments and petty fights.
Just putting on a show!
Not knowing who was right.
Is not the way I wanted this relationship to go.
Talking on the phone for a minute or two.
Just to say goodnight and I love you, too.
My skies are never gray now.
And my day will never be blue.
Because deep in my heart I know I'll never stop
loving you.

God's Nature Cake
Kenneth James Baker
How beautiful are God's garnishings.
The raindrop on a rose, the bird upon a tree,
A gust of wind upon my face, the moods within the sea.
The colours of the rainbow that no artist can re-capture.
The birds, the flowers, the April showers, that fill my
Heart with rapture.
The majesty of mountains tall. The serenity of night.
All those creatures great and small, God got the mixture
right.
He mixed them well in Earth's great dish; they took
six days to bake.
On holy day He made His wish, enjoy My nature
cake.

Whisper In The Wind
Nell M. Wright
Sitting on the porch swing,
As I often do,
I heard him whisper,
"Darling, I love you".

Walking through the meadow,
Grass sparkling with dew,
Again I heard him whisper,
"Darling, I love you".

Standing at the front gate,
Feeling lonely and blue,
Again I heard him whisper,
"Darling, I love you".

Today, standing at his grave,
I heard him once again,
It was soft and low,
Like a whisper in the wind.

Dedication: to William R. Wright

Prayer For Me
Dana Boyd
I hope there's a prayer for me.
Somewhere a prayer for me.

Someone took all my flowers just last spring
leaving me with only sad songs to sing.

The butterflies don't come any more
they say 'cause their wings are sore.

But how helpful they can be when they want to be.
I hope there's a prayer for me.

Why does the sun frown on me
Must only my tears fall endlessly?

All around me my garden grows empty and empty.
Why doesn't hurt have any boundary?

I hope there's a prayer for me.

Why does not hurt have any boundary?

The Writing Workshop
June Mann

There he sat
this disciple of words,
articulate and confident
on a beech Windsor chair,
while she, humbly encased
in past theories of forelock touching,
was unable to free her embryo mind
from a mature body, so prayed
for the contentment of not caring,
for complacency.
But he, gouging and prodding
through her grey, dormant cells
released a flicker of response!

Inner Truth
Grace Bruno

Peeling away
at the layers of pain
peeling away at the levels of strain
shedding the skin that is used
to defend
shedding the armor
that will never bend
Losing the heart
to the unknown soul
Giving and giving
is always the goal
And yet like a child
We run from our fear
we run and we hide
not to look in the mirror
the past and the present
are one and the same
until we find peace
and let go of the game

Dedication: to Rene

Untitled
Andrea Gary-Lopez

With your power and your
might,
you are woman with every
right.
A mother, bearer of child,
bold and beautiful by and
by.

You are woman, that's no lie.

Protector and affector in
your reign, like a tigress does
her plain.
You are woman, hear you
roar.

For all that has been
Mentioned, it doesn't meet all
the fact that...
You are woman and no one
is as good or more.

Alnmouth Evening
Margaret Brewster Watson

The day draws to its close;
A beautiful day, crisp and clear,
A promise of Springtime in the air,
The white-crested sea murmurs along
The shore with a low, soft song
The wheeling sea-gulls, wild and free,
Take up the echoing harmony,
Passing it to the evening breeze
Soughing through the lacy trees,
The sky a kaleidoscope, a blazing show
Of setting sun with vibrant glow,
Who can deny that God exists
When faced with beauty such as this?

Love And Friendship
Timothy F. Russell

Through endless nights, of trusted love,
whispering upon, the stars above.
There's nothing that means, more to me,
than our love for each other, for eternity.

When things go wrong, we make them right,
'Cause we'll always know, our love is so tight.
We built up feelings, that feel so true,
And a friendship to last, all the years through.

We need each other, more than we know,
And the children need us, to help them grow.
We started something, to finish together,
So let's enjoy what we have, now and forever.

Love and friendship, is a beautiful thing,
And I thank the Lord, for clipping our wings.
For all the things we've been through and all we share,
let's show the children and us, we'll always be there.

Dedication: to my wife, Christine Lynn Russell

Untitled
Amy J. Compton

O
Per
Haps it
Was just the
Starlight dust
That was beginning to settle and
Disperse itself in the dark
Atmosphere. Maybe the moon
Had some strange effect
On my emotions, piercing
My heart with its strong
Black-shattering beams of light;
But I like to think
That it was
You that
Kissed
Me
Softly
In that
Quiet
Second.

Enchanted Dreams

An Urban Reality
David Ward Bishop
Weaned from their mothers,
Hip–Hop babies sift through their rubble at trouble's gate,
Seeking the key to a future which lies in dank alleyways among their
brothers.

Shots clear the playground,
Booming a window–shaking beat, gangsta icons of a generation
Looking for souls lost in a shadow of briefcase–toting ghosts in a
dumbfound.

It is not us and them it is WE,
That crowd around the blood–soiled screens of anchors at six
Just to get our fix of a reality unlived, surreal and unfathomable by me.

God's Heavenly Chorus
Carol Taylor
The sorrows in our lives
Are often overwhelming,
But the passion for our music
Gives us depth of understanding.

God tests the timbre of our souls
When He calls those we love,
But we know with deep conviction
That their music rings above.

As we selfishly give in
To the grief within our hearts
Never doubt it for a minute–
All God's angels sing their parts.

So have faith and trust in God above,
Look for laughter in your tears.
Listen to the music of the angel chorus
And hear God's voice say, "I am here."

Dedication: to all members of Barbershop choruses

The Reward
Alyssa Eyzenga
The sun disappears behind the dismal, dreary sheet of clouds.
It wraps around me like a blanket, less the comfort.
The thunder roars, as a lion claiming his territory.
The sound fills the atmosphere, echoing off the hollow, empty hills.
A rushing wind whirls around me, sending a numbing chill
　down my spine as I shiver all over.
The rain begins to pour down, wet, cold, there is no escaping it.
The lightning crosses the sky, sharp, sudden, intense.
Water begins to run down the hills in drones, rushing into me, pulling my
　feet from under me.
The rain begins to slow to a gentle drip and the Earth is left as nothing
but a mound of dirt under a giant puddle.
The sun peeks out from behind the dismal, dreary sheet of clouds
As the clouds disintegrate, the sun emerges, using its friendly rays to
　warm my frigid body.
The rays reach out as far as they can and light the mountainous valleys
　below,
leaving me in awe as I gaze at its wondrous beauty. Everything is new,
　fresh...
ALIVE.
It is the reward of the storm.

He
Jennifer Wooden
He who is true to himself
must be honest to others
He who is caring
must be compassionate
He who is loving
must love the world
You are the "he" I am referring to
For you don't have to do these things
You already have
You have been honest, compassionate and loving
That's why someday I feel as if I could love
you
with all my heart and soul.

Beacon
Luanne Untener
And so it is...
We come into this life.
A defined family awaits.
We grow.
And in that process
We welcome into our soul
That with which
We find strength and courage,
Laughter and joy and
The smiles that embrace and fill
Our hearts to overflowing.

A new family is created.
Our extended family.
Where we often run and are
Always welcome.
Those people that are
Our heart
Our conscience
Our essence
Our FRIENDS.

Texas Spring – Personified
Maria Thelma Tamayo
It's Springtime in Texas –
The birds' melodious songs are heard from every bough,
The sweet perfume of the huisache is everywhere,
And the rain causes a multitude of color to burst,
Like the unexpected "Surprise" of a party!
The trees seem to st–r–et–ch out their branches,
As birds and blooms push out the dreary winter away.
The roadsides are like the fringes of a western shirt,
With billowy white and purple poppies.
The meadows are blanketed with the greenest grass or clover.
Or they are covered with a downy Mardi–Gras quilt,
Of sunny orange–reds and shiny lemon–yellows.
While the sweet–nectared cacti tantalizes the insects,
With their adorned and painted faces,
The steadfast yucca stands rigidly in plumed–white hats,
Their green–pointed spikes ready to tackle anything.
The welcoming sights, smells and sounds are like a smile–
For everyone to enjoy, savor and remember,
Even if it's just for a little while!!

Dedication: to Rachel Kretz – thanks: confidence and motivation

Entombed
Gabriel Dunn
We scaled the garden wall,
Landed in the grass.
The lovers? They are all
In the sunken graves we pass.
Against the tombs, we doze
In each other's warm embrace,
Held together in repose
Within this secret place.

The morning sun, gold
Dances on her skin.
The smell of her hair, holds
A tender, willing sin.

Rage
C. O. Knight
The breath of the Dragon rages; His fierce, formidable body lunges
The Knight negates the blow; He lashes at the beast
THE BATTLE RAGES ON
The Dragon roars in anger; The blade finds it mark
The brave Knight drives his sword deeper; The Dragon reels in pain
THE BATTLE RAGES ON
The Dragon feels the betrayal; The Knight glories in it
Dragon versus Knight; Knight versus Dragon
THE BATTLE RAGES ON
The Knight screams his disapproval; The words bounce off the Dragon's
    scales
THE WORLD RAGES ON
Why all this sadness and pain; Why all this hurt and confusion
Why, Why, Why
Where are we; How did we get here
THE WORLD RAGES ON
The people scream out; The governments close their ears
The poor die; The rich eat and get fat
THE WORLD HAS MOVED ON
THE WORLD HAS MOVED ON
THE WORLD...

The Vine
Stanley J. St. Clair
Up the wall there grows a vine
Until the end of space and time.
Up the chimney flows the smoke
So only soot is left behind.

Out the window stares a girl
Whose charcoal hair is filled with curl,
And the thoughts that press her mind
I cannot read 'cause I'm too blind
To see the words within her heart
Which I pray doth beat for me
That together we will be

Till the vine no longer grows
Up the wall on which it goes,
And the smoke no longer swirls
Through rock chimneys o'er the world...
Yes, together we would be
Throughout eternity—

Up the wall there grows a vine.

My Summer Kiss
Joy Hutton
It was a warm summer day,
Birds were chirping, Kids were screaming,
and the wind was blowing as the trees danced,
him and I were teasing and talking and messing around
as a friend said something to him.
I then felt his silky lips against mine,
and he asked me these sweet words,
"Will you go out with me?"
My heart skipped a beat and I said, "yes!"
as he gently put his hand in mine
and held me close.

Dedication: to my parents for inspiring me

The Misery Of Me
Joshua Sobczuk
For now I watch from a distance,
wanting so much, to be a part
of the dream I see everyday,
that's tearing me apart.

For some reason, I can't let you go.
I wait in silence, so much wanting you to know.

My emotions are crushed daily,
as I fail to realize my dream
of you and I together,
people seeing us as a team.

But for now I stand on the sidelines,
not able to play my own game,
and wishing over and over for you.

With only...
myself to blame.

Dedication: to Rachael, my best friend

All I Need
Beulah M. Nedd
I need to
Fuse my spirit
Stop Static in my life
Switch negative to positive
Cancel my Watts and whys

Lord, I need You to be my Insulator
The conductor of my ways
A breaker of non-truth thoughts
My love—Amplifier
My life—stabilizing Current

Yes, I need to
have You as my Transformer
For with You in total Charge
I'll be a Conduit for Your ways

For with You, Lord
I'll be totally Charged
I'll be Your Can–do–it all my days
And eliminate Resistance to Your call.

Enchanted Dreams

Nobody Else
Annie Sutton
Father God forgive me, for I know not what to do.
About this situation, I know I need to seek You.
I need to know You are close to me, each and every day.
I want Your hand to guide me and Your light to light my way.
I need to feel your presence, today and everyday,
then I know You are so very near to me.
And I am able to see Your way.
I know You are doing something, deep inside of me.
And I know when You're done,
You will have done it perfectly.
Please let me live each day according to Your will
and forget all about these things that make me very ill.
I want to breathe each breath as You as my air
and I want to show people that You do really care.
There is no one in this world, that is as faithful as You are and this I
know, I know by far. You are the only one, that I can count on for
    support,
for if I look to something or someone they will always come up short.
So let me turn to You in everything I do.
Help me to always Praise and to forever worship You.
I need nobody else but You.

Plain
Laszlo S. Sipos
Whitewashed,
just open; thoughts flowing openly
unbiased ordinary.
My mind is flowing with just ordinary
BLANK
Whitewashed,
living in just basic
taking the obvious
the Plain;
later conflictions of,
the Plain.

Dedication: to all our families

Tears Of Joy
Frederick C. LaVoie
Herein lie tears of joy and sorrow.
Each drop – a sign of love from
which no one may borrow.

Tears shared between two people
meeting again for the first time.
What well from which these waters spring?
Is it life itself?
I may not know for many a tomorrow.

Is there love so strong as life?
Is there sadness not so full of strife?

In another time we will know.
From life to life our love continues to grow.
In each heart and soul, a place continues to show.

An eternity from now there will be no tears of sorrow.
We must wait for many a tomorrow.

Dedication: to you, my morning star

Gift
Christine L. Moore
I have a gift for you,
If you want it,
You can take it,
If you don't want it,
I will take it,
And my precious,
Innocent, little heart,
You will break it,
So if you want it,
You got it.

And as for thee,
I may have another one for you,
Let me look in my box and see,
But this will cost you,
No, this one is not for free,
It'll cost you a hug,
All nestled in love,
Or to thee,
A constant bug,
I will be.

Blood Bound
Carl Brown
A drop of crimson hits the brass headstone.
A voice of vengeance is spoken.
The hatred is formed.
The dagger, thrust into the ground to stay.
A constant reminder of the pain.
The scars are his memories now,
And when he finds the one
To help him heal his wounds,
He may be too far gone to reach,
And She may be too far away to touch,
Her healing hand.

Dedication: to Annie, my lover and healer

Sunbeams
Lorraine Fox
Like a morning sunset
You brighten my day.
Clouds can't stay
They just float away.

Your love is a sunbeam
Shining into my heart.
Chasing away the darkness
With a caressing light.

Deeply touching me with
The warmth of your love.
Starting a gentle glow
That spreads to enfold me.

As the arms of my love
Encircle to hold me.
No where else would I rather be
Than right here, just you and me.

Dedication: to Jim, my love and inspiration

Our Special Night
Gail Pandori
Your fingertips are like soft petal tips of a blooming spring flower
Holding me close, feeling my heart beat fast
It beats with excitement
Making each Moment last for an eternity

Long walks along the shoreline
Holding hands, just listening to the waves
Waiting for the evening to turn into night

The stars appear with a full moon
You pull me closer and hold me tight
A sweet kiss soon leads to more

Your touch is gentle and sweet
Waiting for the right time to say all the things you are to me
Hungering for your love
Can't you see my desire?

The morning arrives
The moon departs and the sun appears
And we have the special night we shared

Tryst
Bernice H. Hunt
The moonlight shimmered on an Indian lake
Where timid woodland deer came down to slake
Their thirst and graze along the wooded land.
Long years ago, an Indian youth and maid
Met in the springtime, wandered hand—in—hand,
Enchanted by the spell their love had laid.

Now when the springtime moon rides full and high,
The lake gleams in the hollow of the hill...
Quicksilver quivering. Where shadows lie,
The spirits of the Indian lovers thrill
In ecstasy to meet, to tryst once more.
Beside the water, deer stand by the shore.

I Am The Wind
Lynn M. Tilot
I Am The Wind, I am the wind... that ruffles your hair
And softly caresses your body
Touching, fleeting, teasing

I am the sun... shining down on you
Warming, slowly rising to a fever heat
Glittering, igniting the flame

I am the fire... that consumes you
The raging inferno that engulfs you
Devouring, burning out of control

I am the rain... that slowly cools you
Relaxing slowly into slumber
Refreshing, soothing, smiling

I am the wind... always with you
Blowing gently through your dreams
Here, then not... a memory

I am the wind...

Moment Of Creation
Saleha Chowdhury
Singing in silence
On a bike,
Slowly moves through
Grass and trees.

Through light and shades
I feel
A summery night.

The moving two wheels stop
I lean on it.
Look at the blue sky
Appears a sky—moon therapy.
Wind zips through the trees.

Sky and silence
They grow in me.
A Moment's miracle,
Slowly I open my fist
There is
One of my poetry.

Illumination
Jennifer Esau
Kisses are gifts of golden strands
decorating lacy trees in midnight
with draping, rare beauty encouraged by the moonlight
Lingering illuminated wishes flown by birds
Taken to heights of misty dreams and silent words
Kisses are golden gifts that release fountains of pooling devotion,
dwelling deep within,
sealing its privileged affection of profound emotion
Closing eyes to see with a heart open wide
Strengthens hands to hold knit souls
and let go of expensive pride
Worn in its royal wreath laden of honeysuckle petals
Sweetens the air of where it styles gently rests and settles.

Whose Turn To Cry
Glen Verrier
A baby cries, a mother wakes
Knowing what is to be done.
A creaking door, a thoughtful look.
The crying has stopped for now.

A baby cries, a father's turn
With bottle in hand he goes.
Footsteps and a big, broad smile,
The crying has stopped for now.

A baby cries, the parent's awake,
A beautiful morning has risen.
A laugh, a giggle, a cry of glee.
The crying has stopped for now.

A little one cries, first day of school.
A shout of happiness for graduation.
A diploma in hand, it's off to work.
It's the parents' turn to cry.

Dedication: to Geoffrey and Bradley Verrier

Enchanted Dreams

War...
Bruce Martin Long
Boys, who are now men,
Shake each time the shells come whistling overhead,
Waiting for the one that will drop on them,
Drained of strength,
Unable to show emotion as their comrades die,
Only praying for the end.

Boys, who joined the throng of men willing to defend—
their country,
Not knowing how they will spend their time,
Waiting for the others to move,
Out of their foxholes and into the field of fire,
Hoping they will survive this sortie,
Looking forward to going home, someday.

Boys, who no longer worry about death,
They have seen it all,
Hoping when it comes, it is quick and painless,
War has destroyed their feelings for their fellow man,
Now they live day to day, with no feelings for tomorrow,
Only praying for the end.

The Love Of A Woman Is The Happiness Of Life
William Davis
The women of this world are so beautiful. When we look at
them (we men) as we see her being small, she's so beautiful,
medium built
You're so beautiful, tall and slim you're so beautiful,
heavy—built you're
Just wonderful and beautiful to go with it. God made you all in
Different colors, shapes, hair styles and a great gift of making
a man
Love you, this is the way we see every one of you, so beautiful,
just like a
Rainbow after a big rain, so beautiful to look at.
Remember now we
Know you are the most beautiful thing on this Earth

A Precious Love
J. B. Flynn
I wipe away my tears of grief
With heavy heart I sigh
Treasured memories cloud my mind
Of precious years gone by

I never thought of life alone
We lived our time as one
I think of all the love we shared
Of the laughter and the fun

Often, I can feel you here
Your strength, it sees me through
If only I could hold you close
And still say "I love you"

Waves of grief, they come and go
I know one day they'll cease
When time has come for us to be
United in our peace

Dedication: to whom we have loved

No More
K. Gillion
No more will I wake up
On a morning with you
By my side to hear the birds
Chirping and to enjoy the day
Ho, why did God have to
Take you away
No more parties, outings
Holidays together, yes, we
Both thought we would go
On forever
Life was fun then and no
Strife but there's plenty
Of that now, my dear wife
I loved you so much and
Still do sometimes, I
Seem to feel you touch my
Hand and whisper "I do
Love you so much", it's as
Though you are trying
To make me understand
And then you hold my hand

Kindness
Ruthie Hamlet
Kindness is a little thing that means a lot,
It can easily be sought out,
If only you would give it a try,
To a friend passing by,
It would brighten your day,
In a surprising way.
It will bring a smile to your face,
In every bad case, If you put a little
Kindness in its place.
A smile, a wink, or a cheerful hello
Are always to let your kindness show.
Kindness is a little thing that means a lot,
It can easily be sought out.

Retirement
Jean Wood
Silence, missing the children
Sadness, the passing of years
Quietness, where there was laughter
All too often, the tear
Concern, that used to be passion,
Kindness, that once was love,
Memories thought of often.
Strong need for the Lord above,
Abandonment, without parents, hopelessness, sometimes dread.
Dreams that have reached an ending
A terrible thing to be said,
But life is not yet over,
The third stage just begun,
Still needed by the children
Life's work is not yet done.
God give us strength to conquer
All these fears and dread.
Give us new dreams to strive for.
Show us a new road ahead.

Dedication: to Ken, my husband

Untitled
Dorothy Cooperwaite

There's a submarine sailing far out to sea
There is someone on it who is thinking of me
Though we're apart, I know he'll be true
When we meet, he'll be waiting in Heaven so blue

He is with me always and I know I'm with him
Although at the Moment the light seems so dim
Still burning brightly is the light of his love
Waiting for me in the Heaven's above

When we meet, all the torture and hell of the past
In a beautiful paradise will be surpassed
By a peace oh, so tranquil and strangely divine
With only God, he and I in that wonderful shrine

Until the day I am called to his side
All sorrow and bitterness I'll try to hide
For the day I am offered that tranquility
I'll know it is mine for eternity

Dedication: to my first husband, Thomas

Confusing Thoughts
Shasta Nielsen

Sitting here among my friends of many years,
Remembering our times of laughter and tears,
A strange and confusing thought has just come to me,
Do I really know them, who they are, what they see.
I'm starting to wonder if just maybe,
I know them, but they don't know me.
Sometimes I feel like a stranger in a crowd,
or a new kid who moved in from a different town.
They all look familiar, maybe I saw them at the mall,
or maybe I've never seen them before at all.
I'm still discovering who I am and so are they,
So, no matter what we claim, we really don't know who we're sitting by today.

Tina
Danielle Lennox

Black of body and white of chest
Though with four legs, she's the best —
Friend I've ever really found
My playful, faithful, loving hound.

When I'm feeling down and woes betide,
She never, ever, leaves my side
With wagging tail and offered paw
No more love in an eye have I ever saw.

She doesn't ask for much, just food and a walk
It seems a pity she can't manage to talk
But then she knows her ever-listening ear
Can take away a lot of my fear.

My friend, I know you do understand
By the feel of my love through my hand
Whenever there comes a time to part
We'll both live on in each others' heart.

Dedication: to Tina, my very special pet

The Horse Rhyme
Cassandra Gaeta

Horses are white
and horses are brown
They like to eat oats
and ride you through town!

Horses are friendly
and horses are smart
To people who are kind
they have a big heart!

Horses are fast
and horses are strong
They would love to be brushed
all day long!

So, in the end
I would recommend
You get a horse
Of course...

I LOVE HORSES!

Rain
Renee Suze Baltsen

Deep, white rivers
in splashes of fun
sheets of white
shimmering streams
slicing through my face.
Tiny rings
splashing in silver
dancing in puddles.
Exploding into thunder
the roar of lighting
under my feet.
I soaked in
Nature's embrace

Tim
M. Grimshaw

I gave my heart
To a beautiful bay,
Who came from the land
of the kilt and the sporran.

With a proud young head
and a soft brown eye
He dared me to know him
and keep my heart.

Now I am lost to this
beautiful bay, who came
from the land of the kilt
and the sporran.

A four-year-old
with a star on his head
and hope in his heart
for the love we will share.

Dedication: to our wonderful children and grandchildren

Enchanted Dreams

Hard World
Rachel Jamieson
Pristine,
obscene,
bones that stalk the Earth.
Crude,
and so rude,
plastic love is all we're worth.
Manufactured fears, mirror the tears
that freeze before they run.
Glaze over our eyes, reflecting lies
for a world that seems so numb.
Sold out, sold up and packaged,
with no chance for debate.
Hooked,
and then discarded,
can't swallow
but, it's too late.
We're ready—wrapped, hurt,
wide–eyed and alert,
we're sealed and sent along.
We pray, obey and feed of their way,
and now we sing their song.

My View
Michelle Bernhardt
There are some people in the world today, that make our futures grow,
and there are some people in the world that only love do they show.
Yet, there are some kids and elders, that just don't really care,
because all their thoughts and dreams are completely surrounded by fear.
They say they don't understand, or maybe they just don't want to,
but they realize that things happen and there is a reason that they do.
But no one is perfect, there's always room for mistakes and because of
looking back on what they did, well, that's why their heart so often
aches.
I wish I knew what is better or worse in the world, wish things could be
rewound, see how much we have killed, yet explore how much we have
found!

Hope
Joanne Keith
Shake off your fear; throw away all your doubt
Look to the future, for it's your only way out
Be strong, no matter how hard the road may seem
forget your apathy; nothing is an impossible dream
When life seems content on knocking you to the floor
Don't give up; fight; don't take it anymore

Keep on smiling and you'll pull through
What's past is history; forget it, don't let it keep hold of you
for tomorrow is always a new day
Life's what you make it; so make it go your way
Hold on to your dignity; don't lose your respect
Be what you want to be and not what people expect

So here I write for those who can't seem to find their ground
Keep on hanging on; for your time will come around
When you feel like giving in; don't do it
You'll only look back in anger at one more time when you
blew it
You will get back on your feet again if you believe in it
Just keep on keeping on and don't you Quit!

Nan
Laura Richardson
Here we are in this situation once again
And I find myself asking – is this the end?

However, we know that you are strong and tough,
And all the love we have for you will be enough.

We all see you as a fighter, who we know will not give in.
You can win the battle, if you fight from deep within.

So please Nan, be brave and do not give up hope,
Because, without you, we will not be able to cope.

In my life, you have always been there and played an important part,
And Nan, whatever happens there will always be a place for you in my heart.

Without a doubt, you are perfect and the best a Nan could be,
And this is what shall always and forever be true to me.

You will never know quite how much I love you, as I do not often let it
show.
But I honestly do not know how I will handle it, if you were to go.

Untitled
Cherie DuPlayce–Brown
The day the child starts growing
Is the day the child starts knowing.

The day the child starts to play
Is the day the child gets away.

The day the child learns
Is the day the child becomes concerned.

The day the child becomes obsessed
Is the day the child becomes depressed.
And the day the child starts to rely
Is the day the child starts to die.

A Mi Amiga Adriana Garcia–Macias
Gloria T. Berg
Aurora temprana de un alma sencilla

De la mano del tiempo hemos vuelto a caminar
Reencontrarnos quiso el Sino, recorriendo nuevos mundos
Inventando realiDades, albergando viejos suenos
y en un fugaz instante, abatidas por la ausencia y
Absortas en recuerdos a recorrer los muelles de nuestra feliz infancia,
entre risas y suspiros, hemos vuelto asi a sonar.
Ni en Momentos de tristeza, algunos oscuros... son tantos...
ni sumidas en fracasos, ni en la inevitable distancia,
nuestra amistad pura y santa pudimos olvidar.
Ahora que alcanzamos el zenith de nuestras vidas, se duermen ya las
rondas,
y los cuentos de la infancia... de la niñez y adolescencia solo recuerdos
quedan
y esa firme promesa de volvernos a encontrar,

Graciosa e inolvidable, hermosa AMIGA mia,
hasta que el Momento llegue de volvernos a abrazar,
recibe este poema como promesa eterna del lazo inquebrantable:
de nuestro amor fraternal...

Grave Site
Sandra Schrum

I sit and gaze at the words engraved,

You died at nineteen almost to the day.

How did you die?

Did you suffer terribly?
Did you go Quietly?

Did you scream as the blood
ran out of your veins,

did you lie there quietly,
taking the pain?

did you ever want to run
as the guns sound?

I sit and gaze at the words engraved,

you died at nineteen almost to the day.

Maelstrom
Dyane C. McMahon

I am drawn to you like the tide feels the pull of the moon
helplessly succumbing to your gentle, constant, inescapable gravity
giving way, giving in
the way the sea thoughtlessly tumbles and tosses in a blanket of darkness
the very same creatures it guides lovingly along the journey in the
　　warmth of the sun
no one is safe, nothing is sacred, nothing is spared
for this decision is not mine to make
this decision is no decision,
for there is no option, no other choice to consider
only a true state of being
I am here, I am alive
I am in love with you...

A Sailor's Sunset
J. S. Kelly

It's twilight and high above the surf, a tiny cot'
Framed in whose doorway an old man stands.
A lonely figure time and tide forgot,
He gazes out across the sea and sands.

Time was, when he a sailor bold,
undaunted, would defy those turbulent waves,
But now, a little stooped and growing old,
All he can do is watch and wait the grave.

Yet it's believed among seafaring men,
That as each mariner dies, a seagull's born.
To wing his soul across the sea again,
To tranquil waters far beyond life's storm.

It's darker now, the cottage door is closed,
The sun's last rays to westward tint the sky.
The hush of evening blends in soft response,
With silence, save a newborn seagull's cry.

Dedication: to June and Moo, love and thanks

Untitled
C. E. Dupuy

Lord God Almighty
cares for us all
Every vibrant Moment
of every living day
And when the setting sun
And the growing shadows
lengthen
The twilight turns to night
The grinding world at last
sighs to a blissful halt
The heady fever of life well spent
now ebbs with the tide
The task is finally done
The work forever ended
The Lord God, in His infinite mercy
Provides the lodging, the haven
A holy respite and everlasting
peace Sheep returning to his
Heavenly fold

Amen

My Secret
Cynthia Fenimore

Laying my head down on my pillow at night
I picture angels and doves in clouds of white
My mind is filled with friends and love.
You are no longer what I'm dreaming of.
Holding my bear, I don't think of you
I think of my angels and dreams coming true
I look through my window at the stars outside
They never remind me of the tears I've cried.

If I say it enough, will it all come true?
When I lie to me, when I lie to you?
The truth is buried way down deep.
But you'll never know, it's my secret to keep.

Stale Stillness Stagnant
Sean Takacs

Love.
Found it, had it, lost it.
Miss it.

The moon's just a cheap version of the sun,
and the latter's rise is nothing more than loneliness begun.

I can still laugh and I still cry,
I still brush these rotting teeth
and still smile when there's someone new to meet,
I still talk and dress the same way,
I still drive and take walks to the same nowheres,
loving the same things
and harvesting the same regrets, I still breathe,
the only difference
is now my soul is ready to leave,
it won't look me in the eye anymore
and it makes me shake,
starvation and contamination
both breeding saturation,
and now my soul is ready to leave.

Enchanted Dreams

His Eyes
Patricia Plattner
They say God created this Earth and from the soil He made man;
I know of one man whose eyes are as brown as the fresh Earth below
our feet.
It was his soft eyes that eased my untrusting fears from the
beginning.
They showed me the pureness of his heart.
At times, his eyes have spoken of joy and pleasantry,
But there were Moments when I saw sadness and pain deep within
his eyes.
Both his innocence and his experience lie in the dark pupils of his
Earthen–brown eyes.
Oh, how they shine with all his wisdom.
His eyes sparkle with such life, that it is easy to give in to his wants.
In complete darkness, the gaze from his eyes overpowered me.
One look into his eyes and I become hypnotized; hypnotized into
being his lover, his servant and his guardian angel.
From his eyes, the lights of Heaven do shine and the fires of Hell do
burn.
Even beneath a glassy alcohol daze, his eyes could beg for my
passion and desire.
I didn't love the man, but I worshipped his eyes.

Blue
Elham Khatami
Silky dolphins roam the bright–blue, salty ocean.

A giant blue whale saunters the sea.

Rough blue jeans fill with dirt and dust as they touch the desert
ground.

The dark, rainy sky slowly turns to neon blue.

A blue jay sings to the sunlight and enjoys wonderful spring.

Total blackness fills the air and suddenly the color blue
brightens it up.

Since You Went Away
Iris Hector
The time has gone so quickly,
Since you've been away.
I sit and wait so patiently,
Until you come back and stay

I watch the glowing sunset,
And think of you, my dear.
I dream of having fun,
As I wipe away a tear.

I have always remembered the day you came,
The day you said it's time to part,
But though you are far away,
I miss you with all of my heart.

I wait for you and cry,
With silent tears of pain,
But no one knows the joy I feel,
When I see you once again.

Dedication: to Trevor, Elizabeth, Jessie and Biddy

Musical Jim
Irelee Crosby
There once was a man who lived on a hill.
His name known by all as Musical Jim.
He'd sit on his porch and say very little.
Just sit there all day and play his old fiddle.
The people of his town were so very bitter.
Much in need, he would say, of a very good fiddler.
All he had in his life was ample free time.
Time to sit and fill hearts with rhythm and rhyme.
He told the townspeople there was no need to frown.
Invite in the music, dance and turn it upside down.
With that he played faster and said, "You'll see".
But they looked at him, scoffed and said, "Dancing, Indeed!"
And just like he said, one day came a change.
The townspeople for once had a smile on their face.
Some walked with a whistle.
Others smiled and just sat.
Men greeted each other with a tip of the hat.
And playing festively as ever up on the hill.
With a smile on his face was Musical Jim.

Dedication: to my two Garys

Pain
Heather Mills
Why did he do this to me?
Why did he give me this
terrible pain?
What did I do but ask
For his love in return.
Can he fill the hurt
and pain he put me
through?
Did he use me or did
he really love me?
was that Phrase something
to say to pass the time
away?

What A Beautiful Name
Mary Sutten
What a beautiful name, the name of Jesus,
the name, where demons have to flee,
Where the blind receive their sight,
Where your wrongs are all made right.
What a beautiful name, the name of Jesus.

There is power, in His name,
When you're saved you are not the same,
Old things are passed away, all things are new–
So, stand up and shout, tell the whole wide
world about,
that beautiful name, the name of Jesus

There's healing in His name, His wonderful
name,
He made the lame to walk, the dumb
to talk.
The dead rose again He died to save us
from all sin,
What a beautiful name, the name
of Jesus.

Visionary
Dave Boyce

The rays that bring us life and light,
The beams of heat that cut the night.
We need these solar–power beams,
to build our cities to warm our dreams.

For fields of flowers, corn and maize,
and sunny summer morning haze.
For forest, wood and everglade,
could not survive in constant shade.

So if it dies, this power and light,
and everyday errs into night.
With every shadow drawing near,
and every second filled with fear.

So as I lay me down to sleep,
this frozen hell my soul will keep.
To one day break these chains of ice,
and live again in paradise...

Dedication: to W. J. Boyce, love you forever

To A Dying Soldier
Linda M. Seay

Yes, Mr. Soldier, it's happened to you,
As you lie in the dirt with the men that you knew.
It happened so quickly, that shot in the air.
And now you are dying, does anyone care?
What are you thinking as time slips away?
Are you thinking of home—do you have time to pray?
Remember your friends right there by your side,
Who were fighting for freedom and the ones who have died.
Remember the graveyard and the different tombstones.
Will they remember your name or will you be one of the unknown?

Yes, Mr. Soldier, it's happened to you,
As you lie in the dirt with the men that you knew.

Motivation
Beverly J. Lama

Let it be the hour before
A visitor is due
And greater tricks of magic
No one can show to you

Let it be December
Or the merry month of May
Motivation is the thing
That makes my cheery day

Let it be a something
Never dull and not routine
Let there be that something
To keep me on the beam

When I am old and shriveled
Let the fireflies that glow
Send me secret signals
To keep me in the know.

Dedication: to my children and grandchildren

Mirrors
Neil S. Friedman

I live alone among carnival mirrors
Seeing different shapes
And standards
Different ethics
And values
Seeing different people
Which one am I?

I live alone among carnival mirrors
Looking for a way out
But bumping into myself
And causing pain.

I live alone among carnival mirrors
Looking for the path out
And it eludes me.

I live alone among carnival mirrors
Never seeing what others see
Who am I?
Where am I going?

Search
Sylvia Jump

As we journey, through this life
The path is rarely smooth

But, with each step along the way
A lesson we will learn.

We'll search our soul for happiness
And shed the tears of pain.

Until one day our eyes will open
Seeing "WISDOM" we have gained.

Dedication: to Thomas and Damon, my sons

Untitled
Nigel Paul Walker

O beautiful winds of Heaven
Whose dance set our hearts
Alight with desires
Desires and thoughts that haunt me
And, although uplifting,
They can be so heavy my love
My heart longs to feel again
Your warmth
My eyes thirst for the beauty
Of which they once drank so freely
Am I not to see such a vision again
Except within my dreams
Or in the brief times that my reality allows
It is truly a pain for a man to bear
But I am not totally without voice
Sh! Listen! I cry
O beautiful winds of Heaven
Please dance for us
Once more

Dedication: to Toni, my love always

Enchanted Dreams

Cleaning The Attic
Jean Warwick
I'm cleaning the attic today.
There are so many things I should throw away
There's books, toys, old furniture, odds and ends, too
Where all this stuff comes from I haven't a clue
Now this old wooden crib minus a rung or two
And a wee rocking chair, our children outgrew
This bag of old teddy bears, pink, brown and blue
And all these nice dolls had a name, I once knew
Then these hard-covered books, some pages not there
Here's crayons and pencils and shoes, not a pair.
These puzzles, where's the pieces gone?
Little cars that've been painted and repainted.
Oh, they'll do no harm,
So I dust off the furniture, put the bears back in the bag
And the dolls I once knew I tied with a tag.
The hard-covered books and loose pages
Oh, here's some rocks, I carefully put them all back in the box
The puzzles and crayons, pencils and cars
The unmatched shoes, an egg crate made into a star.
There's too many memories to throw these away, but I cleaned the attic today

---

Keep the Peace
Michael J. Yavorski
A necessity that's blossoming from an opposite concept.
A promise we must make to ourselves and be kept.

Make the most of the present. Keep an eye on the future.
Practice laws of the Heavens. Not the rebellion of Lucifer.
A one-on-one basis, understanding, compassion.
Soon it will spread and become the new fashion.

Forget all the ego. A real person is humble.
Keep that in mind, so you don't stumble.

We may need money, to pay all our bills.
But isn't it funny that greed is what kills?

Desire
Emma Hutchinson
Pearly boy, lips of plum,
So oppressed, under their thumb.
Weeping scars of blackest Kohl,
He's heard the jokes, how very droll.
Baby-black tee, tight across his chest,
Seven sisters but now he looks the best.
Strangled heart, gleam in his eye,
Mirror their eyes, girl or a guy?
Leather skin, such a close shave.
He is the fireboy, no longer their slave.

Flash of passion over his spine,
His mind or his body? He's missing the sign.
Who is this God in fireboy's bed,
He's seen his body, now he's screwing his head.
Androgynous lover, grinding his hips,
Anonymous brother, Babycham lips.
Black plastic hipsters, holding his waist,
Tongue so electric, pure sugar taste.
They said it was evil, this wicked desire,
Licking his face, lifting him higher.

The Wonders Of Spring
Josie Beylerian
Spring creeps up on you like a sassy surprise
all wrapped up in choice colours;
Waiting for the soft rains of April to fall
upon their waiting buds —
To release their rainbow of colours upon us,
Splashing the landscape with their kaleidoscope of
REDS, YELLOWS, PINKS
and ORANGES.

Mother Nature announces that
Spring has left her calling card
and is now holding Open House,
Inviting us to savor the myriad of colours
in our gardens
To feast our eyes and souls on.

Once more,
Spring unfolds its wonders
of the mystery of new birth
and
NEW BEGINNINGS.

Good Memories
Linda Katherine Feagans
When you touched me, I had no strength inside myself.
When you kissed me, I felt the world below me.
When you told me how you needed me, I cried because
I needed you the same.
When you made love to me, there was no one else in the world
Just you and I.
When I looked into your eyes, I saw the promises of tomorrow.
I touched your face, I kissed your lips, I held you so tight
I thought you would never let me go.
When you left me with the memories, I dreamed of you.
When you left, you took my dreams with you.
My dreams are now my memories.
The passion of my memories.

The Lovers
L. E. Maddison
On the large chimney high
Seemed almost to touch the sky.
Two pigeons, or sparrows, maybe blackbirds
Looking from my window, See them merge.
Their beaks they peck and move close.
They chirp up, they seem to float.
Toward each other, they make love.
What is that, another swoops from above.
Feathers fly angry words are spoken
In birdie language, wings flap, are broken.
The female bird looks placidly on
She preens her feathers and is gone.
But back she flies to tend her lover.
Maternal love, she tends as a mother.
Their beaks meet, Kisses are tender.
So proud. He fought for her, she is kinder
Her broken hero, She really loves him
She preens, she kisses his broken limbs
So proud. Her love, his mate forever.
Chimney high. Their home not to leave
Forever.

My Journey
Vera R. Welsh

The time has come, I must begin
The call that comes from my soul within
A need to cherish these thoughts each day
Dear God, help me along the way

I need Your strength and loving hand
To help me draw and process my plan
The thoughts are clear as You do know
But I have a mind that can't let go

I must go back to the temple of love
To sit and listen, like our Morning Dove
Grant me the grace to see the light
To extend my wings for my endless flight

The flight that takes me high above the clouds
So that I can sing my song out loud
A song of joy, peace and caring
That someday we can all start sharing

Dedication: to Margaret, for her inspiration

Waiting For Success
Collette Lambe

I had a dream that I could fly,
when I woke, I found it was a lie,
oh, how I did cry and cry
I had a dream that I could fly
I realized that if I did try, if I reached up high,
with my hands I could touch the sky

I had a dream that I could fly,
now I know if I really try
if I keep on reaching for the sky,
if I really try...
Someday soon I will fly, up in that midnight sky
Keeping on reaching as I try

The Train
Helen Reeve Page

I know that Canadians love their trains
Linking the Atlantic to Pacific
So this poem is, in the main,
My own warm feelings so terrific.

The Moment my feet climb the steps of the train
I am filled with the sense of adventure
And once in my seat, I await that refrain
Of bustling, exciting departure.

My eyes never tire of country or town
And the journey is made resplendent
With the food and service handed down
By concerned and pleasant attendants.

The train will always have appeal
For travel near, or far-away
I love the lullaby of its wheels
That soothe me, from the cares of day.

Dedication: to Kristofer and Kaythin with love

Last Night In A Dream
Avril Furse

Last night so slowly in a dream
Upon the steed of death I rode,
I sat upon his back afraid,
He was so awesome and so tall.
I cried aloud to those around,
"Please help me, hold me or I'll fall."
They turned away and would not look.
They did not heed my pleas at all,
But one beside me rode as well.
I could not see his face but he
Rode never far from me
Through dark woods we traveled on
In such a melancholy way.
Until at last we reached a door
Which turned the darkness into day.
I think one day I'll see the face
Of he who traveled all the way.
And then I'll learn the miracle
Which turned the darkness into day.

Dedication: to James Nelson Arnold, my father

Thorny Red Rose
Constance Timoteo

You have to snuff out the embers
before they start a fire.
It's not so easy to catch.
So you'll have to run before it's spread farther.
Then they'll blame you for the Apocalypse.
When all I wanted was to pick a thorny, red rose.

I'd like to pick it from someone's rose bush.
I don't expect them from some sweetheart
I ain't no romantic.
'Cause I've been stung by thorns all of my life.
And I don't know if I should cry or laugh.
When the blood appears from my thorny, red rose.

Untitled
Sheila Hardwick

You always thought me crackers.
But now I know I am.
The other day, I nearly threw
Coal down the toilet pan.
I think my memory's going.
I keep forgetting things.
I go to put the kettle on.
And then, the shop bell rings.
As the time goes by.
I think! now! where was I.
I'll make a drink.
And have a think.
Or maybe, wash pots, in the sink.
Then I get distracted.
With another job or task.
I should make little notes.
So I wouldn't have to ask.
The problem then would be
Knowing where I'd wrote.
If only I could remember,
Where I put that note.

Enchanted Dreams

Untitled
Sandra Frasier
'Tis time our ties to sever
for soon I'll be gone forever
You haven't a care nor will You ever
cause my memory is one You wished for never

I'm so tired of being hurt
always beaten, thrown in dirt
never getting more than flirt
only loving in a squirt

Will I ever find a guy
one who won't make me cry
and will never get a high
Never will He tell a lie
I'm willing to truly try
to give Him world beyond the sky
up above He shall fly
Never living in a sty
Always willing to apply
I'm so empty and so dry
Me Oh, My Oh, Why Oh, Why

Deep
Marjorie Beatty
Feelings are a gift of love
Which without, we cannot feel,
We look inward into our deepest
Self, if our honesty is real.
The kind of person we'd like to
Be puts our popularity to a test,
Is it more important to be liked
Or is it more important to have
Respect?
This is my message, friend, it's
Real food for our soul, just take
A deep look inside yourself and
Make your person whole.

The World Has An End
Jonathan Ricketts
Our world is simple and sad,
We lust only for power and money,
A friendship is merely a way to achieve this goal and be glad,
We may claim to be helpful and as sweet as honey,
But really are we helping the needy or ourselves to gain
others' realization?
If we were to unite under one flag and forget our fears,
Maybe then, we could rank ourselves in the universal
democratic confederation.
But, Alas, our world is far from free, there are few without their peers.
We have many weapons of destruction yet few of salvation.
Our one human race is worthless.
We take the easy way out and live in anticipation,
Maybe one day someone will try hard to save our dying mess.
The world will end, it is in the book.
You can run from a gun, fly from a bomb but what if the whole Earth
is to end,
Where do we go, to a new planet must we look?
If only God would give the world fifty years to lend,
Maybe an answer would be found.
We have had two thousand years, it is time to stop messing around.

Untitled
Kathy Simpson
To each his own
I always say
Another look
At one more day
I am here but
where are you?
I can't seem to find
A heart that's true.
This one's mine
And that one's yours.
I'm sick of all the selfish words.
My bed too big
For me alone
No one to share with
what I've not been shown
And who makes the rules
To this game we all play
Forfeit my hand
Then again...
No...
I'll stay!

Untitled
Lisa Valkenburg
On a hot afternoon
Wouldn't it be so nice
To enjoy the freedom
Of the wind
However slight
As it dries the skin
Briefly
How refreshing weather
Could be
Without a shirt
On a hot day

Dedication: to Mothers and mothers-to-be

Life Is But A Shadow
David Lang
Life is but a shadow
cast upon the path we walk,
only a ghostly silhouette
it can't laugh, or sing, or talk.

Life is but a shadow
that follows you along,
it comes and goes without a trace,
sometimes it does not belong.

Life is but a shadow
a dark shade of oneself,
sometimes it keeps you company,
sometimes it's on the shelf.

For all of your life's sorrows
your shadow doesn't care,
you cannot hug your shadow,
because it really isn't there.

Dedication: to Susan, love you always

Seasons
Clara Roog

Seasons come and seasons go
Every year we know there will be some snow
Then comes the spring when everything peeks through
The flowers, the bright colors, all come into view
Each season lasts as long as it should
Some we wish would last longer, if only they could
But we know that is not nature's way
And Mother Nature will always have her say
We go through this year after year
And yet we act so surprised
As another season is ready to appear
Or see the changes as they all reappear
Are we not listening, are we not in fear
That we ignore all the signs when they are all here
As once again it is time for one season to come and another to go
It's like Mother Nature putting on a variety show
So why not see a little more of what is around us
And enjoy all the beauty on Earth that surrounds us
For much too soon no longer we will see
The seasons around us, how quickly they do flee

Wishing
Diane Childress

There's nothing here but mountains and snow
And trees all over the land,
I wish I could go where the weather is hot
And wiggle my toes in the sand.

There's nothing here but cactus and sand
And this desert air is so dry,
I wish I could go to the seashore now
And hear the sea gulls cry.
There's nothing here on this one-season island
But sea gulls and wind that blows,
I wish I could go the mountains
With summer and spring and fall and snows.

A Childless Mother
Valerie Axford

In nine long months, she waits in vain
Suffering anguish, worry and the pain
She copes, in the knowledge, it'll all be worth
That final pain, that we call birth

The child, her child so pure, with love
Sent down from Heaven and God above
Will ease, all nine months, she endured
And fill her, so with love, she may be cured

But what if the child, she awaits, does not stay?
Where is the joy, the love, to take the pain away?
What if the loss, the sorrow brings forth more?
How much can a childless mother endure?

Time will heal, some people say
How much time? What of today?
How big is the battle of an emotional drought?
To find the meaning in life, can she do without?

Dedication: to Kristy and John, with love

To A Seashell
Alanna Nattis

Who sculpted your body,
Your twisted nozzle?
Was it the palms of the ocean?
The fingers of the sea?
Who gave you the shine of one—
thousand stars in the night sky?

Mother Nature has carved me,
My nozzle, my body.
And shined me with the love from her heart.
And, within me, lies her presence,
Creating ones just like me,
With her love, her hands.
And soon, she will leave,
As I get washed into the sea.
And, the hands of the ocean,
Will be my home,
Leaving me to forget what it felt like,
To be loved by Mother Nature.

Dedication: to my wonderful and caring parents

To My Siamese
Donna Lundy

Cleo, we are lucky.
We've met a man who doesn't mind
that you are mean and that I can't find
the strength to open mind and heart
to possibilities I've set apart
as things that happen not to me,
but to friends and people who deserve to be
loved and cared for endlessly.
And now it's happening for you and me.
Oh, Cleo!
Truly, truly we are lucky.

Dedication: to Jeff and Cleo

An Artist Revealed
Jonathon Parrish

Let the truth be known.

Let the masque be broken.

We all hide parts of ourselves from sight.

Some in shadows and some in broad daylight.

We live our lives in the eyes of others.

We judge others on what we see.

Now let the truth be known.

Now I let you judge me.

I am Ishmael... And now let the masque be broken...

Enchanted Dreams

My Only Desire Is You
Nancy Ramos
The precious days of our lives.

One meaningful love,
That can last a lifetime.

Who are we to judge,
Or be judged by the way we love.

I stand here before you,
To honor your love and compassion for life.

Who are we, without love.
Certainly not one with peace within our souls.

I cry not for you,
But for the love I deserve to have.

Only you, my love, have the power,
To set my heart on fire.

For you alone, are all I desire!

My Vow To You
Melinda M. Myers
Forever my love, with all my heart.
Your Joy is my Happiness, for we will never part.

For everything you are, means everything to me.
Your Passion is my life, for it helps me to breathe.

To be without you, is more then I could bear.
My life would have no meaning, without you there.

I love you now and I will love you forever.
You're the only one for me, the only one I will treasure.

Dedication: to Terry Young, my heart's inspiration

The Spider's Web
Mary Phillips
Spider, your web is a creation of art,
Lovely to look at, glimmering with dew,
A mesh of woven silver strands,
Decorated with delicate fragile lace,
Like fishnet stockings, every seam always straight.
Fragile yet strong, deadly to all those who enter.

The outer perimeters of your fortress pulsates,
In the gentle undetectable breeze,
While you, the spider, opaque in the moonlight,
Stand guard at the center of the citadel

By day you leave your transparent lair,
You are just out of sight, always vigil, waiting patiently,
Unconscious to everything but your prey
Ensnared in the adhesive filaments.

You wrap the binding fibers, encasing your hostage,
choking the life from this once unsuspecting passerby.
Unwittingly, the struggling victim through death gives you life.
And so the journey begins and ends.

Just Learning To Cook Is Sufficient
Daniel T. Rozman
What have you done, sixty–past man, to insure living
is worth it and after thinking what could have been,
just learning to cook, is sufficient and sustaining.

Pork and beef, roasts and chops, soups and a stew,
or two real, mashed potatoes, the old–fashioned way,
bread, with crust of golden brown, chicken in a pie,
or baked to perfection—and salads singing arias.

Fettuccini noodles smothered in a decadent sauce and
sprinkled with pepper and Parmesan, cool water fish
charcoal–broiled, an absolute joy to hungry mouths.

Dare one say no, to a dark–chocolate cake, enhanced
with rare liqueurs, bitter chocolate threads on top
and a red raspberry sauce, laced with Chambord, the
ultimate treat, a genuine treasure for palates.

An RSVP is never written, coin of the realm is
not exchanged, for Liberal friends and I do agree,
good food and truth is wasted on Conservatives.

Pictures
William Jones
Pictures are worth a hundred words.
Sometimes the words are good, sometimes
The words are bad and sometimes the words
Are silent, because the picture is just two
Beautiful words.
I hold a picture in my hand so gentle like I'm
Holding sand, but I must remember that if you
Squeeze the sand it would fall out and if you
Squeeze the picture it will be ruined and worth
Fewer words.
I would never squeeze this picture, because it is
The world to me.
It is the picture of my very best friend.

The Mongolian Leopardess
Ben E. Weeks
She moves along beside the trail,
With side–wise glance across the vale,
With liquid moves and muffled growl,
The Mongol Leopardess is on the prowl.

She stops to view the distant scene,
With head arched high and senses keen,
Her gaze transfixed, her eyes opalescent,
Her being electric, softly luminescent.

Though sharp and supple, in sinew and limb,
And graceful and dainty and deceptively slim,
There's wit and courage and explosive force
That's hardly hid by her mild discourse.

This Leopardess is little apt to scream,
Or mewl about the trivial and mean.
She seeks her wants without a howl;
The Mongol Leopardess is on the prowl.

Dedication: to Miss Sally Ching Sun

Untitled
D. Myhill

Your golden curls, your pretty smile,
Your little hand resting in mine awhile –
So dear to me.

Your Mummy's curls were just the same.
Another babe – another name –
So dear to me.

And back until the years of war
Those golden curls my mother saw –
So dear to her.

And further, further back until
My father's curls formed a golden frill –
So dear he was.

So darling granddaughter mine
You are the latest in the line.
Those golden curls mark the racing years,
The passing joys and some passing tears –
So dear to me.

Child Of Glass
Carol Joy Attaway

Beloved child, my child of glass
so fragile in the soul of me,
hidden deep within my mind
playing games that I may find
another's face that masks my fears,
another's laughter hides my tears.
And yet, a call so small and still
cries deep within my conscious will.
Speak out, my child, that I may know
so I may take complete control
or deep within my mirrored soul
where there upon the cloudy grass
lies my fragile child of glass.

A Man I Knew
A. Bailey

Let me tell you of a man I knew whose heart was sad and very blue,
I know he tried to make himself well, but due to circumstance, time would tell.
He fought for life but God said, "that's it."
He took his last breath on Earth and then he quit.
He now resides on a star just outside my window, which twinkles, shines and always glows.
Sometimes he makes appearances in my dreams, being with God is Good, it seems.
He lets me know that things are fine and says he'll see me in good time.
I loved this man through it all, we used to laugh and have a ball.
Now all I have is the memory and the wonderful things produced by photography
Through all the bad there is the good, now all my doubts of Heaven Are understood.
This man is in a paradise beyond the clouds, dancing and smiling and laughing aloud.
This man never cries or feels any pain and everything he does is for His gain. I loved this man I called my Dad, he's the best friend I've ever had.

Working Late
Judith R. Haynes

I'm here tonight, cause my man's gone again
He says that he's working late, like most other men.
I'm Lonesome tonight and I sure need a friend.
I'll tell you once more, so that you'll understand.

Ask me no questions, I'll tell you no lies.
We'll be good for each other, there will be no alibis.
Ask me no questions, I'll tell you no lies.
I won't ask for tomorrow, but I'll be yours tonight.

I've children at home, asleep in their beds.
Their Mommy is gone, lonesome again.
I hope and I pray, through the tears and the pain.
My man will never say, "I have to work late again."

Friends
Andrea Christy

Friends are very important
They are always there for you
They help you through tough times
They make you happy when you are sad
They give you advice when you need it
They help you with your problems
You can tell them anything
And not worry that they will ever tell anyone
When you fight with a friend
It hurts deep inside
When you don't have any friends
The day seems to last forever
And you are glad to see it go
When friends start telling you
you shouldn't date who you want
Because they don't like them
Maybe they are not true friends
Or maybe they are looking out for your well–being
True friends wouldn't care who you date
As long as you like them, is what matters
True friends will be there forever

The Chow Chow
I. R. Matthews

Their body rolled from a cooper's yard into a cotton wool factory.
The legs come from a snooker table, which have been covered in Cotton wool.
Their feet are like the paws of a bear.
The cavernous mouth resembles that of a child who has just eaten liquorice.
While their tail is held like a benign Scorpion's tail.
The ears are like camouflaged satellite dishes.
A nose that reassembles an ebony doorknob.
They walk as if they have sore feet,
Ambling, lumbering along like the giant from Jack and the beanstalk.
Their exuberance resembles a lump of granite.
A coat thick like a woolly jumper.
Its colour resembles either a shepherd's warning, a night watchman's shift, a barrel of printer's ink, or a snowy winter scene.
Their temperament is like that of a tree and a cotton plant,
Benign, aloof, affable, soft, innocent, loveable with the heart of a lion – sometimes.
Their origin is as obscure as their description.

Enchanted Dreams

Let's Not Forget
Louise Brunson
Let's not forget there's sorrow and there's
joy

We cannot forget our fellow man
So take a little time and spread
some caring around

A pat on the back, a handshake will do
Even a nod of the head or a tip
of a hat will mean an awful lot

But with a smile and the words "Good day"
Will come a little easier
The good Lord always blesses the
Cheerful giver.

Weeks
Cindy Smith
I am often found wishing
That Mondays won't come.
Or that Tuesday is Friday,
So my work will be done.
I never did want a week
To last a full seven days.
I want longer weekends,
So I have more time to play!
Wednesdays seem to last
More than forty–eight hours.
(Sometimes even longer
When we're having showers!)
And Saturdays always end
Way before they've begun.
One day is not enough
For me to play in the sun.
After all these many years,
You'd think I'd stop objecting
And that a week has seven days
I would just start accepting.

Disclosed
Ruth L. Dixon Helmers
He fell asleep. The moon is in its place,
But, sleeping too, it did not shine upon his face,
But rather shed a misty veil of light
That caught upon some silver hairpins of the night.

The sea was drowsy, too and lulled to sleep
White dreams that bubbled in with secrets from the deep;
And little, hungry birds with running feet
Chased waves and then ran back in fear that they should meet.

He fell asleep. And I scarce moved to see
The wonderment of good which lit that face near me.
As when a tree is stripped of outer bark
To show the inner fineness of the wood and mark
The beauty of the grain that grows inside,
Thus stripped was he in candid sleep that turns aside
The outer shell of consciousness. And I
Could see his soul, as pure as pungent rings that lie
Within the heart of some tall willow tree.
Both, masterworks of God's desire and shown to me!

Hello, Misery
Vinita D. Hall
Misery loves company, that's a saying we've all heard, but misery can work with God up above.

If misery loves company then that company is God because when you're miserable that's when Jesus is heard.

If it takes misery to bring you to God then bring on the misery and welcome the Lord,

He was there in the beginning to be our closest friend so if you trust in Jesus your misery shall end.

If misery loves company then that's what we need...
... Our Heavenly Father and Christ Jesus our closest friend...
... "Hello, Misery"

Lover's Hands
Kimberly Tracy
It was the day we outran the sun.
I wondered if my mother ever closed her eyes.
And remembered exactly
the curve of my father's jaw
the outline of his head
or the wrinkles on the knuckles
of his hands.
If so, "is that how I will feel about
The man driving this car?"
I, seated to his right, still half–drunk
from the day tasting wine in the hills,
asked myself.
We headed south, the burnt–orange rim
fading below the mountains,
behind us, to our left.
We passed Mexicans and orchards,
Oil wells and two police cars
on the way to real life, which felt
so far away from the relevance
of the wrinkles on his hands.

Windowsill, Chin And Seven Blinks
Jonathan Coppola
Green morning wind whipping!
a colony of weak birch in slow
motion agony
Against a weeping window wallowing
in its early impression.
sad squares they are: they think
blinds could cloud the predicted rain
—There's no fate in darkness
only reproduction, a hell just as well,
nevertheless imitated.
Framing intervals of May is always
a winter to bear:
blizzard emotion buries decaying soul
in ephemeral muddiness
Leaving no time for reflection
Fluid, rampant symmetry frozen
in the heart of transformation
God can't catch this fleeting,
couch–ridden thought, neither
can Freud.

My Forever Friend
Darla M. Newman

I knew you were waiting for me
I could see it in your eyes
I knew that you loved me
Like an Angel in the skies
You said that you needed me
to be by your side...
For I could not make you see
And Lord knows, how I tried...
Until we meet in another time
or place
I will always remember the
smile on your face...
For when someday, you'll be
my forever friend...
But until then, this is the end...

A Glimpse Of Heaven
Hubert Hayes

The end of a weary day draws to its close
And as upon my bed I lie in sweet repose
I gaze into the star-spangled night
Hoping the vision I have seen with delight
Will return and I will whisper encore
For in the daylight hours my vision fades
Into some far corner of my mind,
And I am left without recall
Through the many hours that fall.
Perhaps in some quiet Moment
At sunrise or in some high place
The vision will return and I will be enchanted.
As with open eyes I perceive the beauty of that aura
I will rejoice again.
And there upon that summer morn
A most wondrous sight to see was borne
Thrust upon the dazzling scene
A vision transcending all that I have ever seen
Perhaps 'tis a glimpse of Heaven that I see
And I am overjoyed.

Sweet Kolachy
Mary Donovan Vish

It was a kitchen in motion
product of an apron-clad mother
performing yeast, flour, egg rituals
oil-clothed, the table held
towel-covered secrets
as yeast conducted magic
an orchestration known only to those
with patience to endure the worthwhile
odyssey to completion
"Sit down, sit down"
I hear the voice of friendship
warm as the cozy kitchen
an invitation for memory
soon, soon and forever I catalog
this wonderfully delicious gift
as lips, tongue, teeth settle into
the reward, feather-light dough
and filling of cheese, rich, unmatched
the aroma timeless in mind, eye and heart
sweet, sweet, kolachy

Freedom
Justava Nuzum Allison

Oh, mind, you smug gray mass enslaved to Reality — Do you
believe I, the spirit of this body, will leave you in peace?
Do you not know I lead a life that time could not lend?
I run wild and rampant as the untamed sea.
I streak through the night naked.
I call to the shadows of darkness and they embrace me.
I glide though tall grass and it teases my legs.
The dew of the morning kisses my bare-footed feet.
I fly with the wind and it caresses me as you cannot imagine.
My hair is wild and unkempt, spilling over my body onto the
Earth.
I almost die of happiness in my beastly innocence.
You, gray mass, yet unborn, content in the security of your womb.
I will not give you peace, I will bring the pains.
For I run wild and rampant as the untamed sea.

The Only Escape
Gina Martorell

Deep, deep inside the echoes of my mind
I search to find the only escape the Lord can provide
In search of the ultimate release
From the tormenting temptations of the beast
That haunts me day and night
Burning deep within my soul as I struggle to win
What is hidden deep in my heart
The rage of the battle of my secret sin

I surrender myself to You, O Lord
Trusting that You will somehow usher in
The deliverance of my victory draped in gold
True and pure beyond compare

I wait, patiently, I wait
As I cry out in despair
Knowing You are never late
Oh, Lord, You are my only escape

Dedication: to Jesus Christ, who has always been my escape

The Moon And The Darkness
Jessica Wills

I have only one purpose
To survive
I thrive in the darkness
The shadows have become me
The sun is my enemy
And I am a wolf in sheep's clothing
For I fear not
My heart beats with the blood not of my own
Captivation
Desperation
Sensations
The terror that comes with night
Is now flesh and I am the terror
And you are the prey
So beware, my sweet,
For your body will decay
For it is your turn to feel my teeth
Sink deep into your soul and take all that you give
My heart will throb with your blood's sweet cress
And with eternity's kiss, this is the moon and the darkness!

Enchanted Dreams

Recipe For A Grandmother's Love
Stacy Miller
Two bright–blue, sparkling eyes
Two round, rosy cheeks
Two large, caring arms you
could wrap around the world
A peachy glow and shimmer
of gold and silver curls
A cheeky smile, bright–red kisses
dusted with honey powder
grains.
Stir with stories through the
ages and a love bound in
genetic chains
Serve with a heart full of
memories – seasoning with
laughter and joy.

Untitled
Brian Riley
She smiles, not realizing
the bath water she plays in is
filthy.
It is water, nonetheless and
it is Eden to her.
Her mother has scrubbed her,
scrubbed her for countless minutes,
hour upon hour,
but she won't come clean.
Dirt still under the nails
Dust in the hair.
But her bright, young eyes
remain oblivious to the pain
of the depression,
of the ghetto.
These eyes one day will dim
but today,
today in that wonderful bath,
she reminds me of an
angel.

Love
Jana Bronson
What makes you feel up off the ground and
the birds and the bees seem to fly all around

You may think, at first, it was something you
Ate, but your ills go away till he calls for a
date

The Doc gives you pills, but he's only a
Quack, 'cause when that someone comes
'round that old feeling comes back

Now I've learned from experience, so I'll give
you a clue, in case of misfortune, it happens
to you

It's as common and natural as the sky up
Above, you're not really sick, you've just fallen
in love

Dedication: to my special mother

Marching To War
E. M. Budge
The gentle sobs of mother's weeping, as their sons went off to war
Marching proudly heads held high, not knowing what they were going for.
Trumpets blasting, into battle, comes the cry from overhead.
Forward, onward ever onward, to face again the awful dread.

Onward, forward, keep advancing, noises of the battles drone
Guns are booming, bombs a–blasting worn torn soldiers far from home
Bravely fighting, facing danger, up to waist, in mud and stench.
To this life, they are no stranger, home to them is just a trench.

Stretched before them, mud and slaughter, pressing onward they must go,
tired and weary and exhausted, determined they'll defeat the foe.
In hopes they live that soon it's over, then marching homeward
   they will go
But not till they have won the battle, defeating all the awesome foe.

Faith
Mike David Whiteford
I've lived a thousand lives
I've been everywhere and seen everything
I've soared the skies above
I've pursued the Heavens to an infinite end
I've plunged the depths of oceans
And gazed from the highest mountaintops
My soul is rooted upon the soil on which I stand
My breath is the wind, I am one with all
I've been born a sunrise and died in the setting sun
I've fallen like raindrops
And risen like flames, with their fiery scorn
I've slept with the stars
And am old friends with the moon
I am the past, present and future
I have been witness to all things
I have been scarred, raped and wounded
I've been tortured and twisted in ruin
I've been healed and preserved
I am here forever
I am life, I am Earth

I AM THE WALL
Lou Weinstein
I AM THE WALL,
a sculptured sweep of initialed grief,
each letter dug out of me
like a fingernail screeching pain on slate.

I AM THE WALL,
forever entombed in Lincoln's shadow,
cast darker by his perplexity
as to what this latest carnage meant.

I AM THE WALL,
reflecting clear from tortured eyes,
the numbing desolation
of sixty–thousand crucifixions.

I AM THE WALL,
forever moved and yet
in graven immobility, an eternal monument
to your own bitter acquiescence
and need for peaceful resolution.

Flander's Fields
Candice S. Sooknanan
In Flander's fields
Lay the soldiers
That gave their lives
For their country, you and I
They did their part for peace
Paid dearly with their lives
Their souls ascend to Heaven
Where there are no wars and guns
No sorrow, no crying, no dying
They are on holy ground,
With angels all around
Their loved–ones need to mourn no more.
For they are in God's hands.
Dedication: to Aunt S. Gail Sooknanan

Kindness
Lori Ann Kramer
Opportunity for kindness encircles each day.
As sunshine brightens the world,
so can a smile to someone we meet.
Just as colors of a rainbow landscape the sky,
Bright–colored flowers can sure please the eye.
To open a door for a Mom and a child
is a simple gesture without any cost.
A kindness performed is something not lost.
Call a friend to see how they've been.
Run errands for someone who cannot get out.
The joy it brings inside will make you shout.
Send a card for no reason at all, except to say
I thought of you today.
You need not look far, or wonder where to begin
for your family is surely where kindness comes in.
There are little things you can do
to help people make it through.
In a world filled with turmoil,
what is the reason for living each day?
It's opportunity for kindness along the way.

For The Love Of A Child
Shawna Nicol
You stand alone smiling at me,
My heart is overflowing with love for you.
You sometimes ask me things I do not know how to answer.
"Why do clouds stay up in the sky and not fall down?"
"Why does the sun come up?"
Your innocent questions inspire me.
"Why do flowers die?"
With your sweet expressions of wonderment, I realize how exciting it
must be, to be you.
"When will I be a baby again?"
"How old was I when you were three?"
As we walk alongside each other, you reach up and take my hand.
You look up at me and say, "Mommy, how much do you love me?"
For all the questions I left unanswered, your smile told me I made up
for them all when I said: "If I could hug you, the sun, the moon,
the clouds and all the stars in the sky, you would be the one I would
never let go of."
My dear angel, you are the reason the sun comes up every morning.
Dedication: for my dear son Jamie

I Am A Vast Desert
Georgieann Benson
I am a vast desert thirsting for the love that you so miserly
keep in your heart, locked in a box.
Though, your heart within that box will be safe, as you so
wisely keep that box on a shelf, in a room, hidden deep
within your soul.
Be careful my love, for if you are not, one day soon loneliness
will cast a great shadow upon your soul and no light will
dwell within you.
The box upon the shelf that holds your heart and the love
I so desperately crave will become cold and your heart within
it will turn black as a winter's night when the moon
is hidden from sight.
So, open the doors and windows of your soul before it is too
late and let your love rain on me like a monsoon and I will
flourish like an oasis.

Lessons Of The Heart
Rene S. Reidenbach
If I had thought tomorrow
would bring the sun I would've waited.
The days and nights of floods which
accompany your name have become too much.
The silence holds stillness, as though
death has abound all life and ceased time.
The breeze carries a cold chill throughout
the body and soul, leaving the mind thoughtless.
The heart that once loved with joy
now fears love as though it's a disease.
To feel, to breathe, to taste and
drink brings death unto itself.
This nourishment of life also
carries disastrous effects.
As the ocean can be calm and inviting
in an instant it can strike rage and terror.
Leaving insecurity and distrust to
all those it has befriended and then betrayed.
Dedication: to the love I lost

To A Favourite Dog
Frank Probett
O faithful one – when we first met,
I thought of you as just a pet!
How could I know that at the end,
You'd be more than just a friend?
Friend, companion, mentor, guide,
Always ready at my side;
Listening, when I'd want to talk,
Running, when I'd like to walk!
Then they told me you were dead,
And I remembered all I'd said,
And how we'd passed the summer–time,
You, playing games, — me, drinking wine!
When I knew that you had died,
I sat down and softly cried,
Knowing that another friend
Had at last come to the end.
And wondered how I'd pass each day,
With nothing more that I could say
Or do, — and here's the sorrow, —
I'd not be seeing you tomorrow!

Enchanted Dreams

My Danni
Stephen Hughes
Danni, Danni, her face at sunrise,
A vision to sweep a night—mist from my eyes,
To quicken my senses, my heart leaping now,
Like a stag held at bay, like a whispering row,

Danni, Danni, my heart bleeds once more,
Like my lady come lately, it stands at my door,
Uncertain to enter, unable to flee,
It lies in your palm where it ever shall be.

Danni, Danni, a force flows unseen,
Binding us, blinding us, mocking and mean,
To give us the promise of love without end,
Then deny us the right to be lover and
friend.

I can! I can!
Hilda Troyer
"I am going to win a pig,"
Said she, "a piggly, wiggly pig."
She jumped a friendly knoll
And continued her role.
Children heard the noise,
And clamor to the voice.

How can you get a win?
She jumped and flashed a grin.
"Daddy says I can win,
I can," and she jumped again,
"I'm going to win a pig,
A little pig just sooo big!"

"I'm going to win a pig
I'll eat it like a fig!"
Up in the air she went
With energy never spent.
Where will you keep a pig?
"With me, in Winnipeg!"

Family
Ashleigh Bradford
Love in family is very strong,
they stick together when things go wrong.
Children play with one another,
but when things go wrong they run to mother.
Mothers protect with love and care,
when things happen the children can't bear.
Children help hold the family together,
when things go down like a rock on a feather.
Fathers pass the rules around,
then make you listen without a sound.
Parents go and make the money,
so your pantry is full of honey.
Family keeps the hope alive,
and when you're down they make you strive.
Family is made of many people,
it will all start at the steeple.
I have a family, as many do,
I love them and they love me, too!
Keep this in mind,
To your family you must be kind.

End Of Life
Wesley Benge
Why can't we all see,
what Christ said "Follow Me"

Cause our life isn't fair,
but we all still care.

Ya so life is tough,
hard and rough,

But if it was up to me,
we would live worry—free,
with the Lord eternally.

The end of our life has no toll,
so be prepared, the Lord is ready to roll.

The Angel Of Death
Barbara L. Fox
Down the dim corridor walked the angel of death,
With grief, despair and fear; I did not
want it near.
But God in Heaven knew best, for his tired
suffering one must find peace and rest.
As the dark angel hovered near, I begged
God my prayer, to hear.
Alas! It was in rain, my aching heart so
full of pain, cried out once more,
Please, God, don't send this Angel to my door.

Gently on my loved one, the Angel placed
its hand, Come dear one, begin your
journey to a far better land.

Oh! God! I cried. Why must it be?
The whisper of a voice; "You know
She really belonged to me."

Dedication: to my mother, grandmother and English teachers

The Pram Ramp
Pamela Smith
In the year of '81.
Curb was lowered, work begun.
"A drive I'll build", my husband stated.
'82 and still I waited.
Came Sept., first grandchild born.
Still the curb looked all forlorn.
"Ah, but wait" the problem solved
The perfect pram ramp had evolved.
'83. '86. '87. '88. Pram ramp active. Still I wait.
1990 came and went, bringing another happy event.
Passing workmen oft arrive.
Maybe they could build a drive.
Husband totally aghast.
This is his job. It's a must.
'96. Hubby visits son.
Quick, let's start. Work now begun.
15 years. Pram ramp not needed.
One week later we've succeeded.
Holiday over. Husband soon to arrive.
Surprise. Surprise. We have our drive.

There Lies The Letter...
Laura Taylor
Open on my lap and claiming my attention,
Yet my eyes veer away from its call.
Scripted pages blur in my gaze
As my mind looks beyond for escape
On some warmer, softer plane.
A heart tries to withstand
The dagger of the message
Held within the written words;
Soothing phrases are belied
As fast as they arise
By poorly–masked foreknowledge of my pain.
Chilling the soul throughout from inside,
It is the bleakness of this reality of mine.

Dedication: to Jessica, my beloved rose

Heartless Predator
Melissa Kay Stewart
Innocent, shy, daring and bold.
He could be all or none, I was told.

Quite convincing to these virgin eyes,
Telling all those beautiful lies.

It did not take long to find out,
What this mystery guy was all about.

He wrote letters, sang songs, blew kisses and more,
I fell hard and fast, no idea what for.

Never knew him, yet I already wanted something,
Found out in the end, it would be nothing.

Innocence lost and out of school,
He moved on to another love–struck fool

It will not be long until this heartless Predator
Will send your young soul writing a heartbreak letter.

Old Faithful Friend
Marilyn M. Fowler
Old, faithful friend on my rocking chair
Without a sound you sit and stare.
Wise, old man, with straggled fur
Of faded gold, you do not stir.
With glassy eyes and velvet nose
And padded paws in place of toes.
Ragged jacket, patched and worn
'kerchief in pocket, tattered, torn.
You've comforted both young and old
Through generations past untold.
Tucked in nights, 'neath counterpane
Of shelf, 'twixt books and counting frame.
In whispered ears, young secrets said
Your lips are sealed with silken thread.
My cherished friend through bygone years
My childhood dreams, my tender tears.
Now, threadbare friend, we've both grown old
You still look handsome, proud and bold
And memories are always there
Dear, faithful friend, old teddy–bear....

Love—Love
Beulah B. Lippert
Let us sing a song of Love
The most precious gift of all.
It will always be among us
Whether we gain success or fall.
Love comes without counting age
To the young or those growing
older.
And never asks for great reward
It's a loving cape to warm your
shoulder.
You may wander down a lonely road
Or gaze on meadows fresh from
showers
But never, never, give up your love
Let it grow – 'twill blossom flowers.

School
Hayley Forrester
I sit in the corner all on my own
I look at my watch, I can't wait to go home

I feel the tension build up inside
At lunch I locked myself in a room and cried

I feel so lonely, I feel so ashamed
I wish my friends realized I wasn't to blame

I turn to the teacher with a tear in my eye
She asks me what's wrong, but I don't reply

I want to shout out, you are my mates
but what's the point, I'm the one that they hate

The bell finally rings, home at last
I start to run really fast

At school I maybe as lonely as can be
but at least when I go home I've got my family.

Mothers Are A Blooming Rose
Alta Stephen
What a precious and special person
To know and to have is a mother.
She like a blooming rose. She
Stands out there in life, there
is so much to love about her.
In her own special way, she's like
A blooming rose all the time
To us wherever she goes.

Mother, a person we always
Think of, here on Earth and
When she's gone. 'Cause she
Does the nicest things. She
gives us a lot of love. That
Makes her a special person
To us and she stands out like
A blooming rose. She's important
To us all the time, in heart
And many ways, 'cause she's
A blooming rose – a mother.

Enchanted Dreams

The Miracle Baby
Fay De Jesus
He was born so early, weighing one pound and six ounces
He looked so tiny and red as a gel
Doctors thought he would live
But only for ten days!
His condition was up and down
Requiring much of oxygen and medicines alike
He passed day one, day two up to day ten
Fighting with all his might
His condition got better and better
He started putting on weight
His color improved and got nearer to normal
And what more could the parents say
When his medication got discontinued
Made it on his own
And finally went home!

The Last Waltz With You
Sam R. Murphy
When we first met, you were beautiful and Spirit
Free – I smiled at you and you at me.
It was Fate that planned our Destiny.
Our Hearts and Lives crossed and we began our first Waltz
I requested, Dear, that you save the last one for me.
I noticed your hands today, they were
Wrinkled and old, I saw that you
Still wore The Wedding Band of Gold.

As I looked through the window, I could see
In our yard, the big shade tree, how
Stately it used to be – The limbs, are
Now breaking and body decaying,
It seemed to reflect a story about you
and me.

How we once were full of life and Energy.
I looked once again at you, Dear
And I knew you had saved
That Last Waltz For Me.

Madness
William R. Hannon III
Through the land,
Twisted with horror,
Blackened by blight,
He ran.

On and on,
Over a river of blood,
Down a path of sorrow,
Across a plain of death,
He fell.
Kneeling, he wept,

Looking up,
He saw the worms of madness,
Racing toward him,
He knelt there,
And surrendered.

For who can run from the madness,
Of one's own mind?

For You!
Shirley Ledson
Every day I'm thinking of you,
In school, at work, in all I do,
I want you to know how much I care,
I don't want you to suffer, it doesn't seem fair,

God knows what I'd do if you weren't here for me,
If I didn't have you, who knows what I'd be,
You're the reason I'm alive and for that I will love you,
From now till the end, through the old and the new,

You mean more to me than life itself,
As long as you're here, I need no one else,
God bless you forever or as long as you live,
And as long as I'm here, all my love I will give,
TO YOU...

Fading Denial
David McGuire
In my dresser
beneath all my socks
I keep my chains

They hold me down
day after day
Making me numb
making my world insane

Why do I go bad, despite
the heartache
despite the pain

Why do I live
Every day in shame
caused by my own
self–infliction

I don't know ·
could this be addiction?

August Lake
Judith Jaquith
Threatening sky
Gunmetal–gray water
Twilight–blue landscape.

Waves washing up on the shore
A damp, chill wind bends the tall, lake grass.

The sky darkens
Whitecaps dance across the churning water.
Clouds open
Sheets of rain attack the rolling whitecaps.

The wind begins to shriek
Trees thrash and groan under the onslaught
Crashing waves thunder across the shore.
Sea and sky are speaking.

Listen carefully.

Dedication: to Christopher, Amanda, Larene and Gordon

Connections
Claire Howell

I met you last night,
I just knew you were right,
Your smile,
Your Laugh,
Made me feel safe,
I wanted to Dance with you,
I wanted to ask you out,
But I was happy with your,
Legs brushing past mine,
The song came on,
Angel of Mine and you,
Mouthed the words to me,
Now all I want is your,
Lips touching mine,
And your arms around me tight.

Memories
Lynn McIntosh

It took longer than I intended!
How many times have we lamented:
I'm sorry, Hon, I had to work late
and the traffic was moving at an intolerable rate.
I know the game was important to them
but I was later than I should have been.

Our lives are full of late excuses
and feeling the impact of regular abuses.
Not just the others whose lives were affected,
but to ourselves and what is expected:
the missed cheer, or a score and an innocent smile
that has value only now, not after a while.

There are reasons, of course, for the things that we do.
Not always well-planned or even thought through.
But, too often we must do that last little thing,
forgetting about the others and the joy we can bring,
that enrich our own lives with a wealth untold,
that can only be cashed as the years grow old.

Imperfection?
Kevin M. McCoy

Alone in the mind, escaping your world.
Into thought, the soul is hurled.
Endless possibilities of things unknown!
Sharpening skills upon jagged stone!
Galaxies uncharted are shown to me.
Aliens untold of; now have a chance to be.
Everything is real that I wish to make!
I'll stay in my coma, never to awake!
Powers in this state you would not believe.
More than anyone could ever conceive.

Place of constant night, no sunny days?
The question is, would you like to stay?
All that is dreamed of; one may own.
Yes!
I will remain here atop my throne.
Bang! Bang!
I am imperfect!
But in this life who wants to be,
Perfect?

I Did It
J. F. Mitchell

As they grow up like the rest
They know you gave them your best
Keeping them safe and sound
as you teach them the world goes round
Sometimes sad at what they do,
also very glad when they say I love
you.
When you have a minute alone to share
you think about how much you care.
Thinking of them day and night and
of the things done that makes you right
You never complain about nothing done
but you're thankful you were the one.
Thank you, thank you, for your insight
I know I did all things right.

Sad Eyes
Russell T. Richline, Jr.

Look, Miss, into my eyes,
See, my dear, the tears they cry.
All alone, they are set in darkness
design,
their empty stare showing the conflict
that does lurk behind
The madness of a heart deeply
in love,
With a girl sent from Heaven above.
She is like no other that has come before,
she visits my dreams every night, I need
nothing more.
In sleepless rendezvous we meet,
beneath those blankets so deep.
I hold her close in my arms,
she eases closer, letting down her guard.
I try, I try to bring her out,
out of my dreams but I do not know how?
This is the reason for my sad eyes,
the tears of sorrow for which I slowly die.

Sinner Beware
Sharon Vennum

In our world, the devil wants us to be tossed and twirled,
Uncertain of the truth; his ways are so uncouth.
A fiery demise he tries to disguise
By coaxing people into tricks and lies.
He'll try to hurt the worst,
Those who love the Lord the most.
From east to west and coast to coast
He's an evil one—never follows the Son.
He's got tricks up his sleeve
Designed to hurt those who believe.
So we must stay on our guard
So in the end we won't be charred—
Burned in eternal damnation—
We want to bypass that sensation!
The Almighty God gave us His loving Son Jesus
So that we may live, as believers with our lives to give.
In giving we receive; our actions should say we believe.
In loving God, we may be hated by man
But I'll put my faith in the Great I Am.
That's just how it shall be... for me.

A Promise From Within!
Tammy D. Gray
Forever, in my deepest thoughts. You
my friend, shall forever remain, as I remember
how we once embraced one another, never
ashamed to show truest feelings and also
the greatest love we have ever known.
Shining bright among the darkest skies,
our love and friendship, forever will shine on,
no matter where, why or who life has
chosen us to go with, for whatever reason
Our thoughts of one another shall always
remain in our minds and forever in our
Hearts!
For as I've once said, this love we
Share will forever live on, or till Death
Do we part!

Is Life Fair... ?
Jerald D. Porter
Think about life...

Is life Fair? Does it cheat you in a way? Well, how does it cheat you?
You know, if it wasn't for life, I wouldn't be here and neither would you.
You didn't have to wake up this morning but life in
your soul, your spirit, you inner child arose from your cocoon.
Life didn't have to get you through these years. You could have been
dead and gone like other unlucky souls. Bless their hearts, but
you know everyone has to evacuate this beastly world one day.
Matter of fact, will you be happy when you leave?
Where would you go when you leave?
If you go to the land of angels, would you
be happy and elated just to be dancing in the sun?
If you go down to the underworld, you don't get
another chance, you know.
So, the message trying to get through is, live life to your (its) fullest.
Life will go and has gone both ways; good and bad.
Life may not be fair but that doesn't mean you
can't try and make it fair. In my terms, someone has to win and
someone has to lose, but you don't have to cheat to decide.

If I Could Fly
Joan P. Kellawan
If I could fly, I'll fly around the world
in a great big swirl.
I'll start with places that are as far away as,
perhaps, the mighty Himalayas.

I'll fly high and low, even down in the valley of gorges,
then make my way back up in powerful surges.
I'll fly swiftly, then slowly, above all the beauty and glory
searching for verses to tell in my story.

Pausing for long glances and short prances,
I'll travel to places famous for their dances.
I'll fly up and down and over and under
to the land of the Andes, somewhere, yonder.

Moving through the clouds, the wind and the moisture
circling around every green pasture.
If I could fly...

Dedication: to Mikhail, Justin and Brad

King And Queen
Calvin Graham
A King needs a throne
But he is nothing without a Queen
There is no use of power just love, life and trust encrypted within
Children are not used as status symbols but as seeds that will flourish
as a result of knowledge, wisdom and understanding
A King is not a King without a Queen! to provide mental health and
lifetime planning
A King is set forth to rule
A Queen is to do the same
But the misconception of power will lead to a mental mind game
A King needs a Queen to provide balance in his lifetime
Therefore we as Kings must respect our Queens and refine our minds
In this forsaken world where we have doctrines meant to change our lives
A King needs a throne but what cannot be left alone is the fact that a
Queen deserves a throne of her own!

Let Me Be Giddy
Valerie Urbaniec
I think I'm in love with you.
So many infatuations, so many relationships.
But I've never felt like this before.
I feel so giddy.
I think about you all the time
I want to hear your voice, see you smile at me
I want to be with you
I want to be giddy.
We don't know each other well, but I feel so connected
My soul feels so connected to yours.
Are you my soulmate?
My life could be so different with you in it
I can see you in it.
But it's all up to you.
And what do I do when you don't know what to do
Stop this now?
My heart, my soul would never let me.
Life is what you make it
Do what makes you happy
And let me be giddy.

Daddy's Girl
Maria Radau
The word "father" is so formal, it's always been "Daddy" to me.
My Daddy's not Mr. Up—ity, he's down to Earth as he can be.
From the time I was a little girl, my Daddy was always there.
Regardless of how small my problem was, I knew that Daddy would care.
I dreaded the "Lawrence Welk Show" and a "Burt Bacharach" song.
But when it came to my Daddy, no one could say he was wrong.
He couldn't be distracted, when the "McNeil/Lehrer Show" was on.
Only during a commercial, would he notice that I had gone.
If I was going out and I wanted my curfew delayed,
I would wait to ask Daddy, when the program "Nova" played.
My Daddy likes conversation, especially if the talk is deep.
Ask him a simple question and get a sermon that'll make you weep.
My Daddy is very intelligent, but some things I don't understand.
Like how does "Fawlty Towers" tickle, this fifty—three—year—old man.
My Daddy was always so special, eccentric, a stranger might say.
He had his own lifestyle and quite frankly, still does today.
Now that I've grown up, I see that Daddy has grown up, too.
Cuz when he watches "CNN", he will acknowledge you.
Daddy's kinda like "Mr. Roper", a homebody, you might say.
But when it comes to my Daddy, I thank God each and every day.

You
Sarah Eccles

What can I say to you,
The one whose image clouds my mind?
I try to shake free
But it multiplies,
Inhabiting all my thoughts.
Your face is everywhere,
Your voice is in my ears,
Your touch is on my skin.
What can I say to you?
Where can I go?
Your presence rarely leaves me.
Is it right or wrong?
I've ceased to ask –
I simply try to live each day and night
Alone with this constant vision of you.

Oh, America, America
Jesica Schwarz

America the beautiful.
Lush, green hills rolling over her face
Crystal blue water with crisp, white waves
Proud, sturdy mountains saluting her
Bold, bronze bells strongly ringing freedom
Nationalism painted with pride

America the beautiful?
Repulsive litter–decorated highways
Acid clouds devouring the azure sky
Deadly diseases creep in helpless bodies
The homeless cowering in corners
Nationalism dead in some people's hearts

Oh, America, America,
Very beautiful from a distance
But deteriorating inside
How long can these crimes continue?
How much more can people do to her
Before her spirit weakens and dies?

In Perspective
Kitty Druck

The caption reads: A Raging Sea.
I smell the salt
I hear the roar
I see the waves nearing the shore
hiding their strength
behind a screen of foam.

I look again.
I see the uproar pass
into a background of receding waves
smaller, smaller,
calm in perspective.

Tears are like that.
Salty with inner thunder,
they move in waves so violent at first,
but also pass
into a background of receding waves
smaller, smaller,
calm in perspective.

Untitled
Deanna Bove

Love is a feeling you have inside
Most people try to find
You live each day
You live each night
Wondering what love really feels like
You feel for the kids who think they're in love
Knowing they're gonna get hurt by foolish love
You try to teach, but no one learns.
All you can do is sit back and watch
For someday they'll finally learn
Love is a risk of losing all hope.
You try to find the right person
But when you're young, everyone
Seems right.
Soon they'll realize love takes time

I Am The Heartland
Patrick Monnig

I am the heartland,
Rural and sweet,
Just visiting there is a great treat.
Apple pies, yummy cakes,
Down in the heartland, there are no fakes.
In the heartland, Texas and Missouri,
Tornadoes spin in raging fury.
John Deere tractors plow my floor,
To make room for my wheat to soar.
Livestock graze on my dry patches,
And cowboy boots and hats are still in fashion.
Old men talk on their front Porches,
About the weather, how the sun scorches.
Mother and grandma are quilting away,
While father and son are baling the hay.
Children swing on hanging tires,
While men tinker on cars with hammers and pliers.
The family still drives in their '32 ford
And at the end of the day they pray to their dear Lord
I am the heartland, rural and sweet.

Untitled
Salanda Lopez

Putting my thoughts into words. At this time in my life I feel as though
My dreams and ambitions are turning into complete turmoil.
When I think things are going so well and I have such a good head
on my shoulders, something always seems to push me down lower. Why
me?

Trouble, never seen too much of it, but it's all coming back to me
now. Love, my heart was broken in an instance, but when I thought
everything was perfect, a drastic change ended it. A definite necessity
which changed my life, my whole outlook on when I used to say "That
can't happen to me".

Reaching for my future hoping time flies, but the present drags so
slowly... New things come along and I watch them drift right by.
I can't remember where I've been or I don't know where I'm
headed. I guess no one knows at this stage of life. Why can't I
awaken to a new, revitalized lifestyle, secure and sure of everything?

Images pass through my mind of this never–ending point of no return.
Same thing repetitiously. I know I have to change, but will I?

Enchanted Dreams

The Feline Connection
Tara L. Harpis
Silent paws pad across the hardwood floor. No sound as each footfall strikes the bare wood. The cat moves on her coiled springs as she patrols her domain like a policeman on his beat. She hears all things, sees all things and smells all things in her territory. She is the wild animal of the human home. Herself she can provide for.

She rules herself, obeying only her inner urgings. To hunt her prey, to silently kill that which she eats, is her desire. She needs only herself. But it's not only herself she wants.

Liquid muscles slide gracefully under velvet fur. She leaps lightly to a place a mile high to her and gives her contented rumble as five Heaven–sent fingers find her ears.

A Compulsive Cycle
Tanya Gray
A craving, is brewing,
A battle, I'm losing.
My concentration's, being drawn away,
Focusing on bingeing, day by day.
It's getting worse, I cannot stop,
It's one mad rush, to get to the shop.
Chocolates and sweets, I have to buy,
Lots and lots, I'm on a high.
Eating quickly, on my own,
Another diet, I've gone and blown.
I am so full, I'm fit to burst,
Guilt sets in, I feel much worse.
I'll just lie down, for a bit,
Otherwise, I might be sick.
When clothes don't fit, or your legs get sore,
Life becomes miserable and a real bore.
For the millionth time, you start a diet,
Your body's confused and starts a riot.
you still get cravings, now and then,
Like a time bomb it's waiting, you never know when...

My Wife
Bobby E. Farmer
Your eyes
Are like the
Spring
Sunshine

Your lips are
Sweet as
Strawberries

Your love is
Like a fresh
Breath of air
Your beauty
Is beyond
Words

I love you, my
Wife

Dedication: to my wife, Sandy

A Future... And A Hope
Ruth Horton
Autumn days trickle away –
Darkness draws us in.
Hibernation in colourless clothes
Echoes images of leafless trees, lifeless land.
Decay meets death without apology
Hope is arrested... And yet
Within the core of loss exists the seed of new life.
In stillness, in quietude darkness ebbs,
Light returns – slowly at first – then with a gallop,
Horizon glimmers with dawning, with colour.
So, too, pathways trod thro' winter copse
Leave telling footprints of onward journey.
Threads before and aft entwine to weave new cloth
For in darkness there lies a stepping stone to recreation
which promises a future... and a hope.

Insomniacs
Nick Moore
the twang
of him beating
his fist against the water
tower
woke schools of
sheep
arose only to fall under
grizzly steamrollers
toes of grace
song
burst from her
pores
drowned out
arguments minor to violent
struggles were locked
as the sky
opened up
revealing
cities laced with
compassion and true enlightenment

Happy Retirement Days
S. C. Talmadge
When I retired a few years back I wondered how life would be
But I have found so much to do and enjoy
That things couldn't be better for me
I have made lots of friends I go dancing with
Which gives me great fun and pleasure
And I also do lots of knitting in any hours of leisure
I knit dolls and teddies and sometimes a rabbit or two
To raise funds for charity, it's a great thing to do
I also love baking and make lots of cakes
I have made some for parties and even a fete
Voluntary work in a small coffee shop
Is something else I enjoy such a lot
With shopping as well, the days just fly by
You start a new week and before you know it the weekend is nigh
In any spare minutes I make up little rhymes
Another great way of passing the time
So all in all I am very content
Happy times I've certainly been sent
With lovely neighbours and a dear little flat
What more could I want when I'm happy with that

Heartbroken
Susan Brayley

My heart is weeping every day.
I cannot find the words to say,
Why did you leave me?
Why did you go?
The answer is —
I just don't know.

Together we were oh, so good,
I thought that you had understood,
My love for you is everlasting,
My love for you will never die,
All I have is one more question,
Just one word and that is, why?

Dedication: to my love Phil

Loss
Blanche Blevins

You went,
and I cried.
Sorrow so great,
wishing to die.
"Can't go on"
I lied —
I
had
no
choice —
Now my life
is "try, try".
Strength comes slow,
and "WHY, WHY?"
Never quite over it,
I decide —
Only getting
used
to
it.

Your Touch
Raymond Sicard

I feel the delicate touch
of your fingertips
as they caress the palms
of my outstretched hand.
Our digits intertwine —
they yearn to fuse as one —
forming a bridge
through which our spirits pass.
My whole being is focused
in that final point
as I savor every instant
your being touches mine.
An ever-widening chasm forms
as your hand leaves mine!
You are gone from my reality
but will ever haunt my memory.
A fleeting Moment shared,
your life tenderly touched mine;
and forevermore a part of you
will dwell deep in my heart.

Landmines
Frank Savidge

We've heard of hidden landmines and their power to kill and maim.
Our late Princess Diana campaigned to ban the same
Evil devices used by man against humanity —
But what about the landmines of our personality.
It's sad when, just by speaking, we walk down a perilous road
Lest something that we say will cause some person to explode.
It is not honouring to God when our breath must be baited
As, by our words, somebody's mine could well be detonated.
Let's pray that, by God's spirit, we can make a brand–new start;
That He will sweep, de–fuse and clear the mines in every heart.

To Him Who Holds My Hand
Dorothy Hooks

To Him Who Hold my Hand
Who Guides my Footsteps that I didn't plan
Whose Spirit wants to Dwell in Man
That no Soul be Lost, is His plan;
Sometimes we go from day to day
Without stopping and asking God,
Please show me the way.
When times get hard and we cannot see
In His Care is where We want to be.
He only asks this one thing;
That all our problems, to Him we bring.
With Praise and Songs we lift Him up
Forgetting all our needs, wants and buts.
My ways are easy, my burdens are light,
Lay them before me and I'll fix them just right.
On the rising of the Sun, Till the evening of Dawn,
I've fought all your Battles
All Victories have been Won.
So pray for sweet sleep and peace at night
And that God's Love Will Always Shine Bright in your Life.

Untitled
Micheline Pierre-Antoine

Give me love,
give me tenderness,
give me your trust,
give me warmth
You'll give me you
and I'll give you my soul
Touch is life
Touch is warmth
Trust is life
Trust is soul
Touch me, make me warm
Trust me and give me back my soul,
and I'll love you and I'll give you all
with all of that giving,
You'll make me living
again with that warmth
make my body give
Tenderness and love
and I'll thank you for all
Remember giving is receiving!

Enchanted Dreams

The Anfield Dream
H. Leach
I have a young son who is football mad.
He plays the game if the weather's good or bad,
He plays at home and he plays at school,
And he hopes one day to play for Liverpool,
For Liverpool all he wants to do is score a
Goal against Man U.,
And with that goal he'll be so thrilled,
Because his dreams will have been fulfilled.
I have no doubt this son of mine will play
The game and wear number nine,
He'll score the goals that will make his name,
And get himself into the hall of fame
And of this son I'll be so proud,
To have stood and watched him with the
Infield crowd.

Why
Peter Jacob Gavrun
Alone, I reflect, wondering why
Why events happen the way they happen
Why I feel all alone when
a million stand beside me
Why I awaken when I'd really rather be asleep

I often wonder why
Why I feel excruciating pain
Why sometimes I just sit and weep
Why I feel as though life is all
my fault when really I know it's not

I sometimes wonder why
Why it has to be me

Why do I wonder why
Why I sometimes feel I won't make it through tomorrow
Why me, WHY?

Dedication: to Mrs. DenBoer for encouraging me to write

The Keeper
Nita McCoy
I feel as if, I am the keeper of the night
For those, who may awake in fright
Alert, to the night sounds
Listening for the heart that may start to pound
Who — might awake from a bad dream
Always alert for a moan or scream
As darkness surrounds
Like a guard, I'll start my rounds
To protect those, whom I hold dear
To try and keep at bay the fears
For those of us, who walk the night
We learn to live within the fright
For we have the souls of the very old
From the horror stories that we've been told
We must keep away the pain
Or we, ourselves, might go insane
If you awake in the arms of fright
Remember the keeper, who walks at night
Alas the fear, we might share
Rest now, without a care

I Forgot
Mary Devine
Time is slipping by
Thoughts go through my mind
Sometimes I may cry
Memories come and go
What is there to know

Is this the way it's going to be
Now that age has crept up on me?
I went upstairs to—day— for what?
I completely forgot

I looked around to see
What on Earth it could be
I went downstairs again
Without what I went up for.

Honor
Joyce Crawford
Wherein does honor lie?
It lies in respect for our God.
It lies in respect for our parents.
It lies in respect for our country.
It lies in respect for our leaders and
Our authority figures.

Who will lead us on this path to honor?
Can it be found in the hearts of our parents?
Can it be found in the hearts of our politicians?
Can it be found in the hearts of our soldiers?
Can it be found in the hearts of our preachers and
our Sunday school teachers?

If the children are led,
it will be found in our homes,
it will be found in our government,
it will be found in our city streets,
it will be found in our schools and
In our church pews.

Life Is...
Susan Barke
Life is everything you make it
it's what you want it to be
you are an individual
in a place of reality.

Whatever you want
you will make it
it's just others don't really see
that everyone is different
even you and me

Your dreams can be so real
you even think they're true
there is only one person that knows this
that person is you

So be positive about everything
don't let anything get in your way
because life is what you make it
every single day.

The Anthology of Poems

Empty
Kathleen M. Battista
There were nights I spent alone,
I could swear I felt it inside me.
Your presence was unknown to me,
But at the same time, I just knew.
All I could do was wait.
I tried to touch you, get a sense of what I was feeling.
I cried over you some nights,
Afraid all the things I had done to myself,
Might have hurt you, maybe even killed you.
Then that night it came to me.
Everything I felt, cried and feared, flowed out of me.
When I tried to touch you, you weren't there.
When I cried, it wasn't over you.
It was only I.
I was Empty.

My Prayer
Tamara Tigner
Drifting into the night,
my thoughts run wild,
I am now an adult,
but I want my inner child.
Things change from day to day,
making life seem crazy,
I think of how I'll be,
but everything looks hazy.
Maybe life gets better,
at least that's what they say,
I'll never understand it,
so I'll just sit here and pray.
Lord, please make me strong,
for what is yet to come,
let me go on further,
but remember where I am from.
Thank You for helping me,
do my very best,
watch over me throughout the day,
and I will do the rest.

Bad Luck, I Could Not Introduce Myself
Joyce Roach
A frog made it all alone
to the front door
and sat relaxing
with forelegs crossed
on the far end
of the green mat.

Expecting no guest
I opened the door
wearing only my negligee
and came face to face
not with the morning papers
but a pair of peeping eyes,

Piercingly our eyes went
into each other
searching hard for recognition,
while no one extended a hand
or tried to say hello
as strangers usually do.

Me
Cynthia Kastner
I believe, I believe in many things,
I believe there is a reason for everything,
for me to be here at this time of my life, preparing and planning for the future.
Whose future? My future, maybe...
but not my plans, not my dreams, not what I want, not what I love...
but still, there must be a reason.

I believe in love, in new days, new beginnings
I believe in forgiving, I believe in dreams...

I believe in destiny and I believe in myself.
But believing is never enough...

Dedication: to Cecilia and Claire — always believe

Fire
Christopher Jackson
A fire has smoke,
it will make you choke.
A fire has a crackle,
it's hard to tackle.
A fire has ashes,
look at the flashes.
See it blaze,
it will make you gaze.
Look at the red,
it seems dead.
Look at the flames,
while you play games.
Stare at the light,
it's too bright!
Feel the heat,
you'd better retreat.
Watch it smolder,
it's getting older.
Watch it frying,
it looks like it's dying.

The Never–Ending Love
Joan M. May
I think of you, Dear Lord,
When I see a thorned Rose that is red,
With glistening dew from new, morn
I remember the Crown pressed hard on your head
Made up of thistle and thorn.

I see the blood flow down Your Dear, sweet face
And suffering, pain You endure for us.
As You hang in that terrible place.
I stand here at Your cross and can only cry
I feel my heart break as I watch You die.

I suddenly think! You cannot die!
I remember Your words to those standing by
Destroy this temple and in three days it will rise,
They laugh and scorn and can only deride,
I raise my head and there in the skies
God's Holy Angels bear You up to Our Father to sit at His side.
And days when I'm sad and alone, filled with gloom and despair
I lift up my eyes unto Heaven and hear Your voice say, "I CARE."

Enchanted Dreams

Alone
Julie Moyle
Why am I filled with so many questions?
why do they none have an answer?
Why am I so scared to leave, but I know I hate to stay. ?
These questions swim 'round in my head all day long.
with no relief to hold onto at all.
I miss everyone, miss the love, now they're gone.
all that stays is the pain that they leave.
So confused I've become, kinda lost all alone.
I just want someone to love, someone to hold,
someone to show me I'm not alone.
I reach out only to be denied... I look back they all hide.
What'd I do? Where'd I go wrong.
Something's wrong. I just don't belong here anymore.
School's no longer much fun, even leaving is looking glum.
I just wanna go... I just wanna be... I just wanna do... something!

Remember
Erika Nemergut
You were given to me
as I was given to you
2 hearts, 2 minds, 2 souls
each reaching out for the other.
Yours in care of mine,
mine in care of yours.

I look before me and see
a man that has been given to me
to handle with care,
his heart, his mind, his soul
placed delicately in my palms
to nurture and protect, love and console

I look behind me and wonder whether I can
Remember,
be it for today, tomorrow, or for all eternity,
You were given to me
as I was given to you,
with a heart and a mind and a soul.

Killing Eyes
Luther B. Whatley
What I remember most,
about the mansion of the hills.
Is the mansion's trophy room,
displaying all the master's kills.
Where a tiger's skin was placed,
like a carpet on a mat.
With its mouth so wide a–snarling,
it had been a fighting cat.
The room was lit by firelight,
shimmering soft and low.
Giving the eyes of the master's trophies,
a flashing, angry glow.
Just thinking about those creatures,
whose lives were taken from.
That he hung upon his wall mounts bragging,
"see what I have done,"
Still the picture of those trophies,
does not linger in my mind.
It's the portrait above the fireplace,
with eyes of the killing kind...

Through The Eyes Of A Madman
Salvador Solorzano, Jr.
People. People are the core root to the problem. The problem of hatred. Hatred. Like our minds, hatred is a part of us. Parting. Something none likes to do. Do. The reason so many of us are dying. Dying. The number one fear of us all. Fear. It is the one thing that can break us at our hour of need, for none of us are safe from the power of fear.
Can someone tell me how to go to Hell, for I am lost and all is gone. Gone. Like all the innocent people in the world, we are doomed. Doomed. Doomed to a normal life of cruelty and hate. And deception. Deception. Hidden like a stage unseen. We will never know the truth. Truth. Something we can never comprehend for we are all like the lowly creatures that crawl upon the Earth. Earth. Shrouded in mystery. Mystery. Something that challenges the mind. Mind. The one weapon that can destroy everyone and everything. Truth. The truth is out there and we are not yet prepared to understand it. Truth.
The truth hurts.

Reflections Of My Life
Lois Deatherage
If for one brief Moment
my life could begin again
if I could be transported
to the place where I began
would it really make a difference
in who I am today
If I had the courage and the knowledge
to go a different way
would I be a different person?
would my life seek different ends?
If I could turn the sands of time
and live my life again
would the friends that I have gathered
be the friends of yesterday
or would the bright star of their friendship
brightly glow, then pass away?
so the road I took when younger
led me to these caring few
and their strength and understanding
have refreshed me like the dew.

Too Late
Kim Bauder
A cry for help
Heard in the shots
Yet too late, too late

Give us a reason
Help us to share
Don't wait, don't wait

Now your eyes say too much
Of what your mouth
Said too late, too late

Tomorrow will have the memory
Of a Moment
Of hate, of hate

Tears grip my voice because
Yesterday you only acted
And now it's too late
Too late.

Death Angel
Shalimar Chasse
i am the kiss of death, I taunt you with my sweet words and soft lips
come to me now and meet your fate
will you live or will you die, it's all a matter of little time
here we are upon the midnight hour
so come to me and kiss the flower
amidst the darkness and mystery
all that will be there is you and me
do not fear my sweet kiss
i am but a dream that comes of the mist
i come to do no harm
i am just there in the darkness waiting
i come in peace or so they say
please remember not to get in my way
if I come for you then it is your time
no begging, please, it doesn't even effect my mind

The Trail Of Tears
Cindy Thomas
The line grows longer on my eyes,
The mascara is black and keeps growing longer,
The pain in the heart is growing, growing, growing
The question in mind – what was the reason for the tears and why is it me, the only one, tortured.

Days grow longer with the pain,
She grows taller in height and in her hate against me.
It's as though the beautiful girl who was the sweet–smelling scent of holiness of the divine, born to hurt my soul.
She is a demon doll to torture the new fragrances.

Why, why, why me
what did I do, to deserve this kind of discrimination,
the kind from a fellow citizen.
My enemy is a harmonious being, towards me it turns into a witch.
God, forsake her and help me forgive her, I can do it, I can do it.
God, You take my troubles away and make them simple.
I sleep under Your watchful eye, but my mind rests in anonymous anger as daisy dreams are far across the distance.

Artist–Me
Charles Edward Woods
Cannot say what is on my mind
Because it will make you all cry.
Make you all stop and think.
If you all stop and think, you'll make yourself cry.
Cannot tell you all the truth, because you all don't want to know.
Know yourself and you know me also.
Cannot tell you all the truth,
Because you all think I don't care about you all –
Feelings, dreams, religions, country, family.
Want to tell you all the truth
Because I love you all as I do myself –
Mother, Son, Daughter, Brothers, My family, My country, My world.
At last, I thought I could tell you
Like I tell my paintings
They are the loves of my life.
Artist–Me, Just passing through
No need to panic
See you all there down the road.

Dedication: to mother Estelle Long Woods

Untitled
Rhyanna Magee
Crying blank tears,
walking on glass.
Eggshells for floors,
Pain can't last.
Reach out to tomorrow,
promises me a better day.
When feeling is easy,
and sadness fades away.
What is it about me
that scares your mind?
I've never done you wrong,
and my words have been kind.
Lasting forever laughs in my face.
Relationship fades...
without a trace.

What Is A "Senior Citizen?"
Edna L. Maitland
A "Senior Citizen" will be up at dawn
Maybe watch TV or mow the lawn,
Or visit a neighbor or whip up a storm
So independent and fanciful free
They dream and plan over a cup of tea.
They like to be noticed and they'll beam with a smile
Very figure–conscious, they'll walk a mile.
They like to shop and pretend they're immune
To all the loud music and fanciful tunes.
They go to church and offer a bit
And become fast friends with whomever they sit.
They love invitations to go someplace.
For their days are long and they want to see a face.
Sometimes they panic and know great fear
But it's mostly because they cannot hear –
The voice of God, Who is always near.
Their needs are really quite simple, you see
And if they trust in God, His love is free.
A "Senior Citizen" is just a name
For they are just people like you and me.

Friendship
Vanessa Washington Carter
What is a Friendship? Something that's
dear to the heart
It's a bond between you and another person
that should NEVER PART
A friend is someone you can call on any
time of the day
Knowing within your heart, he or she will
never turn you away
But, the best friendship you can have is
with the man upstairs
He knows all your heartaches, your downfalls
and despairs
He'll come to your rescue, in the
time of NEED
And to all your problems, He will
take heed
A friendship from above, should be some–
thing each of us crave
For a friendship like this will follow
you to your grave!

Enchanted Dreams

Family
Blake E. Casselberry-Samuels
My Grandpa, a knight in shining armor, brains like a scientist, hard worker like a farmer. Caring like a bear watching over a cub, not scared to cry and shows a lot of love. Above and beyond, you rise on and on, there's no limit. A hard-working black man tryin' to make a livin'. What can I say, head honcho in Prudhoe Bay, you're really special. You took being black to a whole new level. Willie Casselberry, that's your name; you belong in the hall of fame. You are the bomb, Grandma, Vickie, Stan, Ray and most of all my Mom. Grandpa-slash-father since my biological didn't bother. Pedro is 2 he's doin' what he's gotta do, to be in my life and make Momma his wife, but that's all good, I think he should. It's cool with me, cause then we will finally have a complete family.

Dedication: to my grandpa Willie Casselberry

Instinct
Nadine M. Bushong
They are returning, signaling the weather soon to be
These little, migrating, black-headed chic-a-dees.
Knowing exactly where to look for the seed
Each year returning to the patio for their feed.

When the temperatures begin to drop and get cool
These feathered creatures return as if it's back to school.
Watching their antics is such a great delight
Facing each other, flying straight up, acting ready to fight.

With blue jays vying for the same seed to eat
My lattice obstacle course was for little ones an easy feat.
They land on the vertical cross slats and then pop inside
To the seed-filled box, assured from gobbling jays the lattice will safely divide.

Having the families stay for the winter is a real joy
A little care with feeding, water to drink, bathe and play in like a toy
They flit among the lilacs, rhododendrons and carefully check the ground
These God-sent feathered friends are a pleasure to have around.

Mothers
Kassee Alison Slama
Mothers are caring, loving and bright,
They never let you out of sight.
Mothers are there for you always,
To cuddle up with on rainy days.
To heal a wound when you fall down,
To put a smile in place of a frown.
Mothers protect you from scary things that aren't really there,
To tie your shoes and brush your hair.
To teach you about what is right and wrong,
And at night to sing you a lullaby song.
To punish you when you are bad,
To make you happy when you are sad.
Mothers listen to your woes,
They think about you wherever they go.
Mothers love you no matter what,
They make you feel better when you get a cut.
Love is the definition of Mothers far and wide,
But in my mother I see so much pride.
Your mother may fit this poem,
But I know my Mother's the best ever known!

Autumn Comes To The Heart
Arlene McKinney
Through the window I see a stately, tall
tree dressed in crisp, autumn leaves
Its solitary existence evoking vague,
fleeting feelings of loneliness
A haunting, unidentified emotion stirring
in my heart
Filling me with sadness
And a disturbing sense of isolation
wells up within
Bits and pieces from the past,
A picture in fast-motion flashes
on the screen of my mind,
People, places, events, all unrelated
unconnected
Like the brown and gold autumn leaves
falling, scattering in the wind
To the four corners of the Earth
And I am left wondering what
happened to the ties that bind
Does autumn simply come to the heart?

Autumn
Stephanie Bear
The autumn tree sways
in the wind, its colors are
pink, red, yellow and orange.
The leaves fall and flip in
the air as they land.
The tree starts to get weak and
damp. The day gets shorter as
the night gets longer. The
houses seem green as the
pollen floats in the wind.

Oh, autumn, oh, autumn...
I love autumn

Dedication: to my wonderful mother Christine

Gone Fishin'
Steven N. Taxsar
Gone fishin'. Be back, Lord knows when.
Boots laced, waders suspended
I step upon the stream's bed
Become ensconced, upright
Like a sputtering candle in scudding thunder
I let my soul flow
Dance free on the ululating voice of water
With a flick
A vibrant vector subsumed my bodily rhythm
My lure skims on azure-veined wings
Whirls on undulating currents
Whether it be trout, bass, or salmon
I am hooked
Held entranced by this hydraulic embrace
Reflections of morn's tinted temple surround me
Sensors of balmy Earthen fragrance lift me
Beckon me to cast my feral flesh
In a motion's Moment
I have walked on water.
Gone fishing. Be back? Lord only knows when.

The Winning Shot
Quan Tucker
When I step on the court to play basketball,
A Moment of silence is sure to fall.
I wait for the announcer to say my name,
So the crowd can go wild, but they're not
to blame. When I get the ball, I put on a
show, but that's no secret, you already know.
I shake, then spin and I'm into the air,
Only thing you can't do to sit back and stare.
They say I'm the best ever to play
I think it's the truth, I don't doubt what
they say. It's seven seconds left and we're
Down only by two, I hear the coach say
I'm counting on you.

I get the ball and he jumps in the air,
I take left then go right leaving him there.
I get in the corner and set for three,
Knowing the game is all up to me.
I shoot the ball as fast as a jet,
Close my eyes and hear nothing but net.

Dreamcastles
Kelli Mirelli
Dreams we build
Are like sandcastles
They are beautiful but
Tides wash them away,
Sometimes we walk away
With a tear in our eyes and
A break in our hearts
Future dreams are washed
Except for those who, with
Tears in eyes,
Then bent on knees,
Take grain by grain in hand
Start to form a dreamcastle again.

Dedication: to Caroline, a great mother and teacher

Complete
Bethany Hammond
It is begun.
In the darkness of night, all the cards are on the table
and I have cast away my mask.
No longer is there a reason to hide.
My tears are all I can show,
only remorse over the coldness of reality.
And yet inside I have my strength.
Strength enough to rise from my body,
not unlike the mighty Phoenix and show my beauty.
Beauty like the feathers on a peacock's tail.
But it is too late, I have spent too much time,
used up too much strength, shed too many tears.
I am alone and I now accept that I shall die this way.
My memories wash through me, playing my life again and again
like a music box, never changing.
I chose this for myself.
He's gone and with him went my will to survive.
I am past the point of no return.
And death on his pale horse is now my only company.
It is ended.

Tortured Soul
M. Paul Maffei
My tortured soul,
So loud it screams;
Awakening from,
My darkest dreams.
The twisted sound,
Of the wretched cries;
So sharply stings,
My tear-soaked eyes.
I will not listen!
I will not hear!
Yet in my mind,
The sound is clear.
The agony of,
The truth revealed,
Has taken from me,
My protective shield.
And as my soul,
Shouts out its pain,
I realize now,
It shouts in vain.

Fallen
Andrew W. Reed
As my world falls down,
I hear your voice.
As my world falls down,
I hear your name.
As my world falls down,
I see your face.
As my world falls down,
I see you move.
As my world falls down,
I feel your touch.
As my world falls down,
I feel your breath.
And my world has fallen.

Dedication: to Kelly, the only one

I Came First
C. K. Gemmell
She has always been mine, always, since the dawn of time.
It was her lips I tasted, long before you ever did
Many centuries before, I caressed her skin
I claimed her flower, I was the first; she let in
She was next to me, as we trotted on our way
Down the rocky, dusty roads; those long-ago days
She belongs to me make no mistake.
It was she, I decided to take
Difficult, yet only at first
It was I, who quenched her thirst.
I made love to her on the beaches of white,
Beneath darkened clear and midnight younger skies
Our love has withstood the storms of time.
Departed, yet, not far from my mind
Lord, by a relentless sword which took my life.
I swore again to be with my queen, my wife.
Surrender her now, be a gentleman, a knight
Let her come to me under, age-ed tainted skies.
At this point sir, I'll not say anything more
For her, against You I'll wage war.

Enchanted Dreams

Be Strong
Stacey Whiteman
This is just
a note
to say
I've packed my bags,
I'm going away.
You came to me
in a Moment of sorrow
I hoped that day
we'd see tomorrow.
He lied and cheated
my heart
he broke.
But this day I thought
our love
was no joke.
I have to leave
to give me some hope
maybe next time
I'll be able
to cope.

The Thief Of Man
William Rohr
This candle's light
Does not burn bright
Its flame is the soul of man

From an immortal chill
Or a heart that beats still
The flame changes as only it can

Every candle wails
A different tale
Of who it has carelessly consumed

Flickering just for the wind
Not knowing it's sinned
Stops and then will resume.

Mom
Brenda Wentworth
I Miss you so,
More than you'll ever know.
Life wasn't fair to you.
Why? I just don't know.
You were so wonderful to me
and everyone else.
It was so plain to see.
I know you suffered so,
lying in bed for so long,
and nowhere to go.
Every day my heart ached to see you that way.
I know I can't bring you back.
So I guess, in my heart I'll have to say,
I know I will see you again, someday.
I love you always and I miss you so.
I'll pray for you. I'm sure you'll know.
Look over me, Mom.
You're my ANGEL now.
I hope you're at rest
because, Mom, you're the best!

The Birth Of A Friendship
Christopher Horsford
The day we met; a day with a tomorrow,
And a yesterday.
A day through which the sun rose and later set,
On life lived and memories won.
That day I did not see a friend,
When we passed we did not turn and smile,
With hearts soaring and crying out,
As we do now.
Because that day something was born,
That does not tire, nor fade, nor can be lost.
That will never be seen by anyone except for you and me.
I think of that day, of you and I,
And now, when skies darken and life kicks at my teeth,
I turn my shoulder and walk on tall.
Through my life I will see your face in each setting sun,
And in the wind I will hear you call out to me.
Unlike our friendship, our lives will fade,
So when that Moment comes and life tires and slips from our grasp,
Join me at the ocean's edge,
Where the sunrise meets the day.

Solitary
Vicki J. Rollison
Why do we fight
Why do we kill
Can't we stop the hurting
Do you think we ever will
To put a gun to another one's face
Why risk it all, Oh, what a waste
To take someone's life, in a Moment of
hate
You know that it's wrong, but then it's
too late
You'll be sitting in prison, feeling sorry
and sad
Thinking about the life you could have had

Dedication: to my mom, who inspired me

Words
Leah Laflamme
They are spoken at births,
and at the end of lives.
They unite lovers
and cast-off wives.
They are whispered on the wind
and written in the sand.
They are spoken with voice
and signed by hand.
They are said with gratitude
and yelled in hate.
They are often meaningless,
but some are great.
There are some remembered;
others are forgot.
They cause some to be saved,
while others are not.
Some are without reason,
but others account for something.
But more than anything else,
words are nothing.

The Anthology of Poems

Loneliness
Elise Pimienta
Loneliness was knocking, I refused to let it in.
I let you in before, you will not get in again.

Loneliness was coy and tried to trick me, you see.
But I told loneliness to go away, you shall not have
your way with me.

Loneliness said, "You need me! As I need you.
You have no other choice what will you do?"

I told loneliness, "You will not be my companion this night. "
"I have replaced you with a long yearning for companionship and
    happiness. "

We are too strong for you, can't you see?
You are no longer welcomed here.

SET ME FREE...
Dedication: to Dad – I will miss you

Fairies
Cinde Sullivan
Mystical Fairies deep in the woods...
Tiny little creatures with wings so sheer
and light,
I caught a mere glimpse as I hid out of
sight.
The magical fairies with bells on
their toes, hovered like hummingbirds on
a honeysuckle rose...
The best time to see one is nearly at
dawn,
Perhaps you may catch one riding a
fawn...
As I hid out of sight in the woods that
day, Oh! The joy to see them and watch
them play...

Nothing Compares To You!
Neil Secker
My head sometimes rules my heart
The things I say
It makes me start
To wonder why, I upset you
I made you cry
To make you happy once again
That's all I yearn for
I know I've been down for a while
There's times in life when all you need
Is the love of a good woman
That starts from a seed
You nurture it with feed
You open a book – it lets you read
I don't know whether you'll ever love me
But as time goes by
You sometimes see
There's no charge for love
It's absolutely free!

Dedication: to Pauline McCullagh

Gates Of Heaven
Edna M. Wood
I stood at the gates of Heaven
St. Peter came out with his book
What have you done to gain entrance
I said I've only come to look
I've tried to be friends with my neighbors
With a helping hand
Smile, word or look
Just to show I care
Life's journey hasn't always been easy
Sometimes the burden
Almost too heavy to bear
St. Peter just smiled
Closed his book and said
You've been a liar, cheat and thief
Not always a nice person to know
But I can't see anything
Really evil for you to be sent below
So you can stay here at the gates
Forever or until the good Lord
Himself says come in and hello

Still Am I
Latonya Batchelor
He being so deceiving
And I so young and so believing
Once had a love that was oh, so pleasing
And now barely am I sleeping
And barely am I even eating
Of him is all I'm thinking
Of him is all I'm seeing
In my dreams, of him leaving
Which left my heart full of bleeding
And me in tears and still am I weeping
He left and crushed my mental being
And off a ledge I feel like leaping
But still am I, living, breathing

Dedication: to my heart, Alonzo Copeland, Jr.

Autumn Sunshine
B. McColm
We have hardly seen your face
today.
You almost show, then shied away!
All day the clouds have swept
the sky.
And mocked, you, sun for being shy,
They know not what you have in store
Or even where they're heading for,
Perhaps, by hinting, you make them proud
So now and then become your shroud,

We miss your face when you choose to
sleep,
And just watch the clouds their vigil keep.
We miss your rays straight from the heart
And wish from us you'd never part
Till winter's gone and spring is nigh.
Lord forbid, you'll not be shy
The birds will sing with God's good grace
Pervaded by your Heavenly face

Enchanted Dreams

The Agony Aunt
Rita Kramer

Advice from the media
Is so nice.
The plump adolescent
Panders her problems
Time over again.
In the mirror of her
Helpful magazine —
Spots, pimples, boyfriends, boils,
Rashes and unsightly hair.
Bulges, flab and dreadful wrinkles,
And how to bare the bosom on the beach!

Sadly, the girl scans her inadequacies,
Only five feet two!
A no–hoper.
Can the agony aunt offer any assistance in this
extremity?
The mother of the plump girl
Works in a bread factory everyday.
And is always too busy to notice.

Untitled
Jason Birdsell

Should I think about her tonight? Tonight
when I need her the most. When
my heart aches and my mind fails me.
Should I write these lines? To ease my suffering,
this loneliness. Or hope against hope
that she, somehow, hears these lines.
Should I forget about her? The love we shared,
the infection and eventual transformation
of our souls into one.
Should I open my eyes? To see what we
had for what it was; the flash of a
firefly in the night, a mountain's molehill.

Or maybe, I should just think about her tonight.
Yes, or maybe, I should write some more.

My Silver Birch Tree
Andrew Robertson

I do not think I have a mind to conceive
cherished thoughts I'd print about my Silver–Birch tree.
It stood so graceful, slender and peaceful,
silver–bound branches strong,
spiritual–hands this tree, so wrought.

Heavenward stretching in silent prayer
it seemed clasped in the Heavenly–Father's care.
As one through the foliage gazed
saw windows against the sky traced
and velvet night was also shown
by stars of the Heavenly throne.

One day as I came to see my little Silver–Birch tree
I found her lying on the ground,
and sensed a loss that knew no bounds.
My thoughts and secrets I must store
as to my tree I spoke no more,
until a voice to me did say,
"you will meet in the garden of life one day!"

The Plantation
Sanmi Adegbile

All eyes had looked Heavenwards,
Searching the clear sky for a hope –
Hope hidden in clouds, flitting downwards
Tumid with drops, precious from high up,
And needed for sowing love; and living life.
But failed had these, to Earth, to come;
A land so jagged; cutting like a knife,
On the heels of planters away from home.
Unheralded, had the skies clouded all thro',
Interspersed with life much awaited;
And impregnating the land, where love grew.
In abundance, the planter's mind was elated;
Nature, her most benevolent, had done
On land; to spew forth love manifold,
Tilled and tended to bring back life gone,
And cropped as pretty to behold as marigold.
The harvests of amour'd been bumper
But partakers had failed to hearken to calls,
Bringing to naught, the pains of the planter;
And desolation to all the land in falls.

The High And Low
William C. Cook

The kids just sit, they have
no more to say, All they want
is to get blown away. But is
there a Fib in this magical
high, is life just passing them
by?
But who's to say where their
heads should sit, all those
red–necks who've never been
lit, think about it, you hypocrite.
So mother dears, don't throw
a fit, just sit back and relax
a bit, it's not as bad as you
may think, they could depend
on your alcoholic drink.

Time Well–Spent
I. K. Skinner

Used to make our own enjoyment,
Games we knew, some we'd invent
Sitting there, just watching, tell
Holding on to a nervous belly
Dad keeps shutting us all up.
As he stays watching the World Cup.
Front rooms, were only used for smooching
Now Dad is doing all the poaching
Can't go here, can't go there,
Let's get out, can't stand his stare!
Oh, for good times now gone by.
Doing our own thing, same as the next guy.
Yearning for the good old times,
Did ourselves up, to the nines.
All men then were gentlemen,
Now they're counted, one in ten.
Goodbye to good old days,
Welcome to the modern ways,
If modern ways you count as good
I know better, I'm sure you should

The Royal Flying Corp
Robert J. Joyce
My dawn patrol I must complete over enemy lines
Watching muddy troops be killed by unseen mines
I listen to the wind whistle through my wires
While flying high over tall church spires
And then from a cloud on my right
Two planes came into sight
Painted in that dreaded bright blood-red
My squadron knew what to do, nothing had to be said
With Eddie on my right I turned
And fired my guns and watched him as he burned
Flickering flames making no sound
The red plane spun towards the ground
I looked for some more prey
So that I could today
Put my name among those men
Who had shot down more than ten
Richtofen, Rickenbacker and Ball
I have to say that they all,
Seen through my bloodshot eyes,
Were the aces high.

My Savior
Anna Elizabeth Boggs
My Savior is...
Caring never snaring,
Loving never leaving.
He's always there,
He'll never leave you.
He'll be there when the going gets tough,
And when the waters get rough.
He's the same yesterday, today and tomorrow,
He's the same and He'll never change.
He shares His love between us all,
And doesn't keep it when we fall.
What do you say that He is?
He is my Savior.

Dedication: to Mommy

Twins
Clair Baker
Anthony was the name they chose,
Though why they chose it no one knows,
For he was not a Roman scholar,
All he did was shout and holler,
His teacher said with grave misgiving,
"I can't think how he'll earn a living".
But now he's over six feet tall.
He proudly marches down the mall
In scarlet coat and bearskin grand,
Among the smartest in the land,
He bangs the cymbals in the band,

Twin Adam was the businessman, of acumen he'd
plenty,
But when it came to common sense, his clever brain
was empty,
He phoned his girlfriend every day, when she was busy working,
Just to say "Hello, my love, I hope you are not shirking"
One day she had enough of this, she let him go on talking,
Packed a bag, called a cab and went to live in Dorking.

You Belong To The Sky
April Wicklund
Some day
when the stars are a beam of light
and the sun
is the moon,

I will look up to the sky and say...
I wish I had a rainbow –

So beautiful
I wish I was like it
And I wish it would be mine.

Then on a rainy day...
I would say
Go away!

You are not mine –
ANYMORE

You belong to the sky

Babies
Barbara Schnellbacher
Our children grow up so very fast,
It seems their childhood does not last.

There are many times I wish they were babies;
To hold and rock and read them stories;
To create even more precious memories.

Babies are a great joy,
Whether they are a girl or a boy.

My first grandchild is on the way;
I've waited so long for this wonderful day.

It will be like having my dreams come true;
But this time when I'm tired I can say "Mom, the baby wants you".

In Search Of A Sculptor
H. Himmel
Michaelangelo was our first choice, but we found out he was dead
That really posed no problem, we'd get someone else instead.

We placed a call to Rembrandt, which moved his family to tears
How could we have the nerve to contact someone dead two hundred years

Leonardo Da Vinci was next on the list, on him we were really keen
He never even returned the calls we left on his answering machine

We tried to hire Picasso, but he said we lacked respect
Imagine trying to commission a master by calling him collect

Gainsborough didn't return our calls, Rodan's phone was not in service
Noguchi's number we could not find, we started getting nervous

Thus Charlie was the one we chose and we haggled over the fee
We never should have searched elsewhere, as you all can plainly see

We all are truly grateful and welcome you to this tour
Of a truly beautiful work of art by the future Henry Moore

Enchanted Dreams

Why Did You Come?
Florizella Thompson
Why did you come?
No one invited you
Why did you come?

You took without
Asking
It wasn't yours to take
You took without
Asking

This land was
Mine
My Children's
And
Grandchildren's
But, you came and took it away from us
And now my children have no place to go

I wish you had never come
Why did you come?

Young Love
Evangeline H. Loomis
He said he didn't love her,
That there was someone else,
And he hoped he hadn't hurt her.
With tears in her eyes and pain in her heart
She watched him walk away.
They had promised to love forever,
And now his love was gone.
Does love not last forever?
Or perhaps this was not love.

She saw her daughter's tears
And felt her daughter's pain,
And wished that she could bear the pain instead.
But life goes on — this, too, will pass,
And time will heal the pain and dry the tears.

A Walk Through Christ's Garden
Debra R. Simons
Come, let's walk through Christ's garden.
Let's hold Christ's hand.
Isn't it beautiful, Isn't it peaceful and quiet?
Take in a breath of fresh air.
Smell all the beautiful and fragrant roses.
Feel the gentle breezes as they rustles the leaves on
the trees.
Let's walk the paths as Christ leads.
See all the beautiful colors, see how they mingle all
together.
Christ says, "Watch the thorns, they can be painful, stay
on the path. I will lead you."
Hold His hand and follow His lead.
The roses are beautiful and fragrant and all different
colors, but they live in harmony.
Maybe we should take lessons from Christ's garden.
Stay on Christ's path or it can get painful from the thorns
of life.
Come, let's take a walk through Christ's garden, He
will lead us through.

You
D. G. Cox
You have more to offer than a pretty face,
What you give to others time does not undo,
There is something inside that speaks of the grace
And love that can only be given by you.
The wonder of you.
With warmth and compassion your spirit reflects
There's hope for tomorrow, some brightness to share,
You view all as the same, you see no defects,
Not sitting in judgment, you sincerely care.
The softness of you.
That rarest of talents, a lack of pretense,
Shows that your heart and mind are open to all,
And the difference made by your diligence
Adds new dimension to help someone stand tall.
The realness of you.
Thank God you are you, I thank God that He saw
Fit to bestow you with an angelic heart,
You filled what was empty and you healed the flaw
So one lonely, sad life could find a new start,
The marvel of you.

Empty As Dark
Jessica Hall
Cimmerian darkness swallows the moon.
Silvery whispers of transcendence glide over the erotic night.
A craving awaits upon famine, one which follows chaos.
Existing is enlightenment and I want to experience.
Dying is abortive.
Search me out and find this so-called evil.
Eradicate this burning for a feed in that which I long for.
Snatch me here, quick, without distaste, on this rung of my life, where
no ladder exists, my mortal life. "Make me beautiful."
It is like an itch I cannot reach and so desperately spreading,
I ravage and tear all the flesh surrounding that powerful irritation.
Now I will sleep in my desire of night.
Blood thickens, pulse slows, as does the hour of night.
You leave, I've drained,
and I die as a hunger is born.

Ignore The Differences
Missie Black
Little boy with a lopsided smile
Sat down on the curb awhile
Remembering his mother say
—Sorry, there's no milk today
Catch the bus to head to school
Knowing he'll feel like a fool.

Rich little girl in a pinafore
Patent-leather shoes clicking on the floor.
Doesn't study for the grades she'll get
Always knows she's Teacher's pet.
With a pretty smile and eyes that sing
She gets away with everything.

A teacher must look deep and see
All the differences there may be.
Don't judge your students by their dress.
Don't give up on one if he has less.
Don't educate their money side.
Enrich and liven up their mind.

Offwell Winter
B. Walker

The sleeping trees, 'neath winter's veil.
Leaves carpet ground, sparkling frost,
Ice on pools, buzzards call.
Breath of deer so plain to see,
I walk through woods, crunch underfoot,
alarm call of blackbird warning all.
Door Mice sleep in nests of hay, awaiting
spring and warmer days.
Blossom of hazel so bright to see, in
depth of winter, a delight for me.
Fox on the prowl in winter coat,
Pheasants flee so noisily, into scrub and
under tree, so brightly coloured at their cost.
Down maple walk I make my way,
to meet my friend of bygone day,
he sits upon my hand to feed,
and then he sings a song for me. A Robin
The sleeping trees—(but they must see)

Dedication: to my wife, Una

Ode To Shampoo
Seetharathnam M. Reddy

O', my dearest shampoo,
as thy bubbles tricklest down my visage,
Thou art the smoothest,
As I run thee through my raven, black mane,
I feel soft, silky hair,
tied together by the power of thy beauty!
Art thou not incredible?
Art thou not beautiful?
Yes, thou art the most,
exuberant!
Deadly serious, touchingly beautiful!
The beauty of thee shines,
as bright as the sun.

Dedication: to my family, friends and teachers

My Final Journey
Beverley Lorraine Qassab

I watch my ship come sailing in
No ticket, No Luggage, No friends to bring
The ship that sails to "ETERNAL SKIES"
And here on Earth, my body lies
I think they say "JUST FAT FROM THE LAND"
As I draw nearer that outstretched Hand
All my loved-ones, gone in the past
Am I really "HOME" at last?
Should I fear my Journey's End?
Or am I taking that final bend?
Startled by the dark cloud's formation
Born to die, recycled in life's rotation?
To seek a sanctum, a place to hide
Would I have, then, just merely died?
Surrounded by Earth's mysterious sphere
And in the darkness, young and old fear
Too lovingly say "Good Bye" and kiss my hand
Before I leave this lonely land
And on that day, our final breath
Before us stands "THE ANGEL OF DEATH"

At The Foot Of The Cross
Vanessa Slater

Merky—Muddy—Dirty—And green was the water at the foot of the cross
There were Jesus hung nailed between two thieves
The water was still—but yet in its stillness
Could be heard the ripples of an undercurrent
A sure sign of life
As I gazed from the foot of the cross up to where my Lord hung
Oh, how I wished I could grab hold of Him and hang there
He heard my weak voice as I stood at the mere bank of mud and water
And said He unto me,
When I was hanged on the cross I came not alone,
But, I saw you in the Merky—Muddy—Dirty—Water and I brought all of
your attitudes of rebellion
And your acts of sin
Your fears
Of the unknown
Your desires for love
I brought them all with me so that you would not have to hold to
or carry them
For when I looked down into the Merky—Muddy—Dirty—Green water
Ye, I saw my reflection

Real
Erica M. Chaney

One by one, we ever so gingerly
Cautiously
With a furtive glance
No one's watching
Good
Slip slowly out of our well-worn cocoons
Emerging into personal authenticity like a bride out of the bathroom
Only to slip back again
Wallowing
Close the curtain in slow motion
So no one notices
Imperceptibly
Gone.

Dedication: to my sister Tina

Can It Be?
Anna D. Dodge

Standing alone
Gazing at distant stars
Beautiful, yet so cold.
Glittering diamonds
Scattered on velvet cloth.

Beneath that canopy of light
Our world is insignificant in the vastness
Lonely and alone,
Abandoned in time.

The arrogance of some insisting
That this panorama of creation
Is just for this race of puny beings
Tied to this mudball they call home.

Can it be that Terrans have dominion
Over all the galaxies?
Surely there cannot be a provision
For such a lot of wasted space.

Enchanted Dreams

Christmas Chills
Jayne Johnson
To whom will we go this year
And enact the facade of good cheer?
Shall it be your house, or maybe your brother's
I wonder, if maybe, it might be another's.
Please say, to whom will we go this year?

To whom will we visit this year
And get drunk on liquor and beer?
Then full of Dutch courage, become embroiled in a fight
We'll argue and argue to determine who's right.
Say it true, who will we visit this year?

To whom will we end up this year?
For the message is so very clear.
While we count our presents, demanding better instead
We did not notice our Christmas spirit has fled,
Who cares where we end up this year?

So what shall we all do next year?
For Christmas is cancelled, I fear.

A Mother, A Friend
Jennifer Hannon
Friends and mothers are a lot alike,
They both care for you and
Know what's right.
They're both important but in
Different ways;
Friends may come and go but
A mother always stays.
To have a mother as a friend
You are truly blessed
For you know your love has
Passed all tests.
Not many people connect
The two,
That's why I'm so lucky to have
The both in you.

Untitled
B. Douglas
When God created you, "Mum", it was one of His better days
He took the glow from out of the sun and shaped it in many ways
He took two stars from the skies
And moulded those for your "emerald Eyes"
From the glow of the sun, He was aware
That the fire would be your flaming-red hair
With body complete He looked inside
And gave you feelings that you cannot hide
When you're in pain you show it so
And Oh! when you're angry everyone knows
He gave you all these things that are written above.
And let's not forget a truckload of love
All of these things I can say
For this is how I see you every day.
From a son to his mother
Look at me, do.
Mum, you're the greatest.
And I'll always love you.

Dedication: to Mum, who means everthing to me

The Sword
Graham Sugden
Love is a double–edged sword which strikes you now and then
And when it touches deep within your heart
It may cause rapture and exquisite joy, but then again
The double edge may twist and tear your soul apart

You never know when it will strike or when your turn will be
A brief encounter, words exchanged, or just a fleeting glance
May lead you on to pleasure, sweet enjoyment, breathless reverie
And sweep you off your feet as for a while, to cupid's tune you dance

But have a care for all–too–fleeting love's domain holds sway
And quickly speeds the moon across love's sky
The sword may twist and precious love be torn away
And in reality's gray, watery light, one heart or both may die.

But if the passion's strong and if the love is really true
A love this strong will never be denied
And even though the lovers part and try to start anew
The sword of love which pierced their hearts will keep those hearts
Entwined.

Beverly Troutman
Carolyn McEachin
B oldly approaching her years with grace
E ver so kind and with a smiling face
V ery astute as life passes on
E ven when her heart may not be as strong
R eal in most ways all of the time
L iving her life with a look of sublime
Y ear after year until its her prime.
T urning and Twisting, making decisions
R ealizing her plight with the family physicians
O h, my Lord, you do understand
U nder the light and the hand of a man
T ell me, oh, God what You have in store
M y life is in Your hands and I'm looking for more
A nswer me in my deepest hour
N eeding Your grace and Your awesome power.

The Blackbird
Charles Frederick Gartland
On the grass verge, by the roadside,
Close to the thundering traffic
Not exactly squashed, but flat, very flat,
Feathers matted with its life's dried juices
Pointing in every direction, seemingly in accusation
Empty eye sockets, encrusted, Staring blindly.
Presumably the victim of a type of motor vehicle,
Possibly a potential meal for a hungry cat,
Or a plaything for a like–minded quadruped.
Natural causes seemed highly unlikely.
It won't kill insects anymore.
It won't terrorize worms anymore.
It won't welcome any more sunrises with
Its harmonious vociferousness.
It won't hop and it certainly won't fly.
Anymore.
I assume it was killed by a motor vehicle
But there is no proof.

Dedication: to Mother, with love and thanks

Silence
Jeannette Campbell

Silence is golden but here is the "Pun"
Silence is lonely and dreaded by some
It's said to be healthy, to quiet the mind
To block out our everyday living is fine
Ah, but just for a time
I long for the laughter that made me feel good
For it made me feel useful, needed and loved
So I'd trade you this silence if only I could
For a world without sound is so frigid and cold
When the music is silenced, "it's over, you're old!"
Do you call up a memory from out of your past
Will you have perfect recall, how long will it last?
When the sound of familiar voices are heard
My heart skips a beat, is somebody there?
No longer forgotten in silence therein
For a few precious Moments I'm living again
Peace is no longer a friend but a foe
For silence is deadly, to those in the know!

Dedication: to dad, my heart and soul's author

Anti–Aircraft Radar W. W. II
J. M. Jones

As I have grown "long in years",
Perhaps now is the time to voice my fears.
Fears about things I have done in life,
Actions taken in time of strife.
Long–range killing does not hurt the soul,
It is not for us that bell will toll!
When you defend your Country's skies,
The gunfire lightly upon you lies.
No blazing inferno as down you go,
To meet your Maker on the ground below!
The men you fight you do not hate;
Only their leaders; which seals their fate.

You cheer a "hit" and claim a "kill",
It doesn't haunt you – it one day will!

What Should I Do?
Anthony J. Kroeck

Should I go full speed ahead
possibly to a regretful dead end
through the loss of a friend
or should I keep these thoughts only as mine
telling her only in my next lifetime
Should I confess my thoughts to her
or keep them inside due to fear
Should I risk it all and possibly fall
while answering my heart's call by telling all
or should I keep this feeling inside
and hope it just goes away and dies
Is she my Mrs. right
or just a girl I want only for one passionate night
If she's supposed to be mine
why then has love been so blind
If it's meant to be then I'm sure I'll know
but until that time I'll respectfully go slow
while keeping my dreams on the down–low

Dedication: to J. for being down

Happiness
Amy Robyn Vachon

Where can I go to find it?
Is it just around the corner or,
Do I have to walk a few miles first?
What if I never find it?
Does everyone find it?
Is it down this smooth path here?
Or is it down that rough road, filled with glass?
I am barefoot and I want to choose the smooth road.
But will happiness be there, waiting for me?
Things are always hard and painful.
Should I risk it, should I go down the rough road?
The smooth road seems to be calling to me
But nothing has ever been easy,
Why should happiness be different?
Hopefully, I have made the correct decision.
I shall now walk on with my head held high
Over my bleeding feet.
I will keep my eye out,
And hope I find happiness
Just around the corner.

Woman
Patricia A. Rials

I am a wonder of the world, God made me from man.
I am the most powerful being in the universe.
My mate tries to dominate me, instead of being my partner,
therefore I rule. Because, I can make man.
I will love you. I will make you scream your deepest
pleasures.
I will leave you.
I will give you the worst pain in your heart if you
disobey me.
I will make you marry me, I will make you cry.
I will make you hate, I will make you kill.
I will make you lose your job.
I will make you cheat, steal and lie.
I will make you disown your own children.
God made me from man, they call me woman.

Red Hat At 18
Mary Rogers

A scarecrow pointed wildly,
The children left their play,
As I walked into the village
In my new hat that day.
My hat had a fine feather
That soared to meet the sky;
At one side, it plunged downwards
And quite obscured my eye.
I'd worn it in the city,
And all had looked their praise,
And now I tried the country,
Unused to rustic ways.
A cart horse really skidded:
He'd never seen the like!
A postman cycled past me,
And fell off from his bike,
Unused to such bright scenery
By ploughed or crop–filled land...
When I came back from Claudy,
That hat was in my hand!

Enchanted Dreams

Untitled
Kelly Andrews
I have a secret place inside
where all my fears and dreams can hide
my silent fears that no one sees
my whims and insecurities
my quiet dreams that burrow there
right along my midnight prayer.
like how I wish I could be read
by the thoughts growing in my head
instead of what I wear or who I date
what I seem or how I rate.
in this place that no one knows
my silent little treasure grows
from a little girl
scared and cold comes a great woman
with a heart of gold.
Every day she's growing stronger and the smile is
lasting longer. Until the day will come about
where there will be no more doubt.
then comes the day she holds her head high,
and laughs in the clouds and dances in the sky.

A Letter To God
Lottie P. Denson
Dear God, I write You this letter
Because I know my husband will get better.
I cannot sleep
I lie in bed and weep.
I'm at the mercy of Your feet.
You said by Your stripes
we were healed.
It doesn't matter how he now feels
His physical change will come
According to Your words
it has already been done.
Faith is the substance of things hoped for
The evidence of things unseen.
I believe in You, Jesus
And on Your words, I will lean.

Let's Grow Up Loving
Esther K. Shearer
Let's grow up loving
God's Commandments
And if we do –
The world will love us
If we do
The Lord will bless us
If we do
Our faces will glow
Our souls will shine
If we do
And all the world will know
God loves us
If we do
Let's grow up loving
God's Commandments
And the world will love us, 'tis true.
Let's grow up keeping
God's Commandments
And the Lord will bless us, too.
Let's wait, wait, wait for the Lord.

Heartbreak
Susan M. Betz
I know a heart can break.
For as each tear falls in the dark upon my pillow, I can
Hear the shattering as my heart breaks. The sound echoes
In my ears.

"They" say time heals all wounds and tears wash away your
Fears.

What do "they" know as the images play across my brain–as a
Video on a TV screen.

Our first dance, our first embrace. Our last kiss, the look
That was on your face. A smile, a tear.

The words we spoke and those we left unsaid. How can my
Heart heal? When it's everywhere all around me. Inside and
Out. Will I ever mend?

If I could walk back in time it would be to your arms. So I
Could feel safe and loved once more.

The Scarecrow
Laura Smith
It stands tall, motionless
The wind blows it from side to side,
Standing through dawn and dusk,
Who knows?
It may have a story to tell,
Its straw glistens in the sunlight,
The clothes on its back, old, ragged, jagged,
The hat upon its head dusty and tattered,
Its years of standing all forgotten
Standing,
The wind whispering,
There it stood,
For twenty years of loneliness
Its time has come,
It is no more.

Escape
Carolyn Hernandez
Social blitz
Society schitz
Students of insanity
Somebody help us
Our brains have been blown
There's gotta be a remedy

Positive action
Negative traction
Our planet is coming apart
We're thinking so high
But crawling so low
What we're lacking in is heart

Religious games
Christian shames
Soon it will be too late
We've gotta stand up
And reach for the love
Or our world will die in hate

Musical Evenings
Joan Last

In those days, so long ago, before the time of Radio
We all joined in music making, turn by turn performance taking.
A Piano solo first, by Kate, her fingers went at such a rate
that some notes didn't sound at all, they say "Pride goes before a fall".
Next came Jack, upon the fiddle, tuning with those pegs you twiddle.
He said: "I am a near beginner", but his solo was a winner.
Judith, on the Clarinet, on playing well her mind was set.
My newest piece is by Mozart, to ruin him I've not the heart
I'll play a tune that no one knows in case I miss my highs and lows.
Then there was a lovely cello, with its tone so pure and mellow,
played by Martinez from Spain: we all said "Do play again".
Sopranos came, Contraltos went and Basses, all on music bent.
Accompaniments were played by John who only sometimes got it wrong.
Finally we all joined in, it may have been an awful din
But we knew so many songs and who's to count the rights and wrongs?
Today these tunes pass people by and some of them don't even try
to make real music, only "Pop", bought at the local music shop.
But just a few have evenings still, many with undoubted skill.
They gather round the pianoforte, singing songs, some nice, some naughty.
"Good luck" to them is what I say, I'll come and join you if I may.

A Gift
Jessie Tank

A gift is something that can say a lot,
It touches many lives even if it wasn't bought.

A gift can be anything you want it to be,
It could be a simple greeting,
Like "hello" or "how are you doing."

A gift could be a flower,
Or even your own willpower.

It doesn't have to be something big,
It could be just a small little thingamajig.

It doesn't matter how much the amount,
Just as long as you make it count.

Memories
Alea Wascher

Memories of yesterday,
there are so many I cannot say.

He hurt me badly and could not see,
Just how much he meant to me.

I really did love him so,
But there are some things he did not know.

He lied to me and broke my heart,
And I really started to fall apart.

I realized he didn't care,
And all of a sudden he left me there.

Now I know we weren't meant to be,
But if he only knew how much he meant to me.

I love him and miss him so,
I'm really sorry he had to go...

A Teacher's Life
Suzanne Wordley

Roxanne – will you sit in your seat
Amber – keep your handwriting neat
Hayley – why can I see the back of your head?
Liam – stop yawning, go earlier to bed
Stephen – put your hand down, you'll have to wait
Adam – good morning, why are you late?
Jennifer – please stop sucking your thumb
Roxanne – PLEASE sit on your bum
Jodie – would you please look at the board
Ryan – your pencil is not a sword!
Luke – do not interrupt me anymore
Stephen – what is that puddle on the floor?
Emma – get a bowl if you feel sick
Natalie – help her please – quick!
Laura – just how much tuck have you got?
Alice – why do you talk such a lot?
Michelle – please put your naval away
Roxanne – in your chair – please stay
Out you go children, it's time for our break
Then we have Math, how much more can I take?

Temptress
Marilyn S. Voelker

She has mastered the art of seduction;
Disciple to the name;
Conqueror of the game.

A challenge in submission awaits;
Constricting your heart;
Anticipating the start.

Lust and enticement run rampant in her touch;
Self–control obliterated;
Restraint now annihilated.

Surrender is your climactic resolution;
Quenching ultimate desire;
Feeding the temptress fire.

Final Tributes To A Fireman
Jill Smallfoot

Family and friends gathered to give respectful tribute today,
Reflecting the life this fireman lived in many a way.
As a fireman he'd served his community well,
Of his bravery, there were many tales to tell.
A flag of stars and stripes lay folded at his head,
A symbol of the patriotic life he'd led.
He wore a proud uniform at his rest,
A silver badge upon his chest.
His battered old fire helmet lay at the foot of his coffin;
Evidence, he'd laid his life on the line often.
A uniformed color guard, representative of the best,
Lovingly carried their peer to his final rest.
His widow, gripped a folded flag and shed silent tears,
As she recalled being beside him all those years.
Together his children gathered around him, as well they should,
Living, loving monuments of this man's good.
And the Lord Jesus, He also was there.
He met the departed fireman's spirit in the air.
And they turned, looked down and smiled at those left behind,
And the final tributes to a fireman, one of a kind.

Enchanted Dreams

Searching
Latisha Blades
I go astray looking to find something but I cannot because
I am lost.

So I go deeper to find what I am looking for.

I don't know what it is I'm looking for but I will find it.

I do grow weary but I still search.

I stop for a Moment and think to myself if I'll ever find
what I'm looking for.

I start looking again, this time I look deeper than before.

I finally find what I was looking for.

It was under my nose the whole time — I was looking for
talent — meaning I have the talent to write.

Dedication: to my family for supporting me

One Fine Day In May
Lee A. Hainsworth
While walking through the everglades one fine day in May;
Rooted up through centuries by their seeds that lay.
On a clay-like carpet within a fungi bed;
Poisoned thoughts by the Devil witch that oozed to my head.
A kiss from a beautiful Princess would normally bring back life
But in this case it was too severe and may need a surgeon's knife
To cut away the heartache and replace the love lost;
A love I thought was eternal and would fight for at any cost
A normal man's reaction would be to give up and let it die.
This brave knight's heart was made of steel and he will give
it another try.
Because if it's love and true love, you know it's worth a little
time.
And sure enough, two days later and a fortune on flowers,
She was back in my arms. And mine.

Age
Renee Hodson
This, then, is loneliness; the glass
Behind which one stands to see life pass.
It is the quiet room where sound
Is Time's slow measure moving round.
It is the firelight's gentle blaze
Around scenes and dreams of bygone days.
It is the teapot oft a-steam
O'er willow-patterned cup, a-gleam.
It is the faded photo much
Dog-eared and worn with constant touch;
It is the echo in the hall
of feet that do not tread at all.
The constant wait, for what? who knows!
The heavy sigh at long days' close.
It is the feeling deep and strong
That somehow one does not "belong".
The mind's sad strain to understand
The tremble of a feeble hand.
The turning back of Life's used-page.
This, then, is loneliness – is Age.

Lady Jane Grey
Glenda Whiteside
Her fate was plain
For lady Jane
This nine-day queen
Is hardly seen
The people frown
To a noble crown
Through such power
Beyond the tower
Love and hate
Through traitor's gate
A frightened girl
This precious pearl
A dove which rose
In sweet compose
For blood and lust
A crown was thrust
Build scaffolds high
The nation cry
Upon its lift
Those axes were swift

Displaced
Ann Hutchins
Finding the hairline crack in the foundation,
I leave it.
The house will fall apart anyway, I think,
as we all will.
"Death is real,
Comes without warning,
This body will be a corpse."

When you left, wind blew around my corners.
Through my cracks, life seeps.
The work gets done... slowly.
Forgive me, I'm not quite here today
but wander the universe looking for driftwood
like that piece of me,
the one with your name carved on it.

On Second Thought
Karen White
Imagine and wonder,
Consider and ponder,
The thought of thinking, of how and why
Suppose; anticipate,
Envision and liberate,
Set forth your thoughts unto the sky

Then immerse and acquire,
Observe and aspire,
To conjure the thoughts never called on before
Absorb and regard,
Analyze and discard,
Stand back and move forward on a quest to know more

Now concede and delude,
Understand and conclude,
That this process of thinking was thought up at one time
Realize and decide,
Understand and confide,
In your own mental process; your master; your mind

Loving You
Mary L. Yang

When I think about what made me first notice you,
The thing that brought my attention to you,
I wonder what it would be like if you hadn't.
I wonder what my life would be like now.
Who would I be loving now?
Who would I have loved?

So many have passed by in my life I might have loved.
Yet you were already there in my heart.
You left no room for anyone else to come.
How could I give someone else what you had?
You stole my heart and ran with it.
So now, compared to you, everyone is second best.

It's hard for me to wonder what it would be like without you.
Where I would be if I wasn't loving you now.
But loving you for as long as I have, I wonder,
Do I really love you or is it just left-over passion?
But then all I have to do is look at you and I know,
I know I do still love you.

School
Jamla Rizek

Children screaming, bells
Ringing noise is everywhere
Teachers yelling, lockers
Slamming, voices fill the air
The day is over and teachers
Recover, when they think of the
Past all they do is shudder
Some teachers are mean and some
Are nice,
It doesn't really matter they'll
Still break the ice
The next day comes and here
Comes the bumps
Most of them attend and the
Horror begins again!!!

Missing You
Monique Vasquez

When you died it was
hard to see you go
And while you waited
for your angel to show
Your life was the one
that flashed before our eyes
When all we could do
is lower our heads and cry
The smell of death filled
our homes
And individually we all felt
alone
You were all that was
dear and pure
While they still search for
the cure
And you were the beautiful
creature God had made
But you have died from
that disease they call AIDS.

The Final Climb
Michael Ballard

The body is our only keeper
It's the shell to house our soul
But once exhausted, comes the reaper
To take his prize, is his loyal role
But all through life you know you die
And once you're gone, the soul is ripped
Your time has come, but don't defy
By the hands of God, you will be gripped
Your soul has reached beyond the stars
And you feel the warmth of remembered souls
Peace is freedom, not confined behind bars
All you feel is that your spirit grows
And all things worked for are now gone
They can't be taken to your final rest
And all through life you've hoped you won
With no regrets, you've tried your best
But just remember, that it's just life
And there's always better beyond your time
So just forget your stresses and strife
Because it's faith, that makes that final climb.

Squash Song
Grace Jaqua

O bee!
Have you heard the symphony?
The squash blossom in trumpeting
Golden notes of ecstasy!
O bee!
Come humming musically
And dive into the dusty
Instrument that calleth thee;
And emerge, drunk with the notes
That make your wings so wobbly.
How you would love to lie
Forever and hear the keys!
But you must fly off, headily
To tell others what the squash blossom
Is trumpeting so giddily.

A Mother's Prayer
Stephanie Yunker

A Mother's Prayer
so soft and sweet
"please bless her hands,
please bless her feet"
"Please keep her warm,
and don't let her cry,
and if she sheds tears,
let me wipe them dry"
"Please bless her heart,
to know that she's loved,
and bless her with faith,
that you're up above"
"Last, but not least,
please keep her safe,
keep her in sight,
and out of harm's way"
"One last request,
before my Amen,
bless her, please bless her,
again and again."

Enchanted Dreams

Fall
Priscilla Stark

Fall of the year, is now here. Changing of the trees, all
the colors of the leaves.
Clouds coming in, it is always the same. We know there will
be rain.
There has to be a little rain with the sunshine, too.
The rain keeps the air clean for me and you.
When the clouds lift, the snow will be on the mountain peaks
afar. We know in a short time, it will be down where
We are.
The season will be winter then, our fall has passed away.
But we know it will return to us a year to the day.
Spring and summer will come and then again fall. Our dear
Lord created them all.
We are given all the seasons for God's special reasons.

AMEN.

Shane
Heather Barnak

To make your everlasting dream come true
Is finding someone that is just like you
I found this in you and I won't let it go
You make me so happy, I thought you
should know
I think about you throughout the day
And always by my side I want you to stay
When you touch me with your caressing
hand
It gives me feelings I can no longer
withstand
Once in your life comes along your True
Love
And It's beautiful and pure like a soaring
White Dove
Everything about you is perfect, you see
You are my White Dove and I'll never
set you free

Dedication: to Shane, I love you, Heather

Love Them All
Barbara J. Dockery

Love, love, love. Love them all.
Men, women, children and all.
Open up your heart and let love in.
Love the poor as well as the wealthy.
Love your neighbor as you love yourself.
Every day love knocks your door.
Say yes to love, there is always
Room for more. The more you give, the
More you will receive. This I truly believe.
Never set love high on a shelf.
It is worth more than fame and wealth.
When you love, burdens fall, pressure
Drops and temptation crawls.
Get out of the fast lane before
You hit a brick wall, where burdens are
Heavy and temptation is tall.
Each day just say, I am going to love
More people than I did yesterday.
Then without cease, pray... and go on your
Way. Pray Thank you God for another day.

Drifting
Marjorie L. Competiello

There I was just drifting,
in the endless clouds of
yesterday.

Whereupon I stumbled,
across many a fond memory.

Thinking that they were lost,
I never had gone back.

But as I lay here,
my mind drifting through time,
my inner eye seeing,
my heart feeling,
my senses sensing,
and all the while I am drifting.

A Lost Love
V. Darlene Stilwell

One lovely October night
When the timing was right
He looked at me with eyes so blue
As if I already knew
The question, he was about to ask
Will you marry me at last?
My heart so filled with Love
I know he was sent from God above
Making plans for our special November day
Without any kind of delay
This man I love with all my heart
Just like I did from the start
Only eight more days before we say I do
And he left me for you
The tears slid down my cheek
And my knees were very weak
I knew from this day forward
Life was to continue onward
I truly loved him with all my heart
And now I will have to find a new start

This Feeling
Nate Swearingen

As I sit there, head hung low,
To nothing my face could show.
We are all dregs, my friends and I.
We all feel like we could die.
This is the feeling I try to tell,
This is the state, this state of Hell.

Arising from this state of hollow,
They've done this before, we shall follow.
I am sitting there, safely, sorrow.
We made our mistake with "No Tomorrow"

They will follow, it will go on.
Some will fall. It's the biggest con.
Never think you are condemned,
If you do, you won't ascend.
But this, someone will imply.
When you really want to die.
When and if you decide to live,
My advice you should give.

Lucky Lucky
Lori Miller

I looked out the window of my backyard.
I saw a flower that grew like a star.
And there a bee came from the trees.
And sucked out the pollen in a one, two, three.
And there it stood so pretty and pink.
I came out and watered it in a wink.
And then from the flower came some seeds.
There they sprouted without even a few weeds.
Now I'm watering and giving them feed.
I'm glad I helped these flowers that were in need.
Now I care for each little green being.
They opened my eyes so i could really start seeing.
And now from today till the next day on.
I'll care for these plants until the day they are gone.

Dedication: to family and friends, with love

The Swing
Kathy Amoureux

As I close the gate and start up the walk, the past comes bright
and clear.

On the porch is a swing with children all around. Pushing each other
with joy abound. "Little ones first" they say to each other and turns
are taken.

Off to the side are Dad and Mom. Sitting and watching their children
at play. Holding hands as they did in those days, smiling at each
other. Thinking of times when they were young and she would sit in
the swing with him pushing her.

The days are gone with the swing. We have all grown up and moved
away. The swing is still on the front porch. The chairs are empty
where the folks used to sit and sadness fills my heart.

But maybe tomorrow someone will come to live in this old house. Maybe
there will be children who will swing on the old porch swing with
Dad and Mom sitting near holding hands and thinking of a time when
They, too, would gather around an old porch swing.

I; Alone; You
Daniel Dominguez

and I was so alone as I could be

lost in mists of forbidden memories
echoes of Loves' silent breaths wash o'er my face.

drying tears of lonely falling
become upon airing –
silent screams;
words of purest thoughts;
exploding in breaths of quiet somber,
soundless in the silence of grieving ears.

contorted through an ageless hollow
my echoeless pleading ripples with tears
consumed by a heart–aching tension
groping through realms
of an effortless, yet unreceived
Love.

Dedication: for my Angel

The Volcano
Ryan Myers

As I walk next to this enormous mountain, a volcano,
Could it erupt at any Moment, with me beside it? No.
Suddenly, I feel the ground start rumbling,
Unbalanced, to the ground I start tumbling.
Opening my eyes, with my back to the Earth and my
face to the sky,
I watch the lava and ashes falling from the Heavens
down towards I.
Jumping up and running carelessly,
Lava splashes the floor endlessly.
Seeing my soon–ending life flash before my eyes,
Thinking how everyone lives and everyone dies.
Realizing that running is useless, I turned around,
I peered into the sky one last time and was astounded.
This is the sight I wish to see before I die,
This is the place, the setting, my body shall lie.

Wobbles
Vivienne Griffiths

Wobbles of flesh stare accusingly,
across buttock and tum,
thigh and knee,
Was it there yesterday?
No, definitely not,
I would surely have noticed
I was going to pot.

In acceptance,
I sigh,
may be all is not lost,
I will try, yet again to calorie cost
each mouthful,
each morsel,
each sweetie and choc,
Until sylphlike and slender
I fit size 10 frocks.

No wobbles of flesh will then dare appear
And I need not wonder just what I can wear.

The Road Map To Heaven
James M. Majors

When you know there is a journey, which you have to make,
And you realize that there is more than one road which you may take.
Even in these modern days with all our things of new,
It seems that one must have a road–map if he is to get through.

The Bible being the Map unto which I refer,
Tells of Heavenly guidance received through words of Prayer.
You may face many intersections, but no tolls will you have to pay;
If you follow the Map's guidance
The straight and narrow way.

If you follow the Map's instructions
Which has been proven beyond a doubt,
You may enter the gates of Heaven,
Where all others shall be cast out.

Though your burdens may seem heavy,
Christ will help you bear the load,
And guide you through to Heaven,
For Jesus Christ built the Road.

Enchanted Dreams

Mother
Mary Pryer

They say your job isn't worth a dime
That, I'll say, is a serious crime
Who was there when I cut my teeth
Crawled around and played with my feet
Picked me up and gave me cuddles
O this world is full of muddles

Without you, Mother, where would we be?
You gave us love and laughter – all free
You taught us all we need to know
Without you, Mother, where would we go?
No one to guide us through ups and downs
No one to share laughter and frowns

A Mother's job is beyond measure
My Mother is my greatest treasure
Don't put her as pounds and pence
That would cause a grave offence
Mother you're worth a million to me
I'll never be able to pay your fee

My Secret Wood
Phil Goldman

There was once a wood where I stand,
Destroyed by man's devouring hand,
Around me now are chimneys high,
And concrete towers reach the sky.
Instead of leaves of elm and oak,
The sky is hidden with industrial smoke.
If I close my eyes and stand quite still,
I can see the wood if I do will,
For the chimneys turn into aged trees,
Nodding their heads in gentle breeze,
I hear the leaves for they make a rustling,
And I see I squirrel busy mustering,
Food for his winter store,
My eyes are closed but I see much more,
I know man's hand can destroy a wood,
But my thoughts I know he never could.

Widowed Pensioner's Thoughts
A. Gibson

Dreaming every night and day
Of times long gone and far away
Upsetting my work – spoiling my play
(I wish you'd never gone away)
Remembering how we'd laughed and cried
Things we'd done – and things we'd tried.
(I need you back by my side)
There were summer days in country Greenery
With scents of freshness and beautiful scenery
And winter nights, though dark and cold,
Were never felt when I had you to hold.
All these things I took for granted
While we were together.
It always seemed that life and love
Would carry on forever.
But soon it will be as it was before
And we'll be together once more
Then memories and dreams
Will all come true
Because I will be back again with you.

Untitled
Keanu Young

Sitting here with thoughts
Set heavy on my mind
Of days and dreams of yesterday
that were somehow lost in time
This life has risen to steal
the childhood smile that I once had
It's taken all my happiness
and turned all good things bad
My eyes now burn with sorrow
With many tears to cry
It hurts to know that more will roll forth
As the days go by
The sun of hope that rose for me each day
Is now at sleep
A once-abundant world of life
Leaves nothing more to reap
A game that's lost can be replayed
When it meets an end
But a life that's lost can never be
revived to live again.

Mush
Derek Weatherill

Its four years now, since you've been gone
And life's the same, goes on and on,
I close my eyes and you're still there,
Drinking tea without a care

There's things that happened in the past
That's in our minds are supposed to last
But day by day are getting dimmer,
But life drags on so who's the winner

There's things I said I wish I never.
Will stay with me now and forever.
This Poem I wrote it in a rush,
Forgive me please, I loved you Mush

Dedication: to Sarah Elizibeth Weatherill

Risk Takers
Anne Bell

Living
is a risk.
Risk–
takers are vulnerable.
They
take chances
because
they do not fear
losing
as much as
they want
the unattainable.
Dying
is
a certainty.
Risk–takers
reach for the prizes,
before
they opt
for the sure thing.

The Anthology of Poems

Beacon
Anastasia Lee
Miles across the ocean blue
I saw you standing
Khaki pants damp
with the ocean's salty spray
Surfer–blond hair
flopping in the summer sun.
You looked up from your place
that moss–colored flint
near the beach
You thought no one could see
your chiseled face smeared
with hurt and regret,
Your cranberry lips moist
with salt-stained tears.
You really are alone
amongst your contrived presence
and stoic perseverance,
but, I saw you standing there.

Dedication: to my sweetie, Jesse Pearlman

Special
Darnela G. Miller
Special, that's who you are
You are gentle and tender
with so much passion within.

Your touch has lit a fire
only you can put out.

Your heat has reached deep
inside me uncovering a passion
I have kept concealed.

But when it is revealed you
will feel covered in such passion
you won't be able to sleep
not until you know what you
have come upon.

Destiny
Gail Arlette Service
I have blindly set sail without the consent of my senses
To an uncertain place
To meet an uncertain fate
You, who assail my heart and mind with the force of a
desert wind.
Pommel me unrelentingly with your smiles and glances
Cunning and alluring man–child. What am I to make of you,
of us?
Your demeanor tells me nothing of what I need to know
Is it a challenge you seek?
For I am as the mountains green
As the ageless sea
With heights unclimbed and depths undiscovered
I have not time to be a young man's fancy
Hear me and believe me
Believe me and hear
No eyes will love you more than mine
To no other heart will you be more dear
I have set sail blindly to meet an uncertain fate
With a most–familiar face.

Watch Out Worry
Biagio Iacofano
Star dancing blues
make me pay heavy dues.
Walking down the silently scary street
what should I meet
but crouching relentless red.

Trying to avoid the dead
of the dreadful world surrounding me.

Shots from afar, up in a tall tree.
Missed by close inches,
send him to the lynches.

Saved by the wacky races
which set unbelievable, uncontrollable paces
through my broken, shattered heart.

Looks like I have to part
the unfortunate unforgiving
in the land, that of the lost living.

Happy Daze
Scott Bain
Slip into a dream, forget the here and now
Forgive my isolation, I prefer to be alone
Surrender to the void, just myself for company
At one with my solitude, exploring my open mind
Floating... drifting on the great ocean of peace
A bouyant voyage seeking the isle of thought
Majestic vessel Maria Joanna mooring at the quay of tranquillity
I disembark and venture onward till I reach the town of idea
A place where all my questions shall be answered
Here there are no problems which I cannot solve
Entering the High Hope saloon and offered a cocktail of infinite wisdom
This is where I belong, a paradise of wine, women and bong
Someone shouts my name and now the image is gone
The spell is broken, my dream world now a distant memory
Like a slap in the face, so I answer my call
Then return to the pipe in search of more happy daze.

Precious One
Norma G. Huggins
Sun shines, it's a gray day,
My love has gone astray.
As I weep, I feel the sheet,
Where my love no longer sleeps.
I cannot rest for where I
Laid my head before upon the
chest of a sweetheart beat.
The room is silent, the air is
still, I feel the burden that
Weakens my will. Wishing I
Knew what fate hath sealed.
Birds sit outside my window,
Chirping love songs, with high–
pitched shrills. But my heart
is heavy, my words are not
clever, come home, "Precious
One". I just want to love
you forever.

Dedication: to Charles B.

Enchanted Dreams

You Are Here
Dawn L. Holdridge
One Christmas I was tucked inside my mind
Only here could you spend the holiday with me.
Venturing out to meet others, what would I find...
Happy people, peace on Earth, good will to men, maybe?
I found none of this without you.
You were Christmas, you were everything to this family.
I chose my memories over Christmas that year.

It's six years later, December 25th is near.
Once again, a loss pains my soul.
I remember that one Christmas.
Yes, despite what I said, memories of that year do exist...
And yes, whatever happens this Christmas will be a memory
tucked away as well.
Despite my pain, I thank Jesus for my gifts...
And wish Him a Happy Birthday.
After all, this is the true meaning of Christmas.
Remembering this, love fills my soul,
Drowning out that pain.
Dad, I feel you here with me.

Blind To Salvation
Mike Elkins
It's all out in the open
It's right there in your face
But sadly you're to blind to see
The lies that you embrace
They tell you bits of truth
In the midst of all those lies
But the God of this Earth age
Has covered up your eyes
You're told that we're the deceivers
With our doctrine of deceit
We only want your money
To continue spreading this disease
But have you ever stopped and asked yourself
Why don't they want me to believe
Am I the one living a lie
Am I the one deceived

My Friend's Final Journey
Linda N. Benson
Today I lost a friend of mine.
Someone I've known a long, long time.
Someone who knew me inside-out,
And was still my friend, without a doubt.
I know my heart should be filled with grief,
But knowing Jesus saved her is a great relief.
She only met him Sunday morn,
But into God's kingdom she was born.
There was a glow upon her face,
To know He had saved her by His grace.
He took her home on Sunday night,
He said "My child, give up the fight.
I'll bring you here on wings of love,
To your Heavenly home here above."
She took His hand and entered in,
Leaving behind this world of sin.
For all who knew her, we'll miss her, it's true,
But someday Kathy, I'll be there with you.
Until then my dear friend, will you do me a favor?
Mention we're friends to our Lord and Saviour!

Snowy Winter
Kelsey Bates
After all the turkey's gone,
The clouds open up and snow.
The windows are dark with frost,
And Mr. Wind can really blow.
Children lace up their skates with pride,
Then they fall and slip and slide.
Zipping and zagging 'round all the bends,
Some sledding hills might never end.
As night falls,
We'll have such a ball,
Making cookies of gingerbread
That turns into men instead.
Icing collar 'round his throat,
Skittle button up his coat,
Hot cocoa warms me up,
As I stir the fire up.

Winter is gone,
Spring is coming,
Time to go out and play!

Layers Of Life
Cheryl S. Thompson
The woman in the mirror is new to me
she is strong, soft, persistent, intelligent
she is not afraid of the dark

she sees the light at the end of the tunnel
knows inherently, or from many dark nights of the soul
that life is built outwardly, while searching inward

many layers of self-delusions, masks and walls of protection
must be peeled away, like the onion skin
difficult and slippery

Life has become an adventure of discovery, layer
after layer, recognition and acceptance
delight and dismay, finally, aware of the wonderment and
endless possibilities

Whispers In The Wind
Theresa L. Miner
The wind whispers my name at times,
when I'm alone
I skim the clear blue waters with
a stone
As I think of life's little ups and
downs.
My mind goes wandering back to the
sound
The rain and the crackling leaves
beneath my feet
And the wind and how it smelled
so sweet
I stroll and watch the birds fly
by
In a dark and gray forbidding
sky
It's black and quiet as I walk
back home
I know why the wind whispers my
name at times, when I am alone

The Working Dog
Patricia Currie

I've got a Border Collie,
He's a very precious pup,
His name is Jet, his sister's Jade,
But I usually call him Flup,
I bought him as a working dog
To herd my stock by day,
And training him was easy,
"Come bye" and "Get away"
Jet's black and white,
And quite a fright if met upon his rounds,
He guards so well and faithful,
That's what our neighbours found!!
I get my "Get aways" mixed round
Along with my "Come byes"
He stops and looks his head one side
As if to take the rise,
He gets fed up with my mistakes
And halfway herding sits,
He looks my way and barks to say
"For God's sake, get a grip."

Red Convertible
Ann Kwinn

The Little Man prepared for flight
in my Daddy's red convertible.
Slow it down. Find the right words:
"Come back Sunday."
Show pain or not – what's the call?
What's the difference?
to his false expression, surrounded by red
somethings in the back.
Drive away but you're still here.

Give it sometime.
His mother died.
Her face was yellow; her chest was still.
Forgive me, the first sight, worse than the second.
I have no children.
Just a vision of the red miscarriage.

If A Heart Were To Break...
Martha Kelly

Does a heart break, crumble, or shatter?
No, I hope that it cannot
It was taught hope and faith
And pumps like it were made of steel.
But if it were shattered,
Does it glue back together
Only to become more fragile than before
Or does a heart tear
And stitch back together
Leaving scars
That ache when the weather is rain?
Maybe a heart just deflates
Losing air like a basketball
That can return itself to the same or better form.
I hope it does not
Because I lost my love
It bruised badly like a fruit
And slowly wilted away
Leaving a hole in my chest
And a shell to pass the time of day.

The Spirit Of Racism
Robert L. Owen

Racism is a Spirit,
of colour supremacy,
colour against colour,
it involves you and me,
whether you're black, white,
yellow or brown,
racism is a spirit,
that knocks us all down.
But if we stand and all unite,
in colour, love and creed,
we can rise against the racism,
it's a spirit we do not need,
because racism is a spirit,
that divides us every day,
and causes the most conflict,
in every possible way.

The Night
Jason Cummins

As the sun starts to set,
The pale moon shows its face.
The stars aren't visible quite yet,
But they're starting to take their place.

The sun's warmth is set aside,
For the evening's cool northern breeze.
Sounds of crickets fill the countryside,
While birds flock to their trees.

As twilight's blanket covers us with night,
Everything seems to calm down.
The moon shines with such Heavenly light,
It appears to be wearing an elegant gown.

The night is very calm and serene,
It's like daytime without any light.
There's nothing scary to be seen,
So there's no reason to be scared of the night.

Brightness Dimming
John A. Coles

Leaf tremor echo notes of choirs
gyration of the broken plume
Earthward levers air its rest
to gain darkening pool of our remorse
the heart that powered bird her wing
to shadow continents on pathway of the sun
and eye that held a sea's dimension
that valiant wheeled gold tracery of dawn
extinguished by the schemes of man
small protestations at the end
trawled brightness dimming in the net
then our legacy black sullen tide
on laboured wave last cloying rest
while ever on guns slash at light
dark hail confines the mottled slotted coat
will our chapter deny for others
sweet shimmer on the breasted down
soft rush of bird imperial gaze
mornings unfolding chorus of elation
and immensity of the modest brave.

Unexplained Pain
Dorothy McClure

"Sweet nothings" in the middle
of the night,
Words spoken as free as a
bird in flight.
Bullet down the barrel of a gun
for nothing done.
Kiss me so softly and, pray,
me don't shun!
Soaked and crimson you are
lying so low,
Over you I walk the way the
wind shall blow.

Eyes open sometimes for your
blindness to see;
Other times they provide the daggers
for your enemy.

Wet Dog
Marty Crisp

P. U. Have you noticed? You smell like wet dog.
Did you walk through a rainstorm? Or get lost in a fog?
Well, it doesn't much matter, wherever you were,
You're drippy and soggy and smell like wet fur.

You could roll on your back and I'd unzip your coat,
And remove, yes, completely, your "Eau de Olde Goat."
Then holding my nose, I'd back up a few paces.
But I wonder what you'd do, if we exchanged places?

You sniff out things well, that to my nose are hid,
Yet you don't seem to mind, when I smell like wet kid.
You don't mind if my breath smells like somebody died.
You still snuggle up close and stay right by my side.

I don't care if your breath is all sour and hot,
Or you smell like wet dog, 'cause I love you a lot.
So bring on that wet fur. Come and stink up my room.
'Cause to my nose, wet dog smells a lot like perfume.

Withered Child
Kara Heiser

Growth, watered, nurtured blooms
radiant wills echoing Earth's sounds
of harmony and substance.

Growth; smothered, stifled places
a poison in a soul that leaks
confusion, rage and isolation.

Schools; depleted, sources withered,
struggle to fight a child's soul
of malnutrition.

Parents still yet children—
continue a pattern of birthing
lost youth.

Sounds of "3rd World" nation?
No, herein plenty of children are screaming
to reach for Earth's harmony.

A Broken Christmas
Christopher F. McLemore

It was a jolly time on the streets of New York.
Kids were flying through stores telling their parents
what they wanted for Christmas. In one toy store, there
was a stuffed animal that every kid wanted; they were
selling like melting ice in a stove. There was only one
of these popular dolls left, but it was missing a leg,
and nobody wanted to buy it.

On that misty, foggy, Christmas Eve, a little boy went
into the store with his Mom to pick out his present for
Christmas. He went straight to the dolls and immediately
picked the one that was missing a leg. His Mom asked,
"Tommy, are you sure you want that one?"

"YES!" replied the little boy. The boy's mother
carefully pulled down the crippled doll and gave it to
her crippled little son

Untitled
Canaeke Dixon

Be strong, black woman
Stand your ground, reclaim your identity.
Succumb to no one's frivolous desires,
speak your mind, call their bluff!
Concentrate on you, Queen of the Nile,
speak to your inner self, there is a Nubian queen
in all of us, black woman,
just speak to her and she will appear!
Regal in stature, secure, confident in who you are.
Strong, rooted in your word, standing tall like the
Georgia oak,
weathering the strongest of storms,
the downgrading winds blowing your way.
Come out, come out, black sista of mine,
come out to play among the lilies of the field,
jubilantly stepping with your other sistas.
Singing in unison, "I am woman, hear me roar",
take your place in this world
and reclaim yourself.

Ethereal Freedom
Naomi Ramieri–Hall

Like a host forgotten at her own party, she became
much too fearful to flounder,
sinking again into silky bayous that could not be drained.

While tactile reassurance is divided with erected interest
onto the Mariah rock,
with its wineskin shoes and domelike hard place
always too intense for the soul to bear;
she wanders into his glazed eyes and remembers a time
when she believed his testament.

"Inside deformities are sometimes clear and vague," she says,
Vague as all immaculate, stiletto souls,
Each gathering alongside the other as if in communication,
all sense of talk ceased to exist
evoking time spent alone.

She quit, knowing all went as planned,
sensing again what began as low shall end no higher.

As Perfect As You
Alyssa Rose Goodhart
Are there enough words
Is there enough time
To even begin to tell you
How much I love you

If I searched through eternity
Would I ever be able to find
Someone as perfect as you

Someone to make
My dreams come true
Someone to hold me and love me
In the gentle, loving way you do

If I searched through eternity
Would I ever be able to find
Someone as perfect as you

A Poet's Heart
M. L. Weng
Twisting in the morning
Churning in the night
Leaves of brown are golden
And daffodils in flight
Words flow from my mind
Tears left on your pillow
Angels by the fire
Two paths I follow

Is this a pretty song, all dressed up to go
Is this a song, a sonnet, with nowhere left to go
No web or den to hide in
No musty cave nor dirty hole
I do not wish to die, but I do not wish to be alone

A poem is just a poem with nowhere left to go
But you can give me a home, a place where I can grow
Daffodils and poems, so pretty and so bright
Daffodils and poems, dead by morning's light

Our Differences
Janis Johnson
Father, help me, please.
Not to judge or condemn
Others that may be different than me
But be a good friend

And not be judgmental
In what they say or do
But have love and patience
And become more like You.

Help me be considerate of others' opinions
And have an open mind
To grow and learn by our differences
And be understanding and kind

You are the creator of all things
And love variety
For You made each and every one of us
Not alike, but differently

Wasted Darts
Belinda B. Koss
It was all I needed
Like a shot in the arm
Wasted darts won't do me any harm.

Put down the bow
Put down the arrow
Just watch the dove
Just watch the sparrow
Wasted darts won't do me any harm.

Born carefree and ambitious
Keeping my ideas and my wishes
Wasted darts won't do me any harm.

Giving way to Heaven's mercies
Bring the bow around for good graces
Still wasted darts won't do me any harm.

Bubble Gum
Alex Garner
Bubble Gum
Bubble Gum
I chewed it for a day.
When I was sick of it, I just threw it away.
It blew no bubbles,
It stuck like paste,
It was awful!
It had no taste.

Bubble Gum
Bubble Gum
I need a new piece, I really do.
For after all I've nothing to chew.
The next time I go,
Off to the store,
I'll have my Mom,
Get me some more.
Bubble Gum
Bubble Gum

Canada
Gina D'Agostino
I am glad I live in Canada.
What a wonderful place to be!
There are interesting things to discover
In this great, multicultural nation, including
The beautiful scenery and wildlife,
Nature and its changing seasons.
There is still much to celebrate
And to be thankful for –
Things such as faith, hope, love and peace,
The opportunity for a better life.
It is rich and colourful –
My new home on Earth.
With so much security,
Quiet times and private spaces.
It is best
To preserve spiritual values and beauty,
To follow the Holy Spirit
For the brightest future together,
United with all Canadians.

Enchanted Dreams

Love Says It All
Tameka L. Pounds
How can we express love in words or songs
That without true love – things seem to go wrong
In this wide world of many strifes
True love is hard to find in this life.

We toil to show our love for others who care
Hoping somehow that love will be there
No matter how long it takes
We wait and wait and wait.

All we have is our true fate
Love is delightful
Love is tender
Love is joy
Love is caring
When everyone is sharing.
Love Says It All.

Black Woman
Stephen A. Jones
Peace: To a mother who's been up the hill and didn't fall,
Been on top of the world
and seen it all,
Took a beating
and still stood tall

Love: To a sister who stood by her brother
and didn't lie,
Watched her future taken away
and couldn't cry,
Saw her Father leave
and wouldn't sigh

Rest: To a leader who's been through the valley
and knows the way,
Taught the children
and made them obey,
Fought the battle
and seized the day.

Boy Of The Rain Forest
Laurence Bennett
Dark skin, scorched–blonde hair,
Deep psychosis, strangers beware!
Malnutrition has turned my hair white,
At just eleven years old, I've learned
How to fight.
The scars of a machete are evident on my face,
Where laughter and smiles lived, the tears
Have replaced.
I'm a child of the rainforest, the loggers
Tell us they're our friend, my game is making
Spearheads, a game with no pretend.
Superstition is my ally and the spirits
Speak so clear, I learn from the animals,
I run when danger draws near.
When I sleep at night, I dream of my forefathers
(My spirits who show the way) I dream of us
Together, just living for the day.

Dedication: to little Georgie and beautiful Tracey

Rascal
Beverly Tietz
Rascal is his name
Trouble is the game.

He watches the cat
And says I can do that.

A dog he is supposed to be
But look, he's climbing the tree.

He's outside to be on guard
But he's escaping from the yard.

There he goes down the street
Running fast with those little feet.

If you see a brown dog with a goatee
You will know he belongs to me

Alone On A Tormented Path
Kristy Herrmann
Silently, I sit here
As the tears start to roll
Why they fall so swiftly
I really do not know

The road before me runs
In a very crooked path
And I sit here pondering
How long will my life last?

Cluttered is my mind
Confused is my heart
I know not what I seek for
I know not what I sought

This twisted passage I do follow
Knowing not where it leads
I am consumed by my sorrow
I live inside my dreams

Traces In Time
Mark Feargrieve
The leaves,
That blew over,
Their, traces in time.
With the belief,
Of, all races,
Which, could have been mine.
I can, draw the picture,
But, where do I draw the line.

She leaves,
That, blew over,
Their, traces in time.
With the belief,
Of, all places,
Which, could have been mine.
I can, paint the picture,
But, where do I picture the time.

Dedication: to Elizabeth, the Original Dumb Blonde

Daisy Duck
Lori L. Swanger
Daisy waddles drowsily

Early morning bright,

Washes Mr. Sandman

That visits late each night.

Sets a hearty breakfast

Quacks for her prayers,

Flops on her hat, pecks up her purse,

She's off to the fair.

Dedication: to husband Al and son Brett

A Land Flowing With Milk And Honey
E. McKeown
Ladies and gentlemen
I address this great nation
Think of your brother
And send a donation

I'll be ever-grateful
And turn from being hateful
And bless this great nation
From the depths of my heart

Think of your creator
And don't be a dictator
Learn to respect
Every child in the land

Created in love
Every child it was fashioned
Respect your children
Or your food could be rationed

Romantic Thief
Hereward L. M. Proops
A Sweeter smile I have not seen,
And eyes as deep as green-blue sea.
So warm, so tender, so true to fashion,
A character born for Summer passion.

The waves crash on the sand beach,
Your heart and mine are within reach.
I turn to you, lust is your power,
Our lips soon touch and my heart you devour.

The night soon grows short and gives way to the dawn.
My heart has been taken, my mind starts to mourn.
I look at you and my soul takes flight,
Have you no recollection what happened last night?

I'll tell you what happened, you romantic thief,
You took flight with my heart and left me with grief.
In front of me lies Winter, misery and gloom.
Behind me lies Summer and you in full bloom.

Selfishness
Cindy Leavitt
In every move I make
Selfishness is involved
Wherever I go it follows
I want to put God first
"But what about ME, " I bellows
It's like gum being stuck to your shoe
You try to pull it off and it just gets messier
I is everywhere. You try to remove I and I gets fussier
I want to be noticed
I want to receive some glamour
But where does this get you?
Just deeper in clamor
When HE takes the place of I you will be set free to fly
I is restricted to such a tiny box
He is as free as the universe
He wants to share that freedom with you
But, I... well, he has to say he's through

Pinned
Laura Elmer
As I watch,
The wind moves golden hair about his face,
And stirs brocade upon his shirt.
For the merest instant we almost connect,
Eye to eye and soul to soul.
And then, rapier held high aloft,
He charges into the waiting battle,
A screaming angel in silk and steel.
He is hit!
He falters, falls and bluest eyes flow with pain.
I long to hold him, to soothe his hurts,
To touch silken skin and taste sweet lips,
Slowly, I reach out to envelop him
With aching fingertips......
But, all I hold is my ticket stub,
For although we are both pinned to the screen,
He is far from me,
Who sits dreaming,
On the wrong side of it.

What Is A Poem?
Patricia Guy
A poem from me is what you ask,
But what does a poem mean to me?

Should it be mere lines with nothing to say,
And include empty thoughts of the day?

Should it be correct in all its grammar,
And void of any wild slang?

Should it restrict all lines to conformative rhyme,
And be perfect in every way?

Should it map a life of rosy existence,
Without any human discontent?———or

Should such poem be a patchwork of these,
So that my poem will simply be — me!!

Dedication: to Versella and Gordon, my parents

Enchanted Dreams

The Love Of Life
Sharon Grayston
I'm going to die very soon.
But I don't want to die
I can't stop crying now.
I'll stop when I die.
Who will miss me when I'm gone.
Who will kiss me when I'm gone,
No more tender touches from my husband, no
Or kisses from my mother so.
No more laughter or sorrow, no, not anymore.
The Lord is to take me and close the door.
Is there a Heaven out there or is there a hell.
Not sure, but soon I will be able to tell.
They say, the Lord loves all His children,
So why take me so young.
Each day I ask myself, what have I done?
If I can get back, which I will really try.
Because as I have said before, I don't want to die.

Freedom Is A River
Dian Henson
In the Spring of Freedom's light
A gentle, trickling stream.
Builds its strength from tension,
Cascading into dreams.

Freedom changes as it grows,
Flowing pure and bold.
Pressing over stagnant banks
That ancient dikes won't hold.

Freedom is a river of need,
Swelling like a flood.
Raging through the veins of time,
Bubbling forth life's blood.

All man's goals are freedom—bound,
Floating on the tides.
Where the sea meets river's end,
Is where our freedom rides.

Insanity
Chris Lafferty
Close your eyes, my child
Look inside yourself
See insanity firsthand

Dig deep in your mind
Imagine the worst pain, anguish and fear
You possibly can

And see the demon
That is your soul
Now talk to him for awhile

Dig deeper in your mind
You will hear voices
Fear not, for they are your friends
Listen to what they say

Now sleep, my innocent one
And may dreams accompany your slumber

Heaven
Lisa M. Stanta
I am listening to the
whisper of the ceiling fan

As a feather tickles
my tender tummy

Now my nose smells
sweet succulent love
spices

I taste spicy hot strawberry
fruit roll ups

I see a beautiful bright
light

Is this Heaven?

For The Two
Kimberly Edgemon
The little lights above
and the velvety touch below
enticed two lonely strangers
To find comfort in each other's arms

The moonlight wind complemented
the mysterious sea
Pretending to be somewhere far
for the two who sit on the shore

The midnight sky brightens its eyes
and the sand softens its touch
The sea air mists them gently
Who? The two over there

The moon shines its joyous face
upon the visitors –
He protects by the light
He emits – for only the two there

Windows To The Soul
Betty VanDerHeyden
weapons of destruction,
methods of instruction –
cruel and black as coal,
windows to the soul.

no secret can be kept
when you gaze into the depth
of the countless facts inside –
told through eyes that cannot hide.

windows to the soul,
no secret left untold–
to cry is to concede
the truths they cannot see.

the heart's voice speaks from behind
the infinite chasms of my mind –
lies told to distract my sense,
my head is now a labyrinth.

Untitled
Maria Elena Lobianco

Empty touches, for I know tonight it will
be her body you touch with future promises.
Distant stares, for I know tonight you
will be looking at her – hopefully thinking of me.
Shallow kisses, for I know it's her body you
will be caressing tonight with your tongue.
Lonely hugs, for I know tonight you
will be holding her and whispering, "I love you."
False promises, for it's with her that
you said, "I do."

Tonight and every night emptiness finds
me – caresses escape me and your kisses
leave me dry.

For I know it's with her you will
spend forever.

The Harvest
Melba L. Paul

The farmer stood with hand to his brow
And watched the set of the sun;
Bone—weary and tired from toils of the day,
He was thankful the tasks were finally done.

Contentment glowed upon his face
As o'er his labors he cast an eye;
He knew that all would surely be well
And life in no way had passed him by.

He knew the fruit would later come
For today he had planted the seed,
Which nourished with tender love and care
Would bring a bountiful harvest indeed.

The farmer had discovered a secret
That many people have never found;
In order to reap a harvest,
The seed must fall into fertile ground.

Untitled
Samantha M. Belk

Your pity is no longer breeding through the
depths of my living hell.
So much love, so little time to confess all
you can remember.
Dark, pitiful lies, can never escape a gutted mind.
Dream of a place to live in warm, soft,
velvet beauty.
So senseless the bitter coldness which
consumes.
Tortured, what a waste of my commitment
to solitude. Arise to the voyage of unvoiced
bliss.
Amidst the hollow coldness which envelopes me.
Such scorn to cherish only the dream of
escape.
Thorns grow around my heart and
Spread into my thighs of regret.
Pitiful to think, my life is on the brink.
What sadness, escape is a true virtue.

A Poem For Kitty
Kelly K. Moreau

Such a good kitty, so loyal and true,
Couldn't be better if she were Red White and Blue.
Angel's her name, with such a sweet face,
Just like a baby with ribbons and lace.
Running and playing isn't what it's about,
Snuggling and purring is life... no doubt.
She sleeps and cuddles and keeps your lap warm,
A friend forever to lay on your arm.

Dreaming of mice and rabbits are rare,
Only of hands that will smooth down her hair.
A blink of her eyes will tell you she's happy,
A soft "Meow" to remind you that it's a pity...
To have to wake up from this dream, of cuddles and hugs,
Reminding you again, she wants another rub.
So purr, purr, purr, little Angel so true,
God gave you wings when he brought me to you.

The prize
Richard French

A life so empty and void, how can one love,
They say love can touch even the coldest of hearts,
But first it must be let in to touch the soul,
There are battles that must be fought with oneself,
Battles that most will lose,
Battles, if won, will bring the ultimate prize
The prize of love
For when a child is born, their fate is unknown,
One can only pray they will grow in their life,
They will face many trials and tribulations
But the hardest battle to fight is the one,
Where they must reach down into their souls,
And learn to feel without touch,
Learn to see without sight,
Learn to respond without hearing
For these qualities a person must know,
Before they can gain the prize of love

Dedication: to my prize, Angila Grenier

Aunt Mae
Mary A. Laird

One day, as I was growing up,
I just happened to meet
An Angel sent from up above
With a voice so soft and sweet.

The LORD gave to my Mom, Dad and Me
A very special ROSE,
That only with her special touch
This lovely ROSE does grow.

My Aunt Mae is a pretty woman,
Her sparkle is here to stay,
It makes us sad and blue each day
Because she is so far away.

One Journey I know that she will take
But only GOD knows when
This lovely Angel that HE lent to us
Will be taken home again.

Enchanted Dreams

Walking Down The Lonely Road
Raymond John Price
As I walk down this lonely road
My thoughts turn to a road I once walked
This road I once walked was a road of despair
Each cure brought a new and lonely experience
I remember the time I was cold and hungry
No place to go but down the lonely road
The time I was ill and no one to turn to
Just as I was going to give up on, everything
and everyone, a voice from far above I heard
do not despair my child, for I love you
At that Moment I felt a peace in my heart
For it was my Lord talking to me in my despair
The road I now walk is a road of righteousness
May all the glory be to my Lord, for bringing
from this lonely road

Dedication: to Noreen Foster

Black Wind
Matthew Graybosch
Bend to the Wind, if you would not break
No sense hiding as the black wind blows
All our lives exist for God to take
Are you next, Madam, I do not know

Flames of Hell on wings of destiny
Why do we stand when others fall?
Bother not to cry for mercy
Songs of Angels drown out mankind's call

Careening through life, a human tumbleweed
Any port in a storm, we've nothing to lose
Rush blindly forward to fulfill a need
We are beggars and we dare not choose

Will you stand or fall when Fate's black wind blows?
Madam, do not ask me what only God can know.

Dedication: to Mom, she who understands..

Soul Searching
Penny Jeffrey
I know not what I seek to find?
This dream I cling to holds the key
Yet I am lost within my soul
Oh, won't this life please set me free!
Time is my prison, my cross to bear
From this I know I cannot hide
Only the truth can guide my way
To where I feel deep down inside

Belief will keep this dream alive
Our lonely hearts will beat once more
Your love will make the pain subside
Then my troubled soul will start to soar

Please let my vision touch your life
My true love, only then can we
Transcend the realms of space and time
Leaving a discarded reality
And my search will end – for you will be ME

Urgent
Dave Ehlert
Urgent is a simple word
Get on with it, please
Now!
Run with it, play with it
Let it loose
Make it work somehow
Mail it, phone it
Tell it to someone
Urgent is a way of life
It never stops
Or takes a break
Please move
Hurry up!
I'm loosing valuable time
Urgent can be a friend
Or foe
Or a nightmare in someone's mind.

By Common Bond
JoAnn Jess
By the common bond of experience born,
We find ourselves closer than those sisters born.
By the pain in our hearts we know each other,
And cling to each other, the hurt to smother.

We need each other and we need to talk,
To someone else who has walked the walk.
Someone, somewhere, we know we can trust,
Lest with our tears, our hearts turn to rust.

Before we die, dear Lord, we pray,
Let us find some common bond today.
That common bond that helps us back,
From the brink of despair and nights so black.

There is daylight to find on the other side,
If we find that bond held so deep inside.
Strength from each other we can wrest,
And at last find comfort, peace and rest.

You're The Man I've Been Looking For
Renee Wolfensburger
When we first met, we become friends. As
time prolonged, we came to be one, you understand me
and love me for me, not because of my looks,
body or material things. We often laughed, cried, joked
and sighed, you're the only one I trust, you're my best friend.
I love the way you tell me you love me and hold
me near. When you kiss me, you send shivers down my
spine; your embrace is so warm and sweet, I just
can't speak. You tell me encouraging words so I
can make it in this world. You're the man
I've been looking for. You're everything I've
ever hoped for. I hope it's the same for you.
I share with you my hopes and dreams.
One day we'll be a team. We'll conquer the
world's hardest obstacles. Together, forever,
that's how it'll be, because you're the man
I've been looking for.

Dedication: to John Wikon – love, Renee

The Anthology of Poems

Inner Silence
L. Elaine Potter
Life's hustle and bustle can teach...
Take time to observe.

Silence alone can teach...
Take time to listen.

Walls of fear are gone...
No restraints, no distortions.

All is clear, all is distinct...
Let it flow, let it heal.

Be not afraid, turn not away...
Stay, be quiet.

Look, listen and feel the intensity...
The rocks may even speak.

Destiny
Lorraine Kolesar
I believe in fate
I know with all my heart
If something is meant to be
It will be destined from the start

A fleeting touch of hands
Meeting of our eyes
Tells me you are there for me
When the day's sunlight dies

Across the eons of time
Our minds will come together
United we can face the test
Of life's stormy weather

No matter how I try
To erase you from my mind
You will be there like a song
For me to gently find

If Only...
John Dimailig
Sometimes I stay up late,
On nights I need the sleep
And think of how life would be better
If only I weren't me.

If only I were popular
And had a better look;
If only I went out more
And kept away from books.

Then someone would fall for me
And I would need no longer chase;
Because it seems like I'm the least wanted
Of the entire human race.

But I know that is false,
Because I know that there will be
At least one of the human race
Who would fall in love with me.

Won't You Listen?
Sandra K. Gehrke
God's reaching down His hand to me,
Saying, "Won't you listen? I've set you free."
He does not leave, He does not stray.
He stays with me throughout the day.
He wants to get His message through,
In cloudy skies or skies of blue.
It doesn't matter much to Him,
As long as light from Him shines in.
I open up my heart to God and listen for His voice.
And now it doesn't seem so odd, I really have no choice.
If God does want to work through me, I will then hear His voice.
The freedom He has given me
Was bought by Christ upon a tree.
His love for me so strong and true
Is forever shining through.
God's reaching down His hand to me
Saying, "Won't you listen? I've set you free."

Civil War
Constance Graziano
America wouldn't be losing
her war on drugs,
If more effort were made
to stop dealers and thugs.
Methamphetamines, angel dust, or crack –
Drug dealers abound
can always get a dime.
Rheumatoid arthritis, AIDS, or injured back –
Taking pain medication
is treated like a crime.
The physician's license is threatened –
While cancer patients suffer
and little children cry.
Gangs and machine guns rule the street –
While teens skip school,
get high, steal and die.
Tax money is spent to keep patients in pain –
As we lose the war on drugs,
What a shame.

Day Dream
John Courteau
Crystal delight on my mind tonight, I'll see you in my daydreams.
Green fields where I lay and wait, the flowers fill my daydreams.

All the colors that dance in the sun, just can't compare to a rainbow like you.

Soft, white clouds dance within my thoughts, I'll hold you in my daydreams.
A gentle breeze blows my hair out of place and brings the warmth to my soul.

All the time that drags on and on reminds me of days I've left behind.

Crystal delight on my mind tonight I'm reminded of a daydream.
Green fields where I used to play are now forgotten memories.

Every time I sit among the trees, your voice wears through the stillness of a dream.

Enchanted Dreams

In My Heart
Karen Bennett
You're my rainbow on a cloudy day
My cool breeze in the sun
My full moon on a starry night
When my working day is done.

Though we aren't always together
We spend so much time away
The way I feel about you, baby
I've just got to say...

Know wherever you go...
I'll be waiting here for you when you get back home
Know wherever you are...
my love for you shines brighter than the brightest star
And my love's never–ending
Through the time that we're spending... apart
I always hold you close in my heart

Do Not Give
Lisa A. Kehres
Do not give me flowers
for they always die anyway
but rather let me view their beauty
in the ground where they should stay.

Do not give me candy
packaged in some fancy case,
for my sweet tooth doesn't need it
if I am to look good all in lace.

Do not give me a card
with words written from another's heart,
but whisper to me softly
and tell me we will never part.

If it is a gift you wish to give me
just look deep inside of you,
for all I ever wanted
is for you to love me like you do.

Spring Fever
Elaine Denney
The budding of the trees and flowers
Let's us know spring's on the way
The warm breeze blowing o'er the meadows
Brings the hope of a bright new day.

The dread of all the snow is gone
The winter days forgotten
As we look forward to new life
And the first chirp of a robin.

Funny how soon we forget
The bleak days of winter
All it takes is a little sun
And nature in all its splendor.

Life's like a vapor in the air
It's there, then whisked away
So enjoy all you can
Tomorrow's another day.

The Unicorn's Beauty
Steve Gillespie
Last night when the sky was black,
sometime after midnight, the stars began to shine.
As they sparkled brighter, I awoke.
In the distance, I could see a rainbow.
Its enchanting glow illuminating a castle,
and I could see roses sparkling
From the brilliant colours of the rainbow.
And the beauty, was overpowering.

I moved closer to the castle,
and then I could see the silhouette
of a princess in an upper window.
And as the rainbow's glow grew stronger,
a unicorn was seen standing amidst wild roses
as the princess opened her eyes.
I saw a teardrop sparkling within her eyes.
And the beauty I saw, was overpowering.

Memories
Marjorie R. Hathaway
Gazing out the window...
Many memories seemed to flow;
Of parents I loved so very much,
Who gave me their love, support and such.

They taught many things about life I should know,
Guiding my footsteps in paths, helping me grow.
Living life to its fullness each day at a time;
Enjoying blue skies, smelling flowers, catching sunshine.

In knowledge and rule they planted the seed
To live a good life and eventually succeed.
Find love, raise a family the same way to live,
Teaching them the love and guidance they did give.

I have found that love, married, raised a family;
They have given the title of "grandma" to me.
And I prayerfully hope they pass these memories on,
To future generations after I am gone.

Blob's Of Fluff
Florence N. Troll
Eyes feasting on the water
Swans in beauty grace the scene
Picture–perfect calm and peaceful
sail affront the forest green.

Cob and Pen mate eternal
await hatching of their brood –
oval nest prepared and ready
crafted neatly – never crude.

Cygnets known as Blob's of Fluff
fulfill their Mates' desire –
safely born, it's time to learn
what living must require.

Parental tutoring instilled
the Blob's of Fluff are free
to mate and hatch another brood –
perfect picture – Serenity.

To My Mum
Maria Retter

You may have died and gone
away,
Your love is still here when
we need it most.

When I am alone I sit and
cry and ask myself why you
had to die.

There's no reason why
your time had come for
you to go, but I know
you still love us so.

Mum, you may be far away
but we still love you more
than words can say.

Spilled Words
Colin Leigh Griffin

Sometimes I say words with no meaning,
But you see, they mean so much to me.
Understanding... so much I'm finding,
That knowing, just sets me free.

Words just spill to this paper,
But first they form in my mind.
Like water evaporating to vapor,
With life that you cannot find.

As my hand shakes to write this,
And my eyes study blind.
My heart, deadly clenches bliss,
While my brain, hollowly signed.

This life, made for all of you,
But yet you turn away.
So before my life is through,
Your price, you'll have to pay.

Shoo, Fly, Shoo
Brian Levens

"Some Big Ol' Man is gonna come, so shoo, fly, shoo!
And when he come ya be undone, so shoo, fly, shoo!"
"But how ya 'spects I buzz and run ya 'nan–ny–poo',
'Cause there ain't no door to buzz on through– I'll buzz into!"

"Ya stupid fly just beat ya wings and shoo, fly, shoo!
I'll crack the door to, freedom's yours – NOW, SHOO, FLY, SHOO!"
"POO takes the fan and fans fly to the door SHOO knew,
And SHOO did flew through door POO knew–to FREEDOM–SHOOED!"

When SHOO did flew to POO one day– HIS "nan–ny–poo",
SHOO buzzed his friend, "I thank ya sir!" in "buzzin–boo";
His friend did hear the saddest tale from SHOO, FLY, SHOO:
How Big Ol' Man did crunch the life from SHOO's wife SUE.

And so the tale of SHOO, FLY, SHOO does end quite blue;
But SHOO's young sons did show true love to NAN–NY–POO!
When NAN–NY–POO got crunched one day he Heaven flew –
Was met by all his former friends and shoo-flies, too!

Chasing Butterflies
Margret Holder

Running like the wind
Running through the fields
A feeling of carefree
A motion of no responsibilities
Laughing
No worries
Happiness
The pressures of life absent
for a while
Seeing brilliant greens and blues
Breathing in the freshness
Every flower a different color
Visions of pure beauty
Feeling energetic
Feeling childlike
Innocence
Chasing butterflies.

Two–Timer
Gwendolyn Johnson

That girl over there is getting hip to your plan
You're undermining her and trying to steal her man
She cried a lot of tears about how you used to do
You told her on the phone, "I'll take your man away from you"
So, "shh," be quiet, you're talking too much
You'll never get him, so you might as well hush
You and her man used to sneak around town
After all the bars, you were hotel–bound
Everybody else knows but still you can't see
That man of hers no longer wants to be free
So, "shh," be quiet, you're talking too much
You're like a sinful soul criticizing the Church
So, "shh," be quiet, you're talking too fast
You'll learn the same lesson that I learned in the past
Why don't you go out and find a man of your own
Instead of causing problems in a happy home
So, "shh," be quiet, you're talking too much.

Dedication: to Kathy Stockman, Marvin and Daryl

The Battle Of The Heart And Mind
Ashley R. Epps

Even though, my mind wants to do what is right,
And tries and tries with all its might,
It cannot reach its full height,

So I do what is wrong and bad,
This makes my parents very sad.

But, most important, God gets hurt,
And when I think of this I feel like a squirt.

After Caption:

If you know what you're doing and you know that it's wrong,
You will soon be singing a different song.
So listen closely to what I say,
Because if you don't you'll, someday, pay.

Do what God tells you,
'Cause only He can kill what ails you.

Enchanted Dreams

Riches
Linda Brand
Blood red garnets (are they apples?)
Dangling on a tree.
Polished copper shafts of carrots
Pulled on bended knee.
Amethyst grapes with silver frosting
Dripping from the vine.
Richly ruby–red tomatoes –
Is this wealth all mine?
Emerald peppers, golden pumpkins,
All for me to gather.
Pick them, mound them,
Bring them in!
There's nothing else I'd rather!
Opal–centered heads of cabbage,
Topaz–beaded corn,
Wheel–barrow loads of treasure
Gathered in the morn.

Secrets
Tom Ziolkowski
In sun–drenched daydreams
together we walk
down a road of which there is no end.

In the darkness of night
we gaze upon a star,
and are mesmerized by the sparkles
that we see afar.

For you, my love,
I would slay the wicked dragons,
who haunt you in your wake and sleep.
Cutting from their breast their evil hearts
with a sword from the scabbard of my steed.

You are My Lady and I your Knight,
and oh, how perfect it all could be.
If we could Love and embrace in the reality of life,
than rather through the mist of our dreams.

My Friend...
Dorothy Doore Cole
Please, Just stand there,
Let the light flicker across your handsome face.
In my dreams, I've seen you everywhere,
There's no one who can take your place.

As you walk through my door,
I begin to come alive again,
I could never love you more,
As you are my very best friend.

You are in the stars at night.
You make my sun shine all day long,
You are the one who makes my life so bright,
When you're near, I know things cannot go wrong.

I've never seen the stars so bright,
Those beautiful clouds were never there,
Until you came along and made things right,
Now, I see beauty everywhere.

The Final Frontier
John Seaton
Look upon the stars that shine
Each has a place in space and time
As I have mine.
Ten–thousand–million years of time
Have stars that shine
And each has space in which to nurse
Its own massive, private universe.
Space and time are concepts relative
To those who stand and stare
Who measure, gasp and wonder
At the immensity of – out there.
But three–score years and ten
Are insignificant when
Compared to timeless space.
The much–vaunted human race
Is miniscule, yet audacious
To ascertain what time and space is...

Words
Ezio D. Leite
Come, let's play with words
It's a fun sort of thing I say.
They don't bruise or cut like swords
But, I guess if you want, they may.

The power of words is in the meaning
And whatever it is they convey
So whichever direction they are leaning
Just be certain they are going the right way.

With words you can build up an empire
Or destroy a whole civilization.
What I want is to light up your fire
And with words shake up a nation.

Rough words will start up a war
But gently they may bring in peace
So whatever you say does go far
At the right time speak out your piece.

Pandora And Her Box Of Life
Georgia A. Vickery
I gaze out across this abyss of Hell I call my life,
And I look down into the pit of despair,
And I wonder, is this all there is?
Is there no one out there who knows how to care?

And all around me come the sounds of silence,
Steadily crashing into my ears,
I want to run in panic and hide,
My soul struggles to give in to my fears.

Amazingly, out of the darkness glimmers a small light.
As a solitary being moves through the mist,
Is it my wild imaginings? Do I dare to believe?
This spectacle could now witness a vital twist!

It seems a small thing that changes this mortality
That I call me and maybe it will help me cope,
Yes, the smidgen of light and breath that blows through,
Is a tiny, large thing called HOPE!

The Anthology of Poems

Zombie
Crystal Aldridge
Imposed, but acquainted
The thought lies lifelessly
In my mind
Blank stares are all I give,
And receive nothing but sympathy.
Unwanted sympathy
I have no need for it.
I appear in this world
Physically.
Mentally, I am gone.
Conversation only exists between
Me, myself and I.
My focus maybe toward the wall,
But my vision is clear.
I see more than you'll ever know.
I am lifeless,
But so full of life.

Tobi
Kimberly Kanney
My heart is empty
I cannot speak,
My chin quivers
My legs are weak.

My warm tears
Are rolling down,
I cannot vanish
My gloomy frown.

No one understands
The pain inside,
The fear, the love
That I kept inside.

But now it's time
For happiness to extend,
Because there's nothing worse
Than losing a friend.

Patience
Rozella S. Michael
I waited patiently for God to lift me out of the pit of despair, He set my feet on the right path and gave me a new song to sing, a new prayer to pray.

He has done for me what none other could do. I have learned to trust Him more and more. He didn't give me silver nor gold, but He made me rich in more ways than one, because He heard and answered my prayer and He understands me, that is why I patiently wait on Him. "I've learned to trust Him, because I know God is able."

I've learned the secret of contentment, in every situation. I know how to live on almost nothing or with everything! That's why I go to Him in prayer and Him only.

That's why I wait patiently on Him, because He understands everything I do and say and He loves me anyway. He sent His son Jesus Christ to die for me. I will wait patiently for Him!

Precious Time
Janet K. Justice
Please take the time to understand
and even more time to enjoy.
Before you know it,
they'll all be gone.
It goes too fast, you see,
Much too fast, way too fast and
Then they are off making plans —
wedding bells and future dreams.
They just don't understand.

It takes a generation of the sand,
through the hourglass, you see,
Before your heart is filled so full,
That is when it starts to ache and
then you start to wish —
Why didn't I just understand and
take the precious time we had back then?

Togetherness
Peggy Leaver
Worlds within Our World,
Touching briefly, the diversity
Of Laws and Culture, the hold
On Life, exciting our curiosity.

Dreams of Possession, of Power,
Of other worlds moving,
Within one's own sphere,
Of Creation unending.

Of Love and Understanding,
Of Toleration, of sharing
Beliefs, questioning, marveling
And finally, accepting.

The Unseen Hand of Destiny,
Shaping our lives,
Worlds gradually uniting,
Till all Life thrives.

Woman
Don Ringgold
Of woman there is Life
She knows the Heavens with no thought
And moves with an intrinsic mode that
Maintains the flow of the wine of Life And she, Mother Earth's daughter
The beloved, the beautiful, Knows that she Knows For her world is a
   circular World
One of inner worth and needs no time to fumble with thoughts, words, Deeds
Etcetera, etcetera or the like, For she knows, They all know, Venus Or
Aphrodite, Nefertiti, The mothers, daughters and sisters of eternity know
For she is Love to an infinite degree, She is this, she is that Netae Netae

The sun will rise at five or at dawn,
New generations come up from the lawn
Now see the bright and glorious morning

For she truly knows the sun, She will adorn a rose with her touch
And the rose will reciprocate in the way it knows best, Oh, yes,
The rose Knows, It reveals The Life
Of Woman, there is Life, She Knows, She Knows

Enchanted Dreams

Inner Soul
Kathi Armgard
there's an inner soul,
that soothes a troubled spirit
that allows the sun to break thru
the darkest clouds
to warm the coldest hearts

it seeks the good in all,
when the world
tries to convince us
that all is bad

it believes in love
and all the colors that bloom
in its glow.
And it survives
even in the darkness,
the bleakest of times.

A Letter To My Mother
Rosemarie Shields
When I think of the things we could have done,
I wish I had somewhere to run.
It's so hard to cope with life, I've even had thoughts of using a knife.
Life for me is getting harder; I thank God for leaving me a father.
Ma, if you could see him now, he's getting older but still stays young somehow.
Now the family is getting older, Ronnie's a giant;
you should see his shoulders.
Erick is tall and awful thin, he's forever playing basketball,
trying to win.
Terry's found a great man named Joe, she's finally happy,
believe me, it shows.
Donna gave everyone a big surprise, she came home one day
with tears in her eyes.
Ma, she's going to have a baby, from now on Dad will be going crazy.
Me, myself, as you may know, I miss you more as each day goes.
I feel better letting you know you're missed by one and all!

Dedication: to my beloved mother, Diane Shields

Life
Nila Patel
You're the source of all sorrow
and the source of all joy.
You're the optimist's tomorrow
And the pessimist's ploy.

You're the painter's obsession
and the claymaker's doll.
You're no one's possession,
yet you belong to us all.

You're a dangerous storm.
You're a darkling deed.
You're the prettiest flower
and the ugliest weed.

You're the wing that never flies.
You're a song that's never sung.
You're the hope that never dies
and the war that's never won.

The Timeless Peace
Kristie Gould
It is such a peaceful place
It is a place where the living go to find peace in their lives
And to find solitude in death
It is a place where the dead lay in a forever state of peace
There are so many
They lie like shells on time—washed sand
So many shells
So many people to be forgotten forever
We walk upon them
We cry upon them
Yet they feel nothing and hear nothing
They just lie there in forever peace
As we stand around not knowing or understanding why it is that they lie so peacefully
With no breath escaping their lips
But their peace is heard forever
In the timeless cycle of life

A Life
Leah Hoffpauir
A baby is born,
On the evil night.

A child is forlorn,
It's a horrid sight.

A dress is worn,
In the pale moonlight.

A heart is scorn,
Despite its owners might.

A soul is torn,
From a terrible fright.

Someone is morn,
On this evil night.

Dedication: to my dearest Matt

It's a Sad Day
Pamella Sherman
The sky is ugly – dark
The rain is falling –
People look sad
Running for shelter –
Darkness creeping around us.
The day that was once so beautiful
has now become morose.

It's a sad day
As sad as when you loved someone
It was so beautiful till that love died.
Then it's like today –

Beautiful in the morning
and in the evening –
sour – ugly
That is what happened to our love – my love.

Dedication: to my daughter, Guenet Richards

Reflection
Helena Morgan

She stands awkwardly, examining her curves,
Wind whispers, flitting through the leaves,
Eyes surround her, circling with fear.
Cool air rushes, pressing firmly against her tiny frame,
Carefully caressing,
Hurling confusion beneath the looming trees.
Honesty curtsies, facing disrespect,
Trembling uncontrollably,
Love fades, suffocating in affection,
Cruelty cackles,
Hatred skims the breeze, assassinating kindness,
Doing as he pleases.
Her reflection shimmers upon the glossy lake,
Dark shadows cast their evil dread,
Her tortured, twisted limbs, shiver and shake,
Bleeding, she lunges forward,
Was this forever? or a lucky escape?

Sunrise
Melissa Gill

As a cool wind sweeps the rolling hill
A daisy stirs in the new morning still.
The sun's not up, the dew's still hung,
On blades of grass, sweet succession is sung.

Faint moon shadows dance on darkness still had
The sun's not up, the hills are still clad.
A ripple or two on a nearby lake,
Is the only sound that nature can make.

The color's still dark,
Yet gentle, not stark.
The song of a bird
Is the night's final word.

In a flicker of lightness,
And a flash of brightness,
The meadow awakens to a natural prize;
A wonderfully picturesque sunrise.

Because of You
Marlina Reilly

Beginning...
There is just one
—Alone and afraid
fighting in solitude
struggling to survive
THEN
like gloriously—winged angels
you arrive
NOT gaudy or audacious
but wondrous and
magnificent
Beautiful and terrific
Miraculous and perfect
And then one is two
and there is strength to survive
and courage to face the world
NOT alone—Never alone again
Forever...
All because of you

There Is A Silence...
Susan M. North

There is a silence that speaks all tongues,
It knows all language, past and present,
Has easy parlance in Arabic and Portuguese,
Fluent in English, French and Russian,
Travels smoothly in words of German,
Swahili, Spanish and Hebrew.
Knows languages long dead
Conversing well in Latin and Ancient Greek,
But does not stop its journey there
For techno–speak was easy next to Japanese
And binary numbers, equations scientific
All prepared it for the internet,
The language of the nineties!
This silent language is unique to man
But common to all men:
The eye of agony within the hurricane
The silence of the scream.

My Beautiful Red
Lisa Baldwin

My Beautiful Red –
Sweet and warm,
Lovely and holy –
Come release me,
Bring me to life again.
Make me feel,
Make me cry
And scream as only
The broken ones can.

My Beautiful Red –
Glisten snake–ish
In the dim light –
Breathe into me,
Awaken the spirit.
Arouse the soul,
Soar to the brain
Of this wretched body.
Bring me to life again.

Goodbye
Colleen McGlinsey

Life seemed so sweet
but then death comes
Seems so easy to just
leave.
But think of all that would
be left behind
But I must go. I don't belong
here.
I'm not wanted
But I must go. But why?
Why am I thinking, I must.
This world is not what I
belong to. I wish it were
Nirvana.
But I am in a dream
Please don't wake me
I must die. I must go.
Goodbye, old, sweet life
Goodbye.

Dependant
Kevin Horgan

Feed me, insecurity
Let your false sense nourish.
Lead me, insincerity
From your lies it will flourish.
Fool me with your indifference.
I never see you clearly.
Blindness – my inheritance.
In darkness leave me screaming.

Teach me creativity
I want to know your ways.
Kindness and sincerity
without which I decay.
Love and hate I want to feel
secure and pure in heart.
Be my outlet, not my shield.
In despair I fall apart.

Packer's Widow
Anne Seastrom

Once a month or sooner his laundry comes to visit,
All holes and stains and smelling and usually he's in it.

He'll tell ya 'bout the mountains, the stars so bright and near,
Then whisper, "Come on, Honey," so tender in your ear.

And when the dawn is coming, you feel him getting up,
He whispers, "Hon, I love ya," then walks out to his truck.

You stare out of the window and watch him cross the guard,
Then count the days till winter and curse the messy yard.

The chores are still a-waiting, the grass needing to be cut,
The house needs some painting and ya wanna kick his butt!

Still you count the days till winter and cross them off in red,
And look forward to the morning when he doesn't leave the bed.

Dedication: to my Packer Bob

Lady Of Dunoon
David Sheridan

When first I met you, I could scarce believe it,
My heart was fully captured with your glance.
And after necessary introductions,
I asked you then if you would like to dance.
You nodded "Yes", We glided off together.
I felt like dancing right up to the moon.
I could have danced with you, Sweetheart, forever.
My Dearest, sweetest, Lady of Dunoon.

Whene'er I hear your voice, it sounds like music.
'Tis sweeter than the birdsong in the trees.
Your eyes, they have a gleaming, smiling sparkle.
Your beauty has that something which can please.
And when you're in my arms when we are dancing,
Your body rhythm sways in perfect tune.
'Tis Heaven when we're on the floor together,
My dearest, sweetest, Lady of Dunoon,

Dedication: to Margaret Richmond

A Time For Everyone
David A. Horne

There comes a time for everyone
When life is of the past.
All our senses fade away
And pain no longer lasts.
A plane of life is ended, it is time to say goodbye
This body now will turn to dust
As in this state I lie.

But my soul remains amongst you
As life on Earth goes on.
Although you cannot see me
Does not mean that I have gone.
My spirit is around you, I left this as a gift
To help you through your troubled times
And give your broken hearts a lift.

Dedication: to Miss Hilary Jean West, M.R.C.V.S.

Destiny
Cynthia Oliva

I look in your eyes.
It's breathtaking
Every bone in me vibrates inside.

The sound of your voice.
Puts me at peace.
It's you, I know no other choice

I imagine your touch
A feeling of freedom and ecstasy
Does Heaven mean this much?

It took us an eternity
For us to make a connection
My heart aches at this reality

Even if what we have is not clear
Our time is to be treasured
Destiny is nothing to fear

Alarm Clock
Luann Dallojacono

Alarm Clock, Alarm Clock,
Don't wake me up.
Alarm Clock, Alarm Clock,
Shut up, Shut up!!

All morning long you
beep, beep, beep.
Why can't you just let
Me sleep?

I lay in my warm, cozy bed
As you ring upon my head.
Beep, beep, beep, you go in the morning.
Leave me alone, I'm still yawning!

Alarm Clock, Alarm, Clock,
Don't wake me up.
Alarm Clock, PLEASE,
Shut up! Shut up!!

Echoes Itself
Zach Sussman

I grow tired of the
mind as the sky sinks its
yellow belly into the lake,

and try to find myself,
tracing glazed footprints on
a rainwashed road —

the shock when I realize my
own sturdy feet planted them.

what else can be said with
lips that speak only silence,
like a conch shell's hollow whisper?

(some say it echoes the sea.
I say it echoes itself.)

In Love's Embrace
Helen Pope Bell

It may not be a mansion,
to some may even seem small,
but my home is my refuge,
where I find peace and rest from all.

A place where I can be happy,
or even fret and cry,
Dream about tomorrow,
or reminisce of days gone by.

I can putter in the kitchen,
or sleep 'til dawn is near,
Fill the room with music
so pleasing to the ear.

Home, sweet home,
to me there's no lovelier place,
A place filled with life's treasures,
so sweetly held in love's embrace.

To Mark
Dorothea E. Willson

Caressing the curve of cheek,
Stroking the golden brow,
I feel my heart desert me
For the smile you smiled just now.

I count the golden granules
Sprinkled on your nose
By some angelic artist,
Like pollen on a rose.

Two lips — such pink perfection —
Reach up to kiss my chin.
Beguiling boy, your mother's not
The girl you'll have to win!

So, loose those fingers 'round my heart —
Your pirate's work is done!
My captive heart will follow you
Throughout your life, my son.

Life
Hector O. Sanchez, Jr.

there comes a point in life
when you see everything ahead of you;
dreams, happiness, love.
but then you wake up
and you see your life for what it truly is;
struggles, sadness, loneliness,
and all you get is a "FREE 16 OR 20 OZ. SPRITE".

One day you're just existing
and along comes your dream of happiness and love.
but it turns out to be a different version of your regular life
and like your regular life, it turns out to be a nightmare;
the nightmare where everyone you know,
everyone you care about,
only uses you and doesn't care about you.
but when you wake up from that nightmare
all you wake up to is your regular life.

There Will Be A Call At Dawn
Brandy D. Wood

There will be a call at dawn
Hazy the call will stand
Forcing the distant hold
Filling the morning with greed
Pulling the weight it owns
To lift the awakening scream
And rage across the world,
Piercing the coming light.
It will creep in open seed
That was once my own night
Squeezing the nightly-thrown screech
Feeling the caress of the blackened chill...
The morning will come, fresh
And the night will cease existing
For every moon, there must be a sun
And the night across my face will end
Marching, with my voice strangled
As it claims the need of a new day
There will be a call at dawn.

Life
Dominic J. Fecteau

Looking back upon my life's trials,
I see the follies and mistakes I've made.
Knowing I'm not one for deceitful denials,
I follow my orders and do what I'm bade.

I know I'm not perfect, even in desire,
though I work hard at living and try to create.
Purifying my body by water and fire,
Yet no amount of cleansing my sins can abate.

Being of the type, of peace and of chivalry,
I avoid hostilities and try not to fight.
I watch people try to achieve in futility,
some ask my council for what's wrong or right.

And so my life proceeds night after day,
constantly redundant, never the same.
Searching for meaning, looking for the way,
relying on life to teach me the game.

Enchanted Dreams

God... Who Is He?
Jenny Evely
Is He Light?
the light they say to fill darkness?
... my darkness?

Yes! I'd say He is.
He is glowing light to me—
Radiating Light, intensified Light

God consumes my darkness...
Transmuting it into light.

Light's fullest dimension
Am I Light's fullest intention?

"Light" "Light" "Light"
This is what I want
I want this Light flooding my world.

A Puff Of Smoke
Helen Rodriguez
Smoking may relax your mood
or satisfy your crave for food

Our body's such a maze of nerves
a tranquilizing smoke this serves

But inner–city atmosphere
has smoke enough to last a year

And lighting up just adds more tar
to blackened lungs will further scar

So kick that smoking dynamite
you may gain life and that's your right

Don't let tobacco rob life's hope
in but a single puff of smoke.

Dedication: to Rudy, my life's edge

Cancer's Child
Kirsten Talmage
Tendrils curl beneath
the tainted skin of
fallen angels fighting with darkened wings

Desire Christening minds of virtue
together separate one alone
senselessness, confusion of a

Motherless child
kissing the shaken core
of love's last laugh

Humor fueled by the fire from down under
holds the winning sword of
one final promise

Revealing secrets of the guarded
saint, believing that in the end
this child lives alone

Your Eyes
Lisa Jeanette Hartman
Your eyes are as green as the most purest of forests.
But they are as deadly as the most poisonous flower.
They look so pure and beautiful,
but so cold and deadly at the same time.
NightShade and a Rose altogether.
So horrid, but so beautiful and sweet.
I want to know what's in those eyes.
Those beautiful, deadly eyes of yours.
Do you feel?
Or are your eyes as shallow as a murky pond?
I want to know.
I want to scream and laugh and cry
to get to know those eyes.
But you won't let me learn, you make me so angry.
I wish I could forgive you,
but even the most beautiful of green eyes
won't melt an ice heart.

The Long Wind
Steven J. Chalmers
The Long wind is clear
It's crying in the sky.
It's blowing and blowing
at the tip of my eye.
It takes part of
the beautiful scene
it's powerful wind
for the great, big trees.

We can feel this
powerful wind
but we can't see the wind
because it's so clear.
For once, can we see it
It's so clear
but we can't stop it
but we can feel it.

Dedication: to my mother, Alfreida Chalmers

Motion
Kashmiri Kristina Stec–Neifert
Listening to smiles
Watching for glee
Entertaining joy
And laughing at me

Jumping into dreams
Heading for the sun
This journey brought unto us
Has just begun

Looking for hope
Discovering thought
Years of discomfort
Has been forgot

Smiling faces
Under the sun
Hath reminded me
We are all one

The Anthology of Poems

Darkness
T. J. Hansjon
Black as a never—ending hole
Drifting like clouds
Empty like a continuous desert
Like a cloth covering my face
the night
lightless

Evil, like a hanging tree
in a beautiful forest
Hidden like a fortress from the light.
Secretive whispers pass through the trees.

It is soundless like a barn owl swooping
to attack its prey
without lights,
without sound,
without life.

Restless Heart
Anna Karam
Trapped inside a cage
Racing thoughts and emptiness
Tears fall from my face

I remember when
The sun would shine and birds sang
Now, shade shadows time

When I was a kid
Joy and laughter were for granted
Now, fear killed the child

No more innocence
Jaded by the selfishness
Caught up in pleasure

Too late to change time
Only mend my broken ways
Then I can find love

If I
Jay Marshall
If I had a father, what would I've become?
If I had a father, would I be his only son?

If I had a father, would things change?
If I had a father, would I've stayed sane?

If I had a father, would he teach me the facts of life?
If I had a father, would I be faithful to my wife?

If I had a father, would he show me how to fix a car?
If I had a father, would I not be drunk, stooped over in a bar?

If I had a father, would I've gotten so wild?
If I had a father, would I take responsibility for my child?

If I had a father who was there, would he lend me a hand?
If I had a father, would I be a better man?

I think only If I.

The Heart
Danielle Heeney
Have you ever wondered? Or did you ever care?
How many times must a heart be broken until it's beyond repair?

The Heart is very fragile, So easy to break.
Though time and time again, so many chances we take.

Today in this world, this world that's so unkind.
True love is so important but so difficult to find.

When you find true love, never let it go.
Hold it with both hands and let that person know.

I know the Heart is fragile but love is worth the chance.
For the spirit and the soul, love certainly does enhance.

Love is so special, God's precious kiss.
A little part of Heaven, for our Earthly bliss.

Angel
Yolanda Rivers
When I think of an angel,
I think of blue skies and a message
being of warm heart and truth.
An immortal spirit with the smile of
Heaven on her face with a touch
of rejoice calling out to me with open
arms reminding me of a better day.

When I think of an angel, I think of the
loving—kindness, a tender action
shown where you can't act in a normal way.
It's the angel that gives with great
pleasure and asks nothing in return
But to show you devotion with every word
that's spoken and the goodness of a halo that
should be upon their head.
when I think of an angel, you're always there.

Dedication: to my loved ones

Dreams
Suzanne Zelehoski—Updike
My private world
My sanctuary
My dreams...
I dream of you
Soft kisses
A tender touch...
Walks in the rain
Loving glances
Quiet Moments...
My dreams are a place
of tranquility and calm
Where I go to escape
from an uncaring world.
Moonlight and stars
Rainbows and waterfalls
My gifts to you
In my dreams.

Dedication: to Kevin, keeper of my dreams

Enchanted Dreams

Their Little Boy
Joel Burnett
He used to be a little boy, so innocent and full of joy.
He seemed to grow up way too fast,
where did time go, why didn't the days last?
His struggles seemed hard, his problems rare,
he turned his head and his parents were there.
They showed him the way and that's how he knows
They'll be right behind him wherever he goes.
They dedicate their lives to showing him what's right.
He tries to please them – no matter how hard the fight
People often stare but they can't see within him,
what he would do, how much he loves them.
His parents gave him the will to live
Showing him all that he has to give.
If he owned the stars – they could have any one,
because he knows – they would give him the sun.
He knows he's not perfect – but to them he's not far,
that's why one day – he will give them that star.
So call him a man and look at him with joy,
but if you ask him – he'll always be their little boy.

The Past
Matthew Hohol
The past itself is a prison in which few want to step
For those who live their lives in it will find an early rest

Being present in the past bars the future's mysteries untold
And those who yearn for the past see it is a gem they cannot hold

Yet the past is the ultimate teacher holding all the knowledge you need
Because the lessons you've learned can only dictate the life you lead

For some the past is the ultimate weapon embracing the utmost hurt
Holding enough memories to diminish all self–worth

But for others the past is a tool used on other's minds
To enlighten them of the paths others could not find

Remember that our past makes us who we are
And the time in which the future becomes the past isn't very far.

Under The Influence
Hana Morin
One more second slips by
"Hello sir, can I help you?"
Tarnished lights in tawdry neon
"Yes, sir, you can smoke, here's an ashtray."
The chain of poverty clatters and clinks
"Yes, sir, we do serve beer."
I'm a princess – you in the expensive suit – did you know that?
My handsome prince delivers pizza in a blaze–red chariot
One day he says a real diamond ring will grace my finger
But right now his chariot needs rims and a new oil filter
"I'm sorry sir, but you've had enough to drink."
My dowdy castle holds court to countless fools – I am one
Captive of consumerism, trying on eating disorders like shoes
Maybe this one will rescue me, because my prince is late, again
My castle needs a new roof, I think the one I have is defective
I am cold even in the swelter of summer
I wish I was on TV
Because if I die, they could always bring me back next season
"Sir, you're drunk, let me call a taxi."

Casey
Rose Terrell
You were slowly going
And we moped by your side
You took one short breath
And then you died.

Was it for the best?
We will never know
As you are laid to rest
We know it was your time to go.

Gleaming eyes
Sparkling smile
Things you knew
Only lasted a short while.

But now it's time to say good–bye
As we cry and try to do our best
It's time to let your spirit fly
And it's your body's time to rest.

My Love
Devika Bhagudas
My Love, it's like you cast a spell on me.
My heart beats every Moment for you.
I don't know how I can go on without you beside me.

My Love, you're everything to me, my heart, my
soul, my every breath.

My Love, our hearts beat as one, but, we share
different lives.
Let's run together to that place where our hearts
can be together.

For this is our Moment,
our destiny,
our love.

My tears cry for your love...

Too Late To Live
Qumar S. Sheikh
A heavy medium, locked inside the cage of society
A lost dream, wandering the depths of reality
A true story, told by dishonest storytellers
A false hope and fallen men striving after it

Too many days and just as many nights, passed along as time and
not as gifts
A future built from the past to keep the piece of mind of the present
A lost road leading to the world and a much–traveled road leading
to our death
Timely tempers lost before kept, children of a nation, forgotten before
Their mothers wept

Deceiving fortunes, gathered from the blood of a parent
A healthy wallet put before the blood of a child
A sick world and not a drug to cure it
Insightful sounds, fought in a ghost's dream

Lost in a world, too late to live, or so it seems

The Cancer Prayer
Melissa S. Robertson

First it invaded and then multiplied
Eating him alive from the inside.
Through all of the suffering, I wonder why
Nothing can save him now, my hands are tied.

What do you say when you know it's the end?
When the bell sounds and he loses the fight.
A husband, a father and a best friend.
To take such a man, it doesn't seem right.

The end is approaching, he will soon die.
Future Great-Grandchildren he'll never know.
But now I must tell my Pop-Pop goodbye
And to rest his soul, I must let him go.

My guardian angel, show me the way
So Pop-Pop, I'll see you again someday.

Dedication: to my grandfather Richard Ennis

My Sorrow
Tui Conner

death is a hot red-black fist
in the belly
burning its way upward to the
essence of life
snatching at the pixie sparks of light
in an effort to destroy
to make dark the passions.
punching through where no passageway should go.
lodging in the throat to block the screams.
wrapping 'round the heart
the slowly beating heart
the heart with no emotion
but fear
and panic
and loss.

Too soon.

Let The Music Begin
Pam Rochette

If I had known that I'd get cancer,
I'd have learned to be a dancer.
This, my strange, eccentric answer:
Then I would be free.

Gracefully across the floor,
Spinning, swirling, gliding, more.
Like the waves caress the shore.
Nothing stops the sea.

Like a butterfly in flight,
I'd soar on through day and night,
till the dark yields to the light.
No one would cage me.

Alas, the truth begs to be told.
A dream that can't be bought or sold.
I'll settle for just growing old.
I pray it's meant to be...

Images Of Windham Hill
Mary Beth Mollica

Waves of Snow
Swells crusted and undulating
Rivulets of powder, blown into channels
streaming, flowing,
creating moving shadows
suddenly lifted off the shimmering
crusted surface into blue sky.
Sun pouring down on fields of ice
Pushing light everywhere
Brightness reflected, blinding.
Outline of the golden bounding
then struggling against thick, breaking layers
to keep up with the snowshoes
onward and upward into woods
of gray and brown, green and cinnamon.
Vertical dark patterns against whiteness.
Buds hanging off maples, oaks.
moisture oozing out of trunks
Nature, unplugged.

A Candle
Malacia Smith

I remember my birthday present: a
candle. What a surprise! I put it
on the mantel, but I was afraid it would
get broken. So I made myself a
special lunch and used the candle.
I thought about you a lot during
that afternoon. Thanks for the
beautiful gift. The next time I used
that candle, it broke. Glass was
everywhere and what a mess. That
day meant more to me than any
birthday I could remember. I laughed
so hard, not wanting to choke. While
putting a cloth in the water to soak.
I'd like to see you soon. Just wanted
to say I spent hours cleaning,
and you'll never guess – it was fun.

Broken Hearts
V. Marina Neff

A Broken heart, like broken glass, does not so easily mend
Easier for the blade of grass to cause the oak to bend
The love that I was sure I knew, has given up on me
The pain of loss continually grew, My tears could fill the sea

I told myself "His love was Fake!!!, or lightly given, at best"
and yet my heart was his to take... to beat within his chest
The tears do flow as days go by, at night... the time just slows.
yes, fate has made love pass me by again, as my heart knows

For my Love I wish the best of things, That love and life are kind
that soon we'll both forget the stings, of love, lost in his mind
Till that day comes I'll always hope that he'll return his heart
The tattered remnants for which I grope, will give me faith to start

When that day comes, My heart will leap and dance within my breast
I will endeavor his love to keep till we both enter into rest

Dedication: to James Otto Boyle, beloved brother

Enchanted Dreams

Remember
Jannine Basile

I remember the way it used to be, through good times and bad it was just you and me. But now you lie and you make me cry, sometimes I sit and wonder why. What can I do to make things better for our love and hard times together? When I am without you, I'm as lonely as can be, but still when I'm with you, I'm never complete. I want you to know my love is true and I will always cherish these times with you. But now I see that you don't love me and if you don't, then please just set me free. If you should decide you want me back, it might be too late, but I'll try to wait, because I'll love you today and I'll love you tomorrow, even though you have caused me such pain and sorrow.

So now, my love, the truth is out, my heart is breaking, my knees are shaking and then I realized I was being awakened. It was only a dream, only a nightmare, I turned around to see him there, where he has been all along, singing me my special song. Telling me everything will be alright and holding me close all through the night...

Dedication: to John, my love, my life, my husband

The Making Of The Man
Keith S. Pennington

"Always do your very best," she had told her little boy,
"And when your best is not good enough, be good enough to try!
Always strive for excellence as you venture down life's trail.
Try, try, try again and don't be afraid to fail."

"For failure is a lesson from which we all should learn
That life's joy is in the struggle and true happiness must be earned.
Life's treasures are not reserved for the swiftest,"
she had told her little boy,
While true happiness is not owned by the richest;
but can be yours if you always try.

"Always do your very best," she had told her growing boy.
Treating failure and success alike; if he gave of his best in the try.
In always encouraging him to be the very best he can
She gave him something more than success and
she gave the world a real MAN!

Dreaming
Andrew Admire

Here I am dreaming of you.
I am dreaming of your eyes,
That surround me and keep me secure like a warm blanket.
Of your beautiful hair,
That looks like rays of sunlight dancing in the wind.
Dreaming of your smile,
That is the silver lining to my dark cloud,
I am dreaming of your body that can do no wrong.
Of your wit and humor,
That keeps me company on lonely nights.
I am dreaming of your face,
That is like the sun that warms me on a summer day,
And your voice that cools me like a gentle breeze.
I am dreaming of your kisses that are sweeter than the spring rain.
And of you lying here beside me while I try to sleep without you.

Dedication: to a beautiful lady, Kristyn Gustafson

I Am
Brenda Suzanne Dickey

I am alone and scared.
I wonder if anyone will come.
I hear the sound of my heartbeat.
I see shadows on my walls

I am alone and scared.

I pretend someone will come.
I feel desperate.
I cry when I realize no one will come.
I touch my tears.

I am alone and scared.

I understand solitude.
I say it does not matter.
I dream of someone special.

I am alone and scared.

Enlightenment
Michelle Cook

As long-hidden secrets are revealed, her depthless eyes widen.

Ornate script and faded ink
Grace these hallowed pages.
Answers to unspoken questions and the
Riddles of untold truths are clear.

Pages turn to a rhythm that only the rings can hear.
She pauses now and again to muse over their meaning.
Her inquiries are answered in half-truths and visions seen
Through a veil and heard, as if from a Druid's tongue.

Suddenly, the runes no longer burn with definition and
Confused, her brow furrows with a quizzical look.

The book closes.
The time of her enlightenment is over.

Souls Holes
Jeffrey B. Becker

What is a Soul?
If incomplete, a big hole,
What will hold
And what will mold
Our soul
To be
The way we
Need
Or
Creed
Our souls to be
Does a man
Make his plan,
Or
Does a plan make its man
Who controls who
In this world, this zoo.

Dedication: to JRL

Waiting
Betty E. Venne

My heart is broken
Shattered, too and that is why
This poem is meant for you
Just last year we engaged as two
but now it's over because of you.
I sat by the phone day and night
waiting for you, sometimes past mid–night
I sent you cards, letters, too
I wish you would respond
I would like to hear from you.
Then one day,
you show up out of the blue
just a bit after quarter–past two
You held me tight and kissed me, too,
and you apologized for being so cruel.
Before you left,
that's when I knew,
Your love for me was,
the same as my love was for you.

Broken Trees
Carol Murray

Driving down the road today, going North on 201
the trees screamed at us to look, take notice
The ice is gone, the snow melted, all illusion of beauty is stripped away
Miles and miles, hundreds, then thousands,
of trees brutally broken – disfigured
Bark, like skin ripped away, showing clean, new wood, like bones
Whole tops broken off, branches, like arms, dangling useless
or strewn about – discarded limbs.

The starkness of the landscape on a gray winter's day is grim
But this, this is shocking. Our eyes see, almost look away.
This is strange, not a familiar victim of nature's awesome power.

Young trees, just saplings, mature trees at the height of their beauty
Older, noble trees, none are spared
We grow quiet with respect for what was and sad for what is
We mourn for the trees.

What We Once Had
Mysti Pierce

Turn and look me in the eye,
You owe that much to me.
You Can't explain, don't even try,
This time, I don't believe.

I trusted you with all my heart,
You crushed and ripped and tore.
Then, chewed it up and spit it out,
Just like you've done before.

And though, the time has gone by fast,
The years have made me strong.
For, promises made in the past,
Never lasted very long.

We both agree, it's time to part,
Even though, it hurts so bad.
I still love you with all my heart.
But, need what we once had.

Battle Cry
Phyllis R. Harvey

In the still of night I walk alone, the moon my guiding light
I feel a sense of eeriness around me as I tread,
Thoughts invade my active mind, releasing heartfelt sigh
Such ghastly thoughts are trapped inside my head.

We were as comrades fighting foe in battle's bloody cry
While all around us flesh on flesh lie there as manifest,
With orders ringing in our ears we fought and many died
For queen and country honour and the rest.

On we marched, our spirits low, exhausted and fatigued
In fear of being blown to hell we trod,
Confronted by the enemy, we gunned them down again,
'Twas either that or face the firing squad.

When the war had ended, we returned as broken men
Did politicians pause and count the cost,
Because of just a few, will we pay the price again?
If so... the battle won was really lost.

Family
Mark A. Rogers

Family means caring.
You are there when a
person needs a shoulder
to cry on and a face
to talk to.

Family means support.
You are there for encouragement
when someone needs strength
and guidance to get through
a day of struggle or triumph.

Family means love.
You are there when
someone needs to be understood
and listened to in a time
of trouble or disturbance.

Lost Nursery
K. J. Long

The sunlight streams through the windows
And lights up the dust on the floor
The echoes of long–past laughter
Can sometimes be heard at the door

All the teddies are lined up like soldiers
The dolls' house is empty and still
No more do the toys come and go
Long past is the time when they'd thrill

The rocking horse creaks when you rock it
Its paint's all faded and worn
And all the toys are so very lonely
They miss their friends who have gone

The sunlight streams through the window
And lights up the dust on the floor
Nothing's changed from the days it gave pleasure
But the children don't play here any more.

Enchanted Dreams

Lost In Wonderland
Sean Stallings
Babies and Children crying, Brothers and Sisters dying
Oh! How I wish I were lying
I'm Lost in Wonderland
Sickos, Psychos, Wackos, turning out Crack Hoes
Uneducated, financially unappreciated, are we trying to be eliminated
I'm Lost in Wonderland
Teenage girls strung out on drugs, twenty-something boyz wanna be thugs,
No Harmony, No melody
Y can't they see this ain't the way it ought to be
I must be Lost in Wonderland
Let's turn the table, let's keep it real
Let's make it fun, let's make a deal
Change your life and make a better way and your bloodline
will be here to stay.
Learn your history and learn the truth, learn it well and retain your youth
Get motivated, educated, sophisticated and dedicated
Then ya know where ya headed
Realize this not a part of God's plan
And help me find my way out of Wonderland

Show Me
Erica McNabb-Perry
I wish I could see into
your soul
your eyes reveal nothing about
the person I might see in you
show me the man I need
to love
show me the man that's
truly within you
take me in those arms of steel
make me feel like being with
you is where I belong
show me, show me all that
there is to see
show me all of you, don't
be afraid to trust me with
your soul
I only want to love you

Tears Of A Clown
Richard Fisher
I used to laugh when put to the test.
That same old smile has been put to rest.
In the smile's place is a lonely frown.
Can you see through the tears of a clown.

I remember when love was in my heart.
You were here then, but now we're apart.
You used to hold me up when I kept falling down.
Can you see through the tears of a clown.

I try to hide, when going place to place.
Every time I look up I see your face.
Hearing your voice, but there's no sound.
Can you see through the tears of a clown.

Now you're in Heaven and, I'm alone in hell.
Look from the sky, maybe you can tell.
That the water is from me that covers the ground.
All these puddles are from the tears of a clown.

The Track
Daniel Mitchell
I'm running on a track
That I thought went on forever
But now it gets shorter
The further I endeavor

The brightest blue skies
Become the blackest nights
And the simplest of pleasures
Turn into the darkest of delights

And I see the tears in your eyes
As you see the change in me
You don't hold my hand so tight
Should I just let you be?

I love you too much
To take you far away
Along the winding track of forever
That gets shorter every day

A Little Boy's Prayer
Kathleen Readel
My little boy knelt down to pray,
Then I heard him sadly say;
Lord, please send me a good man to love,
one with the love that comes from above.
One who will play, laugh or cry,
One who will be there to wipe the tears from
my eyes.
One who is strong, but with a loving heart,
One who will stay and never part,
I need a Daddy, Mom needs a man.
Please, dear Lord, send him as fast as you can.
My heart started breaking, my eyes
Started to cry, my body started shaking for
The hurt in his eyes.
I went to my room and started to pray.
Lord, Please send him a Daddy and send him
Today.

Fatal Mistake
C. P. Ward
A stillness descended upon her weary life
As she wrapped her hand around the long, curved knife
The light bounced off that sharp, silver blade
Sweat descended from her brow as she knelt and prayed

"Dear Lord, forgive my weakness, errors I have made"
A life she had so magical, now all spent, nothing saved
By one fatal mistake, her family now ripped apart
Not of her doing, how now could she make a fresh start

Memories linger, photographs sparkle with smiles
Looking at these, she paused for a while
Tears rolled down her cheeks onto her shoulders
She shivered, had the room become colder

She felt numb but had the strength
Taking the knife she gave one final breath
Plunging the blade into her heart so warm
She slumped to the floor awaiting the new dawn.

Precious Moments
Noreen Bagot
As we walk hand-in-hand together
Our troubles disappear
Time it has no limits
Whenever you are near.

We both know there's something special
If we took the time to see
I belong with you
And you belong with me.

Let's put our past behind us
Go forth to share and care
Because, life, it has no meaning
If you are not somewhere there!!

Love is a strange emotion
We just need to take the time
To understand each other
Please, will you be mine?

A Volunteer's Prayer
Clara Lansing
I thank thee, Lord, as a volunteer, for the
chance to serve again this year.
To give myself in some small way to
those not blessed as I each day.
My thanks for health of mind and soul,
to aid me ever towards my goal,
For eyes to see the good in all at hand
to extend before a fall.
For legs to go where the need is great,
learning to love—forgetting to hate.
For ears to hear and heart to cure,
When someone's cross is hard
to bear,
A smile to show my affections truly
with energy plenty, the task to do,
And all I ask, dear Lord, if I may, is to
serve You better, day by day.

Season Of Colours
Jill Brook
When springtime spreads its colours
Green fields greet skies of blue
A rose unfolds in pastel pink
To kiss the morning dew

Daffodils stand in glory
Each with its yellow crown
They play their orange trumpets
And dance above the ground

The hazy rays of sunshine
Pierce through the spreading cloud
It falls with soothing warmness
Spread like a golden shroud

Streams twist like blue silk ribbons
To quench the thirsty Earth
Nourishing blooms and blossoms
As new life comes to birth

Chocolate By The Riverside
Chadley Schmidt
Wet leaves, blades of grass
Holding each other like
Memories on the evening's tide
Secrets sleep in these rain—
Layered ribbons of loneliness

Images, reticent and blue
Behind my eyes to see
Sounds turning like the wind
Searching for my loss
Hearing my wife cry
The selfsame sounds
Repeating in the sable sky.

The riverbank's music is intimate
Like this chocolate on my tongue
Wet leaves rest as the
Moon drifts in comforts
From the sun

Sometimes
Eddie Peabody
Sometimes there's a little light
Shining in my dreams.
Some days I can find the light
That's more than what it seems.

For now I've found the light has changed,
And every day more rearranged,
But sometimes, there it is and I can see it.

Longing for the little light
To shine once more for me.
Wondering if this brilliant light
Can show me how to be.

Today I find I'm all alone,
Tomorrow found me old and grown,
But sometimes, there it is and I can see it.

Prelude To Summer
Deborah Raggett
The crimson petals' leafy shade,
Floats softly down to bed;
On mossy, Earthy head.
The peace of Eden's glade.

The mellow willowed trees.
Bathe the season's days.
In loose and lazy daze,
Of tranquil attitude.

The delicate bud to flower,
Wakes the world in bloom;
Shaking winters gloom,
With breezy, gentle shower.

The splendid beauty bursts,
As nature's dormant eye
Stretches – yawns – to rise.
In prelude to the summer.

Enchanted Dreams

When It's Time To Go
Brenda L. Bradley

When it's time to go,
I will be ready.
How do I know?
My life is steady.

When it's time to go,
I will see Him face—to—face;
Jesus, you know,
In that glorious, beautiful place.

When it's time to go,
She will be there to greet me.
Oh, you know,
The grandmother that loved me so.

When it's time to go,
Will I be ready?
Oh, yes, I know.
Because my life is steady.

A Mother's Prayers For Her Daughters
Vikki Cudmore

Dear Lord, help me to organize my day,
And set aside sometime for play!
Lord, help me shelter them from the cold,
And always have my hand to hold!

Help me teach them not to be afraid of thunder,
Lord, help me, help them through, if they blunder,
Dear Lord, help me teach them how to pray,
And hope their feet never go astray!

Help me to teach them to stand alone,
Let them know, here, they'll always have a home!

Lord, help me teach them good from bad,
Please help me to be the kind of mother I had!

Dedication: to my two loving beautiful daughters

Blind Destiny
Dawn Letourneau

Upon the desert's moon, I realized our strife,
while fleeing from a killer destined for my life.

Lost among the stars above, I left those friends so dear,
entrusted you'll remember I've always been sincere.

Yet these tears of an open womb, unable to create,
are lost among my love and our pre—destined fate.

And now the ones which I have loved and depended on the most,
are only empty thoughts of hauntings and lost ghosts.

You can never understand this, nor understand my fight,
while someone passionately arouses you and makes love to you at night.

So when the summer moon rises up from its grave
and the waves die down on the seashore,
when the wind's shadows silence the night,
we will know what we're here for.

Phantoms Of Love
Nora Graham

I wonder where love goes
When lovers drift apart.
Could passion's fires to cinders go,
When they're burned so fiercely in the heart?

Perhaps somewhere among the Heavens,
beyond where mortal eyes can see;
Shadows of two souls embrace,
as they glide into infinity.

And while we go our separate ways,
only thinking love has gone;
Phantoms of the past still roam,
and memories whisper we are wrong.

In another dimension, as yet unknown,
where Earthly bodies cannot fly;
Lost passions blaze like distant stars;
Proving love, once lived, can never die!

Grandpa (My Happy Pappy)
Kelly Hawthorne

I cried when you died, missing
you so much. Missing your smile and
your touch; love all animals, big and small,
you taught me these things and that's not all,
Teaching me how to fish and to watch
For falling stars and remember to make a
wish. To be a good person in every way,
and it will come back to me someday.
Now you're with Grandma once again, with
a life in Heaven to begin. So, so long For
Now. And please tell Grandma I love and
miss her, too. And someday, in the future,
I'll be reunited with you. Until then, be
very happy and know, I'll always remember
and love my Happy Pappy!!.

Dedication: to my grandpa, Norman Lind

The Hurting Heart
Pat Hocken

Born of woman who cared not,
As a wounded child I prayed a lot.

I asked the Lord to keep me safe,
And guide me to a hiding place.

Throughout the years he heard my prayers,
He healed my heart and dried my tears.

And of the woman who cared not,
It seems the Lord she forgot.

Much time has passed, she's old and gray,
For her soul I now pray.

My heart has grieved an awful lot,
Lord, forgive the one who cared not.

Dedication: to Lee, the love of my life

Room Of Love
M. Jackson

My bedroom was lonely until he came the
Dream of romance has been unlighted.
It comes so fast, it's like a whirlwind whisked
Into different movements nobody knows but me.
I love those eyes, it's like he is my mystery always
There feeling and touching with care.
Dreams of him keep me alive of the special Moments
We have shared.
I love the scent of his beautiful body and running
My fingertips in his hair sends me into an atmosphere
I watch him while he sleeps, eyeing those lines of
Extending skin which are smooth to touch with a
Single tip.
Laying beside him is so warm and tender
Feeling his Scottish chest, wishing to tell him
How much in love I am. I like to hear his voice repeating
So many things.
Paul is my dream come true, if only he knew
How much I cared.

A Military Child's Life
Charlie Mae Braxton

A Military Child's life must seen moveable
But what a happy one,
They travel all around the world
Beneath a shining sun.

II
Sometimes they will ride a big plane
that's strong,
And trees from post to post
But they can see the beauty of this
to get where they belong.

III
While we are riding everywhere,
We'll have a chance to look,
at all the things to see outdoors
More real than in a book.

Thoughts
Shawna Poole

Lying out under the stars
Feeling the breeze flow all over your body
As peacefulness and relaxation cover your body

Thoughts just creep over your mind
You start to wonder about the small things
And to think about the big things.

Hoping and praying
That the good things come your way
And that the bad avoid you.

Realizing that life isn't so bad
That maybe things can straighten out
for you and for others.

Just thank God that you have what you have
And don't mess them up just to be popular
And to fit in.

The Hand
Lil Niven

Hands to do work, hands to play
Hands to show love, hands to pray.
What secrets man's hands can reveal.
Secrets he tries so hard to conceal.

Manicured, pampered, all for show
Tailored nails wafting to and fro.
Hand that greets with friendly grip
Secretly searching for ways to trip.

Hand that steals, hurts and pains,
Interested only in what it gains.
Hand that loves, protects and heals,
Not disguising what it feels.

Hand that prays for sister and brother,
Bidding us care one for the other.
But the hand I trust above them all
Is the hand that is fashioned by honest toil!

The Creator
Pat Murray

As I gazed upon the ocean blue
Just at dusk God's love shines through

The moon shone down like a beacon light
The waves were dancing with delight

As I walked along the beach alone
I thought about my Heavenly home

I felt my Lord, a slight warm glow
It burned within, on my face it showed

His peace and love within I feel
How I know His presence is real

A grain of sand, the rushing sea
God's creations like you and me

Christmas Story
Adelle Jess

People forget what Christmas is all about
Giving and getting presents no doubt
As I lie in my bed at night thinking
Thinking Santa's coming tonight.
Then I think of the real story
As I turn off the light
Jesus was born a long time ago
Laid in a manger
Surrounded by strangers.
The shepherds, the sheep
The night watch keep
Three kings with their gifts are making their way
To find our Lord lying in hay
No newspaper headlines to tell of His birth
Just a bright star above the Earth
So remember to think
Of Jesus and His birth
As you enjoy
your Christmas day mirth

Enchanted Dreams

Black Widow... Beware!
Debra Baldridge
Black widow... beware, beware
They don't hide in dark places
They're here, there, everywhere

Pretending to love and adore you
So nice and sweet they seem

They'll do whatever you want them to
They build up all your dreams

Spreading poison everywhere
That's how they spin their web

Look out, look out, you're being warned
Someone may find you dead

New life insurance is a clue
Look out my friend
Black widow's after you!

Sandy, Sunny Place
Kathleen Williams
In my dreams,
I go to a sandy, sunny place,
It's a deserted island,
In the middle of space.
The breeze is refreshing,
The waves are all splashing.
I see a blue dolphin,
Leaping for the sky,
The sun is going down,
The seagulls flying by.
When I am there,
I do not care,
About anything,
Until I hear the ding.
The alarm has sounded,
It's all erased,
But, I will go back to that sandy, sunny place.

Miss You
Christina-Jean Larson
Grandma to some, she was a wonderful woman...
to seven she was a mother, an excellent advisor.

Great-grandma to many, loved and admired...
Alma Moore to others in which she inspired.

We'll miss you in the winter when the snow begins to fall,
We'll miss you in the springtime when the garden's growing tall.

We'll miss you in the summer when the sun is warm and bright,
We'll miss you in the autumn because the holidays won't seem right.

The year will pass so slowly without your comforting face,
but we will go on knowing you're in a better place.

When you go up to Heaven, when we kneel down to pray,
Please know that we loved you more than words can ever say.

Dedication: to my great grandma, Alma Moore

Norfolk Summer '97
Margaret Archer
The distant horizon gauzed by fret,
Reveals a yacht silently moving through the haze.
The gentle breeze ripples the seed-laden grasses
Which feather our legs as we gaze.

Strange land-locked obelisk shrouded in mist
With sails cruciform against sunlight shaft.
Cows graze where the grass is lushest
Small boats cluster, craft nudging craft.

Soon sand-softened footprints seaward point,
Tide-rippled surface marks the toe-print path
Through dunes and back to sea
Seagulls swoop, squawk and flap.

Window wide, lace fluttered, tabby on sill with Cheshire smile,
Eyes slit-closed against the setting sun,
Table laid with a willow-pattern welcome,
Laden with wholesome treats – sandwich, cake and bun.

The Waiting Room
Kerry Shepherd
Sitting there in your red, plastic seat,
Awaiting your Destiny, one we all meet,
Your hands cling to its wooden sides, your knuckles clenched,
But, only when, the pain is intense.

Muscle fibers cling to your meager frame,
When you catch sight of your reflection,
You know how much time has caused you to change,
The many folds of skin, the lack of hair.
You feel inside you'll soon be there.

Around this room, more chairs await,
For those who have lived and feel they are late,
For the place we all are going,
But here they must remain in this state,
Until their time is called to knock on Heaven's gate.

Untitled
Keith D. Troop
As days go by and time rolls on, I think of days of old.
Of battles fought, both won and lost and their stories left untold.
I think of names and faces and places I wish I'd never been.
I cherish with bitter melancholy scars from fights I did not win.
I try to remember why I was there and the company of friends I
    had known
My thoughts always seem to turn to you, my friend, who did not come home.
We had shared many experiences, joys and sorrows all.
When I'm alone with my private pain, it's you who comes to call.
So I go on, daily dealing with life, trying to cope with the loss,
and trying to live in such a way that the purchase justified the cost.
As memories fade and yellow with years,
As old age comes and I still fight the tears.
I wonder about you and how it will be,
when my time comes and Glory I see.
Will you remember who I was, when I go to that glorious place?
Will you remember the sound of my voice and the shape of my old face?
When walking on those golden paths, will we greet as we pass by?
Will we nod and smile as we did in life and call out, "Semper Fi"?

Majestic Titanic
Tina Hall

A ship so grand sails today
To a promised land far away
Where hopeful souls make their dreams come true
Sailing on the sea, so blue

Dancing and dining all night long
The night so cool, the waters calm
Whispering dangers are in the air
But the people aboard have no care

A`Majestic Structure
A beautiful sight
Sails on through the silent, dark night

Suddenly a thud, the ship hits the ice
People screaming "Please save our lives"
We'll always feel the fear and the panic
Of the people who sailed
On the majestic Titanic

Shattered Dreams
Paul Harris

I throw a picture against my wall
and watch the glass shatter and fall
I remember the first day that we met
Now it's a day I wish I'd forget
I sit and stare at the broken glass
each piece represents a stage in our lives
Jagged yet sharp on any given night
must have been a fool to think it would last

As I pick up the pieces
and move on with my life
Each piece leaves a cut
much deeper than a knife
She was my solid future
but now I recall
She's a shattered dream
thrown against my wall

The Fires Of Time Burn
Tom McGrath

Shadows of me run
Stepping into the sun
Igniting its fury
Upon everyone

Markers of stone
In a resting man's home
Touching the coldness
Poor brittle bone

The countdown is waiting
Sailing ships swaying
The plank is blunt
Forgetting it's falling

Calling of the night
The illuminating light
Like a shooting star's
First and final flight

For P. L. R.
Christy Anne Strike

When I perceive among the flowers
One whose bloom is greater than the others
I step into the garden to inhale its perfume,
Sweeter than imagination.
It inspires me to look deep within myself
And stirs the genius that lies dormant.
However may this flower exist among
Such common flora?
However may its beauty incomparable
With those surrounding it reach my
Senses and resound in my heart
Like chimes in summer?
However may its music be contained
In the shades of colour richer still at
The heart of it, the depth of which is
Unfathomable?
And I see inside myself the conception
Of a bloom in response.
A mere bud to be awakened at its zenith.

Untitled
Elizabeth C. DeBaldo-Thode

Schizophrenic lover is a man of many faces.
He hides behind a mask, but the eyes leave
many traces.

Far too many maybes and not enough answers.
Oh, he knows the script well, it's the truth
he cannot master.

He's a Master Magician with an ace up every
sleeve.
He's a Master of Illusion...
His degree is in deceit!

If you see this detour, do not wander down
this path.
For the laws that govern nature don't exist
behind the mask.

A Mother's Day Gift
Evelyn Spriggs

Why did I wait until this special day
To tell you the things I should say every day?
First of all, thank you for giving me birth,
And teaching me how to survive on this Earth:
To count to ten... to read a book...
To love a child... to clean... to cook...
To plant a seed... to weed... to hoe...
To choose fabric... to cut... to sew...
To sing... to dance... to drive a car...
To make a wish upon a star.
Thank you for tending to all my diseases...
The itches and fevers and boo-boos and sneezes.
Thank you for being there all through the worst,
When I felt like my heart was going to burst.
Thank you for saying our Father's above,
To nurture our souls with His mercy and love.
You were my best friend when I had no other,
So thank you... oh, thank you...
for being my mother!

Enchanted Dreams

Clouds
Lauren Farina

As puffy and white as a cotton ball,
It's as soft and gentle as a melting snowball,
I try to reach it, it's so far up,
They look like marshmallows in a glass cup.

Fluffy little rabbit ears,
My eyes trickling with glistening tears,
Watching them sitting way up there,
I find one shaped like a polar bear.

I want to lay on the big, soft pillow,
But when it moves it looks like a bunch of willows,
Whipped-cream topping for a cherry cheesecake,
I found an oven for it to be baked.

I sat down and looked way up high,
A blanket of snow lay in the sky,
I have to wait for it to fade,
When dark appears, I'm not afraid.

The Fabled Poets
Emil M. Katzer

How long do I have to lie in the sun
With all these fabled poets of Light;
With their thoughts, words and song;
But to hear of honors of Bard's insight.

And often driven out from their lairs
Yet, the learning Elite, heralds of whose Truth,
Lone, wandering and weary and tossed—
About through their lives, age and youth.

Their seeds of imposed wisdom scattered
Everywhere with promises of hope and success.
Then, my own efforts and effects cease not;
Not more nor less.

I stand before the locks of paradise;
Be it ever so humble and so wise.

Cry
Kevin McKeigue

This thing is not effeminate
Yet a gift to get us by.
It does not matter who, where or what you are,
Never be afraid to cry.

Anger makes me weep
Love, brings a tear within my eye
But all I feel is sorrow
For he that cannot cry.

I learned that death is for the living
And life is when you die
But the greatest thing I've ever learned
Was that day I learned to cry.

I express all my emotions with tears
I know the reason why.
For the day my tears stop falling
Upon that day I'll die.

My Mother
Joan James

There is always someone I like to have near,
A person on whom to depend.
We may have our quarrels and shed many a tear,
But she will always remain my friend.

She guides me through the steps of life,
She helps me in every way.
She shows me what is wrong and what is right
Daily, day by day.

She laughs with me when I am happy,
She cheers me up when I am sad.
She always knows when I need her,
She is the best friend I have ever had.

And when the time comes for her to go
To Heaven far above,
I pray to God to give me strength,
To lose the Mother I love.

Life Is A Mystery...
Lynn Weaver

It's about watching a pelican dance with a wave...
It's about a white seagull against a dark gray sky...
It's about feeling the pull to your heart and suspending yourself there...
It's about feeling liquid and feeling the gentle sway...
It's about the gentle giant of the water that springs forth and says
"You are Free"...
It's about the millions of water drops rising into nowhere and you are
but one of them...
It's about tears flowing and washing the skin...
It's about the splash of the wave that drenches you and says
"Enough for now"...
It's about getting into your vehicle and trusting it will take you
where you need to go...

IT'S ABOUT COMING HOME...

Dedication: to Gregory Penn, my teacher

Mother
Gordon Hall

At the start of life none can compare
With a mother's love so gentle and fair
God gave Mary grace of a special kind
To cradle His son at a special time
There was nothing fancy about His birth
For God was sending His son to Earth
But He needed care in His tender years
So His mother was there to calm His fear.

We all need help, so we don't despair
So God sent mothers so bright and fair
To wash the babies and comb their hair
To settle their quarrels and treat them fair
She's only a mother but she is mine
I'll not forget her in my lifetime
Her prayers and tears have set me free
From so many pitfalls of life, you see
When I get to Heaven, I'm sure it will be
Because my mother spent time with me.

Out-Of-The-Way
Larry Foucault

Assuredly;
the sun must shine
to be what it is,
the empire must decline
to be what it was.

So, too;
it is the warrior's time,
to battle the bear with a knife,
to release the internal strife,
it is the warrior's climb.

Away from the mindless habits...
Seeing the unaccomplished run of the rabbits:
full of fear,
deaf to hear.
the treadmills...
the daily drills...
Then fake a smile of happiness.

Beloved Son Of Victory!
Ruby J. Lawson

Oh, Victory! and Valent! One God's Beloved and only, Son
My Lord and Savior, Jesus Christ, who won the Victory,
and paid the price
Knight in Shining Armor, You are
So very Awesome, in Your many ways,
that brighten every waking hour, like the sunlight rays
who gives me everlasting confidence, which is always,
my defense
My precious and Mighty! king, with grace, peace and
joy, that Your presence brings, which always makes me
happy and causes my heart to sing
Oh, precious Prince of Peace,
You make my heart want to feast
Upon the magnificence of Your name,
and the Mighty Glory of Your fame
Makes me Glorify You, my King, for it's You, I hold in
high esteem

Nature's Wonders
Janice Kelly

There's people in a hurry
They're rushing everywhere
They nudge you and they bump you
But do they really care
Shopping bags and brollys
They seem to flail around
And another piece of litter
Being thrown upon the ground
The place we live is beautiful
It's plain for all to see
There are wonders all around you
As far as the eye can see
So take your time and wear a smile
Keep your litter to yourself
Look where you're going
Love what you see
Of nature's boundless wealth.

Dedication: to my grandson, Cameron John Kelly

Never Alone
Loretta A. Hamilton

I feel you entered into the Heavens
Through the pearly gates made of ribbon
After struggling daily to push forward
The Lord had mercy and took you onward

Once upon a time you may of pondered
But now you no longer have to wonder
You never have to strain to see the light
For on you it's always shining so bright

With only good thoughts if any kind
Flying freely throughout the skies
Your halo glistens of a diamond ring
Hearing only the golden harps play

The hurt we all feel will fade away
Yet our memories will always stay
And now you're at peace and rest
For now you lay in the best of hands.

I'll Paint You A Rainbow
Jim Hunsaker

I'll paint you a Rainbow to hang on the wall
To brighten your heart when the shadows fall.
On a canvas of joy outlasting the years,
With a soft brush of sweetness to dry all your tears.

I'll paint you a rainbow with colors of smiles
That glow with sincerity over the miles,
On a palette of words I will tenderly blend
Tones into treasures of sunlight and wind.

I'll paint you a rainbow that reaches so wide,
Your sighs and your sorrows will vanish inside,
And deep in the center of each different hue,

A memory fashioned especially for you.
So lift up your eyes, for, suspended above,
A rainbow designed by the Fingers of Love.

Out Of Sorts
Keith Gems

It's dinner time, I wonder if I ought
To sit and wallow idly?
I don't do this, usually —
Join people puffed with food
And starved of consequential thought.

Wine to halt the tick of time
Served by sycophants who need
The little blood that they can bleed.
Why am I here? Perhaps I'm not,
I have no wish to eat this dish
Or scrape the bottom of the pot.

It's time to go — to leave this place
No point to swim against the tide,
It's time to leave the human race —
Take Rennies home to bed
And hope, to—morrow, when all's said —
I'll get up on the right side!.

Enchanted Dreams

Only You
Steve Russo

You have that special touch,
That can make a flower bloom,
And that magical little smile,
That brightens up a room.

It's how you listen to me,
With your waiting ear,
And how you hold me close to you,
When I'm feeling fear.

And when you open up my eyes,
So that I can clearly see,
The beauty of this whole wide world,
That's right in front of me.

It's all these little things,
That you say and do,
That opens up this heart of mine,
With all my love for you.

Thanks Giving
Megan E. Vanlangendonck

I'm giving thanks to everyone.
Well, everyone I know,
I'm trying hard to think of things,
That I love and cherish, so,
I sat upon my thinking stool,

And after all that thinking.
It came to me at last.
The person I owed thanks to most,
was the one who was always there,
I'm sure he was, because how could
he have answered all those prayers,

'Cause he created all of us,
and is the very meaning of LOVE.

Dedication: to A. J. and Dorothy Vanlangendonck

Lost Love
Diane Hergott

I try so hard to be
A good child in your eyes
And to hope the love you have for me
Will never fade and die

Now would this love fade away
Because I'm not like you
But if this is not the reason
Then, why do I feel so blue

For me to feel so rotten
And I'm just no good anymore
Would be like saying goodbye forever
Just by simply shutting the door

I know I'm not the person
You wanted me to be
But all I really want from you
Is to love me, for being me

My Chestnut Tree
Georges Ware

When I was just a tiny cat my master bought a tree
He said it was a Chestnut and was 'specially for me.
I loved to climb that little tree and play among its boughs
And always chose the highest point to call my proud meows.

As years went by the little tree grew always ever bigger
But still I reached the topmost twigs as easily as ever.
One summer day my master carved my name into that tree.
He said t'would live two hundred years and still belong to me!

Time passed. The tree grew big and strong but I grew old and lame.
My master had to lift me up to let me see my name.
Now my poor broken body lies deep beneath my tree
My spirit, though, still climbs it, playing happily and free.

I think my master knows I'm here for when he stands below
He looks aloft and speaks my name and softly calls "hello".
I've still to wait a little while but then will come the day
When he and I together, will in my Chestnut play.

Alone
Barbara J. Smith

Being lonely and being alone...
There's a big difference.
Sometimes I like to be alone...
to collect my thoughts,
to reflect on the past,
to look to the future.
Maybe just to see where I'm going,
I don't like to be lonely,
When it feels like there's no one who
cares.
Everyone needs another who cares...
to promote the good,
and repress the bad.
Tonight I am lonely and alone –
But tomorrow is a new day.
And there's someone I haven't met,
Just waiting to make things right.

My Angels
Dorothy M. Haltman

Last night I had this wonderful dream
Of angels guarding me.
They were the most, beautiful sight
That I had ever seen.

I counted all, ten of them
As they all smiled down at me
And told me not to worry
They were looking out for me.

They'd guard me, while I'm sleeping
Or when I'm wide awake.
Doing what I do all day
And help me meditate.

So I'll turn my eyes to Heaven
And thank the Lord above
For sending down the Angels
To guard me with His love.

The Anthology of Poems

Untitled
Melissa J. Roder
My love for you shall never waver
On the day of love.
Many express the emotion with trivial objects
And only on this day.
That is not how my love shall be expressed
And not only on this day.
For my love for you shall be evident every day,
Seeing you, being in your presence
That is very much an important thing to me.
The expression of my love may seem different to you.
It is, because that is me.
Your love fills me with happiness
And not is it only on this day.
May fate have with us what it may
On this day.
May our love flourish how it may.
And may you stay as you are
On this day
On this day.

He's Here
Virginia Callaway
He's gone – but no –
his chair, he's here!
He's gone, but no,
the wind whispers
his name – he's here!
He's gone, spring is coming
the garden is waiting
he's here!
He's gone – soft breezes
locust trees bloom
he's here!
He's gone – his hoe hangs
on the garden gate
he's here!
He's gone –
tears fall gently
he's here!

Through The Looking Glass
Katy Richards
Red lights fade into the distance...
I peer, half-crumpled, screwed up as leaves under foot
From under the microscope of my looking glass world.

I am warm, a jittery bug in the heat
Yet freezing cold as I watch the world whirl
On and on in a never-ending cycle of ignoring

Me. I am invisible as I drag my self, empty
Shell along. Wishing on an empty thought
That I could float beyond this, above, away.

The people are smaller. Now they are the bugs
I can stamp on, grind in, spill them over
The edge. I must watch my step.

I am too big, but too small. Too numb
To be. Me. What have I done – not to fit?
The light is fading and I fear I am not bright enough.

When I Was Small
Jennifer Mykolyshyn
I lost my Mom, when I was small
She did the drugs, she did them all
I asked my Mom, about VIP
She said, "Go away, don't bother me"

On that day, on our balcony
She stood right there, so helplessly
I could see, a tear in her eye
Her life was hard, she wanted to cry

She took a step, I did not look
I was so scared, for the life she took
Two days later, I was confused
What happened to my Mom? How badly was she bruised?

I asked my Dad and so he said
"I'm sorry to say
Because of drugs, someone we loved
Has passed away"

Wanted: Just One Valentine
Cynthia V. Key
Cupid sharpens his arrows
and arches his bows
He's seeking two hearts to glitter and glow
He knows the heart is a lonely hunter
just seeking to find
That special someone with
true love in mind
It can happen in an instant
or sometimes, it may take years
It can bring you a smile
or cause a river of tears
When I first laid eyes on you
I knew my hunting days were through
For you are the Valentine
of my life
My happiness, my dreams
Come true!

The Individual
Renee Condon
Rarely today do people observe a true individual,
Willing to risk it all for their own beliefs.
Taught to walk together and not apart,
Dreams become carelessly abandoned in the
Foolish hopes of fitting into society.
Always careful not to bring up issues,
Which raise pondering questions,
Or, dare anyone say it, a heated debate.
For who wants to stand out
In a senseless world where acceptance
Seems the sole key to genuine happiness.
Yet, every so often when the strange appears
An inspiring individual slowly emerges,
With their own thoughts and desires.
Unwilling to have their ideas shot down,
They refuse to accept being pushed around.
To them the world appears as a mosaic of thoughts,
Not a vacant, blank sheet of paper.
Only an individual can fill that paper.

Enchanted Dreams

Pleasure
Milton E. Lampe
I like to walk by the river,
Among the bushes and trees;
I enjoy the pretty scenery,
And the soft gentle breeze.

I usually see some mule deer,
And sometimes a turkey, too;
I look up at the sky above,
It always looks so blue.

I throw sticks in the river,
And watch them float away;
It's such a peaceful pleasure,
To pass the time of day.

I talk to all my horses,
And give them grain and hay;
Then I get in my pickup,
And slowly drive away.

The Visitors
Suzanne Cohen
Youth knocked on my door.
I let her in. We chatted gaily
for a while and then we parted.
I did not see her leave.
I was too busy entertaining.

Middle age dropped by to say hello.
I tried to bribe her with sweets
but she was in a hurry. She slammed
the door rudely behind her
while I was busy entertaining.

Old age crept in.
I never heard her enter,
but only she consented to remain at my party.
She promised to clean up the mess I made
when I was busy entertaining.

A Mother's Haunting
Sheri Spencer
While rest settles in and twilight's hovering
Buried thoughts emerge
Her quiet mind is flooded with waves of anguish
Tears of dread are conjured up
Despair comes haunting
"Your son is not here, he is out in the night,
He loves the darkness better than light"
She fights to sleep and not be consumed
But slips away into another room
Weeping she struggles with the power of thought
Why is he falling? Is it my fault?
She prays to the Father, "I don't understand"
Guilt and Confusion swirling in her head
She cries through the night
Her heart emptied out
Morning awakens with Hope residing
Guilt is hiding, Confusion is still
Faith was poured out – the night is defeated
Haunting is silent 'til another rendezvous

Christine
Judith L. Fischer
Now that you've grown older
and accomplished such a lot
I am so proud of all you've done
and what you are about.

Your gentleness with Christopher
is such a joy to see.
Your patient care with Kymber
is marvelous to me.

You are my first-born daughter
God's blessing from above.
He gave me such a wondrous gift
to cherish and to love.

I love you more than you could know.
I still feel all your pain
and if I could, I'd bear it all
'til you felt good again.

Our Beautiful World
Madge Taylor
Each day as I awake and see
The beauty of this world that
Surrounds me
I know, without a doubt, there
Is someone up there that knows
What it's all about.
The mountains and the seas
Are wonders to behold and the
Beauty and tranquility are
More precious than gold
Always help your fellow man
If he needs help to make a
Stand
Look around at the view, so much
More beauty than we ever knew
Look up, clean up and enjoy
That's what He made it for

Another Soldier
Janice E. Schultz
In the blinking of an eye
In the gasp of a breath
In the stillness of the Moment
A soldier's met with death.

In the echo of a shot
In a lone wolf's cry
In a land far away
A brave soldier did die.

In a grieving mother's heart
In a home filled with love
In a priest's last rites
A soldier's with God above.

In the blinking of an eye
In the gasp of a breath
In the stillness of the Moment
Another soldier's met with death.

Untitled
Michael Birnie

Days go by, not thinking
Of people's ways of life
In countries torn apart
By war and strife.
Children dying, man applying.
Mass-destruction of life
You ask yourself why
Please make it stop
Before it's too late
We are all God's children
To live in harmony
Food for all, it's God's way
No more suffering
No more pain
It's getting late
We should all act now
People of the Earth
Children look up, into the eyes
of adults, thinking, why us.

The Secret Touch
Lillian Galvin

Quietly lay your head upon me, softly close your eyes
Let your fears loose, my Love, they need not here reside

Rest your heart into my hands, Trust with all your Soul
I wish to give you all my Love, with a secret for you to hold

Feel my essence surround you, then gently with Heaven's grace
My heart has entered into yours and it has found its place

Feel the Love, no words describe
Within our warm embrace
It is within where you must go, to dance with me in Love and Grace

This secret, magical touch arrives, when two Souls intertwine
With Love that's pure and truthful.

A Love like yours and mine.

Home At Six
Gladys Fraser

It's grand to be a sailor and sail the world around,
Or yet a mighty fisherman who scores the fishing grounds.
It's great to feel the good fresh air keen against your face,
To challenge all the elements which threaten the human race!

The Clerk, he packs his briefcase and hurries down the road,
He'll be back punctually at six, it's all part of the Code.
His wife has cut his sandwiches and waved him from the door,
And then she'll do her part-time job and fetch the kids at four.

But when your sailor goes to work, he won't be back at six.
He'll have been right around the world, he might be back at six,
But it won't be hours or days or weeks, it's much more likely months,
And those he leaves behind are proud, because, just all at once,

They're part of a much wider world, it's all there at their feet.
Karachi, Penang, Singapore, Malaya and it's sweet
To know how small the world is to the great ships as they roam;
And to know how close we are to them, we wives who wait at home!

The Lost Soul
Jeanne Claire Donald

Look closely, look inside
Bring me out from where I hide
Deep inside there lies a soul
That wants to front, wants to take control
Take the time, believe in me
As there is more than what you see
Everyone deserves the chance
To express, to love, to try
No one should be shut out
and left inside to die

Always seen, yet in the shade
Always danced, yet never played
Always listening, yet never heard
Always for the worst I am prepared
Always the same each and every day
Always the questions that won't go away
Always wanting to shout and be heard
Never taken serious, always scared.

My Wonderful Mother
Tracey Dean Rich

Of All The People In My Life From Beginning To The End,
You Have Been My Special Blessing.
My Wonderful Mom And Great Friend.
You Have Filled My Life With Love And Laughter
We Have Shared Sorrows, Joys And Tears.
We Enjoy Each Other's Company
At Home, At Church And Even Sears.
I Love Spending Time With You, You're The Best Of All
No Matter What We Do... The Movies Or The Beach
But As Always, Nothin' Beats The Mall.
When I Need Someone To Listen, I Know You Will Be There.
No Matter Where You Are. You Always Take The Time To Care.
I Know That I Am Very Blessed, Because No Matter What Life Has To Send,
I Have A Wonderful Mother That I Always Call My Friend.
I Guess My Point Is Simple, Just One More Thing To Say.
I Love You Mom, So Please Have A
Happy Mother's Day!

Sunny Days
Jennifer MacGregor

The sun shines down on the beach,
The morning sun is warm and very bright,
The children put their costumes on,
As they arrive at the beautiful beach.

The calm sea races up the sandy shore,
The children paddle in pools of water,
The waves rush in again,
As the pebbles chase them down.

The gentle breeze blows across the sand,
The beach balls chase the breeze,
The sunbathers look up,
As the sand rushes over the beach.

The tide comes further in,
The people tidy away,
The parents pack the car away,
As the footprints are washed away.

Enchanted Dreams

Wishes
Patricia Hunt
I missed your first breath
I didn't hear your first cry
I even missed the chance to tell you good–bye
I didn't read your first book
Or see the first step you took
I didn't bake your first birthday cake
Or hear the sweet wishes you'd make
I missed the childhood hurts
And the lacy, frilly skirts
I missed the first boy you kissed
So many things have I missed
But remember this, my sweet girl
I always wished for you the world
I wished for stars to light your nights
And the sun to always shine bright
But the most important wish of all
Was that someday you would call
Thank God for wishes and prayers that come true
And for my chance to get to know You

Music Has A Thousand Charms
Florence C. Kehl
Music has a thousand charms,
It holds you, spellbound, in its arms,
A thousand arms, a million fingers,
A tune in your memory that often lingers.

Music takes you floating in the air,
Above the sky, beyond the moon, you know not where.
Sometimes its mood is gay and light and fair,
Sometimes it fills you with a deep despair.
Strange how an oft–repeated tune
Will make you wish again upon the moon.
And as each little note again falls on the air,
Recalls a memory bittersweet and rare.

Yes, music has a thousand charms,
A thousand arms that hold you tight
Or fling you out into the night.

The Dead Poet
Amanda Hillbeck
Lost in time with nowhere to go.

Slowly dying like leaves on a tree.

With no more to give and nothing to say.

Trembling while looking for words.

The poet left each poem she gave,

With a message between the lines.

Put there specially for you.

To hope you will understand the story

that she has left behind.

As the poet can give no more.

A Father's Touch
Cheryl Milazzo
For a father's touch is never very far:
His words still echo in our ears of how much he has
shown us as how to care and the laughter we all still share.

For a father's touch is never very far:
For he has taught us how to love so dear.

For a father's touch is never very far:
For, dear father, how we know your love is so
very near.

For a father's touch is never very far:
For a memory has come to mind of how wonderful
and divine a father's touch can be.

So, dear father, may you know that your touch will always be
known.

For a father's touch is never very far.

Clover Field
Robin Beam
I'm going walking in the clover field dreaming of you.
The emptiness inside of me wishes you were here, too.

The grass is just turning green with spring's sparkling, wet dew,
As it shines in the morning sun, I'm still thinking of you.

Well, I looked into the tall, green grass and it took me by
Surprise,
It was a four leaf clover glistening into my eyes.

I picked it and I made a wish, a wish of me and you,
I'm going walking in the clover field, dreaming of you.

Though dreams are dreams and my wish came true,
I'll be walking in the clover field forever with you.

Dedication: to my husband, Duane, with love

A Woman Full Of Life
Vera Taylor
I'm a woman full of life
I'm a mother, homemaker and a loving wife
My day begins at the crack of dawn
I start the pot, to get the coffee warm
I awake the children, feed and get them dressed
Off to school they go, while the house is a mess
I start my chores and get myself dressed
Only to realize, the family will be home in an hour or less
I burst in the kitchen to start dinner
In walks my husband asking, "What's for dinner?"
This is a ritual, repeated week after week
I thank God for blessing me with joy and meek
I'm a woman full of life, because
I'm a mother, homemaker and a loving wife
I give of myself, nothing but the best
To prepare the children for the REAL world
An even greater test.

Dedication: to God, his love endures forever

The Heart
Patricia A. Nestich
Words and words and words —
Words are such a powerful force,
They make melodious the heart.
Kind words – softly spoken,
Heart it sings – the touch of love,
For sweetness has come – grace, new–given joy to thee.
My heart feels emotion, too;
But words can darken sadly – touch and hurt.
They are so powerful.
Oh, word of God, abide in my heart.
Now let's see – with God in my heart,
Direction I have – for we should love one another,
How pleased the "Lord Must Be".
Heart of light, Jesus loves you —
So be happy, glad and peaceful, too.
This tune in my heart,
For the Lord can do anything.
When we trust and love one another,
As He told us to!

Angel Of The Bridge
Mary Cogley
We will meet someday, on the bridge...
Between East and West...
Our worlds will blend...
Or melt and fuse.
We'll stay awhile...
And Listen...
Hear the drums...
First still... then louder...
Calling... throbbing...
Insistent... pounding...
All–pervading.
Do they call us together?
Or draw us apart...
Or is it the beating of my heart?
The thrill to see you...
Once again...
Oh, Angel of the bridge.

Just Another Day
Richard D. Becerra
Another day of hearing your voice sweetly caressing the inner
depths of my heart. How the day grows long as I wait to just get a
glimpse of your radiant smile and drown in the sparkle of your
blue eyes. Each day brings anew the hope of seeing you again for
the first time. You are a constant reminder that spring will be
upon us before we feel the warmth of the noonday sun. How I
yearn to hold you close and feel the beat of your heart next to mine.
Still is the night as I walk in the solitude of knowing that you are
resting in the quiet and comfort of your own home. Slowly the
night returns to the light of a new day and my thoughts are still
fixated on that imprint of you on my mind, I dream, that this day
will come to pass, to see a love so pure, so innocent, so sweet that it
will melt the hardest of hearts. And your blue eyes sparkling like
the stars in the evening sky across the vast reaches of the Heavens
to warm my heart from the cool night air. But I'll stay put, focused
on what is right for you and I. Because who knows what
tomorrow will bring, if we miss what's here today.

Dedication: to luv of my life

Victims
Beata M. Kulawiak
Victims of the prison we created
weeping into the depths of night
as moonlight silently lingers
Over the flames we chose to ignite.

Swept into insatiable passions
Mutual decision to refuse control
Frolic acts of raging passion
The exquisite journey has taken its toll.

Deceptive laughter beyond reproach
A futile attempt to divide
Two souls resisting fate
A love that will never subside.

After a tragically–resisted separation
Acknowledgement roughly settles in
A period of adjustment is in order
Our eternal contrition will now begin.

Death Valley, 1998
Karin Dovring
I saw the desert blooming
Because disaster struck
When storm and flood were coming
And all seemed out of luck.
Then – seed that had been buried
Decades in torrid Earth
Suddenly it hurried
To light and fruitful birth.

My soul in arid sorrow
In apathy stood still
With no hope for tomorrow
It paralyzed my will.
Disastrous rains kept flowing
And swept my buried soul
Then – hidden seeds came growing
And gave my life new goal.

The Heart Of A Woman
Thelma J. Gooch
The heart of a woman which every man seeks;
It will make him happy, other times to weep.
In the heart of a woman, a child will dwell;
To find comfort for a Moment, a delightful story to tell.

When tribulations prevail as they will appear;
Reach out from beneath for refuge is near.
We cannot recapture youth once it is gone;
But the heart grows stronger as the years pass on.

The depth of the heart stretches from sea to sky;
It concludes matters and sometimes asks "Why?"
The heart makes room for heartaches, joy, or sorrow;
Regardless how dark the night, it seeks tomorrow.

As we grow in years, we all will be admired;
The love of a woman every person would like to acquire.
The strength of the heart, though small it may be;
It carries great power, in the end you will see.

Enchanted Dreams

For True Love
L. S. Edwards
Some men walk upon God's Earth
in search of worldly riches,
But!
If I searched and found a flower
that bloomed the whole year round,
If I searched and found a perfume
that never lost its fragrance,
If I searched and saw a sight
that never looked more lovely,
If I wrote such music
that sounded so angelic,
All of these and more, much more
I would forfeit
just to find true love.
For two hearts as one
Two lives as one
brings true joy
brings true happiness.
I've found that love.

My Love Affair With Life
Tamyra Brooks
6 months into existence, I fell upon sickness.
2 Years, as a toddler, my skin burned from a coffee mess.
4 years, as a preschooler, a loss impacted me.
10 years, as I approached preadolescence, I learned of my identity,
12 years, as I entered teenhood, I saved young girls from the male
Clutches of sexuality.
16 years marked a turning point, I entered duality — bore a life and
Almost lost mine, simultaneously.
17 years I graduated, with a high school degree, entered into
Motherhood with a goal of college decreed.
20 years marked devastation — physical and verbally, the sexual
Ravages of a deviant had overtaken me.
21 years was my escape into reality.
From the 20's to the 30's, the bumps of life I bore.
The 30's to the 40's marked a much better score.
What was torn and tattered has become a success.
And now is experiencing only happiness!

Oddity
Bryant A. Evans
Oddity — I am
Just a statement
Just a fact.
Not to conform to sanity
As one man would see it
But live with a good heart
As all men should see it.
To meet another is truly amazing.
Who knows that the trivial and taxing
Are not things to base one's life on.
To lay your beliefs on the table
And to feel no need to conform.
For your grandfather told your father
What my grandfather told mine.
To coexist, filtering fact from fiction
Is defined as friendship.
Oddities we are.
Just a statement
Just a fact.

Four Seasons
Alex Padfield
Bursting with pride and the spirit of life
A March maple springs a surprise
Along her sweet branches she opens her hands
Dappling some shade upon where she stands

The light beams through her crimson leaves
You can hear her whistling in the summer breeze
Every day and every night
She fills our hearts and souls with delight

Weeping gracefully, she stands so proud
Casting her figure above the ground
Ablaze with colourful Autumn falling leaves
Returning to Earth without a sound

Winter shows the end of an era
Just a silhouette of her outlined figure
Cold, frosty days with her robin friend
To keep her company until Spring's here again.

No Storms In Heaven
Gladys Brucker
There'll be no storms in Heaven fair
No lightning flashes there
To be dimmed by the glory of our Lord;
No claps of thunder can e'er rift asunder
The beauty of God's choir in sweet accord.

No more restless sea,
All there calm will be
As the saints of all ages come ashore;
No sorrow or crying, no sickness or dying
For Christ has conquered death forevermore

There'll be no temple there,
We'll worship everywhere
With the saints and the prophets of old;
There'll be no more night for Christ is the light.
Sin can never enter God's fold.

My Three Angels
Bevy D. Bice–McFarlin
I have three little angels
Up in Heaven in God's care,
So I don't need to worry about them
Cause I know they're safe and loved up there.

Jesus took them home to be with Him
And the reason, I'll never know why,
I know what He did must have been for the best
But I'm a mother and I still sometimes cry.

For a while they grew and were a part of me
But their faces I never did see,
So when my life down here on Earth is over
I know in Heaven they're waiting for me.

I think of my angels quite often
And wish they were here on this land,
But I get comfort just in knowing
That Jesus is holding their hands.

Treachery And Treason
Nevada McIntosh
Beyond reason
She gave me pain
It drove me insane
She wasn't charming
More like harming
She gave me marks
It drove me apart
Behind her smiles
She was vile
Behind her sighs
Were more lies
She kept on funning
I kept on running
She seemed so nice
But that was just her
Vice
I knew we had to
part but that was better
Than being in the dark

Nature's Greatest Show
Ann Tork
The wind was rain as I gazed in awe
Nothing stirred but this tiny bird
Oh, what a wondrous sight to see
The busy flight of the sweet chickadee
First at the feeder and last to go
It couldn't be daunted, not even by snow
Not just in winter, but all year long
I watch the birds and hear their song
The cardinal, Blue Jay, Nuthatch and Wren
Visit my feeder again and again
There is no admission for nature's great show

The props are four seasons that come and go
A standing ovation I owe my small friends
May their engagement here never end

Dedication: to Alice Brostowitz – she helped me understand birds

---

Confusion
Jessica Poropat
Lost in a world of Euphoria
Is it better to ask no questions
Acting on feelings... nothing planned
But then a whole new look
New emotions never felt
For an instance no confusion
Then lost even more once again
Not knowing what will come next
Wanting one more, but never having enough
Knowing you're not sure
But when that Moment comes, you know it's what you want
Telling yourself no, but acting on instinct
Being spontaneous; A feeling never felt before
Never this magical
Confusing things more, but loving it all
Trying to search, a heart too full
Finding love everywhere; Loving too much maybe
About to overflow
But letting some out is the hardest of all

My Vision Of Heaven
Jennifer Brown
My vision of Heaven
Is very beautiful indeed
God is with them and taking care
Of their every need.

A place where people gather
After they die
Where angels are present
And unicorns that can fly.

A place with peace
And people who smile
Frowns don't exist
They're out of style.

A place where
Everyone is free
From sin and greed
Where all Christians shall be.

Is This The Real Beginning
A. H. Dickinson
Is our world now breaking
Like arctic icebergs are
And old volcanoes burning
And spitting out their fire
Our seas are getting bigger
And so the floods begin
Oh, what a mess we live in
How did it all begin
We are well into this year
And our climate's changed its course
And so have several rivers
Been broken with its force

Oh, what a mess we live in
Let's pray that it soon stops
And we get back to normal
Before it starts to rot.

Untitled
Mary Ann
A person is someone who carries themselves like gold,
Silver and diamonds, they mind their own affairs and
don't cause trouble for others and are a person you can really
trust who will try to help, in most cases.

A person is someone who knows when to talk and when
Not to talk, to be all they can be out of life and not
bring others down for their own doings

A person is someone you can reach out to who knows
What's right and wrong and gives support when it is
Needed, no matter what's the problem

A person is someone who has real answers and does not
talk about another behind their back and pretend
in their face

And finally, a person knows real love; how to make people
Love them and spread the love out to others

Enchanted Dreams

I Can't Tame Your Love
Roy Tindle
If I could ride the sun and control its fire
I could stand the heat of your desire
But I can't tame your love

If I could direct the winds across the land
I could resist the power of your hand
But I can't tame your love

If I could hold back the water in all the oceans
I wouldn't cry from my emotions
But I can't tame your love

If I could shield the world from lightning and thunder
I could protect my mind from your mystery and wonder
But I can't tame your love

If I could stop the Earth from turning
I could control the fire of your love that is burning
But I can't tame your love

Untitled
Sara Dawson
Her pure, white plumage gains a single, black feather,
This temporary mark that scars her for a lifetime,
A wasted breath that creates her purpose,
To love the cement that holds her name,
Set firm in the base of her stomach.
She reaches up to gain something below her being,
Just to end the permanent reminder of illusion,
And the panic that strays beyond her control.
The forgotten truth that courts guilt and wins,
The battle against fate, her destiny goes untold,
Unlived.
The shallow expression that states the life
that she has been made, by others,
To live through their perceptions and stop
the sins that they created.
The harmful voices that scratch tangled matter,
The birth of the deprived spirit.

Home Again
June Schott
Sometime I would like
To just go home again
To where I would be free
And know no hurt or pain.

Where I could sit and talk to Mom
And spend sometime with Dad
Where things would just stand still awhile
I wish all this I had.

Where life would be so simple
Where there would be no strife
Where I could be a kid again
For a little time in life.

But the years have come and gone
And time does not stand still
And no matter just how hard I try
I guess it never will.

What Happened To Yesterday?
Rachel Bruner
What happened to yesterday?
When love was ours and so true,
When our fears were lost,
When hope was all we needed,
When dreams came true.

What happened to yesterday?
When it was just me and you,
When together we were perfect,
When us being apart was unthought of,
When love sparkled from our eyes.

What happened to yesterday?
When all we needed was each other,
When we were a perfect symbol of love,
When anger never raged into our lives,
When love was what kept us going.

What happened to yesterday?

To Be Strong
Sandra Kalina
I never knew I could be so strong,
I don't have to be sorry if I've done nothing wrong;
I can say no to someone when I'm not in the mood,
Who cares if they get mad, it's up to me to feel good;
People may talk and say things that aren't true,
Rumors are for fools who are really jealous of you;
It's when we search for strength to get through the woes;
The strength is within us, though it may be hidden deep,
We each have our demons that try to keep us weak;
Face these fears by remembering where did it all start,
Write them all down and release them from your heart;
List them all, no matter how harsh or mild,
Then let no one see them, not even a child;
Hide it in a place that's safe from others' view,
Go back to it later and have your mind read it through;
Once you read it, burn it, don't even leave a shred,
From this Moment on all your fears are dead!

Twins
Earline J. Brown
My sister and I never wondered
Why we have the same taste
Why mother dressed us the exact same way
Why we have the same face.

We never questioned when one was ill
Why the other was sick, also
We never gave it a second thought
Or, had the need to know.

Why we communicate without speaking
And, when we speak it's the same
Why we know each other's inner thoughts
Why we feel each other's pain.

Some are mirror—like images
Twins are more than just a few
GOD had so much love for one
HE decided to share it with two.

Life's Toils
Joseph W. Brown II

The pains we endure, to fight the good fight.
The struggles we suffer, both day and night.
The boundaries we have, keep us in stride.
Our feelings will change and thoughts will collide.
We all walk alone, in life's wicked style.
Only strong people survive, this wretched trial.
Assert yourself, for knowledge is prosperity.
Pass through life, with truth and great sincerity.
Life will throw curves when unexpected.
So stay on your feet and keep it collected.
You'll see then how life does unfold.
For the burdens you bear, will take their toll.

Queen Of The Flowers
Randy Lee Abdallah

You are the Queen of the flowers
Thoughts of you pursue my hours
I watch for a sign, I gaze from a tower
I assay to be bold but before thee I cower
I feel the dew I sense the shower
Yet antagonistically it all seems to devour
When I behold apprehension and your state of power
I hide in the trees, I lodge in the bower
Like foods that are tart and lemons that are sour
My emotions precarious and my day too dour
So when considering all her endowments
Rhonda blossoms the Queen Of The Flowers

My Angel
Lynda Olson

My angel came one night to me and with gentle softness said,
"I know you've had a tougher road than most along the way,
some are easy, some are not, but all of us are led,"
He touched my cheeks with satin hands and continued on to say.
"The Lord above has heard you cry and also heard you pray,
for strength, for peace and for His helping hands.
But all of this that's happening, is all that He has planned."
"Sweet child," he whispered, as a smile came to His face,
"you've got to gain your own rewards and not to have them given.
One life the Lord has given you, the other one you live in."
Now with reasons coming clear to me, I know just what to do,
look not away from all the gifts, that are right in front of you.

The Bath
Jo Ann Streeter

sinking into the welcoming warmth
lost beneath the luxurious blanket of bubbles,
embraced in a cocoon of sheer refuge

the scent of summer's strawberries
belie the winter winds howling without,
while the morning sun peeks in the window, in a game of hide and seek,
teasing of spring's imminent arrival

a baptism at daybreak,
washing away the grime of self–sufficient striving,
streaming out bone—weariness,
softening the calluses of hand, heel, heart

the suds are gone, as into thin air,
the water tepid, then cold,
plunge through the frigid air into the inviting folds of terry cloth;
the day awaits

Drinking and Driving Nightmares
Don Chamblee

I can see, now that I'm getting old
Can't you understand
For I am going to die
A boy, grown up like a man
I do not wish to go
I do not wish to stay
So, hopefully, I'll end up in a better place
Full of dreams of yesterday
It's not so that the dying hurts
It's no one's left to care
It's just I'm lying in this hearse
and it's a lonely, dark, nightmare!

My Grandma's Rocking Chair
Alex Alois

Rocking back and forth
the way my grandma did
when I was little
daydreaming to a place
that never was
falling asleep
remembering great things
but the best one,
Grandma rocking me on her lap
in that same rocking chair

Dedication: to Grandma Evelyn

Retrospect
Terra Lesack

Angry questions
left without answers
on the abandoned porch
of the house where I grew up
So I climb the creaky stairs
to my childhood apartment
and upon opening the door
to my ancient wonderland
I find the unlocked chains
that I discover
were only holding me back
from the monsters under their bed

Untitled
Lisa A. Mastrucci

Saying good–bye
to someone you love
could be the hardest task
to ever achieve.
The pain felt inside
the memories held tight
Are all that is on the mind.
Though a thought crosses by
of a sweet memory,
or a chuckle that was shared,
And for that one Moment
your pain may be eased
even forgotten about.
And that is why
time makes it better
even makes it easier
as more memories are cherished
and more chuckles are remembered.

Enchanted Dreams

One Of Those Days
Debbie Hruby
Morning glories tangle in the weeds,
sprouting on the Earth its new seeds.
The brown soil drinking the rain,
that the Heavens poured from its veins.
As the breeze from the wind sway,
down comes the sun's powerful rays.
The clouds looking a bouncy white,
drifting away and out of sight.
Thunder bangs its final good—bye,
as the lightening bolts the sky.
It's times like these Mother Nature can say,
"It's gonna be one of those days."

Revelation
Richard Huhn
I've inhaled the breath of humility,
Been taught the lessons of fear,
Been plagued by the wrath of futility,
Whose tune echoes deep in my ear.
I've chosen the path of humanity,
For my road was tainted with wrongs.
I've rejected the laws of my vanity
And now sing a humble man's song.
For all that I've learned of divinity
And the life of my love and my faith,
I'm indebted for all it has given me
And I know now it's never too late.

Day And Night
J. C. Fuller
The day was bright, sunny and warm,
The night was filled with a vicious storm.
Oh, the brightness, where's my shades?
The storm, it brings a thunderous rage.
A perfect day with a sunny glow,
The dead of night and lightning show.
Soothing and warm, enjoy the view,
'Cause with the storm, comes the down—pour, too!
It's all over, a new day begins,
And the wait to see what the night sends.
A constant circle that continues to be,
Each one different from the other, you see.

The Journey
Nancy Raimondo
The flight from fear to love
departs at gate 4.
I have been given
first class seats for this journey.

I've taken this flight all my life,
and have accumulated
a lot of frequent flyer miles.

I usually miss the
connecting flight
from love to trust.

I pray that I will lose
my bags on these flights.

Someday I will use all my miles
for a one—way ticket home.

The Poem From The Heart
Sue H. Scholl
The poem of all poems
Is the one that's not wrote
There are no words
It could never be spoke
You hear it inside
Deep down in your heart
Must never be shared
Must never part
So to me the best poem
Is the one you can't write
Made up of true feelings
You just can't recite

Heartaches
Tamara Shewmaker
A teardrop rolling
down my check.
A whimpering cry in the
dark.
My love for you is
still known.
Not a depressive Moment
goes by
My heart aches for
You, my love.

Dedication: to my four beautiful children

Broken Heart
Mike A. Rendino
I'm his box he lay so still,
to no one was left a will,
dreaming forever of the past,
Love he had that did not last,
tears would streak down his Face,
Knowing his heart had no place,
nieces and nephews he had galore,
hoping for a child of his own to adore,
having no wish to be alone,
though to himself did he condone,
his truest words were known as Art,
but still he died of a broken heart.

Soleil de Black Sand
Linda Christian
While I lay on a horizonless beach of black sand

I am enveloped in shower of pure gold

I do not move, for I want each droplet to replenish me

To induce my fantasy, fulfill my ecstasy

My skin begins to glisten as I bow my head in silent submission

While shimmering, golden drops cascade down my spine

A gentle breeze blows to pirouette golden swirls on tiny ebony granules

As time and I dance together, the sky darkens and Ra, the sun God, whispers to tell me

To begin my sojourn again when morning comes.

Silence
Brenda Lungley
Imagine the shouting at the match,
Or the sound your nails make when
you scratch,
The car horn tooting on the road,
Mums washer chunking with a heavy load,
Take away the sounds you always hear,
Replace comforting noise with feelings of fear,
Silence is a wall, where nothing is heard,
Not a whisper, a shout or the singing of a bird,
Silence is a feeling, smothering and pressing,
Sometimes though, just sometimes,
Silence is a blessing.

Yesterday And Tomorrow
Doris Scudder
No more yesterdays.
No more tomorrows.
Perhaps there will be happiness
In the vale of no tomorrows.
The days of youth so enjoyed,
When one ran through the woods
With hair flying like the wind.
On our way home from school.
With never a thought that the
Tomorrows would consume us.
And all the brain could do
Would be remember.

Orbit Of The Sun
Alan Edwards
Repose gave way to dreaming; dreaming searching.
Searching for her in seductive warmth of darkness.
Searched and beheld her upon clouded moon.
But morning found her vanished with the rising mist.

Awakened by cool light of sunrise, I rose;
Rose and turned my gaze upon the revolving horizon.
Revolved and watched each mark upon it vanish and return
And with the passing of each, imagined her waiting beyond.

Beyond and beyond and ten thousand more,
Each beckoning with deceitful promise anew.
Quiet taunts allowing but one hope,
That this nomad star might find her, too.

Man At The Clavichord
Marion Schoeberlein
There is an antique Sunday
afternoon in his fingers.
He touches the delicate things
of a dead era.
His notes become a wall,
then a cathedral.
They drop like silver water
into a bucket.
Even a man's coarse thoughts
twinkle like stars here.
In Mozart's parlor where
tiny shoes and tiny gloves
wait to welcome us; the man
at the clavichord
is like the first singing
peacock we have ever heard.

When The Wind Blows
Frances Strickland
I sat outside
watching the sun go down
Painting the sky liquid gold
As the cool wind blew
Across my skin
My spirit flew
As the shadows came out
And began to dance
My spirit danced, too
Oh, what a feeling
To fly when the wind blows
To set my spirit free
And guide through the sky
When the wind blows

Untitled
Tracy McInnis
How will we teach our children, the freedom of our shame
a world in constant turmoil, where nothing stays the same
Born into a tragic shadow, in a life they will defend
In a world we are destroying, what message do we send
Do we teach them to be strong, do we teach them to pretend

How will we teach our children, the value of their heart
Rendering our evils, will their God be torn apart
Reaching for their souls, a spirit they may find
The wisdom and the guidance, to see where we are blind
Lost in the adult playground, we choose to leave them behind

How will we teach our children, they are born to recreate
a world in which their lifetime, is all that we forsake
Will they know about love, as they move toward
The hands of desperation, will you pray for their reward
Have we sacrificed the future, as we've sacrificed the
Lord.

Christmas Is Coming
Ben Howell
While it is still only November, with pilot night already gone,
The house will be busy from now on, with the undertaking
of Christmas; baking the puddings and cakes, the smell of dried fruit
marinating, as the mincemeat Becky's making, a true declaration,
of Christmas preparation, my son and his wife will be doing, a special
batch of home brewing, complementary, to help Christmas be merry,
fortunately, in bottles not barrels, it aids one to join in singing the
carols, the sitting room, although use–accustomed, to constant
adjustment, rearranged it will be, to accommodate the Christmas
tree, its position should be, quite centrally, according to tradition,
the symbol of our celebration, the sight should delight, everyone's
observation, decked–out in coloured lights and with Becky's added
decorations, how can it fail, to win everyone's admiration, with
the cards to write and send, even then, there's no stopping,
remember the toughest task of all, there's the Christmas Shopping,
even then, there is no time for napping, yet to begin, the gift
wrapping, no wonder you hear folk say, "No, I'm not ready for
Christmas, but I'm ready for the holiday."...

Enchanted Dreams

Going Home
Damien Massey
As one lonely soldier walks along the dead bodies
He wonders why he was the only one who had survived;
Then he hears a voice saying, "don't forget me, here I am."
As the soldier looked around he saw one lone figure with his hands in the air,
The soldier thought he was talking to him,
Then he noticed, the man's head was turned the other way;
The soldier runs to the man and asked who he was talking to?
The man answered, "You don't hear them, they're calling our names?"
Then the soldier realizes the man was talking about going home.

Dedication: to Lenard O. Stevens

Hello J.
Malacia A. Smith
I met a man who was so
Joyful.
Even though he had to put
Ointment on his skin.
Outside of an empty room
Was a place for him to
meet people.
Either I was seeing something
different.
I thought he was standing in
a hallway.
After that morning I went
For a long walk.
As time passed, I thought to
myself, who was he.
I would like to have known.
But, I could not remember
how he looked.

Thinking And Drinking
LoriJean Hildebrandt
There once was a man
Who decided to drink,
He climbed in his van
and He did not think.

After the sun went down
After the sky was pink,
The car crashed in the town
When that man did not think.

Three people died
As fast as a blink,
Now their families have cried
Because that man did not think.

I Still Wonder
Pamela Systermann
My head rose slowly
Our tears fell together
I then felt your heart.
I wonder what you thought of mine,
Which came from deep inside.
I wonder what your Dad
Thought back then of you.
My generation, differs from yours
Years my past, I cannot change.
We had to grow, I can't take away.
Could feelings be changed, now
I wonder how.
Rest in peace, they say
In our final days.
With all the hurt, deep inside
I still wonder how.

Dedication: to Mr. and Mrs. Delfrate, whom I love dearly

Remembering
Darlene Shaw
I would like to walk along the beach in Corpus Christi.
That's my home town and it's very dear to me.
Now that I am grown and live so far from home,
I'd like to just reflect on all the memories.

It all seems more like a dream, or a movie I've seen,
Of a small girl growing up by the sea.
The many friends I had that I vowed always would be close and dear
They've grown up, too and none are here.

All the silly games we used to play and the arguments, too,
Are meaningful only to me and who?
Just to walk along the beach, barefoot in the sand.
I can close my eyes and see it all again.

North-Eastern Blackouts
Adam Caravaglia
I have always found myself profoundly Imprisoned
In the relentless grip of horror
During the blackouts
In our timeworn, northeastern home.
The silent darkness appallingly creeps up
And crawls beneath my obscured flesh.
The dull, forlorn flicker of candlelight
Rhythmically dances upon the stone-cold
Faces of loved-ones.
So very silent and ominous—
Conjuring up the mass chaos
Of the middle ages.
In the dark corners of the room
Sitting by the gloomy, starlit window
I watch the family dwell
Distorted and fall helplessly
Victim to their faces of erosion,
With the fall of night.

The Anthology of Poems

What Am I
Fiona Montgomerie
C is for the little Child
laid in the manger, meek and mild;
H is for the clear blue Heaven
where our Jesus Christ is living;
R is the initial that starts Religion
but Faith is also another description;
I is for all the information
spread to others throughout the nation;
S is for our holy Sunday
but praying shouldn't stop because it's Monday;
T is the beginning of the word Trust
which between all people is a must;
I can also mean Immoral
which no deed we do should be at all;
A begins the word Amen
it ends our service and leaves our hearts open;
N is for the New Testament book
where inspiration and answers are found when we look.

Untitled
Uhron Robinson
If humans were all telepaths,
there would be no dumb or smart.
No keeping knowledge hidden,
no thoughts kept apart.
I'd know what
You know and,
She'd know what
He knows and
We'd all know the same thing.
And finally we'd understand what it means to be
human beings.
But humans are not telepaths
and thoughts are kept apart,
from strangers
from loved–ones
but mostly from our hearts.

Dedication: to my sun Rapheal

A Poem
Marie Goodwin
A poem is life, we want to share
we want to share our life with you today.
Each and every one of us has
a poem to tell.
A poem is a teardrop, a poem is
a smile, a poem is a kiss,
a poem is a sigh. A poem is loving
a poem is dying. A poem is being born.
A poem is sunshine, a poem
is the rain, the thunder and the lighting.
A poem is a tree, a poem is
you and me.

Dedication: to my children and grandchildren

The Statue Of Liberty
Ordy J. Daff
In the harbor of New York, there
stands a statue with her arm outstretched
toward Heaven, she holds
in her hand the torch of liberty for
you and me and freedom throughout
all the land.

She stands there in the harbor as a
statue to guide the ships day and
night, when they see her friendly
hand reaching up from the land and
guiding them by her light.

She stands there in the harbor with
the torch held high to guide the ships
by her light. She's an assembly of
freedom and liberty, God Bless Old
Glory and the land of the free.

Pictures In The Sand
Arnold Frost
Walking on the shores of sand
a masterpiece come to my hand
of rocks of different shape and size
the beauty there before my eyes

As I looked with pride and fear
I knew the Master was quite near
and as I looked once more with pride
The Great Creator by my side

There were no words that I could say
that could enhance that joyous day
for to my heart came words most clear
where are you? I am quite near.

Untitled
J. A. Orton
If only I could speak my mind,
But, alas, I cannot do,
For all the things you mean to me
I always will be true.

You really are my valentine
And this I've got to say
We've been together a great many years
Loved every minute of every day

I know this card's the very first
Never bothered in the past
Although we've been through thick and thin
Your love will always last

Enchanted Dreams

Changed Days
Helen Johnson
I remember well the teacher's belt
And I know exactly how it felt
Oh, yes! I've been at the receiving end
On the odd occasion, the teacher I'd offend
Please don't think I was unruly and wild
I was not that kind of child
More likely I made an ink blot on the page
And that certainly did put teacher in a rage
Or I might have made a spelling mistake
For just one wrong word, the belt I must take
The teacher's word was law in those days
But the government saw fit to change its ways
So sadly that discipline having been withdrawn
Now chaos in the schools appears the "Norm".

Enlightened
Jane R. Harwood
Another night to write
about the way the light
turns my staid cut–crystal
into ice–minded figures
that dance across the glass
and brass coffee table
after balcony curtains are parted
to let the sun's rising smile in
while mine begins to match it
and lines of grief retreat
until the sun falls asleep again
yet even then–yes, even now
Life's promise, light–winged,
hovers.

Just A Thought
Debi Sheridan
I write from my heart, my soul, my mind.
You need not understand me, today or in time.
But if you can feel from a word or a line
Then you open your eyes wide on the world for a time.

Sit in the center, breathe and take in.
The warmth of a blanket or pillow or friend.
Open your life to it, all or a bit.
Wallow in sunshine today where you sit.

Feel for the first time, joy or true pain.
Allow it to enter upon your domain.
Accept all you can in your mind and your heart.
Move on in your life, you've made a good start.

Calling Time
Darren Wells
His infant humour turns to tasteless evenings,
His subtle flirting to public complications,
And now the TV does the talking,
And now he sleeps instead of sharing himself.

Her playful whispers turn to stifled laughter,
"I Love You" giggles to tricky situations,
And now the pillows do the dreaming,
And now she hides instead of sharing herself.

The years go by,
"Under–the–table–touchings" are gone,
Fleeting kisses that never were fleeting before,

And now they make plans,
To cast aside the gloom,
Wishes to wash away,
Like a wave returning to Neptune's arms.

She
Charles Murphy
She makes my day.
She's all a woman could
Ever be and more, sometimes
She is hard, so very hard,
to please.
She gives me such blissful,
shelter, solitude away from
an uncaring world, she's
cupid's finest, playful tease.
Time, sweet time only adds
To the flame, when by
her side, I long to be near.
I love her more than all
the raindrops falling from this
quietly–passing storm, she's my
funny Valentine year after year.
She's still the only girl for me.
God bless her and keep her safe.

The Greatest Compliment
Clara Beth Negoro
When I was 5, the greatest compliment
I could get was telling me I was a cute baby.

When I was 15, the greatest compliment I could get was
telling me I was so sophisticated I looked 21.

When I was 35, the greatest compliment I could get
Was telling me I looked 21.

When I was 45, the greatest compliment I could get
Was asking for my ID before getting a drink.

Now I'm 65, the greatest compliment I could get
You look so young, you must be 45!

Foregrounds
Carol Trinder
Eminonou Harbour:
the gristly, fishy bustle,
faces of the Baltic
facing East.
Boarding the ferry to Uskador,
no other European features
look back at us.
Soldiers, countenances of seasoned plums,
Tibetan eyes searching ours.
Asking,
"What vast echoes separate us?"
Birds screeching off the Bosphorus,
flapping, cries fusing
with the call to prayer.
Bodiless man, shuffling on his hands
in among the feet.
My heart cries with the gulls
in Eminonou.

The Birth Of A Grandson
S. M. Mitchell
There was a time in our lives which was filled with darkness
and sadness

Now we have laughter in our lives with the birth of our beautiful
grandson

He taught us lots in his first year with all his trials for one so young
fighting hard to survive

He still kept laughing and smiling through it all.

Now the days and weeks are shorter because of this beautiful child

With this blond–haired, pale blue–eyed child

Which brought the laughter and happiness

Back into our lives, we thank God for our ANGEL.

Me
Mary Clark
My heart is so heavy and my mind is a
blank. I'm so mixed up that I just can't thank
I try to live the way God wants me to but
Sometimes Satan makes it so hard to do.
He's around every corner and behind every door.
He was even there when I entered the store.
You have to be strong and avoid doing wrong.
I walk around singing Heavenly songs. If you're
true to God and confess your sins, there's no way
that Satan can win.

Sometimes my life seems such a mess, it's even
hard for me to rest. I know that God knows
best but I feel like I'm just failing the test.
I do unto others as I want them to do. But from
what I can see, that's even falling through.
God loves me that much, I know. Because if He
didn't He would just let me go.

When
Norbert Atherton
When you walk through life on the brink
its tempting magnet—drawing—drawing
Other forces—full of tears—pulling—pulling
with hearts that sink.

When you win the battle of being alone—but not lonely
eyes that accuse—forever anti-belief—
Oh, if only we could stay within ourselves——
——Oh, if only !

When we sleep do we die—floating in time—
being judged daily—of sins unspoken
Awaken—reprieved again——everything logged
Another day–another life to live–everything prime.

My Best Friend
Ruth Whitehead
My best friend has changed over the years
When in school it was one of my peers.
As I age it is now someone wise
She is marvelous and has green eyes.

She is fun and makes life worth living
And never, ever stops the giving.
She's bright and witty and makes me laugh
As we sip our tea by the carafe.

She's more than a friend could ever be
Because she loves me just to be me.
I'm glad I'm not born to another
This wonderful person is my mother!

Untitled
R. Horrocks
I went fishing one fine
Day,
The sun was shining
As I went on my way.
The fish were rising.
To the fly and the birds
Were
Singing in the sky
The heather with its
Purple flowers was like
A carpet full of colours
I was happy to be there
breathing in the country
Air. When the sun sank
In the west. A beautiful
Day had gone to rest
Sending my troubles
Far, far away.

Enchanted Dreams

Green Love
Anthony Rizzi
A man in search of love nonexistent
Can see the many faces it can hold.
Undecided yet remains persistent,
The world is a garden of fruit and mold.
A budding beauty, his euphoric state,
The thoughts he covets, he dare not confess.
For as his orbs dilate, he can't dodge fate,
As her body twines with lovers' caress.
Seeds from many others journeyed within,
This man's time is close for he knows her ways;
The spring sun rises, her cycle in spin,
It is too late and it's his heart she slays.
His life is like a fish trapped in a mesh,
One way to kill the pain; steel into flesh.

Jungle Symphony
Katie Jantzi
Fronds of palm trees bow to each other in a ritualistic dance
To welcome the rain.
Green leaves rustle and swish in harmonious response.
The sighing of the wind increases in intensity
until it encompasses the listener's entire being.
The prelude to the Master Composer's symphony ends
with a distant tympani.
The staccato beat of rain drops accelerates in tempo
Until all nature participates in this symphony of sound.
Thunderclaps reverberate in the distance;
They become louder and louder until only the bass notes are heard
The music softens and swells and fades again.
Raindrops gently plop from the leaves in a soothing melody.
Sweet-voiced birds trill in a chorus of joy;
Their praises echo from every tree
Because their world is refreshed again.
Can we as humans harmonize in our position
In the Master's symphony of life?

Silent Killer
Roy Kenneth Pallett
A drug addict lies dying alone in filth and misery,
a young man in an old man's body, barely twenty-three.
A life of self-destruction, he waits at Heaven's door,
reflecting upon his life, a life he wants no more.
Images of his parents, once more he's just a boy,
cuddles from his mother, his father's pride and joy.
At school he was a scholar, distinction with every grade,
his life was mapped-out clearly, the foundations had been laid.
Sport was his forte, athletics, he was king of the track,
he would represent his country one day, his parents were sure of that.
University was a different story, here he could not cope,
stressed and under pressure, the young man turns to dope.
Falling victim to the pushers, the boy was easy prey,
he had everything to live for, but he threw it all away.
Trading university for cardboard city, the gutter now his home,
blankets made of paper, his pillow a block of stone.
To feed his ever-growing addiction, he leads a life of crime,
Heaven's door opens, cut short in his prime.

The Crossing
Vicki McConnell
Death comes as a silent partner
To guide us forward on our voyage
Through timeless shadows
That veil the distant shore.
Our heads turn the other way
Our hearts heavy with pain
We will not look.
We cannot bear the parting.
But what is there to fear?
Death is but a friend.
A silent angel from beyond
Who calls our name and helps us
Make our passage through the unknown.
A mystical crossing
To the far side of the universe
Where we have been called
Out of this dream—like haze
To continue our spiritual quest.

In My Head
Matthew Dilley
In my head is a sports car,
A chocolate bar,
A football team,
A heat-sensing beam,
A private pool,
That's what's cool,
My own zoo,
A funfair, too,
A Kawasaki motorbike,
A dog called Tyke,
A jumbo jet,
A basketball net,
My very own sports shop,
So I can buy a football top,
A CD shop,
With Jazz and Pop,
Lots of things are in my head,
But now I've finished it's time for bed.

A Perfect Rose
S. Plumb
Love is like a perfect rose,
Where it goes to nobody knows,
All at once its colours bloom,
Like a delicate bird in full tune.

Then as the wind blows, the petals fall,
Scattered amongst the trees so tall,
Love was here in all its glory,
Only the rose thorns can tell the story.

Year after year the rose will grow
Like love it has another go,
To bloom as beautiful as the time before,
To love one person more and more.

The River
Roy Taggart
Oh, beautiful river tumbling down from your mountain high source.
Rushing at speed,
Through wood, valley and field,
Slowing down as you reach the much—lower ground.
Now gently flowing, over pebbles and rocks,
Glistening like silver, on bright sunny days.

Oh, beautiful river so tranquil you flow.
Meandering along so peaceful and slow.
At times hardly moving
With waters so still.
But with abundance of life, we know that you yield.
The flowers and trees that grow on your banks,
All thrive with the goodness, that only you can provide.
The colours and sounds are there night and day.
To enrich body and soul, as we go on our way.

Reflections At Sunset
Joan C. Anderson
The sunset in the western sky
Foretold the end of another day,
In quietness I pondered——
Had I reflected God's loving way?

Or had I added to some distress
Neglecting to share a joy worthwhile?
Had I given my best to others?
Taken time to give a smile?

My tangled thoughts unraveled
As I sifted through the dross,
Humbly I asked forgiveness
In the shadow of the cross.

Never Again Will It Be The Same
Chloe' Thompson
A wonderful castle made of all that was beautiful to her,
It rested in the heart of her most—treasured memories and
existed in a glorious past.
She knew its every secret and all the magic it possessed.
In its halls she danced,
The rooms were a sanctuary of her laughter, its walls were
the guardian of her dreams.
The castle was her security, her strength, her glory, her hope,
her everything.
The sun fell behind the clouds, rain began to pour, lightning flashed,
A plane zoomed through the turbulent skies, her feet mid—air,
she looked down on her
castle...
It was gone.

The Little Shooting Star
Alyene Yaws
There once was a star high up in the sky
Who always wanted to learn how to fly
He hung around in the same old places
He'd always seen the same old faces
Then one day just out of the blue
The little star just started to move
At first it was just a little bit
But before he knew it he became fit
As the days went on he became bright
And before he knew he was in full flight
He flew from star to star and then passed the moon
He was headed for Earth very soon
As the Earth became closer it looked like a big ball
Before he knew it he started to fall
As he fell to Earth at a terrific speed he burst into tiny stars for
everyone to see
So the little star served a great purpose
Made everyone smile on Earth's bumpy surface

Life Of A Teenager
Niki Linn Butler
Life of a teenager is like Hell,
many of us buy and sell,
marijuana and crack cocaine,
our lives will never be the same,
Why should we be caring,
when this life of ours is so daring,
we run against the world,

because it's us against the world,
everyone against this teenager's life,

Why don't I pull out a gun or a knife,
run with the thugs, gangsta's crew,
is more than what I plan to do,
I got mixed up with the wrong teenagers,
now my life is in constant fear,
every noise or ring of a bell
life of a teenager is like Hell.

First Day Of Spring
Cecil L. Griffith
The morning creeps on pussycat feet up to my window
and rapping lightly whispers, "I am here."
The virgin sun, smiling above the distant horizon,
promises to do its share
To make the day an enjoyable one for all.
On jumping out of bed, blanket and pillows fall
Scattering on the floor.
I flex my arms, rush through the door
Into the almost—empty street
On eager, springing feet,
Through the deserted park down to the shore,
Take a quick plunge into the sea before
Returning home. A warm soak in the tub,
A vigorous toweling rub;
Then sitting down to coffee, toast and marmalade,
while birds outside in the garden sing,
I give thanks to the One who gives us everything.
Now I'm prepared to face the world on this first day of Spring.

Enchanted Dreams

Nightfall
Ian O'Reilly
Shrouds of darkness fall like bitter rain,
Pondering which life is worth its salt.
This endless shock of realization,
A constant reminder of loves won and lost.
With heart in hand we walk that path,
An ever–twisting crossroads of choices.
Thunder echoes in time with my baited breath,
Each rattled whisper falling on the next.
These beads of sweat that mark my confusion,
They sing and dance their litany of fear.
For no man can truly gaze inside,
And find peace in what he sees.
Boundless oceans of dreams and good intent,
Locked away until oblivion.
That time when light itself will hide like a scared child,
Running from the demons of the night.
And my heart that shines this candle's glow,
Is destined to flicker and then fade to black.

One Way Love
Amina Shaffie
One way love can hurt you
One way love can desert you
But always remember my little friend
This world is not gonna come to an end
Until you find your true love
Just hang in there and he'll show up
You'll fall in love and won't realize
Someone special will take you by surprise
It's gonna happen someday, somehow
Just believe in yourself and go with the flow
There's a person out there who needs your love
He needs your smile and he needs your touch
So, whatever you do, don't forsake
Because one way love is always a mistake.

Love Me
Vincent Duarte
Passing Moments, right love?
Can you share that blood–
stained rose with I?

Your white, pastene lips
left burning impressions on
the night sky.

Touches of insanity through
our sweat–filled nights. Left
senseless in the violet darkness
of our passion. Awakened by
your cynical kiss upon my
chest. Cold fingers dripping
Outburst of flame on my
Cheek.

Annette Lafond
Steve Gillespie
As the moon shines,
nearby stars twinkle and
next to a river, stands an
elegant princess with eyes
that sparkle, forever enhancing
the beautiful smile which
enlightens a glow within.

Left on a rose,
a sparkle of beauty
frees a unicorn, but
only in a dream
next to a river, as
discovered by a princess.

Hawaii
Joyce Malaske
Oh, how I love to visit Hawaii, especially in December.
The beautiful decorations in the hotel lobbies and the outside
Displays, are things that you will always remember.
The warmth of the golden sun, the vastness of the ocean, the scent of
A plumeria lei
These are some reasons that make you want to stay.

Both Christmas carols and hula melodies hang in the air
You truly feel the presence of God everywhere.
Gentle trade winds blow, so blue is the sky, the emerald waters are
Full of God's creatures.
Spinner dolphins and snapping turtles are also Hawaiian features.

The most beautiful, vibrant rainbows and crimson sunsets are lovely
And free.
The beauty of it all are God's gifts for you and for me.
The beauty of life and variety of things in our sight
Makes everything seem so wonderful and spiritually right.

Have You Thought Of Suicide?
Granville Solloway
How can I help you, lonely one?
Behind your self–constructed barricade,
Repulsing all advances, rejecting all who give you aid.
Has life gone wrong? Or is it just the way you're made?
Do you want to end it all tonight?
If that's your answer, you have the right.
But think, think deep,
Before you forever sleep.
Have you thought the sleep may not forever be?
You might return in some other body, strange and wee,
And have it all to again to face,
Maybe in another place.
So stay and make a fight
Instead of ending it tonight.

The Anthology of Poems

The Ring Of Power
Marya Davidson
The Power is mine to do anything,
It was given to me with my wedding ring;
I can cook and clean and I can sew,
And all at the very same time, you know!
I can fix a broken toy with glue
I can nurse a husband in bed with 'flu.
I can fix up my daughter's tangled, long hair,
Whilst also re–covering a dining room chair;
I can walk the dog and feed the cat;
It only takes two minutes flat!
At home no one has this Power but me –
At least not as far as I can see!
My warning, then, to you ladies fair,
Is be on your guard and always take care
Don't let you heart's delight be sold;
For the Power that comes with a band of gold!

Dedication: to Bert, my source of inspiration

Frozen Teardrops
Karina Dibble
Frozen teardrops drip from her eyes
As out in the rain she cries and she cries,
Dropping to her knees like a mourner in prayer,
She lifts her arms to the Heavens in relief and despair.
Frozen teardrops run down her cheeks,
The icy–cold warmth brings the comfort she seeks.
Lightning flashes, lighting the scene,
A brief ray of hope in the dark that had been.
Frozen teardrops melt and are gone,
A life of fear has at last moved on.
She gets to her feet with an easy grace,
A beautiful smile touching her face.

Dedication: to my family, my inspiration

A Religious Divide
Ian MacLean
No passive eye could fail to chill,
to see two bairns walk side–by–side,
like Siamese twins, towards the
learning land.

And there, there came the swift
conclusion, to split apart their
heart–felt bond, by religion's archaic
scalpel.

Yet to justify incision, we may
tranquilize their pain, but
tell us brother, tell us plain,
how can we heal division?

Passed Judgements
Kerry Polk
If I asked you to search deep within my soul and take away all of my pain,
could you be brave enough to face all of the ghosts?
Would you chance it all to know me and all of my wretched mistakes?
To love a woman with so many scars?
Could you love me, anyway, if you could see my past?
Would you hold my hand as we walk down this road
and protect me from all who have hurt me?
If I told you all of my secrets, could you still look into my eyes and
love more?
Or would you look to the floor and love me no more?
Would you walk away and not look back,
holding all of my secrets deep within your soul,
knowing I need you,
but never telling a soul?
And if the ghosts you faced came for you,
would you run from them, too?

Shelby
David Renner
As your child grows and
Your gray hair begins to show

You begin to wonder what life has in store.

Then you're given this wondrous gift of life
From your son and especially his loving wife.

For grandparents there is no greater sight,
Than this loving gift, the gift of life.

Thank you both for what you have given us.

Dedication: to Shelby, my first granddaughter

Lady In White
Karen Hahn Findley
Ice crystals sneaking upon limb and frond
Nature's way of descending with her magic wand
Quietly in the night on cold winter wings
Changing lumps and bumps into beautiful things
Weeds bending their weary heads
Dressing in sheaths of crystal instead
Reflecting the sun's morning rays
Giving color and splendor to their icy displays
And quickly as she came
Silently she leaves
With the gentle warmth of a caressing breeze
She makes her exit till next frosty night
When to reappear with different designs
And more dresses of white
As she bends and kisses the Earth farewell
Her icy breath casts another gossamer veil

Enchanted Dreams

Innocence
Kenneth R. Tober, Jr.
Growing older, I cannot be that which I was.
Having lost all that separates the heart from the soul.
The charred remains of dignity washed away
with tears of regret.
When the little boy within the man
has forever lost his innocence.
A small victim of human passion.
Now I face a sure and systematic decline,
spiraling endlessly towards confusion and anarchy.
Mother cannot patch the wounds.
Her gentle kiss cannot ease the pains.
The tales of Gods and men were spun of lies
into this tapestry that is our lives.
The loose threads gnawed and chewed,
slowly consumed by the demons we possess.
We are after all... only human.
Perhaps true happiness hides within ignorance,
and joy... within stupidity.

Essence
Theron Clarke
The smallest speck, in which is contained the rivers of the world.
Flowing into the seas, whose waves propel breath, crumbling mountain
Forming, white, red and black beaches that dance beneath the pale, gossamer
moon, in presence of, lavender and jasmine, mulled honeysuckle,
crimson–hearted
Aches, roses blushing, dewdrops kissed by morning sunlight, echoing,
crashing
Crescendos waves. Small-handed children running sparkled-eyed and
hooray into dewberry patches where forlorn sounds; foghorns call wanting
for departed lovers.
A biting sun! And hearing my fears of unimportance, the telephone,
a great rush of emotion, the whir of ceiling fans, the drip of candle
wax and unmailed intention. Tides call back and ebbing moons that
dance to Rumbas in old San Juan, on red, black and white beaches.
Where atoms form, falling faster than light on an outstretched child's
hand.

Dedication: to the lady who

Don't Cry
Monica Wood
Look up and live, God will forgive.
For you have life still.
There are many hills, you will climb
So don't cry.

If you keep on trying and choose to live
Instead of dying.
God will stop you from crying.

Don't try to understand, what the Master plans
Just put your life in His hands.
So don't cry

Tears will not wash away our fears.
It's only when we pray, will God hear
So don't cry.

Memory Remains
Wanda M. Bell
When I think of you, I've done this for a long,
I listen well and remember that song,
No matter what I do,
I'll never be able to forget you,
Things I see,
Just everything reminds me,
To have known you, I hold that honor,
This town may someday grow founder,
I'll always wonder, something I'll never see,
Will you ever think of me?
You're always in my thoughts,
I will always miss you, LOTS!

Dedication: to Chai Chai – love and miss you

Untitled
Bill Mackay
One May Think That Winter
With Its Dark And Chill
Would Be The Ideal Haven
For The Desolate Spirit Soul

But This Is Never So
For When One Is Level Low
There Is No Upside Downside
Everything Is Level Low

Made Worse By Snow–Whiteness
Blinding Shining Moonlight
To Glisten Tears
In Sad, Unseeing Eyes.

Dedication: to a lost lover

Untitled
Juliet Dean
Thinking happy thoughts that dim
while staggering through my mind.
Pacing my emotions in my personal
courtroom where my heart's being tried.
My body now weakened by the daybreak's
Violent, seemingly endless light. Night
will soon fall upon me and comfort
those and I, who know pain hides
in moonlight. Not knowing when I'll
see the next cloudy day that
brings no clarity of reality in sight.
I await to comply to my nocturnal
longing where stars are reminders that
only friends are near. People who
show no interrogation of words inducing
tears to reappear.

Dedication: to remembrance of Patrick Terry Topping

Father (A Nursing Home Dirge)
Doris J. Blazy

A waiting station for death is where my father lays...
along with some of life's other castoff strays

It is a depressing sight, poor souls... lying, riding, gliding, shuffling,
none bustling... no, never bustling

I abhor going there
seeing him in his chair
just sitting with a glassy-eyed stare...

IT ISN'T FAIR, IT ISN'T FAIR!!!!

He hardly talks, doesn't walk, can't hear at all,
slurs his speech, it casts a pall

on me

I feel so mad, bad, devastatingly sad... sad... sad... sad... sad

---

My True Love
Erica Burch

Do you believe in love at first sight?
I do, because I met my true love at first sight.

My true love is kind, sweet, caring and loving.
He is all that I have ever wanted in a man.
He is everything that I ask for.

My true love is always there for me when I need him.
He is always by my side when I am feeling down.
He always helps me when I am in need of help.

My true love is a man who is not afraid to show his
true feelings, not even to me.
He loves me for who I am, not for anything else.
Just as I love him for who he is, not for what he is.

Do you believe in love at first sight?
I do, because I met my true love at first sight.

The Essence
Sara M. Bodner

I look with wonder and,
I am filled with awe...
As each glorious colour the breaking – dawn
Casts across the sky
Arcs gently and lingers, in pure beauty
For a fleeting heartbeat;
Then, spreads ever so gracefully, over a
Widening arena.

The colours moving,
Alive and vibrant
Then, subtly molding into the
Next phase of depth,
And hues of magnificence.
My heart fills with joy, as I witness
This breath-taking scene...

Man Child
Janette Jackson

I knew you as a small boy, chasing the sun and laughing out loud,
Head thrown back toward the sky.
I saw you fall, scrambling, not caring, skipping through the sun-soaked
    fields.

I heard your laughter in the quiet rain after a summer's storm, alone and
unobserved. I shared your pain at being shy – not asked to join the games,
yet making all the rules.

I walked the paths of your dreams, touched your lips, danced on your
covers till dawn. I knew you as a small boy with tousled hair and
running nose, full of ebullient wonder and unending curiosity.

I know you now as a man full-grown.
Still running, laughing out loud, falling, not caring, through the
sun-filled days of our lives.

Dedication: to Stan – my best friend!

Ofz
Selig Gertzis

I live in a world of mental disease
Can it be this horror will never cease?
Who can relate this unbearable time,
Living amidst an unchanging crime?
Seeing the depths
Bearing the burden
Watching the failures
Of love's closing curtain.
Try as I will the monster to please
Try as I will the insults deter
Greater the hurt, never the ease
Helpless to seek the illness refer
Never an answer, never a cure
Never a hope, but more to endure.

Changing Of The Tide
William D. Sharp

The morning waves extend their fingers on the
shoreline, as the strength of the tide erodes
yet another landmark. Raw clams, mussels and
saltwater shells placed by the strength of the
sea, slowly start their counter-clock roll with
the changing of the tide. April winds slowly
warm the shoreline as the gliding gulls
search for deposits to complete their food
cycle. Long, narrow, sharp-ended boats scatter
across the shoreline to relieve the waters of
the plentiful that once existed. The once
plentiful, becomes now a dark abyss and
further extends the void that exists
between man and the sea.

The Warrior
Alan Hopkins

Cascading darkness of the night
Blinds the lighting of my sight
The shroud of fear as a partner would
With evil fingers freeze the blood.

Oh, courage of light where have you fled
Voices of the dark skies whisper in my head
I am the warrior that now lays dead

I stood my ground, held it fast
While all around others breathed their last
When the final blow did come
Naught I heard but the muted drum

My Celtic fathers lean to me
And take my hand to guide
Across the threshold of death's door
Forever to abide.

The Three Bears
Suzanne Adams

I had four golden teddy–bears, when I was a child.
If one ever strayed, Oh! how I wailed.
Four faithful friends, my small heart's extension.
Companions at bed–time and every excursion.
Then, one day, the ultimate tragedy occurred,
One got left on a bus, ne'er again to be heard.
Of his whereabouts now, I can only surmise,
Recalling lost childhood, thro' the remaining
six eyes.
But, question I do, did an omen lay hidden?
In that childhood past that was never forgotten.
When adulthood presented another loss to encounter,
A thousand times worse in compared disaster.
For I had, four golden–haired children born to me.
And now, just like the Bears,
I can only hold three.

Dedication: For Max

Summers Of My Youth
Derek Commerford

Of long, hot days of brilliant
summer sun.
Of beaches topped with golden sand
where sparkling tides had run.
Of fields so green and flowers
of a dazzling hue.
Of mornings bright and clean
A sky so clear, so azure blue.
Of evenings in a garden, its flowers
still unfurled.
The calm, the beauty, the peace, it
seems so long ago, perhaps it was
a different world.
Of a country village unspoiled
by modern rage.
These were the summers of my youth
So lovely, so etched forever in my heart
The were of a bygone age.

Alone On Walberswick Beach
M. E. Johnson

Way out to sea the horizon lies gray,
and puffing along, with black, billowing smoke
are two sturdy coasters at work night and day,
made now of iron, not good British oak.
Next when I look, they are way out of sight,
and I'm left with the gulls with their feathers so white.
I thrill to the cry of the gull in the sky
and the feel of the sand on my feet;
I'm watching the waves as they hurl and unfurl
and rattle the stones on the beach.
It's a wonderful day in the wind and the spray
and the roar of the sea makes a silence for me
that holds and enfolds me and goads me to sing—
"Glory to God, to Christ, Holy Spirit, our Heavenly King."

Circumstances
Torderick Curry

We take the most of that which comes,
and the least of that which goes,
Circumstances sometimes cause a wrong turn
when a better way can be chose,
Circumstances may cause us to miss
the beauty of the lowest times,
When we miss the best that comes
an exact match is hard to find.
I've been struck by circumstances
with not much to say
But always remember,
You're the every thought of my day
Forgive me for the shortcomings
forgive me for the change,
Even though I face these circumstances
My love is still the same.

Daniel
J. Corr

We had a precious little love
Jesus called him from our side
To live with the angels in Heaven
Across the great divide
We know he's always with us
When we look to the sky above
We see a star alight with love
It's Daniel watching over us.
We know not, Heavenly father,
Why you took our little boy
But we thank You for his time on Earth
He brought us so much joy
We pray, dear Lord,
When our days are through
We shall join our precious little love
In Heaven with the angels and You.

Dedication: to Danny and Marie

Carlisle Station 1986
Susan Kirby
The woman on the platform
Momentarily panics:
The man on the train
Has disappeared from view.
But then he strides purposefully
Into the compartment, into view.
She catches his eye
Through the window
And smiles.
He waves.
She can see him once again.
But her smile fades fast.
In her heart of hearts she knows
That she has lost him forever.

Summer Days...
Amber Roach
Well, here we are in Summer.
And enjoying what it brings.
Like chilblains on our fingers,
And armfuls of bee stings!

With barbecues and picnics,
Attracting all the flies,
With sweat running down your trousers,
And sand inside your eyes.

Well, here we are in Summer,
With insect–repellent spray.
Our "kiss me quick" hats and coconut mats,
And we wish you all "gooday"!

It's Not So Bad
Joe Plank
It's not so bad, being six
Even though you can't get your kicks
Playing football with the other lads.
You never actually hear the awful thud,
When a mine goes off beneath your foot.
"If it's got your number on it, son, there's nothing you can do"
– or maybe it's your Dad's?

It's not so bad, out playing
In curiosity to pick up a toy
Even though it may destroy your hand.
"Life is what you make it"
when your limb's been amputated?
You get on and endure
If you've quietly concentrated
On living with three limbs instead of four.

Dedication: to Brenda, who helps the crippled

Autumn
Diane Langridge
The air has changed, the colours, too;
From Summer's sun to Autumn tune,
The golden leaves fall gently down,
And collect like paper parcels on the ground.

The birds are leaving for sunnier shores,
While the squirrels are busy collecting Winter stores.
All farmers have gathered in their crops,
And the old man's beard now smothers the hedgerow tops.

This is my favourite season of the year,
Its smell and sounds delight my nose and ear.
These thirteen weeks are soon to pass,
And then I'm left to my memory's grasp.

Best Friend
Linda Shacklady
A poem I send to my best mate
I think she's Bill and just so great
We work together, we get on well
Her name is Jacqui L
You never take the Mickey
or ever put me down.
If I have a problem
you always understand
If I am sad or feeling blue
I know I can depend on you
I couldn't find a better friend.
No matter how I try
We laugh, we joke, work so well together
I hope we'll be the best of friends forever

Ode To The Major Oak Of Sherwood
Pamela Hayes
Centuries have passed you by,
Majestic, there you stand.
So regal and so graceful.
Your arms embrace the land.
In winter you are barren,
Your weathered bark is cold,
But life still stays within you.
The bell has not yet tolled.
In spring your buds do open,
And blossoms soon burst forth
With acorns you are laden,
Yet soon fall down to Earth.
The time will come so sadly,
When you will be no more.
And I'll remember gladly,
When I passed through your door.

Dedication: to my sons, Gregory, Christopher and Timothy

Enchanted Dreams

Untitled
Diane Kerswill

The good Lord came to visit me
He thought my hill too high to climb
He laid His hand upon my heart
And said peace now be thyne.

With arms of love wrapped round me
He lead me by the hand
Into the holy kingdom
They call the promised land
A place that's filled with kindness
Love and peace is all around
No words can describe the beauty
Of this treasure that I've found.

Shed not a tear for my sake
Instead just give a smile
When your thoughts allow you
To think of me once in a while.

Land Lover
Jean Bailey

I would Love a little cottage on a little
plot of land with a stream of running water
flowing clearly through the land.

I would wake up in the mornings at the sight
of meadows green—at the poppies in the fields
so red and much to glean.

I would enjoy the sunsets from my window in
the evening time and early in the mornings
lie and listen to nature calling time.

I would listen to country sounds, the birds
singing in the trees, I would watch the seasons
changing as I gazed into the breeze.

I know the sounds of the country would be pleasing
to my ears and the smell of new mown–hay when July is here.

A Lullaby
Megan Livermore

Dreamer of dreams, your life is sweet, you have nothing
to fear, in your growing years life will be full, full
of dreams.
Hopes and frustrations as you grow older, older and
bolder, your dreams getting stronger.
Oh, dream of life, my little one.
Love and charm, you'll have it all, Those blue eyes,
warm and so bold, that charming smile, so lovely to
use, used to charm life and whatever it holds.

Dream, oh, little one, dream sweet dreams
life is full of love for you, your eyes so blue,
how can they fail to make laughter shine, Shine
all round you now, now and forever.

Redemption
Eileen Kettle

I was lost in a dark, foreboding wood,
Where fearful shapes around me stood.
Knowing not which way to turn,
Where is the "point of no return"?
I felt I just could not go on,
Then suddenly, a bright light shone
Small and far away it seemed,
But, somehow, I felt I'd been redeemed.
I stumbled on towards its ray,
Not knowing how long, but many a day,
Then I was standing in the light,
The sun was shining, clear and bright.
An angel of Mercy did appear,
And I felt, once more, that Life was dear!

The Legacy
Margaret Andrew

Your fingerprints are everywhere
It is too soon for you to be a ghost.
And yet you linger
In corners that were once yours,
Cradled by yesterday's laughter.
Time banishes, laughter breaks
And yet you linger,
Smiling out from old photographs
Reassuring in gentle, faded loveliness.
To me you sang old songs and lullabys
I have not lost you,
Your fingerprints are everywhere
It is too soon for you to be
A ghost.

Dedication: to Wilf, my dearest love

My Childhood
Beverley Kavanagh

When I look out of the window,
I dream of days gone by,
The clouds, they look like pictures
floating in the sky,
I think about my childhood,
The fun that I once had,
I've always got those memories,
I'll keep them of my Dad,
I know that I was lucky to have him for a while,
I think about the good times,
They often make me smile,
My Mum is very special, she is always there for me,
I never could replace her,
She means everything to me.

Dedication: to Bridie, my mum and friend

Love On High
Pauline Wisdom

Every evening as the sun goes down,
A secret meeting does take place.
Two lovers embracing one another
At long last, face to face.

Nothing unusual about that, you cry,
Gazing around for more proof.
Well, look beyond the garden fence
High upon the roof.

For these are no usual lovers
Who are necking high above.
The two sweethearts in question
Are pigeons filled with love.

The Forecast
Grace Davis

What will the stars forecast to–day,
Will you go, or will you stay,
That girl you've met, could she take my place,
Or will you forget her without trace,
My love for you is so strong,
Could that forecast be right or wrong.

We've been together for quite awhile,
Had our sorrows and our smiles,
The world around us is in a state,
Please don't let me add to the hate.

I sit and wait in the gloom;
Whilst the neon signs light up the room,
The dancing shadows on the wall,
They try to say, don't be a fool,
But tomorrow is another day,
And there is hope and I must pray.

In Reply
V. M. Broadbear

You've asked me to find a rhyme
Applicable to Christmastime?
I've hunted through books galore,
There was no Santa in that store.
So now I'm racking my brains
To hear the jingle of those reins!
I walked around the London store
Searching for gifts by the score,
No coloured lights to guide my way
Not even the star of the shepherd's day!
Yes! The Christmas spirit is fading fast
What can we do to make it last?
Christ was born to make it men gay
Strife and warfare rule to–day.
Can we follow where Christ has led
Beginning humbly within that shed!

An Anvil Wedding At Gretna
Stephen A. Yow

Bitter cold and early morn,
The last fifty paces,
From the Hall to the Blacksmith's shop,
A gathering of related faces.

Mist quivers with floral euphony
As The Piper cuts the northern air,
Timbered roof stood guard to yesterday's young bride,
Far away, other loves left unaware.

This is it.
Tears when fears fall,
Flashes of white flutter the flock,
Soft, Scottish intonation soothes the shop,
New titles given in trust and hope,
A clash of steel seals the deal.

Sonnet 1
Pete Whitcomb

How many sleeps
Can we go to the fair
Swimming or the park to play

How many sleeps
Can we stay
for days and days

I know where school is from here
You can still go to work
as I know the way
How many sleeps.

Dedication: to Jasmin and Demi – love, Dad

Ode For The Occasion
Ann–Marie Troup

A poetry contest – just send in a rhyme?
I couldn't resist – I do it all the time.
For friends and relations I try very hard
to include a poem in their birthday card.
If one gets married I get out my pen
I can't help it, I'm at it rhyming again.
Passed an exam or your driving test?
I can't wait to send you a rhyming jest.
My friends all like them and say they're funny
so now I'm trying to win some money.
My eyes lit up at your advert today
inviting one to make ones' writing pay.
So now I'm filled with hope and tension
to hear if I've won cash or honourable mention!

Enchanted Dreams

Mother Earth
Joan Egre
What price to place on our greatest treasure?
With all its creatures, both great and so small,
Tender care by all hands beyond measure,
For due respect and true love, it does call.
To keep all its glory and beauty so fair,
To labour lovingly, for it is our wealth,
Protecting forests, its life, some most rare,
Seek good husbandry practice for its health.
Keep pure our rivers, seas and little streams,
Try keep the very air pure everywhere.
To continue all our abundance dreams,
With glorious beauty, joy and peace there.
We hope, protect the world's atmosphere right;
Wonder mother Earth, mantled in her might.

Music Emotions
Kristin Sasse
I take a deep breath and my lungs fill with air
I slowly breathe into the shiny tube with keys they call a
flute
The beautiful notes reach the listeners' ears
Making them imagine an orange and pink sunset over the
Pacific Ocean
The music acts as the waves washing onto the listeners' ears
It's as if my heart and soul are reaching out to these
people
Telling them all my dreams and fantasies in a beautiful
language from a distant planet of sunsets and beaches
And when the song ends and my soul's speech stops
The memory of that Moment when my whole being was
exposed to the cruel world will live on
And I hope that with the music I love so much
I some how have enriched the listeners' spirit and soul

Wondrous Life
Brian Miller
Oh, wondrous life in which I am but me
What can be found to lessen clouding haze.
The need in me to grow and yet to see
Will in hope veil the me and yet amaze.
Are we to ponder on the life of One,
To rack the thoughts and bruise the tired brain
Or nestle soft and let the One become,
To come to life and live this life again.
There is but me to stop this righteous course,
To leave the loathsome memories behind.
In time whatever shields the precious source
Will bring the light to eyes before so blind.
Perhaps try not to work at seeing more
And let true light pervade the closing door.

Dedication: to my dad, Bill

Rainbow
A. J. Hughes Aubney
The spectrum bridge is in the air,
With the real sun shining through,
Fine drizzle is a–falling down,
With colours of every hue.

Morning had a bright blue sky,
And a smiling difference made,
The light of afternoon has changed,
The scene now looks afraid.

When the rainbow returns with a majestic light.
And it seems ethereal, too,
The grey has gone, its colours bright,
And it's true for all the view.

Life's Cycle
Clare Jewell
Harvests come and harvests go,
Love's cycle comes full swing,
Life, birth, marriage, death,
Are placed upon a wheel.
Yet death is not an end,
But a passing between worlds,
And life and love, hate and fear,
Will always come full swing.

Debts must be paid,
Labours rewarded,
And what we sow shall we reap.
Life is what we make it,
Choice and free will are ours.
So open your hearts,
Children of the Earth, sun, stars and moon,
Know your heart is a divine spark
Of God's loving wisdom in you.

Life
D. Palmer
Faster than a flying arrow,
Swifter than a bird in flight,
Speeding on towards tomorrow,
As quick as time goes by at night.
In the blinking of an eye,
A blur of light too fast to see,
Like lightning bolt in thundery sky,
It comes and goes like you and me.
Our lives are but a fleeting shadow,
Hopes and fears condensed by time,
Dreams and goals of then and now,
Too soon our light will cease to shine.
Let each day be one to treasure,
Who knows when our span will end,
Take what life's prepared to offer,
Ere the reaper's scythe descends.

Dedication: to Sandy Que Sera Sera

The Anthology of Poems

To Odgen Nash – One Poem Is As Good As Another
Mary Louise Ho
Dear Mr. Nash, I truly do say
That you most certainly have a peculiar way
Of making your line–alies
Strangely Rhymilie.

And many people must often stop and
Ponder again and again without fully
Understanding exactly what in Heaven's name you mean!
Tell those people to go eat a stringbean!

For certainly it cannot be denied
That nothing is not unright with your mind.
To you I say hurrah! Hurrache!
And now to bed, you've given me a headache.

In A Cloud's View
Forbes Jackson
In a cloud's view
the Earth seems fresh and new
passing over land and sea
giving life to dreams so easily

High up in the air
clouds are so unaware
of the love and sorrow below
they just follow where winds blow

it's not for clouds to care
what happens down there
floating along so gracefully
seeing things so happily

The Woman Within My Dreams
Tony R. Watret
I dreamed a dream.
A dream so colorful and wondrous, it was.
A dream of the lust of a woman to be.
The lust of the passion I shared with the woman of my dreams,
Is one of a fire from within my heart and soul,
Fueled by a flame of passionate love,
That would last beyond life itself into eternal afterlife.
The rhythm of the love we had within my dreams,
It was like the waves of the sea crashing upon the shore, so fresh, so beautiful,
And in perfect harmony with life itself.
But alas, the cruelty of the dawning of the day comes upon me,
I am awakened to go through another day of life,
Alone on the path, I travel into the darkness of times to come.
The woman within my dreams,
Will she ever be?

Time And Distance
Julee Carlson
It separates me,
from a person I care so much to see.
He stole my heart, I steal time to hold him close.
I want him to be mine.
Power of love, stronger than me,
takes me where I want to be.
High on a mountain, above the clouds.
Places I dream, away from the crowds.
Fogged–up windows, hidden places,
passionate kisses in enclosed spaces.
Can one person, full of life, fill my soul and end my strife?
Dreams of laughter
Dreams of play
Dreams of hope make my day.

The Giving
Amanda Lynn Darling
If
I could
give the world
a gift, I would give
food to the poor, I would
give peace to the world, I would
give homes to the people who have no
homes so their children can get warm by the
fire
and
the tag
would say
Love
Amanda D.

Dedication: to my third grade teacher, Mrs. Zoerb

You're The Woman I Love The Most
Brandon Lee Hartfield
You're the woman I love the most
You're the woman I'm only trusting
You're the woman I still love
You're the woman each day I love more
I can't stand being without you
Everything I am is because of you
I'll love you till the day I die
but death can't take away my love
I used to pray for you every night
now every night I hold you tight
I see you in everyone
but you are my only one
No one have I loved more than you
You're the woman I love the most

Enchanted Dreams

Him
Erin Girby
His eyes were strong, such a muscular build. But there on that night he stood alone. His body frail and his heart broken, knowing there was no looking back at what had happened. The words still burned through head, heart and ears. What was he to do now, he had just learned to love and trust again and he
Had finally let someone over the wall he had built. This person helped him slowly tear it down, piece by piece, but now he once again put up a border or boundary against love, at least for a while. How could he forget the love and
Feeling that they had. But now he walks off into the moonlight and cries himself to sleep at night, praying and hoping that it's all just one big nightmare and he'll wake up soon.

Dedication: to my big brother Michael

My Uterus
Timothy M. Forry
are you one of the boys
who says
women are beautiful?

I've scraped my knees on carpets
for boys like you before
you scream your mother's name
when you fill my mouth
with a million
half–children
I choke
as you walk out the door
my mouth is a womb
I can spit out babies
just like a beautiful
uterus.

A Spirit Breaks Free
R. Meo
My soul cries out into the night,
Seeking the passion of a lost day.
Ears strain, poised, waiting
for the answering call.
In the distance, an echo grows,
Waves of passions wash over me.
The blood in my veins rises to meet it,
like the river rushes to join the sea.
My spirit strains, trying to break free its Earthly bounds.
The pulse of the echo moves below me,
lifting the wings of my being, giving it the joy of flight.
There is a Moment of pain, as spirit and body part,
it is wiped out in an instant, as the body gives up its fight.
Firelight dances in the chamber of joy as the echo becomes a flame,
glistening with the light of a new day.
Born on the wings of an echo, my soul has found,
not the passions of lost a day,
but the promise of a better day...

Emotion Called Poetry
Andrea Thompson
Creative words stimulate our mind...
Open thoughts ready to explode,
Bleeding feelings of Black ink,
Screaming words waiting to be witnessed
Threads of emotion woven together,
this loose–leaf paper loom.
A flooded mind of memories,
The undertow of tears...
flowing through the hand
into puddles of nonsense.
Comprehended in a splash of chaos,
Conformed only by a label.

Dedication: to Salena, an inspiration

Time
Brad A. Manis
Life and years keep moving past
Time runs our days and nights
Time's like a thief that gets his way, we just can't win this fight
Like the wind and burning sun turn green shrub to brown sage
Time takes the colors of our youth and turns us gray with age
But don't pass down your judgment based on what you've read
Till now
Time also has some good points and I'll tell you of them now

Time doesn't really steal, in fact it's more a compromise
A young mind's thoughts are foolish. But with time a mind grows
Wise
And for the sake of time I feel more good things should be
Spoken
For time's the only cure that heals your heart when it's been
Broken
The clock now strikes the hour and the bells begin to chime
There's so much I could tell you – if we only had the time.

The Voice Of The Willow
Sadie Rose Terral
The sun shines here
The wind blows there
Willow stays in a spot
Thousands of arms go only where the wind says
Loudest voice among all trees
Not a single person can hear

Yippidy fox waits
For the threatening wind will pass
He dances about and sings his songs to make cheer
The wind goes from here
The sun shines there
The fox lies silently asleep
Loudest voice among all trees
Fox can hear
Not a single person can

Silent Scream
Nathan Lawyer
Feelings my heart put to bed
Once forgotten, left for dead
Mingle with my thoughts and fears
Behind a shroud of faceless tears
Lips so close beyond my reach
Cloud my eyes, my thoughts, my speech
Brief encounter, skin touch skin
Fire roars and screams within
Heart is heavy, screams the name
One to save me from my pain
Hold me close in arms so warm
Save me from myself and harm
Cradle me against her breast
Lay my aching soul to rest

Dedication: to my beloved Victoria

Psychotic Lament
Julia Chastain
A wave of vengeful intent, nothing more than a word of regret.
Dark and sleepless is the night, like the heart filled with discontent.
A woman walks down the forbidden street, the man passes in a car.
Somewhere on the road, loneliness and tragedy are destined to meet.
The back alley behind a park, maybe an empty room in an apartment block.
Is it real? It matters not, both will play their worthless parts.
Cries of pleasure, then cries of anger, sounds of pain.
A blade of death draws near, "walls have eyes" the brain again assures.
Flee once more into the comforts of mind, the tortures of home, away from being satisfied.
Let the light of day awaken to, what is actual, what is sublime.
The heart of discontent, beckoned back into the night.
The blade of death strikes, with no word of regret, in a wave of vengeful intent.

Scared Heaven
Gabrielle Herbst
If Heaven is so great,
How come no one ever wants to go there?
Is it a big torture chamber,
filled with the things that you never had,
but always wished you'd owned?
Do the angels scare you with their beautiful, pale faces and soft wings?
The feeling of a white, satin robe against your skin,
does it itch?
The warmth of the soft clouds,
do you dislike comfort?
Eternal bliss and harmony,
does it seem impossible?

If Heaven is so great,
How come no one ever wants to go there?
Do you cry of loneliness?
Is it truly filled with the pain of perfectness?
Is Heaven really a Heaven?

Reunion
Kathy Hallak
Carpets of wildflowers
Ceilings of blue sky
Walls draped in Spanish moss
Surrounded by a ring of trees
She waits for my arrival
With baskets of fresh strawberries
We eat and laugh until our lips are red and hearts are full
Her silver hair is long and thin
Noble like the horse's mane
My fingers touch her wrinkled skin and I gaze into her eyes
Her face tells stories words could never share
Love surrounds her like sweet sunlight
She died when I was only eight
Thank goodness for the beautiful eternity of memory

Dedication: to my father

The Rose
Bethany Hartle
with all its beauty
is only as strong as its stem
Its thorns protect it from harm
yet in doing so
it keeps it all alone
we can reach out
and touch its soft petals
but never hold it close to our heart
if we try to cut away the thorns
it will wither and die
we must accept it as it is
with its thorns and great beauty
forever
The Rose

Fireside Vigil
Loni Pham
Laughing out into the moonless night
Slowly dying by the fireside
Searching for the guiding light
Looking for a soul unto confide
Learning about life from isolation
Slipping from society's grip
Losing sight of civilization
Ignoring words uttered by other's lips
Growing lonelier with the days
Wondering why life went uninspired
Not knowing what to do or say
Hoping life will soon expire
Dying by the burning fireside,
Laughing at all there was to hide.

Enchanted Dreams

In The Winds
Jennifer M. Garcia
In the winds floating in the clouds
and flying with the butterflies
are lost sounds.
Sounds, voices, broken promises of love,
wishes and dreams
lying in the wings of a dove.

Love is a word that is very abused.
Look in the clouds, do you see images
of broken hearts and lovers who were once confused?

Love is a word that is very abused.
Love is a word,
we should watch how we use.

The Flash Of Faith
Tim Stevens
As the moon shines out on the cold, dark sky
You sit and look deeply into the never-ending specks of an
unknown world
Where the peacefulness is mesmerizing and the beauty is
unthinkable
Then a thought from the deepest part of your soul rises up
Why are we here? And what are we doing?
Then more thoughts arise
Where did we come from and where are we going?
Just then a light flashes in the sky
"Where did that come from" you say quietly to yourself
And then your brain goes numb
And you realize that all your questions have just been
answered
By one flash in the sky
That makes the outcome of your life
different
For the rest of your years to come

Why I Hold You Dear To Me
Dianne Renze
You're honest and compassionate
You have a heart a mile wide
You don't condemn, you never judge
And you encourage me to try
You love me unconditional
With not one string attached at all
Give me courage to take a chance
Without the fear that I might fall
You give me faith in who I am
And all the things I want to be
You give me strength to stand alone
That's why I hold you dear to me

Dedication: to Craig, for believing in me

Untitled
Antonio Marcello
Souls of a tainted garden,
memories, without gleam.
Hearts have become hardened,
unheard and unseen.

Look into the eyes,
the gloom is plain to see.
Many will not notice,
unless you have been.

So as for living life,
be sure to take a glance.
The children are our future.
This may be your last chance!!

Dedication: to the children of the world

A Poem For My Grandmother
Cyndi Hug
One bright, sunshiny day,
Grandmother, Aunt Minnie and Dorothy went out to play.
Down the sidewalk, through the flowers they walked.
The birds were singing as they talked.
As the trio started up the stairs,
Their laughter turned into scares,
Grandmother fell into the grass,
Aunt Minnie fell upon the lass.
To the hospital she was rushed,
Her right hip bones were badly crushed.
Now with a new hip she is mending,
And to her this poem I am sending.

Dedication: to Angela Schwartz

Diana
Casey Parker
rising star
shining bright
cutting through
the darkest night
when it falls
it's unaware
of all those
who truly care
emotions
it can't see
deaf to all
the agony
time too short
life too long
a shadow over
the new dawn

The Anthology of Poems

The Testament
William W. Collins III
Through life we meet people; see them come and go.
Loved-ones and acquaintances long lost by time.
But, once in a lifetime we find someone who can change even the meaning of time. I have seen you and never knew of you till now; your very essence flows around my soul like a warm blanket in this wintry day of life.
I know loneliness no more, for that void is filled with your very being. In your eyes, so beautiful and warm, I see my soul held so very high. You have the gift to bring out the best of my heart, for which you will always have a place; a promise that can never be broken. You make an angry man smile and a sad one laugh. Your love is beyond that which can be spoken of any reason or cause. I am so very grateful that you are by my side to walk with me in my time of need

---

Waves
Michael Pavlovic
Some use boards of fiberglass
to propel themselves along,
to keep from a wipeout crash
they need to be skillful and strong.
Then there are the kindred souls
that wish to view the negative,
as they go for submerged strolls
to explore the alternative.
They all fight for space
with native inhabitants,
gliding with ease and grace
but losing most entanglements.
I'm glad we look to the Heavens
to make our next conquest,
let's leave the waves to the dolphins
and allow them their noble infiniteness.

First I Love You
Jessica McLelland
A young girl watches her Daddy go to work.
A young girl watches her Mother go to sleep.
A young girl watches her sister leave.
The beast enters for a visit
A young girl watches as her clothes are ripped from her body.
She watches her tears fall down in the crevasse between her breasts.
She hears his growl in her right ear and feels the heat of his panting breath.
She feels his claws rip into her soft cotton skin.
She dares not make a noise – a scream – a cry – she is dying inside.
The beast is tired.
He removes himself from the innocent lamb and retreats to his cave.
Before he leaves he whispers – I love you...
Father comes home from work – Goes to say goodnight to his child.
Goodnight– I love you – he whispers.
The daughter sits and cries.

Dr. King's Dream
Rochelle Harris
Dr. King had a dream for all mankind
His dream was for equality, so we all could be free.

He was a peacemaker and a dreammaker.
For the world to see.
He believed in equal rights for you and me.

Dr. King was a minister, teacher and a father, too.
He stood for justice for me and you.

Peacemaker and dreammaker, that was his legacy, as a man.
He tried to spread love, peace and unity across the land.
That was Dr. Martin Luther King, Jr.

Untitled
Svetlana Zakharova
It's better if you will not let me come in,
Then I will not open these doors.
It's better if you will lie to me,
Then I won't believe in your words.

It's better if I'll be disappointed in you,
Then you'll be disappointed in me.
It's better if I'll stay with no clue,
Then you'll be mixed up and lose a key.

While I am alive, while you are alive
I'm praying for your benefit.
Let me be the sun of your life,
The soil under your feet.

Yesterday's Loneliness
Laurie McLaughlin
People don't understand why I feel so alone,
Because my hurt has never shown.
It's little things that always get me down,
Killing my smile, making me frown.
There are just a few things you fail to realize,
This mean, big fighter has tears in her eyes.
Maybe you need someone, maybe you don't.
Maybe we'll get along, maybe we won't.
I feel there are things you really want to say,
But you just can't seem to throw trust my way.
I want to share your laughter and all of your tears,
All of your happy times and erase your world of fears.
To help and hold your heart if ever it should bleed
I really want to be there when you are in need!

Enchanted Dreams

Thirst
Mike Lege
I have a thirst
A thirst deeper than that of man lost for days in the hottest desert without water
Nay, lost for a lifetime on the face of the sun without any water
A thirst not for water, though
It is not a physical thirst, but a mental thirst
A craving for the love of a woman
A thirst not from the stomach, but from the heart

My thirst is for Love, the true love that bonds people for all eternity
My hunger is for a woman who will always fill my stomach
For if I had the love I crave, I would need nothing else
My stomach would be filled and my thirst would be quenched
All would be well

Tears In My Heart
Sarah Schroeder
Although I am not crying, there are tears in my heart.
They come from deep within my soul where a sea of pain rages against my
Will to survive.
Each tear holds a lifetime of pain.
I wonder why I am still breathing as tears of blood flow like a river from
The broken pieces of an innocent heart.
I am weak now as each tear takes its toll on the remnants of my strength.
I long to be cradled in the loving arms of peace but the tears in my heart
Are like chains.
I am bound to my pain.
It is my destiny,
Although I am not always crying, there are always tears in my heart.

Dedication: to all the tender souls

Lost Love
Jerome Sellars
It's the middle of winter,
yet I think it's summer.
It's been only weeks since
I lost my life.
And yet, I wait patiently
for my resurrection
but it's seemed
to be denied.
Having no life, soul, or body,
feels like death
that comes every day.
I'll continue to wait patiently,
for my resurrection is what
my patience will pay.

Pain
Melissa Sciullo
Pain is an experienced feeling
Emotionally or physically felt.
It can be the hatred of others,
Or the knife in your back.
Whatever it may be,
Do not feel alone.
We are all in it together,
But there is much more to learn.
You cannot experience joy
If you have not any pain.
Listen to others more seriously.
They may be suffering more than you.
We must reach out and help.
It is the pain's turn to suffer.

Treasuring
Susan L. West
Beyond the tall trees where the grasses swished,
We stood together and prayerfully wished,
"Dear God, we place our lamb in Your keep
With our steadfast love..." and we did weep.
It's been a year now, our dear Love,
Since you joined the angels up above.
While down below we've tried our best,
Though, at times, it's been quite a test.
We've missed your smile, that breath of spring,
Your kindness, humanity... just everything.
You taught us a manner of living,
The blessing of unselfish giving.
How easily you mastered that key
While we still struggle diligently.
God surely needed your gentle touch;
But how we miss you, oh, so much,
Please rest well in your Godliness,
We'll treasure always your loveliness.

My Unicorn
Gordon Burch Watson
Wonderfully, a creature of beauty,
affectionately, eyes brightly gleam,
surrounded by tales of mystery,
My unicorn, magical he seems,

Majestically, cantering alone,
secretly, under the moon's bright light,
from a world seemingly unknown,
My Unicorn, spirit in the night,

Free as the whispering wind,
Strong, courageous and bold,
from now 'til eternity's end,
My Unicorn and his horn of gold,

Reflections Of Love
John C. Zimmerman
I look and see the roses in the garden
as the incandescent rays emitted by the sun
illuminate their beauty,
memories arise of a love so warm,
a love so true, a love not to be forgotten
alas, the only love I knew
the love of an Angel, Goddess or
is she just a maiden, as the rose
is just a flower? She cannot be,
for thou has stolen my soul and
the heart I wore upon my chest,
just as a rose remains in a garden until
torn from its roots of home or until
the rose perishes, as someday
my heart will less, I find my love
so warm, a love so true.

Dedication: to Candace, my lost love

The Vineyard's Virtuoso
Nancy Moller
Green leaves, weather–gilded
Sun, shade, shadows, silence
Fragrant fruit, hard, soft, sour, sweet
Lavender luminaries, purple pearls

Oval ornaments, baubles, beads
Clustered on climbing, curving, curly vines
Brave branches gently growing
Robust roots, through Earth, nurturing

Flavors, colors, scents, senses
All in full concert
Quietly conducted by Creation
The vineyard's Virtuoso

Today My Smiling Cowboy Went To Heaven
Rickie Jean Cassady
Looking For His love of His Life
The Smiling Cowboy in my Life
is gone for now.
But I know the Smiling Cowboy
is a Smiling Angel Cowboy now.
And he is with the love of his life.
And I'll see my Smiling Cowboy
named Jack again one day.
His spirit is strong with us all.
So there's no need to say good–bye
to my Smiling Cowboy
But to say hello each and every day
And I love you, my Brother
Dear.
So hello and I'll see you
Soon.

Dedication: to Jack McPherson (my smiling sibling)

Untitled
Scott B. Sherman
I lay alone at night and stare into space,
Then I see an image of your pretty face
Down my cheek rolls one lonely tear,
I don't want to blink, because you'll disappear
I fight back the urge with all of my might,
I don't want to lose this beautiful sight
I reach out my hand to try to touch your cheek,
My hand goes right through you and your image grows weak
Finally I blink and you are not here,
I smile to myself as I wipe off the tears
Your image stays with me, though we're apart,
I carry it with me, here in my heart
The day will soon come, when you'll be my wife
And we'll be together, one heartbeat, one life
So then when this image comes back to me
I'll just roll over and there you will be,
Where I can reach out and hold you so tight
Here in my arms, for the rest of our nights.

The Master's Gems
Jeanette L. Estrada
The stone that lays on the cutter's bench
is rough and not very trim—
But he knows, that with a little work,
there is beauty deep within.
He cuts and grinds, to give it rebirth—
and, now, it's a gem of the greatest worth.
Polished, it is and very fine—
because the cutter took the time.
So it is with God's own jewels
that are rough and unpolished, but fine—
With loving care He cuts and grinds—
until they are ready for service divine.
The Master knows the worth of His own—
He knows, deep inside, they are more than stone.

Dedication: to Sherman and Edna Hales

Sweeping Through Me
M. David Ficarelli
Blowing through my mind,
The winds of life dance.
They tickle my soul gently,
And push me toward my fears.
The winds of the changing world,
Are here to show us how
And when and where and why,
The reasons that we're alive.
I'm angry that those winds,
Have yet to blow my way,
All the joys of love
And the blessings that love holds.
But without the taste of love,
I might not feel the power
Of the connection of two souls.
And while I long for love,
I still feel the winds of life,
Gently sweeping through me.

Enchanted Dreams

Mirror
Carmen Garcia
I look in the mirror, who do I see?
A youthful expression smiling at me.
My future wide—open, clear with
no bound.
I could be anything, happy and proud.
Today I woke up, looked in the mirror
Who do I see? Just an older version
of me.
The child I was, the mirror took away,
Stolen from me day after day.
Give it back, it's not fair!
The mirror just laughed without a care.
I look in the mirror, that day
it took my hand.
Told me it was time to leave this
land.
Mirror, I ask, do you ever change?
No not me, only the reflection you see.

Celebrating Men's Day
Jeanette H. Jefferson
Marshals and ministers of our wondrous Universe
Explorers innately of Earth and space
New inventions — seeking new dimensions.
Conceived in mind by our Almighty God.
Men — the rough, tough exterior, a man—made protective facade.

Women do not generally agree that this is a man's world.
However, today's celebration of men, a Man's Day flag we unfurl.

Men celebrating life, love, family and friends
Men who know how to draw on the power within
Men doing the right thing from beginning to the end of this day
Celebration of life and love
Our Creator lives within, not in some obscure "above".

Dedication: to Husband John, my brothers — Men of St. Paul

Did You Ever??
Steven Nahoum
Take a look at the sky when the sun is setting, disregarding anything
    commercial?
Gaze at the lips of someone you love and realize you've waited too long to
kiss them again? Swim with your eyes open underwater in the clear
blue—green surroundings of a tropical retreat?
Watch the wind play havoc with trees, plants and shrubs?
Stare at your almost—grown children sleeping and remember
when they came out of the womb?
Think about how old you are, how much time has passed and
what's in store for the time you have left?
Hope that someone can feel more wonderful than they've ever felt
in their life, because of you? Stop and think that a little,
white lie is still such when you claim to be totally honest?
Contemplate if someone can truly be at ease about death
when you possess life's most precious gifts — children,
grandchildren, great—grandchildren?
Come to the realization that life is so short and yet such
an abyss of experiences and feelings?

You Are So Fine
R. L. Fincher
When I think of you
I think of the morning dew
So clean, so bright, so full of life
I've been waiting for my whole life
With hair as dark as the sky in the deep, dark sky at night
Your eyes so deep, so dark, so bright
In your arms all my love I would surrender
To feel your lips touch mine so warm, so soft, so tender
To hear your silken voice ask, "Will you be mine?"
I'd give my soul to you for all time
I'd give you my heart
For it was yours from the start
To hear your voice whisper, "I love you," as your lips touch mine
Is all I need to be yours until the end of time

Dedication: to my special friend forever

Dreamin'
Roosevelt Neal
I slipped into your room last night, you
didn't see me there. I kissed your lips and
touched your face and ran my fingers through
your hair... I felt such comfort in my mind,
I heard your beating heart. I looked into your
Dream, my dear and saw I played a part... As I
gently lay beside you, I couldn't help but cry,
the dawn was soon in coming and my dream with
you must die... I whispered softly in your ear
and told you how I feel, you seemed to smile with
pleasure as if this dream were real... I slipped
away before the dawn and if only I could stay.
My dreams are all I have with you while I'm
so far away.

Christmas Prince
Ray Posada
The holidays are here! That's great. This time is very enjoyable.
But when I think of my Grandpa, it brings back memories of his
favorite day, CHRISTMAS.
I think of Christmas's past, when he was alive. I remember him
telling stories of how he heard bells and hoofsteps on his roof and
how surprised he was when he woke up. Then he would put my sister
and I to bed, tuck us in and wish us goodnight. As he closed the
door and the room turned dim, we laid motionless, listening for every
little sound, only our anxiety kept us a wake.
But soon the darkness took us over and we fell asleep.
The next Christmas, when he was gone, we missed his stories and
his spirit. On Christmas eve, we lay in bed, not listening for sleigh
bell or hoofsteps, but his laughter and his voice, which rang with joy
around this time of the year.
The next morning there was no spirit, there was no joy.
I miss my Grandpa, the Christmas Prince.

The Anthology of Poems

The Stream
Jacqueline Rue
The stream in the mountain,
Trickles and gleams like a fountain.
The water is so crystal clear,
It's a wonderful thing to hear,
Rushing over the stones so near.
Listen to its little moans,
See its sparkle, hear its groans.
It's full of excited, jumping fish,
I throw in a penny and make a wish.
But one day all of the fish disappear,
The water turns gray instead of clear,
That beautiful fantasy slowly smears.

My only wish is to find a solution,
And kill the pollution,
Before it kills all of the beauty of the world.

Dedication: to Mom, Dad, Evanne, Haley and Belle

The Eyes Of A Child
Shelley Hewes
You are so dear, so special to me.
And, in my heart, you always will be.
So tiny at first, but bigger each day,
No words will express what I need to say.
Growing in ways I never knew I would,
You've changed my life as only you could.
Always there with your ready smile,
You help to overcome each new trial.
You are the shadow at my side,
So curious, so wonderful, so much left to try.
A world of marvelous things to explore,
Amazed to discover secrets by the score.
The world must seem, indeed, very wild
When seen through the laughing eyes of a child.

Middle Of June
Ernest Allen
When the middle of June comes by each year
It takes my angel far from here
Austin, Texas, is where my angel goes to stay
Three full months with her Dad, night and day

I know he's happy but I'm so sad
She's seeing her father and for that I'm glad
My teardrops fall 'most every day
Worrying about my angel at play

Writing her letters and using my phone
Keeps me busy while she's away from home
At the last of August, it's great to learn
That to California, she will soon return!

Wanderlust
Joel Boush
Violet, booming violence,
Runaway wind chases dreams,
Running wild like a raging child,
Boisterous blows, unutterable things.
Crashing, crushing bane;
Slicing, slashing rain
Slipping down the drain,
Driving the very drops insane.
Thunder rolls; that thunder rules;
Dark'ning screams, unchangeable themes;
Brewing pot, boiling hot,
Bowing to th'crimson blot.
Lightening sparks screaming blue,
Roaming skies, scheming hues.
Unsearchable seams, unalterable scenes,
Feverish pleas from souls unfree.

Apache!
Ardis Kent
In the long ago, but not so far away from here
Lived a young Apache brave, who knew not the word fear
By the age of twelve, in the eyes of the tribe, he was a man grown
He'd wander in the woods each day; he liked being alone
While hunting for small game, one morning, free of any care
He chanced upon a white man's camp; he hadn't known it was there
They took one look at his painted face, he had no time to run
They drug him off to a nearby fort, they reached by setting sun

They cut his hair, dressed him in jeans, taught him white man's ways
He sat in school learning lessons, but dreaming of happier days
He longed for the cool forest, for the soft rain upon his face
He pined away for freedom; he didn't like this white man's place
He escaped one Sunday morning while the rest of the fort still slept
He remembered his Apache training, as over the wall he silently crept
He tried in vain to make it home, but he died in the winter cold
As he closed his eyes in death, he smiled,
"at least I'm free of the white man's hold"

Time Dance
Jerry Laub
Although life has insured its powerful presence be felt.
We have been dealt the difficult task of taming our tormented hearts
in living our lives defiantly apart.

Maintained only through mesmerizing memories of times gone by;
on occasions I'm taunted to comply, uncontrollably I'd cry.
Your lips, laughter and love will never die;
for it will be carried on as long as I'm alive.

Be Bold as Brave Knights,
Pacing Solemn, Cold Nights;
Awaiting their Painstaking Fights!

Rewarding in its valored attempts, you may retain a glimpse of we at will,
presently as I of you; sitting near with only your face in place,
suddenly I appeal to the way only you can make me feel.

Enchanted Dreams

Kitchen Girl And Feather
Priya Bhakta
oxidite armour shine
the cry of dear damsels
covered by the fall of charging horsemen.
the oblong fancies on Earth–
jarred in her mouth
like fireflies in a stone grave
let them shine, give them shrine
o holy wreath of holly and tart berry
watch the rise of a rose red
flickered up with free thorn
stifled with countless stem
oxidite armour shine
filmy cream and churned light beam
races to their rush
and makes it–
a cape.

Dedication: to my wonderfully inspirational Shruti Masi

Me And My Motorcycle
Thomas E. Harris
I wear my helmet on my head
And on my shirt "go big red"
It feels like a bit of Heaven to me
Riding my cycle and feeling free
Our big, wide state is awaiting me
For the splendor and beauty for me to see
The thrill and excitement is hard to explain
Riding along in the sun and the rain
Riding my cycle is riding in style
But without my helmet, I dare not smile
For the wind and the bugs would hit my face
And I would need to drive at a slower pace
Me and my cycle are always together
Going places in all kinds of weather
My great cycle is my best friend
And together we will stay to the end

Untitled
Roberta A. Lieberman
I gather my greatness
from deep within.
I have no beginning
and I'll have no end.
I can be your enemy
or your best friend.
I can be gentle and soothing
or angry and mean
I can give things life
I can take it away
Some come to me for work
While others come to play.
I was here with you yesterday
I'm here with you today.
Everyone knows I'm rolling and free
Everyone knows my name is the Sea.

Dedication: to my husband, R.J.

Infinitesimal The Moment
Teri Casey–Hentges
That which cannot be held,
harnessed, nor put into form
That which cannot be bottled,
Chained, nor contained without harm
As uncontrollable as the wind
that comes before a storm
As inexplicable, the same
Winds that shall blow
Only the wind will pass
to leave nothing behind
have what forever blows
across the mind
With the wind, it will return
a relentless reminder
of that which has been
if only once more... to be again

Kentucky Morn
Paulette Cosden
Woke to a whinny one misty morn
A tiny foal had just been born
Outside the barn I saw a stallion
Solid black and very gallant
Running around the barn with joy
As if he knew he had a boy
It wasn't long the foal appeared
his mother, of course, was very near
his legs were shaky but oh, so tall
he'd be running the pastures in no time at all
with mother's assistance, it steadied him some
in a few minutes more, he was off in a run
Kentucky bluegrass as far as he could see
that little foal knew what he was meant to be
I closed my eyes and what I did I see, but
A tall, black horse at the Kentucky Derby

Dedication: to my husband, Curtis

The Wolves' Echo
Michelle Davis
'Tis to my night friend that I call,
When the sun has left the azure sky,
and darkness descends over God's land,
while the stars shine bright in my lonely eyes,
like lovers, forever lost from one another.

'Tis to him that I call.
When the pains of this world
Weigh a heavy burden on my shoulders.

'Tis from him that I wish comfort and security.
'Tis him that my heart beckons,
though I hear no answer,
only the wolves' echo of my lonely cries.

The Anthology of Poems

Abortion
Catherine L. Thomas
It isn't time... It isn't time!
I'm only beginning to take form—
Yet I hear/I feel/I know/I am known.

I don't have a name and I never will
I'll never belong to anyone.
I'll never feel the warmth of another human being,
nor feel the brush of your lips on my cheeks
I'll hear no lullaby — or the beating of your heart
I'll never know the touch of a mother's hands
And your face will always be a blank to me.

Such a struggle/I'm being pulled/torn/
Ripped/separated from my life source
I feel... I feel... I am gone
Child... I am dying... I am dying...
I am dead!

Hope
Peter A. Gracey, Jr.
The world is a wave
and I am a boat
I float through life
with only my hope

In goodness and wisdom
which the Lord will protect
for my sorrow and sadness
no one will detect

Except at times
one so loving and true
who can understand me
all the way through

Your Love
Patricia Powell
Your love I've known, Your love I've had,
Your love was more than just a fad.
Your love was mine, why was I so
blind as to let it go? I will never know.
If I could go back in time, I would
make you mine. If only I could go back
in time, you, Babe, would still be mine.
Your love I'll always remember, I'm trying
not to cry, but it's hard when the month of
July comes by.
Your love was always so dear to me, only
Then, Babe, I was too blind to see.
As for me, I sometimes wonder what could
have been for you and for me.

Books
Rachel E. Sellers
Books, books are everywhere
All the kinds to read.
I see the one with Moby Dick
The whale in the sea.
The one about the Dragon,
The one about the Knight,
The one about the Sword,
All the books of fright.
The books you read are like seeds, seeds, seeds.
They make your imagination grow.
They take you to far-off places,
Places I'd like to go!
I can go to Africa or sit by the sea.
If you read a book and believe!

Waves In The Water
Amanda Lynn Ramseyer
Standing by the water here
Waves crashing against the pier
And as the waves go passing by
I just stand here and wonder why
Why do the days go by so fast
How can the present, so quickly, be the past
But time seems so irrelevant here
So do loneliness, emptiness and fear
The waves carry promises about the day
That I'll get by, somehow, some way
So, not knowing what's in store for me
I simply stand here by the sea
For there is one thing I am sure
There will always be an open door

Dedication: to my whole family

How Special You Are
Danny Martinez
One Look at you
is all it takes
for me to fall in Love
Something in your smile
Makes me feel things I've never felt before
it's as if
I've discovered you, feeling Love.
For the first time
One kiss from you
is all it takes
To remind me how special
You are to me.

Dedication: to my mother and lovely girlfriend

Enchanted Dreams

Listen, My Child; A Holocaust Story
Casey Smith
Listen to the story, my child,
Listen to my tale.
Listen with open ears, my child,
can you hear their pitiful wail?
For they were just like you and I, my child,
People without a care.
Their only crime, my child,
was they wanted everything to be fair.
So they were taken away, my child,
To a place known only as death.
Where six million of them, my child,
would take their final breath.
So listen very closely, my child,
so this will never happen again.
There will be peace and happiness, my child,
there will be love in the end.

Forever
Jill DiNicola
We need to sit
And talk things through
So I can prove
That I love you
Sure we have problems
I know this is true
But all that matters
is I'll stand by you
Even though we fight
I know you care
I love you too much
To never be there
You may call me crazy
You may think I'm insane
It doesn't matter
our love will remain.

A Christmas Call
Dorothy L. Carter Fain
A little girl dressed in frills and bows
Talked on the phone as she stood on her toes.
The picture of this child was on Mother's wall.
It belonged to Grandma when I was small.
Grandma passed on, then Mother claimed to be,
That little girl on the table, near the tree.
Long curls down her back,
With a bow to hold it in place,
If she would just turn around,
I could see her face.
She must have a smile as she completes her call.
This was a long conversation,
Because she's now on my wall.
Many Christmases have come and gone,
But the tree looks the same,
Next to the little girl on the phone.

Dedication: to Mother Christmas 1997

The Fields Of Snow
Bryan Sztukowski
I see upon the fields, the snow
Whereon my love and I did roam
She full of promise and aglow
In her the sun called home
And we would play and she would smile
In those waving fields of green and gold
The best in me could she rile
To be my wife the thought I sold
But no longer does that sun shine
And its warmth bathes me no more
I am now in slow decline
My life pulse all but obscure
Mine eyes doth close upon where we had trod
In hope my fate doth move God.

Chloe
Amy Irene Anderson
Chloe Girl's ghost bops and darts around,
up in the air sometimes, defying gravity.
I see her in Ambrose's yellow–cat eyes, transfixed
in motion, I feel her playing with wild abandon,
sweet sprite, glorious in her dexterity.
She can fit into all the nooks and crannies
that used to be too small; she can make even more
amazing leaps to high places, go everywhere
with me: my beautiful tortoiseshell girl with the bird–chirp
purr, blithe, adroit, like a thousand suns
in the night sky. Dark Chloe from
the void, teeny, tough, scrawny stray
come to bring my heart back to life—
dearest friend, stay, or go if you must.

The Cycle of Human Needs
Christina Baldwin
I'm a child– rear me, I'm talking– hear me
I'm hungry– feed me, I'm human– need me
I'm defenseless– protect me, I'm a person– respect me
I'm loving– embrace me, I'm playful– chase me
I'm fleeting– sustain me, I'm bored– entertain me
I'm doubtful– assure me, I'm interested– allure me
I'm distant– reach me, I'm ignorant– teach me
I'm lost– find me, I'm forgetful– remind me
I'm frightened– hold me, I'm selfish– scold me
I'm rebellious– police me, I'm grown– release me
I'm broken– restore me, I'm your wife– adore me
I'm wild– tame me, I'm yours– claim me
I'm gentle– caress me, I'm faithful– test me
I'm exposed– accept me, I'm innocent– inspect me
I'm complicated– dissect me, I'm torn– connect me
I'm aging– cling to me, I'm afraid– sing to me
I'm contented– believe me, I'm hurting– relieve me
I'm dying– surrender me, I'm gone– remember me.

Happiness
Garry Crawford

An unknown shadow dances in the wind
Whisping and flowing, her hair weaves and spins

Across a barren field of dreams
She silently sits, praying for a sunbeam

A ray of hope, illuminates the skies
As her arms turn to wings, she ups and flies

She soars over the mountains and glides through the air
Hovers over a river where the fishermen stare

To see such a beauty shimmering in the sun
Makes you glad to be alive when all's said and done.

Dedication: to my darling wife Donna

Spring's Beginnings
M. Johnston

The winter sun glistens no more
there is no sudden flurry of snow
Just a light sprinkling of frost
Much to the gardener's cost

Bulb tips peek thru frosted soil
and buds on trees start to uncoil
Shrubs and hedges burst into life
sunlight cuts thru clouds like a knife

As April showers start to croon
spring flowers dance to the tune
Butterflies and birds prance around
and insects crawl from the ground
A rainbow appears in the morning light
what really makes this spectacular sight
No one knows 'bout the pot of gold
but that's another poem to be told

Seeing, Not Thinking
Roy Whittaker

In those eternal shades of mind which sometimes we can glimpse,
In flashing inspiration for seconds at a time,
We see the truth of nature without obscuring mist,
And only then can we revere a beauty so sublime.

If we, when wandering through our days
Can put aside our thoughts and ways,
And softly, silently, give way to thoughtless feelings from inside,
Then, our fleeting images expand
And so reveal what we can truly understand:
Thus, understanding all alone, can bring to one what many seek,
And seeing clearly from the source, enables one to sometimes speak.

The riches of the ghostly self which we can now explore,
Will then unfold and we will see our God
and what is more;
In this silence and with great joy,
We learn that this is love, so true, so pure.

Away From You
Ben Elkanah ADad

A beauty encompassed in light, auburn hair,
Whose beauty compels me, I transparently stare.
Each step that she falls, is flooded with grace,
I look purely dumbfounded, I, feeling so base.
Compare me to such virtue? What challenge be I?
Lips sewn by fear or exile, on inside I die.
Yet, then, how express myself to such marvel?
No, I think not, lest I return to that ancient civil squabble.
Call me a coward, encumbered by fright?
Then again, who but I, can care for my plight?
No courage with such beauty? I admit to fault,
Nevertheless her beauty, still constant, assault.

Dedication: to Evann

Listen To The Silence
Todd Groves

The path to God is an arduous one
Lined with pain, guilt, fear and love
Followed by voices both human and failing
Their hearts mean well and keep me sailing

Look no further than the path within
For the fear to end and the love to begin
While words can both heal and soothe
Allow the soul to recognize the truth

Trust that God has given you all you need
And you will surely find the peace you seek
Listen to the silence, to God within
And you will find in this Moment... a new life begins.

Otto's Biography
Dustin Andrews

I think that it's all but obvious, that his tears soak these pages!
Like paint soaks the canvas, his work displays fears of ages!
But it's the purest thing he knows!
About the only thing to prosper from his heart and soul!
I think it's all but obvious, that his fears soak these pages!
Like paint soaks the canvas, his work cites uncomfortable rages!
But its the only thing he knows!
About the best plant to bloom from his dark hole!
So I guess I'll let him rain, I guess I'll let it pour!
He'll talk of pain and I'll talk of horrors!
So let it pour and let it rain!
With hopes these thoughts will far steer you from pain.
I think it's all but obvious, tears of his own soil the roots he lay!
Like paint soaks the canvas, His work is often drowned in ways!

Enchanted Dreams

Miss Teenage Suicide Queen
Hillary Zaer
Love this hate that she never really cared
but something crept upon her that she never wanted shared
walking down an empty road
covered in feet of snow
thinking about that monster that she never wanted shared
she wonders why the people fear
to lose another and want her here
here she walked and contemplated life
she reached into her pocket and pulled out a knife
as she crumbled and fell to the ground
she hated the world; no love was found
now she lied upon the street
her world had crumbled, her heart took heat
as her soul rests, her new name being,
without consent
Miss Teenage Suicide Queen

Dedication: to my cousin Kristina

He Needed An Angel
Linda Robinson
As I watched the clouds drift by and heard the birds singing,
I knew you were here with me and that eased my pain a
little today.

Our hearts are heavy, for our loss is great, but the memory of your
love and kindness will never fade, it's like an everlasting light that
shines for all the world to see.

God gave you to us for only a brief, brief stay and we know he
must have needed an angel or he wouldn't have called you home
that day.
There are things we here on Earth do not understand and I guess it's
supposed to be that way.
Our comfort is knowing that we'll all be together again someday...

Yes, God needed an angel, so he called you home that day.

Fences
Carrie Coleman
We never know whether they're meant to keep
strangers out or wanted people in

but we must realize that sometimes wanted people
don't want to be kept and sometimes strangers are
the only people who share the inside of our fences

fences, borders, barriers, walls
they are all the same...
lines drawn by people to determine space that isn't
theirs to designate, or maybe as humans we share an uncontrollable desire
    to close things off

and it all starts with our minds.

Dedication: for Josh, love sister

Untitled
Charlene K. Gallardo
You and I are connected at the heart
Nothing will ever keep us apart
Life would hold no meaning without you
You and I share a love that is true
You have it all—my love, my heart, my life
I am so lucky you chose me for your wife
You bring my life love and happiness
I give my heart to only you to possess
You are my life, my love, my precious heart
I'm blessed that it's your life I am a part
A lifetime will never be long enough
To share ourselves and celebrate our love
Love me, hold me, never let me go
I am yours only—heart, body and soul.

Dedication: to Rick, whom I love

A Living Treasure
Sean George
Who brightens our day with a warm, loving
Smile?

It is you, who is willing to go the extra mile.

Who is the one who is as nice as can be?

It is you, the one who brings glee!

Who cares a care that cannot be measured?

It is you, God's gift and our living treasure!

Dedication: to my grandmother Georgia Whaley

Husband
Peggy Witt
You are my best friend, my amigo, companion and my lover
Without you, there could be no other

You are my strength in time of need
My knight upon a steed

Though at times we are apart
You're always with me in my heart

I want to thank you for the best of life
and now for making me your wife

I love you, you're the only one for me
From now and through eternity

Dedication: to my husband, Larry David Witt

Seven P. M.
Jessica M. Wahlberg
It's seven p. m., another day after.
I feel the feeling that has been given to me on
A sad day of loss.
I look up through the air and see Georgia's cross
With a heart.
I realize what the loss has given me.
A sincerity to loved-ones who practice what they preach.
In a glossed gaze I am taken back to my past,
An angered child left with the burden of life's test.
A tear falls to my lips, frozen to the touch.
My eyes are my breath and silence my language.
It has been Hell and Heaven stuck on suction cup
Fingertips.
Spontaneity and chaotically inspired.
I am caught on a cloud with Heaven on Angels,
Feathers for thoughts and wings for feet.

Dedication: to my great uncle Gary O'Keefe

Me And You
Lisa Fow
We've been through our ups as well as our downs.
We've shared a lot of smiles and a few frowns.
But one thing has always held true.
I could never regret there being a "me and you".

I would like for us to always be friends,
in some shape or form.
Even though we are considered "ex's" and that
probably isn't considered the norm.
But I really care a lot about you and would like
you to somehow always be a part of my life.
Friends forever, even down the road,
when I have a husband and you have a wife.

Sure we have a history, but I feel the bond we
share is rare and to me extremely special, too.
So no matter what happens in our future days,
I hope in some capacity there will always be a "me and you".

Passage Of Time
Shirley Butler
The looking glass in which I see
What passing years have done to me.
Time will not cease, for this I know;
So, gracefully in age I grow.

Where have you gone, oh, youthful face
That once was smooth like satin lace?
But now has changed to lines of love
And wisdom brought from up above.
The silver peeking through my hair
Like weightless feathers in the air,
Reveal in essence, years gone by;
Respectfully, but do not cry.

Accept the change with strength and grace
Of time gone by upon thy face.
As long as those I love are there,
Endless beauty within I'll share.

Angels Choice
Christopher Stetler
Sleeping among the clouds
Heaven's angels secluded in a shroud.
Floating in a baby's laughter
with a sweet-smelling scent that lingers after.

Smells of roses, candy and joy
float off and down upon the Earth
to a mother giving birth.
She sees her child, a baby boy.

The mother smells the angel's rose and candy scent
and realizes the child is Heaven scent.

Dedication: to Erik Neil Stetler, baby brother

Not In Sight
Thelma Cheesman
As I stood there in the night
I held your hand so very tight.
I closed my eyes and I softly
prayed, please don't go so far
away. But I knew, deep, down
inside, that God had wanted you
by His side. I gently leaned
and kissed your cheek, I softly
cried and said goodbye, I heard you
whisper in the night, "I'll still be
here, but not in sight." I see you
often in the night, I hear your
laughter, I feel you near, I see
your smile. It helps to know
that you're still here, even if you're
not in sight.

Dedication: Jenny

The Assault On Rhythm And Rhyme; Who Did It?
Shirley Hart
Who stole the rhythm and the rhyme out of poetry? Who attempted to
    obliterate it from line and verse forever?
I know Chaucer didn't do it; Sir Walter Raleigh wouldn't think of such a
    thing, nor would William
Shakespeare. It wasn't Edgar Allen Poe, John Keats; Percy Shelley;
    William Wadsworth-Longfellow, nor was it Paul Dunbar; by far!
I can't imagine Emily Dickinson; Carl Sandburg; Mark Twain
or Charles Dickens ever committing such an unscrupulous act.
Ebenezer Scrooge nor the Grinch who stole Christmas wouldn't
be so cruel as to attempt to annihilate rhythm and rhyme from poetry
    forever.
So; who attempted to crush rhythm and mash rhyme by replacing them with
    Traditional, Contemporary and Haiku Poetry???
STOP! WAIT!
We all need some rhythm and rhyme in our life.
POETRY: there's plenty of room for all styles.
I'm here to declare that rhythm and rhyme is going nowhere.
They are here to stay; come what may!

Enchanted Dreams

Winter Arboretum
Helen Pitt

As we trample through the rustling leaves
past swaying, naked, majestic trees,
Our noses cold, our cheeks aglow,
The frosty breeze strokes us as we go.
The wood seems silent and almost dead
Until you spy a snowdrop head,
Even in the cold and gloom,
The oriental cherries bloom.
You realize life does abound
By taking in all sights and sounds,
As we talk, our words take shape and
plumes of white—like smoke escape.
We speak in awe of all we see
Nature surrounds us, what Beauty is she.
Small saplings wait impatiently,
For their turn to come,
To stretch their branches t'ward the sky,
For future generations as they walk by.

The Yellow Bird
Janet Spooner

A yellow bird Perched high upon a branch of a tree
She looked down below sadly at the other beautiful three
And watched them Cawing angrily

Beautiful, Shining, blackbirds wanting to be free—
Free of the color they saw in ME

Not wanting to share the same sky with ME
or the same branch of the same TREE
And in their angry Cawing pushed the Yellow Bird
Further and further up the Tree.

But soon the winter will come
And Circumstance will cause us to move on
And then, perhaps, would you share the sky with me
Or perhaps the same branch of another Tree—

Fresh Air
Sarah Louise Winch

I look up bravely, in despair
at her long, brown, flowing hair
her dark—brown eyes, her deep—tanned skin
That slinky little dress she's in.
I look and think, "that should be me"
it's not that I feel jealously,
it's just that she's dancing with he,
He, the man, my destiny.
All the promises that he was mine
But, that was once upon a time,
If I'd have known, that he'd be here
I think I would have stayed well clear.
For I am now, the me, once more
the next man has so much in store,
And here he is, walking up to me
A new—found and chosen destiny.

Sunset
Rossline O'Gara

Did you see the wondrous sight, last night,
When the Earth was bathed in a shimmering light,
And ribbons of color wrapped the sky,
Like a gift from the sun, on saying goodbye.

Did you feel the mood of the eerie glow,
That filtered around the horizon's bow,
While filigree fingers of rippling rays,
Pierced the hypnotic, Heavenly haze.

Did you lose your cares and find your dreams,
Deep in the sunset's silken streams,
In those magical Moments 'twixt day and night,
Did you see, did you see the wondrous sight.

Trapped Within
John May

Trapped in a body that does not work,
People look and think, "what a jerk,"
But beneath this skin and twisted bone,
Lives a perfect mind, but so alone,
I can see the beauty of trees and sky,
I cannot tell anyone, even though I try,
I try to form words, but they won't come out,
All that happens is that I scream and shout,
I would love to tell people just how I feel,
I'm not some monster that is so sick and ill,
I would love to play Football and support the teams,
But this can only happen in my dreams,
Wish I could do all the things normal people should,
But it will never happen; my body's no good,
So next time you stop and give a stare,
Remember I am a prisoner with my own despair.

God's Gift To Everyone
Dolores Feurer

Legend tells of a pot of gold
At the rainbow's end;
But the pot of gold is nothing
But an extraordinary blend
Of a Kaleidoscope of colors
In constant vibration
Sending healing rays of color,
Of love and stimulation.
Though our eyes do not perceive it
The energy's still there,
Touching you with healing
As we walk with Him in Light.
With faith and trust allow Him in
On the path you trod,
For what you need is always given,
Your special gift from God.

Untitled
Inkham Mone Vongpanya

I look into the eyes of yours that
seemed so cold,
Like a knife stabbed into my heart
as if the truth had been told...
You don't look at me the way
you look at her,
You gazed at her as if your heart
she has conquered...
I know my thoughts are true,
You have set your heart on
someone new...
You're not the same person anymore,
And our love is not like before...
I know that I don't have much choice,
but to let you go,
Even if I still love you so...

No Doubt
Cynthia Brooks

To picture life without you
And your love I hold so dear
Brings such grief and sorrow to my heart
And to my eyes a tear.

You are the reason I arise
To meet each passing day.
To sleep each night in your embrace
I want no other way.

So please don't doubt my love for you
My love, it runs so deep and true.
A love that's in my heart to stay
Growing stronger with each passing day.

Dedication: to my beloved husband, Robert

The Fan
Ed Guziewski

Metallic petals
Like a GIANT sunflower
Spin endlessly in a blur.
Flashing brightly, they whirl
Around
And hum
Like a swarm of bees.
Swishing, swirling,
This flashing frenzy
Whips whirlpools
Of cool air
Against my face.

Dedication: to family – Louise, Steve, Teri and John

Untitled
Tami Washington

Our baby boy crawls into our bed,
He jumps in—between us and lays down his head.
He drifts off to sleep almost instantly,
I lie watching him curiously.
I look to my husband and son cradled in sleep,
I lovingly kiss them without making a peep.
In those still, quiet Moments my love overflows,
My heart effervesces and my spirit glows.
As their quiet slumber in darkness transcends to light,
I thank God they slept peacefully through the night.
I lie in wonder as the sun's rays grin,
I whisper good morning, please come on in.

Dedication: to my beloved husband and son

Freedom
Robert H. Shipman

We wait each day and hope we'll hear,
The voice far off and yet so near,
Speaking those awaited words,
We've dreamed about and never heard.

The wish for freedom, oh, so near,
The things we miss and hold so dear,
They seem to float all through the air,
They come and go without a care.

When that special voice appears,
We are released of all our fears,
Knowing we were all alone,
Finally, friend, we're going home.

Dedication: to June and Jeannie Shipman

America
Ruzica Gilich

Like a blanket,
With beautiful flowers
Colors and shapes,
That's the promised land.
Open your hands,
Feel the power,
Breathe the fresh air
Fragrant that you smell.
Hug her tight,
Don't let her go,
Lots of people, are missing
Missing her soul.
Teach the kids
To treasure the land
With beautiful flowers
Black, white, yellow and red.
America is the
Promised land.

Enchanted Dreams

Dad
Maureen Grayston Gander
What is a Dad, he's always there,
To lend an ear, when others don't care.
You feel downhearted, you feel sad,
You have a problem, talk to Dad.
He is your Dad, your best friend, too,
Really Dad, I do love you.
Now Dad has gone, he's left us here,
We're all alone, but feel him near.
He was the mainstay of our life,
He left his daughters and a wife.
He had a smile right to the end,
To you, my Dad, my love I send.
He broke my heart on that sad day,
When he was cruelly taken away.
I miss him so, he's now at rest,
I love you Dad, goodnight, God bless.

Country Churchyard
D. Perry
Sundays are the days we meet
So much sadness beneath our feet
Yet lovers walk arm in arm
A Moment of such rural charm
Thoughts of loved–ones not
long passed.
And of a love I hope will last
Oak and elm reach out to touch
Upon the wooden cross
Look upon past loves.
Of stone's encrusted moss, in footsteps
Life–twisted track.
Yet hope, walks arm in arm
Amongst such rural charm.

Dedication: to Prim. Perry

Hit, Miss Or Maybe
Gareth Morgan
Here it comes, here it comes.
Where will it land? Desperate, dumb.
But why say?
When deny it next day.

Quite a walk from end to womb,
Spinning through the endless vacuum.
Where will I be? Plus thirty years.
Will I watch the finish, drink the tears.

Will time forget, now that it knows,
Public eye surely can't close.
So if the news tries to drown it out,
"Don't forget the meteor!" You'll hear me shout.

I'm Free
Sherri Beam
Don't grieve for me, for now I'm free. I'm
Following the path God has laid, you see. I
Took His hand when I heard Him call. I
turned my back and left it all. I could not
Stay another day, to laugh, to love, to work
Or play. Tasks left undone must stay that
Way. I found that peace at the close of the
Day. If my parting has left a void, then fill
It with remembered joys. A friendship
Shared, a laugh, a kiss, oh, yes, these things, I
Too, will miss. Be not burdened with times
Of sorrow. I wish you the sunshine of
Tomorrow. My life's been full, I savored
Much. Good friends, good times, a loved
One's touch. Perhaps my time seemed all too
Brief. Don't lengthen it now with undue
Grief. Lift up your hearts and peace to thee.
God wanted me now; He has set me free!

Mother
Gloria Morgan
I looked upon the face of white hair
And aging beauty,
Time and years have taken away her
Health and youth.
How can time be so cruel?
Her arms that once held me, now ache
With arthritis,
Her kiss could make a bee sting disappear,
Her smile would warm my soul.
A kiss good night would take away any fears
I had,
This woman, I call MOTHER.

Dedication: to my mother, Berta Douglas

Glow
Ginger Stoffel
The whispery soft touch of the early morning
Breeze reminds me of the serenity I have with
God.
The bright morning light is the glow I have
In my heart.
The silky feel of the sand on my feet
Reminds me that every day is really real.
The blue–green of the water reminds me
Of the way the words flow from my head
to my heart when I talk to God.
And the seashells lying on the shore
Remind me of bad times that have
Been washed away.
And the humble flight of the gulls
Reminds me that there are many more
Years of peace and serenity.

Dedication: to all my friends

Dancing With Light
Megan Kathleen Geuss

Dancing with light,
Wondrous rays,
Leaping with joy,
Flowing away.
Dancing again,
Echoing songs,
Laughter once more,
No rights or wrongs.
Dancing once more,
Under the sun
Under the moon.
Joyously fun.

Dedication: to my family and friends

Early Springtide
Mary Ellen Kolodziej

The brave little crocus just poked its head out,
As it looked around, I'm sure I heard it shout:
"Come on, you sleeping beauties, I'm calling your bluff;
Let's wake up Mother Nature so we can strut our stuff."

The long, winter months cause many to whine,
While others just sit around and pine;
Get up, go out and take a walk,
Listen to the birds sing; they might even talk.

It seems Mother Nature and God walk hand–in–hand,
When they spread their glory over all the land;
As surely as the sun will rise and set,
Spring will come — it hasn't missed yet!

A Child Taken Away
Estella Ritter

A child taken away is a promise not kept,
a gift taken back,
independent from my body,
now wrenched from my soul –
a loss felt twice.

A child taken away is the past not appreciated,
the present, not real
and the future not seen.

My child is missing and my heart has gone to
find him.
My arms ache from the weight of not holding.
I will not dull the pain that protects my senses.
Nor mask my horror and cover my eyes –

For forever I will be listening to the sonant silence
that stunned, at the Moment when he died.

War Of Day And Night
Matthew Sullivan

As the day comes to an end
Will our hearts beat again?
Darkness falls, there is no light
The day's betrayed by the night.
I hear no more, I can't see the light.
Will we give up or win the fight?
Darkness falls all around
Nothing about, not even a sound.
Will we live another day?
Or will the angels take us away?
In our eyes, we see no more
Will we live to even the score?
The light is afoot
The sun is at rise
Darkness is fading
And everyone dies.

Renewal
Katherine G. Lee

Concentric circles of watery shapes,
Scudding Clouds, barometers foretelling.
Portents unheeded, sheets draped
Ignominiously. Sacrificed crispness unwillingly.

Playground jungle tamed into silence,
Plows abandoned, woods stilled.
Swelling pools sharing affluence
With desiccated furrows in arid fields.

Sated Earth of replete greenery
Gratefully quickens freshening air,
As life gathers in puddles silently.
The cycle of Ceres—a wonder most rare.

Dreaming
Kristi Cobb

Swiftly, swiftly I say
Into the night I went, swiftly;
Beyond the stars and the moon
Beyond the Heavens and the Earth.

Swiftly, swiftly I say
My everlasting wings took me, swiftly
To a place known only to me
Oh, so swiftly.

But upon the climax of my flight,
I began to descend;
And I realized
I don't want this dream to end.

Enchanted Dreams

Sonnet Of Mirrors
Ben Smith
The silent evening surface of a pond
Reflects the unknown passion of the moon,
And waiting, wakens with the kiss of dawn
And craves the soothing warmth of afternoon
The same, I feel, was mirrored in your eyes.
It moved in growing ripples from your heart
And followed sunlight's map from Earth to sky,
Where you and I will never now depart.
If I were like a stone thrown in your pond,
If I sank deep – not wanting to return,
If I could only gaze at you 'til dawn,
Then I would never cease to feel love's burn.
When poets die, the world still feels their words.
When lovers die, their spirits fly with birds.

Dedication: to Shelley Jackson, editor and friend

The Old Farm
Charlotte Easterling
No one was there, but me.
No one felt the chill in the air;
or saw long, straight roads and barren hills.
I was alone and could see for miles.
I heard the wind whisper to the Jasmine climbing the gate;
And saw it kiss the giant oaks, making them sing.
The grasses danced.

A tattered hammock clung to the porch,
As the old house breathed secrets from the past.
Thirsty cows drank from the blue pond,
Knowing I was there. . . watching.

Huge birds flapped their wings and led me away.

Untitled
Eileen Howard
He Smiled —
I knew it was for me,
And I wanted to know him more.

He Smiled —
A soft, quiet smile,
That caressed my heart.

He Smiled —
Like warm rain
It was familiar.

He Smiled —
And I was forever changed.

Mum
Beverly M. Pickles
Who is so sweet, so gentle and kind
Displaying only a pureness of mind?
Who is so lovely, with thoughtful mood
Doing only that which is good?
Who is so precious, loved and adored
By all who know her, here and abroad?
Who is this person who's my best chum?
It is my dearest, my darling Mum.
Thanks go to her for helping me
All through my life, so tenderly.
She's wiped my tears and eased my hurts,
Not just when little and holding her skirts,
But now I'm older she still helps to calm,
Those upsets and fears which can often alarm.
So thank you Mum for being "you",
Gentle, warm and always true.
I hope this verse will play its part
In saying "I love you" with all my heart.

Tread Softly
Joan A. Thomas
Tread softly round this fragile peace
'til all atrocities shall cease,
And we can rest from mortal fear
Of dying.

Tread softly till all talk is done,
And victory for peace is won;
Then we can walk from bloody fights
And crying.

Tread softly on this new—won day,
Let love and joy now be our way,
And Christians join in one accord,
Of living.

Ode To A Sleepy Black Dog
C. E. Marshall
Can sleeping dogs be taught new tricks,
While canines dream of chasing sticks,
With twitchy limbs and wagging tail,
They chase the rabbit down the dale,

Faster, under, over, through,
Quickly find a bone to chew,
Splash in water, stand on bank,
Shaking limbs all wet and lank.

Sleeping dogs can dream, it seems,
Of running single or in teams,
But we shall never really know,
Where in their doggy dreams they go.

The Anthology of Poems

Heartbreak
Sylvia I. Wood
Sorrow never waning
Heartache and despair
Pray to God for help
How much more to bear
Don't want to see tomorrow
Future bleak and grim
Hand over mouth in panic
Life nothing without him
Family friends leave when over
Suddenly alone
Dog, thank God, still living
Blessings son at home
Though the years go over
Yet can you measure time
True, it is a healer
Pray God it will be mine.

The Seed Of Love
Susan J. Barnes
Love is unpredictable,
for the seed that first you sow,
may not be destined to survive,
to blossom or to grow.
It may not have the staying power
and is plucked early from the vine.
A very short–lived kind of love,
like frothy, sparkling wine.
But if you tend that special fruit
that has the stamina to remain,
it will mature to such a precious love,
like a rare vintage champagne.
Shower it with tenderness.
Cherish it day and night.
For if it's rooted deep within you,
it will be your heart's delight.

Untitled
Maria Daleo
You didn't believe it, did you? no, you didn't.
You were surprised, weren't you?
Yes, it's dead, it's broken, blown away,
It's nowhere, everywhere...
Flying in pieces all over the universe,
To the life again, to regain the shape it had lost,
To the Goddess, to the stars,
You didn't believe it, did you? It's finally dead.
Didn't you ask for it?
Didn't you do anything possible to destroy it?
Here you have it,
Pieces flying all over the universe,
Aren't you happy now? You said you were going to be.
So be happy and cry alone, if you ever cry,
If you ever have the courage to cry,
If you ever have the courage to look in the mirror
And watch those tears run down your face
And pray for the God you are still looking for.

Feathered Friends
Joseph P. Harrington
Who will feed them when I'm away
My feathered friends who come each day?
From whence they come I do not know.
Their nesting place is hid' by snow.
Yet one I see on chimney high.
I think it's come to sit and spy.
When winter's white is on the ground
To give them aid, I'm duty bound.
Not silver, gold, but these instead;
Seeds, cracker crumbs and bits of bread.
By ones and twos, then flocks of more
They fast descend and track the floor.
With softest bits to nests they fly.
Perhaps to silence baby's cry.
Then back again in frenzied haste
To bite and toss 'til there's no waste.
At last that steady stream is gone.
But they'll be back at crack of dawn.

By My Baby's Grave
Maggie Williams
I've gathered a bunch of wildflowers
To lay on that tiny green mound
Where my little boy is sleeping,
All lonely and cold in the ground.

His blue eyes are closed fast forever,
And I know that he cannot see
The mother who weeps here beside him,
The Daddy who bends on his knee.

I believe in a distant hereafter,
In a land with no pain or sin –
We'll find our darling son waiting,
And we'll all be a family again.

Life
Brenda R. Hamlet
Life can be long or short
Though not measured in years
Life can be good or bad
Though not measured in tears

Life can be rich or poor
Though not measured in gain
Life can be great or small
Though not measured in fame

Life can be what you make it
Easy or hard
Life is measured
By your closeness to God

Dedication: to my husband, children, and grandchildren

Enchanted Dreams

Friend
Cathy Fazio–Lerner
Although the miles keep us apart,
You're with me every day
For friends are not a part–time thing,
You're in my heart to stay.
Gone are the days when we could
sit and have a cup of tea,
But trust me, friend, you're in my heart
and there you'll always be.
God blessed me when He gave me you,
I couldn't ask for more,
I loved you then, I love you now,
just like you were next door.
So please don't think because I'm gone
so many miles away,
That I don't treasure such a friend,
You're in my heart to stay.

Dedication: to my sister Mary – my friend

Repression
Patricia Ridpath
Lost touch with my "self" over passing years,
Bury the feelings, don't shed the tears.
Live up to the standards set by someone else,
Approval gained from others, but never myself.
"Wonderful daughter", "wonderful wife",
"Wonderful mother", still I cried for my life.
A cry from the inside, never set free,
'Til unexpected love came to rescue me.
Is it too late now to forgive and forget?
Are the patterns so molded, so dried and set?
Soul–deep emotions kept in military check –
How to crack that mold? Will emotions wreak
Havoc upon you, my dear man?
Shall I take a chance? Perhaps now I can.

Dedication: to David, who understands

The Day
Michael Opuszynski
Connecting box – cars scream.
Church bells always ring.
Stray cats at your window scratch.
Old cars passing by smoke.
High grass in the meadow whistle.
Water from a faucet drips.
The old rusty gate squeaks.
The summer winds howl.
The bottles from the milkman clatter.
The floorboards on the porch creek.
Smoke from the chimney billows,
Logs in the fireplace crackle.
I wake up in the darkness yawning.
As the pot of coffee starts perking.
The dog out yonder is barking,
In the distance the dawn is breaking.

Instant Recall
Ellen Hastings Janosik
The clamor and the clinging
Have vanished overnight,
But I remember passion
And Moments of delight.

I am older than springtime
My mirror says so.
But a girl lives inside me,
Refusing to go.

She preens and she stretches,
She laughs and she cries
And sometimes I catch her
Looking out of my eyes.

Pray To The ATM God
Frances Daacola
Begin your prayer with,
I remember my pin number.
Pray it doesn't eat my card.
Pray that I have enough cash on hand.

Then it demands a tithe.
Either we pay or begin our prayer again.

Then we raise our hands to get our cash and receipt.
or we feed it more tithe.

Then it asks if we want more.
To which we pray no.

We should show such faith and love.
to each other and the real God.

Outside
Keith Feinberg
The sound of the airplane rumbles through the atmosphere.
The field is covered in a light black blanket.
The black–top burns like a red–hot stove.
The flowers blow in the gentle breeze.

The shiny silver fence stands tall and still.
Yellowjackets buzz and zoom in on bushes to find pollen.
The light peach sand blows with speed and power
down a hot metal drain.

Cool crisp air whips the side of my face.
The hard, cool bricks lay still against the wall.
Oceans of colors fill the bright sun–covered flowers.
I turn my head away from the fiery ball of lava in the sky.

Outside.

The Anthology of Poems

Here He Lies!
Ruth J. Scott
Here he lies today, cold and dead
Shot by an assassin in the head.
The world is filled with sorrow and regret,
For John F. Kennedy it will never forget.

Though from us he is now gone
In our hearts he still lives on.
Though now he lies cold and dead
His work and deeds march ahead.
"Dear God," the nation prayed
"Why was our leader taken away?"
Hurt and dismayed, the nation cried
"Why did he have to die?"

In honor of the man whose love was deep
Today is a time to weep
For even though his deeds live on
Our great leader is gone.

Tears
Stephen P. Gifford
Tears are but mem'ries of faded dreams,
So many heartaches, too many schemes.

Tears hold the visions of future past,
Painful the truth fate has cast.

Tears are those words never said,
Crying forgiveness from the dead.

Tears are all gone, no going back,
(May there be) forgiveness for all I lack.
I pray

Dedication: before I encountered Jane

You
Cynthia Hobby
I let you touch me
in more than one way,
that no one has ever touched me before.
Your body has claimed mine,
my heart has claimed yours.
You may not love me,
our time together may be brief,
but I shall never forget
even in my grief
that you have touched me twice.
No one will ever be able
to touch me in quite the same way.
Thoughts of you and what
has been and what could never be
will always get in the way,
but until that time
I wait breathlessly to see, touch,
and talk to you again

My Sister, My Friend
Candice F. Walters
We have known each other for a while
and shared many happy days and smiles.
Through first crushes, high school fears,
driving scares and baptism tears;
You have been my sister, my friend.
I watched you grow from a young girl
to the beautiful young lady that I now know.
Even though we had our differences
and we didn't always see eye to eye;
You have been there, my sister, my friend.
Now this most special day of your life is near
and though I will not be standing beside you;
You always know that I am here.
As you start your new life together as
husband and wife in eternal marital bliss, know this,
I love you because you are my sister, because you are my friend.

Dedication: to Tameka Lewis Igbonegun, my friend

A Little Peace
Daria Gionta
All I want is a little peace
to lay my weary head.
A chance to be alone
with no outsiders looking in.

A time to collect my thoughts
and find sanctity within.
A few captured Moments
to come and heal.

No tugs on my sleeves,
no people to please.
Just a quiet place
all by myself.

He Only Takes The Best
Michelle Cunningham
God saw they were getting tired
and a cure was not to be.
So He put His arms around them,
and whispered "come with me,"
with a tearful eye we watched them
Suffer.

We saw them fade away.
Although we loved them dearly,
we could not make them stay.
Many golden hearts stopped beating,
hardworking hands to rest.
God broke our hearts to prove to us;
HE ONLY TAKES THE BEST.

Enchanted Dreams

A True Friend
James T. Bingert
Your friendship has been angelic
It has shined white light
And brought back hope
I know now that which is right

It is hard to believe
So great a prize
Should come my way
My spirit had to rise

The friendship I have sought
Will never be forgot
You have added genuine meaning to my life
If you ever need a friend – I'm yours for life!

Mother's Eyes
Eleanor Drum
I never saw a pair of eyes,
So beautiful, clear blue,
Showing a load of cares and sighs,
but somehow smiling through.

They watched over me and brothers,
Through years of toil and strife.
they taught us, be happy and to love one another,
no matter what comes in life.

These crystal, blue eyes belong to Mother
who showed us love and many things kind,
Her beautiful eyes – T'will be no others,
will shine in my heart for all time.

Shades And Shadow
Rachel Kowalsky
Shades and shadow of the night, they call
As she sits in quiet corners
Passing over the sands of time
She's seen it all before her eyes
Still she looks onward
And the sun shall rise
Much the same
She'll smile
If you see her drifting by
On shades and shadow of the night
She's just passing through a dream
Worlds unseen, she dances by
Still looking onward
And the sun shall rise
Much the same
You'll smile

Disguised
John Crawford
"Who am I?" you ask, as if I would even know,
The person that I am is not who I like to show.
I'm very strong, when I'm not terribly weak.
Truly optimistic, unless circumstances seem bleak.
Extremely sympathetic, except when I'm insensitive.
Courageous to a fault, until fear is more definitive.
Humble to the core, if pride is not too apparent.
Always charming, when I'm not being transparent.
Honest to a fault, lest the truth seem unnecessary.
Alert to circumstance, ignorant of what surrounds me.
Intelligent of thought, unconscious in my manner.
Noble of character, undignified in my candor.
I cannot be who I am, for that is a contradiction.
I am not guilty, yet I'm deserving of conviction.

Daughter
Constance R. Suber
To my heart, my soul, my friend
I don't know what to say or where to begin
I know I haven't spent as much time with you like
I used to do
But no matter where I'm at, I'll continue to think
of you
I will tell you as many times it takes that I
Love you
I will find a way to prove my love is true
Please let me know how to get things right
And I promise you I will do it, day or night
Whenever you need me, I will be there
I will always love you and keep you in my
prayers

Angel and Harp
Bonnie Hall
I'm just a little angel
fluttering over a cloud.
Trying to play this harp,
but yet not too loud.
I don't really know how
or why, but what's an
angel to do, up here so high.
I've been told that it's
one of my chores. But
sometimes it sure is a bore.
So, I guess I'll keep on
playing until I get better.
'Cause I want to grow up
to be an Angel jet–setter.

Dedication: to my recently deceased parents, Hank and Helen Sullivan

The Anthology of Poems

A Dream Come True
Nicole Medina
I wish that dreams can
come true but, I'm too old
to dream about a dream come
true.
I will keep on believing my
long lost dreams, even though
I know they won't come true.
I will keep on believing until
I've done enough so one day
one of those dreams will
come true.
Everyone has a special day
when nothing goes wrong and
a dream comes to life.

Dedication: to the Medina family and pets

Untitled
Gloria Jean Marshall
In the deepest throes of sorrow
With all defenses down
It is so important to know
That God sends His angels around
To lift you when you're sad
To truly make you strong
You seek to find His messenger
In every word and song
So thru my time of sorrow
I seek to see His face
And find the beauty of God's love
And see His saving grace
So thank you, Lord, for friend and foe
I pray You guide me as I go
Help me to see Your strong hand
That picked me up and helps me stand.

The Prairie
Joseph Jay Finkbeiner
Buffalo herds on the prairie,
Roaming wild and free,
Out in wide–open spaces,
It feels like home to me.

Here in the Great Midwest,
You're 'bout worry free,
Out here in the prairie,
Nowhere near the sea.

E'er since the 1800s,
The prairie's been unique,
And when you are out here,
There's nothing more to seek.

One Sweet Day...
F. Hannacho Lutu
As the sunset sprays the sky with its colored rays
I watch with falling tears as you drift away
Never to be seen again, you departed with the angry tide
Why did you leave? I feel so empty inside
I looked up to see your light beckoning at me
I crept closer and then you made me see
Look inside you and there I will find
The spirit of the beloved, stronger than any kind
You gave me strength and undying love
You told me you will always watch over me from above
Soon I will be with you at that happier place
So we can drink in the juices of life at a much slower pace
Where visions of the sunset are seen in the sky
Where the flute flies and the violin cries
Your soul and endearing spirit are here with me to stay
As I await to be united with you on that One Sweet Day.

Untitled
Eric Wright
Hello, Mr. Froggy. Have you seen my Uncle John?
He drowned here long ago and now lives beneath the pond.
If by chance you meet him, please tell him I said "hi!"
Greet him with a smile, "I'll see him in July."
I've been practicing my breathing and I think I've got it now.
I can hold it twenty minutes, any longer I might drown.
My time is very scarce, so I'd better use it well.
The extent is very small and I have so much to tell.
So please, Mr. Froggy, please direct me to my goal.
Look under every rock, examine every hole.
Talk to every fish that swims among the light.
Confront every creature that slithers in the night.
Now I'm sorry, Mr. Froggy, but I must be on my way.
I should be getting home before the night steals the day.
Now all my bags are packed and I think I'm ready to go,
To live with Uncle John, in the pond... down below.

Untitled
Holly Alison Bernu
Goosebumps from the chill of the fall wind
makes our fire we sit around small,
telling of what we DRIP see for
our future or what was in the past.
Moving to Northern Iowa, where the land DRIP is flat as a pancake
DRIP our house is surrounded by other DRIP
houses with DRIP windows peeking
in DRIP other windows knowing all of our DRIP
neighbors and what they are doing or
DRIP where they are DRIP going, going
to shop at the mall and DRIP pick up their
child at soccer practice DRIP DRIP
because there DRIP would be no DRIP game, we put
out the fire DRIP to DRIP run inside DRIP
DRIP to drink hot drip cocoa DRIP DRIP and
to DRIP look DRIP DRIP out DRIP the DRIP DRIP window DRIP

Enchanted Dreams

If It Not Be Love
Tina Anderson
Like the candle has a flame, so goes my heart every
time you speak my name, when I look into your eyes, I
feel dizzy; when you walk into a room, I become breathless
what is this wonderful feeling, if it not be love?

My every thought is of you, about you, or because of you.
If I go for days without seeing you, It feels like an eternity
What is this power you have over me, if it not be love?

I have seen many oceans and mountains and truly they can't
compare with the awe I feel when you are near, so what is this
magic, if it not be love?

As the flame of my heart grows hotter and the room starts to
spin, as the oceans of my thoughts start to drown, you somehow
become an eagle and fly me over the mountains, so you see, my
friend, this can only be the one true love that was meant for
me!!!!

Wishes For Life
Lanette Dauster
I wish you happiness in all you do. Joy and peace your
Entire life through.
Solitude and calm when you've had a rough day; patience and
Truth on the road you pave. Storms will pass and clouds
Will fly; thunder and lightning will excite the mind's eye.
Sunshine and daisies to blanket your path, only to comfort
Your destiny from wrath.
Love and faith will strengthen your soul: Those who truly care
Shall help keep your heart whole.
Confidence and stamina while you work and play: Security and
Protection while consciousness is at bay.
Success and wisdom will come to pass; as will time to relax in
Emerald grass. Intelligence and honesty in choices made;
These are important to shield you from the blade.

Tomorrow The Sun
Lisa Martell
Rain splashing the cold windows
Trees dancing as the harsh wind blows
The sky is so cloudy, muddled and gray.
Glum and damp is the mood for the day.

Kitty's curled on the bedroom sill.
Sleeping peacefully, Oh, so still
Cozy warm, no need to wake
Life goes by, nothing at stake.
Chill, rain and air sealed from my home.
With failed penetration, they continue to roam.
Flowers and plants, quenching their thirst
Tomorrow the sun, their beauty will burst.

The town is scampering to escape the wet.
Errands to run and things to get
Ducking and dodging the drops as they run
Tomorrow so dry, tomorrow the sun.

Lost Dog
Amber Dietrich
A lost dog named Ringo,
was looking for his home;
when he wandered onto my lawn,
and saw my dog alone.

They fought for a while
then called it quits;
when I came out the door
with a handful of biscuits.

I looked at his collar
and found his owner soon;
now he's lost again.
Will he be found with you?

Fading Memories
Jeanne Bryant
In the distance, I heard A child crying
And as I looked up to the sky
I saw a bolt of lighting;
Thunder roared

Tears rolled down an old woman's cheek
There were no stars
Yet it was bright
It was frightening

Fading memories
Only darkness
Images
Flashes

Missing You
Sue Lotz
Oh, friend of mine.
I miss you so.
I am drained, hollow inside.

I wait for the sound of your voice.
The emptiness fills my heart.
I reach for your hand,
Only to find, a nothingness.

Our Moments together can never be again.
How do I fill this void?

Will it be another kind of love I find?
Love of mankind, love of life itself.
Whatever I choose, I pray it will be soon.
For the days are long and lonely.

Dedication: in loving memory of Ken

Beauty In Decay
Quintin Peterson
Saw a walking corpse today
shaking violently as it fell prey
to the violent shaking that comes
from not taking to the skies

I knew her, once, during the time
when I believed that beauty never dies,
long before the tracks marked her arms
and
the veins of red cracked her eyes

Yes, I did know her... once

Baffling: how anything could make her
that way
Nothing is more heartbreaking
than witnessing
a thing of beauty in decay

Hopeless Dreams
Annie T. Miller
Don't you wish that dreams came true
That's what I wish for me and you
A place where you could sit and rest
Find a song to sing and really feel blessed
I wonder why it's so hard to find
Rest for the body and peace for the mind
When there's no way to escape trouble, it seems
Must we wait to die to achieve these things
I would settle now for just one day
Just to be with you again, just to have the chance to say
The many things left unsaid of all the wonderful schemes
And all the plans we had, now lost forever in a hopeless dream
For you're not here, you've gone on before
And I wish, how I wish, when I open the door
You'd be waiting for me in your favorite chair
And we could live all our dreams— oh— but you're not there.

Dedication: in loving memory of Bill

My Love
Suzanne D. Regan
My heart is awake
with the joy and love of you,
My heart sings a song
that I swear belongs to you.

My arms reach out
for a star that can't be reached,
My life is a vessel
that needs its share of fill.

My soul is captured
by your strength and tenderness.
I promise that no one
will love you more than I,
I promise that I'll love you
with each and every breath.

The Magic Circle
Kristina Sveda
On the night of the full moon
The evening glows with starlight
Shadows in the forest of trees
And the creatures of the night
Shafts of moonlight on the silvery, glimmering woodland carpet
The stillness of the night,
The gentle whispering of the leaves in the zephyr of a breeze,
A soft melody drifting from somewhere, melodious and sweet
In the forest glade, a circle of maidens dancing so lightly and
free,
Singing so sweetly to the tune of nature and the moonlight night
Spiritually at one with all
Barefoot in long, white, flowing, gossamer gowns, with flowers in
their long hair
The magic of the rites of spring, the renewal of life and love of
Nature and spirit as the Earth awakens from its winter sleep.

What I Dream
Vita Zadura
I'm gonna sit up in my room
And think about you
I see you and your wonderful smile
I'm gonna dream about you for some while.

I'm gonna wait for my phone to ring
I wonder what your dreams will bring
But that's only what I dream
I wonder if you're really as nice as you seem.

When you need me, I'll be there
I'll be waiting in my room up here
It may not be in anytime soon
So I'll just sit by my window and dream of you.

Tarnished Soul
Tami M. Snyder
I sit here quietly, listening to the tears in my soul
Every cry of anguish longing to break free and be heard
I have tried to silence them long ago
But they did not die
They live like a fire burning within my very being
Their flames being fueled by the hatred within me
I have tried to extinguish the hate
But it still burns
The scars I carry are not visible to any other
They are wounds only I can see and feel
I have tried to make them heal
But they do not disappear
I search within myself to find the courage buried long ago
Sifting through the ashes of my tortured heart
I find my courage,; although tarnished, it lives
And that will never die

Dedication: in memory of David Snyder, Sr.

My Dad
Susan Dorn

As I watch my Dad grow old
his heart remains pure of gold

His mind is feeble, his knees weak
But he holds the wisdom wise men seek

He's been the stable force in my life
Even when I filled his one with strife

And although Mom is gone for many a day
I wonder why God takes the stronger and, alone, the weaker stay

We both realize he's in the twilight of his years
But the memory of his smile will wash away my tears

Deaf
Helen Denham

Personalized by shape, flexibility and bone
speaking a language distinctly their own.

Painting a picture in a sentence or less
like a seasoned artist, the air its canvas.

Fingers as brushes in a quick, sweeping motion
the canvas decorated with vivid emotion.

Look quickly! You shall hear the echoes
distant, yet so near.

In the air, words slowly disintegrate
one of those words is... communicate.

The Rose
Lorea B. Shaffer

Ah! So fair the lovely rose, soft velvet is her gown.
Petals pink with youth, she wears no frown.
In stately grace, reigns o'er the garden bed,
Where balmy breezes sway her lovely head.

Elegant and fragile, there for all to gaze upon,
The honey bees kiss her tenderly and fly on.
A cloak of green surrounds this quaint array
As do the flowery clusters on display.

Her scent so delicate, deliciously subdued,
Blends with the rest of nature's subtle hues.
To enhance the garden, does fair rose aspire –
But at night she peacefully sleeps in leafy, green attire.

Ode To The Grim Reaper
David W. Noah

I've died inside, I can't get out
It's driving me insane
Whatever happened to me
I simply can't explain

I know it happened long ago, when I was not aware
I know it happened very slow and I didn't seem to care
I dredge through life from day to day
with cinder blocks for feet
My heart is cold, my body's old,
I'm tired but I can't sleep

So bring it on and let me die
I'll go out with a grin
Because no matter how hard you try,
It's death that always wins.

Faraway Friend
Richard R. De Lillio

The sky seems so far away.
Yet, how beautiful it looks,
so blue and comforting.
I want it closer
wrapping me
in its deep, luscious folds.

My arms reach out,
embracing only air—
longing to feel
this pure, azure blanket.

Yet, distant and vigilant
my loyal, loving friend watches—
sending cloudless, cerulean comfort,
from afar.

Dedication: to lasting friendships

The Archer
Phyllis Ann Taphorn

Twice he had used his bow,
Then thrice he had let fly
The swift arrow to go
Arching through the blue sky.
It hit the maiden's heart
With such a stinging blow,
She vainly strove to thwart
This third one in a row.
The archer hit his mark
And she beheld her man
With love, hit by the spark
Shot from the bow of Pan.
Oh, woman, playful, coy
Playing as Cupid's toy!

In Retrospect
Joyce G. Milne

In retrospect, I ponder the vastness
of the sea;
The grandeur of the Earth and sky
surrounding you and me.
In spite of all magnificence we
mortals richly share,
In narrow minds we sometimes
live— excluding those who bear
The scars of sad indifference that
we've inflicted there.
In retrospect, I wonder, if we
can ever be
As open and as giving as Earth
and sky and sea.

Dedication: to my beloved grandchildren

Painted Moon
Dallas J. Kahlhamer

Cradled within her arms
I lay myself to rest,
Pain and anguish lurk at the door
riding upon winter's icy breath.
The wind whispers in my ear
to let me know I am not alone,
as chariots of fire capture my heart
for the journey home.
The moon's rays pull at tides
of emotion that run deep,
her flowing rays lighting the way
toward the answers that I seek.
The ocean mirrors her painted face,
that is when I see,
the door to Light within us all
and our soul... the key.

God's Love
Connie Myers

Would you lay down your life for a friend
Loving them to the very end
Giving your all so they might live
Baring the cross, His blood He gives

He said to go and sin no more
Preach My gospel to the poor
Bring the halt and lame to Me
So my mercy they will see

The thief will come to kill and destroy
But I have come to bring you joy
So cleave unto me and no other one
For my name is Jesus, God's only Son

While Widows Walked
Clark Hunter

While widows walked in lighthouse beam,
Hearts cast toward the sea,
Echoes of a last farewell seem
but a memory.

How stout the hearts, how brave the souls
Who sailed on distant mast,
With hopes, the beam in search of life,
Will draw them home as last.

A fearful chill surrounds the night,
As shadows touch the shore.
The beam of life shows no return,
and widows walk no more.

Easter
Stacie L. Bezon

Easter to me is all about new beginnings.

New blossoms of beautiful flowers to fill our
flower gardens with beautiful colors and smells.

New fields of green grass to run our feet
through on a warm, spring day.

New, bright smiles on our children's faces as
they fly their kites in that new, warm breeze

A new look at what our Lord, Jesus Christ,
did when they hung Him on that cross on that sad
day. He gave His life for us so we can be
forgiven our sins. And on Easter day, He arose
again. Oh, what a beautiful new beginning Jesus
gave us.
So to me, Easter is all about new beginnings.

Apollo
Jo Ann Roberson

He touched me
and I lost control
turned into a black panther
and padded confidently through the jungle
I felt my panther muscles flex
smelled the rotted vegetation stirred up
by my passing
Saw through the eyes of a cat
Smelled through the nostrils of a cat
Heard through the ears of a cat
Jumped... and climbed a tree above a pond
Laid out on a branch, I retracted
and untracted my claws and licked my paws
felt the bark beneath my skin
felt the slight breeze that rippled the pond
screamed in triumph at the moon!
I was instantly there... in the jungle... in a cat's body
when he touched me

Enchanted Dreams

Through A Child's Eye
Amy Kuschka
Everything to look at, is a wonder.
How it works, what things do.
All the colors and hue,
Is pure fascination to ponder.

A child is full of love and trust,
And accepts everything as is.
Curiosity is a must,
To get into everything, a child is a whiz.

A wide world to roam, using the imagination.
Turn the ordinary into Kings and Queens –
or pure science fiction.

Always questions, asks why? Why? Why?
A thirst, can never be quenched.
To live through a child's eye.
Imagine.

Conflict
W. R. Trahan
The clouds moved across the skies with
Their usual grace —
Gathering, amassing, forming into
A natural panorama of imaginary
Faces and figures to the human eye.
The jealous winds pushing, swirling in
Their everlasting attempts to shovel
Them out of the Heavens so they,
The winds, could be the masters of
The skies.
The winds prevailed, but still a tiny wisp
Of a cloud continued to evade the onslaught
And settled in western borders of the
Earth and skies to form a halo for the setting sun.
Darkness crept in and over the landscape, causing
Shadows to form without pattern or meaning —
Whatever the eye or mind felt comfort to
Precede.

He's Everywhere
Shawna Heslop
I can't see the wind as it hits my face,
I can't see God but He's everyplace,
And the stars disappear in the daylight
you know, though they're still in the
Heavens waiting to glow.
I can't see God, but I know He's there,
His love surrounds us everywhere.
We see the sunrise each morning
So bright and the moon and the stars
in the Heaven each night.
We see the seasons change, year after
year, but whatever may happen, we
know He is near.
So why should I worry, fret or
care? He takes care of my problems,
He's Everywhere!

Dedication: to Lyle and Crystal, thanks for everything

My Prayer To Cheryl
Clara Alverson
I said a special prayer for you because
you weighed heavy on my mind.

So I asked the Lord to give you
strength,
joy and inner peace that you are
trying to find.

I asked the Lord to gently wrap you
in His loving grace and calm your
roughened sea.

I am glad you are my sister and friend
because you mean everything to me.

Descent
Mark E. Fane
Instinct dies.
Its final breath gives birth,
To knowledge,
Born, into the abyss.
Pregnant, the void inhales inquiry.
Exhaling silent answer.
Curls of smoke sail seas of sound.
Beautiful music of ocean waves pounds,
Shorelines, of my belief.
Inventing fine, white sands of question,
From boulders.
Who once resolved my appeal.
Their truth,
Carved in stone.

Don't Be Afraid
Ilona Taft
No regrets, you took my heart by surprise
High expectations, no compromise
The situation is harmless, this thing is strong
Conquer your fears and we can't go wrong.

Go on and enjoy it, swallow your pride
Live life to the full, tell no lies
Say only the truth, be grateful, be real
This emotion's called love, don't make a big deal.

Our strengths speak for us, keep the promise, be great
Take the chance now it's here, tomorrow's too late
Make a fool of yourself, be hopeful, stay high
I love you now and forever, be peaceful, don't cry.

Destiny
Jacob Lucan

A trick of light, a cosmic rift?
A sleight of hand, a twist of fate?
What microcosm brought me here,
And filled my empty plate?
Should I have held a different key
That opened some remembered door,
I would have walked another track
And crossed ten thousand more!
Had I but changed one fateful step,
Or ventured by another street
What hat, would not, adorn my head?
What shoes, upon my feet?
I've traveled life's great labyrinth,
I've made my mark along the way
A chance in billions, brought me here,
I celebrate, this day.

I Do It For You
Flem Combs, Jr.

I speak on behalf of a people who need protection.
So I build toys, stockpiling them in toy boxes.
The toys of my foes must not bring them harm.
I look for the time when I can play with my toys.
In time I will, when it is in my interest to do so,
As well as the interest of a people.
Little green men with guns. Only a few good ones.
Weapons of war! Toys for the protection of a people.
They will accept what I say. If said enough times.
I am right, our foes wrong. So let's slaughter them.
Then rejoice in our guilt, confetti in the streets.
While the superiors of the green men smile and wave.
You must trust and follow me so our foes won't do this.
You are a people and I speak on your behalf.
I will answer your questions, tickling your ears.
Then a voice speaks out,
"But what if no one followed you, or your foes?"
My foes and I then shot him, in protection of a people.

Stone Speaks
Ruth Partington

My veins throbbed with trembling pulse
where now you see me solid;
I was alive.
The liquid colours gleamed
beneath the Earth
where no light shines;
I was alive.
Swift–flowing water
carved my curious shape
you hold.
Your skin meets mine,
its warmth enclosing cold,
but hold me long,
you'll feel the life that formed me.

Uncle John
Robert Bryan

High in the Carolina Hills
I knew a man whose life instills
Respect in me, though he his gone.
(Most folks knew him as Uncle John).
A rippin', scripture quotin' man,
In his own way an artisan
Who worked hard at the job
Of livin', his big heart a–throb
With love for all his fellow men.
He went to school just now and then
When he was young, but after all,
He learned to love and live so tall
That he garnered greater knowledge
Than most of us who went to college.

Dedication: to my deceased son, Douglas Scott Bryan

The Freak Storm
Terence C. Curran

No one knows what was in the
Storm that night, as it rolled
In from the East Coast across
Manhattan, block by block, the
Lights went out, as people in
Apartments began to shout;
All types of city dogs began
To bark, because they'd never seen
A city so dark, cars, trains, planes
Ceased to move, as the storm
Reached the Bronx, it began to
Stop, It started to go back out
To sea, the lights began to
Flicker and old men in bars
At last start to see their
Liqueur, no one knows what
Was in the storm that night,
The night of the freak storm:

Untitled
Flossie Evans

She is like a little sparrow,
darting to and fro.
Working and helping others
as through the day she goes.
And like the little sparrow
with a broken wing, she needs
A helping hand, "Lord", to get
Through each day.
Her body is frail now, "Lord".
But, Oh, what inner strength.
Please reach down and heal her,
"Lord, I ask of You, AMEN."

Dedication: to Carol Stone, my friend

Enchanted Dreams

Untitled
Ellen K. Stine
Dear Lord,
My prayer is to linger with You,
At the close of the day;
To love You, honor You,
In such a beautiful way,
That joy bells will ring,
And angels sing;
And glory to You I'll bring.
In my solitude, dear Lord,
Your strength abides with me
To overflowing ecstasy.
In the sweetness of Your nearness,
Let me sip the nectar from Your cup.
This, my Lord, enfolds me to Your bosom,
To bask in the glory of Your love,
For me at last and mine for You.

Another Place
E. Ann Taylor
There is a place I've been to
that a few people know
of dark, light and peace
where violence does not go

You leave the pain behind you
Your heart is filled with joy
A place that will accept you
no matter what your story

But if there's something you need to do
or maybe another test
you will come back to finish it
before your soul can rest

Sunrise Service
Kathy Dorn
While I sit here alone on this beautiful Easter morn,
I anticipate the sunrise as a new day is born.
As the sun peaks over the treetops and the sky begins to glow,
the birds begin their singing, as if, somehow, they know
of the young man who died for me many years ago.
I think about my Savior and how He suffered for me,
as He hung, nailed, upon that cross from a gnarled dogwood tree.
He did not understand and questioned, as would we,
"My God! My God! Why hast thou forsaken me?"
As the crowd roared, "Crucify him!", little did they know,
He was the Son of God and it was time for Him to go.
He was sent here, with a purpose, from our Father above,
to live, teach and die for us as a symbol of His love.
That Someone cared enough for us to give His only Son,
that we may have eternal life when ours on Earth is done,
is more than I can fathom, but question, I will not,
as I return His love and give Him praise
for the Son whom He begot.

The Way It Is
Ralph Davies
Politicians foil, while workers toil.
Bankers scheme to aid the regime.
They hoard the gold, while folks go cold.
All the nation's assets sold.

An island rich, with oil and coal,
Where miners and seamen sign the dole.
The wealthy invest in trusts abroad.
British skills they can not afford.

Tempt the workers into debt,
and afraid to strike,
Then unto them,
they will do as they like.

Women
Raymond Doersam
When I was 12, women frightened me
They still frighten me at 103
Some women are cute but never mute
Why are the mute ones never cute?
Some women have acts that are funny
To this drone, some feel like bee's honey
Women reminded D. H. Lawrence of fruit
Unfortunately, he looked like a newt
D. H. was right —oh, those honey dews!
Invariably they light my fuse
Women have always been part of my life —
Cousins, my sister, my daughter, my wife
And my mother — thank you for having me
Without you, where would I be?
Oh, yes, my father was a help
Without him, I'd never been whelped.

In Halls
Rebecca Allcott
I will not remember
This first year
For the nights of hedonism with friends who never seemed as real
During the day,
Or the long hours of conscientiously laborious studying,
Blue words on white, endless
Constructed terms.

Instead I will remember
Those eternal days and nights
of excess–fuelled apathy,
Which prevented us from either building a temple to Dionysius
Or consciously experiencing mundane life,
But somehow, between the intensity of play and the barrage of work,
Seemed to us; far from home but still not alone,
To be completely normal.

Virulence
Jase Botting

Am I to speak in multiple forms to impeach upon your brow,
the many destructible virtues you possess
and control with your speechless beauty?
There are no rainbow reflections with coughing walls,
along in surreal magnet vibrations.
and there is no view of poison pride
from watery archway nations.
There is no feathered moonlight,
with photons of gray and gold.
and there is no rhythm in borderline weaver,
for one to behold.
Take on the world with a rusted finger,
for my ignorance has cascaded.
One cellophane thought,
One plastic wish,
for the soul who remains unfaded.

The Rain
V. A. Lyons

The rain comes fast and furious,
washing away my lonely thoughts.
It leaves me feeling clean, wild and free
at it gently washes over me,
the rain so clean,
the smell so sweet,
makes everything seem so right
the rain falls slowly,
gently now.
Making me feel alive somehow
who cares if it's cold?
not me, I won't be told
It makes my soul wild and free
as it gently washes over me.

Dedication: to Andrew and my daughter Allyson

Dancing With Deception
Rick Adams

I walked a weary walk and failed the fearsome fight.
I sought nothing and nothing was my reward.
Reaping all that I had sown, I reaped nothing.
I floundered in my faith, gasping and gulping on fear,
As wave after wave, like days of the year
Flowed over and over and over...
Shadows chased me into the valley of Baca,
As hope in hope and faith in faith offered little victory.
Glimpses of a happier past were but stumbling stones to the future.
I courted fear, danced with Deception and when the music stopped...
I was just as I was before.
Pity, the painful prison, parts possibility from opportunity,
And binds the prisoner; for Fear and Deception are steps to destruction.
But invisible Hope, can break, dissolve,
Destroy invisible Fear and Deception.
And Joy comes singing when Hope has had its way.
So hope...

A Love Like Ours
Ruth R. Sasala

Thinking about you, Baby,
Every day and night.
Holding you close to my heart,
When you're nowhere in sight.
Just want to thank you
For coming into my life,
You made me feel special,
You light up my life.
Hold me close to your heart,
And never let me go,
You were made for me,
My heart's telling me so
When I hold you in my arms,
And feel you close to me,
I know deep inside my soul,
This is the way it's supposed to be.

Hyacinth
Chris Burkhardt

... but only half of her sensuality I love,
or at least the potential of it.

And the other half, a stern, proud look
—a reassurance: like a sea who knows its
eminent return upon the shoreline.

Small lips, yet solid, in squinting eyes,
her cheeks are the suns of an endless day.

On these nights, with her hair pulled back, jet black,
frays exposed only shyly,
she is a woman in soft nude bathing half–bent slanting
in a silent morning light

looking directly at you, unrelenting.

Ribbons
Amanda Arsenault

I walked into school today with ribbons in my hair,
The kids don't really look at me, it's just empty gawks and stares.
The kids at school, they laugh at me, but why, I do not know,
I haven't been here all that long, yet still I want to go.
I met someone and asked her why no one will talk to me,
She turned around looked me in the eye and this is what she said:
"You're not like the rest of us"
"You're not like us at all"
"You're not black"
"And we're not white"
"A friendship that will never be"
"For color is all anyone will ever see"
And with that said she walked away,
And once again I was alone, alone as one can be.
But what she said had made me think,
Of what the world would be.
If we weren't so quick to judge,
Of who we are or what we someday might be!

Enchanted Dreams

A Stone For The Living
Joyce Hendres
Down the narrow, winding path, nettle–edged,
we picked our way
past rhododendrons waving their party pom poms
to a fanfare of foxgloves
into the heart of the untended part
of the old cemetery

A stone with weathered words and dates
ideal accommodation for our picnic
we danced to the music of its environment
amid forgotten lives

Through sand–like particles of biscuit
to unseen fish in the slime–green pond
played party games on our stone table
a stone for the living
to our party of innocence

Lovetime
Robert Donald Spector
From the Moment I first met you,
Time itself stood still.
I knew that nothing else
In this wide world mattered
Since you became at once
My present, past and future,
My hourglass in which
No grain of sand would ever move.
I dismissed with ease
What ordinary clocks and watches
Kept telling me that I must do.
I didn't have the slightest doubt
That I could do away with everything,
Except my love for you.

Mother's Day Tribute
Melanie Pace
Cantankerous old woman, decrepit and full of spite
We battle through the day and bicker through the night
I'm in her jurisdiction and under her command
I am the worthless daughter she loves to reprimand
I am an onerous burden she's forced to schlep about
And I'm unable to rebel, her rules I cannot flout
Oh, she is an avid slaver, I'm on a ball and chain
Give her sufficient reason and she'll gladly cause me pain
I'll start a revolution to obviate her rule
I'll enlist Saddam Hussein, 'cause that guy is pretty cool
Compared to that nefarious hag, Saddam Hussein's a saint
Hitler is a gentleman and the Ripper's habits quaint
Yet she smiles at the neighbors and wears no army boots
Instead she wears her elegant pumps, with her Sunday suits
No one can see through her facade, they're all duped by her spell
She seems the perfect mother
But she's a demon straight from hell!

If I Were An Artist
J. McLaughlin
If I were an artist
I'd never tire
Of the colour red
I wouldn't be able to get enough
Of rowan berries or
Those laser streaks
In a summer sunset or
Apples in a bowl
or wine in a glass
I wouldn't be able to get enough of it
The life colour
It draws like a lover's lips
Everywhere
As desire.

A Heaviness In My Soul
Robbin Christein
There's such a heaviness in my soul—
this heaviness the world will never know
We stand and pray and wait for the return of
our Lord Jesus Christ – and again the
heaviness in my soul.
The world doesn't understand and they know
Him not– A heaviness in my soul
As we stand before God Almighty –
no more heaviness in my soul
This heaviness – the world still will never know–
You see – our Jesus came and took His
children home —
Sadly enough — a home the world will never
know.

The Nightmare
Stacy Allan
Nightmares, screams, horrible dreams,
Ugly, hairy, weird and scary.
Thunder, lightening, all things frightening,
You'll be in luck if you wake up!
Most folk don't, you probably won't,
You scream and shout but don't get out.
Until, at last, the nightmare's passed.
You need a drink, but just can't think,
Then you get up to find a cup.
The tap is dry, you want to cry.
Water, wetter, something better,
Your neck is tight, you're still in fright.
You ache with pain and feel insane,
When soon you see a cup of tea.
You drink it quick and feel quite sick,
Then sit down stiff and wait until...
Your head is clear, there's no more fear,
You'll sleep once more, with no more GORE!!!

My Father, My Friend
Debra A. Weidman
Each evening I sit while time slides by,
Wondering why he had to die;
My good–by was said to him at the end,
The day I lost my Father, my Friend.

When I visit his final resting place,
In peace and in tears streaming down my face;
I look to the sky and in the clouds I see.
My Father, my Friend watching me.

As the years go by I'll miss him so,
Peace will come easier, this I know.
When my life is over and God takes me home in the end,
I know I'll be with my Father, my Friend.

Divorce
Mary Alice Orazen
Why live in a dream that used to be?
I'm still young and certainly free.
Free from all vows I ever made,
Yet beneath it all I'm so afraid.
Afraid the mistakes that I made then,
Will happen to me again and again.
Am I doomed to live in this life alone
And possess a heart that's made of stone?
Or was it fate and meant to be,
And somewhere someone waits for me?
If this be so, I do not know,
How will I tell? How will I know?
Shall I pass it off as a silly joke,
And watch my dreams go up in smoke?
No! From this time on I solemnly vow
To forget the past and think of NOW.
And in time, I hope and pray
That God will help me find my way.

Looking For My Angel
Beth J. Hohensee
I'm looking for my angel with the light and love of God.
My angel that has helped me with every step I've trod.
I want to see her clearly – with eyes so bright they shine,
And a smile that's warm and friendly and a heart that's good and kind.
I know that she is out there – for my heart says it is so.
And the fact that she is with me, is so comforting to know!
But I'm still looking for my angel – for I want to really see
That she is there and watching and taking care of me.
So many others have seen theirs – so why can't I see mine?
Could it be I'm so unworthy – or is it not yet time?
I'll keep looking for my angel and pray that others see...
My angel's light of goodness shining right through me!

Dedication: for Sissy – watch over me

October 15, 1997
Dennis J. Cornelius
Around the storm–blue moon
Glowing just atop the trees
Before the dawn has broken
I beg my heart to please
Find its pieces.
To nurture happiness.
To forsake vanity and pride
And know as I was mystified
With your love
And distracted by your charm
That the iridescence was the sunlight
Colliding with the dew
Dancing on the long–stem roses
I had not sent to you.

Memories
Annie Sammons
I sit and stare out the window onto the farm.
The pecan trees stand their ground
while the blue birds fly south for the winter.
The deeper I stare, the brighter the light becomes......

I can see the vague figure of
a little girl skipping rope through
the trees in her eyelet lace dress
and white ribbon in her hair.

I can almost smell one of
Grandma's apple pies in the oven
and smell of sweat and
grease as Grandpa comes in
from the fields.

As I sit and stare out the window onto the farm,
I sip my coffee and cover up with Grandma's old quilt.

A Funeral Mask
Mary Pickin
Why do you ask me "cleanest?"
Western woman with a Harpic smile.
We are from different continents
Different cultures
Yet I speak your language
If you can't speak mine
I will tell you the cleanest thing
That I ever found
It was a mother's grief for her dead child.
She had lost so many children
To the filth of disease
Keenest, cleanest pain wiped her heart clear
Grief white and strong like bleached bones
Tears as sterile as your strongest disinfectant
Burned her mother's face
And cauterized her spirit.

Enchanted Dreams

After Asphodel
Ronald Pies
For WCW
In snowless late December,
you tug me through the yard
to see how life persists:
hardy cyclamen, Russian sage,
and wisps of sweet woodruff
have kept their growing edge.
Yellow dead–nettle
is anything but dead,
and even columbine
has lingered.

So why this view
of death–bed winter,
when there is you—
elfin as early spring—
to bless the green pulse
of our land?

Unreality
Lisa Klassen
Break out of the confines
Of your porcelain–white world,
Where wandering eyes mask blank souls.
Once I held out my hand
To induce your metamorphosis.
But you muttered an insubstantial threat
And would not accept.
Stay trapped in your clinical existence, then.
Smooth white walls that smother thoughts.
Whereas my reality intertwines
With the misty webs of dreams.
No darkness gathers there,
In the vacuous interludes between truth and fiction.
Look far into my eyes,
Soar higher and higher.
Drift away with me
On the blue dreams of my desire.

I Recall
Michelle Seib
I recall sitting beneath a tree so many years ago, it could
only be tomorrow, basking in the silent songs of the first
sentient benefactor with whom I sought shelter from home.

I remember lying prone amidst damp foliage in moist mother's
flesh, amazed at the peace I felt then as undetectable chords
and rhythms helped salty sweet fluids find passage through
straining eyes from a too–soon bitter heart.

I remember my wonderment also, watching this ancient androgynous
being dancing with a gentle, equally–sexless breeze in a
passionate, soulful ballet as it rained pink and cream blessings
upon me almost unintentionally.

The solace I felt then returns to mind, too, the peace that trickled
into my child's hardened heart as I witnessed the subtle union
of that vagabond breeze and the stoic elm, both content
with their silent song and brief time that they shared.

First Passion Of Youth Is Passing
Lonny Harrison
First passion of youth is passing.
Where blood once boiled in my veins
flows a thinner syrup
diluted with grief and disappointment.
No longer would I sell my soul
to catch a glimpse
of her curious brow
or the capricious smirk
playing at the corners of her mouth.
No more romantic visions of exotic adventure
and wild abandon.
Let Homers write the epics
and Beethovens write the symphonies;
I'm through with chasing shadows.

To The Universal New Year
Sylvia Major
Budding, a green leaf
incipient–forming,
Tight
to a fine point
like
tissue, twirled
by
nervous
fingers...

Identity pubescent,
quasi–bud, quasi–leaf,
tremulous,
winsome and proud,
Unfurling flag,
salute
to a New Year!

CHAPTER TWO

Poet Profiles

The following pages comprise concise personal profiles of many of the poets featured in this book, including pen names, occupations, special honors, other published writings and even personal goals and philosophical viewpoints. You will find that some are professional published writers, while others are appearing for the first time ever in print. But all of these poets have one thing in common: they are all compelled to reveal their feelings about life through creative expression in the form of words and verse.

EDITOR'S NOTE: *Please keep in mind that not all poets who have contributed to this book will appear in this chapter. All biographical information presented is specifically at the behest of each person listed.*

Enchanted Dreams

Author: Stacey A. Adams; **Pen Name:** Stacey Ann Adams; **Birthplace:** River Falls, WI; **Occupation:** Clean Tour Coaches; **Hobbies:** Poetry; **Memberships:** Poetry Guild; **Spouse's Name:** Randy Adams; **Education:** High school and Eau Claire, WI Vo-Tech; **Published Works:** Mother's Day poem, Even Then Even Now and Raeseto Remember; **Personal Statement:** Writing poetry for other people makes me feel inspired to go on in life and to enjoy it to the greatest ability.

Author: Kelly Ahlstrom; **Birthplace:** Jersey City, NJ; **Occupation:** Homemaker; **Hobbies:** Writing, reading, gardening and singing; **Spouse's Name:** Kenneth Paul Ahlstrom; **Children:** 3; **Education:** High school and going to college for writing; **Personal Statement:** Poetry is an intimate glimpse into one's soul and their gracous decision to share it with others. I thank God for all my inspiration.

Author: Masir Ahmed; **Birthplace:** Assam, India; **Occupation:** Security representative; **Hobbies:** Swimming and playing the flute; **Memberships:** Allied International Union; **Spouse's Name:** S. Ahemd; **Children:** 5; **Grandchildren:** 1; **Education:** High school and 2 years of college. Also SGT Education Air Force; **Published Works:** The Exquisite; **Personal Statement:** Knowledge should not be limited to restricted few. Instead, it should be delivered to all for the good of mankind.

Author: Robert W. Anderson; **Birthplace:** Clear Lake, WA; **Occupation:** USMC retired and Police Sgt. retired; **Hobbies:** Bowling and music; **Memberships:** USMC Association and Intl. Police Association; **Spouse's Name:** Audrey M. Anderson; **Children:** 3; **Grandchildren:** 2; **Education:** Assoc. Degree in Law Enforcement; **Honors:** President's List; **Published Works:** Your Time Account in Leatherneck Magazine; **Personal Statement:** Influenced early by music and literature, channeling activities into sentimental and sensitive matters.

Author: Tina Anderson; **Pen Name:** Andie Anderson; **Birthplace:** Venice, FL; **Occupation:** Pharmacy tech; **Hobbies:** Writing, reading and swimming; **Education:** LKD High School; **Personal Statement:** In June of 1995 I was injured and started losing the use of my hand and couldn't work any longer, so I followed my dream and started writing poems and I'm starting a book.

Author: Margaret Andrew; **Birthplace:** Doncaster; **Occupation:** Housewife; **Hobbies:** Painting, craftwork, travel and reading; **Spouse's Name:** Wilfred Andrew; **Children:** 2; **Grandchildren:** 4; **Education:** Rossington Secondary Modern School; **Personal Statement:** Poetry has enhanced my life and is a wonderful way of expressing my own personal vision. I admire the poets Brian Patten and Sylvia Plath.

Author: Margaret Archer; **Birthplace:** Keswick, Cumbria; **Occupation:** Retired; **Hobbies:** Reading, drawing, painting and heritage issues; **Memberships:** Friend of R. A., Birmingham Museum and Art Gallery; **Spouse's Name:** John Villiers Archer; **Children:** 2; **Education:** Grammar, higher education at Birmingham College of Art; **Published Works:** Poetry by the Poetry Guild and Poetry Today; **Personal Statement:** Retirement after a busy career in Art Education offered me the opportunity to write. I had been encouraged to quit school and consider writing as a career.

Author: Vernon Archer; **Birthplace:** Auglaize County; **Occupation:** Retired refinery worker; **Children:** 4; **Grandchildren:** 8; **Education:** High school, Navy Medical TDW and management school; **Personal Statement:** This poem was written by my oldest brother (Leonard Melvin Archer). It was written when he was in the 3C's in 1933. He passed away Nov. 1971.

Author: Calvin A. Austin; **Birthplace:** Philadelphia, PA; **Occupation:** Postal clerk; **Hobbies:** Coaching track and field, drawing and writing; **Memberships:** Deacon Board and UAGTCA; **Children:** 2; **Grandchildren:** 1; **Education:** 2 years of college

Author: Jean Bailey; **Birthplace:** Wolverhampton; **Occupation:** Housewife and mother; **Hobbies:** Dog shows, breeding and writing; **Memberships:** RSPCA; **Spouse's Name:** David Bailey; **Children:** 3; **Grandchildren:** 3; **Education:** General; **Personal Statement:** I am passionate about animals, but I can see that it's necessary to not be oversentimental. There needs to be control over wildlife.

Author: Scott Bain; **Birthplace:** Stirling; **Occupation:** Production operator; **Hobbies:** Playing guitar, keeping fit, fishing and music; **Education:** Wallace High School; **Personal Statement:** I wrote this piece while bored on a nightshift. My influences are singer songwriters Ozzy Osbourne and Neil Young.

Author: Nancy L. Baker; **Birthplace:** West Allis, WI; **Hobbies:** Writing poetry; **Personal Statement:** With all eternity, I still couldn't tell how Todd, my destiny, has influenced and inspired me and helped me find my true self.

Author: Shayne P. Baldwin; **Pen Name:** Shayne P. Baldwin; **Birthplace:** Camden, NJ; **Occupation:** U. S. Navy; **Hobbies:** Writing, woodworking and golfing; **Personal Statement:** Inspiration can be found all around us. We just have to open our hearts to see it.

Author: George Ball; **Pen Name:** Damien; **Birthplace:** Seivierville, TN; **Occupation:** Student; **Hobbies:** Video games, writing and building models; **Education:** Ninth grade student; **Personal Statement:** Anything said from the heart never sounds wrong and is always touching. My inspirations are Shakespeare, Stephen King, Dean Koontz, Mom and the night sky.

Author: Lynnette Barclay; **Pen Name:** Lynn Barclay; **Birthplace:** Baltimore, MD; **Hobbies:** Reading, writing, music and spending time outside; **Education:** 10th grade and pursuing GED; **Personal Statement:** As a newly published author, my goals are to see more of my work published. I'm influenced by what goes on in my everyday life.

Author: Ryan Barrios; **Birthplace:** San Antonio, TX; **Occupation:** Student; **Hobbies:** Dance, theatre and writing songs and poetry; **Education:** High school diploma; **Personal Statement:** My writing is my way of releasing my emotions. My inspirational influences range anywhere from Edgar Allan Poe to Maya Angelou to Jim Morrison.

Author: Latonya Batchelor; **Pen Name:** Tonya; **Birthplace:** Hampton, VA; **Occupation:** Telemarketer; **Hobbies:** Shopping; **Spouse's Name:** Alonzo Copeland, Jr.

Author: Diane Netherland Baxter; **Birthplace:** Kingsport, TN; **Occupation:** Wife and mother and former social worker; **Hobbies:** The Arts, music, scenic bicycle riding and others; **Memberships:** Choir member and infrequent soloist; **Spouse's Name:** Van David Baxter; **Children:** 2; **Education:** Bachelor of Science with honors from University of Tennessee; **Honors:** Several honor societies while in college; **Awards:** Fred M. Roddy Academic Merit Scholarship; **Personal Statement:** This is one of my first poems. I have mournfully cried for children in this society. I hope that my work will be shared again.

Author: Stephanie Bear; **Pen Name:** Demita; **Birthplace:** Augusta, GA; **Occupation:** Student; **Hobbies:** Writing, gymnastics, jet skiing and swimming; **Memberships:** 4-H, Hayden's Gymnastics, Meskwaki Nation Isa & Fox Tribe; **Education:** Fifth grade student; **Honors:** Honor roll; **Awards:** Scholar of Destination Award and Creative Writing Award; **Personal Statement:** My goals include going to college, becoming a marine biologist and writing poems about dolphins and the ocean.

Poet Profiles

Author: Richard D. Becerra; **Birthplace:** Kansas City, KS; **Hobbies:** Writing, reading, gardening and riding motorcycles; **Children:** 1; **Education:** BFA degree Dramatic Arts

Author: Thomas Beechey; **Birthplace:** Butler, PA; **Hobbies:** Writing and music; **Education:** High school and 2 year degree in Journalism; **Published Works:** The Flag and Inside and Outside; **Personal Statement:** The writings of Robert Frost and Dylan Thomas, the lyrical geniuses of Bob Dylan and John Lennon are my influences and life itself with all of its splendor is my inspiration. My utmost desire is to bring peace and joy to at least one soul.

Author: Samantha M. Belk; **Birthplace:** Pensacola, FL; **Occupation:** Hair and makeup artist; **Hobbies:** Art, antiques and yoga; **Education:** High school, beauty school and various for cosmetology; **Personal Statement:** My heart and soul are released into my poetry. I would like to share my thoughts and feelings in the hope to touch someone.

Author: Sarah E. Benson; **Birthplace:** Wheeling, WV; **Occupation:** Student; **Hobbies:** Reading, crafts and chorus; **Memberships:** Triadelphia Middle School Band and chorus; **Education:** Going into high school

Author: Gloria T. Berg; **Pen Name:** Arion; **Birthplace:** Colombia, SA; **Occupation:** Teacher; **Hobbies:** Astronomy, writing, aerodynamics, aviation and gardening; **Memberships:** Planetary Society, Smithsonian Inst.; **Spouse's Name:** Anders Henrik Berg; **Children:** 1; **Education:** Business Management Pontifical Javeriana University in Bogota, Colombia; **Honors:** Poem published and registered; **Awards:** For poetry

Author: Stacie L. Bezon; **Birthplace:** Canton, OH; **Occupation:** Housewife; **Hobbies:** Gardening, bowling and writing; **Memberships:** Woman's Club; **Spouse's Name:** Corrie; **Children:** 5; **Education:** High school

Author: Georgia Taylor Bidwell; **Birthplace:** Hartford, CT; **Occupation:** Disabled; **Hobbies:** Reading, writing, sewing, crafts, birds, movies and walking; **Education:** One year college, one year business school; **Personal Statement:** For me, writing poetry is like painting with words.

Author: Jason Birdsell; **Birthplace:** Naerville, IL; **Occupation:** Marine Corps, Reservist and student; **Hobbies:** Hiking and writing; **Education:** Graduate of Tustin High School

Author: Dennis W. Bishop; **Pen Name:** D W Bishop; **Birthplace:** Saginaw, MI; **Occupation:** Dreamer; **Hobbies:** Yoga, nature, golf and pondering; **Education:** Old age; **Honors:** My guru; **Awards:** Life; **Personal Statement:** Poetry is the wine of words. It has color, fragrance and a mellow high.

Author: Norma J. Boyll; **Birthplace:** Toadhop, IN; **Occupation:** Housewife; **Hobbies:** Walking, crocheting, gardening and writing poetry; **Memberships:** YWCA; **Spouse's Name:** Rondel L Boyll; **Children:** 2; **Grandchildren:** 6; **Education:** Graduated Honey Creek High School; **Awards:** Shorthand and typing; **Personal Statement:** I always liked poetry, not like MacBeth, but the more down-to-earth and from-the-heart-poetry. My mother always liked poetry. She passed away: that was when the first poem came. I have had cancer, this added to my writing. They keep coming.

Author: Brenda L. Bradley; **Birthplace:** Chester Park; **Occupation:** Special Education Instructor; **Hobbies:** Music, poetry and ceramics; **Memberships:** Alpha Kappa Alpha Service Sorority; **Spouse's Name:** Julius E. Bradley; **Education:** Graduated Millersville University; **Personal Statement:** I thank God for the many gifts He has bestowed upon me. Through His love, grace and mercy, I have been inspired to place my thoughts and feelings on paper and to share these feelings with all.

Author: Tarrahal Branch; **Pen Name:** Tee; **Birthplace:** Saratoga Springs; **Occupation:** Homemaker; **Hobbies:** Writing, drawing and reading; **Education:** High school graduate; **Awards:** Art award, poetry & drawing award from F. Donald Myers Boces; **Personal Statement:** I believe feelings and thoughts are easier to write down on paper than being said to the one you're thinking of.

Author: Tamyra Brooks; **Birthplace:** Detroit, MI; **Occupation:** Social worker; **Hobbies:** Writing all forms; **Memberships:** Nat'l. Assoc. of Social Workers & Board Member; **Children:** 1; **Education:** Master of social work from Wayne State University; **Honors:** ACSW; **Personal Statement:** There is no such thing as an excuse. There is always a creative solution to any dilemma encountered. Find the source and utilize it.

Author: Joseph W. Brown II; **Birthplace:** Toledo, OH; **Occupation:** Construction; **Hobbies:** Model building, poetry and writing; **Spouse's Name:** Evelyn M. Brown; **Children:** 4; **Education:** High school graduate; **Personal Statement:** I have always been fond of poetry.

Author: Kristen Browne; **Birthplace:** Long Island, NY; **Occupation:** Student; **Hobbies:** Dancing, playing the violin, singing and swimming; **Memberships:** Science Club, Art Club and Dix Hill United Methodist Church; **Education:** Grade 4 at Forest Park Elem. School; **Honors:** Citizen of the Month; **Awards:** Pat Hannafin's Dance Studio 5th, 6th and 7th Year Awards; **Personal Statement:** I will add writing to my list of hobbies, and I am influenced by my parents and teachers.

Author: Robert Bryan; **Birthplace:** Marshall, NC; **Occupation:** University faculty; **Hobbies:** Woodwork, poems, photography and others; **Memberships:** National Assoc. Retired Federal Employees and MENSA; **Spouse's Name:** Elizabeth Scott Bryan; **Children:** 4; **Grandchildren:** 4; **Education:** BS Degree Animal Science; **Honors:** Rural Safety Promotion Award and NC Rural Safety Council; **Published Works:** Numereous poems published; **Personal Statement:** I plan to write a book about my mountain, about University life and its faults. About the future.

Author: Jeanne Bryant; **Birthplace:** Missouri; **Hobbies:** Travel, reading and gardening; **Children:** 2; **Education:** Student at Southwest Missouri State University; **Personal Statement:** Writing opens a world of feelings. It is a way I can relate to anything, Like a song without notes; it flows by the tone, of the voice.

Author: E. M. Budge; **Birthplace:** London; **Occupation:** Receptionist and secretary work; **Hobbies:** Reading, knitting and writing poems; **Spouse's Name:** Derek John; **Children:** 2; **Education:** Ordinary; **Published Works:** Poetic Thoughts, Elizabeth M. Budge and various anthologies; **Personal Statement:** Influenced by life in general and the world of nature.

Author: Joel Burnett; **Birthplace:** Atlanta, GA; **Occupation:** Student; **Hobbies:** Golf, soccer and travel; **Education:** Majoring in psychology; **Honors:** Honor graduate of Lexington High School; **Awards:** 1st recipient of E. Chandler Owen Scholarship; **Personal Statement:** This poem was written and given to my parents when I graduated from high school in 1996. If they could not see my appreciation and admiration towards them through my actions, I hoped that they could somehow see it through my words.

Author: Daniel Ray Cano; **Birthplace:** Colorado Springs, CO; **Occupation:** Student; **Memberships:** National Hispanic Institute; **Education:** Currently in 10th grade

Author: Adam Caravaglia; **Birthplace:** Morristown, NJ; **Occupation:** Sales; **Hobbies:** All sports; **Memberships:** MH

Enchanted Dreams

Football, wrestling, lacrosse, baseball little leagues; **Education:** Graduate Morristown High School; **Published Works:** In The Shadows of the Night

Author: Vanessa Washington Carter; **Birthplace:** Houston, TX; **Occupation:** Supervisor for Environmental Services; **Hobbies:** Reading, writing, camping and trail riding; **Memberships:** Wild Bunch Riding Club; **Education:** J. L. McCallough High School and Houston Community College; **Honors:** A and B honor roll in high school; **Awards:** J. W. Marriot appreciation award; **Personal Statement:** To the younger generation: keep your hand in God's hand.

Author: Rickie Jean Cassady; **Pen Name:** Sissy; **Birthplace:** Roswell, NM; **Occupation:** Cashier; **Hobbies:** Gambling, writing, reading, and poetry; **Spouse's Name:** James E. Cassady; **Children:** 1; **Education:** Two years of college; **Awards:** Never Late; **Personal Statement:** One of my younger brothers went to Heaven five years ago. It still feels as if it was yesterday. I do miss his smiling face! I think of him every day.

Author: Lydia Castillo; **Birthplace:** New York, NY; **Occupation:** Retired secretary; **Hobbies:** Reading, travel and writing; **Spouse's Name:** Caesar M. Castillo; **Children:** 2; **Grandchildren:** 5; **Education:** High school and Business Secretarial School graduate; **Personal Statement:** Pity we show so little interest in reading. A thought well penned and a verse well phrased can illuminate the mind and nourish the soul.

Author: Steven J. Chalmers; **Birthplace:** Harvey, IL; **Occupation:** Student; **Hobbies:** Band, basketball and bowling; **Education:** 7th grade student; **Honors:** National Honor Society; **Awards:** Academic and band; **Personal Statement:** I wanted to write this poem, "The Long Wind," because I have wanted to be a poet someday. I have felt it in my heart.

Author: Theron Clarke; **Birthplace:** Richmond, VA; **Occupation:** Artist, writer and social worker; **Memberships:** National Writers Union; **Honors:** Silver Reel Award; **Awards:** Association of Community Broadcasters; **Personal Statement:** We need wish and hope that words approach genesis, creation manifests a truthful reality, our senses open to the full potential of justice and humanity.

Author: Evelyn Cleghorn; **Birthplace:** Berwick-On-Tweed; **Occupation:** Retired; **Hobbies:** Writing; **Memberships:** Atticus Writers Group; **Spouse's Name:** William Gleghorn (deceased); **Children:** 2; **Grandchildren:** 4; **Education:** England and Canada; **Personal Statement:** My writing is deeply influenced by my belief in God, my life and my surroundings.

Author: S. M. Collins; **Birthplace:** Hatfold, Hertfordshire; **Occupation:** Manufactures penmorer; **Hobbies:** Art, music, football, golf, snooker and steam engines; **Spouse's Name:** Marcia; **Children:** 2; **Education:** Chace Secondary, short course on creative writing; **Personal Statement:** I had to write something today because when walking my dog "Connie" I realised I would not see her for the next five weeks.

Author: Amy J. Compton; **Birthplace:** Dover, NJ; **Occupation:** RN; **Hobbies:** Writing and hand stamping; **Spouse's Name:** David Compton; **Children:** 2; **Education:** AAS; **Published Works:** Poem entitled Rick

Author: William C. Cook; **Birthplace:** Vale New Haven; **Occupation:** Master Tech Commercial Engine Division; **Hobbies:** Reading, bird watching, landscaping, NY Yankees & Giants fan; **Memberships:** Smithsonian Institute; **Spouse's Name:** Doreen B. Cook; **Children:** 2; **Education:** High school; **Awards:** Employee of the Month; **Personal Statement:** Be careful what you write, you may have to come back and live it.

Author: Bettie Cooper; **Birthplace:** Raceland, KY; **Occupation:** Day care worker; **Hobbies:** Reading and house plants; **Spouse's Name:** Lee Cooper; **Children:** 10; **Grandchildren:** 7; **Education:** High school graduate; **Personal Statement:** Two of my favorite writers are Grace Livingston Hill and Helen Steiner Rice.

Author: Helen E. Cooper; **Birthplace:** Aldenham, Herts; **Occupation:** Retired; **Hobbies:** Writing, reading and crossword puzzles; **Spouse's Name:** Walter Cooper; **Children:** 1; **Grandchildren:** 4; **Education:** Watford Grammar School for Girls; **Personal Statement:** My life has been varied and interesting and I have spent most of it caring for others, working for the social services.

Author: Eboni Cooper; **Pen Name:** Nytia Drummer; **Birthplace:** Milwaukee; **Occupation:** Student; **Hobbies:** Basketball, writing and inventing new things; **Spouse's Name:** Michael James Stephens; **Children:** 1; **Education:** San Leandro High School graduate; **Personal Statement:** I am a person with billions of thoughts and feelings. They only seem to clear when I write them down. Am I alone?

Author: Cynthia Cooper; **Birthplace:** Richmond, VA; **Occupation:** Special Education teacher; **Hobbies:** Reading and oil painting; **Memberships:** Showers of Blessing Christian Center; **Spouse's Name:** Divorced; **Children:** 3; **Grandchildren:** 1; **Education:** Elizabeth City State University and MA Ed., East Carolina University; **Honors:** Student of the Year in Psychology and Dean's List; **Personal Statement:** To God be the glory for speaking directly to my heart in order to benefit others and me.

Author: Evelyn Cope; **Pen Name:** Eve Mathyson; **Birthplace:** Milton, Stoke-on-Trent; **Occupation:** Retired Pensioner; **Hobbies:** Painting, landscapes, flowers, writing and family history; **Spouse's Name:** Alfred Cope (deceased); **Children:** 3; **Grandchildren:** 9; **Education:** Left school at age 15, some additional courses; **Honors:** For English under the Adult Education Course; **Published Works:** Poem which was composed in The South EastTimes; **Personal Statement:** I was brought up by an aunt and uncle from the age of four months until fifteen years, in lovely Warwickshire which I never forgot after migrating.

Author: Lia M. Corey; **Birthplace:** Rhode Island; **Occupation:** Student; **Hobbies:** Basketball, drawing, writing; **Memberships:** Middle School Basketball Team; **Honors:** Grade Seven Student; **Personal Statement:** My goal is to become a famous writer.

Author: Dennis J. Cornelius; **Birthplace:** Cincinnati, OH; **Occupation:** Parking enforcement officer; **Hobbies:** Golf; **Spouse's Name:** Peggy; **Children:** 2; **Education:** 12th grade

Author: Shane Cullen; **Birthplace:** Portsmouth, OH; **Occupation:** High school student; **Hobbies:** Playing guitar, drum and basketball; **Memberships:** Planetary Society; **Education:** Sophomore in high school; **Awards:** 2nd Place Astronomy, Ohio Regional Science Olympiad; **Personal Statement:** This is my personal quote, "Follow your heart and stick to your morals, no matter what happens."

Author: Luann Dallojacono; **Birthplace:** Long Island, NY; **Occupation:** Student in middle school; **Hobbies:** Tennis, softball, acting, singing and golf; **Education:** Presently attending Catholic school; **Honors:** High Honor Roll; **Published Works:** Anthology of Poety by Young Americans; **Personal Statement:** I started creative writing when I was eight years old. I enjoy writing poems and childrens stories. I like to read mystery novels.

Author: Amanda Lynn Darling; **Birthplace:** Fountain Valley, CA; **Occupation:** Student; **Hobbies:** Beanie Babies, tether ball, sports & collect porcelain dolls; **Education:** Elementary school 4th grade

Author: Adam Dave; **Pen Name:** Christopher Davidson Adams; **Birthplace:** Los Angeles, CA; **Occupation:** Writer; **Hobbies:**

Poet Profiles

Reading, travel, jogging, weightlifting and movies; **Memberships:** Blockbuster Video, LA Fitness and Extravaganza Video; **Education:** BA in History and Business from UCLA; **Honors:** Having a wonderful family & extraordinary woman that love me; **Awards:** This life on earth and the ability to enjoy it; **Published Works:** Lost and Found in The Land of Seduction; **Personal Statement:** The responsible writer does not create simply to entertain but also to instruct and uplift. The skillful writer accomplishes this without its being evident.

Author: Tony Wayne Davis, Jr.; **Pen Name:** T. J. Davis; **Birthplace:** Knoxville, TN; **Occupation:** Student; **Hobbies:** Guitar, football and writing; **Education:** Currently in high school; **Personal Statement:** Poetry is the only way I can express how I feel about life. I love that.

Author: Sara Dawson; **Pen Name:** Louie Sherrati; **Birthplace:** Sussex; **Occupation:** Student; **Hobbies:** Crystal healing and songwriting; **Education:** 10 GCSE's awaiting results for A–Level Psychology; **Personal Statement:** With all my work, I look to nature for simple inspiration which can then be mixed with illusion and exploded to create a dream.

Author: Richard R. De Lillio; **Birthplace:** Wilmington, DE; **Occupation:** Priest; **Hobbies:** Jogging, publications and whitewater rafting; **Memberships:** National Catholic Development Conference; **Education:** Doctorate in Ministry; **Honors:** Outstanding Secondary Education in America; **Published Works:** Articles on spirituality; **Personal Statement:** During my ministry I've held the belief that the secret of our desire for happiness and holiness lays in the present moment of our lives. I encourage others to face this moment and move forward in faith.

Author: Lois Deatherage; **Birthplace:** Lake City, AR; **Occupation:** Nurse; **Hobbies:** Reading, camping and writing poetry; **Spouse's Name:** Kenneth R.; **Children:** 2; **Education:** Nursing education and Bachelor of Art; **Honors:** Graduated Cum Laude from Northwest Christian College; **Awards:** Dean's List; **Published Works:** Mirror Image and Beauty in a Soul; **Personal Statement:** I've always loved to write, it is usually about how I feel about myself or how I view the world. My only goal as a writer is the hope that the words in the poems I write might have a positive influence on the people who read them.

Author: Brad Deifer; **Birthplace:** Whitehall, PA; **Occupation:** Various; **Hobbies:** Basketball, golf, movies and music; **Memberships:** Comet, West End and Zephyr Club; **Spouse's Name:** Shelly Denise; **Education:** Temple University; **Published Works:** Circle of Friends and The Tower; **Personal Statement:** Everybody is so strung up on the future they rarely remember the present. Is it so horribly easy to convince people what is good yet so insanely impossible to expose something creative.

Author: Nellie Ruth W. Demons; **Birthplace:** Barnesville, GA; **Occupation:** Retired teacher; **Hobbies:** Reading, writing and photography; **Memberships:** Retired Teachers Association and AARP; **Spouse's Name:** Divorced; **Children:** 2; **Grandchildren:** 3; **Education:** College Bachelor of Arts, BA in Secondary English; **Awards:** 1988 Teacher of the Year; **Published Works:** Sharing, First You Worry... Then You Pray... Never Panic; **Personal Statement:** My goals as a writer are to make people feel better, to stir the imagination of those who like to read, to be honest in my thoughts, truthful in my words and always maintain God's presence in my life. My inspiration Gibson, Rice and Angelou

Author: Simon P. Dennis; **Pen Name:** Simon Peter Dennis; **Birthplace:** Stafford; **Occupation:** Chef; **Hobbies:** Singing, writing, producing, DJ and basketball; **Education:** O Level English and maths. City and guild catering; **Honors:** NEBS Management Cert. Hygiene Cert.; **Published Works:** Tribute to Princess Diana and Towards 2000 Life; **Personal Statement:** It is nice to know my work is being recognised. My goals as a writer are to produce my own book, write a song, make a record and just keep on writing. Princess Diana was a big inspiration to me.

Author: Cristoval Diaz; **Birthplace:** Salt Lake, UT; **Hobbies:** Poetry, writing, enjoying life and nature; **Personal Statement:** Enjoy life, for it's so short and not savored by most. It comes and goes day in, day out not enjoyed by most, only a few.

Author: Karina Dibble; **Birthplace:** Cardiff; **Occupation:** Student; **Published Works:** My Dad and Waterfalls; **Personal Statement:** Truly great poetry comes from the heart, the soul and is inspired by anything which really moves you.

Author: Heather Dorman; **Birthplace:** Newport News, VA; **Occupation:** Paramedic; **Hobbies:** Flower gardening and enjoying life to its fullest; **Memberships:** The Picture Rocks Volunteer Fire Department; **Education:** Albemarle and the Williamsport Hospital and Medical Center Paramedic Training Institute; **Personal Statement:** Through sharing laughter, tears, dreams and love we are forever connected in our heart and soul. The two of you will walk with me where I go.

Author: Nadia Alicia Douglas; **Pen Name:** Alena; **Birthplace:** Fort Worth, TX; **Occupation:** Lab assistant; **Hobbies:** Reading, music and writing; **Memberships:** National Honor Society, NABSE Conference; **Spouse's Name:** Jermond Johnson; **Education:** High school graduate and attending TWU Fall Sem.; **Honors:** Tandy Scholar top 10% of graduating class; **Awards:** Full scholarship to Texas Wesleyan University; **Personal Statement:** My pen name is a variation of the name of my late aunt, Alena Jefferson. I only met her once, but she made a lasting impression.

Author: Dolly Dowker; **Birthplace:** Lincoln, AR; **Occupation:** Bookkeeper; **Hobbies:** Writing, cooking, gospel singing; **Memberships:** U. C. T. (United Commercial Travelers); **Spouse's Name:** Robert Dowker; **Children:** 3; **Grandchildren:** 7; **Education:** High School, Cosmetology, Accounting; **Personal Statement:** My writings are inspirations by God. I enjoy writing poems and tributes for my church. It would be a dream come true to get published. My husband always encourages me to write & praises my works. I owe my talent to God.

Author: Vickie Dunlap; **Birthplace:** Conneaut, OH; **Occupation:** Student; **Hobbies:** Reading, writing, bowling, poetry, bicycling and sewing; **Children:** 3; **Education:** Working towards a BA in Social Work and minor in Counseling; **Personal Statement:** I just started writing this year and realize that I have a talent for it. I am furthering my college education to include this area. I am a year away from my BA. My poetry reflects breaking up with a boyfriend who was also a longtime friend

Author: Whitney Durham; **Pen Name:** Minnie; **Birthplace:** Miles City, MT; **Occupation:** Student; **Hobbies:** Titanic, Heaven, writing poems, journalism and basketball; **Education:** Third grade student; **Personal Statement:** God is my inspiration.

Author: Susanne Eaton; **Birthplace:** Worcester, MA; **Occupation:** Teacher; **Hobbies:** Traveling, running, exercising and reading; **Memberships:** Delta Sigma Pi, Professional Business Fraternity; **Spouse's Name:** Richard T. Eaton, III; **Education:** Northern Arizona University, BS Hotel, Rest. Management and National University CA teaching credential; **Personal Statement:** I did not create this world; therefore, I do not have all the answers, but I do know life is a gift to be treasured.

Author: Carla F. Ellis; **Birthplace:** Chatham, England; **Occupation:** Housewife and mother; **Hobbies:** Drawing, painting, writing poetry and songs; **Spouse's Name:** Graham Stuart Ellis; **Children:** 1; **Education:** Highfield Secondary School; **Published Works:** Blue, in the junior school children's paper; **Personal**

Enchanted Dreams

Statement: Poems are out there waiting to be written; you just have to listen.

Author: Jeanette L. Estrada; **Birthplace:** Belton, MO; **Occupation:** Retired; **Hobbies:** Travel, baking, poetry, cake decorating and resin tables; **Memberships:** Women's Club, Sun & Fun Club, senior center and church; **Spouse's Name:** Deceased; **Education:** High school and some college; **Awards:** Milton O. Wilen Award for service to Educational Excellence; **Personal Statement:** Avenal is nestled at the foot of the Kettleman Hills, where Clark Gable made the movie Boomtown. I think poetry is a better way to express what I want to say, and I have done all poems since living in this little town.

Author: Rosanna Fabrizi; **Pen Name:** Rose Fabrizi; **Birthplace:** Bridgeport, CT; **Occupation:** Writer/poet; **Hobbies:** Reading, writing, weight training, dancing & interior design; **Memberships:** Distinguished Member of the International Society of Poetry; **Education:** Notre Dame High School; **Awards:** Poetry Merit Award '97 and '98; **Published Works:** Two poems published in two anthologies; **Personal Statement:** I have discovered that personal happiness must come from deep within. This happiness will be enhanced one thousand-fold if your soulmate is in your life.

Author: Joseph Fahy; **Birthplace:** Washington, Tyne & Wear; **Occupation:** Retired plant operator; **Hobbies:** Writing, walking and gardening; **Spouse's Name:** Jean; **Children:** 3; **Grandchildren:** 3; **Education:** Standard; **Personal Statement:** My viewpoint is to be able to continue to share my own work with all and to enjoy the work of others.

Author: Alan Fait; **Pen Name:** Garven Dreis; **Birthplace:** Shaw, SC; **Occupation:** Student; **Hobbies:** Starware CCG, computers; **Memberships:** Boy Scouts, Roy Christian Church and Order of the Arrow; **Education:** Tenth grade student; **Honors:** Commanded a Wing; **Awards:** Drug-Free Committee and Student of the Month; **Personal Statement:** I wrote this poem for my English assignment. I never thought it would have gotten to this!

Author: Bobby E. Farmer; **Birthplace:** Dayton, OH; **Occupation:** Retired; **Hobbies:** Gardening; **Memberships:** VFW; **Spouse's Name:** Sandra; **Children:** 4; **Grandchildren:** 9

Author: Donald J. Ferguson; **Pen Name:** Don; **Birthplace:** New Haven, CT; **Occupation:** Retired business administrator; **Hobbies:** Reading, writing, travel and swimming; **Spouse's Name:** Bette Ferguson (deceased); **Children:** 3; **Grandchildren:** 4; **Education:** Graduated Northeastern University BA and graduated US Army Command and General State College; **Honors:** Fellow AAMR, Military Bronze Star, Purple Heart & Deans List; **Awards:** Edgar Doll Award for Outstanding Service to disabled; **Personal Statement:** Have admired great poets and authors: Robert Frost, Emily Dickinson and many others. I enjoy writing as means of self-expression. Never sought publication.

Author: Pasquale Ferrucci; **Pen Name:** Paddy; **Birthplace:** Brooklyn, NY; **Occupation:** Jockey Agent; **Hobbies:** Writing and sports; **Spouse's Name:** Lois Ferrucci; **Children:** 2; **Education:** High school; **Personal Statement:** Whatever trials and tribulations come in life, there is always love in your heart – learn how to express it and God will reward you.

Author: Dolores Feurer; **Birthplace:** Plymouth, WI; **Occupation:** Tailor and seamstress; **Hobbies:** Drawing and writing; **Memberships:** United States Amateur Ballroom Dancing; **Children:** 2; **Education:** High school and self-educated; **Published Works:** Short articles in newspapers and spiritual magazines; **Personal Statement:** In 1968 I experienced a spiritual awakening which opened me to new vistas, and have practiced Metaphysical Science since then. I receive intuitively through the spiritual realms.

Author: Rhonda K. Fleming; **Birthplace:** Windsor, MO; **Occupation:** Operating room nurse; **Hobbies:** Painting, writing, sports and crafts; **Memberships:** Aorn, Kimball Art Museum, Smithsonian Institute; **Education:** AA and BSN; **Published Works:** Several poems published by the National Library of Poetry

Author: Christopher Foley; **Pen Name:** Robert Grey; **Birthplace:** Philadelphia, PA; **Occupation:** Comedy writer; **Hobbies:** Poetry and helping people; **Education:** High school; **Personal Statement:** I've always believed that poetry is an art form. It can help people see new things.

Author: Barbara L. Fox; **Birthplace:** Lawrenceville, IL; **Occupation:** Retired; **Hobbies:** Dolls, hats, floral designs, reading, writing and poetry; **Memberships:** IROC, Rebekah Lodge, MO Keups, Bonniebrook Ch. Gardening; **Spouse's Name:** Norman; **Children:** 5; **Grandchildren:** 7; **Education:** High school graduate and 2 years of business college; **Personal Statement:** As a poet I would like to leave a legacy to all to have the appreciation and love of poetry. I had Browning, Frost, Kipling, Tennyson and Poe to influence me, and many more.

Author: Kevin Patrick Fram; **Personal Statement:** For one moment, when I have the attention of another through my writing, they will walk into my soul. The moment that they feel what I have written, then I walk into theirs. So we are stealing from each other.

Author: Tony Franks; **Pen Name:** Tony Ynot Franks; **Birthplace:** Birmingham; **Occupation:** Painter and decorator; **Hobbies:** Travel, fishing, pool, darts and coin collecting; **Memberships:** Cannon Hill Poetry Club; **Children:** 4; **Education:** Secondary Modern; **Published Works:** Jokes and limericks, A Brummie in Amsterdam; **Personal Statement:** Enjoy life, love meeting people. Proud to be a brummie, world traveler, born the day James Dean died 1–10–55. Member of Cannon Hill Poets and happy-go-lucky.

Author: Arnold Frost; **Birthplace:** Horbury; **Occupation:** Retired; **Hobbies:** Photography, videography and poems; **Spouse's Name:** Renee (deceased); **Education:** General

Author: Noriko Fulmer; **Birthplace:** Osaka; **Occupation:** Scientist; **Hobbies:** Writing, piano and travel; **Spouse's Name:** Andrew Fulmer; **Education:** Ph. D., MS, DVM and BS from Osaka Prefecture University; **Published Works:** Scientific papers in Endocrinology, J Dermatol Sci and Arch Dermatal Res; **Personal Statement:** This is my first poem, although I have read and admired many poets. I wanted to express how much I appreciate my mother.

Author: Avril Furse; **Birthplace:** Hampton, Middlesex; **Occupation:** Farmer's Wife; **Hobbies:** Gardening, swimming; **Spouse's Name:** Kenvyn Furse; **Children:** 4; **Grandchildren:** 7; **Education:** Stella Maris Convent Biddeford 'O' Level; **Personal Statement:** To me, writing poetry is the ultimate form of expression. I have always greatly admired Wordsworth and Matthew Arnold.

Author: Lillian Galvin; **Pen Name:** L. D. Cook; **Birthplace:** Teaneck, NJ; **Occupation:** Investigator; **Hobbies:** Computer, dried flower arrangements and poetry; **Children:** 3; **Education:** Graduated St Mary's High School and some college; **Published Works:** Emotions in Mindfire Magazine and The Sky's The Limit in National Library of Poetry; **Personal Statement:** Life, a beautiful gift to be fully experienced. I live, I love and I will write about it.

Author: Charles Frederick Gartland; **Pen Name:** Henry Alexandre; **Birthplace:** Stevenage; **Hobbies:** Reading (occult, fiction, horror, true crime), poetry; **Memberships:** I. E. C. Wine Society; **Education:** Secondary School, Life's Experiences; **Awards:** Red Cross Cert, Basic and Higher Cert–Wine/Spirits Ed Trust; **Personal Statement:** Inspired by the hectic, traumatic lifestyle and the trials and tribulations of which I have so far conquered with determination and expulsion of self-doubt.

Poet Profiles

Author: Andrea Gary-Lopez; **Pen Name:** Dre Lopez; **Birthplace:** Miami, FL; **Occupation:** Student; **Hobbies:** Singing, writing, volleyball, tutoring and dancing; **Memberships:** Academy of International Business and Finance; **Education:** Ninth grade student; **Honors:** Ambassador of AIBF; **Awards:** 5. 0 by Florida Writes and Outstanding Writer; **Personal Statement:** Nothing comes to a sleeper but a dream. Through my works I like to open the eyes of the world.

Author: Peter Jacob Gavrun; **Birthplace:** Allegan, MI; **Occupation:** Student and nurses' aide; **Hobbies:** Swimming, rollerblading, drama, writing and going to races; **Education:** Junior at Allegan High School; **Personal Statement:** If you have a dream don't let anything stand in your way of achieving it. Anything is possible when you put your mind to it.

Author: C. K. Gemmell; **Birthplace:** San Francisco, CA; **Occupation:** School bus driver; **Hobbies:** Writing, sketching and reading; **Spouse's Name:** Glen Burungame; **Children:** 1; **Personal Statement:** I know there must be more than what is seen.

Author: Keith Gems; **Birthplace:** London; **Occupation:** Architect, painter, adventurer; **Hobbies:** The art of living and the sea; **Spouse's Name:** Pam Gems; **Children:** 4; **Grandchildren:** 2; **Education:** City of London School, Manchester U. V. Buildhall U. V.; **Awards:** Assoc M. C. T., Yacht Master–Dih Mech Engn–Dih Fine Arts & Des; **Published Works:** Various Poetry Mags, Daily Press, Yachting Press; **Personal Statement:** If you can think, you can write, draw and paint. That is our difference to the rest of nature.

Author: Dean E. Gerry; **Pen Name:** Deano; **Birthplace:** Sioux Falls, SD; **Occupation:** Retired; **Hobbies:** Hunting, fishing and writing poetry; **Spouse's Name:** Bonnie Lee; **Children:** 2; **Grandchildren:** 5; **Education:** High school and some college courses; **Personal Statement:** I have written numerous poems but have never sent any to contests or publications. I love to write and share my poetry with others.

Author: Megan Kathleen Geuss; **Pen Name:** Megan Kathleen Geuss; **Birthplace:** Santa Monica, CA; **Occupation:** Student; **Hobbies:** Volleyball, spoon collecting and reading; **Memberships:** Girl Scouts and school choir; **Education:** Going into 6th grade; **Honors:** Honor roll every year; **Awards:** Best Poem Award; **Published Works:** Enlightenment Poetry; **Personal Statement:** I get inspired to write through beautiful places in nature. My love of reading helps to inspire me to write the words in my poetry.

Author: Ruzica Gilich; **Birthplace:** Yugoslavia; **Occupation:** Quality control and student; **Hobbies:** Writing poetry and gardening; **Children:** 1; **Education:** High school; **Personal Statement:** Writing poetry is feeling the touch of art, expressing your own feelings with best pictures admiring every corner and share with others.

Author: Erin Girby; **Birthplace:** Mobile, AL; **Occupation:** High school student; **Hobbies:** Singing, playing the flute and writing poetry; **Education:** Junior in high school; **Honors:** Advanced diploma and varsity concert marching band; **Awards:** Superior rating on a solo w/flute at state contest with band; **Personal Statement:** My inspirations have come from many heartaches and from other people's problems that they tell me about.

Author: Bertha Givins; **Pen Name:** B Givins; **Birthplace:** St. Paul, MN; **Occupation:** retired microbiologist; **Hobbies:** Writing, reading and keeping busy; **Children:** 4; **Grandchildren:** 8; **Education:** Graduated Medical Institute of MN; **Honors:** Honorable mention 2 times; **Awards:** Two Golden Poets and 1 Platinum; **Published Works:** Today's Greatest Poems and Best Poems of 1985; **Personal Statement:** I believe that poetry is a God-given gift. And I think if young people have this gift, they should pursue their natural talents and dreams to the fullest.

Author: M. Goodman; **Birthplace:** St. Neots; **Occupation:** Retired; **Hobbies:** Pets, grandchildren, writing, sci-fi and Star Trek films; **Spouse's Name:** Ronald; **Children:** 2; **Grandchildren:** 4; **Education:** Local school in St. Neots and Cambridge College; **Personal Statement:** Since retiring I now write poetry. I am inspired by Gene Roddenberry. My hobbies are Star Trek and science fiction.

Author: Marie Goodwin; **Birthplace:** Indianapolis, IN; **Occupation:** Retired; **Hobbies:** Reading, jewelry-making and crochet; **Memberships:** St. Gelasius Church; **Spouse's Name:** Charles; **Children:** 3; **Grandchildren:** 5; **Education:** College Kennedy King graduate; **Honors:** High honors; **Awards:** Art, Honorable Merit Award and 1st place ceramics; **Published Works:** Waiting and He's Gone; **Personal Statement:** Never give up your dreams. Reach to highest level that you can in education. People are like water; it reaches its own level.

Author: Kathy Graff-Nelson; **Birthplace:** Dunkirk, NY; **Occupation:** Caseworker; **Hobbies:** Travel, aerobics and baking; **Spouse's Name:** Rev. David Nelson; **Children:** 1; **Education:** BA in Sociology, teaching certification for elementary education; **Honors:** Dean's List and National Dean's List

Author: Matthew Graybosch; **Pen Name:** Matthew Lovelace; **Birthplace:** Bay Shore, NY; **Occupation:** Student; **Hobbies:** Music, writing, reading, computers, cycling, heavy metal; **Memberships:** VFLW Local 1500, Metallica Fan Club; **Education:** Student, Briarcliffe College; **Honors:** Dean's List; 1992 National Finalist, Nat'l Geography Bee; **Published Works:** "Razor's Edge" in Sayville HS Literary Magazine Collage; **Personal Statement:** A light shines brightest in utter darkness. Too many people forget this and turn away from their dark side. The result is a life of twilight.

Author: Karen D. Green; **Birthplace:** Gary, IN; **Occupation:** General Maintenance; **Hobbies:** Writing and communication; **Memberships:** Entertainment Travel Advantage and American Income Life; **Spouse's Name:** Dennis D. Green, Jr.; **Children:** 4; **Grandchildren:** 3; **Education:** Special education and word processing; **Awards:** Young Scholars Award; **Personal Statement:** All things are possible to him that believes.

Author: Leroy Grier; **Birthplace:** Shelby; **Occupation:** Retired truck driver; **Hobbies:** Traveling and reading; **Spouse's Name:** Betty; **Children:** 3; **Grandchildren:** 4; **Education:** High school; **Personal Statement:** I claim no creative style. I have been touched by many poets and authors. I pray I can reach out and touch someone through the written words, maybe be an inspiration.

Author: Richard S. Griffith III; **Birthplace:** Abington, PA; **Occupation:** Student; **Hobbies:** Lacrosse, football, wrestling and reading; **Education:** 8th grade in junior high; **Honors:** Presidential Scholastic Award

Author: M. Grimshaw; **Birthplace:** Blackburn; **Occupation:** Retired designer dressmaker; **Hobbies:** Reading, gardening and show dogs and ponies; **Memberships:** Cocker Spaniel Club of Lancashire; **Spouse's Name:** Vincent Grimshaw; **Children:** 4; **Grandchildren:** 10; **Education:** Blackburn College of Design; **Published Works:** Rosy; **Personal Statement:** I reflect my love of animals and people I have cared for. I have had a love of poetry all my life.

Author: Patricia Guy; **Birthplace:** Gloversville, NY; **Occupation:** Retired; **Hobbies:** Grandchildren, travel, community service and needy children; **Spouse's Name:** Divorced; **Children:** 4; **Grandchildren:** 4; **Education:** High school; **Awards:** Frank C. Moore Award and American Society for Public Admin.; **Personal Statement:** Living life, as we know it, should include giving to

Enchanted Dreams

others, whether it be through our writing, tithing or more. Importantly giving of our time.

Author: Ed Guziewski; **Birthplace:** Ft. Jackson, SC; **Occupation:** School principal; **Hobbies:** Travel, sports, collecting, reading, computers and music; **Memberships:** Optimist, Principal Association; **Spouse's Name:** Louise; **Children:** 2; **Education:** University of Wisconsin Ph. D, MS, Dominican College BA; **Honors:** Dean's List; **Awards:** Sports Editor of college newspaper, Student Council VP; **Published Works:** Ph. D. Relationship of School Management Instructor Magazine; **Personal Statement:** Poetry is another form of music for the mind. Our family enjoys the thoughts and depth of feelings conveyed by the lyric/narrative of poetry. My favorite poets are Browning, Frost, Longfellow and Whitman.

Author: Roberto Guzman; **Birthplace:** Barcelona, Spain; **Occupation:** Book maker; **Hobbies:** Painting, fine arts and poetry; **Memberships:** Handyman Club of America and Latino Arts Council; **Spouse's Name:** Julia C. Gueman; **Children:** 5; **Grandchildren:** 1; **Education:** Master degree of Fine Arts and Graphic Arts Industries; **Honors:** Diplomas, certificates in fine arts; **Awards:** Several at galleries of fine arts and museums; **Published Works:** Oro Malo (Bad Gold) short story published in Spanish; **Personal Statement:** Based on my last poem, Time is a Clown, we all lived funny lives. In time of trouble we stumble, in times of success we make fools of ourselves.

Author: Delores Hagerich; **Birthplace:** Johnstown, PA; **Occupation:** Homemaker; **Hobbies:** Crocheting, knitting, sewing, writing, bowling and reading; **Memberships:** Scattered Thirties Bowling League; **Spouse's Name:** Clair; **Children:** 2; **Grandchildren:** 8; **Education:** Franklin High School graduate; **Honors:** Number six in graduating class; **Awards:** English award; **Personal Statement:** Helen Steiner Rice is my favorite poet. I would love to publish a book of all my poems. My grandchildren encouraged me to send you a poem. Jesus is my inspiration.

Author: Ruthie Hamlet; **Occupation:** Retired; **Hobbies:** Writing, songs, crocheting, quilting, embroidery and cooking; **Spouse's Name:** Elbert K. Hamlet; **Children:** 3; **Grandchildren:** 2; **Education:** High school graduate; **Personal Statement:** In all my hard life, I worked, enjoyed life, loved children but always wanted to get somewhere in life, make a lot of money, if it is the Lord's will, and writing poems is one of the things I want to do.

Author: Brenda R. Hamlet; **Birthplace:** Roanoke, VA; **Occupation:** Reading and writing; **Spouse's Name:** Scott; **Children:** 3; **Grandchildren:** 3; **Education:** BA from Bennett College; **Personal Statement:** The ability to learn is a gift. With an open mind and a caring heart, one learns from every book read and every person met.

Author: Brenda Hammersley; **Birthplace:** Bedford; **Occupation:** Optician's receptionist; **Hobbies:** Dancing, swimming, aerobics, cycling, walking and keyboards; **Memberships:** International Society of Poets and The Writers Club; **Spouse's Name:** Brian Hammersley; **Children:** 1; **Education:** Cuckee Hall County Secondary School and Herford Regional College; **Published Works:** Seven poems published; **Personal Statement:** Writing poetry is an enjoyable way of expressing my thoughts and feelings. My ultimate goal is to have my own book of poems published.

Author: Robert Harniman; **Birthplace:** Tunbridge Wells; **Occupation:** Pupil in Grammar school; **Hobbies:** Warhammer 40, 000, computer games and writing; **Education:** Tunbridge Wells Grammar School for Boys; **Awards:** Commended by WH Smiths Young Writers' Competition; **Published Works:** Autumn published by Poetry Now; **Personal Statement:** Although I'm only 12, I believe anyone of any age can write poetry if they feel inspired.

Author: Rochelle Harris; **Birthplace:** Chicago, IL; **Occupation:** Teacher; **Hobbies:** Reading, cooking, horseback riding and skating; **Memberships:** National Organization of University Women; **Spouse's Name:** Lynard Harris; **Children:** 2; **Education:** BS in Education from Chicago State University; **Honors:** Dean's List; **Personal Statement:** I enjoy reading and writing poetry. It is the best form of written expression and creativity. My favorite poets are Gwendolyn Brooks and Maya Angelou.

Author: Paul Harris; **Pen Name:** Pea Jay; **Birthplace:** Las Vegas, NV; **Occupation:** Casino services; **Hobbies:** Screenwriting and poetry writing; **Education:** Set to attend UNLV; **Honors:** Poems appearing in Anthology; **Published Works:** Poems in Time and Tide; **Personal Statement:** My heart set goal is to become an accomplished screenwriter and actor. I currently have two completed screenplays, Poetry helps me express my feelings.

Author: Thelma Hart; **Pen Name:** Zara Beth Windsor; **Birthplace:** Ririe, ID; **Occupation:** Bookkeeper; **Hobbies:** Reading, writing, piano and interior decorating; **Memberships:** Pine Mtn Writers Club and P. V. H. O. A.; **Spouse's Name:** Raymond Olin Hart; **Children:** 4; **Grandchildren:** 7; **Education:** Completed two years of college; **Personal Statement:** Poetry is the language of the soul. It gives words to those thoughts that whisper in your head, then your spirit is still for awhile.

Author: Lisa Jeanette Hartman; **Pen Name:** Liliyan; **Birthplace:** Voorhees, NJ; **Occupation:** Employee at KennyWood Park; **Hobbies:** Reading, writing and role playing; **Education:** Graduate of Steel Valley High School and in 2nd year at Clarion University; **Personal Statement:** I was a senior at high school when this was written and this was about my best friend, Marty. He is my main inspiration.

Author: Janis Harvey; **Birthplace:** West Virginia; **Occupation:** Bluestone State Park employee; **Hobbies:** Quilting and writing songs; **Memberships:** BMI; **Spouse's Name:** John R. Harvey; **Children:** 8; **Grandchildren:** 17; **Education:** Graduated from Hinton High School; **Personal Statement:** A special thanks to the Lord, my husband John, my family and friends. You have always been there for me. I am richly blessed.

Author: Dave Hatcher; **Pen Name:** T. M. P. (The Master Poet); **Birthplace:** Akron, OH; **Occupation:** Amateur Writer; **Hobbies:** Wood Crafting and Chess Playing; **Education:** Shawnee, and Ohio State University (Non-Grad) (Pyschology Major); **Published Works:** Two First Time Lovers; **Personal Statement:** I believe the greatest motivator of human volition is the desire of one to express him or herself.

Author: Gary L. Heck; **Birthplace:** Des Moines, IA; **Occupation:** Maintenance mechanic; **Hobbies:** Gardening; **Spouse's Name:** Sharon Heck; **Children:** 1; **Education:** High school graduate; **Published Works:** The Illustrated Adventures of Sven & Oley, Poetic Ponderings; **Personal Statement:** Inspiration by observation of people, animals and nature.

Author: Danielle Heeney; **Birthplace:** Philadelphia, PA; **Hobbies:** Swimming, writing poems, friends and roller-skating; **Education:** Sophomore at Saint Hubert's High School; **Honors:** First Honors; **Awards:** American Legion Award; **Personal Statement:** My family and friends greatly influence my poetry, especially my best friend. I am fortunate to have great friends who are always there for me.

Author: Michael Hendrix; **Birthplace:** Ft Collins, CO; **Occupation:** Mergers & Acquisitions; **Hobbies:** Farming, travel and reading; **Education:** BS Purdue University and MS Colorado University; **Personal Statement:** Hospital, doctors, medications, loneliness, fatigue and fear all front and center with multiple sclerosis. Maybe reading and writing poetry will help ease the pain and difficulties.

Author: Karen Hennessey; **Birthplace:** Ayrshire, Scotland; **Occupation:** Secretary; **Hobbies:** Cycling, aerobics and travel; **Spouse's Name:** Richard; **Children:** 2; **Education:** St. Michael's Grammar School; **Personal Statement:** Love makes the world go around; with the hectic hustle and bustle of life we forget to stop and look through the eyes of love.

Author: Brenda Henson; **Birthplace:** Chenowee, KY; **Occupation:** Registered nurse; **Hobbies:** Writing, reading, gardening, travel, fishing and sports; **Memberships:** Phi Theta Kappa; **Spouse's Name:** Ralph Henson; **Children:** 2; **Education:** Graduated from Lees College; **Honors:** Dean's List, Who's Who Among Jr. Colleges and Cum Laude; **Awards:** Chemistry Award, 2 awards for volunteer work; **Published Works:** Several selections in Lees; **Personal Statement:** Poetry is a very personal form of communication, to be able to express what we often cannot say. It is a great release of energy and emotions.

Author: Dian Henson; **Birthplace:** Ypsilanti, MI; **Occupation:** Employee of EMU; **Hobbies:** Reading, writing, photography and needlework; **Education:** Currently a sophomore at Eastern Michigan University; **Personal Statement:** My inspiration comes from falling in love with poetry in college. My favorite poets are Walter de la Mare and Dante.

Author: Shawna Heslop; **Birthplace:** Wheeling, WV; **Occupation:** Painter and secretary part–time; **Hobbies:** Reading and working out at the gym; **Memberships:** Doubleday Book Club; **Spouse's Name:** Lyle Hart; **Children:** 3; **Education:** High school diploma; **Personal Statement:** I hope this will be the beginning to a lifelong dream I've always had to be a writer. I've been writing poems since childhood.

Author: Pat Hocken; **Birthplace:** Newark, NJ; **Occupation:** Owner of Walk–N–Comfort Shoes; **Hobbies:** Professional artist and sign carver; **Spouse's Name:** Lee Hocken; **Children:** 1; **Education:** Doven High School; **Published Works:** This Child Of Mine; **Personal Statement:** I've accepted what can't be changed, and I've changed much for the better. This journey called life had been truly guided by a higher power.

Author: Terry Holmes; **Pen Name:** Tigger; **Birthplace:** Oakland, CA; **Occupation:** Sugical technologist; **Hobbies:** Writing, music and love; **Children:** 1; **Education:** High school, OR School and U. S. Air Force; **Personal Statement:** A tele–source for life... I write, and for a moment, there's freedom and pride... An encyclopedia of lessons learned and love's losses.

Author: Kevin Horgan; **Birthplace:** Brooklyn, NY; **Occupation:** Student; **Hobbies:** Music, poetry, sports and dancing; **Education:** Bachelor of Science in Psychology from Sacred Heart University; **Honors:** Psi Chi National Honor Society for Psychology

Author: Christopher Horsford; **Birthplace:** Farnborough; **Occupation:** Student; **Hobbies:** Cricket, sailing and travel; **Education:** Oxted Country School and Staffordshire University; **Personal Statement:** The experiences I shared with the crew of the tall ship Astrid changed my life. This poem is for them.

Author: Diane M. Hubiak; **Birthplace:** Trenton, NJ; **Occupation:** Marketing; **Hobbies:** Crafts, creative writing; **Spouse's Name:** Bruce Hubiak; **Children:** 1; **Published Works:** Ethos Of Her, River Of Fears; **Personal Statement:** Daughter of Earl and Berdella Walker, mother of Denise Freeman. My inspiration is found through the love of my family and my trust in God.

Author: Jim Hunsaker; **Birthplace:** Afton, WY; **Hobbies:** Writing poems; **Spouse's Name:** Janis Hunsaker; **Children:** 2; **Grandchildren:** 2; **Education:** Finished 8th grade; **Awards:** Editor's Choice Award

Author: Joy Hutton; **Birthplace:** Poughkeepsie, NY; **Occupation:** Student; **Hobbies:** Poetry, drawing, reading and computers; **Education:** Currently in 9th grade and have 2 college credits; **Honors:** Honor roll; **Awards:** Soccer Award; **Personal Statement:** I would just like to say that poetry is your feelings, inner emotions, hopes and fears. It doesn't need to rhyme or make sense to anyone but you.

Author: Irene Jackson; **Birthplace:** Workington, Cumbria; **Occupation:** Process Worker; **Hobbies:** Writing poetry, gardening, flower arranging, dogs, psychic; **Spouse's Name:** Stephen; **Children:** 4; **Education:** Secondary Education, received 9 C. S. E. Certs, 2 'O' Level English; **Honors:** Pianoforte; **Published Works:** A Broken Heart, Take Time Out, Love; **Personal Statement:** I write poetry mainly for pleasure. Since the unexpected loss of my twenty–four–year–old son "Jimmy" in 1997, the words seem to flow naturally.

Author: Forbes Jackson; **Pen Name:** Peaken; **Birthplace:** Pottstown, PA; **Occupation:** Electronic and mechanical technician; **Hobbies:** Outdoors, music and special relationships; **Children:** 2; **Education:** AST Electronics Technology; **Awards:** The International Poetry Hall of Fame; **Published Works:** A Winter's Solstice and Heather; **Personal Statement:** I hope I reflect in my poetry the need to appreciate the little things that can make our world special. Thanks.

Author: B. J. Jackson; **Birthplace:** Brooklyn, NY; **Occupation:** Self–employed; **Hobbies:** Sewing, needlepoint and photos; **Memberships:** Children's Cancer Society, North Shore Animal League; **Children:** 1; **Education:** Prospect Heights High School; **Published Works:** Church Girl and The Morning Rain; **Personal Statement:** My goal as a writer is to reach as many people as possible to show that life goes on. But always remember that life is the best teacher in the world. You learn from your own mistakes.

Author: Helen J. Jarvis; **Birthplace:** Prince George, VA; **Occupation:** Retired; **Hobbies:** Gardening, baking and writing poetry; **Memberships:** Mississippi Poetry Society, National Federation of States; **Spouse's Name:** Deceased; **Children:** 4; **Grandchildren:** 5; **Education:** High school graduate; **Honors:** President's Award for Iliad Press 1997; **Awards:** 3rd place in MPS 1996 Fall Festival and 2nd, 3rd, in Fall 97; **Published Works:** Numerous poems and church newsletters; **Personal Statement:** I have been writing since high school but with a family and a job, as I worked in fast food starting at age 45 and worked for 20 years. I sent in a poem to ISP and then started turning my stories into poems.

Author: Jeanette H. Jefferson; **Birthplace:** Charleston, MO; **Occupation:** Nurse, Retired, Disabled; **Hobbies:** Reading, writing, poetry; **Memberships:** St. Paul AME Church – Int'l Society of Poets, NLP; **Spouse's Name:** John L. Jefferson; **Children:** 3; **Grandchildren:** 2; **Education:** A. S. Nursing Ret. and RN; **Honors:** Outstanding Achievement in Poetry, 1994, '95, '96, '97 – NLP; **Published Works:** Save The Children, Hate A Deadly Disease, Letter From Beyond, Somebody Said, Mirthless Parody, Family & Friends Salute; **Personal Statement:** As a stroke survivor, if I can just help somebody then my living will not be in vain. Faith will carry you through anything.

Author: Aleshea J. Johnson; **Pen Name:** Joy; **Birthplace:** California; **Occupation:** Retail; **Hobbies:** Sports and reading poetry and horror stories; **Spouse's Name:** Eddie L. Johnson; **Children:** 5; **Education:** International Correspondence; **Personal Statement:** Writing is a very relaxing enjoyment. I've always admired people like my dad for being creative and others like Robert Frost and William Blake.

Author: Gwendolyn Johnson; **Birthplace:** Atlanta, GA; **Hobbies:** Sewing, raising tropical fish and interior decorating; **Children:** 2; **Education:** LPN training at Carver Voc Tech and Clinical training at

Enchanted Dreams

Grady Memorial; **Personal Statement:** My love of poetry stems from music and my belief in the power of love.

Author: Cynthia Yvonne Jones; **Birthplace:** Marietta, OH; **Occupation:** Secretary for Bureau of Public Debt; **Hobbies:** Yoga, reading, creative writing and aromatherapy; **Memberships:** National Arbor Day Foundation & Editorial Board of Interest; **Education:** BA English, Berea College; **Honors:** Dean's List; **Published Works:** Zephyr in literary magazine; **Personal Statement:** The most wasted day is that in which we have not laughed.

Author: Robert J. Joyce; **Birthplace:** London; **Occupation:** Student; **Hobbies:** Writing, model rockets and computer-aided aircraft designs; **Education:** Woolwhich Polytechnic Technology College; **Honors:** Completing course of 12 GCSES; **Personal Statement:** I have always dreamed of becoming a pilot, and a poem about the Aces of First World War conveyed my admiration for their bravery.

Author: Verna L. Kammen; **Birthplace:** Polk County, MN; **Occupation:** Retired; **Hobbies:** Knitting, crocheting, writing poetry and flowers; **Spouse's Name:** Deceased; **Children:** 5; **Grandchildren:** 10; **Education:** High school graduate; **Published Works:** A few poems published locally; **Personal Statement:** My goal is to share my poems, but not to be under any obligation. My influence is God and His beautiful creation and my family.

Author: Elham Khatami; **Birthplace:** San Francisco, CA; **Occupation:** Elementary school student; **Hobbies:** Reading, writing, swimming and learning foreign languages; **Memberships:** Basketball; **Education:** Fifth grade student; **Honors:** Many high honor roll awards; **Awards:** Excellent Author Award, Reading Award and Citizenship Award; **Personal Statement:** Writing poetry is the best way to express my feelings. My goals as a writer vary. I'd love to write about my native country, Iran.

Author: C. O. Knight; **Birthplace:** Wausau, WI; **Occupation:** Photographic lab technician; **Hobbies:** Role-playing, fishing, reading and writing; **Memberships:** Thespian Guild; **Spouse's Name:** Nicole M. Knight; **Education:** 2nd year of college; **Personal Statement:** Today is the future, tomorrow the past. Think of this and all is well.

Author: Lorraine Kolesar; **Birthplace:** Chicago, IL; **Occupation:** Disabled; **Hobbies:** Crochet, American Indians and visiting nursing homes; **Spouse's Name:** Donald; **Children:** 1; **Grandchildren:** 4; **Education:** High school; **Honors:** Won 2 poetry contests; **Published Works:** Dream of America, God's Smile, Lake Superior and a song, What is Love; **Personal Statement:** I try to encourage children to write their thoughts down on paper. I can't believe what I wrote 40 years ago.

Author: Theresa Kollefrath; **Birthplace:** St. Louis, MO; **Occupation:** Chemist; **Hobbies:** Gardening, sewing, crafts, writing, computers and animals; **Spouse's Name:** George; **Children:** 2; **Education:** Senior at University of Missouri; **Personal Statement:** Writing is my outlet. Words seem to flow from my pen freely. Particular inspiration has come from Poe, Dickinson and Nash.

Author: Frank Komer; **Birthplace:** Cleveland; **Occupation:** Retired; **Hobbies:** Reading, hiking and gardening; **Spouse's Name:** Deceased; **Education:** High school; **Personal Statement:** Ability to love my fellow man.

Author: Rachel Kowalsky; **Pen Name:** Wolfmoon Dancer; **Birthplace:** Malden, MA; **Occupation:** Radio Producer; **Hobbies:** Music, reading and performing arts; **Education:** BS Communications Lyndon State College; **Published Works:** A Picture of Elegance, Cherished Poems of the Western World;

Personal Statement: Poetry lies in everything you do... Your surroundings... the people that touch your life in every way. Life breeds poetry.

Author: Claudia Kowkabany; **Birthplace:** Jacksonville, FL; **Occupation:** Volunteer; **Hobbies:** Spa, walking, different social events and activities; **Education:** Assumption Catholic School, Landon High School, Florida Junior College and Community College; **Honors:** Thespians; **Awards:** Ladies Auxiliary; **Published Works:** Article, poems, a Mother's Day special newspaper heading and article; **Personal Statement:** This is a great honor for me to be one of the semi-finalists in your poetry guild.

Author: Beata M. Kulawiak; **Birthplace:** Chicago, IL; **Occupation:** Legal secretary; **Hobbies:** Reading, travel, baking, poetry and the Mob; **Spouse's Name:** Joseph; **Children:** 2; **Education:** Maria High School graduate; **Personal Statement:** My writing is a reflection of all personal experiences, and my strength comes from my husband and children.

Author: Sota Kurylo; **Birthplace:** Lublin, Poland; **Occupation:** Educator; **Hobbies:** Music, literature, nature and science; **Memberships:** New York Academy of Science, Polish Inst. of Art and Science; **Spouse's Name:** Widow; **Education:** MSC, PhD in Bio-Chemistry; **Awards:** Editor's Choice Awards and Honorable Mentions; **Published Works:** Island of Memories and number of other poems and a book of poems published in Polish; **Personal Statement:** Researching in the field of natural sciences opens the window to the better understanding of the world and the human nature. Writing poetry to share my feelings and experiences with others to improve human relationships.

Author: Joan Last; **Occupation:** Retired professor of Royal Academy of Music; **Hobbies:** Writing, piano and music; **Memberships:** National Trust Incorporated Society; **Education:** What is now called A Level Godolphin School; **Honors:** Honorable RAM 1961 and OBE 1988; **Published Works:** Noah's Scrapbook, The Young Pianist, Freedom in Piano Technique and others; **Personal Statement:** My first love is music, and I do not let a day pass without playing the piano. To be in a house where there is no piano is like the loss of something precious – inspiration for music and poetry comes in the country.

Author: Frederick C. LaVoie; **Pen Name:** P. T. Thumpp; **Birthplace:** Hudson, NH; **Occupation:** Electronics; **Hobbies:** Painting, gardening, astronomy and cooking; **Spouse's Name:** Divorced; **Children:** 3; **Education:** 100-plus hours toward a BA in English Literature; **Honors:** Dean's list; **Personal Statement:** With knowledge, common sense and an ability to use language, I feel as if I hold the key to all that is in my soul.

Author: Tom Lawrence; **Birthplace:** Bletchley, Bucks; **Occupation:** Resident engineer; **Hobbies:** Chess, painting, landscaping and gardening; **Spouse's Name:** Carole June; **Children:** 8; **Grandchildren:** 14; **Education:** Grammar-high school Harlington Middx; **Personal Statement:** "Oh for the Breeze" a reminder that God's gifts give peace and tranquility to us all.

Author: Anastasia Lee; **Pen Name:** Anya; **Birthplace:** Illinois; **Occupation:** Student; **Hobbies:** Dance, skiing, writing and looking at the stars; **Education:** High school graduate; **Honors:** AP Photography student with highest honors; **Personal Statement:** The more simple a poem or phrase seems, the more complex it truly is.

Author: Yukwor Lee; **Birthplace:** Burma; **Occupation:** Retired; **Hobbies:** Travel, sports, photography, natural history and music; **Memberships:** Distinguished member of the International Society of Poets; **Spouse's Name:** Shui Ming; **Children:** 1; **Grandchildren:** 1; **Education:** Northcole College of Education, College of Commerce and Engineering and Institute of Education, University of London; **Awards:** Civil service scholarship and Editor's Choice

Poet Profiles

Award; **Published Works:** Poems published in Day Break on The Land, Best Poems of 1997, In The Land of the Midnight Sun and others

Author: Amy Lefler; **Birthplace:** Davenport, IA; **Occupation:** Student; **Hobbies:** Playing softball and golf; **Education:** 11 years of education; **Honors:** Presidential Academic Award; **Published Works:** Love; **Personal Statement:** My goal as a poet is to write about how I feel and to make sure I express all my feelings.

Author: Celena Lewis; **Birthplace:** Tacoma, WA; **Occupation:** Student; **Hobbies:** Rock collecting, reading, singing, and hanging with friends; **Memberships:** Southbend Boys and Girls Club; **Education:** Seward Elementary and Stewart Middle School; **Honors:** Bookworm and honor roll; **Awards:** Kiwanis Club; **Published Works:** Memorial Day; **Personal Statement:** I love writing poems and I like all authors. I've written two little books, when I was in 2nd and 3rd grades. I also wrote another poem, "Memorial Day," which was selected for publication.

Author: Ethelyne H. Lewis; **Birthplace:** Virginia; **Occupation:** Retired from Dept. of Social Services; **Hobbies:** Crocheting, reading; **Memberships:** Bridge St. Ame Church; **Education:** Thomas Jefferson High School; **Awards:** Recg as Christian Ed by Dept of Christian Ed of above church; **Personal Statement:** My talents are my gift from God. I try to use my writing to His honor and glory. My goal is to publish a small book of my poetry. My inspiration has always been my mother, now deceased. I have been influenced by my family and church.

Author: Catherine Lindsley; **Birthplace:** Tallahassee, FL; **Hobbies:** Reading Shakespeare and writing poetry; **Children:** 2

Author: Lorraine K. Lines; **Birthplace:** North East, England; **Occupation:** Resident warden for elderly; **Hobbies:** Singing, reading and computers; **Spouse's Name:** Chuck Lines; **Children:** 6; **Grandchildren:** 11

Author: Megan Livermore; **Birthplace:** Balham, London; **Occupation:** Semi-retired accounts officer; **Hobbies:** Gardening, crosswords, World War II planes and air displays; **Children:** 2; **Education:** Secondary modern, technical college and City and Guilds Catering; **Honors:** Top of class in English and Math; **Awards:** Passed City & Guild 150/151 and also swimming awards; **Personal Statement:** I've worked hard all my life. Now I look forward to my dream bungalow by the sea, with a faithful dog companion, relaxing.

Author: Bruce Martin Long; **Birthplace:** Bridgewater; **Occupation:** Acting senior care assistant; **Hobbies:** Poetry, short stories, bowling, photography and crosswords; **Memberships:** International Library of Poetry, Mensa and British Legion; **Education:** Heles School and Plymouth University; **Awards:** Editor's Choice Award; **Published Works:** Ode To Falklands Island, War and Star Laden Sky; **Personal Statement:** I have found over the last 20 years that my collective works have been created from desperation and inspiration. This is foretold in my work.

Author: Sue Lotz; **Birthplace:** McKeesport, PA; **Occupation:** Self-employed; **Hobbies:** Music and graphics; **Memberships:** Junior Achievement, East Allegheny Business Assoc.; **Spouse's Name:** Ken (deceased); **Children:** 4; **Grandchildren:** 7; **Education:** McKeesport High School; **Personal Statement:** My goal as a writer is to touch the heart of the reader.

Author: Eboney Love; **Personal Statement:** I was influenced by my brother Johnny Love, my mother Merrian, aunt Jo Jenkins and the rest of my family who believed in me. I always admired Maya Angelou's poetry.

Author: Joyce MacGillivray; **Birthplace:** Dundee, (1939–1997); **Spouse's Name:** John MacGillivray; **Children:** 2; **Education:** MA English and History, University of Dundee, 1991; **Personal Statement:** We found this poem after my mum's death. Her love, passion and strength are simple. She lived for my dad, and for us. That love will forever remain in our hearts.

Author: Bill Mackay; **Birthplace:** Aberdeen; **Occupation:** Retired; **Hobbies:** Golf, riding, yoga, massage, Taize singing, conversation; **Children:** 2; **Grandchildren:** 3; **Education:** B Sc, Hants; **Personal Statement:** I am interested in personal growth, change and harmonious integration of the mind, body and spirit. Also health, diet, xercise and physical well-being.

Author: Gordon W. MacKenzie; **Birthplace:** Massena, NY; **Occupation:** Retired GM process engineer; **Hobbies:** Sports, study history texts and medical newsletters; **Spouse's Name:** Josephine; **Children:** 4; **Grandchildren:** 2; **Education:** Clarkson College of Technology, BCE Degree; **Personal Statement:** The last few decades have shown remarkable shift in many of our social institutions away from a centuries-old proven value system. The arts, media and the written word should portray man's more enabling traits rather than baser instincts.

Author: Rhyanna Magee; **Birthplace:** Westerly, RI; **Occupation:** Caterer; **Hobbies:** Rollerblading, nature and reading; **Memberships:** Mystic Community Center; **Education:** High school graduate; **Honors:** Principal's Award and Most Improved Award; **Personal Statement:** We shouldn't take life for granted. We should enjoy every sunrise, every sunset. We should appreciate the life we are given.

Author: Jackie Magnuson; **Birthplace:** Los Angeles, CA; **Occupation:** Homemaker; **Hobbies:** Canning, making musical dolls and enjoying my family; **Spouse's Name:** Donald Wayne Magnuson; **Children:** 6; **Grandchildren:** 16; **Education:** 10th grade; **Personal Statement:** My writing is a way of events being remembered. Therapy, a way of bringing out my innermost feelings.

Author: Edna L. Maitland; **Birthplace:** Lynnfield, MA; **Occupation:** Retired; **Hobbies:** Reading, knitting, dancing and baking; **Memberships:** Mother of Twins Club and Evening Garden Club; **Spouse's Name:** J. Richard Maitland; **Children:** 3; **Education:** Wakefield High School; **Honors:** Married 58 years and Poets of MA, Clan Maitland Society; **Awards:** Blessed with twin sons; **Published Works:** Clan Maitland Year Book; **Personal Statement:** I'm one of 12 children, wrote my first poem in 4th grade and nothing until I was in my 50's. I am in 80's and a Pisces, work with children in the church and a very giving person. My poems usually tell a story.

Author: Sonja Mardi; **Birthplace:** Wales; **Occupation:** Teacher; **Hobbies:** Reading, music and travel to France; **Memberships:** Teaching profession; **Spouse's Name:** Michael Alan Strode; **Children:** 2; **Education:** Newbridge Grammar and College; **Honors:** Won Fellow Award to do research degree; **Personal Statement:** Poetry an inspiration in my life, a reminder I am human, that feelings matter, its source an eternal secret? I am humbled by its power.

Author: Alicia Rosalinda Marquez; **Birthplace:** Houston, TX; **Occupation:** Student; **Hobbies:** Poetry, reading and volleyball; **Education:** High school freshman

Author: Kimberly Jo Marshall; **Pen Name:** K J Miller; **Birthplace:** Mt. Clemons, MI; **Occupation:** RN; **Hobbies:** Writing; **Children:** 2; **Education:** Bachelor of Science in Nursing; **Honors:** Dean's List; **Personal Statement:** Special influences are the beauty and strength of the mountains and its people of Eastern KY.

Author: Gina Martorell; **Birthplace:** Bronx, NY; **Occupation:** Administrative assistant; **Hobbies:** Reading, piano, music and playing; **Education:** Fordham University, working towards Master's in education; **Personal Statement:** Writing poetry to me is

Enchanted Dreams

the ultimate release and at times gives me a great peace within my spirit.

Author: Christian Masot; **Birthplace:** Bellville, NJ; **Occupation:** Aspiring tattoo artist; **Hobbies:** Drawing, surfing, snowboarding, martial arts and music; **Memberships:** Lead vocalist of band and Black Belt in martial arts; **Education:** High school and three yrs of college; **Honors:** Graduated high school with high honors; **Awards:** Several martial arts accomplishments; **Personal Statement:** As a writer I try to relate to people, to make them say, "Wow, this guy knows what he's talking about."

Author: Charlotte McCann; **Birthplace:** Kansas City, MO; **Occupation:** Retired; **Hobbies:** Crocheting, square dancing and travel; **Spouse's Name:** Raymond L.; **Children:** 7; **Grandchildren:** 23; **Education:** GED; **Awards:** Typing and computer achievements; **Personal Statement:** Having retired from Hallmark Cards, Inc., after 30 years, I love reading beautiful works.

Author: Cassandra McCanse; **Pen Name:** Anjelz Ize; **Birthplace:** Tucson, AZ; **Hobbies:** Swimming, weight lifting, travel, writing and singing; **Education:** Eighth grade student; **Awards:** Essay contest 1st place plaques and trophies for swimming; **Published Works:** Lighting, a poem; **Personal Statement:** I feel as though each moment should be cherished. Love with an open heart for life to love you back. It's all about spirit, mind and body.

Author: Stuart McDonald; **Birthplace:** Glasgow; **Hobbies:** Music, drums and Morris Minors; **Spouse's Name:** Linda; **Children:** 1; **Education:** Balornock Primary and Albert Secondary; **Personal Statement:** It just takes a certain thought, the first line appears, it seems quite taught. Inspiration great mountains and scenes. Influences are Linda and my dreams.

Author: Joshua McDowell; **Pen Name:** Josh; **Birthplace:** Kankakee, IL; **Hobbies:** Writing and drawing

Author: Carolyn McEachin; **Birthplace:** Newville, AL; **Occupation:** Revenue collection specialist; **Hobbies:** Writing, singing, sports, gardening, travel & floral design; **Memberships:** Volunteer Fulton; **Spouse's Name:** Leroy McEachin; **Children:** 3; **Education:** High school graduate, 2 yrs. of college, trade school graduate in Business and Clerical; **Honors:** Outstanding Public Service and Employee of Month; **Awards:** 1st place floral design, beauty pageant and sewing for 4-H; **Personal Statement:** This poem was inspired by a co-worker who has cancer. I am inspired to write by the experiences and request of others and by subject matter.

Author: Christine McGinley; **Birthplace:** Bayshore, NY; **Occupation:** NY Police Officer; **Hobbies:** Reading and cooking; **Education:** Two years of college

Author: Jimmy McGrath; **Pen Name:** Jimmy McGrath; **Birthplace:** Bayshore, NY; **Occupation:** 6th grade student; **Hobbies:** Baseball, basketball, fishing, writing poetry, WWF wrestling; **Education:** 6th Grader at Lindenhurst Middle School; **Honors:** Principal's List (90% or higher grade average)

Author: Dyane C. McMahon; **Birthplace:** Bergen County, NJ; **Occupation:** Health care consultant; **Hobbies:** Travel, reading, gardening and the Arts; **Memberships:** NACH, HHANJ, HFMA, ASCA and Women in Healthcare Management; **Education:** Rampao College of NJ and NY Medical College; **Honors:** Dean's List; **Personal Statement:** Having this poem published has reaffirmed my belief in the following quote from Nellie Bly... "Energy properly applied can achieve anything."

Author: Sarah Mendoker; **Birthplace:** New Brunswick, NJ; **Occupation:** Student; **Hobbies:** Soccer, reading and writing poetry; **Education:** Junior in high school; **Honors:** In Creative Writing and English; **Awards:** Rutgers Soccer Camp Most Outstanding Defensive Player 2 yrs

Author: Tim Meyer; **Birthplace:** Mt. Kisco, NY; **Occupation:** High school student; **Hobbies:** Reading, writing, journalism and swimming; **Education:** Senior at Horace Greeley High School; **Personal Statement:** Writing is about exploring and defining yourself and coming to grips with who you are.

Author: Marilyn Y. Meyer; **Birthplace:** Lockport, NY; **Occupation:** Housewife and mother; **Hobbies:** Volunteer as a foster home for stray or abandoned animals; **Memberships:** Save–A–Pet; **Spouse's Name:** Daniel A. Meyer; **Children:** 2; **Education:** High school graduate; **Personal Statement:** Poetry is beautiful to read. I write to relieve my thoughts of all the images that I see in those thoughts. It's a creative hobby.

Author: Lori Miller; **Birthplace:** Tacoma, WA; **Occupation:** Student; **Hobbies:** Writing, modeling, swimming, and hanging out with friends; **Education:** Entering Middle School; **Honors:** Honor Roll; **Awards:** Reflections (Writing Contest); **Personal Statement:** I would like to write children's books.

Author: Annie T. Miller; **Birthplace:** Vivian, LA; **Occupation:** Retired; **Hobbies:** Reading, sewing and painting; **Memberships:** Benevolent and Protective Order of Elks, Amigos Dance Club; **Spouse's Name:** Billy S. Miller (deceased); **Children:** 3; **Grandchildren:** 7; **Education:** High school and some business college; **Personal Statement:** After reading a C. S. Lewis book on grief, I was inspired to write, thus releasing my own grief somewhat. Writing helps heal.

Author: Kelli Mirelli; **Birthplace:** Memphis, TN; **Occupation:** Caterer; **Hobbies:** Art, theatre, reading and fashion design; **Education:** High school Shelby State and Memphis State; **Awards:** Art – Nazarene Church 1st and 2nd for Art scholarship

Author: Erick Moffatt; **Pen Name:** Innocent; **Birthplace:** San Diego, CA; **Occupation:** Student; **Hobbies:** Computers and writing; **Education:** 11th grade in high school

Author: Bertha J. Moore; **Pen Name:** B J Moore; **Birthplace:** Boggy Depot, OK; **Occupation:** Retired secretary; **Hobbies:** My children, grandchildren, reading, writing and all sports; **Spouse's Name:** Widow; **Children:** 10; **Grandchildren:** 20; **Education:** Draughon's Business College; **Honors:** Mother of the Year; **Awards:** All American Basketball Team 1944 for Dallas Hornets; **Personal Statement:** Reading and writing poetry restores the peace in my soul.

Author: Arlene M. Moore; **Birthplace:** Orrville, OH; **Occupation:** Retired RN; **Hobbies:** Yard, gardening, birds, flowers, fishng, sewing and travel; **Memberships:** Genealogical Society; **Spouse's Name:** Cyril E. Moore; **Children:** 1; **Education:** BS Nursing; **Personal Statement:** Writing this poem helped me to heal and press forward as I struggled to find my place within the established family I had married.

Author: Phil Murray; **Birthplace:** Aberdeen; **Hobbies:** Educational reading, counselling, medicine and music; **Education:** Windsor School; **Awards:** Regimental Support Unit cup for service; **Personal Statement:** My wish as a poet is to reach the deep emotions of any reader, using this link to give them encouragement, appreciation, understanding and pleasure.

Author: Ryan Myers; **Birthplace:** Scottsbluff, NE; **Occupation:** Student; **Hobbies:** Wrestling, judo and computers; **Memberships:** National Junior Honor Society; **Education:** Sophomore in high school; **Awards:** AZ State Judo Champ 1997 and Honor Student

Author: Melinda M. Myers; **Birthplace:** Kendallville, IN; **Occupation:** Quality auditor; **Hobbies:** NASCAR Racing and

Poet Profiles

shooting pool; **Children:** 3; **Education:** High school graduate; **Personal Statement:** I receive my inspiration from my children, Jenelle, Corey and Brandon, my boyfriend, Terry, and my great uncle Arther Franklin Mapes.

Author: Beulah M. Nedd; **Birthplace:** Trinidad, WI; **Occupation:** Nurse; **Hobbies:** Writing, swimming, reading, arts, crafts and travel; **Memberships:** YMCA, Mt. Carmel Spiritual Baptist Church; **Children:** 3; **Grandchildren:** 2; **Education:** Mercy College, Modern Academy; **Published Works:** In the Driver's Seat

Author: V. Marina Neff; **Birthplace:** Fuerth, W. Germany; **Occupation:** Cosmetologist manager; **Hobbies:** Reading, singing, writing, outdoors and water activities; **Spouse's Name:** Lou; **Education:** High school; **Personal Statement:** Poetry is a song that is sung by the eyes and heard in the heart.

Author: Carol R. Newingham; **Pen Name:** Angelica Rose; **Birthplace:** Decatur, FL; **Occupation:** Pharmacy tech; **Hobbies:** Writing, reading, crafts and computers; **Spouse's Name:** Robert L. Newingham; **Children:** 2; **Grandchildren:** 3; **Education:** High school graduate; **Honors:** English; **Personal Statement:** Writing poetry is a way I can express myself and enjoy the feeling that I have accomplished something. My favorite poets are Shakespeare, Browning and Byron.

Author: Kelly Nicholson; **Birthplace:** Queens, NY; **Occupation:** Administrative assistant; **Hobbies:** Writing poetry and fiction; **Memberships:** National Psoriasis Foundation; **Education:** Martin Van Buren High School and Bachelor's from Adelphi University; **Published Works:** You and Me and Wintertime Quiet; **Personal Statement:** Special thanks to Marnie; you helped me look inside and turn feelings into words. Thanks also Mom, Mike and Dad for constant love and support.

Author: Brian O'Dell; **Birthplace:** Newburgh, NY; **Occupation:** Student; **Hobbies:** Chess, writing and snow boarding; **Education:** Currently in 9th grade; **Personal Statement:** At only the age of 15, I hope I can grow up to inspire the youth to write, as Robert Frost inspired me.

Author: Angel Ocana; **Birthplace:** Brooklyn, NY; **Occupation:** Student; **Hobbies:** Basketball, drawing, acting and football; **Education:** 6th Grade student at IS77Q; **Personal Statement:** Writing poetry is fun and relaxing for me.

Author: SueAnn Ohagan; **Birthplace:** Brooklyn, NY, USA; **Occupation:** Housewife; **Hobbies:** Knitting, gardening and movies; **Spouse's Name:** Barry

Author: Cynthia Oliva; **Birthplace:** San Antonio, TX; **Occupation:** Student; **Hobbies:** Music and people; **Education:** Close to getting Associate Degree; **Personal Statement:** I am a disabled person who loves life. I enjoy writing because it's an opportunity for me to share a different viewpoint with others.

Author: Mary Alice Orazen; **Birthplace:** Hoopeston, IL; **Occupation:** Retired nurse; **Hobbies:** Poetry; **Spouse's Name:** Deceased; **Personal Statement:** I love poems that tell a story, down to earth sentiments. My favorite author is James Whitecomb Riley.

Author: J. M. Organ; **Pen Name:** Joyce Marian Organ; **Birthplace:** Dagenham, Essex; **Occupation:** Hairdresser; **Hobbies:** Interior decorating, tapestry, crafts, sewing and poetry; **Spouse's Name:** John Organ; **Children:** 2; **Education:** Secondary education followed by hairdressing apprenticeship; **Personal Statement:** Writing a poem for my daughter's 30th birthday in 1997 inspied me to express my experiences of life through poetry. I haven't stopped writing since.....

Author: Julie Ori; **Birthplace:** Skokie, IL; **Occupation:** Student; **Hobbies:** Reading, music and collecting Beatles; **Education:** Sophomore at Johnsburgh High School; **Awards:** English Merit Award

Author: Imara Vanessa Otero; **Birthplace:** Los Angeles, CA; **Occupation:** Accountant; **Hobbies:** Reading, gardening and cooking; **Education:** UCLA applied mathematics; **Honors:** Honor student; **Personal Statement:** I was inspired to write this poem after my father's death due to liver disease. Writing poetry has helped heal some of the wounds.

Author: Candice Pappas; **Pen Name:** Candy; **Birthplace:** Chicago, IL; **Occupation:** Cashier; **Hobbies:** Reading and writing; **Education:** Schurz High School; **Personal Statement:** My goal is to one day become a successful writer. A special inspiration of mine happens to be my grandmother for all of her encouragement.

Author: Casey Parker; **Pen Name:** Paris Parker; **Birthplace:** Grand Rapids, MI; **Occupation:** Student; **Hobbies:** Tap dance, riding, reading and writing; **Memberships:** 4-H; **Education:** Currently student of Lowell High School; **Honors:** Academic, sportsmanship and literacy; **Personal Statement:** If the eyes are the window to the soul, poetry is the key to the heart.

Author: Jonathon Parrish; **Pen Name:** Ishmael; **Birthplace:** Fort Morgan, CO; **Occupation:** Waiter and student; **Hobbies:** Ham radio, cars and playing pool; **Education:** High school diploma and certified EMT; **Honors:** Who's Who Among American High School Students and Honor Roll; **Awards:** Academic Scholar Graduate; **Personal Statement:** A special thank you to Mrs. Barbara Keenan for support and help with grammar. Also a special thanks to Gwen, Brandon, Okra and B. K.

Author: Kathleen M. Parsons; **Birthplace:** Saugus, MA; **Occupation:** Certified home health aide and student; **Hobbies:** Poetry, short stories and doll collecting; **Education:** Associate degree in Business Marketing; **Honors:** Graduated from college with honors; **Personal Statement:** My goals are to be published and to do something I really love... writing. Nothing could give me greater joy or satisfaction in my life.

Author: Michael Pavlovic; **Birthplace:** McKeesport, PA; **Occupation:** Self-employed; **Hobbies:** Reading, kayaking, writing, painting, woodworking and sports; **Education:** BS degree in Hotel, Restaurant and Institutional Management; **Published Works:** "M" Lady in the Music of Silence

Author: Frank Pellegrino; **Birthplace:** Niagara Falls, NY; **Occupation:** Retired; **Hobbies:** Gardening, writing, classical music, sports and cooking; **Memberships:** DAV and CSEA; **Spouse's Name:** Theresa (deceased); **Education:** 11th grade; **Awards:** Six poetry awards and one Beautification Award; **Published Works:** Over 15 published with National Library of Poetry; **Personal Statement:** My goal as a writer is only to fill empty hours. Life itself inspires me. God's power and creations, life's surroundings give me life.

Author: Keith S. Pennington; **Birthplace:** Westbromwich, England; **Occupation:** Retired scientist; **Hobbies:** Hiking, biking and cross country skiing; **Memberships:** Fellow IEEE, OSA and IN&T; **Spouse's Name:** Theresa; **Children:** 3; **Education:** Ph. D. and B. S.; **Honors:** Albert Rose Medal and Charles Ives Award; **Awards:** Several for outstanding contribution and tech achievement; **Published Works:** Many technical papers, Scientific American paper and four book chapters

Author: Denise G. Penny; **Birthplace:** Erwin, NC; **Occupation:** Cost Analyst; **Hobbies:** Horse riding, decorating, reading and playing with puppies; **Memberships:** Energy Information Forum; **Spouse's Name:** Tim; **Personal Statement:** This poem was an

Enchanted Dreams

anniversary gift to my husband many years ago. I think it describes his soul and his unlimited understanding during times of adversity.

Author: Bernice Weddington Pernu; **Birthplace:** Virginia, MN; **Occupation:** Retired teacher; **Hobbies:** Travel, crochet, painting, writing, music and piano; **Memberships:** Church of Christ, VFW, KTA and DAVE; **Children:** 4; **Grandchildren:** 9; **Education:** BS, MA, MS rank in education; **Honors:** Who's Who Worldwide; **Awards:** Volunteer Service, tutoring and others; **Personal Statement:** I've had influence from a dear friend, Dr H. A. Smith, to publish a book I am writing. My Life Wayward Journey.

Author: Ryan Petrilli; **Birthplace:** Wilmington, DE; **Occupation:** Operations manager; **Hobbies:** Hiking, running, sightseeing, camping, skiing and writing; **Memberships:** Contemporary Poets International, International Society; **Education:** AI DuPont High School and High Point University; **Honors:** A couple of honorable mentions; **Awards:** 2nd and 3rd place in poetry contests; **Published Works:** Passing By and Wisdom; **Personal Statement:** I write from my heart, for it will see and feel more than my eyes and hands ever will.

Author: Jeff Phillips; **Birthplace:** Bradford, PA; **Occupation:** Food service; **Hobbies:** Magic the Gathering, comics and football; **Education:** Graduated 1998 Hickory High School; **Honors:** Eagle Scout; **Personal Statement:** Writing serves as an outlet for the soul, in which each person is responsible for themselves and are only limited by their imagination.

Author: Audrey Pilcher; **Birthplace:** Huddersfield; **Occupation:** Retired; **Hobbies:** Reading, writing and Scrabble; **Spouse's Name:** Widowed; **Children:** 4; **Grandchildren:** 6; **Education:** Longley Hall Secondary School; **Published Works:** Poem "Collecting Day" in Yours Magazine; **Personal Statement:** My thanks to the Deighton Creative Writing Group for their encouragement and criticism.

Author: Suzanne L. Plein; **Birthplace:** New Rochelle, NY; **Occupation:** Writer of poetry and fiction; **Hobbies:** Reading, gardening, needlework, art history and poetry; **Memberships:** Weekly Poetry Workshop; **Spouse's Name:** Lee Plein; **Children:** 6; **Grandchildren:** 4; **Education:** MA in writing Manhattanville College; **Honors:** Rec'd Distinction Mast Theses; **Published Works:** Poetry at Gertrude White Gallery Exhibit and poem published in Inkwell Magazine; **Personal Statement:** I began writing poetry 3 yrs ago as a student of Barbara Holder, a published poet. Taking poetry workshop in September and studied poetry fiction with June Gould. My goal: to submit more poems for publication and publish children's books.

Author: Kerry Polk; **Birthplace:** Lynn, MA; **Occupation:** Nanny; **Hobbies:** Writing, computers, reading, and music; **Spouse's Name:** David Palmer; **Children:** 2; **Education:** High School Diploma, 1 year of college; **Published Works:** Colloquial Hyes "Intimate Sorrows"; **Personal Statement:** When I write, it just flows from within me. The words, they simply come from my heart.

Author: Nora Porrata; **Birthplace:** Chicago, IL; **Occupation:** Secretary; **Hobbies:** Running and gardening; **Children:** 1; **Education:** High school graduate; **Personal Statement:** Natalie and Arthur give me reason to love and trust. Becky teaches me not to fear and to have faith in life. Treasure the moments.

Author: Elizabeth A. Powell; **Birthplace:** Akron, OH; **Occupation:** Teacher and special educator; **Hobbies:** Painting, writing, walking, singing, woodworking and history; **Education:** BFA from the University of Akron, Graduate work at Kent State University; **Honors:** Certified by Ohio Department of Education; **Published Works:** The Hunter a short story and Zebras a pencil drawing; **Personal Statement:** Poetry is a painting in words

Author: Caroline Rae; **Birthplace:** London; **Occupation:** Healer; **Hobbies:** Restoring old furniture, various crafts, antique shops; **Spouse's Name:** Grahame Rea; **Children:** 3; **Education:** Secondary Schooling; **Personal Statement:** I enjoy all types of reading. I only started writing poems whilst my father was dying of cancer. To experience the excitement of writing is wonderful.

Author: Amanda Lynn Ramseyer; **Birthplace:** Pontiac, IL; **Occupation:** CNA; **Hobbies:** Poetry, singing and debates; **Memberships:** HOSA Health Occupation Students of America

Author: Kenneth V. Randall; **Pen Name:** Kenneth Randall; **Birthplace:** Nazirabad, India; **Occupation:** Retired sapper officer; **Hobbies:** Gardening and learning about desktop publishing; **Memberships:** C Biol, MI Biol, ML Mgt and Inst of RE; **Spouse's Name:** Margaret Randall; **Children:** 4; **Grandchildren:** 8; **Education:** RMA Sandhurst and Keele University; **Honors:** TD; **Awards:** BA; **Published Works:** Pipe Bridge Crossing of River Teme at Graham's Cot.; **Personal Statement:** Good poetry is to writing what the finest liqueur is to wine: A distillation and condensation of emotions and experiences that profoundly affect the reader.

Author: Sharon Redington; **Pen Name:** Malk; **Birthplace:** Walton-on-Thames; **Occupation:** Housewife; **Hobbies:** Gardening, decorating; **Spouse's Name:** Mark Anthony Redington; **Children:** 3; **Education:** Secondary Modern; **Personal Statement:** My husband deserted me on 6th Sept. '97, which inspired me to write the poem. It comes from the bottom of my heart.

Author: Andrew W. Reed; **Birthplace:** Torrance, CA; **Occupation:** Student; **Hobbies:** Soccer, coaching, writing, surfing and reading; **Education:** High school student; **Personal Statement:** I have found writing to be an escape from any and all worries in my life. When I find myself in turmoil and I cannot talk about it, I write. My emotions are expressed through my poetry.

Author: Larry D. Reeves; **Pen Name:** Lairdreves; **Birthplace:** San Jose, CA; **Occupation:** Land surveyor; **Hobbies:** Bicycling, hiking, camping and rafting; **Spouse's Name:** Leslie St. Ives; **Children:** 1; **Education:** Graduated Santa Rosa Junior College; **Awards:** MVP Track and Cross Country; **Personal Statement:** I asked Leslie what she wanted for Valentine's Day. She said, write me a poem.

Author: Mike A. Rendino; **Birthplace:** Syracuse, NY; **Occupation:** Sales and Distribution; **Hobbies:** Chess, sports and herbalism; **Memberships:** Blockbuster; **Education:** Physical Therapy Major; **Honors:** Dean's List and Honor Roll; **Awards:** Track and field and various artwork; **Personal Statement:** This poem was meant for those who may be alone, One day you'll turn around and someone may be there.

Author: Dianne Renze; **Birthplace:** Ft. Dodge, IA; **Occupation:** Bookkeeper and payroll manager; **Hobbies:** Fishing, camping and writing; **Children:** 3; **Personal Statement:** I am inspired by those near and dear to me to express what is in my heart.

Author: Patricia A. Rials; **Birthplace:** Hughes, AR; **Occupation:** Contract painter; **Hobbies:** Cooking, drawing and writing; **Children:** 4; **Grandchildren:** 2; **Education:** Robert Morris college; **Awards:** Minority Business Award, Certified Protection Officer Award; **Personal Statement:** My writing ability is a gift from God. God sent John Rowell in my life to inspire me to write poems, short stories and novels.

Author: Don Ringgold; **Pen Name:** Rahim Rabb; **Birthplace:** Philadelphia, PA; **Occupation:** Tennis professional; **Hobbies:** Contemplation, concentration and meditation; **Memberships:** Screen Actors Guild and United States Tennis Assoc.; **Education:** Graduated Temple University School of Communication; **Honors:** Dean's List; **Awards:** Four Chaplains Legion of Honor Membership; **Published Works:** Self-Determination; **Personal Statement:**

Poet Profiles

Consider the heart and what makes it beat. Light life and love are the joys to meet.

Author: Rebecca Rising; **Birthplace:** Holyoke; **Occupation:** Senior at Agawam High School; **Hobbies:** Writing, reading and roller skating; **Memberships:** International Society of Poets and Unicorn & Mirror; **Education:** Eleven grades in the Agawam Public School system; **Honors:** Nominated for Poet of the Year in '96, '97 and '98; **Awards:** Four Editor's Choice Awards and Poet of Merit; **Published Works:** National Library of Poetry published 5 poems and Iliad Press published 1 poem; **Personal Statement:** Everything around me inspires me. I hope to be an author and/or journalist. Poetry and writing allow me to express myself and say what I want.

Author: Jo Ann Roberson; **Birthplace:** Vallejo, CA; **Occupation:** Administration Aide; **Hobbies:** Gardening, reading and science fiction; **Spouse's Name:** Divorced; **Children:** 4; **Grandchildren:** 2; **Education:** High school; **Personal Statement:** For me poetry is a means of expressing fleeting moments and captured feelings that I might otherwise forget. It helps me remember a memory.

Author: Hilda Roberts; **Pen Name:** Kim Roberts; **Birthplace:** Davao City, Philippines; **Occupation:** English teacher and part-time novelist; **Hobbies:** Reading, writing, golf, cooking and travel; **Spouse's Name:** John Watson Roberts; **Education:** BA degree in English, Ateneo de Davao University; **Published Works:** Pacific Rim and a collection of contemporary poems; **Personal Statement:** My wonderful English husband has been a special influence and inspiration. He encouraged me to join the competition. Perhaps he really believed in me.

Author: Andrew Robertson; **Personal Statement:** A "Life Energy" interpenetrates all things physical, trees, etc., supporting given minute life to animals and humans. States of consciousness separate each species.

Author: Lynn S. Robinson; **Pen Name:** L S Robinson; **Birthplace:** Jasper, AL; **Occupation:** Receptionist; **Hobbies:** Writing, bowling, gardening and viewing sports; **Spouse's Name:** Harold; **Children:** 4; **Education:** High school graduate; **Personal Statement:** Writing is my way of expressing the emotions of everyday living. Whether it stems from happiness or sadness, it's all from within the heart.

Author: Helen Robinson-Romeo; **Birthplace:** Rome, NY; **Occupation:** Piano stylist; **Hobbies:** Writing, music composer and antiques; **Memberships:** Right to Life Group, Our Lady of the Snows Missions; **Spouse's Name:** Gerard Rocco Romeo; **Children:** 5; **Grandchildren:** 8; **Education:** U. S. Navy and Antone's School of Beauty Culture; **Honors:** Appearances at several concerts as guest pianist; **Awards:** Certificates of merit for poetry and music; **Personal Statement:** My beloved mother always said, "Do the very best job at everything you endeavor. If you do, then angels can do no better." Tremendous inspiration.

Author: Helen Rodriguez; **Pen Name:** Har; **Birthplace:** Santa Monica, CA; **Occupation:** Cake decorator instructor; **Hobbies:** Poetry writing, bowling, reading and music; **Memberships:** California Cake Club; **Spouse's Name:** Rudy; **Children:** 3; **Grandchildren:** 4; **Education:** High school and one year of college; **Personal Statement:** Father's a published songwriter, musician and philosopher. Raised by loving overindulgent grandmother. Pre and adolescent years formed by patient, stable aunt, uncle and irrepressible cousins.

Author: Jacqueline Rue; **Birthplace:** Hartford, CT; **Occupation:** Student; **Hobbies:** Softball, reading, writing, swimming, saxophone and clarinet; **Education:** 6th grade student; **Honors:** Math Olympics; **Awards:** Writing and reading awards; **Personal Statement:** One September day, I was sitting on a high hill in the woods with a stream below. I wrote some descriptions about the stream, then put them away. In March I took them out again and wrote a poem. That's how "The Stream" came about.

Author: Timothy F. Russell; **Birthplace:** New Jersey; **Occupation:** Harvey Industries; **Hobbies:** Deep sea fishing, camping, hiking and writing poems; **Spouse's Name:** Christine Lynn Russell; **Children:** 3; **Education:** Graduated from Gloucester City High School; **Personal Statement:** I would like to thank my family and friends for enjoying my poetry over the years, and my wife Christine for inspiring me to write again.

Author: Hector O. Sanchez, Jr.; **Birthplace:** Houston, TX; **Occupation:** Military USMC; **Hobbies:** Art, designing aircraft and model airplanes; **Education:** High school and graduated military training; **Awards:** 2nd place Houston Independent School District Visual Arts; **Published Works:** Chance, Love and I am Your God; **Personal Statement:** Life is not what's given to you or what you suffer, it's what you take control of.

Author: Wanda E. Sanders; **Birthplace:** Ford County; **Occupation:** Public relations manager; **Hobbies:** Painting, reading, writing poetry and gardening; **Memberships:** DAR, Civic Club and Legion Auxiliary; **Spouse's Name:** Robert Sanders; **Children:** 4; **Grandchildren:** 11; **Education:** High school and nursing degree; **Honors:** National Honor Society of Phi Theta Kappa, Dean's List & 4.0; **Awards:** First prize in art and photography; **Published Works:** My Daily Prayer; **Personal Statement:** You're never really dressed until you wear a smile.

Author: Joanna MacDonald Sapp; **Birthplace:** Fairmont, WV; **Occupation:** Nursing Aide and Home Health Care; **Hobbies:** Gardening, crafting Nativity Scenes w/Votive candles, sewing; **Memberships:** Home Makers Club, Church (Free Methodist); **Spouse's Name:** Vernon Lee Sapp (deceased); **Children:** 1; **Grandchildren:** 1; **Education:** 2 years of college; **Personal Statement:** I am very optimistic. I try to find a "silver lining" in even difficult circumstances. I love my neighbors and try to be a good example.

Author: Frank Savidge; **Birthplace:** Forrest Gate, London; **Occupation:** Dispatch administrator; **Hobbies:** Birdwatching, music, playing guitar and keyboards; **Memberships:** Baptist Church, RSPB and London Wildlife Trust; **Education:** Leyton Country High School for Boys; **Published Works:** Thank God for Beauty; **Personal Statement:** The millennium to get excited about is the thousand years whn the Lord Jesus Christ reigns on earth, not the one everyone's talking about.

Author: Liz Scantlin; **Pen Name:** Roision Steele; **Birthplace:** Conroe, TX; **Education:** BS in Animal Science and Entomology from Texas A & M University; **Personal Statement:** The personification of emotion.... this is what is called poetry.

Author: Casey Schuler; **Birthplace:** St. Joseph, MO; **Occupation:** Student; **Hobbies:** Writing and dance; **Awards:** Dancing Awards for 1st and 2nd place; **Personal Statement:** Our lives are like puzzles. There are a lot of pieces to be put together. Sometimes if pieces don't fit, find the right ones.

Author: Melissa Sciullo; **Pen Name:** Melissa; **Birthplace:** Pittsburgh, PA; **Occupation:** Student; **Hobbies:** Rollerblading, softball, violin and music; **Memberships:** National Honor Society and Gifted Opportunities; **Education:** Freshman at North Allegheny High School; **Honors:** Nominee for Outstanding Young Citizen Award; **Awards:** Highest Scholastic Achievement and Principal's Honor Awards; **Personal Statement:** My poems are simply my feelings, thoughts and emotions put into words on a sheet of paper for me to reflect upon.

Author: Jeremy Senske; **Birthplace:** Ishpeming, MI; **Occupation:** Student; **Hobbies:** Basketball, psychology and writing; **Education:** Diploma from Westwood High School and freshman at Northern

Enchanted Dreams

Michigan University; **Honors:** Academic honors and Board of Controls Scholarships; **Personal Statement:** Life leads us down many roads, roads that are all too often difficult. To combat these tough roads, sit back, relax and know that right where you are is where you belong.

Author: Linda Shane; **Birthplace:** Evansville, IN; **Occupation:** Foster parent; **Hobbies:** Oil painting, drawing and writing; **Memberships:** Birthday Club; **Children:** 1; **Grandchildren:** 1; **Honors:** Youth group leader; **Awards:** Missionary Award for working with children; **Personal Statement:** I have already started on writing a poem for foster children.

Author: Qumar S. Sheikh; **Birthplace:** Pakistan; **Occupation:** Sales associate; **Hobbies:** Music, poetry, writing and drums; **Education:** Fashion Institute of Design and Merchandising; **Personal Statement:** My goal as a writer is to never forget how to use my pen.

Author: Kerry Shepherd; **Pen Name:** Kes; **Birthplace:** Aldershott; **Occupation:** Company Director, toys; **Hobbies:** Football, reading, tennis; **Memberships:** Blackbrook Orchard Football Club (coach); **Spouse's Name:** Tim; **Children:** 2; **Published Works:** Beauty Abound; **Personal Statement:** Life is worthless without love and friendship

Author: David Sheridan; **Birthplace:** Glasgow; **Occupation:** Retired taxi driver; **Hobbies:** Photography, singing, dancing and crosswords; **Memberships:** Pentax Club; **Children:** 6; **Grandchildren:** 15; **Education:** Basic education at country school; **Personal Statement:** I like all things beautiful – music, poetry, paintings, etc., but have no special aims in any of these fields.

Author: Aubree Silver; **Birthplace:** Fairfax, VA; **Occupation:** Student; **Hobbies:** Writing, reading, theater, outdoors, animals and friends; **Memberships:** International Society of Poets and PETA; **Education:** High school Notre Dame Academy and Sophomore at East Carolina University; **Honors:** English, Campus Ministry, Drama, SODA and Dean's List; **Awards:** Nat'l English Merit and Editor's Choice; **Published Works:** Where's Perfect and Redemption, both in National Library of Poetry; **Personal Statement:** Thanks to Billy for being my inspiration and for seeing the best in me. I love you. And to Randal and Dave for the encouragement.

Author: Laszlo S. Sipos; **Pen Name:** Laz; **Birthplace:** Szekesfehervar, Hungary; **Occupation:** Injection mold set–up apprentice; **Hobbies:** Home brewing, walks and cooking; **Memberships:** American Homebrewers Association; **Spouse's Name:** Marion E. Sipos; **Children:** 2; **Education:** WCTC; **Personal Statement:** I would like to thank all the people who have had an influence on a positive mental attitude.

Author: Ellis Skoglund; **Birthplace:** Grossmont, CA; **Occupation:** Electrician Apprentice; **Hobbies:** Basketball, writing poetry and just having fun; **Education:** High School; **Personal Statement:** As a writer I hope to express how I feel and possibly influence others to do the same.

Author: Vanessa Slater; **Birthplace:** Cincinnati, OH; **Occupation:** Administrator in child care; **Hobbies:** Writing short stories, poetry, plays, singing and volleyball; **Memberships:** Assoc. of Ministers United in Christ, W. O. M. B. and M. A. H. A.; **Children:** 2; **Grandchildren:** 1; **Personal Statement:** Life is a maze until confusion transforms into clarity and the power of clarity becomes your road to destiny.

Author: Ana M. Sloan; **Birthplace:** Miami, FL; **Occupation:** Elementary school teacher; **Hobbies:** Reading, writing and cooking; **Memberships:** Professional Association of Georgia Educators; **Spouse's Name:** Edward Sloan; **Education:** Graduated Florida International University; **Honors:** Graduated with honors; **Personal Statement:** Reading and writing have always been my passion. As a teacher, I strive to instill love of books in young minds.

Author: Susan L. Smith; **Pen Name:** Sunny Day; **Birthplace:** Denton, TX; **Occupation:** Executive Assistant; **Hobbies:** Art, Bears and antiques; **Spouse's Name:** Fred A. Smith; **Children:** 3; **Grandchildren:** 3; **Education:** Art major; **Personal Statement:** Combining a love of writing and illustration late in life I find myself developing a series of short stories and a second children's book.

Author: Thomas Smith; **Birthplace:** Sunderland Co. Durham; **Occupation:** Retired; **Hobbies:** Light classical music, history and metal detecting; **Spouse's Name:** Joan Smith; **Children:** 2; **Grandchildren:** 4; **Education:** Bolt Street Boys Elementary School; **Published Works:** Nine short stories over the years; **Personal Statement:** I'm hoping to get my autobiography published, titled Snakes and Ladders.

Author: Tecia Lanese Smith; **Birthplace:** Chicago, IL; **Occupation:** Administrative assistant; **Hobbies:** Music and nightlife; **Education:** Attended Southwest Missouri State University; **Honors:** Dean's List and Honor Roll; **Awards:** AllState Field Hockey Goalie; **Personal Statement:** Writing is the best form of emotional release for me. If I need a reality check on my life, I just reread past writings.

Author: Laura Smith; **Birthplace:** West Midlands; **Occupation:** Student; **Hobbies:** Writing poems and stories; **Personal Statement:** I live in Devon with my parents and i find my inspiration from the beautiful countryside I live in and the places I've been.

Author: Wanda T. Snodgrass; **Birthplace:** Menard, TX; **Occupation:** Retired Shakespeare Theatre Publicity Director; **Hobbies:** Writing, Scrabble, card games, fishing and camping; **Spouse's Name:** Elisha Snodgrass; **Children:** 2; **Grandchildren:** 5; **Education:** Menard High School and Alamo City Business College; **Published Works:** Odessa 100, Where Are We, Melody in Winter, Liberty Shamed; **Personal Statement:** I tell it my way standing alone if I must. God is ever beside me.

Author: Sharon L. Sobczak; **Birthplace:** Chicago, IL; **Occupation:** Care management representative; **Hobbies:** Writing, music, dancing and outdoor activities with family; **Memberships:** The International Society of Poets; **Spouse's Name:** Mark Thomas Sobczak; **Children:** 3; **Education:** High school graduate and some college; **Awards:** Editor's Choice Award; **Published Works:** Love On the Net and Me; **Personal Statement:** I hope my writing is fun for all to read, as much as I like reading everyone else's poetry.

Author: Kimberly Souza; **Birthplace:** Weymouth, MA; **Occupation:** Housewife and mother; **Hobbies:** Reading, crafts and dancing; **Spouse's Name:** Stephen J. Souza, Jr.; **Children:** 3; **Education:** High school graduate and certified home health aide; **Personal Statement:** "Love is anterior to life, posterior to death, initial of creation and the exponent of breath." Emily Dickinson

Author: Missy Spaulding; **Birthplace:** Boston, MA; **Occupation:** Aspiring writer; **Hobbies:** Reader, knitting and my golden retriever; **Memberships:** Boston Fine Arts Museum; **Spouse's Name:** Dr David C King; **Education:** BA Art Education and working toward a Masters in Metaphysics; **Personal Statement:** Science is my religion, the universe is my inspiration and nature is magical. And like the universe, my writing skills are expanding.

Author: Evelyn Spriggs; **Birthplace:** Tecumseh, OK; **Hobbies:** Reading, writing, sewing and walking; **Spouse's Name:** Deceased; **Children:** 1; **Education:** Tecumseh High School; **Honors:** National Honor Society; **Published Works:** Small local publications; **Personal Statement:** My poems are little pieces of my soul, written for family and friends. I have only recently started sharing them with the rest of the world.

Poet Profiles

Author: Stanley J. St. Clair; **Birthplace:** Clayton, GA; **Occupation:** Insurance Agent and manager; **Hobbies:** Writing, video and art works; **Memberships:** Church At Sunset Hills and Warren County Kiwanis Club; **Spouse's Name:** Rhonda; **Children:** 4; **Grandchildren:** 7; **Education:** BRE from Covington College; **Honors:** Most Talented Senior Boy in high school; **Awards:** Several ribbons from art fair; **Published Works:** Bessie White, The Farmer & The Black Birds, When I Slow Down and The Still Voice of Nature; **Personal Statement:** My mother and grandfather were inspirational and encouraging to me in early years of forming values and goals. I have never given up my dreams, and my Christian faith has kept me strong.

Author: Lois A. Steir-Lewin; **Birthplace:** St. Ann, Jamaica; **Occupation:** Claims Adjuster; **Hobbies:** Writing, reading and gardening; **Memberships:** New Life Seventh Day Baptist, Holiness Church of God 7th Day; **Spouse's Name:** Mansel Lewin; **Children:** 3; **Grandchildren:** 2; **Education:** College, high school and business school; **Honors:** Dean's List; **Awards:** Golden Poet Award; **Published Works:** Reach Out; **Personal Statement:** Throughout the years my faith has had its share of uphill climbs but though I've had good and bad days, the good ones far outweigh the bad. So I refuse to complain. God has been good to me.

Author: Christopher Stetler; **Pen Name:** Christian Lore; **Birthplace:** Wayne, MI; **Occupation:** Student; **Hobbies:** Computer, writing, drawing and roller blading; **Education:** Sophomore in high school; **Awards:** MEAP Achievement Award in math and science; **Personal Statement:** Writing comes naturally. We don't have long to make an impact. Start young; otherwise you won't accomplish anything. Pick something you love and work hard.

Author: Melissa Kay Stewart; **Occupation:** Housewife; **Hobbies:** Fishing, hiking, reading and watching Guiding Light; **Memberships:** Gardening Club and Janette Oke Book Club; **Education:** Enrolled in ICS Home Schooling; **Published Works:** Two in the Dialysis Newsletter, The Lord Knows and My Life; **Personal Statement:** I have learned that it helps to write down how you feel. It has helped so much that I decided to write poems, I never thought I would become a semi-finalist! Just a point for the beginner, write how you feel.

Author: Ellen K. Stine; **Birthplace:** Orange County, VA; **Occupation:** Retired; **Hobbies:** Sewing, cooking, poetry, recording, preaching and writing; **Memberships:** Christian Fellowship Church; **Spouse's Name:** Deceased; **Education:** Eighth grade; **Personal Statement:** Poetry has always been dear to me but only as an outlet for my innermost feelings – especially for my Lord and Savior.

Author: Ginger Stoffel; **Birthplace:** South Lauguna Beach; **Hobbies:** Art and association; **Education:** High school; **Honors:** Honor roll; **Personal Statement:** When I became sober I was told I had a rare gift.

Author: Ray A. Strawser; **Birthplace:** Ephrata, PA; **Occupation:** Retired Army Chaplain; **Hobbies:** Writing and gardening; **Spouse's Name:** Elva Jean Stranger; **Children:** 3; **Grandchildren:** 5; **Education:** Doctor of Ministry; **Honors:** U. S. Army Bronze Star and Legion of Merit; **Personal Statement:** Everything could be verse.

Author: Cinde Sullivan; **Birthplace:** Fulton, NY; **Occupation:** Homemaker; **Hobbies:** Knitting, reading and writing; **Spouse's Name:** Michael; **Children:** 5; **Grandchildren:** 1; **Education:** High school; **Personal Statement:** I collect fairies and love them, which prompted me to write about them.

Author: Ginger Sullivan; **Birthplace:** Readford, VA; **Occupation:** Teacher; **Hobbies:** Computers, gardening, reading and hiking; **Memberships:** National Education Assn., VA Education Assoc. and 4-H leader; **Education:** Bachelor of Science graduated from Lincoln Memorial University; **Honors:** Outstanding Young Woman of America & Outstanding 4-H Leader; **Awards:** 4-H Clover Award for 20 yrs of service; **Published Works:** My First Class published in Lincoln Memorial University Alumni Magazine; **Personal Statement:** My mother, grandmother and aunt had great influences in my life towards being an educator. I feel writing poems expresses one's thoughts deep within the soul.

Author: Gail M. Sutton; **Birthplace:** Bemidji, MN; **Occupation:** U. S. Forest Service Information Receptionist; **Hobbies:** Biking, volleyball, softball, tennis, hiking and reading; **Education:** Blackduck, MN High School, University of Minn., Duluth, Campbellsville College and University WI – Lacrosse; **Published Works:** Seashell Friendship; **Personal Statement:** The enjoyment of nature and the preservation of the wilderness for today and for future generations to enjoy behind us is a necessary objective for inspiration from nature to continue and for the restoration of the soul after work and toil.

Author: Annie Sutton; **Birthplace:** Sacramento, CA; **Occupation:** Daycare provider, mom, foster mom and wife; **Hobbies:** Softball, boating and camping; **Spouse's Name:** Jeffery Sutton; **Children:** 6; **Personal Statement:** As a writer of poems, I plan to keep writing them, the Lord willing. The Lord is my inspiration and my friend Judy encourages me. I am thankful for both.

Author: Cindy Sutton; **Birthplace:** Boulder, CO; **Occupation:** Newspaper Carrier; **Hobbies:** Crocheting, reading, surfing the net; **Spouse's Name:** Vincent Sutton; **Children:** 2; **Published Works:** Seasons (Poem)

Author: Jessie Tank; **Pen Name:** Jessie; **Birthplace:** Milwaukee, WI; **Hobbies:** Playing basketball and writing poems; **Education:** Park View Middle School in 8th grade; **Honors:** Honor Roll; **Awards:** Presidential Education Award; **Published Works:** Blue Christmas; **Personal Statement:** When I am older, I would like to publish my own book of poems.

Author: Lora Taylor; **Birthplace:** Barberton, OH; **Occupation:** Insurance underwriter; **Hobbies:** Backpacking, camping, hiking and photography; **Children:** 1; **Awards:** Who's Who in American High School Students; **Published Works:** Wadsworth Bruin; **Personal Statement:** Poetry allows me the chance to express my innermost feelings and my views on life.

Author: Carol Taylor; **Birthplace:** Golden, CO; **Occupation:** Retired; **Hobbies:** Barbershop music and 4-part harmony; **Memberships:** Sweet Adelines Int'l and Beta Sigma Phi Sorority; **Spouse's Name:** Dwight Taylor (deceased); **Children:** 2; **Grandchildren:** 5; **Education:** Business college; **Personal Statement:** Families can be loving, honorable individuals when they spend their lives making memories that last a lifetime.

Author: Joseph S. Taylor, Jr.; **Birthplace:** North Carolina; **Hobbies:** The Old Testament and translating foreign dialect; **Education:** General education GED and some college courses

Author: Toni Terry; **Pen Name:** Lexus; **Birthplace:** St. Paul, MN; **Occupation:** Firefighter; **Hobbies:** Exercising and weight lifting; **Memberships:** River of Life Christian Center; **Children:** 2; **Personal Statement:** When in doubt write it out! Write daily if you can.

Author: Theresa Lynn Thomas; **Pen Name:** Theresa L. Thomas; **Birthplace:** Houston, TX; **Occupation:** Record Administrative Supervisor; **Hobbies:** Reading, drawing, writing poetry, bowling and painting; **Memberships:** New Light Christian Center Church; **Spouse's Name:** Eddie C. Monroe Jr.; **Children:** 2; **Education:** Ross Sterling High School, Texas School of Business–Paralegal Study; **Honors:** Certified to minister to women who have husbands

Enchanted Dreams

on drugs; **Published Works:** Farewell My Love, Women; **Personal Statement:** Poetry is a tool for me to reach out to hurting people who have experienced times in their lives with loved ones, due to drugs or tragedy.

Author: Andrea Thompson; **Birthplace:** Arizona; **Occupation:** Student and artist; **Education:** High school student; **Personal Statement:** "I am a part of all that I have met, yet all experience is an arch wherethrough gleams that untraveled world." Alfred Lord Tennyson

Author: Wanda S. Tobola; **Birthplace:** Austin, TX; **Occupation:** Bookkeeper; **Hobbies:** Sewing, fishing, gardening, painting and hunting; **Memberships:** Gardening Club, National Rifle Assoc. and Sewing Clubs; **Spouse's Name:** Edmond A. Tobola; **Children:** 3; **Grandchildren:** 1; **Education:** Woomera High School; **Honors:** 2nd place Valentine's Day Poem; **Published Works:** High school newspaper; **Personal Statement:** I would like to be a published poet and writer someday. I've loved poetry and writing ever since I could remember. I wrote poems to family members and my husband who pushed me forward in my ambition to write.

Author: Ann Tork; **Birthplace:** Essex, England; **Occupation:** Housewife; **Hobbies:** cooking, gardening and bird watching; **Education:** High school; **Honors:** All A's in senior year in high school; **Personal Statement:** A novel is my dream.

Author: Hilda Troyer; **Birthplace:** Edgerton, OH; **Occupation:** Retired; **Hobbies:** Art, children's stories, crochet, research and gemology; **Spouse's Name:** Deceased; **Children:** 3; **Grandchildren:** 2; **Education:** High school and RN College; **Published Works:** Troyer Family Book

Author: Sally Truss; **Pen Name:** 185546; **Occupation:** Day care owner and operator; **Hobbies:** Cooking and crocheting; **Memberships:** International E-Mail Club, Muskegon Economic Growth Alliance; **Spouse's Name:** Deceased; **Children:** 2; **Grandchildren:** 1; **Education:** Two years of college; **Personal Statement:** Poetry, for me, comes from the soul.

Author: Steven Tungate; **Pen Name:** Steve; **Occupation:** College student; **Hobbies:** Writing poetry and short stories; **Spouse's Name:** Teresa; **Education:** Sophomore at Lindsey Wilson College; **Honors:** Award of Merit for The Lost Lamb; **Awards:** Outstanding Achievement; **Personal Statement:** A poem is a reflection of one's self. We must constantly wipe the mirror clean. Let nothing impinge on the mind.

Author: John Turner; **Birthplace:** Stapleford, Nottinghamshire; **Occupation:** Truck driver; **Hobbies:** Walking, swimming, writing and poetry; **Spouse's Name:** Jessie; **Children:** 2; **Education:** Secondary Modern School; **Personal Statement:** I have always had a wish to write and be published, in both poetry and novels. A creative writing course put me on the way.

Author: Lisa Valkenburg; **Birthplace:** Palas Park; **Occupation:** Homemaker; **Hobbies:** Family, sports; **Spouse's Name:** Matthew Valkenburg; **Children:** 2; **Education:** A. S. Morgan Valley C. C.; **Published Works:** "Egger" drawings in Chicago Sun-Times Comics; **Personal Statement:** I want to grow to be an asset, to reach out to what is happening now and to aim for the best future.

Author: Wesley G. Vaughn; **Birthplace:** Seattle, WA; **Occupation:** Surface mount assembly operator; **Hobbies:** Songwriting, fishing, stamp collecting, singing & astronomy; **Spouse's Name:** Patricia; **Children:** 3; **Grandchildren:** 7; **Education:** BA Warner Pacific College and studying for MAR Liberty University; **Awards:** Quarter Finalist Award in lyric competition; **Published Works:** Article in "Of Such Is the Kingdom"

Author: Kristy Vega-Park; **Birthplace:** New York, NY; **Hobbies:** Writing and music; **Spouse's Name:** Steven Park; **Children:** 1; **Honors:** Hispanic Culture Club; **Awards:** Writing awards; **Personal Statement:** Writing is a great, gratifying and fulfilling way to express myself. I've always enjoyed reading and writing poetry and stories.

Author: Nigel Paul Walker; **Birthplace:** Barton-on-Humber; **Occupation:** Archivist; **Hobbies:** Reading, mysticism, supporting Chelsea F. C.; **Education:** Baysgarth Comp.; **Personal Statement:** Let all our thoughts sent forth be of love and warmth, knowing that the universe will act and return that love and warmth tenfold.

Author: Cynthia F. Walker; **Pen Name:** Cyndi Faye; **Birthplace:** Southampton, NY; **Occupation:** Letter carrier; **Hobbies:** Writing and poetry; **Children:** 2; **Education:** High school; **Personal Statement:** A dear friend inspired me to start writing again and I'm glad they did.

Author: Shirlene Wallingford; **Birthplace:** Portland, OR; **Occupation:** Cashier; **Hobbies:** Singing, dancing and writing poems; **Children:** 1; **Personal Statement:** The only thing I can say is keep your head up and never lose faith. When you think every one has walked out remember there is always someone to guide you home.

Author: Nicola Walsh; **Birthplace:** Hemel, Hempstead; **Occupation:** Housewife and mother; **Hobbies:** Drawing, reading and writing poetry; **Spouse's Name:** Stephen Walsh; **Children:** 3; **Education:** Public school and have 6 CSE's; **Personal Statement:** I have always loved writing, especially for the people who are special to me. When you are surrounded by love and inspiration, the pen follows the heart.

Author: Candice F. Walters; **Birthplace:** Columbus, OH; **Occupation:** Teacher; **Hobbies:** Playing the flute and writing; **Education:** Northwest High School; **Personal Statement:** I write what I feel and it comes from my heart. That is what makes my poems so special.

Author: Tami Washington; **Pen Name:** Amelia Clemson; **Personal Statement:** Life and love, cherished gifts from God to us, are my inspiration.

Author: Antoinette Washington; **Birthplace:** New York City, NY; **Occupation:** Greyhound Bus Driver; **Hobbies:** Reading, traveling and music; **Spouse's Name:** Steve Watkins; **Children:** 2; **Education:** 12th Grade, Kensington H. S.; **Personal Statement:** My inspiration for "Pass Me By" came from being homeless myself. It was how I felt at the time.

Author: Kevin Watts; **Pen Name:** Jazz; **Birthplace:** Fort Jackson, SC; **Occupation:** Future band director; **Hobbies:** Playing in band, writing poetry and short stories; **Memberships:** Music, percussion camp, honor roll, Jim Gainey Martial Arts; **Education:** Pelin High School; **Honors:** Honor roll and captain and leader of marching band; **Published Works:** The Ocean Breeze; **Personal Statement:** I am a spontaneous person when it comes to poetry because when I'm inspired by my true love or something special, I write about it.

Author: Ben E. Weeks; **Birthplace:** Dalton, GA; **Occupation:** Psychiatric social worker; **Hobbies:** Southern mountains, folktales, singer, guitarist and band; **Memberships:** NOW, Greenpeace, Nat'l Wildlife Fund, ACLU, ACSW and PPA; **Spouse's Name:** Genie A.; **Children:** 2; **Grandchildren:** 2; **Education:** Masters degree from Florida State University; **Published Works:** Fall, a four-stanza lyrical poem published in The Progressive Farmer

Author: Debra A. Weidman; **Birthplace:** Lebanon, PA; **Occupation:** Medical Records Tech; **Hobbies:** Bowling, photography, handbells and flower garden; **Memberships:** Grace United Church of Christ and WIBC; **Spouse's Name:** Donald C.

Poet Profiles

Weidman; **Children:** 1; **Education:** High school graduate; **Honors:** National Heath Care Hero; **Personal Statement:** During my years as a child I loved to do poetry; I wrote poems as a child. Recently losing my father from cancer inspired me to write a poem to put in a local paper on the anniversary of his death. I really miss my father, my friend.

Author: Gloria Jean West; **Pen Name:** Gloria Jean; **Birthplace:** Sterling, GA; **Occupation:** Atlantic Engineered prod.; **Hobbies:** Writing poems and speaking in public; **Memberships:** Zion Rock Missionary Church; **Children:** 3; **Education:** Glynn Academy High School; **Honors:** Most Outspoken; **Personal Statement:** Writing poetry allows me to express what I feel in my heart. I thank God I have more to write.

Author: Emily Wheeler; **Pen Name:** Emily Rose; **Birthplace:** Los Angeles, CA; **Occupation:** Mother and housewife; **Hobbies:** Art, poetry and writing; **Spouse's Name:** Ron Wheeler; **Children:** 5; **Education:** High school graduation; **Personal Statement:** Through writing I'm able to express and allow the trial and error in my life as a manic depressive, to become a source of strength rather than weakness.

Author: Elga Haymon White; **Birthplace:** Flatwoods, LA; **Occupation:** Retired; **Hobbies:** Writing, music and outdoor sports; **Memberships:** International Society of Poets; **Spouse's Name:** Rev. N. J. White; **Education:** Attended University of Colorado and Denver University; **Honors:** International Poetry Hall of Fame Museum; **Published Works:** Poems in Anthologies, National Library of Poetry and also in American Poetry Association; **Personal Statement:** A brush in the hand of an artist is like a pen in the hand of a poet, both portray beauty.

Author: Andrew Wilds; **Birthplace:** Glendale, CA; **Occupation:** Student; **Hobbies:** Sports; **Education:** Freshman at Glendale High School

Author: Riva Marea Williams; **Pen Name:** Riva Marea; **Birthplace:** Brooklyn, NY; **Occupation:** High school English teacher; **Children:** 1; **Education:** Graduated University of California, Riverside; **Honors:** Dean's List and Academic Excellence Scholarship; **Published Works:** Through the Backstreets Window; **Personal Statement:** I am a woman living with AIDS. My poem and upcoming novel are expressions and facts of my experiences.

Author: Kathleen Williams; **Birthplace:** Chicago, IL; **Occupation:** Student; **Hobbies:** Swimming, playing violin, hanging out and drama club; **Memberships:** Tuskawilla Middle School Drama Club; **Education:** St. Luke's Lutheran School and Tuskawilla Middle School; **Honors:** Honor roll and Principal's List; **Awards:** Class Superlative – Most Intelligent Girl; **Published Works:** Sandy, Sunny Places Anthology of Poetry by Young Americans

Author: Connie M. Wilson; **Birthplace:** Baltimore, MD; **Occupation:** Secretary and student; **Hobbies:** Writing, reading, sewing and hiking; **Memberships:** Crell in United Brethren in Christ; **Spouse's Name:** Luther M. Wilson, Jr.; **Children:** 1; **Education:** Sr. in college at Frostburg State University; **Honors:** Volunteering; **Personal Statement:** Writing is a gift to be shared with the world, a direct gift from God the Father.

Author: Pamela Wisher; **Birthplace:** Paignton, Devon; **Occupation:** Community Development Manager; **Hobbies:** Boating, reading, listening to music, travel; **Children:** 2; **Grandchildren:** 2; **Education:** Rushcliffe Technical Grammar School for Girls and Demontfort University, Leicester; **Personal Statement:** Poetry is like personal luggage; you take it with you wherever you go.

Author: Peggy Witt; **Birthplace:** Rochelle, VT; **Occupation:** Secretary; **Hobbies:** Travel, wine and food; **Spouse's Name:** Larry Witt; **Children:** 4; **Grandchildren:** 2; **Education:** Some college and secretarial certificate; **Honors:** Dean's List and National Honor Society; **Personal Statement:** My influence is received from my husband's undying love and dedication. My children inspired me with their outlook on life. My love for my family is my life.

Author: Kathy Wood; **Birthplace:** Poughkeepsie, NY; **Occupation:** Student; **Hobbies:** Shopping, writing poetry, reading, skating and music; **Education:** Home-schooled; **Personal Statement:** Love is the world's best inspiration. To have just a little is all that you need to live life at the fullest.

Author: Jean Wood; **Birthplace:** Saddleworth; **Occupation:** Housewife; **Hobbies:** Reading, gardening and music; **Spouse's Name:** Kenneth Wood; **Children:** 1; **Grandchildren:** 2; **Education:** Uppermill High School; **Personal Statement:** Poetry is a garden of thoughts endlessly flowering, challenging the reader's imagination.

Author: Bryan Scott Wood; **Birthplace:** Kirbyville, TX; **Occupation:** Sales; **Hobbies:** Writing poems and short stories; **Education:** High School; **Personal Statement:** I have always wanted to be a writer, but I didn't think I was good enough, but my mother says I was. She always said I could do anything I wanted to if I put my mind to it. My mother is my best friend; she is always there for me.

Author: Charles Edward Woods; **Pen Name:** Know; **Birthplace:** Natchez, MS; **Occupation:** Poet-artist-soldier; **Hobbies:** Gardening, fishing, cycling and sculptor; **Memberships:** Disabled American Vets and American Merchant Marine; **Children:** 3; **Grandchildren:** 2; **Education:** Govilan College, trade college and Navy; **Honors:** National Defence Service Medal Korean, Vietnam; **Awards:** Editor's Choice Award and National Library of Poetry; **Published Works:** Buffalo soldier and America; **Personal Statement:** Foundation of a country is the establishment and endowment of an institution and underlying principle. If that is injustice, then that country is also injustice.

Author: Elizabeth Woolcott; **Birthplace:** Redmond, WA; **Hobbies:** Singing, writing, reading and just plain having fun; **Education:** Sophomore at Lake Washington High School; **Honors:** Honor Roll

Author: Eric Wright; **Birthplace:** Kankakee, IL; **Occupation:** Full-time student; **Hobbies:** Writing poetry, music and short stories; **Education:** Elementary Education Major at Western Illinois University; **Honors:** Dean's List; **Awards:** Rockford Poetry Guild Award winner; **Published Works:** Arachnophobia, DUI; **Personal Statement:** Writing poetry is an excellent way to relieve stress while creating an artistic outlet for personal expression.

Author: Tina L. Wyatt; **Birthplace:** Gallipolis, OH; **Occupation:** Recreation and wildlife field; **Hobbies:** Fishing, hiking, camping and woodwork crafts; **Education:** Wellston High School, Hocking Tech. College and ICS Learning School; **Published Works:** Crack Free, Why and God Cares For Me; **Personal Statement:** There's only one true inspiration, that's God in heaven who made this creation. Do you believe that Jesus is God's only son, sent from above? If so, you realize what it means when you say true love.

Author: Zai O. D. Yates; **Birthplace:** Nottingham; **Occupation:** Retired civil servant; **Hobbies:** Writing poetry; **Spouse's Name:** Deceased; **Children:** 1; **Grandchildren:** 3; **Education:** Elementary; **Personal Statement:** A great love of words and the profound messages they can convey.

Author: Brian Yoder; **Birthplace:** Millersburg, OH; **Occupation:** Carpenter and musician; **Hobbies:** Writing and playing drums; **Education:** Dalton High School and YWAM Cambridge; **Personal

Enchanted Dreams

Statement: As a writer I wish to express the grace, love and beauty of God. I have been and will always be inspired by these three things.

Author: Stephen A. Yow; **Birthplace:** Liverpool; **Occupation:** Taxi driver; **Hobbies:** Golf, parachuting and football; **Memberships:** British Parachute Association; **Children:** 1; **Education:** Glenburn High School; **Personal Statement:** I hope my poem can touch the emotions of those having visited Gretwa. My favourite poem is HighFlight by John Gillespie McGee Jr.

Author: Melisa Zahn; **Birthplace:** Smithtown, NY; **Occupation:** Student; **Hobbies:** Photography, guitar, sports and yoga; **Spouse's Name:** Paul Zahn; **Education:** Currently getting Liberal Arts Major; **Awards:** Gold Medal Jr. Olympics 1985; **Personal Statement:** I feel that the best way for me to express myself is through poetry and short stories. My inspirations are Maya Angelou, Sark and my husband Paul.

APPENDIX

Index of Poets

This easy-reference index of poets is an alphabetical listing of each author whose poem appears in this anthology. A quick scan of the Poet Index will tell you the full name of every poet featured in the book, followed by a page number on which their poem can be located.

A

Abdallah, Randy Lee, 271
Ackroyd, Elizabeth, 136
Acland, Roy K., 74
ADad, Ben Elkanah, 301
Adams, Diana H., 156
Adams, Rick, 321
Adams, Stacey A., 43
Adams, Suzanne, 284
Adegbile, Sanmi, 216
Adlparvar, Hasty, 165
Admire, Andrew, 252
Ahlstrom, Kelly, 81
Ahmed, Elias, 51
Ahmed, Masir, 121
Akizaki, Doreen H., 118
Aldridge, Crystal, 243
Alexander, Pearline, 87
Allan, Stacy, 322
Allcott, Rebecca, 320
Allen, Ernest, 297
Allen, Maggie L., 158
Allison, Justava Nuzum, 197
Allwright, Janet, 88
Almond, Joan, 107
Alois, Alex, 271
Alverson, Clara, 318
Amoureux, Kathy, 227
Anderson, Amy Irene, 300
Anderson, Connie, 25
Anderson, David, 146
Anderson, Debbie, 59
Anderson, Edwin E., 153
Anderson, Joan C., 279
Anderson, Laurie, 100
Anderson, Robert W., 66
Anderson, Tina, 314
Andrew, Margaret, 286
Andrews, Alethea, 108
Andrews, Dustin, 301
Andrews, Kelly, 222
Andrews, N. L., 81
Andrews, Stephanie J., 100
Ann, Mary, 269
Antonacci, Philip Anthony, 23
Archer, Margaret, 258
Archer, Vernon, 28
Armgard, Kathi, 244
Arneil, D. E., 82
Arroyo, Deana L., 35
Arsenault, Amanda, 321
Askew, Richard, 61
Atha, Justin K., 44
Atherton, Norbert, 277
Atkinson, F. E., 76
Atkinson, Maxine, 68
Attaway, Carol Joy, 195
Aubney, A. J. Hughes, 288
August, Helen, 114
Austin, Calvin A., 58
Averill, Sheila P., 150
Awberry–Beck, Claire, 17
Axford, Valerie, 193

B

Bacal, Vanessa, 165
Bagot, Noreen, 255
Bailey, A., 195
Bailey, Jean, 286
Bailey, Shirley, 125
Bain, Scott, 229
Baker, Clair, 217
Baker, D. C., 82
Baker, Eric W., 91
Baker, Kenneth James, 178
Baker, Nancy L., 157
Baker, Paul J., 77
Baldridge, Debra, 258
Baldwin, Christina, 300
Baldwin, Lisa, 245
Baldwin, Penny, 160
Baldwin, Shayne P., 104
Ball, George, 145
Ballard, Michael, 225
Baltsen, Renee Suze, 185
Barclay, Lynnette, 176
Barke, Susan, 208
Barksdale, Joyce, 9
Barnak, Heather, 226
Barnes, Susan J., 309
Barnett, Jill, 161
Barnett, Linda, 127
Barnett, Melanie, 49
Baron, Adam H., 86
Barrios, Ryan, 167
Basile, Jannine, 252
Bass, Martha D., 123
Batchelor, Latonya, 215
Bates, Kelsey, 230
Bathurst, Brandi, 152
Battista, Kathleen M., 209
Bauder, Kim, 210
Bauman, David, 80
Baxter, Diane Netherland, 29
Beach, Sean, 157
Beam, Robin, 266
Beam, Sherri, 306
Bear, Stephanie, 212
Bear, W. W. Fardels, 129
Beatty, Marjorie, 192
Becerra, Richard D., 267
Becker, Jeffrey B., 252
Beechey, Thomas, 121
Beedell, V. M., 109
Begamen, Tammy, 139
Belk, Samantha M., 237
Bell, Anne, 228
Bell, Elizabeth, 138
Bell, Helen Pope, 247
Bell, Wanda M., 282
Bellows, Diane, 141
Benge, Wesley, 200
Bennes, Arlene R., 38
Bennett, Karen, 240
Bennett, Laura, 113
Bennett, Laurence, 234
Bennett, Mark, 66

Benson, Georgieann, 199
Benson, Linda N., 230
Benson, Marcia, 133
Benson, Sarah E., 168
Bent, Rima, 160
Benton, Penny K., 94
Berg, Gloria T., 186
Bernhardt, Michelle, 149, 186
Bernu, Holly Alison, 313
Bersch, Danielle, 118
Betz, Susan M., 222
Beylerian, Josie, 190
Bezon, Stacie L., 317
Bhagudas, Devika, 250
Bhakta, Priya, 298
Bhola, Shelley A., 141
Biagini, Sherilyn, 53
Bice–McFarlin, Bevy D., 268
Bidwell, Georgia Taylor, 163
Bilello, Stephanie, 97
Billingham, Mary, 76
Bingert, James T., 312
Birdsell, Jason, 216
Birnie, Michael, 265
Bishop, David Ward, 180
Bishop, Dennis W., 155
Black, Missie, 218
Blades, Latisha, 224
Blankenship, Sarah Jane, 106
Blazy, Doris J., 283
Blesing, Debra A., 122
Blevins, Blanche, 207
Bodner, Sara M., 283
Boggs, Anna Elizabeth, 217
Bogle, Linda Frances, 20
Boldue, Colette, 35
Bonesho, Sharon M., 72
Bonner, Paul, 106
Bonsper, George, 94
Boone, Amy, 138
Borgheiinck, Andrew L., 19
Bossen, W. M., 120
Botting, Jase, 321
Boucek, Jane V., 39
Boush, Joel, 297
Bove, Deanna, 205
Bowers, Eugene, 136
Bowers, Susan, 18
Bowler, Maurice G., 143
Boyce, Dave, 189
Boyd, Dana, 178
Boyll, Norma J., 27
Bozanic, Gloria, 166
Bradford, Ashleigh, 200
Bradford, Ruth, 164
Bradley, Brenda L., 256
Branch, Tarrahal, 64
Brand, Linda, 242
Brate, Amy, 115
Bratt, D. J., 73
Braxton, Charlie Mae, 257

Brayley, Susan, 207
Brewer, Teresa, 104
Brigham, Angela C., 67
Brindle, F. M., 73
Broadbear, V. M., 287
Brock, Jr., Pope F., 128
Bronson, Jana, 198
Brook, Jill, 255
Brooks, Cynthia, 305
Brooks, Tamyra, 268
Brown II, Joseph W., 271
Brown, Ardeda, 162
Brown, Carl, 182
Brown, Carol, 10
Brown, Dana Sue, 58
Brown, Earline J., 270
Brown, Jennifer, 269
Brown, Kenneth, 131
Brown, Stephen, 131
Browne, Kristen, 80
Browns, Patrick T., 134
Brucker, Gladys, 268
Bruner, Rachel, 270
Bruno, Grace, 179
Brunson, Louise, 196
Bryan, Robert, 319
Bryant, Jeanne, 314
Bryant, Mary Sue, 147
Budge, E. M., 198
Buedel, Jennifer, 68
Burch, Erica, 283
Burch, Kathy, 152
Burkhardt, Chris, 321
Burkhardt, Sheri L., 26
Burnett, Joel, 250
Burnette, Pamela L., 55
Bushong, Nadine M., 212
Butler, Alf, 113
Butler, Bebe, 13
Butler, Jeffrey, 99
Butler, Niki Linn, 279
Butler, Shirley, 303
Butts, Shannon, 4
Byerley, Dana D., 127

C

Callahan, Betty, 132
Callaway, Virginia, 263
Calloway, Peggy Guynn, 46
Camacho, Linda, 134
Camarda, Antonella, 95
Campbell, Dawn, 142
Campbell, Jeannette, 221
Canisales, Donis, 116
Cano, Daniel Ray, 92
Carada, Faye, 151
Caravaglia, Adam, 274
Carlson, Julee, 289
Carlson, Maryann, 43
Carlton, Erin, 79
Carolan, Melody J., 50
Carreiro, Bob, 56
Carruthers, George L., 61
Carter, James, 125

Carter, Ruth, 58
Carter, Vanessa Washington, 211
Casey, J. P., 120
Casey-Hentges, Teri, 298
Cash, A. C., 102
Cash, Michael J., 132
Caskey, Josh, 176
Cassady, Rickie Jean, 295
Casselberry-Samuels, Blake E., 212
Cassidy, Cathy, 54
Castello, Nathan, 144
Castillo, Lydia, 107
Castro, Darla, 144
Caswell, Stephanie, 161
Centric, Carol E., 6
Challinor, Ian, 110
Chalmers, Steven J., 248
Chamblee, Don, 271
Chandler, Jackie, 16
Chaney, Erica M., 219
Chaplick, Michael J., 133
Charnock, Charles, 90
Chasse, Shalimar, 211
Chastain, Julia, 291
Chaussee, Alice, 74
Cheesman, Thelma, 303
Chermely, Priscilla, 64
Chesebro, Marjorie, 148
Cheyne, Louise Marie, 109
Childress, Diane, 193
Chowdhury, Saleha, 183
Christein, Robbin, 322
Christian, Linda, 272
Christian, Ron, 29
Christy, Andrea, 195
Clapton, Gemma, 78
Clark, Evelyn, 76
Clark, Mary, 277
Clarke, Edward G., 146
Clarke, Niki, 151
Clarke, Theron, 282
Clarke-Brown, Carmen K., 102
Clary, Jennie, 27
Clayton, Cadge, 75
Claytor, Aulia, 55
Cleghorn, Evelyn, 87
Click, Lauren Melissa, 105
Cobb, Kristi, 307
Cody, Dale, 42
Coffey, Alpha Corrine, 46
Cogley, Mary, 267
Cohen, Suzanne, 264
Cole, Dorothy Doore, 242
Cole, Edward P., 70
Coleman, Carrie, 302
Coles, John A., 231
Collier, Crystal M., 73
Collier, Elaine, 99
Collins III, William W., 293
Collins, Gaylyn, 86
Collins, S. M., 176
Combs, Jr., Flem, 319

Commerford, Derek, 284
Competiello, Marjorie L., 226
Compton, Amy J., 179
Condon, Renee, 263
Conner, Tui, 251
Conrad, Danielle, 110
Conrad, John, 112
Conroy, H. E., 149
Conte, Frank S., 84
Cook, Michelle, 252
Cook, William C., 216
Cooper, Bettie, 163
Cooper, Cynthia, 135
Cooper, Eboni, 69
Cooper, Helen E., 135
Cooper, Susannah, 25
Cooper, William A., 137
Cooperwaite, Dorothy, 185
Cope, Evelyn, 39
Coppola, Jonathan, 196
Corbier, Myrtha B., 142
Cordingly, Cassandra, 86
Corey, Lia M., 110
Cornelius, Dennis J., 323
Corr, J., 284
Cosden, Paulette, 298
Coupland, N., 47
Courteau, John, 239
Courtney, Jennifer Liles, 32
Coverly, Doug, 114
Cox, D. G., 218
Crabtree, Tommy, 84
Crawford, Garry, 301
Crawford, John, 312
Crawford, Joyce, 208
Crisp, Marty, 232
Crosby, Irelee, 188
Cross, M., 166
Cudmore, Vikki, 256
Cuellar, Lisa, 32
Cullen, Shane, 148
Cummins, Jason, 231
Cummins, Melinda Kaye, 39
Cunningham, Michelle, 311
Curran, Terence C., 319
Currie, Patricia, 231
Curry, Jana K., 171
Curry, Torderick, 284
Custodio, Suzy R., 129

D

D'Agostino, Gina, 138, 233
Daacola, Frances, 310
Daff, Ordy J., 275
Daleo, Maria, 309
Dallojacono, Luann, 246
Dang, Phung Kim, 61
Daniels, Roger, 124
Dannug, Perrin Antonio, 41
Darling, Amanda Lynn, 289
Dauster, Lanette, 314
Dave, Adam, 44
Davidson, Marya, 281
Davies, Cynthia, 103

Davies, Dennis C., 119
Davies, Judith, 50
Davies, Ralph, 320
Davis, Anne, 23
Davis, Carolyn A., 36
Davis, Grace, 287
Davis, Jr., Tony Wayne, 62
Davis, Michelle, 298
Davis, Regina, 163
Davis, William, 184
Dawson, Sara, 270
De Jesus, Fay, 202
De Lillio, Richard R., 316
Dean, Juliet, 282
Deatherage, Lois, 210
Deaver, Patricia Lynn, 132
DeBaldo-Thode, Elizabeth C., 259
Decroy, F., 169
Dee, Diane, 122
DeGennaro, Christine, 101
Deifer, Brad, 126
Demons, Nellie Ruth W., 92
Denham, Helen, 316
Denney, Elaine, 240
Dennis, Simon P., 168
Denson, Lottie P., 222
Desgroseilliers, Jerrie, 40
Devine, Mary, 208
DeWulf-Sellers, Shelia, 139
Diaz, Cristoval, 115
Diaz, Luis R., 111
Dibble, Karina, 281
Dickerson, Paul W., 90
Dickey, Brenda Suzanne, 252
Dickinson, A. H., 269
Dickson, Kimberley, 83
Dietrich, Amber, 314
Dilley, Matthew, 278
Dimailig, John, 239
DiNicola, Jill, 300
Dixon, Canaeke, 232
Dockery, Barbara J., 226
Dodge, Anna D., 219
Doersam, Raymond, 320
Dominguez, Daniel, 227
Donald, Jeanne Claire, 265
Donato, Debra Ann, 58
Dooley, Julia C., 42
Dooley, Mary Jane, 130
Dorman, Heather, 14
Dorn, Kathy, 320
Dorn, Susan, 316
Doty, Susan E., 165
Douglas, B., 220
Douglas, Nadia Alicia, 63
Dovring, Karin, 267
Dowker, Dolly, 131
Down, Robbin E., 28
Driver, Pat, 139
Druck, Kitty, 205
Drum, Eleanor, 312
Duarte, Vincent, 280

Duffield, Fred, 53
Dugan, Jr., Wallace, 167
Dunlap, Vickie, 71
Dunn, Gabriel, 181
Dunn, Jr., Robert W., 100
DuPlayce-Brown, Cherie, 186
DuPlayee-Brown, Cherie, 55
Dupuy, C. E., 187
Durham, Whitney, 131

E

Easterling, Charlotte, 308
Eaton, Susanne, 134
Eccles, Sarah, 205
Echols, Betty L., 124
Edgemon, Kimberly, 236
Edwards, Alan, 273
Edwards, L. S., 268
Egan, Sherry, 86
Egre, Joan, 288
Ehlert, Dave, 238
Eichhorst, Kaleigh, 89
Ekdahl, Virginia, 120
El-Yousseph, Yousef Michael, 67
Elkins, Mike, 230
Elledge, Lana, 137
Ellis, Carla F., 164
Elmer, Laura, 235
Embro, Patricia, 113
Enck, Crystal, 69
Endreson, Jana, 22
Epps, Ashley R., 241
Epstein, Paulinerose M., 114
Erickson, Sally, 56
Esau, Jennifer, 183
Essig, Ashley, 15
Estrada, Jeanette L., 295
Evans, Bryant A., 268
Evans, Dorothy Jean, 139
Evans, Flossie, 319
Evely, Jenny, 248
Eyzenga, Alyssa, 180

F

Fabrizi, Rosanna, 161
Fahmy, Nahed, 19
Fahy, Joseph, 108
Fain, Dorothy L. Carter, 300
Fait, Alan, 93
Fane, Mark E., 318
Farina, Lauren, 260
Farmer, Bobby E., 206
Farnsworth, Robin, 116
Farrell, W. H., 18
Farris, Glenn, 56
Fazio-Lerner, Cathy, 310
Feagans, Linda Katherine, 190
Feargrieve, Mark, 234
Fecteau, Dominic J., 247
Feinberg, Keith, 310

Fenimore, Cynthia, 187
Fenton, Enid, 40
Ferguson, Charity Ann, 174
Ferguson, Donald J., 45
Ferrucci, Pasquale, 159
Feurer, Dolores, 304
Ficarelli, M. David, 295
Fincher, R. L., 296
Findley, Karen Hahn, 281
Finkbeiner, Joseph Jay, 313
Fischer, Judith L., 264
Fisher, Hannah, 161
Fisher, Richard, 254
Fitzgerald, Dorothy, 142
Fitzpatrick, Richard, 22
Fleming, Rhonda K., 33
Fletcher, B. N., 70
Flournoy, Christon, 103
Floyd, Fanci, 140
Fluharty, Edith T., 118
Flynn, Dave, 174
Flynn, J. B., 184
Foley, Christopher, 58
Forcaro, Joseph M., 66
Ford, Natalie, 175
Ford, Rosanne, 70
Forrester, Hayley, 201
Forry, Timothy M., 290
Forsyth, W. P., 2
Forty, Olga, 94
Foucault, Larry, 261
Fow, Lisa, 303
Fowler, Marilyn M., 201
Fox, Barbara L., 200
Fox, Lorraine, 182
Frahm, Jolene, 175
Fraize, Paula, 173
Fram, Kevin Patrick, 11
Franks, Tony, 47
Fraser, Gladys, 265
Fraser, Rena, 106
Frasier, Sandra, 192
Frazier, Caitlin, 133
Freeman, Cherrin Tessitore, 127
French, Cathy, 141
French, Richard, 237
Friedman, Neil S., 189
Frost, Arnold, 275
Frost, David, 22
Fulle, Tab, 119
Fuller, J. C., 272
Fulmer, Noriko, 74
Fultz, Deborah A., 89
Funk, Matthew W., 57
Furse, Avril, 191

G

Gabriel, Brandy D., 59
Gaeta, Cassandra, 185
Gallardo, Charlene K., 302
Galvin, Lillian, 265
Gander, Maureen Grayston, 306
Garcia, Carmen, 296
Garcia, Donna Marie, 83

Garcia, Jennifer M., 292
Garner, Alex, 233
Gartland, Charles Frederick, 220
Gary–Lopez, Andrea, 179
Gavrun, Peter Jacob, 208
Gehrke, Sandra K., 239
Geiger, Virginia C., 116
Gemmell, C. K., 213
Gems, Keith, 261
Gennaro, Marie, 97
George, Barbara Caldwell, 51
George, Sean, 302
Gerry, Dean E., 84
Gertzis, Selig, 283
Geuss, Megan Kathleen, 307
Gibson, A., 228
Gifford, Stephen P., 311
Giles, Martha, 78
Giles, Terence, 21
Gilich, Ruzica, 305
Gill, Melissa, 245
Gillespie, Maureen, 101
Gillespie, Steve, 240, 280
Gillion, K., 184
Gilmour, Jillian A., 73
Gilsdorf, Annette, 90
Gionta, Daria, 311
Gipe, Sharon, 92
Girby, Erin, 290
Givins, Bertha, 30
Glanville, Rhoda, 88
Gledhill, Kathleen, 126
Glenn, Jane, 95
Goldman, Phil, 228
Gomes, Alisa, 64
Gooch, Thelma J., 267
Goodhart, Alyssa Rose, 233
Goodman, M., 19
Goodwin, Deane P., 106
Goodwin, Marie, 275
Gore, Samantha, 19
Gorman, Sharon, 119
Gorton, Angi, 98
Gould, Kristie, 244
Goulden, Mark John, 136
Gracey, Jr., Peter A., 299
Graff–Nelson, Kathy, 63
Graham, Calvin, 204
Graham, Nora, 256
Gray, Brad, 171
Gray, Tammy D., 204
Gray, Tanya, 206
Graybosch, Matthew, 238
Grayston, Sharon, 236
Graziano, Constance, 239
Greathouse, Lee, 171
Green, Karen D., 48
Greenacre, Joyce C., 125
Grier, Leroy, 28
Griffin, Colin Leigh, 241
Griffin, Mary, 18
Griffith III, Richard S., 150
Griffith, Cecil L., 279

Griffiths, Jason R., 71
Griffiths, Vivienne, 227
Grimshaw, M., 185
Groves, Todd, 301
Guinn, Chris C., 55
Gurley, Joshua, 129
Guy, Patricia, 235
Guziewski, Ed, 305
Guzman, Roberto, 68

H

Habrovitsky, C., 96
Hadley, Joanne, 136
Haehle, Dawn C., 146
Hager, Cynthia T., 110
Hagerich, Delores, 24
Hainsworth, Lee A., 224
Halcrow, Ellie, 89
Hall, Bonnie, 312
Hall, Gordon, 260
Hall, Jessica, 218
Hall, Tina, 259
Hall, Vinita D., 196
Hallak, Kathy, 291
Haltman, Dorothy M., 262
Hamilton, Jayne, 37
Hamilton, Julie Kite, 15
Hamilton, Loretta A., 261
Hamlet, Brenda R., 309
Hamlet, Ruthie, 184
Hammersley, Brenda, 95
Hammond, Bethany, 213
Hammond, Michelle, 167
Hammond, Vera, 161
Hampton, Vince, 160
Hankins, Stephanie Rhiannon, 152
Hannon III, William R., 202
Hannon, Jennifer, 220
Hansjon, T. J., 249
Haq, Samarah, 95
Harbidge, Roger G., 122
Hardwick, Sheila, 191
Harniman, Robert, 177
Harpis, Tara L., 206
Harpster, Dorothy J., 113
Harrell, Rebecca, 17
Harrington, Joseph P., 309
Harrington, Kay, 149
Harris, Paul, 259
Harris, Rochelle, 293
Harris, Thomas E., 298
Harris, Vanessa, 167
Harrison, Lonny, 324
Harrison, Ty, 152
Hart, Shirley, 303
Hart, Thelma, 154
Hart–King, Cicely M., 170
Hartfield, Brandon Lee, 289
Hartle, Bethany, 291
Hartle, DeLoris, 15
Hartman, Lisa Jeanette, 248
Harvey, Janis, 10
Harvey, Phyllis R., 253
Harvey, Tim, 101

Harvey, Vonnique, 154
Harwood, Jane R., 276
Hatcher, Dave, 80
Hathaway, Marjorie R., 240
Hawkins, F. C., 125
Hawthorne, Kelly, 256
Hayes, Charlene A., 29
Hayes, Hubert, 197
Hayes, Lynne, 119
Hayes, Pamela, 285
Hayes, Wanda, 112
Haynes, Judith R., 195
Haywood, Andrew, 90
Hearty, Kristen, 167
Heath, Kristin, 117
Hebert, Mark, 56
Heck, Gary L., 45
Hector, Iris, 188
Heeney, Danielle, 249
Heiser, Kara, 232
Heller, Suzanne R., 81
Helmers, Ruth L. Dixon, 196
Henderson, Mandy, 89
Hendres, Joyce, 322
Hendrix, Michael, 109
Hennessey, Karen, 109
Henry, Charlotte, 57
Henson, Brenda, 162
Henson, Dian, 236
Hepburn, Anna, 96
Herbst, Gabrielle, 291
Hergott, Diane, 262
Hernandez, Carolyn, 222
Hernandez, Virginia C., 101
Herring, Gathelma J., 150
Herrmann, Kristy, 234
Heslop, Shawna, 318
Hewes, Shelley, 297
Hicks, Cristy, 72
Hicks, J. J., 79
Hicks, Neil, 155
Higgins, Vivienne, 106
High, Margaret, 110
Hildebrandt, LoriJean, 274
Hill, Dorita C., 170
Hill, Melody, 9
Hillbeck, Amanda, 266
Himmel, H., 217
Hip, Jay, 51
Hirschy–Boutwell, Wendi, 170
Ho, Mary Louise, 289
Hobbie, Jenniffer, 134
Hobby, Cynthia, 311
Hocken, Pat, 256
Hodson, Renee, 224
Hoerl, Jennifer Lynn, 172
Hoffpauir, Leah, 244
Hohensee, Beth J., 323
Hohol, Matthew, 250
Holdaway, Lori Dawn, 5
Holder, Margret, 241
Holdridge, Dawn L., 230

Holm, Alma M., 60
Holmes, Terry, 158
Homes, Irene C., 165
Hooks, Dorothy, 207
Hopkins, Alan, 284
Horgan, Kevin, 246
Hornbaker, Valerie, 88
Horne, David A., 246
Hornung, Fred, 62
Horrocks, R., 277
Horsford, Christopher, 214
Horton, Ruth, 206
Hough, Chrissie, 72
Hough, Jean, 71
Houle, Harvey, 176
Howard, Eileen, 308
Howell, Ann L., 123
Howell, Ben, 273
Howell, Claire, 203
Howell, Nikola, 8
Hruby, Debbie, 272
Hubiak, Diane M., 129
Huffman, Kelly, 132
Hug, Cyndi, 292
Huggins, Norma G., 229
Hughes, Colleen, 31
Hughes, Connie E., 177
Hughes, Stephen, 200
Huhn, Richard, 272
Hulick, Lester M., 133
Humphrey, Ann, 91
Humphreys, Eleanore, 65
Humphries, Valerie S., 105
Hunsaker, Jim, 261
Hunt, Bernice H., 183
Hunt, Emma, 108
Hunt, Patricia, 266
Hunter, Clark, 317
Hunter, Judy, 67
Hutchins, Ann, 224
Hutchinson, Emma, 190
Hutton, Joy, 181
Huxter, Joan, 108

I

Iacofano, Biagio, 229
Illguth, Cathrine, 135
Isakow, Richard, 105
Isham, Shelley, 46
Ives, Aeron, 130

J

Jackson, Alicia, 96
Jackson, B. J., 156
Jackson, Christopher, 209
Jackson, Crystal, 90
Jackson, Dora, 122
Jackson, Forbes, 289
Jackson, Irene, 93
Jackson, Janette, 283
Jackson, Kathleen, 145
Jackson, M., 257
Jagiello, Luke, 76
James, Joan, 260
James, Peter, 171
James, Sara, 72

Jamieson, Rachel, 186
Janczak, Nicole, 146
Janniello, Teresa, 137
Janosik, Ellen Hastings, 310
Jantzi, Katie, 278
Jaqua, Grace, 225
Jaquith, Judith, 202
Jarvis, Helen J., 13
Jefferson, Jeanette H., 296
Jefferson, Jeanette Harris, 141
Jeffrey, Frances, 13
Jeffrey, Penny, 238
Jensen, Denyse, 130
Jess, Adelle, 257
Jess, JoAnn, 238
Jewell, Clare, 288
Johnson, Aleshea J., 98
Johnson, Darlene, 158
Johnson, Gwendolyn, 241
Johnson, Helen, 276
Johnson, Janis, 233
Johnson, Jayne, 220
Johnson, M. E., 284
Johnston, M., 301
Jones, B. V., 98
Jones, Carla J., 167
Jones, Cynthia Yvonne, 140
Jones, Gloria A., 53
Jones, J. M., 221
Jones, Jan, 48
Jones, Ricky, 112
Jones, Stephen A., 234
Jones, William, 194
Jordan, Norman, 171
Jordan, Philip K., 135
Joyce, Robert J., 217
Judge, Louise, 54
Jump, Sylvia, 189
Justice, Janet K., 243

K

Kahlhamer, Dallas J., 317
Kaihani, Lotti Maria, 41
Kalina, Sandra, 270
Kamiel, Lauri, 158
Kammen, Verna L., 27
Kane, Kathleen, 7
Kannepalli, Srinivas, 170
Kanney, Kimberly, 243
Kappes, Denise Ann, 96
Karam, Anna, 249
Kastner, Cynthia, 209
Katzer, Emil M., 260
Kavanagh, Beverley, 286
Kavanagh, Bill, 170
Kearney, Helen, 172
Keaton, Randalee J., 78
Keel III, W. Ben, 71
Keeney, Jennifer, 12
Kehl, Florence C., 266
Kehres, Lisa A., 240
Keiser, David, 82
Keith, Joanne, 186
Kellawan, Joan P., 204

Keller, Jr., Rick, 128
Kelly, J. S., 187
Kelly, Janice, 261
Kelly, Martha, 231
Kemmerer, Harvey M., 149
Kemp, David A., 154
Kent, Ardis, 297
Kerswill, Diane, 286
Kerton, Joyce, 174
Ketron, Tommy L., 87
Kettle, Eileen, 286
Key, Cynthia V., 263
Khatami, Elham, 188
Kiddle, M. A., 99
Kiedaisch, Danielle, 16
Kimchuk, Pete, 146
Kirby, Susan, 285
Kirkham, Alison, 87
Kirtos, Pamela N., 78
Kitchener, J., 75
Klassen, Lisa, 324
Klausner, Dorothy Chenoweth, 138
Knapp, William D., 153
Knight, C. O., 181
Kolesar, Lorraine, 239
Kollefrath, Theresa, 122
Kolodziej, Mary Ellen, 307
Komer, Frank, 150
Koss, Belinda B., 233
Kowalsky, Rachel, 312
Kowkabany, Claudia, 127
Kramer, Lori Ann, 199
Kramer, Rita, 216
Krapf, Russell A., 40
Krisher, David B., 23
Kroeck, Anthony J., 221
Krohl, Gina, 59
Kulawiak, Beata M., 267
Kuntz, Bernie, 57
Kurylo, Sota, 128
Kuschka, Amy, 318
Kwinn, Ann, 231
Kylloe, Nancy, 62
Kyriacou, Claire, 161

L

Lacey, Kristy, 112
Lafferty, Chris, 236
Laflamme, Leah, 214
Lafreniere, Linda, 115
Laird, Mary A., 237
Lama, Beverly J., 189
Lambe, Collette, 191
Lambert, S. E. Alan, 166
Lampe, Milton E., 264
Lanasa, Joseph Michael, 82
Lang, David, 192
Langridge, Diane, 285
Lansing, Clara, 255
Laqualia, Judy, 24
Larmer, Rachel E., 38
Larsen, Sandra, 5
Larson, Christina-Jean, 258
Lasala, F. J., 20

Lashomb, Brain, 85
Last, Joan, 223
Laub, Jerry, 297
Lauder, Jr., Charles G., 10
Lauersdorf, Charles, 83
LaVoie, Frederick C., 182
Law, John, 73
Lawrence, Rebecca, 3
Lawrence, Tom, 114
Lawson, Ruby J., 261
Lawson, Sally E., 164
Lawyer, Nathan, 291
Leach, H., 208
Leach, Phillip D., 166
Leal, Anthony, 177
Leaver, Peggy, 243
Leavitt, Cindy, 235
Lebron, Natalie, 131
LeChance, Phillip, 54
Ledbury, Christine, 54
Ledesma, Jo Vanna, 77
Ledson, Shirley, 202
Lee, Anastasia, 229
Lee, Katherine G., 307
Lee, Linda, 140
Lee, Yukwor, 163
Lefler, Amy, 159
Lege, Mike, 294
Legg, Angela, 160
Leighow, Susan Rimby, 21
Leighton, Angela, 103
Leite, Ezio D., 242
Lemos, Roger, 121
Lennox, Danielle, 185
Lesack, Terra, 271
Letourneau, Dawn, 256
Levens, Brian, 241
Levy, Alexander W., 65
Lewis, Celena, 74
Lewis, Cynthia B., 176
Lewis, Ethelyne H., 61
Lewis, Shirley Ann, 86
Lieberman, Roberta A., 298
Liik, Judy, 148
Lilley, Jr., Gregory J., 93
Linares-Crilly, Anne P., 42
Lindsley, Catherine, 157
Lines, Lorraine K., 120
Lippert, Beulah B., 201
Livermore, Megan, 286
Llewellyn, A., 107
Lobianco, Maria Elena, 237
Loch, Michael, 153
Lominac, Gene, 170
Long, Bruce Martin, 184
Long, K. J., 253
Loomis, Evangeline H., 218
Lopez, Salanda, 205
Lorenzano, Ashley, 108
Lotz, Sue, 314
Love, Eboney, 101
Lovelace, Bonnie, 138
Lucan, Jacob, 319
Lucas, David W., 12

Lucas, Jason, 83
Lucia, Peggy Shafer, 166
Lundy, Donna, 193
Lungley, Brenda, 273
Lupa, Jo, 100
Luster, Elaine, 45
Luth, Ashley, 71
Lutu, F. Hannacho, 313
Lyons, Ethyl, 140
Lyons, V. A., 321

M

Mabee, Nancy, 94
MacDiarmid, Gordon, 121
MacGillivray, Joyce, 90
MacGregor, Jennifer, 265
Mackay, Bill, 282
MacKenzie, Gordon W., 75
MacKenzie, Ken, 25
MacKinnon, Renny V., 111
MacLean, Ian, 281
Maddison, L. E., 190
Maffei, M. Paul, 213
Magee, Rhyanna, 211
Magliocco, Olga, 13
Magnuson, Jackie, 93
Mahon, Cassandra, 162
Maiorino, Cynthia, 118
Maitland, Edna L., 211
Major, Sylvia, 324
Majors, James M., 227
Makower, Martine, 130
Malanczyn, Colleen, 83
Malaske, Joyce, 280
Manis, Brad A., 290
Mann, June, 179
Mann, Susan, 105
Manning, Connie, 41
Marcello, Antonio, 292
Mardi, Sonja, 38
Marian, Oana, 15
Marquez, Alicia Rosalinda, 70
Marquez, Junior, 36
Marrero, Juan, 104
Marshall, C. E., 308
Marshall, Gloria Jean, 313
Marshall, Jay, 249
Marshall, Kimberly Jo, 98
Marston, Deborah J., 88
Martell, Lisa, 314
Martenia, Tamara, 36
Martin, Jan, 87
Martinez, Danny, 299
Martinez, Salvador Lee, 152
Martorell, Gina, 197
Martucci, Christopher, 97
Maruca, Deanna, 119
Marx, Diana, 20
Masot, Christian, 49
Massey, Damien, 274
Mastrucci, Lisa A., 271
Matejin, Mira, 92
Matthews, Hazel, 144
Matthews, I. R., 195
Maunders, Cyril, 114

May, Joan M., 209
May, John, 304
Mayer, Debra, 157
Mays, Joseph R., 166
Mayville, Jenna, 103
McCann, Charlotte, 16
McCanse, Cassandra, 159
McCarthy, Denise, 79
McCarty, Fred B., 76
McCarty, Mary, 94
McClenan, M. E., 160
McClintick, Hazel J., 77
McClure, Dorothy, 232
McColm, B., 215
McConnell, Vicki, 278
McConville, James, 117
McCoy, Kevin M., 203
McCoy, Nita, 208
McCumber, Barbara, 81
McCurley, Margaret, 3
McCutcheon, Kimberley, 137
McDonald, Stuart, 162
McDowell, Joshua, 79
McEachin, Carolyn, 220
McGary, Gloria M., 99
McGinley, Christine, 69
McGlinsey, Colleen, 245
McGrath, Jimmy, 145
McGrath, Michael J., 173
McGrath, Patricia, 48
McGrath, Tom, 259
McGuire, David, 202
McIlwraith, William, 143
McInnis, Tracy, 273
McIntosh, Lynn, 203
McIntosh, Nevada, 269
McIntyre, Hope, 21
McKeigue, Kevin, 260
McKeown, E., 235
McKibbin, Monica, 147
McKimm, Michael N., 139
McKinney, Arlene, 212
McLaughlin, J., 322
McLaughlin, Laurie, 293
McLelland, Jessica, 293
McLemore, Christopher F., 232
McLennan, Roberta, 91
McMahon, Dyane C., 187
McMinn, Regina, 109
McNabb–Perry, Erica, 254
McNeil, Christopher William, 85
McNelly, J., 168
McNerney, Dolores, 147
McNicol, W., 35
McStay, Amanda, 106
Medenwaldt, Paul, 140
Medina, Nicole, 313
Mendoker, Sarah, 132
Meo, R., 290
Meola, Nick, 62
Merrick, Julie, 8

Merriwether, Karen Charrise, 76
Meyer, Daniel, 138
Meyer, Marilyn Y., 154
Meyer, Tim, 157
Michael, Rozella S., 243
Middleton, J., 115
Mifsud, Melanie, 100
Milazzo, Cheryl, 266
Miles, John P., 175
Miller, Annie T., 315
Miller, Brian, 288
Miller, Cathy, 64
Miller, Darnela G., 229
Miller, Lori, 227
Miller, Michael, 173
Miller, Stacy, 198
Mills, Heather, 188
Milne, Joyce G., 317
Miner, Theresa L., 230
Minton, Danny, 145
Miranda, Krista, 12
Mirelli, Kelli, 213
Mirkovich, Melissa, 126
Mitchell, Daniel, 254
Mitchell, J. F., 203
Mitchell, S. M., 277
Moffatt, Erick, 12
Moller, Nancy, 295
Mollica, Mary Beth, 251
Monnig, Patrick, 205
Montgomerie, Fiona, 275
Moore, Arlene M., 36
Moore, Bertha J., 39
Moore, Christine L., 182
Moore, Nick, 206
Moreau, Kelly K., 237
Morgan, Gareth, 306
Morgan, Gloria, 306
Morgan, Helena, 245
Morgan, Ron, 128
Morin, Hana, 250
Morrell, Heidi B., 143
Morse, Marjorie J., 67
Mosley, Tiffany, 178
Mount, Stephanie, 49
Moyer, Amy L., 116
Moyes, Stephen, 75
Moyle, Julie, 210
Mucha–Kangas, Felina–Marie, 140
Mueller, Jewell Rita, 168
Mulvenna, Davina, 141
Mumford, Alicia Marie, 68
Murphy, Charles, 276
Murphy, Sam R., 202
Murphy, Susan Fila, 123
Murray, Carol, 253
Murray, Pat, 257
Murray, Phil, 162
Myers, Connie, 317
Myers, Jessie, 122
Myers, Melinda M., 194
Myers, Ryan, 227

Myhill, D., 195
Mykolyshyn, Jennifer, 263

N

Nahoum, Steven, 296
Nashtar, S. Suhela, 56
Nattis, Alanna, 193
Neal, Roosevelt, 296
Nedd, Beulah M., 181
Neff, V. Marina, 251
Negoro, Clara Beth, 276
Nemergut, Erika, 210
Nestich, Patricia A., 267
Newby, Elizabeth B., 54
Newingham, Carol R., 84
Newman, Darla M., 197
Newman, Leona, 41
Nichols, John, 105
Nicholson, Kelly, 177
Nickol, Roger K., 77
Nicol, Shawna, 199
Nicolson, Janice, 10
Nielsen, Shasta, 185
Niishimura, Lisa, 103
Nitsche, Eric G., 75
Niven, Lil, 257
Noah, David W., 316
North, Susan M., 245

O

O'Brien, Troy M., 61
O'Dell, Brian, 104
O'Gara, Rossline, 304
O'Grady, T. J., 151
O'Hara, Meghann, 119
O'Malley, Jr., Martin J., 2
O'Reilly, Ian, 280
Ocana, Angel, 72
Ohagan, SueAnn, 136
Oliva, Cynthia, 246
Oliver, G. G., 72
Oliver, Maurice, 23
Olmos, Eric James, 81
Olson, Charlotte G., 85
Olson, Lynda, 271
Opuszynski, Michael, 310
Orazen, Mary Alice, 323
Organ, J. M., 174
Ori, Julie, 112
Ortego, Juanita, 143
Orton, Gregory B., 18
Orton, J. A., 275
Osborn, Jonathan James, 78
Osmond, Chris J., 63
Ostle, Helen, 66
Ostroff, Elaine, 11
Otero, Imara Vanessa, 32
Otto, Jr., Richard W., 20
Owen, Robert L., 231

P

Pace, Melanie, 322
Padfield, Alex, 268
Page, Helen Reeve, 191
Palfrey, W. Herbert, 97

Palladino, Jackie, 7
Pallett, Roy Kenneth, 278
Palmer, D., 288
Palmer, Rye, 52
Palmore, D. J., 172
Pandori, Gail, 183
Pappas, Candice, 33
Pardoe, Jill M., 32
Parker, Casey, 292
Parker, Joseph A., 128
Parker, Kathleen Mullen, 4
Parker, May, 57
Parker, Melissa, 145
Parlin, Richard, 133
Parravano, Julie, 144
Parrish, Jonathon, 193
Parsons, Kathleen M., 97
Partington, Ruth, 319
Patel, Nila, 244
Patlan, Amy L., 31
Paul, Melba L., 237
Paulsen, Christina, 126
Pavlovic, Michael, 293
Payne, Peggy, 136
Peabody, Eddie, 255
Pellegrino, Frank, 33
Penagos, Elizabeth, 134
Pennington, Keith S., 252
Penny, Denise G., 33
Perkins, Jacqueline, 145
Pernu, Bernice Weddington, 47
Perry, D., 306
Perry, J. T., 160
Peterson, Helen, 30
Peterson, Quintin, 315
Petitt, Brodi, 124
Petrilli, Ryan, 98
Petrillo, Dana, 104
Pham, Loni, 291
Phillips, Barbara, 74, 169
Phillips, Jeff, 104
Phillips, Mary, 194
Philp, Cassandra, 120
Piazza, Karen A., 169
Pickin, Mary, 323
Pickles, Beverly M., 308
Pierce, Mysti, 253
Pierre-Antoine, Micheline, 207
Pies, Ronald, 324
Pilcher, Audrey, 107
Pimienta, Elise, 215
Pitt, Helen, 304
Plank, Joe, 285
Plattner, Patricia, 188
Plein, Suzanne L., 156
Plumb, S., 278
Politziner, Dorothy, 98
Polk, Kerry, 281
Pond, Dianna M., 93
Poole, Shawna, 257
Poropat, Jessica, 269
Porrata, Nora, 37
Porter, Jerald D., 204

Posada, Ray, 296
Potter, L. Elaine, 239
Pounds, Tameka L., 234
Powell, Elizabeth A., 141
Powell, Patricia, 299
Powell, Sarah M., 110
Pratt, Calvin, 57
Preuss, Linda, 163
Price, Raymond John, 238
Probett, Frank, 199
Probett, Frank W., 102
Prokop, Sheila, 3
Proops, Hereward L. M., 235
Pryer, Mary, 228

Q
Qassab, Beverley Lorraine, 219
Quain, Peter K., 162
Qualls, Loren L., 117
Quinn, Jenny, 28

R
Radau, Maria, 204
Radzwilowicz, Laurie, 65
Rae, Caroline, 77
Rafajko, Regina M., 34
Raggett, Deborah, 255
Raimondo, Nancy, 272
Raine, Raymond, 26
Ramieri-Hall, Naomi, 232
Ramos, Cristine Maria, 42
Ramos, Nancy, 194
Ramsey, Gladys, 97
Ramseyer, Amanda Lynn, 299
Randall, Kenneth V., 96
Ratler, Natasha D., 176
Raymond, Elizabeth Ann, 132
Raymond, Raianne A., 129
Readel, Kathleen, 254
Reardon, Georgette M., 125
Redd-Preston, Leslie, 123
Reddy, Seetharathnam M., 219
Redington, Sharon, 63
Reed, Andrew W., 213
Reed, Deb, 126
Reesey, Sharon, 65
Reeves, Larry D., 50
Regan, Suzanne D., 315
Reidenbach, Rene S., 199
Reilly, Marlina, 245
Rendino, Mike A., 272
Reneau, Marie H., 2
Renner, David, 281
Renze, Dianne, 292
Retter, Maria, 241
Reyna, Linda, 147
Rhetta, Wandasha A., 70
Rhodes, Virginia, 84
Rhymer, Bryce W., 17
Rials, Patricia A., 221

Rich, Tracey Dean, 265
Richards, Katy, 263
Richardson, D., 169
Richardson, Laura, 186
Richline, Jr., Russell T., 203
Ricketts, Jonathan, 192
Ridpath, Patricia, 310
Riffle, Jessica K., 85
Riggs, Dustin M., 4
Riley, Brian, 198
Ringgold, Don, 243
Rising, Rebecca, 93
Ristow, John, 59
Ritchie, Sandra Jean, 147
Ritter, Estella, 307
Rivers, Yolanda, 249
Rizek, Jamla, 225
Rizzi, Anthony, 278
Roach, Amber, 285
Roach, Joyce, 209
Roadruck, Marlene Wenger, 34, 173
Robbins, Tiana, 148
Roberson, Jo Ann, 317
Roberts, Anne, 153
Roberts, Hilda, 89
Roberts, Karly, 164
Roberts, Kristine S., 153
Robertson, Andrew, 216
Robertson, Melissa S., 251
Robinson, Linda, 302
Robinson, Lynn S., 81
Robinson, Markeeta, 124
Robinson, Uhron, 275
Robinson-Romeo, Helen, 64
Rochette, Pam, 251
Rockwell, David A., 6
Roder, Melissa J., 263
Rodriguez, Helen, 248
Roffe, Linda L., 65
Rogers, Mark A., 253
Rogers, Mary, 221
Rohr, William, 214
Rollison, Vicki J., 214
Roog, Clara, 193
Rose, Shayna Leah, 111
Roser, Mary Elizabeth, 34
Ross, Heather, 157
Rozman, Daniel T., 194
Ruble, Anna M., 129
Rue, Jacqueline, 297
Rush, Trey, 101
Russell, Angella, 92
Russell, Jan, 96
Russell, Timothy F., 179
Russo, Steve, 262
Ryan, Tamara, 107
Ryczek, Lori L., 169

S
Saggers, Julie, 53
Salernitano, Santy, 35
Salmons, Ronnie, 86
Salvatore, Alice, 178

Sammons, Annie, 323
Sanchez, Jr., Hector O., 247
Sanchez, Reymundo, 142
Sanders, Maryann, 142
Sanders, Wanda E., 54
Sandler, Douglas, 82
Sapp, Joanna MacDonald, 59
Sasala, Gary J., 5
Sasala, Ruth R., 321
Sasse, Kristin, 288
Savage, Kathleen, 168
Savidge, Frank, 207
Scantlin, Liz, 63
Schaffter, Todd, 143
Schellhamer, Terrie, 44
Schleis, Jennifer, 134
Schmidt, Chadley, 255
Schmidt, Teresa, 7
Schneider, Ailene Hayes, 8
Schnellbacher, Barbara, 217
Schnittker, Nicholas L., 128
Schoeberlein, Marion, 273
Schofield, Joann, 112
Scholes, E. A., 154
Scholl, Sue H., 272
Schott, June, 270
Schroeder, Sarah, 294
Schrum, Sandra, 187
Schuler, Casey, 22
Schultz, Janice E., 264
Schwarz, Jesica, 205
Sciullo, Melissa, 294
Scott, Jo, 30
Scott, Mary F., 80
Scott, Ruth J., 311
Scott-Marak, Ronda, 3
Scudder, Doris, 273
Seastrom, Anne, 246
Seaton, John, 242
Seay, Linda M., 189
Secker, Neil, 215
Seddon, J. C., 150
Seevers, Nicole, 56
Seib, Michelle, 324
Seide, Ruth A., 111
Sell, S. J., 25
Sellars, Jerome, 294
Sellers, Rachel E., 299
Senske, Jeremy, 158
Service, Gail Arlette, 229
Seuberling, Ron, 60
Shacklady, Linda, 285
Shafer, Judith, 43
Shaffer, June Roberta, 88
Shaffer, Lorea B., 316
Shaffie, Amina, 280
Shane, Linda, 60
Shannon, Luverna Stella, 137
Sharp, William D., 283
Sharpe, R. L., 130

Shaw, Darlene, 274
Shearer, Esther K., 222
Sheikh, Qumar S., 250
Shelfer, Gee Gee, 118
Shepard, Scarlett, 37
Shepherd, Kerry, 258
Sheridan, David, 246
Sheridan, Debi, 276
Sherman, Pamella, 244
Sherman, Scott B., 295
Shewmaker, Tamara, 272
Shields, Rosemarie, 244
Shimmel, Brenda J., 94
Shipman, Robert H., 305
Short, Kevin, 111
Sicard, Raymond, 207
Sietman, Melba, 113
Silver, Aubree, 29
Simonetti, Rosaria, 155
Simons, Debra R., 218
Simpson, Kathy, 192
Simpson, Lecy Marie, 103
Sinnott, Jessieca, 82
Sipos, Laszlo S., 182
Skinner, I. K., 216
Skoglund, Ellis, 102
Skreslet, Tabor, 7
Slama, Kassee Alison, 212
Slater, Vanessa, 219
Sloan, Ana M., 55
Slough, John, 105
Smallfoot, Jill, 223
Smith, Barbara J., 262
Smith, Ben, 308
Smith, Casey, 300
Smith, Cindy, 196
Smith, Joan T., 31
Smith, Jonathan, 159
Smith, Laura, 222
Smith, Malacia, 251
Smith, Malacia A., 274
Smith, Megan R., 158
Smith, Nina, 8
Smith, Pamela, 200
Smith, Shanna, 169
Smith, Susan L., 21
Smith, Tami, 99
Smith, Tecia Lanese, 69
Smith, Thomas, 68
Smith, Tracey, 164
Smith, William B., 49
Snodgrass, Wanda T., 61
Snyder, Tami M., 315
Sobczak, Sharon L., 108
Sobczuk, Joshua, 181
Solarski, Sharon Ann, 2
Solloway, Granville, 280
Solorzano, Jr., Salvador, 210
Sommer, Penelope F., 92
Sooknanan, Candice S., 199
Sookoor, Basdai, 114
Soria, Andrea, 47
Soucie, Edith, 58
Souder, Ann M., 14

Souza, Kimberly, 151
Sparks, Lawrence, 137
Sparks, Rebecca, 52
Spaulding, Missy, 146
Spector, Robert Donald, 322
Spencer, Nicholas, 60
Spencer, Sheri, 264
Spilker, Susan, 144
Spooner, Janet, 304
Spriggs, Evelyn, 259
Squires, D. M., 85
St. Clair, Stanley J., 181
Stafford, Will, 24
Staley, Hank, 118
Stallings, Sean, 254
Stanta, Lisa M., 236
Stapleton, Helen, 17
Stark, Elizabeth, 151
Stark, Priscilla, 226
Stark, Stacey, 135
Starks, Wanda, 52
Starks-Veliz, Thelma, 100
Starry, Lawrence R., 5
Stec-Neifert, Kashmiri Kristina, 248
Steen, Elsie B., 175
Steir-Lewin, Lois A., 102
Stephen, Alta, 201
Stetler, Christopher, 303
Stevens, Tim, 292
Stewart, Donna Marie, 74
Stewart, Melissa Kay, 201
Stilwell, V. Darlene, 226
Stine, Ellen K., 320
Stoffel, Ginger, 306
Storey, Douglas, 125
Strain, Ian, 51
Stranger, Alison, 52
Strawbridge, Shane, 44
Strawser, Ray A., 155
Street, Gloria, 89
Streeter, Jo Ann, 271
Strickland, Frances, 273
Strike, Christy Anne, 259
Stroud, Dawn Michelle Hawkin, 6
Strouse, Mary Lou, 37
Suber, Constance R., 312
Subia, Brandon, 121
Sugden, Graham, 220
Sullivan, Cinde, 215
Sullivan, Ginger, 24
Sullivan, Matthew, 307
Summers, Jax, 156
Sunshine, Bill, 139
Sussman, Zach, 247
Sutherland, Sandra, 79
Sutten, Mary, 188
Sutton, Annie, 182
Sutton, Cindy, 95
Sutton, Gail M., 9
Sveda, Kristina, 315
Swanger, Lori L., 235
Swann, Dianne R., 124
Swearingen, Nate, 226

Systermann, Pamela, 274
Sztukowski, Bryan, 300

T

Taft, Ilona, 318
Taggart, Roy, 279
Takacs, Sean, 187
Talmadge, S. C., 206
Talmage, Kirsten, 248
Tamayo, Maria Thelma, 180
Tank, Jessie, 223
Tanzola, Christopher, 11
Taphorn, Phyllis Ann, 316
Tassell, Rhys, 115
Tawse, James E., 111
Taxsar, Steven N., 212
Taylor, Anna O., 67
Taylor, Carol, 180
Taylor, E. Ann, 320
Taylor, Jr., Joseph S., 168
Taylor, Laura, 201
Taylor, Linda Ann, 30
Taylor, Lora, 85
Taylor, Madge, 264
Taylor, Micah, 80
Taylor, Ruth, 27
Taylor, Teresa, 11
Taylor, Vera, 266
Tedesco, Adam J., 148
Terral, Sadie Rose, 290
Terrell, Rose, 250
Terry, Toni, 83
Tetter, Marcellus, 71
Theobalds, Shawn, 64
Thomas, Catherine L., 299
Thomas, Cindy, 211
Thomas, Joan A., 308
Thomas, Lisa, 55
Thomas, Theresa Lynn, 151
Thompson, Andrea, 290
Thompson, Cheryl S., 230
Thompson, Chloe', 279
Thompson, Florizella, 218
Thompson, Mark, 165
Thrumble, Ned, 177
Tietz, Beverly, 234
Tigner, Tamara, 209
Tilot, Kathy, 40
Tilot, Lynn M., 183
Timoteo, Constance, 191
Tindle, Roy, 270
Tober, Jr., Kenneth R., 282
Tobola, Wanda S., 133
Toftely, Nora, 142
Toney, Drew, 14
Tork, Ann, 269
Torres, J. Benhur R., 171
Tracy, Kimberly, 196
Trahan, W. R., 318
Traudt, Cicily, 123
Trepanier, Theresa, 117
Trevino, Stephanie, 16
Trinder, Carol, 277
Tripp, Lia, 154
Troll, Florence N., 240

Troop, Keith D., 258
Troup, Ann-Marie, 287
Troyer, Hilda, 200
Truss, Sally, 153
Tucker, Quan, 213
Tungate, Steven, 63
Turner, Alisa M., 120
Turner, John, 150
Turner, Sharolyn K., 152
Tutko, George A., 127
Two Eagles, Bruce, 159

U

Udell, Joy, 135
Unger, Barbara, 9
Untener, Luanne, 180
Upton, Katherine J., 115
Urbaniec, Valerie, 204

V

Vachon, Amy Robyn, 221
Valenzuela, Carolyn, 113
Valkenburg, Lisa, 192
Van Dyk, John, 149
VanDerHeyden, Betty, 236
Vanier, Khristian, 70
Vanlangendonck, Megan E., 262
Vasquez, Monique, 225
Vaughn, Earline, 62
Vaughn, Robert W., 46
Vaughn, Wesley G., 178
Vega-Park, Kristy, 148
Venne, Betty E., 253
Vennum, Sharon, 203
Verrier, Glen, 183
Verstraete, Kerri Lynn, 123
Vickery, Georgia A., 242
Vigil, Penelope, 67
Vish, Mary Donovan, 197
Vivian, Val, 147
Voelker, Marilyn S., 223
Vongpanya, Inkham Mone, 305
Vowles, Craig, 109

W

Wade, Frances, 156
Wahlberg, Jessica M., 303
Waldron, Linda J., 45
Walker, B., 219
Walker, Bill, 149
Walker, Cynthia F., 172
Walker, Nigel Paul, 189
Walker, Vickie Lynn, 131
Wallace, Bob, 173
Wallingford, Shirlene, 69
Wallis, Elizabeth, 57
Walsh, Nicola, 66
Walters, Candice F., 311
Wamhoff, Sareen, 159
Ward, C. P., 254
Ware, Carolyn, 117
Ware, Georges, 262
Warren, Sherri, 65

Warwick, Jean, 190
Wascher, Alea, 223
Washington, Antoinette, 48
Washington, Tami, 305
Waters, Freda, 99
Watret, Tony R., 289
Watson, Gordon Burch, 294
Watson, Kirk Antony, 68
Watson, Margaret Brewster, 179
Watts, Kevin, 91
Weatherill, Derek, 228
Weaver, Lynn, 260
Webb, Bob and Catherine, 84
Webb, M. E., 124
Webber, Danyelle M., 88
Weeks, Ben E., 194
Wegienka, Matthew, 77
Weidman, Debra A., 323
Weinstein, Lou, 198
Welch-Thorson, Camerone A., 60
Wells, Darren, 276
Welsh, Eileen H., 143
Welsh, Vera R., 191
Weng, M. L., 233
Wentworth, Brenda, 214
Werner, Kari, 14
Werner, Laurin Ashley, 62
Wesley, Mae Frances, 173
West, Deirdre Maria, 107

West, Gloria Jean, 53
West, Susan L., 294
West, T. Earl, 91
Westberg, Sandra, 177
Westbrook, John, 4
Whatley, Luther B., 210
Wheeldon, Brian, 91
Wheeler, Emily, 6
Wheeler, Muriel, 59
Wheeler, Wayne D., 26
Whitcomb, Pete, 287
White, Deborah J., 78
White, Elga Haymon, 66
White, James R., 144
White, Karen, 224
White, Susan, 117
Whiteford, Mike David, 198
Whitehead, Ruth, 277
Whiteman, Stacey, 214
Whiteside, Glenda, 224
Whittaker, Roy, 301
Wicklund, April, 217
Wilds, Andrew, 127
Wilk, Carol, 116
Willard, Graham, 87
Williams, Kathleen, 258
Williams, Maggie, 309
Williams, Nathan, 60
Williams, Riva Marea, 34
Williams, Sadie N., 43
Wills, Jessica, 197
Willson, Dorothea E., 247

Wilson, Candelee Woodward, 52
Wilson, Connie M., 38
Wilson, Jo Ann, 163
Wilson, Lorna, 155
Winch, Sarah Louise, 304
Winter, Barbara J., 69
Wisdom, Pauline, 287
Wiseman, Kathryn Ann, 75
Wisher, Pamela, 174
Witt, Peggy, 302
Witter, Edith, 73
Wolfensburger, Renee, 238
Wollesen, Heather, 165
Wood, Brandy D., 247
Wood, Bryan Scott, 155
Wood, Edna M., 215
Wood, Jean, 184
Wood, Kathy, 95
Wood, Monica, 282
Wood, Sylvia I., 309
Wooden, Jennifer, 180
Woods, Charles Edward, 211
Woolcott, Elizabeth, 164
Woolridge, Loretta N., 116
Wordley, Suzanne, 223
Wright, Eric, 313
Wright, Julie H., 121
Wright, Nell M., 178
Wright, Tricia Le, 175
Wyatt, Tina L., 102

Wyles, Natalie, 172
Wynn, Lisa, 156

Y

Yaltiligil, Rebecca, 126
Yancey, Carla, 130
Yang, Mary L., 225
Yates, Zai O. D., 175
Yavorski, Michael J., 190
Yaws, Alyene, 279
Yisrael, Ammayeh, 79
Yoder, Brian, 172
Yoder, Myron E., 53
Young, Keanu, 228
Young, N., 174
Young, Parrish R., 50
Young-Powell, Alice Elaine, 31
Yow, Stephen A., 287
Yunker, Stephanie, 225

Z

Zadura, Vita, 315
Zaer, Hillary, 302
Zahn, Melisa, 80
Zakharova, Svetlana, 293
Zelazny, Dennis A., 26
Zelehoski-Updike, Suzanne, 249
Zimmerman, John C., 295
Ziolkowski, Linda J., 52
Ziolkowski, Tom, 242